...from the dawn of aviation

THE QANTAS STORY 1920 ~ 1995

FOCUS PUBLISHING
PTY LTD

Enquiries should be addressed to the publishers.
Published by Focus Publishing Pty Ltd ACN 003 600 360
PO Box 557, Double Bay NSW 2028.
Telephone (02) 327 4777 Facsimile (02) 362 3753

Steven Rich Chairman
Jaqui Lane Publisher
Jane Blaney Production Manager
William E Munt Project Manager

Sally Moss Editor

Designed by The Brochure Production Company Pty Ltd,
Brian Hutchinson and Jon Howe
Printed by Griffin Press
Film separations by Litho Platemakers Pty Ltd
© 1995 Qantas Airways Ltd.

I S B N 1 - 875 - 359 - 23 - 0

...from the dawn of aviation

THE QANTAS STORY 1920 ~ 1995

by JOHN STACKHOUSE

Contents

This book has been published as part of the proud celebration of the 75th Anniversary of Qantas. As the title suggests, it relates how Qantas took off from the dry, flat plains of central western Queensland 75 years ago, and rose to the forefront of the international civil aviation industry.

The text focuses on people, their foresight, skills, enthusiasm, determination and plain hard work to overcome every challenge they met along the way.

Respected aviation writer, John Stackhouse, has talked to hundreds of Qantas people, old and new, to breathe life into and around the framework of the history of the airline.

The trail led him to veterans such as George Roberts, whose love of flying pre-dates Qantas, and whose memory has been the source of invaluable information.

John Stackhouse spent countless hours scanning old newspaper files, news releases and published histories to piece together the story of the airline. But whenever he drew a blank, he went straight to such people to draw upon their personal recollections and experiences.

This approach has been successful, as the story of Qantas is ultimately about the people who have created its long and exciting history—the staff, the customers and the excellence of key supply companies.

The success of Qantas is really a tribute to their efforts and performance, often in very difficult and challenging circumstances.

Paul McGinness, Hudson Fysh and Arthur Baird had to overcome what must have seemed to be insurmountable scepticism in the early days. But they never wavered in their belief that aviation would become an essential and major industry, and this determination laid the foundations for the standards of Qantas.

Their successors have carried the baton they passed with pride, meeting the challenges of distance, weather, war, regulations and competition to develop the company into a national icon.

They brought the airline to the point in this, its 75th year, of being successfully floated by public share offer which saw Qantas shares traded for the first time on the Australian Stock Exchange on 31 July 1995.

This book recognises all the people who have contributed by their efforts over the years.

It is the way in which they have done their jobs, the way they have behaved and supported the airline, that has made Qantas what it is today.

James Strong

JAMES STRONG

Managing Director, Qantas Airways Ltd

Aviation artist Robert Taylor's romantic recreation of the company's first aircraft, the Avro 504K.

Introduction

'Qantas has become integrated into the very fibre of the Australian nation.
It has grown to perform a diverse and often critical role in the development of the state.
The nature of this role is such that it encompasses: transportation, balance of payments, employment,
defence, social and cultural development, trade, economic development, national emergency.'

Keith Hamilton, General Manager of Qantas, 1976

The late Keith Hamilton, one of the important figures Qantas has fostered, set out his thoughts in a note to his Board at a time which was to become a watershed not only for Qantas but for Australia as well.

More than half a century after the company was founded in outback Winton in 1920, the Qantas he guided occupied a landmark building in the commercial heart of Sydney, next to its great hotel The Wentworth. Its fleet of Boeing 707 jets had spanned the world, bringing Europe within a day's journey of Australia. The airline had earned a reputation throughout the world for its reliability, quality of service, technical excellence, and above all for safety.

Australia was a country of 15 million people, three times as many as in 1920. Qantas was restlessly looking ahead. It was establishing a fleet of Boeing 747-200 jets, the world's biggest commercial transports, which also had the longest range. As with each previous generation of aircraft that preceded it, the 747 was changing the climate in which Qantas operated. The Jumbos ushered in an era of mass travel that caused unprecedented strains—within Qantas itself, and between Qantas and the nation—which were to lead to a fundamental re-alignment of Qantas. Such strains took their toll. Hamilton was to die from a heart attack. But the course Qantas was to follow, one which Hamilton had helped to pioneer, would focus increasingly on Asia years before Australia began looking north.

In fact, had it not been for the physical links which Qantas had established, Australia's 'part of Asia' outlook of the 1990s is unlikely to have developed as a national focus.

Today the physical realities of the birthplace of the founders of Qantas have not changed. But Australia's population has more than tripled, its make-up changing largely through migration from Europe and Asia. Australia, the only single nation to occupy a continent, is bigger than western Europe and about the same size as the continental United States of America. Its population is clustered in cities around the periphery or in tiny settlements separated by vast distances. For most of the last 75 years, its main national characteristic has been isolation. It lies on the opposite side of the globe from the sources of its main traditional culture—Europe and North America—and many thousands of kilometres away from its trade partners, even the most recent in Asia.

Hamilton selected his points well when, in 1976, he listed the ways in which Qantas had become part of the fabric of Australia.

'Transportation: Safe, reliable and fast and lowering in price as the mass travel market was developed.

Balance of payments: Qantas itself is a huge earner of foreign exchange. But without the network it established, tourism to Australia—which is now this country's biggest export earner—could not have developed.

Employment: Apart from its own workforce (then about 12 thousand), Qantas created jobs directly in supporting industries, and fostered many, many more in hotels, restaurants and tourism generally that flowed right through the community's prosperity.

Defence: Then, with the Vietnam War still in memory, Qantas was demonstrating its ability to keep open the nation's links with Europe despite repeated troubles in the Middle East and, in the previous decade, in South-East Asia. Hamilton could also look back to the Pacific War, when Qantas had supply-dropped to frontline soldiers in New Guinea and provided the expertise that delivered essential Catalina flying boats across the Pacific. The expertise in times of crisis also bore fruit when Qantas itself was to fly Catalinas direct from Perth to Sri Lanka (then Ceylon) and re-open the link that the Japanese had cut. Qantas engineering excellence had helped support the Australian and allied forces and continues to do so to the present day.

Trade and economic development: Fast Qantas air freight has opened the way for whole export industries to Asia, the Pacific and the Middle East. Qantas is the cornerstone of the tourism industry. It has also been the national leader, not only in aircraft engineering, but also in bringing computers into use in all facets of business. Qantas has also led the way in electronic technologies such as the use of 'clean rooms' for precision repair and maintenance of equipment. And operationally, it is still pioneering new techniques of flying.

National emergency: Fresh in Hamilton's mind in 1976 must have been the Qantas effort in the relief of Darwin after Cyclone Tracy struck. One Qantas 747 lifted to safety more than 600 people, including babies and children, in a single flight, then a record'.

At 75 years of age, Qantas has turned another page in its history. In 1995 the airline was returned to the hands of private shareholders after decades as a government entity, sacrificing some financial and flag advantages but leaving behind much political and bureaucratic influence. It was the weight of these pressures which had been on Hamilton's mind when he sought to clarify the role of the airline in the words quoted above. At that stage, a return to the private sector could not have been imagined. Now, some 20 years later, it has become a reality.

But the basic challenges remain—among them competition against some of the best airlines in the world; staying abreast of technology; making the right choice of aircraft and engines from mere patterns on designers' computer screens; control of costs that run into millions of dollars; in daily operations, ensuring that the service is friendly, open and equal to the best in the world. And, finally, facing up to the fundamentals: servicing a country that is also an entire continent, its population scattered, its distances huge—a long, long way from the major population centres of the world.

In writing this book, I want to acknowledge the work of my friend John Gunn, who chronicled the Qantas saga up to 1988 in four huge volumes (one, still unpublished). I also received help from many Qantas and former Qantas people including Bernard Shirley, Jim Eames, George Roberts, Ern Aldis, Captain Ian Wyndham and others. In particular, thanks to John Tilton, who contributed the brief history of TAA/Australian for this project.

JOHN STACKHOUSE

Sydney 1995

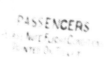

Chapter 1

Outback days

THE WONDER OF FLIGHT

'Be dammed to the doubters.' Quote from first passenger carried by Qantas—Mr Alexander Kennedy.
Here he proudly poses alongside a Qantas aircraft at Longreach.

When Paul McGinness and Wilmot Hudson Fysh flew the first flights for Qantas in biplanes in western Queensland, the public still considered aviation an adventure. Less than two decades before, Wilbur and Orville Wright had flown at Kitty Hawk. Aircraft had blossomed as a weapon of war. Those who had survived war could see how to use aeroplanes for transportation in peace; although, for many, flying seemed a fantasy, a remote dream.

Everyone associated with Qantas was a pioneer: they were creating an airline with no model to follow. They all had to learn from scratch—the pilots; engineers like Arthur Baird, who worked in corrugated iron hangars that became ovens in the blazing Queensland heat; the agents who learnt how to take reservations and sell tickets; and, in the back room, Fergus McMaster, who as chairman and director took time off from his property and business interests to steer Qantas through its difficult birth until it was firmly established.

It was hard work. But, for the public, it had glamour. Fysh, in his reminiscences, recalled that the landing of a stuttering aeroplane on the local racecourse and the emergence of airmen in goggles and flying suits brought children and parents running. *'It created the sensation an astronaut in a space suit would make if he suddenly appeared in a country town'*, he said.

Flying in the Outback demanded special skills. Engines were unreliable and, as each plane had only one, a breakdown meant a forced landing. During the onset of the wet season and its inevitable storms, the wood-and-fabric aeroplanes were like thistledown. It was imperative to begin flying in daylight, when the air was relatively still, and complete the first leg of a journey by the heat of midday.

The first scheduled Qantas flight, on 2 November 1922, strictly obeyed this rule. With 'Ginty' McGinness as pilot, the Armstrong Whitworth FK-8 left Charleville at 5.30 a.m., refuelled at Blackall, then went on to Longreach for the night. Next morning 'Huddie' Fysh climbed into the cockpit and flew on to Winton, refuelled again and travelled to McKinlay for a brief stop before completing the journey in Cloncurry. On arrival, there were three cheers for Fysh and three more for the only passenger, the indomitable 84-year-old pastoralist, Alexander Kennedy.

That first trip was 580 miles (933 kilometres), or about the distance from Sydney to Brisbane. It had taken seven and three-quarter hours of flying, over two days. Aircraft in the modern Qantas fleet would routinely cover that distance in about an hour, carrying up to 400 passengers and 20 tonnes of freight and mail.

This was the inauguration of a route which for years would see wire-braced, wood-and-fabric biplanes laboriously building an airline. It was a rigorous and uncomfortable training ground, with both pilots and passengers putting up with extremes of heat, dawn cold and altitude chill. As the pilots, the engineers and the airline itself learnt the trade, they gained the skills of maintenance, safety and reliability which laid the foundation for Qantas traditions. At the outset there was the network that became the

Queensland and Northern Territory Aerial Services. From Winton it relocated first to Longreach then to Brisbane, and finally to Sydney. Qantas expanded services to Singapore, then to London. The war intervened, but Qantas was to return in the late 1940s, the 1950s and beyond to weave its 'aerial services' around the world.

Western Queenslanders accepted the discomfort and risk of those early days because a journey which had once taken days, weeks or months could now be accomplished in hours. That first passenger, Kennedy, for instance, had travelled for eight months to get to Cloncurry when he established his property. To drive from Charleville to Longreach could take several days or even weeks in the wet season. By rail, people had to take the narrow-gauge line to Brisbane, change for Rockhampton, and finally catch the inland train to Longreach.

The landing of a stuttering aeroplane on the local racecourse and the emergence of airmen in goggles and flying suits brought children and parents running.

The birth of Qantas came at a time of restlessness for Australia. A generation had survived a war and brought fresh minds to bear on many of the nation's problems. The three founders of the airline had all served in the Australian Imperial Force (AIF) in World War I, two of them—Fysh and McGinness—seeing combat together. Hudson Fysh and 'Ginty' McGinness met for the first time on the battlefield at Gallipoli, where 'Ginty' had won the Distinguished Conduct Medal for bravery. They both transferred to No. 1 Squadron, Australian Flying Corps (AFC), which flew in the Middle Eastern campaigns against the Turks. 'Ginty' was already serving as a pilot when Hudson arrived as an observer and chose to fly with him. Fysh had volunteered to become a pilot but was not trained until after the war ended and learned to fly in Egypt.

Three visionaries.
Paul McGinness, pilot;
Hudson Fysh, observer;
and below, Arthur Baird.

Hudson Fysh (left) and Paul McGinness in 1919.

Local manpower pushes Fysh and McGinness' Model T Ford through a dry river bed in the Gulf country.

A weary-looking Model T Ford gets some running repairs during the 1919 air route survey conducted by Fysh and McGinness.

Ex-service pilots with dreams of long-distance flights jumped into action in March 1919 when the Prime Minister of Australia W M Hughes announced a £10,000 prize for the 'first successful flight to Australia from Great Britain in a machine manned by Australians'. Those who took part had to provide their own aircraft and the flight had to be completed within 720 consecutive hours before midnight on 31 December 1919.

McGinness and Fysh by that time were aboard ship on their way home from Egypt. Fysh went back to his old trade of wool classing at Launceston, in his native Tasmania, while the restless McGinness decided to try for the prize and headed off to the mainland to look for a sponsor.

In the AFC squadron, one of the Bristol fighters had been paid for by a wealthy grazier, Sir Samuel McCaughey. McGinness rushed off to Yanco in western New South Wales to talk to McCaughey, whom he persuaded to back him for a flight from London. McGinness telegraphed Fysh and rushed back to Melbourne to line up their former mechanic, Arthur Baird. Fysh sold his car and Baird his garage business. They were set to leave for England when McCaughey died and their great adventure was off.

However, the story was far from over. The Defence Department, which was in charge of aviation, offered McGinness and Fysh a chance to survey the route across northern Australia from Longreach, through the Gulf Country to Katherine, and north to Darwin. They were back in uniform again as airmen and, in August 1919, arrived at Longreach to acquire a Model T Ford and their first taste of the Outback. Station owners told them no car had ever been through on the northern route via the Gulf of Carpentaria, and warned of the hazards of the black soil plains and the danger of getting lost in the featureless country.

The locals ridiculed them but the trailblazers learnt that a drover was going to Borroloola with twenty horses, so they prudently arranged to use these to pull the loaded Ford across rivers and through soft sand, reaching Borroloola and their cache of fuel.

They drove on, with an ailing Ford, to the Roper River and to Katherine, where they took the train, *Leaping Lena*, to Darwin. Their experiences and information from a group of motor cyclists who had ridden from Sydney had convinced the pair that,

when the planes arrived, they should follow a route to the south, across the Barkly Tableland. McGinness set off back to Cloncurry to survey the route. He organised a party to build an aerodrome at Newcastle Waters, cleared stones away from a paddock at Brunette Downs for a landing strip and checked out another at Camooweal. McGinness then waited for the fliers at Cloncurry.

Fysh had stayed in Darwin to build a landing ground. It was ready in time for the successful Ross and Keith Smith team when they landed in a Vickers Vimy on 10 December 1919. The Vimy then headed south on the route McGinness had surveyed and flew on to the state capitals to enjoy a triumphant welcome. The flight awakened the entire nation to the possibilities of air travel and planted a seed for the notion of an 'empire' air route between London and Sydney. This was only 16 years after the first flight by Wilbur and Orville Wright. In the next decade, the first Australian plane would be flying north through Darwin and what was then Batavia to Singapore, and linking with a British aircraft to make the Empire Route a reality.

Hudson Fysh (third from right) met Ross and Keith Smith (first and fourth from right) at Darwin to certify that they were eligible for the £10,000 prize for winning the London–Australia air race.

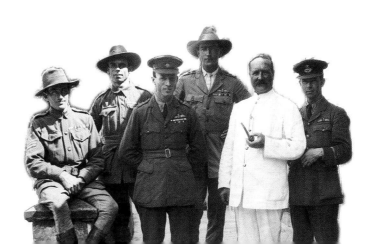

Refuelling the Vickers Vimy at Charleville on 23 December 1919.
Keith Smith stands in the cockpit as the Shell representative on the ground oversees the operation.

The Vickers Vimy at Charleville, December 1919.

TRAVEL BY BIPLANE

In the early days of Qantas, passengers were just as much pioneers as the pilots who flew them from one Outback town to another. Arthur Affleck, who joined Qantas in 1927, wrote nearly 40 years later, in his autobiography *The Wandering Years*, about the hardships the passengers endured. Dawn take-offs, and long stopovers at country pubs when conditions got too hot and too bumpy to fly, were normal.

Hudson Fysh signing for the mail at Longreach. Arthur Baird looks on in the background between Fysh and the Postmaster.

'Considering the extreme discomfort for which they were paying, these people must have been in a desperate hurry to go somewhere', he wrote.

In those days the only alternative means of transport [involved] days of bumping over dusty, pot-holed roads followed by an equally uncomfortable train journey. The travelling public was beginning to look for a degree of comfort and convenience. However, the passenger paid for his own accommodation and meals en route and it was only by the purest chance that he was ever provided with a cup of tea at any of the intermediate stopping places.

'At not one of the hotels where we stayed overnight did the publican consider it worthwhile to supply early breakfast to passengers or crew and the pilot, in addition to flying the aircraft and in many instances refuelling and servicing it, was required to wake his passengers, rush down to the hotel kitchen and make a cup of tea and toast for them, help handle their baggage, collect mail from the agent's office, pick up any passengers from their homes or other hotels and then get out to the aerodrome in time to open up the hangar, push the aircraft out with the assistance of any of the passengers who felt strong enough to help at that hour of the day, start up, load up and take off at the first crack of dawn.

'All were obliged to wear flying helmets and regardless of age, sex or physical condition, were forced to scramble up and over by means of foot inserts in the side of the fuselage'.

Flying helmets were obligatory in the early days.

EARLY AIR TRAVEL AND CONDITIONS

Along came the DH50, which had an enclosed cabin—a huge advance for that time. But it remained a work horse rather than a luxury transport. Describing flying from Normanton on the Gulf of Carpentaria to Cloncurry, Affleck wrote:

'Passengers were required to make themselves as comfortable as possible, jammed into the cabin with among other items three or four large cornsacks full of wriggling and twitching fish. Our normal weekly fishy load weighed in at 500–600 lbs. In addition to this there were two or three passengers, suitcases, swags, saddles, rifles, mailbags, sundry items of freight and a couple of savage cattle dogs travelling with their drover master. All had to be fitted into a small four-seater cabin and the resultant congestion had to be seen to be believed'.

Flying in western Queensland had its compensations. Affleck, for instance, describes the good times as 'group captain's weather', compared with routes around Melbourne where he trained. He experienced moments of joy—for instance, after a take-off from Cloncurry at first light, on a medical flight to Camooweal, before returning to Cloncurry for his wedding the next day.

'I set course and climbed to 4000 ft. I could see behind me in the east the faintest lightening as the piccaninny day was born. The sky above the eastern horizon took on a deep pinkish tinge which gradually spread and became fainter. And then, as I looked ahead again, the tops of the higher hills began to glow as though lit from within. This effect lasted only momentarily then, as the sun rose, the whole countryside showed up clean and fresh in the light of the new day. Always since this trip the newborn day, when seen from aloft, has had a special fascination'.

By contemporary standards, the pay was good. When the company was launched, Fysh was paid £500 a year as a pilot, or £10 a week in round terms. The basic wage was then about £4. In 1922, Fysh—still employed as a pilot—went up to £550. When he took over as general manager, his pay went up to £750 and he still routinely flew services, although his time in the air diminished as the airline grew.

Qantas carried its first baby passenger in 1923.

Recalled home from Darwin in May 1920, Fysh decided to return overland. The rainy season had begun and Fysh, blocked by a roaring, flooded river near Cloncurry, was given bush hospitality in a homestead called *Bushby Park*. This was the property of Alexander Kennedy, who was to become a supporter and the first Qantas passenger. Kennedy was full of the ideas he had heard from McGinness, who was still in Cloncurry and who was drumming up interest in forming an air charter company.

McGinness had not been letting the wet-season grass grow under his feet. The young flier and returned soldier, involved in the excitement of the flight from London, had cut a swathe through north-west Queensland's squatter society. One Sunday afternoon, on his way to a picnic, he chanced to meet another leading grazier, Fergus McMaster, who had been driving back to his Devoncourt Station when the front axle of his car broke. McGinness abandoned his excursion and volunteered to help McMaster repair his car. The young airman scoured Cloncurry for parts, then worked with McMaster until the car was running again. His initiative and drive greatly impressed McMaster.

After being reunited in Cloncurry, Fysh and McGinness headed south for the Queensland capital, Brisbane. McGinness was bubbling with enthusiasm for a scheme to start an air-taxi business. As they travelled south, they developed their plan.

McMaster, too, had gone to Brisbane and the pair called on him at the Gresham Hotel to explain their proposal to him. McMaster, a returned soldier and a power in the grazing industry, had political influence as well through the new Country Party. The two fliers could not have found a better and more influential friend.

'*I was quite prepared to assist*', McMaster later wrote, '*not only personally but to raise sufficient capital for the venture.*' He lobbied friends from army service and also his fellow graziers, and the money began to trickle in. McGinness demonstrated his faith in the scheme by putting in £1000 and Fysh invested his savings of £500.

McGinness and Fysh then went to Sydney and ordered two Avro 504K biplanes, the popular training aircraft of the day. They planned to modify them with reliable Sunbeam Dyak engines. The Avro was about 8.8 metres long and had a wingspan of just under 11 metres. It could carry a pilot and sometimes two passengers, cramped into a tiny, open cockpit, at just over 62 miles (100 kilometres) an hour. But the engines were delayed and they had to cancel one of the orders.

Paul McGinness (left) and an aircraft inspector pose with the first Qantas aircraft, an Avro 504K biplane which was delivered in 1921.

15th Feby 1921.
Q'sland & N.T. Aerial
Services Ltd.:
Flying B.E. Aeroplane
Richmond to Longreach
                    130 . 0 . 0
Flying 3 days 4 hours
@ 5.5.0 day . 12.18.4
Petrol & oil . 38.15.7
£81 . 13 . 11

15 : 2 : 21.
Hudson Fysh
bonus for flying
aeroplane to
Longreach from
Sydney :
£5 : 0 : 0

An early record of the costs of the flight from Richmond to Longreach
and a £5 bonus paid to Hudson Fysh for flying to Longreach from Sydney.

By now the embryo company's first brochure was being printed, and McMaster was firmly behind it. The original plan for joy-riding and aerial taxi work had blossomed out into plans for an airmail service from Longreach to Darwin, linking the settlements in between. At that time, it would have been the longest air service in the world. On 16 November 1920, the company Queensland and Northern Territory Aerial Services Ltd was incorporated. It adopted the acronym Q.A.N.T.A.S. (complete with full stops) which, McMaster wrote, had been created *'with Anzac as its inspiring factor'*. McGinness flew the Avro to the new headquarters at Winton, departing Sydney on 31 January 1921. In the absence of any other available aircraft, Fysh flew to Longreach in a BE2E bought by a local stock-and-station agent. Forced landings, storms and the unreliability of the aircraft made it a risky trip.

But the infant airline badly needed a passenger aircraft to start services. It ordered a five-seater Avro triplane, which was dangerously underpowered. McGinness crashed it in Sydney on a test flight, writing off half the capital of the company. Qantas now faced

ruin. Fysh, in the BE2E, was desperately trying to bring money in by offering joy-flights. McGinness rejoined him and, with the Avro, won some lucrative charters and operated even more joy-flights.

It was at this point that McMaster, McGinness and Fysh changed focus again and proposed a plan for an air service to link the western railheads of Longreach and Winton. Captain Edgar Johnston of the Air Board invited them to apply for a subsidy for the service. Qantas rushed out a second prospectus for 15,000 shares at £1 each, to take advantage of what it claimed was an available Commonwealth subsidy of £25,000. Johnston's boss, Lieutenant Colonel H C Brinsmead, the controller of civil aviation, chided the Qantas Board, saying the promise of a subsidy was 'premature'. Notwithstanding, the prospectus pulled out all the stops. *'The service is part of a scheme for the Aerial Defence of the Commonwealth'*, it claimed, *'and from a patriotic standpoint and in the interests of the Commonwealth, it should be supported by all good Australians.'*

Although McMaster had promised to refund money subscribed if the Commonwealth contract was not approved, he used all his political clout to make sure it was. More than a dozen Queensland shires and towns, plus five chambers of commerce and a political group, sent telegrams to the Prime Minister, W M Hughes, urging that it go ahead. Every Queensland Member of the

Hudson Fysh, investor, pilot and aircraft cleaner.

House of Representatives and the Senate joined McMaster to lobby the Prime Minister. Hughes rejected their approach.

A few days later, McGinness seized the opportunity to take a trip on the Melbourne–Sydney train when Hughes was travelling. The persuasive pilot reached a deal. He called McMaster in Brisbane to say that, if the Country Party eased its opposition to the Government's estimates, the Government could find the money for the western Queensland aerial service.

'To support civil aviation', the Country Party in the House a few days later voted with the Government and the estimates were passed. The Air Board delivered with a subsidy of 'up to £12,000' for an air service from Charleville to Cloncurry. Qantas again canvassed its supporters for capital to buy better aircraft, and began planning the new service.

The Air Board demanded that the infant airline buy an untried, heavy British aircraft, the Vickers Vulcan. With strikes at the British plant and other impediments, the Vulcan's arrival was repeatedly delayed, effectively closing down the first Qantas route. As the paymaster, the Air Board called the tune, even insisting that, as no local pilots had experience with 'heavy aircraft', Vickers should supply a pilot from Britain. This recruitment proved difficult, as McMaster had insisted that all Qantas pilots sign a pledge to abstain from alcohol. Not a single Brit with experience was prepared to migrate to the outback to work in the heat and dust without so much as a refreshing ale at the end of a flight.

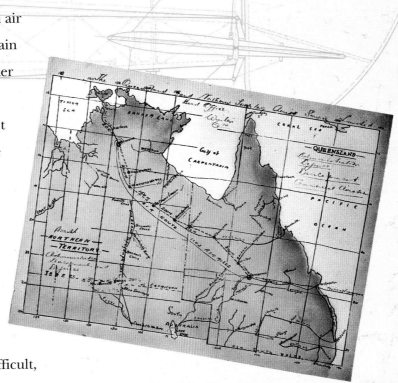

The original route map for Qantas from Darwin to Longreach, marked with all the refuelling stops.

25

Fysh had bought some smaller aircraft, including a DH4, which carried two passengers in a tiny cabin. Two Armstrong Whitworths, slightly faster and bigger than the Avro, carrying three passengers, also became available. The Air Board gave Qantas permission to buy them and it was with one of these, registered G-AUDE (in the old format that gave Australian aircraft British registrations), that they launched the first service with a single passenger and 108 items of airmail.

The restless McGinness flew only two more flights with Qantas. He resigned in mid-November 1922 over McMaster's no-drinking rule (McGinness wanted to be able to have a beer after work). A new pilot, Fred Huxley, was engaged, followed by a third, T Q Black. Then came another resignation which was to have personal significance for Hudson Fysh. Marcus Griffin, the company manager, left. The Board decided Hudson Fysh should 'be given a trial' in the manager's position. He was to remain at the top of Qantas as managing director, then chairman, until 1967.

Meanwhile, the pressure to take the Vickers Vulcan was worrying the Qantas Board and management. But it enabled them to establish the basic principle of technical excellence and the priority of safety which live to this day. Qantas could not allow an outside body to dictate its equipment choice.

Already Arthur Baird, as engineer, and the pilots recognised that the western Queensland

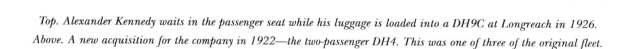

Top. Alexander Kennedy waits in the passenger seat while his luggage is loaded into a DH9C at Longreach in 1926.
Above. A new acquisition for the company in 1922—the two-passenger DH4. This was one of three of the original fleet.

conditions ruled out inadequate aircraft. The Avro triplane had crashed and the Beardmore engines in the Armstrong Whitworths (known as the 'boiling Beardmores', until Baird fitted them with larger radiators) also gave trouble.

On a January day when the temperature in the shade was 110° F, Fysh wrote to Brinsmead, a Vulcan supporter, saying that Qantas had already discovered it was *'positively unsafe'* to fly either the Avro or the Armstrong Whitworths between 11 a.m. and 5 p.m. in summer, so *'could there be any hope for the Vulcans on a hot day?'*

Qantas prudently contracted that the Vulcan must be able to reach a maximum altitude of 10,000 feet and additionally climb to 6000 feet, fully loaded, in 13¹/₂ minutes. The company was prepared to accept a weight restriction to four passengers in summer,

although the Vulcan was supposed to be a six-seater. Fysh wrote: *'The first aim of this company is absolute reliability of machines and safety to passengers. It is only on those conditions that commercial aviation can be built.'*

The Vulcan had a spacious, richly fitted cabin with dove-grey upholstery, hat racks and satin braid. In his history of Qantas, John Gunn describes it as a flying palace for its day. With its swollen fuselage the shape of a great pear, and a single engine and propeller at the pointy end, unimpressed Australians irreverently nicknamed it 'the flying pig'.

The British pilot sent out to demonstrate this 'heavy aircraft' to the Australians was Geoffrey Wigglesworth, who flew in carpet slippers. When the struggling 'pig' eventually reached Longreach for its acceptance demonstration to Qantas, Wigglesworth, covered in grease and dirty after working on the

The Beardmore engines in the Armstrong Whitworths.

Rolls-Royce engine, walked into the local hotel, surveyed the populace in the bar and roared: *'What are all you convict bastards drinking?'* The awed citizens of Longreach quietly named their drinks.

On 27 March, still in the hot season, the tests began. The Vulcan took off with the chairman and directors of Qantas aboard, just clearing the end fence. One observer noted that the engine revolutions were on the emergency figure of 1950 rpm (1850 rpm was the design maximum, with 1950 rpm allowed for only five minutes). There was no way the pig could climb any more than 500 feet. Wigglesworth saw some circling kites, denoting a current or rising air, and joined them. After 45 minutes, at only half payload, the Vulcan had not exceeded 5750 feet. Wigglesworth decided to call it a day and landed the wallowing pig.

Contemporary reports say the directors rushed out as soon as it stopped and, without a word, headed for the Longreach Club. Two days later, the Board met and declared that, as the tests of the Vickers aircraft had proved unsuccessful, the offer was refused. Qantas was to receive £1000 in damages.

The money went into buying a Bristol fighter, a sturdy single-engined aircraft that could lift 1000 pounds (454 kilograms) and carry a pilot and one passenger in an open cockpit. There was a drawback. The Hispano-Suiza engine was lubricated with castor oil, which sprayed back on the passenger, who was invariably nauseous after every trip.

What Qantas had wanted all along was the DH9C, a de Havilland aircraft developed from the DH4. As a bomber, it was one of the most successful combat aircraft of World War I. The order Qantas had placed was not due to be filled until November 1923; meanwhile, the company had problems. Its aircraft were unsuitable and prone to making forced landings when

After 45 minutes, at only half payload, the Vickers Vulcan (above) had not exceeded 5750 feet. Wigglesworth decided to call it a day and landed the aircraft. Contemporary reports say the directors rushed out as soon as it stopped and, without a word, headed for the Longreach Club.

their single engine failed. They were also underpowered. On one trip from Longreach to Cloncurry, Fysh flew the Avro when the shade temperature was 114° F and, in the thin air, could not get the plane higher than 1000 feet for the whole journey. Fortunately he had no passengers aboard.

At the end of September 1923, Qantas's vice-chairman, Dr Hope Michod, warned that the company might have to close. McMaster surprised the Board when, immediately after the DH9s arrived, he suggested Qantas should buy DH50s, which were just completing flight tests in Britain. But the arrival of the DH9s seemed to revitalise the company and Qantas started to struggle back. Spirits were further

lifted by a letter from Brinsmead announcing that the government subsidy of four shillings a mile had been renewed.

The first DH50 arrived in September 1924. Fysh, flight testing it, found it had all-round better performance and a much better payload. For the passengers, the four-seater cabin put an end to the need for cap and goggles. The prime minister of the day, Stanley Bruce, was one of the first to benefit from the new aircraft. At the end of the month, an official party visiting Longreach was cut off by early rains. Fysh flew the prime minister and his party in the new aeroplane while another pilot lifted the luggage and the lesser lights in the DH9.

Above: The first DH50 arrived in September 1924 and was used by Qantas for the Flying Doctor service.

THE FOUNDERS OF QANTAS

Qantas emerged from two crucibles: World War I, and the heat and dust of the Queensland outback. The honours for starting Qantas belong to four men, two of whom—Fergus McMaster and Hudson Fysh—were knighted for their contribution. Fysh, McMaster and the engineer Arthur Baird stayed on and shared the credit for the emergence of Qantas as a world airline.

But it never could have happened without Paul J. ('Ginty') McGinness, the dominant character at the birth of Qantas. His partner Hudson Fysh was to stay with the airline as a pilot, general manager, managing director and chairman until 1967.

Fergus McMaster, who had also served in the AIF, owned western Queensland grazing properties. He contributed the vision that Qantas should become 'an aerial service' rather than a ply-for-hire air-taxi. He took on the grinding pressures of directing the airline through the good years and bad until his retirement in 1947. For nearly all that time he was chairman.

Arthur Baird was a sergeant mechanic when he met McGinness and Fysh. He joined them in Winton and Longreach in the early days, working under harsh conditions to keep the original, old aeroplanes in the air. Later, he was to grow with the airline, developing in capability, until he was managing the maintenance not only of an international airline but also of US and RAAF aircraft throughout the war.

McGinness came from country Victoria and, like Fysh, joined the Australian Light Horse and served on Gallipoli as a sergeant, winning the DCM for bravery. He was a natural leader and in the Australian Flying Corps distinguished himself in the air war.

Fysh, from Launceston in Tasmania, transferred from the Light Horse to the AFC as an observer. It was not until the war had ended that he trained as a pilot. He had relatively little time in his logbook when he was called to fly the second Qantas aircraft from Sydney to Longreach, then to run joy flights and later fly scheduled services.

Those who knew Fysh agreed that he was a dedicated and resolute man. His success was in sticking it out at Qantas, providing first the tenacity, then the continuity that the venture needed as it matured.

A portrait of the first chairman of Qantas,
Sir Fergus McMaster painted by William Dargie.

Born in 1895, Fysh was eight years old when the Wright brothers first flew. In his lifetime he was to see this beginning culminate in a moon landing, the Boeing 747, mass travel and supersonic flight in the Concorde.

McGinness successfully sold his dream to start an aerial taxi service in western Queensland to McMaster and other graziers in the west. He invested his life savings in Qantas at the start-up, then vigorously flew air charters and joy flights in the early days. He also took to the road to sell shares in the fledgling company throughout northern Queensland. At the critical time, it was McGinness's lobbying of Prime Minister William Hughes that won a subsidy for the first Qantas route and allowed it to start scheduled flight services in 1922.

But his restlessness made him move on. For one thing, he objected to McMaster's edict that pilots could not drink, even off duty. Later, McGinness said he felt as though he had been pushed out of the infant Qantas, even though over the years McMaster and Fysh were unfailingly generous in recognising his contribution.

McGinness went on to launch a primary producers' bank in Perth, which later had to be rescued. He took up a property about 450 kilometres north of Perth but drought and depression drove him off. He searched for gold, using a plane to carry out the first mining survey from the air in Western Australia. But nothing came of this venture.

In the mid-1930s, McGinness returned to the eastern states and tried for a job back in aviation, including the Civil Aviation Department; without success. During World War II, he went into the RAAF to train pilots at Point Cook near Melbourne in Victoria and, after he took his discharge, returned to Western Australia to start a farm on a soldier settlement property near Albany. But again the venture failed.

McGinness suffered a heart attack on Christmas Day 1951 and died at the end of January in a Perth hospital.

Paul 'Ginty' McGinness
at Longreach in late 1926.

Lt. Hudson Fysh with the
Australian Flying Corps in Palestine.

Take a "Qantas" Air Taxi

As Cheap as Car Hire
and Four Times as Fast!

QANTAS
GAZETTE

Devoted to the Advancement
of
Commercial Aviation

No. 70—NOVEMBER, 1930

Chapter 2

Longreach to Brisbane

THE GROWING DAYS

The November 1930 edition of an early Qantas magazine.

By 1926, Qantas was firmly established, with a permanent base in Longreach. Its services were operating regularly, despite initial problems with war surplus aircraft that kept breaking down, necessitating forced landings in remote places. The airline's first DH50, with its relatively comfortable cabin, was proving its worth. Arthur Baird and his fitters, fabric workers and mechanics had become expert in sending out the old Talbot truck to salvage a damaged plane and bring it back to the hangar to be repaired.

Operating in such a remote location, Qantas needed a big support staff to respond to emergencies. But when things were going well—which became the norm as the older aircraft were phased out or written off—there was insufficient work. Hudson Fysh and Arthur Baird thought they could keep their skilled staff busy building their own aircraft in the Longreach hangar, instead of retaining them only for emergencies.

The aircraft type chosen was the versatile DH50A. To import one from England cost £2400. Hudson Fysh reported he could build it in Longreach for £2350. Qantas imported engines, tanks, radiators, instruments and most metal parts from England; rolls of linen for the fabric covering from Ireland; and spruce from Canada for the wing spars and longerons, and Queensland maple for the propellers.

Construction of the first Qantas DH50A at Longreach in 1926.

The Qantas office at Longreach in 1921.

The first of these aircraft was rolled out in August 1926, in time to be christened *Iris* by Lady Stonehaven, wife of the Governor-General. The vice-regal party was on a tour of North Queensland, departing next day in the new plane. Maintaining the tradition of named aircraft, Baird's team made two more of this model, *Perseus* and *Pegasus*, the latter christened by Mrs S M Bruce, wife of the prime minister.

Fitted into this production run was another model, a single DH9C which was the development of the successful World War I bomber. While it was a useful aircraft, its cabin seated only two people and there were problems with its centre of gravity. Baird modified the seating to address this problem, making loading much easier and operation even safer.

The original DH50A had some problems during Outback flying. Notably, it was underpowered in the heat of the day. Baird suggested fitting a much more powerful Bristol Jupiter 450-horsepower engine. As Fysh noted, the cost of the modified DH50J was twice as much as the DH50A. But the speed improved from 120 kilometres per hour to almost 170 kilometres per hour and it could carry an extra 136 kilograms. Qantas built three of these: *Atalanta* and *Hermes* in

Passengers wait to board Iris,
the first Qantas DH50A in 1926.

1928 and *Hippomenes* in 1929. Because the engine was more durable and reliable, the DH50Js gave Qantas a remarkable record of safety and reliability.

In a stronger financial position and now confident of operating a scheduled air service, Qantas looked for expansion, south and east to Brisbane and north and west into the Northern Territory. The Empire route from England via India and Singapore to Australia was occupying the minds of many in Australia and Britain. Qantas saw itself strategically positioned on this route.

The company ordered two new eight-passenger DH61 aircraft from England. Hudson Fysh said this meant the end of aircraft construction in Longreach because the aeroplane was too big for the facilities there, and he doubted whether de Havilland would license the design. When the Government finally agreed to permit the route extensions, an old rival for routes and subsidies, Lasco of Victoria, also submitted bids. The DH61s saved the day for Qantas on the important Charleville–Brisbane route, but Lasco was granted the subsidy to fly from the Qantas terminus at Camooweal to Daly Waters in the Northern Territory.

Above: At work fixing the damaged DH50 Pegasus.

Top left: This DH50J, Hippomenes opened the first regular Australia–Britain service on 10 December 1934, flying the Brisbane–Darwin sector.

Bottom left: 'Save days of travel'. Some early Qantas marketing brochures.

To secure its future—in a time of drought and with a receding economy—Qantas badly needed to anchor itself in a State capital and planned to move from Longreach to Brisbane. However, there was a setback in September 1928 when the DH50J *Hermes*, on a charter flight, crashed in the hills north-east of Parafield, the then airport for Adelaide. An engineer was killed and the pilot, Charles W A Scott, was eventually dismissed. His faults were flying blind in cloud, which was forbidden under company rules, carrying cans of petrol in the cabin and his failure to attain 'the standard of care and safety' Qantas required. Scott, heavyweight boxing champion of the Royal Air Force, had been regarded as an excellent pilot. He was later re-employed as an instructor when Qantas launched a flying school in Brisbane. In 1934, Scott won the Centenary air race to Melbourne in the de Havilland Comet racer. The loss of the *Hermes* delayed the Brisbane start-up until after the arrival of the DH61s in April 1929.

P H ('Skipper') Moody took out DH61 *Apollo* from Brisbane to Charleville on 17 April, the day after Lady Goodwin, the governor's wife, had christened the aeroplane. What fascinated the travellers as well as the general public was that this was the first aircraft with a toilet on board. The first Qantas passenger, Alexander Kennedy, by then 91, was on that inaugural flight, wearing a three-piece suit and a felt hat for the occasion. Soon afterwards Qantas became involved in

The first Qantas DH50J, Atalanta, *was completed in March 1928 and operated on all the company's routes.*

The mail arrives at Mount Isa with the ubiquitous Alexander Kennedy looking on.

one of the great dramas of aviation history. The famous Sir Charles Kingsford Smith and Charles Ulm, who had flown the Pacific and twice crossed the Tasman, had gone missing in their Fokker tri-motor *Southern Cross* en route to England. They were eventually found safe near the Glenely River in the north-west of Western Australia at Coffee Royal,

An early version of 'in-ground' refuelling.

and were helped to fly out. But double tragedy struck when Lieutenant Keith Anderson and his mechanic H S Hitchcock took off in the ill-equipped Westland Widgeon *Kookaburra* to join in the search, developed engine trouble on 10 April and were forced down near Wave Hill in the north-west of Western Australia. Qantas provided the DH50J, *Atalanta*, specially fitted with radio, to join in the search. It was flown by Lester Brain (later to become chief pilot) with a two-man crew, engineer Phil Compston and wireless operator Fred Stevens. They spotted *Kookaburra* and the body of one of the aviators and radioed the grim news from the remote cattle property.

A month later Brain was involved in another search in *Atalanta*, finding an aircraft flown by Muir and Owen that had crash-landed at Cape Don lighthouse, south-west of Darwin, after crossing the Timor Sea. Brain, a Point Cook graduate and a RAAF reservist, was awarded the Air Force Cross for his achievements.

Qantas used the DH61 Apollo *to fly the mails to Brisbane.*

39

SUBSIDIES

Australia's network of air services exists today only because of what were, for their time, heavy subsidies. The aircraft available until after World War II could not operate scheduled services economically.

Subsidies were also the order of the day internationally. In the USA, airlines could not operate with economic confidence until the arrival of the Douglas DC 3. This aircraft allowed ticket prices to drop to a level which could attract a market big enough to make the industry viable.

In Australia, subsidies were paid to carry mail, at first on a per-mile basis (initially Qantas received four shillings a mile). In the early 1920s, when the memory of World War I and the importance of military aviation were still fresh, the existence of a strong civil aviation industry was regarded as a defence necessity. Another form of support was an ambitious Government program to build landing fields around the country.

As a result of the subsidy system, the Government's

aviation authority (until the formation of the Department of Civil Aviation, known as the Civil Aviation Board, which grew out of the Defence Department) was highly interventionist in the establishment of air routes. The Government would approve a service, down to specifying the frequency of flights and even the type of aircraft to be used, then call for tenders for its operation.

The process became highly political, particularly as the emphasis on subsidies shifted from building a defence reserve to the requirements of faster transport. Fergus McMaster and Hudson Fysh devoted a disproportionate amount of their time to lobbying local pressure groups, Members of Parliament and Ministers. Strong opposition to air services came from the State railways, which did not want competition. Many air services fed into the railways or linked railheads, as with the original Charleville–Longreach–Cloncurry flights. The height of absurdity came with the early Empire Route from London to Australia, which terminated not in Sydney or Melbourne or even Brisbane but in Cootamundra in southern New South Wales, with passengers and mails being picked up in the early morning by the Melbourne–Sydney express.

Interventionism worked to perpetuate the need for subsidies. The Government and public opinion actively supported the British aircraft industry and its products. The authorities would register for use in Australia only aircraft that were certificated under a European

Air Ports & Agents.....◉
Agents.........................●
Air Lines......................▬
Proposed Air Lines....----
Rail Connections......+++++

convention. US aircraft were certificated by the US authorities and hence were not allowed to fly commercially in Australia until this protection was abolished in 1935. British aircraft were slower and smaller, and their technology lagged behind that of the USA. They tended to have a shorter range, and were more expensive to operate. So they required subsidisation. There were also defence implications in the 'buy-British' policy.

When a route was approved, the authorities would call tenders to operate it. The bids were highly competitive and Qantas's very existence depended on bidding a subsidy lower than its opposition, particularly the Victorian Larkin group (Lasco).

In 1928 the Government called for tenders for two routes which Qantas had promoted (and which were highly strategic for the young airline). One was from Charleville to Brisbane and took the airline's main western Queensland route into the State capital. The other was from Camooweal (to which Qantas had already extended from Cloncurry) to Daly Waters in the Northern Territory. Even at that time Daly Waters was seen as a step along the eventual air route to Darwin, then on to Singapore.

For the Brisbane sector, Qantas bid new DH61 aircraft, carrying eight passengers, twice the capacity of the DH50s that were then in service, for a subsidy rate of three shillings and three pence a mile, reducing by twopence a mile the second year and by another

threepence in the third. Lasco's bid started at the lower rate, but it lost the tender because Qantas's DH61s were superior to the aircraft Larkin proposed. For the Daly Waters sector, Qantas bid four shillings and threepence a mile, reducing to four shillings. Larkin bid three shillings and fourpence, reducing to three shillings. Qantas won the Brisbane route but Lasco was awarded the Daly Waters connection. The Government had made a serious mistake. It had assumed that the Northern Territory railway would extend as far south as Daly Waters; in fact, it stopped about 50 miles (80 kilometres) short at Birdum. Larkin refused to operate the extra distance and Qantas eventually had to fly this isolated sector, building up goodwill with the authorities. Later, as the nation's needs changed, government support for the airlines came through payments to carry airmail, which attracted a surcharge; but in the early days the extra payment for mail did not cover the cost of carrying it.

Until the 1950s, airmail was an important priority for all the governments of the British Commonwealth. However, gradually the rates were set by international agreement (using a gold Swiss franc as the basis for calculations). The mail is still a valuable revenue earner but it has been overtaken by passengers and freight.

In 1929 the gloss was beginning to rub off the bright Qantas picture. The later-model Jupiter engines in the DH61s were costing the company money as well as disrupting its services. As enthusiasm for an air link to Britain grew, West Australian Airways (WAA) began flying from Perth to Adelaide. A strong lobby publicised the fact that the route from the eastern states through Perth to Wyndham and on to what is now Indonesia would be the shortest route and therefore the most logical service to support. WAA was granted a five-year contract based on the weight of mail carried at the rate of twelve shillings and eightpence a pound with guarantees which took the effective subsidy to 760 pounds per flight. WAA ensured that heavy postings from Perth of material such as catalogues provided a maximum load every time. Qantas was told that its subsidy for a considerably smaller amount was being renewed for only six months, with a chance that the Royal Australian Air Force might take over its operations. The rival Lasco was dumped, removing the barrier to Qantas's expansion at the northern end of the route. But more competition was quick to arrive.

On 1 January 1930, Kingsford Smith and Ulm, with the first Australian National Airways (ANA), posed another threat to Qantas by opening an unsubsidised service between Sydney and Brisbane, and in June extended this with a Sydney–Melbourne service. One airline start-up flew along the Queensland coast to Townsville and another started operating to towns in northern NSW.

In 1930 Qantas moved its office to Brisbane. The battle lines were drawn for the next big contest in Australian airline development: which company would fly the Empire Route to Singapore and London, and what path would it take across Australia?

Longreach—Brisbane in 10 Hours.

Modern Travel this—and as SAFE and COMFORTABLE as it is FAST.
Try it—you will agree it is the "ONLY WAY."
THE AIRLINERS 'APOLLO' or 'DIANA,' leave LONGREACH every SUNDAY at 5.30 a.m. calling at BLACKALL, TAMBO, CHARLEVILLE, ROMA and TOOWOOMBA, arriving BRISBANE at 3.30 p.m. the same day. THE RETURN TRIP is carried out on TUESDAYS, BRISBANE being left at 5.30 a.m. and LONGREACH reached at 3.30 p.m. the same day.

REDUCED FARES

Longreach—Charleville	£6/13/	Longreach—Toowoomba	£13/5/
Longreach—Roma	£8/16/6	Longreach—Brisbane	£14/16/

FULL INFORMATION FROM—

Q.A.N.T.A.S. LTD., LONGREACH.

Agents for AUSTRALIAN NATIONAL AIRWAYS, Brisbane, Sydney, Melbourne and Perth.

Right: The first Qantas office in Brisbane on the floor of the Wool Exchange building, situated at 43 Creek Street.

FLYING DOCTORS

The genesis of what is now the Royal Flying Doctor Service can be traced to World War I. A young medical student, Clifford Peel, enlisted in the Australian Flying Corps and brought together his experience in aviation and medicine. From France, he wrote to the Australian Inland Mission (AIM) and outlined how medical services could be brought to the inland using aircraft based at Oodnadatta, Katherine or Cloncurry. Peel was tragically killed in action two months before the Armistice, but his idea survived and flourishes today.

The Reverend John Flynn, who headed the AIM, published Peel's letter in his journal, *The Inlander*. With personal experience of young men injured and killed in accidents in the remote Outback, of women dying in childbirth and the aged languishing because

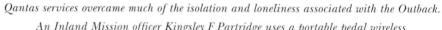

Qantas services overcame much of the isolation and loneliness associated with the Outback.
An Inland Mission officer Kingsley F Partridge uses a portable pedal wireless.

The Rev Dr John Flynn OBE, founder of the Flying Doctor Service.

they could not get care and attention, Flynn started crusading for 'an aerial ambulance service'.

Peel's vision required an aeroplane which could fly safely and reliably into isolated properties, which could carry a medical attendant and a patient on a stretcher. He also saw the need for radios on which the isolated stations and settlements could call for help.

Flynn and Fysh were brought together by their work. The minister kept interrogating the aviator about what the Qantas aeroplanes could do. Eventually, when Qantas took delivery of its DH50As, Fysh wrote to Flynn and told him that a suitable aeroplane was now available. However, it was to be another two or three years before a simple radio transceiver—an ingenious pedal-powered station

invented by Alf Traeger of Adelaide—was built. At first, transmissions were in Morse code, which was not satisfactory as few station people were trained in this method of communication. Traeger invented a typewriter keyboard which allowed senders to punch keys to transmit their messages.

In March 1928 Flynn signed an agreement with Qantas to provide an aircraft and a pilot for the service out of Cloncurry. If a trial of one year proved the concept, Qantas was guaranteed 20,000 flying miles at two shillings a mile. Any unflown miles would be refunded at tenpence a mile. The Civil Aviation Authority, as it then was, offered to pay a shilling a mile towards the cost. One of AIM's great benefactors who helped back the experiment was industrialist Victor McKay, of Sunshine Harvester, who died in 1927. To honour him, the DH50A *Hermes* was renamed *Victory*. Legend has it that, whenever Flynn was photographed alongside the aircraft, he raised his hat to obscure the 'y' making the name of the plane appear to be '*Victor*'.

The first pilot chosen was Arthur Affleck, the first doctor, St Vincent Welch. The work was divided into two categories: visits to bush nursing centres and clinics, and emergency calls. The district was the north-west of Queensland, the Gulf Country and across into the Northern Territory.

One of the many hundreds of patients to be unloaded from a Qantas aeroplane into a waiting ambulance at Brisbane Airport.

Welch was a dedicated medical man whose overriding priority was the patient. Affleck was a careful and cautious pilot, who heeded the perennial Qantas rule: 'Safety is paramount.' The pair often disagreed, particularly when Welch would not accept that an instant take-off would mean landing in the dark on an unknown strip or flying into severe weather. *'What's the use of saving a life if we all die in the process?'* Affleck would challenge him.

There were unusual lighter moments. Affleck and the doctor once landed at Alroy Station, followed closely by another Qantas DH50. Charles Scott emerged to ask his startled colleague, *'Quickly, Arthur, where in the hell are we? I've got the Governor-General on board and we're supposed to be at Brunette [Downs].'*

There were many urgent incidents. Affleck once landed in the main street of Urandangie, passing beneath the telephone lines as he put down between the hotel and the store to care for an old man who had had a heart attack. Other emergencies included appendix operations, accidents among stockmen and a range of life-threatening illnesses. The flying doctors saved a gold prospector who wandered into a property on the verge of dying of starvation and patched up a sleepwalker who stepped off the six-metre-high balcony of a hotel in Mount Isa and woke up in the main street with a fractured pelvis.

Qantas played an important role in bringing medical services to the Outback.

Enlightened, the suave Scott opened the door to let out Lord Stonehaven and his party. *'Your Excellency'*, he said, *'knowing the flying doctor would be here at Alroy, I took it on myself to bypass Brunette so you might meet him and learn something of the work of the service'*. Affleck later recalled that the Governor-General was so delighted that *'he almost decorated Scottie there and then'*.

The aerial ambulance experiment was a success, proving Flynn's wish that it would throw a 'mantle of safety' over the Outback. It was expanded into all States—Victoria and Tasmania supporting units in Western Australia—and began using twin-engined aircraft when they became available. Qantas was eventually to operate aircraft out of Normanton and Charleville, as well as Cloncurry.

After Affleck came Eric Donaldson, the consummate bush pilot, who earned a Distinguished Flying Cross with the Royal Flying Corps during World War I. Donaldson was to take over the Flying Doctor work and also fly for Qantas in north-west Queensland for many years.

Flynn died in 1951, when the 'aerial ambulance' had become the Royal Flying Doctor Service and a national institution. He is remembered by the Flynn Memorial Church at Alice Springs which was opened in 1956. Hudson Fysh, Affleck and many associates of those early days of aviation paid tribute at the dedication ceremony of the Church.

DIANA CLASS

Used by Imperial Airways on certain of its Continental and Empire Routes, by Qantas Empire Airways on the Empire services between Singapore and Brisbane, and by Railway Air Services on internal services in the United Kingdom. The latter Companies are in association with Imperial Airways

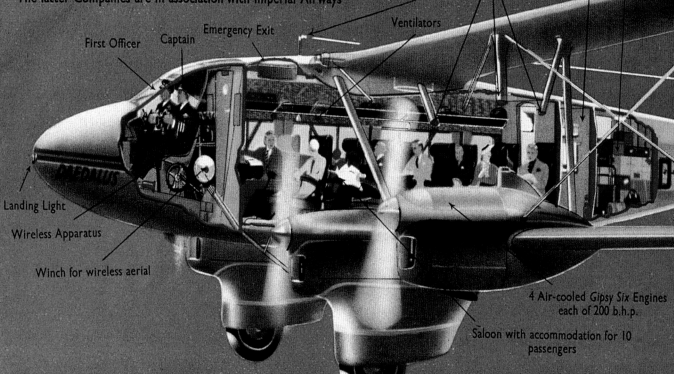

First Officer
Captain
Emergency Exit
Landing Light
Wireless Apparatus
Winch for wireless aerial
Ventilators
Fixed Wireless Aerial
Struts cut away to show cabin
Mail and Luggage Hold
Lavatory
4 Air-cooled Gipsy Six Engines each of 200 b.h.p.
Saloon with accommodation for 10 passengers

The main routes of
IMPERIAL AIRWAYS
and companies in association

○▬▬ Projected routes
●▬▬ The service from Johannesburg to Cape Town is operated by South African Airways.

Imperial Airways	
Delphinus	G-AC
Delia	G-AC
Dorado	G-AC
Daedalus	G-AD
Dione	G-AD
Dardanus	G-AD
Dido	G-AD
Danae	G-AD
Dryad	G-AD
Denebola	G-AD
Demeter	G-AD

Qantas Empire Airways

Canberra	VH-
Brisbane	VH-
Sydney	VH-
Melbourne	VH-
Adelaide	VH-

Span, 64ft. 6ins.;
46ft.; Height, 12ft.
Weight fully loaded, 4
Speed, 175m.p.h.

Aeroplanes and Engines bu
de Havilland Aircraft Com

Chapter 3

First steps overseas

EXPANDING HORIZONS

An international air service becomes a reality for Qantas.

The 1930s saw the maturing of commercial airlines in Australia. The decade was to bring a rationalisation of the older domestic operators, the launching of some new companies and the inauguration of international services.

The 1930s began with a valiant attempt by two of Australia's most renowned pilots, Sir Charles Kingsford Smith and Charles Ulm, to launch their own airline, the first Australian National Airways (ANA). The company's maiden flight was between Sydney and Brisbane on 1 January 1930. The service, in an eight-passenger Avro X aircraft, was scheduled to take five hours but, because of strong headwinds, took seven hours. The fare was £9 13s—more than twice the basic weekly wage. But the venture proved popular and initially profitable. The airline opened up a second service between Sydney and Melbourne in June, which also carried freight.

ANA brought a powerful new force into the highly politicised world of airlines. Unlike the others—Qantas in Queensland, WAA in Western Australia, Jim Larkin's company Lasco, based in Victoria—ANA had no subsidies from the Government. For all of them, economic conditions were tightening. Qantas, particularly, was feeling the pinch because there had been a severe drought in Queensland.

Behind the public interest in aviation lay the Australian feeling of isolation. It took about six weeks by ship for Australians to visit Britain, which many of them regarded as home. Fast air transport would overcome their isolation. Individual fliers cut the time

The 1930s began with a valiant attempt by two of Australia's most renowned pilots, Sir Charles Kingsford Smith and Charles Ulm, to launch their own airline, the first Australian National Airways.

of the Britain–Australia journey from the weeks of that first flight to a fortnight in 1919, then to a Kingsford Smith record of 10 days in October 1930. The exploits of the record-breakers fostered intense Government and general interest in the question of when an air link would be established, predominantly to carry mail.

From the first days, Fergus McMaster and Hudson Fysh had realised that, because Qantas operated over the potential 'inland' route from Sydney to London, an extension to Brisbane was an essential part of this greater strategy. Similarly, Qantas looked north-west to Darwin. Lasco's money-losing intrusion into the Camooweal-Daly Waters segment was seen as a block to this long-term ambition. The Qantas operation over the 80-kilometre gap, from Daly Waters to Birdum,

which was needed to link the air service to the Northern Territory railway but which Larkin refused to cover, cost Qantas money but established it in government eyes as the natural airline over the entire route to Darwin.

The big threat to the Empire came from the Dutch. Albert Plesman's KLM Royal Dutch Airlines had established a route to Batavia (now Jakarta) as early as 1929. It needed only a relatively short, 820-kilometre hop across the Timor Sea to link Australia with Europe. Norman Brearley, the great Western Australian pioneer, pressed for this easy option. But for Australians, brought up with a British Empire inked red on the maps and forming a geographic chain from Australia to Britain, the idea of using a Dutch carrier was unthinkable.

The biggest player in the Empire air game was Britain's Imperial Airways, created when the British Government forced the amalgamation of many of the struggling carriers which emerged after the war. Using British aircraft from makers such as de Havilland and Vickers, powered by engines from Bristol and Rolls-Royce, Imperial Airways reached eastwards towards Australia when it extended its Middle Eastern route to India in 1929.

In 1931 the British Post Office fired the public imagination by announcing two experimental round-trip airmail services between Britain and Australia. In April 1931 Imperial was to carry the mail to Delhi, then to Darwin. Qantas would fly it to Sydney. On the first flight, the DH66, *City of Cairo*, carrying the mail from Karachi to Darwin, ran short of fuel and crash-landed near Koepang in Timor on 19 April. Qantas was helpless to go to the rescue because it had no multi-engined aircraft to fly over water. Kingsford Smith and pilot G U ('Scotty') Allan flew to Timor and brought the mail into Darwin on 25 April. On that day the Qantas DH61 *Apollo* left Brisbane with the return mail, which was loaded into *Southern Cross* in Darwin and carried to Akyab in Burma to connect with Imperial.

The second experimental mail left London also on 25 April. Imperial flew to Akyab and connected with *Southern Cross*—which flew back to Darwin. Captain Russell Tapp met it there in the DH61 *Apollo*. Imperial had bought a multi-engined DH Hercules from WAA and carried the return mail back to Britain. Because of the *City of Cairo's* accident, the first London–Brisbane onward trip was completed in 24 days, the second in 18. The return mails took 19 days and 16 days respectively.

The *Southern Cross* rescue mission showed that Qantas had neither the aircraft nor the experience to fly long, over-water routes. Kingsford Smith and Ulm were capitalising on the publicity when their ANA, on a flight from Sydney to Melbourne on 21 March, lost the Avro X *Southern Cloud*. Despite a huge search it was not found until discovered by chance in the mountains in 1958. The loss of the aircraft and falling passenger numbers caused mainly by the worsening depression eventually sent ANA into bankruptcy.

McMaster, a long way from Brisbane on his property, *Moscow*, near Longreach in western Queensland, and even further away from London, was thinking and planning about the future of Empire services. In May he wrote to Hudson Fysh with the first suggestion that a joint venture between Imperial and Qantas would be the best tool for the job. McMaster always saw Qantas as being an equal partner in the venture, operating through to Singapore.

Later that year, fighting to make a comeback, Kingsford Smith and Ulm mounted an all-Australian

The first stage of the Britain–Australia air journey.
Passengers boarding an Imperial Airways aircraft at Croydon, London.

return flight to London with Christmas mail. Under the command of Allan, carrying 52,000 items of mail and one passenger (the controller of civil aviation, Colonel Brinsmead), the Avro X *Southern Sun* left Melbourne on 21 November and made good time as far as Alor Star, in Malaya near the Thai border. Attempting a take-off from a water-logged airfield, the aircraft's central motor failed and it crashed. Unhurt, Brinsmead decided not to wait for the relief sister aircraft, *Southern Cross*, which 'Smithy' was readying, travelled on to Bangkok and caught a KLM aircraft. This also crashed on take-off, killing five. Brinsmead was severely injured, became incapacitated and died several years later, in 1934.

Southern Cross continued, collected Allan in Alor Star on 5 December and delivered the mail on 16 December. On the return journey, this aircraft was damaged at Croydon and the departure was delayed until 7 January. It arrived in Sydney on 21 January.

At home, Brearley in Western Australia floated the idea of a merger between ANA, WAA and Qantas which would operate at home and overseas. Later he proposed involving the Government and possibly a railways representative in the company. The amalgamation proposal was to be debated many times over the next two years but eventually collapsed because of financial and personal clashes.

The first airmail bags from Melbourne to London being loaded for the journey on 24 April 1931.

The political stew, stirred by frequent media comment and agitation from Larkin supporters in Melbourne, behind the front of an organisation calling itself the Air Convention, was placed before a new controller of aviation, Captain Edgar Johnston, also a Light Horseman who served in Gallipoli, then in the artillery and finally as a pilot with the Royal Flying Corps. Johnston was to be a major figure in aviation development over the next 30 years.

In February 1932 Hudson Fysh met Sir Walter Nicholson, the government representative on the Board of Imperial Airways. They reached a 'gentleman's agreement', even then an old-fashioned description of how Qantas and Imperial were eventually to work together in one form or another until about 1970. The eventual agreement, which saw Imperial and the old Qantas establish the jointly owned Qantas Empire Airways (QEA), contained the clause: *'It is the intention of both parties that each shall have a "square deal" in the sense that expression is understood by fair and reasonably minded men.'*

In June 1932, Australia established an inter-departmental committee, which Johnston chaired, to evaluate the claims by Imperial, KLM and the various

C A Fisher, Superintendent of Mails, Brisbane, proudly holds the inaugural Brisbane–Singapore Royal Mail bag.

Australian groupings to operate an overseas air mail service. There were basically three proposals. One was to let the Dutch service to Batavia connect to Australia at either Wyndham or Darwin. Another was to extend the Imperial service to India through to Australia, perhaps by linking up with an Australian carrier at Singapore. The third was to subsidise an Australian company, which would link with Imperial at Singapore. The committee reported to the Minister for Defence in November. It recommended that there should be an air mail service to Britain. And it also called for the Commonwealth to sponsor the service from Darwin to Singapore. Internally, there should be connecting services from Katherine to Perth, Darwin to Cootamundra, New South Wales (on the main railway line between Melbourne and Sydney) and a service mainly along the existing Qantas route to Charleville, extending to Roma which is linked by rail to Brisbane. Johnston advocated the extension to Brisbane but the other departments overruled him. It also called for a Melbourne–Hobart service, via King Island. In December a cabinet sub-committee accepted the report.

The first Qantas step in February 1933 was to rule out an alliance or merger with the other Australian airlines in favour of the partnership with Imperial.

Throughout 1933 there was public ridicule in Australia and Britain at the concept of terminating the service in Cootamundra. But the Government remained adamant when it called for tenders for the new services in September. The tenders made it clear that an Australian

company was required, so the name of Qantas Empire Airways was chosen, and the company was registered on 18 January 1934. The old Q.A.N.T.A.S. was to become a holding company.

With the tenders due on 31 January, the most important step was selecting an aircraft for the new service. Qantas chose the DH86, which was offered with either the Gypsy IV or Gypsy VI engines. The former was considerably cheaper but slower and included in one of the tender options because the price was lower. But the preferred option was five DH86s, with the more powerful engine.

This model weighed 6000 pounds and could cruise at more than 230 kilometres an hour. The fuselage was basically a plywood box and the wings had wooden spars. On 19 April the Prime Minister, Joe Lyons, announced that Qantas, with the faster aeroplane and lower subsidy requirement, had been chosen to operate the Darwin–Singapore service for five years. Qantas also won the Darwin–Brisbane via

The DH86 Commonwealth Class aircraft could carry
10 passengers and two crew and flew the Australia–Singapore
and Brisbane–Darwin air mail routes.

The DH86 was the flagship of the Qantas fleet when
the company launched its international services.

The interior of the DH86 which
flew the Brisbane–Singapore leg of the
journey to London in the 1930s.

Charleville route but the connecting flight from Charleville to Cootamundra was awarded to Butler Air Transport. Unasked, Qantas had bid for a combined operation. The Government accepted this to achieve a minor saving.

Hudson Fysh was later to produce strong evidence to support the choice of the DH86. The previous year he had visited both Britain and the USA to look at new aircraft and had been mightily impressed by both the Boeing 247 and the prototype DC1, later to be developed into the DC2 and DC3. US aircraft were still banned in Australia because imports were restricted to those certificated under the Paris Convention of 1919, which barred US-certificated aircraft. But, Hudson Fysh was to write, the DH86 compared in speed with the Boeing and, while nominally much slower than the DC2 or DC3, proved to be about the same in operations. It was, however, the only new aircraft available with four engines, which he regarded as essential for safe operation over water.

Refuelling and loading a cargo of Phillips valves in Batavia.

While the Government was faced with spending large amounts of taxpayers' funds over the next five years, it considered it had won a bargain. Under the new system, route mileage rose by 95 per cent but the subsidy by only nine per cent. Anticipated airmail revenues would in fact reduce the total by 30 per cent. Johnston and his fellow committee members badly underestimated the public's demand for faster airmail. The volume grew so much after the service started that it swamped Qantas. At peak mail times, the airline could carry only one passenger on the flight to Singapore, which hurt it because, under the agreement, Qantas received the passenger fares and any freight earnings. In the first year of the service, during 1935, Hudson Fysh was to calculate that the Government was 'breaking even' as mail surcharges balanced payments.

Until 1934, Qantas had operated only single-engined aircraft and then over land in flying conditions which, while sometimes uncomfortable, enjoyed generally clear weather. If engine problems arose there were plenty of places where the aircraft could land. The introduction of overseas services was to change Qantas's operations forever. It had to train pilots in new techniques of flying and navigation, establish new workshops and build a support organisation in Darwin, at several points in Indonesia and in Singapore. Qantas also had to establish a traffic organisation to handle a long-distance air route. To improve its accounting and lessen the burden on Hudson Fysh, it brought in a new accountant, Cedric Oban Turner, who eventually succeeded his boss as the head of the airline.

Captain 'Scotty' Allan in mid-1935.

The build up to the launch of the airmail service in December 1934 was a period of frantic activity—and also disaster—for Qantas and a second airline.

The first came when the DH50J, *Atalanta,* flew low over McMaster's property *Moscow* outside Longreach to drop papers and mail. The burned out wreck was found later a short distance away. An inquiry surmised that the pilot, Norman Chapman, was tired, had lost concentration while flying low and crashed into the ground, killing himself and two passengers.

Now there was trouble with the new DH86. Qantas and Imperial had agreed that de Havilland could sell the DH86 type to the winner of the Tasmanian services, which turned out to be Holyman Airways, run by the shipping family. The first of these, *Miss Hobart,* was to disappear on its second flight across Bass Strait. The only wreckage recovered was a seat. Then the second Qantas DH86, at the end of its delivery flight from London, crashed after leaving Longreach on 16 November. The aircraft type was grounded.

Servicing the DH86 at the Qantas maintenance depot at Archerfield aerodrome near Brisbane.

With the service due to be inaugurated in Brisbane on 10 December, Qantas made available a DH61 flown by Lester Brain and a DH50 flown by Russell Tapp. The Duke of Gloucester, in Australia for a royal visit, cut a ribbon which 'released' the first aircraft, after speeches by the Prime Minister and Minister for Defence. An Imperial Airways aircraft *Arethusa*

and strengthened the fin post fittings and the rudder tab. Allan and Brain, two veteran pilots with experience of the type, suspected that the cause may have been the way the aircraft was loaded. So, with the modifications and rigorous attention paid to weight distribution, the DH86 returned to service.

On 29 January RMA *Canberra*, commanded by

Testing the rubber dinghy in the hangar at Darwin.
It was stored on the DH86s for emergencies.

received the mails at Darwin. Augmented by services from Cootamundra and Perth, it loaded 55,967 items of mail, which reached London on 24 December.

Baird had stripped the first DH86 after studying reports from two kangaroo shooters who saw the Longreach accident. They said the plane had turned in a wide flat circle and had then crashed into the ground. Baird suspected the variable fin was at fault

Brain, left Brisbane for Darwin, where Imperial was still collecting the mails. On 26 February, again with *Canberra* but with Allan in command, the first Qantas multi-engine, international service was cleared for take-off to Singapore. That wood-and-fabric biplane was the forerunner of the Super Constellations which were to circle the world 23 years later, establishing Qantas as a leader among international airlines.

FLYING IN THE 1930s

To modern readers accounts of the first DH86 services from Brisbane to Singapore are a nostalgic reminder of things past.

After a seven o'clock departure, the first of six stops was at Charleville, where often there would be a wait while Arthur Butler arrived from Cootamundra with the Sydney and Melbourne mails. Then to Cloncurry for an overnight stay at the Post Office Hotel. Everyone had to carry their own suitcases up to the bedrooms on the first floor. Next morning, they continued their flight to Camooweal to refuel and to Katherine, to pick up more mails. A 300-kilometre flight to Darwin completed the day.

Passengers and crew stayed overnight at the Qantas rest house, a cottage in the grounds of Vesteys meatworks on the edge of a cliff overlooking the sea. It cost £2 a week to rent—which Hudson Fysh thought excessive—but passengers and pilots wrote warmly about the hospitality and the pleasure of sitting on the verandah and enjoying the ocean view at the end of a long day in the air.

Early next morning came the departure from Australia. Ahead lay the Timor Sea: the 820-kilometre over-water haul for which the four-engined DH86s had been bought.

'Scotty' Allan later wrote about using Cape

Refuelling at Koepang in Timor.

Fourcroy, about 160 kilometres from Darwin, as a positional check. For much of the journey, the sea lies over the shallow Australian continental shelf.

'On days of fine weather the 350-odd miles [about 560 kilometres] of shallow water revealed easily seen whales, enormous turtles, flying fish and very large sharks', Allan wrote in a note to Hudson Fysh.

'The shadow of an aeroplane on the sea ... [provided] an accurate and easy measurement of the length of whales and sharks ... One shark was observed to be just short of 40ft [13 metres] long.

'...the extremity of the Australian shelf is easily observable as it rises to within six or eight feet [2–2.5 metres] of the surface within 140 miles [about 225 kilometres] of Koepang. Immediately after crossing this strip of cheerful light green, the bottom of the sea falls away to an awe-inspiring black depth of about 6000 feet [about 1820 metres]'.

The flight was never boring. The winds were seasonal and Allan found that they blew in one direction on the surface and another at altitude. So by crossing below 30 metres in one direction and coming back about 275 metres in the other he could get tail winds each way.

The cloudscape was always interesting. In the monsoon, when aircraft could not climb over the storms, they would fly around the rain columns marching across the sea. Darwin weather helped with observations, aided by the release of little rubber balloons carrying a lantern that could be tracked. Qantas pilots bought the balloons for the equivalent of $1.50 for a box of 144 in Singapore. These observations, incidentally, laid the foundation for one

Aboard a Qantas DH86 over the Timor Sea on the Britain–Australia service in 1935.

of the great meteorological discoveries of the 1980s and 1990s: the temperature of the sea and wind patterns north and west of Darwin constitute one of the engines of the Southern Oscillation, the weather pattern that drives the El Niño currents and brings droughts or floods to Australia and other parts of the world.

Fuel consumption was an obsession with Allan, perhaps from Scots parsimony but more likely to ensure that he had endurance for any emergency. He was constantly fiddling with the mixture, his first officers noted. At Koepang, 'Scotty' learnt, petrol was cheap and he could get a few precious extra gallons into the tank by turning the aeroplane round to face downhill.

Koepang was a refuelling stop set up by the Shell company. From there it was on to Lombok Island in the Indonesian chain for an overnight stop. Hudson Fysh later wrote that there were only three bedrooms, and passengers had to share the big beds with 'dutch wife' bolsters separating them. For bathing there were the 'chatties', the big earthenware jars of evaporation-cooled water. You stood alongside and dipped water out for a splash-bath.

The only navigation aids were radio stations such as those at Koepang and Darwin. To check the course over the sea, pilots used a drift sight. They would line the sight up on some flotsam or a white patch left by a breaking wave, then track the angle as the aircraft flew on its track. They would do the same thing again, flying across the track at 90°. From the two, they could calculate how much the wind was pushing them off

All the 'mod-cons'. Adjusting the air vents on board the DH86.

course, and correct accordingly.

Qantas was not cleared for night flying, other than between Cloncurry and Longreach, which was the night stop southbound. On this 500-kilometre sector, there were revolving beacons every 100 kilometres or so. Only very limited operations were permitted in cloud. On one occasion, when a DH86 was delayed and Darwin radio had gone off air, the crew tuned in to the commercial station in Darwin as bad weather hampered visibility. (With direction finding using one station, the transmitter can lie either on one bearing or the opposite, the reciprocal. It can be hard to determine which is which.) The pilot, running low on fuel, started flying along one of the bearings, measuring the strength of the signal, which fortunately increased as he got closer. In Darwin, Allan had taken to the air in another aircraft and circled the aerodrome firing rockets. As dark gathered, the lost aircraft saw the lights and came in for a successful landing.

Cabin service consisted of the first officer coming back to chat with the passengers, getting out the thermos of tea and handing around sandwiches. The meals along the way were on the ground—and to Australian palates of the 1930s they tended to be exotic. The Dutch in the Indies put dinner on the table as late as 10 p.m., and 'Scotty' earned company displeasure by taking the head of the table wearing his pyjamas. Hudson Fysh remembers the 'sumptuous' breakfasts, such as the fried eggs, bacon and bananas at Koepang. One passenger had high praise for 'Jim Synnott's breakfast, put on at Camooweal'.

*Qantas Empire Airways route map
for the Darwin–Singapore section.*

IMPERIAL AIRWAYS

EUROPE · AFRICA · INDIA · CHINA · AUSTRAL

Chapter 4

Flying boats

LUXURY ALOFT

Left: An Imperial Airways brochure from the 1930s illustrates passengers embarking at a foreign port.

Despite continuing worries on the part of the Civil Aviation authorities about the airworthiness of the DH86 following the loss of another Holyman aircraft, the Brisbane–Singapore service was a complete success. Adopting a cautious approach, the authorities did not clear the over-water flights to carry passengers until April 1935. On the first service, the passengers were Lady Mountbatten, the wife of Lord Louis, and Major A Philips of the Coldstream Guards. However, because of the success of the Singapore flight and because the same aeroplane was also serving the Outback, the people who had supported Qantas from its start were being deprived of service. Qantas began lobbying its paymaster, the government, to 'duplicate' the service. As Hudson Fysh pointed out, mail revenues were three times the budget and earning more than £45,000 a year above estimates. A departmental study confirmed this financial bonanza but it was not until February 1936 that the Government allowed the second weekly flight to proceed. The first of the new services was not to leave until May because Qantas had to recruit and train extra pilots.

Captain G U 'Scotty' Allan, commander of RMA Canberra *on 17 April 1935.*

From left to right: Squadron Leader A E Hempel, Flight-Lieut. C S Riccard, A R McComb and Sergeant Elder at the Roper River in Arnhem Land the survey of the flying boat route in May 1936.

Meanwhile, Imperial Airways was pushing an ambitious scheme to carry all Empire mails by air at surface rates, and had commissioned Short Brothers to build an all-metal, four-engine Empire-class flying boat for the task. The airline ordered 28 of them off the plan. Imperial wanted Qantas to become a part of the scheme but the Australian Government worried about the cost and the loss of sovereignty in the British plans. There was also strong opposition within the Australian Government to flying boats. The Royal Australian Air Force (RAAF) did not want a bar of them, sending on a survey mission an expert who claimed that landing areas that met the conditions for the big Short boats did not exist. The controller, Captain Edgar Johnston, thought the future lay in US landplanes.

Taking the practical view, Hudson Fysh realised that by 1939 the DH86 contract would have ended and there were no four-engined landplanes immediately available for over-water operations. Pan American, increasingly regarded as a rival encroaching from the Pacific, had pioneered its routes with the big Sikorsky, and later Martin, flying boats to Asia. Fergus

Passengers experience some of the luxury aboard the Short S23 C Class flying boat.
Quoits or clock golf could be played on the promenade deck.

Refuelling the first flying boat, Coolangatta, *at Groote Eylandt during its first flight to England in 1938.*

McMaster returned from Britain confident that flying boats were the only answer. And Lester Brain, as chief pilot, wholeheartedly endorsed them.

In Singapore in May 1936 Hudson Fysh joined Major H G ('Brackles') Brackley, Imperial's operations director, for the start of a flying boat route survey to Australia using a Short Singapore III boat. It was the first time Fysh had seen an automatic pilot. They found landing areas near Banka Island, Surabaya and in the open sea off Koepang. The Indonesian waters were generally so calm that even on open beaches fishermen could launch their nets and prahus into a sea that rippled, almost without waves.

At Darwin, the survey selected an area of the harbour near the town. Travelling across Arnhem Land, they found that the lonely Roper River had ideal reaches of deep water, although it was virtually uninhabited. They flew on, landed at Mornington Island and Karumba, then continued to Townsville, down the coast to Bowen and finally landed on the Hamilton reach of the Brisbane River. The choice in Sydney was the harbour at Rose Bay.

The politics were complex. But Qantas and the Australian Government were able to get guarantees of control of the route from Singapore, even though the flying boats would be operated interchangeably between the Imperial and Qantas fleets and fly to Britain.

In January 1937 Prime Minister Joe Lyons announced Government agreement for both the Empire mails and flying boat schemes, with a contribution to the capital as well as operating costs under a 15-year contract. However, the Government would not agree to mails being carried at ordinary rates and insisted that the surcharge continue. Qantas said it would need a fleet of six flying boats and sought £480,000 ($960,000) new capital from its shareholders to pay for them.

Meanwhile, in the financial year to 31 March, it was plain that the landplane service was under pressure. Passenger miles were up 114 per cent (the passengers had included Noel Coward and Charlie Chaplin), mail carriage was up 48 per cent and freight was up 87 per cent.

Lester Brain led the Qantas contingent of seven pilots and two engineers, plus engineering manager Arthur Baird, to Britain to train on the flying boats.

They had already experimented with yachts and had flown a floatplane in Singapore as a taste of the very different techniques that lay in store. For Qantas, the flying boats were to open a new era.

At first the intention was to do all the maintenance and overhaul in Britain. There was a sniff of war in the air and Hudson Fysh prudently lobbied to get an engine overhaul base in Sydney. Otherwise, he said, any engines that were removed would have to be sent by ship to Britain and returned, taking about four months. The lessons learnt in the Queensland Outback were applicable to operating at the far end of the world's longest air route.

Interest was mounting in New Zealand for a trans-Tasman air service. The crossing of just under 2000 kilometres compares with the 3180-kilometre flight across the Atlantic from Newfoundland to Ireland, which was not to get a regular air service until 1939. Pan American was to reach Auckland from

Corio *takes off.*

Honolulu in early 1938. The Tasman service was agreed in March 1938.

Preparing for the flying-boat service, Qantas started moving its headquarters from Brisbane to Sydney in May 1938, taking space in the Shell building. For the first time Qantas also began planning to provide cabin service on the new aircraft. It recruited Bill Drury, a former Imperial Airways steward, who arrived as crew on the first flying boat delivery and began training locally-recruited men as stewards. As Fysh wrote: *'They developed in the first few years a standard of attention which was destined to lead the world and lives on today in Qantas service aloft'.* The 15 passengers in three cabins were to enjoy quality meals with a drinks service, even though the boats did not have a galley. Cold drinks and mixes came aboard in ice-boxes; hot foods—from poached eggs to roasts— were carried in Thermos and vacuum flasks. A speciality, at least on the early stages of flights from Sydney and Brisbane to Singapore, were trays of

oysters kept on ice. The helpings were so generous, that often the passengers could not finish them.

The first two flying boats, *Coolangatta* and *Coogee* flew to Rose Bay on 10 June, as part of the move. However, the government which had pledged to build the support structure for the flying boat service had done little construction. At Rose Bay, neither the slip nor the hangar had been started. The agreement for Qantas to run three flying boat services a week from Sydney to Singapore (which Imperial would take through to Britain) was signed on 23 July 1938.

The first service preceded the official agreement. Under the command of Captain Lynch Blosse, Empire flying boat *Cooee* departed Rose Bay on 5 July 1938 for Singapore, from where an Imperial crew took it on to Southampton. The Imperial flying boat *Challenger* arrived in Darwin on 4 July, under the command of Captain 'Scotty' Allan, in darkness and during a gale. The arrival was disastrous. Passengers, left in the aircraft as it tossed at its moorings, became

A common sight in the 1930s, the three flying boats Champion, Calypso *and* Coolangatta *moored in Rose Bay, Sydney. Maintenance crews work on* Champion *and* Calypso.

(Following pages) 'The inside story'. A diagrammatic representation of the interior of the flying boats in a Qantas brochure.

seasick and had to be taken ashore up the gangway of a ship in port.

The Empire Airmail scheme was inaugurated, departing Sydney on 4 August and Britain on 6 August. On arrival at Sydney, the mail load was found to be 2.5 tonnes. According to Hudson Fysh, for Christmas 1938, 240 tonnes of mail were sent from Britain on the Empire Route, with incoming mail at about the same level. Thirty-three landplane flights, along with 31 flying boat services and a seaplane, were enlisted to carry the mails along the route. Not all came to Sydney, but 42 services operated into and out of the New South Wales capital in the five-week period. Many of the flying boats were stripped of all their passenger fittings so that they could lift more mail.

The journey from Sydney to Southampton took nine days, a day longer than the rival Dutch KLM/KNILM (the Indonesian subsidiary) service. Although the Dutch had accidents and delays, Albert Plesman, the visionary KLM boss, announced plans for a three-day service by 1941. But the war was to interrupt this timetable.

Qantas lost its first flying boat, the *Coorong*, which was moored at Darwin for the overnight stop on 12 December 1938. As the wind strengthened in the evening, *Coorong* strained on the cable and the station engineer, Norm Roberts, went aboard to run the engines and take some of the strain. Later the mooring line broke and the big aircraft blew ashore on the breakwater. *Coorong* was salvaged, dismantled and sent to Shorts in England for rebuilding. A few months later, in March 1939, the Imperial flying boat *Capella* was taxying into Batavia harbour when it struck a submerged wreck, ripping out the bottom of the hull. The aircraft was written off as a result.

The flying boat service to Singapore and Britain operated for just over 13 months, until the outbreak of war on 3 September 1939. In that time, with few

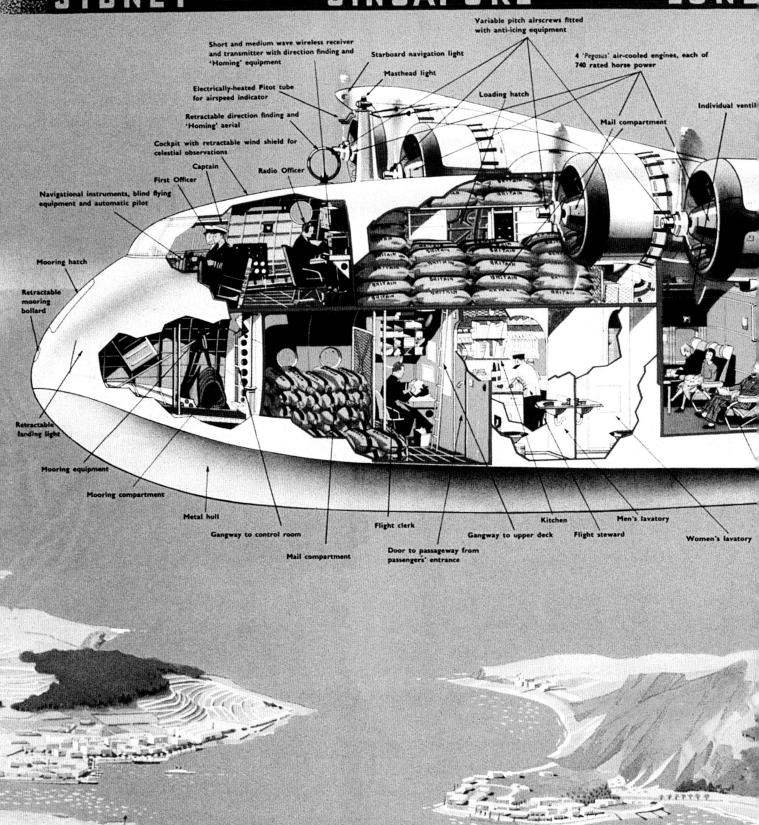

Fixed aerials

All-metal wing

Port navigation light

Freight hatch

International registration marking

Mail, freight and baggage hold

Adjustable chairs

Aft cabin

Flaps fitted to trailing edges of the wing

Promenade cabin

Wing tip float

IMPERIAL AIRWAYS

EUROPE · AFRICA · INDIA · THE FAR EAST · AUSTRALIA · U.S.A. - BERMUDA

*The cockpit of the Hythe flying boat
introduced into service in 1946 by BOAC.*

interruptions, Qantas flew three services a week in both directions, carrying more than 5000 passengers, about 500 tonnes of mail and about 100 tonnes of freight. The cargo service marked the start of what was to become a huge industry: the export of seafood, which started with three dozen oysters to Singapore and built up to 400 dozen a week.

As it went into World War II the RAAF changed its attitude towards flying boats. An Australian squadron was in Britain training on Sunderlands and the Government made these available for Coastal Command for the duration. Consequently, the RAAF urgently needed flying boats at home. It took over two Qantas flying boats, *Coogee* and *Coolangatta*, and also two Imperial boats which were in Sydney, *Centaurus* and *Calypso*. These were fitted with long-range tanks and machine-gun mounts. Fifteen Qantas pilots, air crew and engineers went with them.

The war ended an era for Qantas and for flying boats, an era that had hardly begun. But it was a valuable interlude for Qantas, which had to develop advanced engineering facilities and also a passenger service system to support the flights. In particular the engineering bases that had been—and were to be—established ensured the survival of the airline throughout the war and laid the foundation for its aggressive resumption when peace returned. For Fergus McMaster and Hudson Fysh, running an airline had a steep learning curve as Qantas, at first a mere outback carrier, expanded to the metropolitan centre of Brisbane and finally overseas.

In the maintenance hangars, Arthur Baird faced a parallel engineering task. Not only had the emphasis changed, since the patch-and-mend days, but the technology was advancing at a headlong rate. At the same time, the number of staff he needed to manage grew at a rate that was to become exponential during the war years and the rapid airline expansion that followed. Australia had no huge pool of trained and licensed engine and airframe mechanics like the USA and Britain. Neither did it have the relatively big military services of the Europeans and Americans, which trained thousands of maintenance staff.

Even in the early days at Longreach, Qantas had taken the decision to develop its own trained personnel. Baird recruited Dudley Wright who was later to succeed him as chief engineer and set up an apprenticeship scheme in 1927. Jack Avery, the son of a local garage proprietor, was the first apprentice; Bill Bennett the second. Two years later, when Qantas had established a flying school in Brisbane and extended its services to the Queensland capital, Eric Kydd also started an apprenticeship. Baird recruited two brothers, Norm Roberts in 1934 and George in 1936. All of these people, initially hands-on, hangar-floor workers, developed into senior executives in an engineering and maintenance organisation. Keeping hundreds of Allied aircraft in the air through the war years helped Qantas to become a top-ranking international airline with an engineering staff numbering about 6000.

Not all Qantas engineers were home-grown. Ern Aldis, who had served his apprenticeship with the Kingsford Smith and Ulm Australian National Airways, went to Britain to qualify for flying boat licences and was given a job with Imperial at Hythe, the flying boat base. He was assigned to check inspection of the new Shorts flying boats and later remembered how, working on a wing behind an engine one day, he heard a gruff voice call: *'G'day, what's your name?'* Aldis gave it. Then the voice went on: *'Come out and talk to me. My name is Arthur Baird. I'm looking for bloody Australians with licences to work for us on flying boats in Sydney.'* Aldis was to become one of Baird's strongest executives.

In the early days, the Qantas planes had wooden airframes and wing structures, covered with linen. They began to acquire radios, then gyro instruments for night and 'blind' flying. George Roberts set up a one-man overhaul shop for instruments.

With the flying boats came all-metal construction, advanced radial engines, passenger amenities such as galleys, and in the cockpits delicate instruments such as automatic pilots. Each of these advances required special training, and involved greater degrees of

difficulty which with flying boats and float and hull damage was a problem. Baird had to find people to send to Darwin, Surabaya, Batavia and Singapore. An inspired choice was Eric Kydd, who was based in Surabaya but flew the service from Koepang, through the overnight stop at Rambang on Lombok Island, to Surabaya, then back again with the returning flight.

Even in Sydney, where the Government—which promised to build the facilities—took more than a year to complete the slipway and hangars at Rose Bay, the engineers had to work on the wing, out in the open, to change engine components. A spanner that slipped from grasp into the water was gone forever.

With war obviously threatening in Europe, Fysh pressed strongly for engine overhaul shops in Sydney and Qantas put up a two-storey building at Sydney Airport, Mascot. In contrast to the Government's poor performances, the facility was completed in 39 days. Not only did it provide a workshop environment to dismantle engines and overhaul them, there were also test rooms in which checks could be run. The Bristol Pegasus 10C engines caused some problems but the engineering effort was able to tame them.

After war broke out, the Government set up a Department of Aircraft Production, which built maintenance shops at Rocklea, Brisbane, and at Randwick, Sydney. Qantas was asked to manage these. Staff numbers climbed quickly into the hundreds, for the first time including women.

Aldis, running the Randwick plant, was aware that engine run-ups in a built-up area 'annoyed the neighbours'. He solved the problem by devising a

Connie Jordan, aircraft engineer (and also a pilot) stepped in during the war years.

muffler made out of a 44-gallon drum with an inner cylinder and rockwool insulation, into which he ran the exhaust.

Avery ran the Rocklea facility, which supported the Lodestars and other aircraft Qantas used to supply the frontline in Papua as the Australians and Americans drove back the Japanese from the Owen Stanley Ranges. The only person qualified to 'sign out' the completed Lodestars was a woman, Connie Jordan, so Henry Williams, the Brisbane works manager, put her in charge. The 250 men on the site promptly went on strike. Avery called in the union organiser who organised a mass meeting of the strikers. He agreed they had a grievance. *'Who's got a licence to sign out this work?'* he asked them. *'I'll see he gets the job.'* There was much shuffling. *'Well, if none of you has the bloody intelligence to get a licence, you'll have to have a woman boss'*, he shouted. The men went back to work.

Jordan won her engineering credits the hard way. She is remembered as a pre-war woman pilot who maintained her own aircraft, and also as a racing-car driver.

The Qantas hangar at Archerfield, Brisbane, which had been kept to support the Queensland services after the move to Sydney, was also overwhelmed. One task was to repair and modify US Army Air Corp B24

Liberator bombers and install gun turrets with twin .50-calibre guns, greatly increasing the firepower. Skills learned in this work were not wasted. At the end of the war, when Qantas acquired Liberators which eventually replaced the Catalinas, the airline's engineers were able to rip out many of the military fittings and install seats and cargo space in the former bomb bays, raising passenger capacity to 15 on the long-range flights.

George Roberts came to Sydney to set up his instrument shop at Rose Bay. It was called on to handle hundreds of gyros and auto-pilots a month from the US and Australian forces. Roberts and his team built a Scoresby, an advanced instrument which checked and calibrated auto-pilots two at a time. The workload was crushing. *'The department went out and manpowered all the jewellers and watchmakers in Sydney and we used them to repair and overhaul the instruments'*, he later remembered.

The Rose Bay facility was also inundated, maintaining and overhauling RAAF and US Consolidated Catalina flying boats that were patrolling the south-west Pacific.

The practical grounding from those early days was invaluable when Qantas expanded to Nedlands, Perth, to run the Catalina flights across the Indian

Maintenance crew George Williams (left) and George Roberts, work on the engine of Centaurus.

Ocean to Koggala Lakes, Ceylon (Sri Lanka). Norm Roberts went over to support the flights. When he arrived, his only stocks were 50 spark plugs. He designed and built a hangar at the head of the slips so the Catalinas could be run up into it, allowing the engineers to work under shelter. As they were delivered, Roberts and his team gradually replaced the standard engines with Pratt and Whitneys, built under licence at Lithgow in New South Wales, which were more powerful and reliable than the original equipment. There were only six in-air shut-downs in the months during which the service ran—which was just as well, as the aircraft were operating in radio silence and at emergency weights a non-stop flight of 3,513 miles.

Even bigger challenges lay ahead. The power plants that were to come when the Constellations and Super Constellations were bought after the war were of a new order of complexity and notoriously fickle. The postwar aircraft had radar and a new generation of avionics. After them came the Boeing 707 jets—two generations of them, followed by three models of 747s, and instrumentation and communications that had not even been dreamt of when Arthur Baird recruited his lads.

The philosophy from day one had been self-sufficiency because of remoteness and isolation, backed by Baird's motto: *'Near enough is not good enough.'* The engineering establishment was to maintain this philosophy right through the years in which Qantas changed. They contributed one of the essential elements in the proud Qantas safety record.

Engine testing on the four wheel mobile test stands at Randwick in 1943.
The ingenious muffler system, a 44-gallon drum at the far left, is connected to the exhaust outlet on the engine.

Chapter 5

Qantas in World War II

SUPPORT AND SACRIFICE

Left: A Qantas poster depicting the airline's support role during World War II.

After a brief pause to overseas flights in the first six days of the war, the flying boat service to Singapore was resumed. In late April 1940 the trans-Tasman service started between Sydney and Auckland, also using two Shorts Empire flying boats, *Aotearoa* and *Awarua.*

A poster promoting TEAL

Tasman Empire Airways Ltd (TEAL), formed by Qantas, Imperial (which re-emerged as British Overseas Airways Corporation—BOAC—in April) and a partnership of Union Airways of New Zealand (19 per cent) and the New Zealand Labour Government (20 per cent), did not want the private enterprise operator, owned by a shipping company, to hold the NZ stake. New Zealand owned 39 per cent, BOAC 38 per cent and Qantas 23 per cent, with individual directors holding token shares. The governmental body, which controlled the licence and paid the subsidy, was based in Wellington; the service in Auckland. Hudson Fysh and the Australians regarded it as an awkward, unwieldy organisation. The first flight took nine hours and 15 minutes.

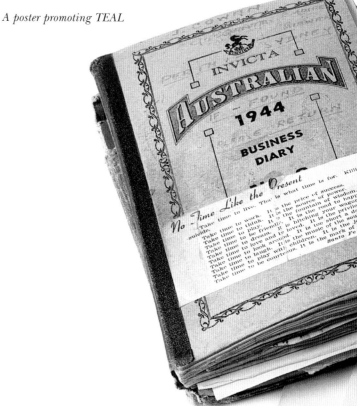

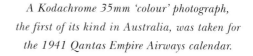

A Kodachrome 35mm 'colour' photograph, the first of its kind in Australia, was taken for the 1941 Qantas Empire Airways calendar.

BOAC, now wholly government owned, had a new chairman, Walter Runciman. As the German offensive rolled through Europe and Italy came into the war, closing the Mediterranean to the through service, Hudson Fysh wrote to Runciman: *'No doubt the flying boat service is in the lap of the gods. My object is to keep at least a portion of the QEA organisation together.'* It was an uncomfortably true prophecy. Runciman wrote back congratulating Hudson Fysh on getting the engine overhaul shop up and running. *'I do not*

EMPIRE FLYING-BOAT 'CAMILLA' FROM DARWIN, 19TH FEBRUARY, 1942

METEOROLOGICAL REPORT & FLIGHT PLAN

DECEMBER 1943

know how we should be faring without it today', he said.

Initially while Qantas operated through Singapore to Karachi, BOAC flew a 'horseshoe' mail route from Karachi to Cairo, then south to Durban, where the mails were despatched on a ship to Britain. To do this, Qantas engineers fitted their boats with long-range tanks and stripped the passenger-comfort furnishings from the aircraft to lighten them. A B Corbett, Director-General of Civil Aviation (who came from the Post Office and was a bureaucrat of the old school), chided Fysh for going against the letter of the government contract by making the aircraft uncomfortable and noisy.

As the British influence waned, the USA started to flex its aviation muscle in what Hudson Fysh and others regarded as American imperialism. Pan American, which was serving Auckland, wanted to fly to Australia via Noumea. Refused rights unless the USA was prepared to reciprocate, Pan American talked about putting passengers aboard a chartered yacht in New Caledonia and sailing them to Australia. At best it was a hare-brained scheme and nothing came of it. But the threat worried Fysh and McMaster.

One of the first big tasks Qantas was called on to organise was delivery of 19 Consolidated Catalina flying boats for the RAAF during 1941. The USA was then neutral, so it required civilian crews. Engineer Dudley Wright left for the USA in December and Lester Brain was put in charge of the program. Scotty Allan, by that time in the RAAF, was an air force representative.

The first delivery flight, which departed San Diego in January 1941, was only the third flight across the Pacific (after Kingsford Smith and Ulm's Southern Cross epic from east to west and Kingsford Smith and P G Taylor's west-east journey). The first leg of the flight amounted to just on 6000 kilometres, an indirect route because of weather patterns, which was the longest over-water route operated up to that time. It took 22 hours and five minutes. A pilot from Consolidated joined them for that leg with two US engineers. Brain, Taylor and Allan flew to Phoenix Island, Canton Island and Noumea, then to Sydney. Later Russell Tapp flew direct from Canton Island to Sydney—6400 kilometres, a flight which provided invaluable experience for when Qantas began looking at an Indian Ocean operation later in the war.

The Government asked Qantas to begin a service to Dili in (then) Portuguese Timor, which had already been visited by a Japanese flying boat and was coming under Japanese influence. The fortnightly Qantas service began in January 1941.

As the war spread, Qantas was becoming enmeshed in the war effort. The RAAF had taken over two BOAC boats which were in Sydney, but did not, as planned,

commandeer the fleet of five and form it into a RAAF squadron. In December 1941, after Japan struck south through Malaya, Singapore and the East Indies (now Indonesia), the Qantas world imploded. Fysh had flown to Singapore on 4 December for talks with Runciman and was woken on 10 December by the sound of falling bombs and gunfire. Immediately, Qantas stopped flying to Penang and Bangkok. Fysh flew to Batavia on 14 December and back to Sydney a week later. Aircraft were still flying through Indonesia and as far west as Rangoon but it became increasingly hazardous. The captains reported hostile planes and chose to refuel in isolated bays of the Indonesian islands, sometimes hidden under trees.

On 6 January Qantas started a shuttle from Singapore to Batavia, carrying mainly refugees. When air raids were in progress, their aircraft landed in an out-of-the-way spot called Thomas's funk-hole (after Captain Frank Thomas) and waited for the all clear.

The first casualty came on 30 January when Captain Aubrey Koch was flying RMA *Corio* from Darwin to Surabaya to pick up refugees. Seven Zero fighters riddled the flying boat. Koch dived for the water at best speed, heading for the beach, but the cannon fire disabled two engines and filled the cabin with smoke. Koch landed the plane on a holed hull and was thrown through the windscreen by the jolt. The aircraft burned and the seven survivors of the 18 on board started swimming ashore. Only five made it, Koch with an injured leg. First officer V Lyne, grazed by a bullet, was one of the survivors. Three other crew died.

In their retreat from Java, some of the allied forces and refugees gathered on the south coast at Tjilatjap, which was to become a port for flights to Broome, Western Australia. Captain Bill Crowther took the last Qantas flight out of Singapore on 4 February 1942 Less than two weeks later the island fell. The flying boats started operating from Batavia through Tjilatjap on 8 February. Captain Russell Tapp, who was at the far, western end of the service at Karachi, started the last flight home, landing at Burmese ports with Japanese aircraft frequently raiding the coast. At Port Blair he had engine trouble. Fortunately he had as a passenger BOAC's engineering superintendent for the area, who worked on the engine until it was running. They took off at 4 a.m. for Sibolga in Sumatra and were warned out to sea because of alleged air raids. When they realised that their aircraft was causing the alarms, they went in and refuelled.

Next day they flew down the Sumatran coast. With Japanese aircraft reported blocking the entry point to Java, they landed at a small island, pulled into a tiny, tree-shaded backwater and anchored until the way was clear. They were able to get into Batavia and returned to Broome through Tjilatjap with refugees, two days after the destructive air raid on Darwin on 19 February. Crowther then had the doubtful honour of commanding the last flying boat to leave Batavia on the same day.

In hospital in Darwin after his rescue from Timor, Koch found himself once more under fire. As Darwin was being raided by 188 carrier fighters and bombers from the same strike force that had devastated Pearl Harbor, 54 more land-based bombers from Ambon joined them. The assault sank nine ships, damaged 13 others, destroyed a number of military aircraft and killed and wounded many civilians and service people. The Qantas hangar at Darwin was destroyed, as was the flying boat jetty. Two Catalinas on moorings were sunk. The flying boat Camilla came through unscathed, except for a couple of shrapnel holes in the elevators.

Two ships were burning at a nearby wharf. When Crowther and Captain H B Hussey learnt one of these was loaded with munitions, they climbed aboard the flying boat, started the engines and hurriedly took off again, keeping low. Eight minutes later the ship blew up. They flew on to Groote Eylandt, refuelled and returned to Darwin in radio silence, to pick up a load of passengers, including Koch, and return to Sydney.

Meanwhile, in Broome, an array of aircraft, including Dutch flying boats, civilian land planes and military bombers and transports, had assembled. Most had come from Tjilatjap, almost 2000 kilometres and eight flying hours away. The town was crowded with 8000 refugees, many of whom had dengue fever. In one day, 57 aircraft arrived.

Captain Lester Brain, the Qantas chief pilot, later general manager of TAA.

Australian troops disembark from the
Coriolanus *at Port Moresby in 1943.*

Broome had only a single jetty and notorious 10-metre tides. Qantas flying boats made 10 crossings on the shuttle. One of the last aircraft to leave was *Circe*, on 28 February. *Circe* reported when 320 kilometres off Java but never reached Broome and presumably was shot down, with the loss of Captain Bill Purton, three of his crew and 16 passengers. The last flight was *Coriolanus*, which flew out almost at the same time and arrived without damage. Earlier Captain Lew Ambrose had escaped when he encountered a Japanese reconnaissance flying boat and fortunately was able to hide in cloud.

Brain, distinctly uneasy at the vulnerability of Broome, wrote: *'I shall not be surprised if all this activity brings on an air raid.'* The Japanese arrived in gleaming silver Zero fighters on 3 March. There were 15 flying boats in the port, several of them Dutch Dorniers loaded with women and children, awaiting refuelling. The Qantas (ex-BOAC) flying boat *Centaurus* was the first to go as the lead fighter blew it apart. Also destroyed was *Corinna*, which was at the jetty being refuelled. Six landplanes were lost on the airport, and a US Liberator which struggled into the air, crashed and blew up. The Japanese also shot down a US DC3 about 100 kilometres north of Broome.

Brain had sent out one of his boats, *Camilla*, to rescue 25 passengers off the steamer *Kulama* and told Captain E C Sims not to get back before 11 o'clock, when he anticipated *Corinna* would have departed. Brain thought—rightly—it was unwise to have two flying boats in port at the one time. Sims heard radio reports of the air raid and swung inland to miss the Japanese attackers.

The DH86s were to emerge with honour in the last of those 1942 rescues. A Catholic priest and pilot, Father Glover, crashed while he was rescuing people from the areas on the coast of Papua New Guinea which the Japanese were invading. He walked behind Japanese lines to Alexishafen, commandeered a light plane and flew it out to Australia, where he told authorities there were about 90 refugees in the Mount Hagen and Ramu areas.

Captain Orm Denny, who knew Papua New Guinea well, took one DH86 and, accompanied by Sims in another, flew into the Highlands and refuelled during an air raid alarm at Horn Island, off the tip of Cape York. They landed at Mount Hagen to find a small

A wounded Australian soldier is loaded aboard the Coriolanus *at a northern Australia flying boat base in 1943.* Coriolanus *was the last C Class flying boat to be withdrawn from Qantas service with a record 2.5 million miles flown.*

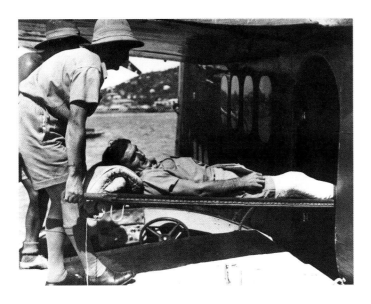

crowd waiting for them. One party of 18 soldiers had walked from Rabaul, the length of New Britain, captured a launch and crossed to the mainland, then trekked into the Highlands to escape the Japanese. The 1000-metre strip was very soft and the DH86s could not use it when fully loaded. Denny set about organising the local people into a 'sing-sing'. Some 2000 people, dressed in feathers and finery, sang and stamped on the ground all one day and into the night. This compacted the ground so that the aircraft were able to leave. Between 13 and 24 May, 18 flights rescued 78 evacuees to Horn Island.

When the confusion had ended, the home front became frustrating for Fysh. With George Harman as general manager and Cedric Turner as chief accountant, together with Arthur Baird as works manager and Lester Brain in charge of flying operations, he had a strong executive group but no airline for them to run, except for a couple of routes in western Queensland. There was also a service to Darwin with a Lockheed 10, the first US aircraft Qantas had used.

The workshops were working full time on war work developing the skills they would need after the war ended, but most of the aircraft had either been destroyed or taken over by the RAAF. All the engineering and the flying was at the direction of the military, through the Department of Civil Aviation and the Director-General of Civil Aviation, A B Corbett. Fysh was concerned about the disintegration of the organisation that he and Fergus McMaster had built up. There were indications that the aggressive US airlines, notably United and Pan American in the Pacific, planned to dominate postwar aviation. They were working with the US military, most of the air transport officers being former airline executives, and had access to the powerful, big new aircraft flooding off the wartime assembly lines. There were twin-engined DC3s and C46 Curtis Commandos; the C54 Skymaster was just coming into service; and moving into prototype was the lovely, long-range Constellation from Lockheed. Qantas could not obtain any of these.

The internal rivals Ivan Holyman and Reg Ansett seemed to have the ear of Corbett and the military. The other power was the Australian, Harold Gatty, who represented the US airlift commands and was a Pan American man. When Fysh wrote to the Minister for Civil Aviation, A S Drakeford, he was rapped over the knuckles by Corbett.

The Qantas flying boats were put on to the Noumea and Townsville–Port Moresby services, but the RAAF would not return those it had taken over. Fysh began lobbying to begin a flying boat service across the Indian Ocean, to knit together the severed Empire link. Corbett angrily rejected the idea, even though Prime Minister, John Curtin, had not by any means dismissed it. With the pilot force under-utilised, Reg Ansett began tempting some of them to join his operation, which was running a busy courier service for the US Army.

A call to help supply the Australians and Americans attacking Buna, plus two Lockheed Lodestars and a Lockheed 10A together with two DH86s, allowed

Qantas to enter into the war. Captain Orm Denny was in charge of the civilian supply group. Qantas was told that three million pounds (about 1360 tonnes) of war supplies were needed on the other side of the Owen Stanley Ranges from Jackson's Airfield in Port Moresby. Denny's RAAF opposite number was Wing Commander Alec Barlow, who was to become a senior Qantas executive after the war.

Hudson Fysh, who visited the team in October 1942, wrote: *'I had seen Chicago Airport, then the busiest in the world. I had watched Germany's Tempelhof and London's Croydon at their peak hour; but all were as nothing compared with the feverish animation of Port Moresby's airstrip with a continuous stream of aircraft flying in, being flagged to their loading positions while others were waved into the air in aircraft carrier fashion.'*

Hudson Fysh flew over the 4000-metre peaks of the Owen Stanleys with Frank Thomas and landed at Popondetta from the south because the Japanese were holding the northern Buna approaches. Very shortly, they took off again with a load of sick and wounded. In areas where they could not land, the crews of the 'biscuit bombers' kicked supplies out to the troops on the ground. On his return, Fysh took to the slit trenches during an air raid. His first such experience had been the surprise attack on Singapore. Returning to the airstrip next day they found that a bomb had fallen near their Lodestar but buried itself deep in the ground. When it exploded, the force was upwards, covering the aircraft in dirt and denting but not damaging it. Another bomb fell nearby but it failed to explode.

Apart from the Lockheeds, the flying boats were still operating where the action was. They made seven flights into Milne Bay, which the Japanese invaded—to meet their first defeat on land in the war—only an hour after Denny had flown one of the flying boats out.

At home, McMaster, in poor health and soon to be knighted, was doing his utmost in political circles— even though the Country Party now sat in Opposition—to secure a future for Qantas. His main emphasis was on the Indian Ocean service. Curtin failed to respond to his request for a personal interview. In May 1943 Fysh flew on US transports across the Pacific and Atlantic oceans to Britain to talk to Runciman. Corbett remained indomitably negative. The flying boats were still operating,

Hudson Fysh (left) and Sergeant Bird stand in front of a Lockheed Lodestar which was operated by Qantas for the US Army at Dobodura during 1942.

The Engine overhaul shop at Randwick in 1943 which was provided by the Department of Aircraft Production
for the overhaul of aircraft engines for the Navy and RAAF. Qantas supplied the expertise and key staff.

notably rescuing downed US air crews from remote places such as the Trobriand Islands in Papua New Guinea.

In April, Fysh met the BOAC directors, who said the British Government had agreed to re-opening the Empire route with Catalinas. Admiral Mountbatten had taken over the South-East Asian command based in Ceylon and wanted to see a link with Australia established. Britain was prepared to supply four

Catalinas for a civilian service. Fysh lobbied one of Churchill's 'ears' and also spoke to the Canadian Prime Minister about the need for Commonwealth air cooperation.

Bad news reached Fysh in London. Captain Aubrey Koch, who had been shot down off Koepang, had been flying *Camilla*, the Broome survivor, into Port Moresby when the weather closed in. Running out of fuel, he tried to land after dark on the open sea. He was descending on automatic pilot but at about 30 feet the aircraft stalled onto the water. The craft sank. Koch and four others swam towards land until the afternoon of the next day, when they were rescued. A further 13 passengers were brought to shore in boats. Two crew and 11 passengers, including RAAF airmen and US soldiers, were drowned. Water landings, with aircraft striking obstacles or stalling in, claimed one flying boat in 1939, three in 1942—in Townsville (RAAF charter), Darwin (bottom ripped out of hull), and Daru in Papua (hull collapsed landing in a rough sea)—and two in 1944 at Rose Bay as a result of heavy landings through stalling.

The good news was that Japan was retreating. The Indian Ocean was still a danger zone, but with secrecy the flights agreed by the British air ministry and Qantas would get through. Fysh, staying in Britain until summer, was notified that he could return by Qantas. In August 1943 the long-awaited Indian Ocean flights had started.

Wounded Australian troops from the Buna-Gona Campaign
about to embark on a Qantas Lockheed Lodestar at Dobodura during 1942.

Chapter 6

The double sunrise epic

THE MOST FASCINATING AND ROMANTIC UNDERTAKING

Left: A Catalina flying boat low over the Indian Ocean.

Above: A celebration of flying with Qantas over the Indian Ocean from Perth to Ceylon, more commonly known as 'the Kangaroo Service'.

Early in 1942, weeks after Singapore had fallen, Hudson Fysh and his chairman, (now Sir) Fergus McMaster, had concluded that a thin link between the two ends of the Empire Route could be forged using Catalina flying boats. The service would carry mail and official documents reduced to microfilm, plus the odd high-priority passenger and perhaps urgent freight.

The distance from Koggala in Ceylon (now Sri Lanka) to Perth is about 5620 kilometres. Proof that it could be flown lay with two Royal Netherlands Navy Catalinas that had escaped to Australia from Java in 1942 and had then flown back to Ceylon, the escape destination of their unit. In the next two years, three more Dutch Catalinas made the journey from Ceylon to Australia, one operating the return trip non-stop. Approval for the civilian service to be resumed came from the British Government, which initially made available four Catalinas. The RAF squadron at Trincomalee, the British base in Ceylon, surveyed the route. The first flight was made by a Canadian, Wing Commander J E Scott, with a second flight made nine days later. On the last of a programme of survey flights, the first two Catalinas were delivered to Qantas in Nedlands, on the Swan River, Perth in Western Australia.

The first Qantas flight left Perth on 29 June 1943, returning the RAF crew that had delivered the aircraft. Russell Tapp was in command. In Qantas hands, the flying boats were all named for stars used in celestial navigation—*Altair Star, Vega Star, Rigel Star, Antares Star* and *Spica Star*. Each was maintained under British registration. The return flight was on 10 July. It carried only 23.6 kilograms of diplomatic mail. The

Left: Captain Russell Tapp using an astro compass on a Qantas Empire Airways Catalina in 1943.

Above: The astro compass.

The Secret Order of the Double Sunrise certificate presented to those passengers who flew on the Qantas service between Perth and Ceylon. This one was presented to Brigadier N W Weir in August 1944.

Koggala–Perth flight took 28 hours and nine minutes.

The service got off to a bad start. The first flight was scheduled for 7 July but, three hours out from Koggala, Tapp and Captain Bill Crowther, who was acting as navigator, found they had left behind two sextants. They turned back, only to have to sit out a spell of unfavourable weather.

As each flight departed in the still air before dawn and lasted longer than 24 hours, participants were awarded a 'Secret Order of the Double Sunrise' certificate. Because the Japanese were capable of intercepting the lumbering, slow, overloaded aircraft, they flew in radio silence.

Captain R J (Bert) Ritchie, later to become general manager and chief executive officer of Qantas, was one of the pilots on this service. Later he recalled how the aircraft were so heavily loaded with fuel that they lifted off in ground effect—air was cushioned between the wings and Perth's Swan River, providing more lift. He had to fly down course of the wide stream because he could not break clear to lift over a narrow peninsula of low ground some kilometres away. It was not until some fuel had burned off that he was able to climb. And he was often eight to 10 hours into a journey before the aircraft was light enough to fly on one engine, should there be a failure.

Fysh departed Koggala at 8 a.m. on the eighth service. Crowther was commanding, with two assistant pilots. Jim Cowan, one of the finest navigators Australia has ever produced, charted the course. (Cowan was eventually to survey the routes for many new Qantas services over the Indian Ocean and the Pacific.

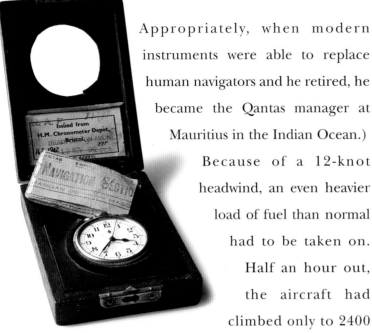

A standard issue deck watch from HM Chronometer Depot in Bristol that was used on Catalinas during the 1940s.

Appropriately, when modern instruments were able to replace human navigators and he retired, he became the Qantas manager at Mauritius in the Indian Ocean.) Because of a 12-knot headwind, an even heavier load of fuel than normal had to be taken on. Half an hour out, the aircraft had climbed only to 2400 feet and, Fysh noted, would not have an effective single-engine performance for another 11 hours. The wind worsened and Crowther flew at an angle to it, to minimise the effect. At 11 a.m. he was able to climb to 5500 feet. At 5 p.m., while there was still daylight, Cowan dropped a smoke bomb to check on the wind. The smoke streamed dead behind, indicating that there was still a headwind. At midnight, Crowther and Cowan could see the Catalina's namesake, the star *Vega*. During the night, they tried flame floats to check wind drift but to no effect. At 11 a.m. (Colombo time) they sighted the coast and had to fly along it to reach Perth. At about 3.45 p.m. the Catalina touched down on the Swan River. The official duration of the flight was documented at 32 hours and nine minutes, a record for the service.

In the following months, with new engines and a rigorous weight reduction programme on the aircraft, Crowther lifted payload to 1000 pounds, approximately half of which was mail.

About midway between Koggala and Perth, there was an emergency landing place, the Cocos Islands (which are now under Australian control and are regularly used by RAAF Orion and F-111C aircraft). The British kept a small presence on the atoll and the Japanese failed to invade because they felt they could not hold the islands. However, they often sent air patrols to check activity.

In February 1944 Tapp was sent to the Cocos to collect a Royal Navy officer and take him back to Ceylon. In radio silence, this was a tricky navigational task and Tapp used a technique of flying down the sun in the early morning to bring up the low islands under the aircraft's nose. Tapp and the crew were about to start refuelling when a Japanese bomber roared over at about 1000 metres. All those aboard the Catalina went overboard into the lagoon. But there was no attack, so they resumed refuelling. Then, without warning, a bomb landed about 60 metres away. The crew went overboard again. The Japanese aircraft was so high that it was out of sight. The Cocos garrison, a tiny group, said they were tracking the bomber at some distance off and at a height of about 2000 metres. Tapp concluded that the aircraft must have been on a navigational exercise and lacked bombs or guns. So the Qantas crew finished refuelling and took off after dark.

Qantas made two other visits to the Cocos at that time. In January 1945 Captain Frank Thomas in *Rigel*

Star, was close to the islands when one engine began vibrating. He was able to make a night landing using a technique, developed by Crowther, of flying down wind and dropping seven flares at regular intervals. The aircraft then came round to touch down on the impromptu flare path. Ritchie commanded a relief flight, arriving in the vicinity early in the morning to use the technique of running the sun line. But the weather was overcast. Fleeting sights of the sun enabled him to hold on course. Flying through heavy showers from storm clouds, he dropped down to 600 feet (about 200 metres). An hour later, they burst through a black squall to find one of the islands dead ahead.

The Catalinas completed 271 crossings before the flights ended on 18 July 1945, two weeks before the defeat of Japan. In June, Qantas had been given two four-engine, 16-passenger Liberators to re-open a landplane service. Departing from Exmouth Gulf, considerably closer to Asia, these were faster and had a bigger payload. With the Liberators, the airmail service resumed on 24 August, just weeks after the war ended, symbolising the civilian resumption of the former Empire Route from Australia to Europe and Britain.

A memory of the Catalinas lives on today when 747s cross the world in less than a day. When the Indian Ocean flights started, the Qantas people in Perth gave it the name of the Kangaroo Service.

Passengers boarding a Liberator LB-30 at Guildford Airport near Perth,
Western Australia in 1944 for the flight across the Indian Ocean to Ceylon.

Chapter 7

Back
on track

THE POSTWAR WORLD

Left: The partnership between QEA and BOAC gave passengers a choice in flying.

As the war drew to its end, there were several blueprints for the future of air transport. The Americans thought they should run it. At the Chicago conference of 1944, which was to shape the rules for international air transport, Australia and Britain, whose joint interest was what had become the Kangaroo Route, agreed that the Australian and British flag carriers should cooperate but fly in parallel between Australia and Europe. The Q.A.N.T.A.S Board, as distinct from the Qantas Empire Airways Board, favoured a return to sectoral operation—QEA would fly to a point such as Singapore, with BOAC responsible for the rest of the service to London—mainly because of the huge capital cost involved in buying new aircraft.

The Australian Government, through its Minister for External Affairs Dr H V Evatt advocated a monopoly controlling all aircraft on international routes. The Labor Government favoured socialisation of air transport, along with other key industries, which the public had rejected in a referendum. Blocked from nationalising the privately owned Ansett and ANA, the Government set up Trans-Australia Airlines (TAA) to operate within the country, and recruited Lester Brain as the first general manager. Qantas continued to operate internal flights in its traditional heartland of western Queensland and the Northern Territory, as well as the Flying Doctor Service until April 1949. It initiated a civilian service in Papua New Guinea in 1945, buying the assets of Carpenter Airways, which included hangars and a Lockheed 14 aircraft.

In August and September 1946, Hudson Fysh and Fergus McMaster negotiated with the Australian

A Qantas Lancastrian on the tarmac at the Cocos Islands in 1945.

Government on a takeover, first of the British interest in QEA, then of the private shareholders on the Australian side (Q.A.N.T.A.S.). In declining health, McMaster resigned as chairman in May, although he was to remain a director. Fysh succeeded him as executive chairman and managing director. The acquisition and establishment of a government corporation to run Qantas, with a company structure, was completed by September 1947. The original company that began as Queensland and Northern Territory Aerial Services was liquidated. Fysh was the only member of the old Board to transfer to the new one, retaining his two positions. C O Turner, whose financial judgement had won respect at home and in the United Kingdom, was to become assistant general manager.

While all this had been going on, Qantas was also establishing its technical independence. Prime Minister John Curtin had told Australians that new ties with the United States (which was using Australia as a base to mount its counter-attack against Japan) superseded the old dependence on Britain. But the World War I generation including chairman Sir Fergus McMaster and managing director Hudson Fysh regarded the British connection as paramount. During the war, when the Australian Government and bureaucracy seemed intent on seeing the Qantas organisation disintegrate, Britain and BOAC had provided first Catalinas and then Liberators to reopen the world's longest over-sea crossing and end-to-end air route.

However, this emotional and practical bond did have its limits, which were eventually reached under the pressure (applied by the British Government to BOAC, which in turn passed it on to QEA) to use

The Lockheed 749 Constellation Harry Hawker. *The 749 carried 38 First Class passengers along with 10 crew.*

British aircraft. The Australian Government was reluctant to commit funds to buy the four-engined Douglas Skymasters and the Lockheed Constellations which were now rolling off the civilian aircraft production lines.

Soon after the war, Qantas flew Liberators and then 13-seat Lancastrians (the civilian version of the Lancaster bomber), on the Kangaroo Route. It also began operating to Norfolk Island, the Australian Territory in the Pacific about 2000 kilometres east of New South Wales, and, under RAAF charter, to Japan via Darwin and Manila to support the Australian Occupation forces. But these aircraft were uneconomical. The British industry had developed Lancaster derivatives, the York and on the drawing boards the Tudor II, which looked capable of operating the Britain–Australia service. BOAC was intent on procuring the Tudor, but it began to fall well behind schedule. Qantas engineers and pilots sent to the United Kingdom to monitor technical trends said it was unlikely to deliver the economics or

performance needed. BOAC also suggested a Sunderland III (Hythe) flying boat as 'extremely comfortable'. But it was also uneconomical, and Qantas memories of the hazards of operating off water were still very fresh in the minds of pilots and engineers. The inescapable conclusion was that the answer lay in the USA.

Initially the Government gave Qantas permission to buy two surplus C54s and convert them into civilian Skymasters. Faced with competition from US carriers flying Constellations and the big Boeing Stratocruisers, Qantas opinion hardened on the Constellation. The fact that KLM had ordered the four-engined Lockheed aircraft for use on the Batavia route was an added incentive because the spectre of Dutch competition had always hung over the Empire duopoly.

At a conference in London, BOAC and the British Government on the one hand and Qantas (through Turner) and the Australian Government (through Captain Edgar Johnston) on the other agreed to differ but still work together. Qantas would operate two Constellation through-services to London, and BOAC would use Lancastrians to carry mail and flying boats for passengers on the parallel service until British aircraft became available. They would pool revenue and share it on a formula based on the capacity (weight multiplied by distance flown).

But, as the reality of tightening government control became apparent, acquiring the Constellations

Qantas had applied for permission to acquire two Lockheed Constellations in 1946 on a basis of 25 per cent down and payments to be spread over three years. The aircraft had a speed of 400 kilometres per hour, a range of 4000 kilometres and could carry about 64 passengers. Later that year Turner reported that four Constellations was not an economic number and eventually the order was to grow to six. These proposals horrified the British, who mounted what

The 749 Constellation Horace Brinsmead *painted in a later Qantas livery.*

was proving anything but easy. At the stage where the Commonwealth owned the BOAC shares but the former Qantas company was still privately owned, the new Board suggested issuing additional shares to pay for the aircraft. Treasury countered with a proposal that the Department of Civil Aviation buy the aircraft and lease them to Qantas, which was clearly unsatisfactory. The situation showed that the hybrid ownership was not going to work, and culminated, later that year, in the Government's acquisition of all the shares.

Fysh was later to describe as a 'diplomatic blitz' to coerce Qantas to 'buy British'. It went as far as the prime minister. Hudson Fysh was called to Melbourne one day for a meeting with Ben Chifley. On the desk in front of him was an urgent cable from the British Prime Minister, Clement Attlee, *'begging us'*, Chifley told him, *'not to go ahead with those Constellations you want'*. Fysh wrote that Chifley paused, smiled, then said: *'Well, anyhow, I have decided. Let's give it a go'*.

After the pressure put on Qantas by the British, Fysh was surprised firstly to receive an enquiry

Qantas Constellation Lawrence Hargrave
delivered in October 1947.

from BOAC asking whether Qantas could acquire Constellations on its behalf—the Qantas order had excellent prices and conditions—and secondly to learn a few days later that BOAC had gone ahead with an order for the bigger and more expensive Boeing Stratocruisers.

Preparing to put the Lockheeds into service fully occupied Qantas. It sent pilots and engineers to California to train on the aircraft, which was the first pressurised type in the fleet, and to Curtis Wright on the East Coast to train on the complex 2500-horsepower engines. Qantas also introduced two new categories of flight crew: flight engineers and

hostesses. When the latter jobs were advertised, 2000 applications were received for nine positions.

Towards the end of 1947 the first postwar aircraft, the Lockheed 749 Constellation, arrived. It left for a survey flight to London and back. On 1 December, the *Charles Kingsford Smith* inaugurated the first modern passenger service on the Kangaroo Route to London, carrying 29 passengers and a tonne of food parcels. The elapsed time was just under four days. Passengers spent two nights on the ground, in Singapore and Cairo, and two in the air. Initially the frequency was monthly but it increased to three a fortnight. There were problems with the engines. Sixteen spares had been positioned along the way but it became clear that another four would be needed. Back in Sydney, Ron Yates, a university qualified engineer—the first in the airline—who was later to become chief executive, had developed the unique Qantas contribution to this era of postwar aviation. He designed and built a clamshell pod under a Lancastrian. Into this protuberance an engine could be loaded and carried.

THE BCPA STORY

An almost forgotten—and tragic—player in the Qantas story was British Commonwealth Pacific Airlines. BCPA had its origin in 1946 when senior aviation officials from Britain, Australia and New Zealand met in Wellington to discuss the pattern of postwar air services across the Pacific.

From Australia and New Zealand to Britain, there is little difference in time or distance between travelling eastbound across the Pacific or westbound via Asia and the Middle East on the Kangaroo Route. The fear about Pan American World Airways, which started flying to Auckland before the war, was that it would siphon off Empire traffic. With its 'sleeperettes' and glamour, Pan American began to do this after it started flying into Sydney in March 1947. From the Qantas point of view, it seemed logical for the experienced international airline, which had demonstrated its capabilities on the Pacific by delivering 19 Catalinas to the RAAF during the war, to operate the route. What completely defied logic was that the Australian Government, which had just bought Qantas, was to own 50 per cent of BCPA so it would be competing with itself.

The last British Commonwealth Pacific Airways departure on 12 May 1954. This DC6 flew the Sydney to Vancouver route.

The new airline had no aircraft and no rights to pick up or set down in US territory, although it could go through to Vancouver in Canada. Its first initiative was to contract with Australian National Airlines to fly the route on its behalf. ANA used Skymasters. When the air services agreements with the United States were signed in 1946, BCPA, through ANA, started a regular weekly service from February 1947 through to Vancouver via Honolulu and San Francisco, increasing to three fortnightly later in the year. Paying a fixed charter cost to ANA, BCPA found that it was getting little traffic and began to lose heavily. It bought the two ANA Skymasters in 1948 and two more from the infant TAA to operate its own flights from April 1948. TAA provided BCPA with engineering and other support.

Later that year, BCPA was lucky to buy four Swedish-owned DC6s that had been in storage at the Douglas plant. This helped the airline around the cash shortage that was restricting Qantas ambitions at that time. The faster, pressurised DC6 reduced flight time to 40 hours, which made the link across the USA to Britain much more competitive.

By 1950 it became clear that BCPA was costing the three governments big money, largely because it had no mail contracts. Qantas began to look for an opportunity to realise its ambitions to extend east as well as west from Australia, which was to culminate in its round-the-world service later in the decade.

BCPA's general manager was Alec Barlow (who in the RAAF had hosted Qantas Port Moresby operations in the war and after the BCPA takeover was to become a senior Qantas executive) and its secretary Ivan Lawson. Both were regarded as capable. But the airline was heavily dependent on TAA, it had no opportunity to expand routes and, Qantas told the Australian Government, it 'lacked depth'. The Board of Qantas proposed acquiring the airline.

However, BCPA was ambitious. Spurred on by TAA's very able technical director John Watkins, BCPA in 1951 initiated talks with de Havilland about buying the Comet, even though it would have a ludicrously low payload departing Honolulu on a hot day because of the characteristics of its jet engine and the heavy fuel load required.

By 1952, Qantas was doing its sums about the acquisition and getting a generally sympathetic hearing from the Government. Qantas put the argument to Britain and its partner, BOAC, that it could then link up on the west coast with BOAC services and also in London, establishing a Commonwealth round-the-world link. Qantas suggested to the Australian Government, that merging BCPA would reduce overheads and allow it to become profitable. The argument to New Zealand, was that Tasman Empire Airways Ltd (TEAL), which needed new aircraft, could acquire the DC6s.

The end came in late 1953 after one of the BCPA aircraft crashed on approach to San Francisco Airport. Although BCPA was eventually cleared of blame, the accident destroyed the little morale that was left in the airline. Qantas took it over the following year, after the Australian Government, which had acquired the New Zealand and British shares, vested them in Qantas. It flew on in name for a few months, in accordance with the naming of the licences for the route. But in May 1954, the first Qantas Super Constellation, named *Southern Constellation*, took off from Sydney for San Francisco, inaugurating its flights across the Pacific. The way was clear for Qantas, with its beautiful new aircraft, to girdle the world.

A BCPA poster from the 1950s.

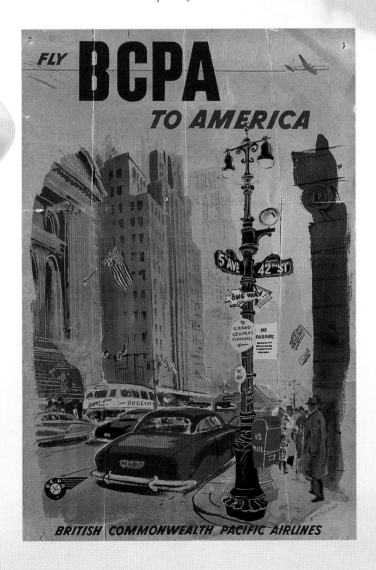

Chapter 8

Papua New Guinea adventures

PIONEERING ADVENTURES

Left: The rescue of a US bomber crew as reproduced from a watercolour by Walter Jardine.
The Coriolanus *was under the command of Captain H B Hussey.*

Before World War II, Qantas saw expansion through north Queensland to Papua New Guinea as a logical path for the airline, which had moved its headquarters to Brisbane. It failed to get a government contract to operate a service from Sydney through to Rabaul. This went to Carpenter Airways, the subsidiary of the big Islands trading company. However, with experience of Papua New Guinea operations during the war, when Qantas flew or air-dropped supplies right into the frontline assault on Buna and Salamaua, and with the recruitment of senior captains such as R J (Bert) Ritchie, Ken Jackson and Dick Mant—who came from Carpenters—the company began talks to acquire the air assets of the airline.

The main assets of Carpenters were a Lockheed 14 aeroplane, some spares and hangars. For 44,000 shares, Sir Walter Carpenter sold the airline to Qantas and took a seat on the Board. In October of that year, Qantas was given the rights to the route and in April 1945 began flying the service to Lae with two

Qantas in Papua New Guinea.

converted DC3s. In the following years, the flights extended to Rabaul, Madang and Wau, with a frequency of five a week, and became the Bird of Paradise Service.

As the war ended, former Qantas pilot, Arthur Affleck (who had been involved in the beginnings of the Flying Doctor Service), led a Department of Civil Aviation team committed to making air transport the mainstay of Papua New Guinea communications in the postwar effort to reconstruct and develop the country. Affleck had flown in Papua New Guinea after leaving Qantas, operating into the Wau goldfields. At the time this was by far the heaviest air cargo lift in the world. He recognised that many of the strips and facilities would be inadequate by Australian standards but, given the special developmental role, regarded them as operational. One of Affleck's recommendations was to make Madang the air centre to service the Highlands from the coast and this was greatly to influence the pattern of postwar air transport.

Flying conditions in Papua New Guinea were a complete contrast to those in Australia. The central spine of mountains rises to almost 4700 metres, with broad highland valleys between its the high ridges. The north coast is wet and tropical, while much of the south is as arid as northern Australia. Crossing from one side of the country to the other involves using mountain passes, in which cloud builds up in most seasons. There is always a local wet season somewhere in Papua New Guinea. Visual flying is not possible at most times of the year after about 10 o'clock in

Locals roll away empty petrol drums from an airstrip in Papua New Guinea.

the morning, if at all, in many regions. In Affleck's day, ground aids were virtually non-existent and today they are scattered and challenged by the terrain or weather. In Papua New Guinea the pilots say: *'The clouds are like a box of chocolates. Some have soft centres and some have hard ones, and you don't know which is which'. Cumulus graniticus* is the generic description of such cloud formations.

At the end of the war, there were some huge airfields. Civil operators needed only a fraction of the vast complex just outside Port Moresby. There was a similar maze of taxiways and runways in the Markham Valley and at places like Salamaua which were

abandoned. On the coast, crushed coral provided a good surface. Inland there was a choice of grass, dirt (which turned to mud in the rainy season) and in many places, the steel surfaces called Marsden matting, some of which survive even today.

The local airline—which also had routes between Adelaide and Darwin—had been Guinea Airways, formed by Guinea Gold in the 1920s. Guinea suffered the fate that almost befell Qantas. Its aircraft were commandeered by the RAAF and after the war it was denied permission to return. Left with only skeleton Australian routes, it was absorbed in the postwar expansion of Ansett.

This left a vacuum in Papua New Guinea at a time when air services were an urgent priority of reconstruction. Qantas had stationed two light aircraft in Lae as early as 1946 for domestic services. But in 1948 the Australian Government, now the shareholder in Qantas, nominated the company to develop air services under contract to the Australian administration. It was like a return to the pioneering days of 20 years before, as the company built up a mixed fleet of twin-engine de Havilland DH84 biplanes, DC3s and other types of aircraft. There was a Catalina, which flew to remote coastal centres, islands and the Highland lakes, single-engine de Havilland Canada Beaver and Otter landplanes and floatplanes, and three-engine Australian-designed de Havilland Drovers, a type built for the flying doctor service. The latter had serious deficiencies that were to result in accidents. Four-engine Douglas DC4 Skymasters took over the Sydney–Port Moresby–Lae service in 1950.

By mid-1952, Qantas had 14 aircraft and 172 Australian staff and flew to more than 100 places in Papua New Guinea. Twenty-six pilots flew 35,000 passengers and almost 1.5 million ton-miles of freight per annum.

Qantas was to operate in Papua New Guinea for just over 11 years. Its opposition came from Mandated Airlines, which bought out Bobby Gibbes' Sepik Airways—and was to be taken over by Ansett, plus other operators of light aircraft from missionaries (one pilot was a Catholic bishop) to fiercely independent pilot-entrepreneurs. The domestic hubs were Port Moresby, Lae and Madang. One DC3 flight from Port Moresby flew to Wewak, then round the outer islands such as Manus and New Ireland to Rabaul. In the early days, just like during the war,

Left: A Catalina in the background being unloaded after arriving at Milne Bay in Papua New Guinea in the 1950s.

Below: A Lockheed 10 Electra is prepared for departure. These aircraft were first introduced into the company's service in 1941.

passengers had to strap themselves down as best they could on air freight. It was a reassuring experience to share a bag of potatoes with an Anglican bishop in purple-fronted tropical rig. Many of the aircraft still had the military webbing seats that let down from the cabin walls and were hitched up again if cargo had to be loaded. There were no flight stewards. The cabin attendant was more of a load master. In-flight service consisted of a big cardboard box containing meat, salad, bread, fruit, and tea or coffee in a thermos.

Aircraft became very hot on the ground and very cold at altitude. Occasionally the DC3s had to climb as high as 12,000 feet and a glance around the cabin would show passengers huddled in blankets to protect themselves against lack of oxygen and the unaccustomed cold.

But Papua New Guinea was a marvellous training ground for pilots and engineers. While their colleagues flying the Constellations and later the Super Constellations on the international routes habitually assumed considerable status, the Papua New Guinea pilots knew everybody on the outstations and would carry messages and do shopping if required. They also had to do their own inspections, work out their own loads, and balance and fly with a cautious eye on the weather. On the Otter floatplanes, travelling along the coast to places such as Samarai, the water could be so transparent and still that establishing where the surface was could be difficult.

Young engineers were sent to outstations on their own. They faced plenty of challenges, including damage from rough strips and gravel thrown up into propellers or engines. They had to become masters of impromptu repairs, using whatever tools and material were available.

By 1959, the Papua New Guinea services had become an important part of the Qantas financial and operational structure. Its revenue was the equivalent of A$3.7 million, or about eight per cent of the total. Of this about a third came from the internal services. However, the government of the day, responding to lobbying, had decided that services to and from Papua New Guinea were domestic in nature, and licensed TAA and Ansett to run them. TAA took over the Qantas facilities and Ansett took over Mandated Airlines.

Another pioneering era had ended.

The de Havilland Otter was introduced into the company's service in 1958.
Qantas used four Otters for its Papua New Guinea operations as landplanes or amphibians.

Loading catering supplies on board a Qantas DC3 at Archerfield Aerodrome in Brisbane in 1947.

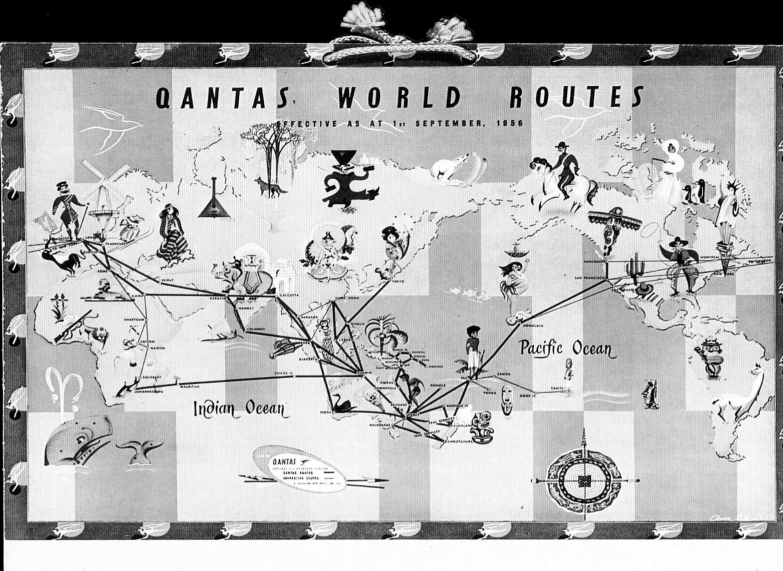

QANTAS WORLD ROUTES

EFFECTIVE AS AT 1st SEPTEMBER, 1956

QANTAS EMPIRE AIRWAYS LIMITED

AUSTRALIA'S OVERSEAS AIRLINE

YOUR
QANTAS CALENDAR
FOR 1957

Chapter 9

The battle of the jets

AND AROUND-THE-WORLD

Left: The front cover of the Qantas Empire Airways Limited 1957 calendar shows the world route flown by the airline.

Launching the Pacific service linking Australia and North America at Sydney Airport on 15 May 1954

The pre-war Empire Route flights launched Qantas as an international airline. Wartime achievements demonstrated Qantas determination, ingenuity and the myriad of values that built its operational and engineering strength. The government's indifference to Qantas in those years, which could have let its expertise disintegrate, placed a heavy management load on to Hudson Fysh, George Harman and the ailing Fergus McMaster. The war and the years immediately afterward cemented Hudson Fysh's already considerable achievements. When peace returned and the rapidly developing aviation industry turned to civilian production, a generational

change in aircraft took place. The new era required a management free from the inhibitions of the past.

In Qantas, there was a changing of the guard in July 1951 when C O Turner was appointed general manager. He succeeded George Harman, who had been Hudson Fysh's loyal aide since Brisbane days. Hudson Fysh remained chairman and managing director.

Turner was determined not to be just a day-to-day manager of Qantas affairs. He had been recommended to the company as chief accountant about the time of the move to Brisbane before the war. He had been in Europe and involved in helping to clean up one of the huge European financial scandals of the 1930s. His analytical skills went far beyond juggling figures and he rose to become assistant general manager. Turner's financial analysis of routes, operations and aircraft performance fitted closely with the technical instincts of pilots such as 'Scotty' Allan and Bert Ritchie and the engineering ability of Ron Yates. Turner developed the vision and ambition to power the company into the top layer of international airlines and a growing force in world aviation.

Unfortunately, the cost was tension between Hudson Fysh and Turner. They disagreed on matters of policy and international and government relations. Turner was forceful and aggressive when it came to industrial relations. The Qantas pilots started pursuing pay and conditions which were comparable with those enjoyed by US pilots, with whom they mingled on stopovers in the finest hotels around the world. They were losing touch with Australian values and government wage policies of the day. The official approach was to keep a lid on the wage expectations of the community and to

control a tendency towards inflation. Turner was inclined to meet the pilots head-on, while Fysh, himself a pilot, believed he could reason with them, despite crippling industrial stoppages which Qantas faced in almost every decade.

Throughout the 1950s Qantas services expanded, with the takeover of BCPA and the Southern Cross routes to the USA and Canada, and new flights into Asia and across the Indian Ocean to South Africa.

At that time, the world was an uncertain place from the Qantas point of view. Until 1953 Australia had forces fighting in Korea. There were communist insurrections against the colonial powers in Indo-China and Malaya. Australian forces were to be committed to Malaya in the 1950s and 1960s and to Vietnam in the 1960s and 1970s. The independence of India and Pakistan had been hard-won and the future of the independent Indonesia—which was to experience its own conflicts in the 1960s and which lay across so many Qantas routes—was uncertain.

A strategic consideration was to find alternative routes to keep open the services to Britain and Europe. It had been only a few years before that the Japanese thrust had cut off Australia. Fysh had pressed the RAAF to build an airfield on the Cocos Islands, which were a strategic base in the Indian Ocean and a refuelling point on the South African service, which operated via Mauritius. An Indian Ocean route to Europe was seen as one of these alternatives, as was the route across North America.

If the first priority was to secure Australian air routes, the second was expansion. Turner's leadership

The Lockheed Constellations were the backbone of the Qantas fleet during the 1950s.

was to take Qantas strongly into Asia, the Middle East and parts of Europe. These countries, still hung over from the war, did not seem likely to develop airlines which could seek reciprocal services into Australia. These were the years which set the pattern of growth for Qantas. They were also to leave it open to greater competition in the future. One thrust came from the Asian tigers, which grew in economic strength under the western, anti-communist umbrella. The other was from the USA, which gained what were later regarded as excessive rights when Australia made the concessions that gave Qantas its round-the-world services.

But the key to the Qantas growth was in choosing the right aircraft. They needed to be fast with a long range and sufficient payload to carry mail and cargo. And they had to appeal to passengers. 'Scotty' Allan's

work, which had led to the dismissal of British claims to supply postwar aircraft, had started a culture of comprehensive aircraft evaluation that had no place for sentiment.

The Qantas relationship with Britain was at two levels. On one hand there was the airline partnership with BOAC. The economic basis of Qantas rested on the pooled revenues for the Kangaroo Route. At times, there were other and lesser players in the pool, such as India, but the agreement to share revenues remained until well into the jet era. The other relationship was with the aircraft industry. For Britain, aircraft projects were a matter of national prestige. Australia's political leaders were still 'British' in outlook and shared British pride in the first jet airliner, the Comet 1. Qantas was not impressed by the aircraft's performance and economics and also had

Whether the passengers were dining, reading, sleeping or simply enjoying the flight, the 'Super Connies' had it all.

some reservations about its handling. By this time Qantas had emerged as a world leader among the smaller, national airlines and its choice was seen as an endorsement of equipment. Although BCPA was enamoured of the Comet 1 in the 1950s, Qantas calculations showed it could not carry an economic payload over key sectors of its routes.

Because jet engine performance diminishes with rises in temperature, the Comet 1 had virtually no payload available after loading fuel to fly on Pacific routes, particularly when fuel reserves were taken into account. The British manufacturer, de Havilland, claimed that this basic rule of flight planning was 'unfair' to the aircraft.

Britain put pressure on the Australian Government to buy a second version of the jet, the Comet II, which had better payload and range. But the project was put on hold when a series of crashes in 1953 and 1954 showed there was a fundamental problem with the design. By then Qantas had already won the battle to order the bigger Super Constellation, the Lockheed 1049C. By the end of 1953 it had eight on order and by 1955 there were 12 in service. The aircraft was to be the mainstay of the airline's routes until the Boeing 707-138 jets took over in 1959.

Hudson Fysh was personally knighted by Queen Elizabeth II during her visit to Australia in 1954, having been recognised in the coronation honours of the previous year. He stepped down as managing director of Qantas in June 1955 on reaching the official retiring age of 60. Turner took over as general manager and chief executive.

By this time, Qantas was faced with making decisions on new aircraft for the next decade.

1957-58 SOME GOLDEN MONTHS

Six weeks after the 35th anniversary of its first scheduled flight of 750 kilometres in November 1922 Qantas launched its new round-the-world service, the first ever scheduled, with a spectacular prelude. The take-off, on 20 December 1957, was a little later than the 2 November anniversary. And the distance was somewhat longer: 40,000 kilometres. Instead of a single passenger in an open cockpit the airline took 32 editors, senior commentators and radio and television stars from around the world to meet the Pope, the Archbishop of Canterbury, the Prime Ministers of New Zealand, India and Thailand, the Presidents of India and Pakistan, Singapore's Chief Minister, top US officials and world business leaders.

Shortly before the anniversary, the Australian Prime Minister, Robert Menzies, opened Qantas House in the heart of Sydney. Symbolically, a new Lockheed Super Constellation L1049G completing a delivery flight from the USA circled Sydney as the ceremony took place.

The regular scheduled round-the-world services began spectacularly on 14 January 1958. Two Super Constellations took off from Melbourne and flew to Sydney. After a second farewell, one turned east and flew the Pacific through Fiji, Honolulu, San Francisco and New York to London. The other went westbound through Jakarta, Singapore, Bangkok, Calcutta, Karachi, Bahrain, Athens and Rome. Both returned to Sydney on 20 January.

In 1957 the number of passengers using Australian ships and aircraft was about the same, at just over a million each. In 1958 there were 1.3 million air passengers, while 964,000 people travelled by sea.

Queen Elizabeth II and the Duke of Edinburgh came to Australia by ship in 1954. The Queen Mother travelled by Super Constellation *Southern Sea* during her February 1958 visit.

£115/10/-* DOWN flies
this happy couple right around the world
with QANTAS

* Deposit on two Tourist Class Round-World Tickets

£57/15/- each is all that is needed to set them or anyone else—including you!—off on a round-world trip with Qantas.

Under the Qantas Credit Travel Plan you can fly to almost anywhere in the world and back on a deposit of 10% with up to two years to pay the balance.

See at right how little you need in cash to take an overseas trip right now. You may choose from comfortable Tourist Class travel in huge radar-equipped Super Constellations or First Class travel in the same magnificent aircraft, but with more room and amenities.

Whichever way you fly, you can be sure of world-famous Qantas courtesy, care and attention all the way—in the air and on the ground.

Why delay that overseas trip when it is so easy to start now! Let Qantas or your travel agent tell you all you want to know. and help you to plan your journey in every detail from departure to return.

If you prefer, you can pay for your trip by Lay-by and earn 3½% interest on your money. Send the coupon at right for full details of Qantas Easy-Pay Travel Plans.

Increased sterling and dollar allowances for tourists

Recent relaxation of currency restrictions now makes it permissible for overseas tourists to take with them up to £1,300 in sterling, in any period of twelve months, half of which may be converted into dollars or other non-sterling currency.

BOEING 707 JETLINERS
COMING TO QANTAS

During the next six months, Qantas will start taking delivery of its fleet of Boeing 707 Jetliners, which will completely revolutionise air travel out of Australia. and put Qantas years ahead

Take a week — or a year
Stop over at no extra air fare

Listed alphabetically below are some of the places to which you can fly direct by Qantas Super Constellation without changing airlines. Those marked with an asterisk (*) are ports of call on Qantas round-world flights via New York and London. Side trips to adjoining cities and countries are simple to arrange—often without extra cost. Get the facts from your Qantas travel agent.

MELBOURNE to:	Tourist Class Round Trip		First Class Round Trip	
	Deposit	Full Fare	Deposit	Full Fare
Around World	£57 15	£573 15	£79 5	£785 5
*Athens	£52 5	£515 5	£71 5	£704 5
*Bangkok	£27 8	£269 8	£38	£371
*Bombay	£34 15	£339 15	£46 15	£465 15
*Cairo	£46 10	£463 10	£64	£639
*Calcutta	£31 15	£312 15	£43 15	£429 15
*Colombo	£31 5	£308 5	£43	£423
*Djakarta	£19	£189	£26 19	£259 19
*Fiji	£12 15	£120 15	£16 10	£164 10
*Frankfurt	£56 10	£562 10	£77 15	£771 15
Hong Kong	£29 5	£287 5	£36 17	£362 17
*Honolulu	£37 8	£365 8	£50 7	£497 7
*Istanbul	£51 10	£508 10	£70 15	£699 15
Johannesburg	£48	£477	£60 5	£596 5
*Karachi	£36 5	£362 5	£50 5	£497 5
*Kuala Lumpur	£22 12	£219 12	£30 13	£301 13
*London	£56 15	£564 15	£78 5	£776 5
Manila	£25 10	£253 10	£31 17	£317 17
Mauritius	£42	£414	£52 15	£519 15
*New York	£54 16	£541 16	£75 9	£752 9
Port Moresby	£10	£97	£12 2	£113 2
*Rome	£54 10	£535 10	£73 10	£733 10
*San Francisco	£44 19	£448 19	£61 9	£611 9
*Singapore	£20 18	£207 18	£28 19	£285 19
Tokyo	£36 10	£361 10	£46 2	£455 2
Vancouver	£44 19	£448 19	£61 9	£611 9

QANTAS EMPIRE AIRWAYS LTD.
341 Collins Street, Melbourne. (Phone MB 5501)
Please send me full details of Qantas Easy-Pay Travel Plans.

NAME

ADDRESS

I AM INTERESTED IN TRAVEL TO

ON CREDIT ☐   ON LAY-BY ☐

QANTAS EMPIRE AIRWAYS LIMITED (INC. IN QLD.) IN ASSOCIATION WITH B.O.A.C., TEAL AND S.A.A.

The Southern Constellation *was the first Super Constellation purchased by Qantas
and was officially handed over on 29 March 1954 in San Francisco.*

There were a number of choices. One was to stay on the Constellation track and acquire a faster and longer-range Lockheed 1649. This aircraft had a longer and narrower wing, basically to carry more fuel. The engines were further out on the wing, reducing cabin noise. But its piston engines, which still were causing maintenance problems, were obviously about to be superseded by turbo-props and jets.

Bristol in Britain had a turbo-prop, the Britannia, which initially looked attractive, but its flight development was slow. Lockheed was also developing a turbo-prop—which became the Electra—and it was soon evident that this would be available before the Britannia. Qantas believed it had been well served by

Lockheed and was attracted to the company and its products. But emerging were two American jets, that were to become the Douglas DC8 and the Boeing 707. And in Britain, the fatigue problems of the Comet solved, de Havilland was now offering a superior Comet IV which, in the event, was to beat the 707 across the Atlantic. A Qantas evaluation in 1955 said that, at that stage, the Boeing and Douglas were 'very large' aeroplanes and could not be considered. The evaluation said the Comet IV appeared to be the most promising although it still had payload problems. The studies intensified when, later that year, Pan American and other airlines placed big jet orders for both the DC8 and 707 which were to inaugurate the jet era in air transport.

Just as the aircraft and engines scene was ever changing and needed constant study, so was the Qantas route structure. The strategic problem of political turmoil along the Kangaroo Route worried both Qantas and BOAC in 1955. Jointly they pointed out to the British and Australian governments the need for the two airlines to operate via North America, a route which would require new negotiations with the USA.

Edgar Johnston, who had retired from civil aviation to become a Qantas adviser, recommended that the two airlines should have parallel end-to-end services over North America as soon as possible. The target date he suggested was mid-1956. The Director-General of Civil Aviation, Don Anderson, began talks with the USA and found that, although sympathetic, the officials asked that formal negotiations be held over until after the late 1956 presidential election. The rights were formally agreed in 1957. But Anderson had to trade off permission for

The Prime Minister of Australia, Robert Menzies with the chairman of Qantas, Sir Hudson Fysh and the company's chief executive, C O Turner, at the opening of Qantas House at Chifley Square, Sydney, on 28 October 1957.

US-designated carriers—effectively Pan American at that time—to fly into Australia from Asia, beyond Australia if they wanted to, and to have traffic rights across the Tasman from New Zealand. The agreement meant that Qantas could fly to the United Kingdom and Europe either via Asia and the Middle East or across the Pacific. Effectively Qantas had round-the-world rights, paving the way for the historic service it was to launch in late 1957.

Meanwhile the aircraft selection process had become intense. The orders from Pan American in particular had placed Qantas on the spot. The big American airline would be operating jets by 1959. If they deployed them against Qantas, with propeller-driven 'Connies', they would cream the traffic with a faster, bigger and more comfortable aeroplane.

At this stage the 120-passenger 707s were regarded with some awe. They were about twice as big as the early Constellations and more than 200 kilometres per hour faster. Apart from shortening journeys, the speed made them much more productive. As one Qantas executive put it, recalling the first apprehensions: *'It was like a flea going to his bankers to buy his own dog.'*

When Turner's executive group in Qantas began to report that the Boeing 707 looked a strong prospect, he called William Allen, the president of Boeing. It was a personal touch that led, as historian John Gunn noted, to the long and close friendship between the big US manufacturer and the medium-sized Australian airline. Turner asked for Boeing to give him a letter setting out the options to buy

Sir Hudson Fysh at his investiture by the Queen in the State Ballroom of Government House, Sydney, on 6 February 1954.

the model which had intercontinental range. He also wanted a comparison between the Pratt and Whitney and the Rolls-Royce Conway engines. Turner warned Allan that Qantas could not act independently; it had to seek government approval for aircraft orders and this was not easy.

The 1049 family of Constellations (by now they had reached the 'H' variant) were facing a competitive threat from a piston-engined Douglas DC7C (the Seven Seas), which was faster and had more passenger appeal. Lockheed proposed a 1649 model which, its salesmen promised, *'would beat the pants off the 7C'.* But this could not be delivered much more than a year or so earlier than the jets.

Douglas stepped in, suggesting a combined DC7C and DC8 jet order.

Lockheed and Boeing went into frantic consultations. They proposed that Lockheed trade in 1049s for up to eight 1649s and buy them back again from Qantas two years later at about half the new price. Bob Walker, a Qantas engineer trained in aircraft evaluation, was stationed at the Lockheed plant at Burbank in this period. Walker, keeping abreast of the DC8 and the 707 technically, reported that there was little to choose between them.

What finally proved a decider was that Qantas singled out the Nadi–Honolulu route as the critical one for jets on its network. Douglas was not prepared

to alter its standard aircraft, designed as it was for domestic US routes. However Boeing proposed shortening by 10 feet their standard domestic aircraft (the 100 series) to 128 feet 10 inches. To this they married the more powerful US military version of the Pratt and Whitney engine which gave extra thrust and which the USA would be prepared to release in December 1958. This ability to meet the problems of an individual airline persuaded Qantas.

In September 1956, the Minister for Civil Aviation announced that Qantas would buy seven Boeing 707-138 jet aircraft. In the event Qantas decided not to go ahead with the Lockheed 1649; instead it upgraded its L1049s by adding weather radar and wing-tip tanks for extra range over the Pacific and bought two more, which Lockheed would trade back. When the jets were delivered in May 1959, the plan was that Qantas would have 16 Super Constellations.

This order meant also that the Australian airline would become the first non-US carrier to operate American jets. The new aircraft would carry 104 passengers, cruise at 880 kilometres per hour, reducing the flying time between Sydney and London from 48 to 27 hours and between Sydney and San Francisco from 28 hours to 18 hours. These journey times were to remain essentially the same for some years, shortened only by the longer range of later aircraft which eliminated refuelling stops.

The new aircraft dictated a big expansion of the Sydney Jet Base, with new engine shops and test cells. There would also be simulators to train pilots and new catering facilities.

While the jet selection absorbed management time, it was not the only issue to do so. Britain, France and Israel invaded Suez. There were riots in Singapore, where Chinese youths stoned the air terminal and also in Malaysia. There were strikes in Jakarta. With the fighting, Qantas had to re-route its aircraft through Iran, Turkey and Greece. The difficulties lent urgency to the talks about rights over the USA, which were about to get under way.

Qantas was leaping ahead by the end of 1956. Passenger numbers were 161,000—up 19.25 per cent for the year. On the Kangaroo Route, where a fourth weekly flight had started, loadings were up 30 per cent. Passenger traffic across the Pacific was up 50 per cent. Although the military charters to Japan had ended, Skymasters were flying to Hong Kong twice a week. And the first year of Super Constellation services across the Indian Ocean to South Africa had strong acceptance of the service.

The airline had just completed its first quarter-century, with 23 years of scheduled services. Qantas now had a fleet of 14 Super Constellations, two of which were strengthened to carry heavy freight, five Skymasters, eight DC3s, four DHC Beavers, a DHA Drover and two Catalinas. On order were two more L1049Hs and seven Boeing 707s.

The jets were not only to change the way Qantas—and the airline industry—operated as well as the structure of the airline itself. By shortening journey times, they would also bring Australia much closer to the population centres of the northern hemisphere. Singers, concert performers and other artists who once were deterred by the long journey to Australia would include the country in their tours. In the next decade, the British group the Beatles was to rock Australia even before they were at the height of their popularity in North America and Europe. Politicians and business people began routinely flying to Europe and North America. Australian business began expanding its enterprises internationally and investors came to Australia to discover opportunities. Air freight became part of the transport equation.

At the end of 1959 'the jet set' was the popular label given to a high-living elite. Eventually, most Australians became potential jet-setters and popular travel came to dominate the future of Qantas.

A Qantas Super Constellation with wing-tip fuel tanks. These planes were in service between April 1954 and May 1963.

Chapter 10

The jet age begins

NEW FRONTIERS

Qantas enters the jet age—the Boeing 707 V-Jet.

Qantas chairman, Sir Hudson Fysh, and Boeing president, William Allen, walk through a guard of honour representing every department of Qantas on their arrival in Sydney on the first 707 delivered to Qantas in July 1959.

T he first Qantas Boeing 707-138, appropriately named *City of Canberra*, arrived in Sydney from the Boeing plant in Seattle on 2 July 1959. The delivery flying time from San Francisco was 16 hours 10 minutes. The previous fastest journey, in a DC7C, had taken 27 hours 30 minutes.

For Boeing, the Qantas aircraft was a variant of the -120 series, the -138 being the manufacturer's designation for Qantas aircraft. Apart from a cruising speed twice as fast as that of the Super

The interior of the Qantas sales office in London in the early days of the jet era.

Constellation, however, the jet provided another big advantage for passengers. The 707 would cruise at above 10,660 metres, compared with the 6,060 metres of the Constellation, literally flying above most cloud and weather.

But the noise of the Pratt and Whitney pure jets and their black smoke trails disturbed Sydney residents. Qantas was also concerned at their high fuel consumption. The engineers were already looking at a new type of engine: a by-pass or fan engine. A big fan in the front ducted air around the body of the engine, increasing the thrust and encasing the noise from the jet exhaust, making it much quieter and more efficient. The fans increased engine thrust by a third, to 18,000 pounds, greatly increasing performance and reduced the need for water injection on take-off from short runways. Qantas became the second airline in the world (after the USA) to order the new engines to retrofit its first six aircraft and they came as standard on future orders. The modified V-Jets were designated -138Bs. Eventually Qantas operated 13 of the type.

While the jets were being acquired, Qantas made another equipment decision. It chose the turbo-prop Lockheed Electra to replace the Super Constellations on routes that were not suitable for jets. TEAL—with some acrimony, as it had initially favoured Comet IVs —also ordered Electras. (Qantas was to remain a shareholder in TEAL until 1961 when it withdrew, following an agreement by both governments that each airline should operate its own services.)

The Electras were similar to the Orion maritime patrol aircraft, which the RAAF was to order later. The engines came from the same Allison family as the power plants on the Lockheed Hercules, which was to be the RAAF's main transport aircraft. The number of engines allowed Qantas to overhaul Allison engines in Sydney, alongside the Pratt and Whitneys for the 707s.

It was a period of exciting change for Qantas, driven by the faster, bigger and more productive new aircraft. Passenger numbers and revenues were growing every year. The Mascot Jet Base had turned into a big industrial enterprise employing several thousand people. More Australians from Qantas were being sent overseas to open offices and handle services as they passed through. Qantas had a big presence in London and San Francisco, together with a number of crew and engineers in both regions. Although the professional service ethic was not part of the Australian psyche, Qantas in-flight and airport service was winning plaudits from international travellers—and from rival airlines as well. Inside Qantas the baton had passed from the pioneers to the new generation of managers, technicians and pilots. Australians were justifiably proud of Qantas and it was considered prestigious to work for the company.

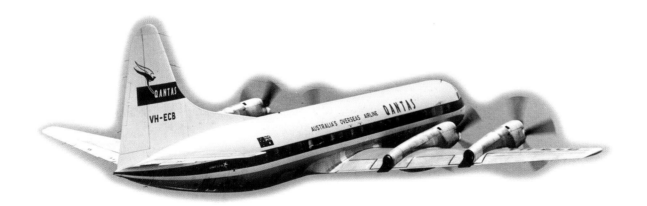

The Pacific Explorer, *the first of four Lockheed Electra aircraft is pictured on its inaugural flight to Sydney on 7 November 1959.*

Qantas was directly affected by the social development of Australia, particularly through postwar migration from southern Europe. It was a period of prosperity for Australians. As people earned more, air fares were becoming cheaper relative to wages and salaries. Until about 1960, when most Australians thought of travel, they thought of passenger ships. The journey still took more than a month each way by sea, so a visit to Europe was out of the question for many. For others it was a once-in-a-lifetime experience. The postwar migrants, from Britain and northern Europe, from Italy, Greece, what was then Yugoslavia and increasingly from Turkey and the Middle East, prospered enough to fly home for family reunions. And they were beginning to press for lower fares to allow them to do this. As far back as 1954 Qantas had provided a tourist class on its Super Constellations. Within two years this had grown to take 44 per cent of the traffic. By the 1960s tourist class travel dominated on Qantas and other carriers. First class passengers occupied only a small area of the aircraft. By international standards, Qantas had a higher than average first class traffic, at about 23 per cent of the total passenger miles flown in the mid-1960s.

Passengers disembark from the turbo-fan powered 707, City of Perth.

The relative cheapness of air travel and the much faster travel times brought Australia closer than ever before to the cities of the USA, Britain, Europe and Asia. The 1960s were a time of a broader international outlook and the feeling of a greater involvement in world affairs. This was partly because events had moved closer. South-East Asia had become one of the world's trouble spots. Jet aircraft turned long-distance travel into a reality for growing numbers of people, and there was the influence of migrants.

Qantas sought to join in carrying migrants from Europe to Australia, quoting special low fares. It also contracted for traffic and chartered aircraft from other airlines to do this. By 1966 migrant traffic had become an important part of the airline's business. In the financial year ending March 1966 Qantas carried 18,500 migrant adults and children on scheduled flights and organised charters for another 23,200. In the following year, on both scheduled and charter flights, the number had grown to 47,600.

Although in May 1967 Qantas formally dropped 'Empire' from its name to become Qantas Airways Ltd, BOAC and Qantas continued to work in partnership, sharing revenues through a pool agreement. In the 1960s Air India was admitted to the pool. There were similar agreements with South African Airways across the Indian Ocean and TEAL across the Tasman. Pools predominated on world air routes, except for those to and from the USA which did not permit its airlines to pool because of anti-trust laws. With pools, airlines maintained their own identity and controlled their own costs. They were

A close-up of the Pratt and Whitney JT 3D turbo-fan engine.

able to coordinate features such as departure times and days of travel, sell one another's services and carry out work for their partners in handling aircraft

Most governments supported the system and backed the airlines' International Air Transport Association (IATA), which met regionally to agree on fares and conditions. Governments approved fares and generally endorsed the IATA-set levels.

However, this arrangement was beginning to break down in the early 1960s. More airlines were buying jets and flooding their huge increase in capacity onto markets. Discounting of published fares began. As IATA required unanimous approval of fares by operators in and between each region, a single airline could veto agreement. As the 1960s progressed, this led to increasing 'open-rate' situations where the only limits on fare-cutting were the requirement for governments at each end of an air route to approve fares. The slump in prices for piston-engined aircraft led to a huge growth in charter airlines, mainly in Europe. As fuel prices were still low, old aircraft became cheap to operate.

While such influences were beginning to affect Australia, IATA was the most powerful force in world aviation. It held its 17th annual meeting in Australia in 1961. There were 400 delegates from 92 airlines of 57 countries. Ironically, the difficulty of accommodating these people and providing conference space highlighted the Qantas plea to build a new hotel in Sydney, which cabinet had twice refused but would now approve. Meanwhile, Sir Hudson Fysh—the trooper who had fought on Gallipoli, the observer and gunner who had fought in the air in the Middle East, the pilot who had started one of the world's leading airlines which had grown to the seventh biggest in the world—was honoured by his peers with the chairmanship of this international organisation.

Qantas Flight hostesses, 1950s.

The Boeing 707-138B City of Melbourne *in flight. 707s were used on services across the Pacific from 1959.*

But the airline business was falling on hard times. The Australian economy had slowed. The boom in jet purchases had brought too many seats onto world air routes. Qantas had achieved expansion through government negotiation of air rights, which inevitably recognised the right of the other country to fly to Australia. The jets gave them the reach to fly the long distances. And the ethnic communities in Australia held the promise of markets. Qantas had lost the advantage of being the sole jet operator on its main routes—as it did when it first bought 707s—and had to work much harder to maintain its advantages.

Long before benchmarking became fashionable, Qantas had measured its performance against that of its rivals. It identified high labour costs as the most worrying feature of Australian operations. But in terms of staff productivity, it rated second only to the big US operators with their economies of scale. On the raw figures, its investment in maintenance, overhaul, and training costs and staff numbers was above average. But this was a factor of the distance between Sydney and manufacturers in North America and Europe. Qantas, like other Australian airlines since the 1920s, had to pursue a high level of self-sufficiency in all its activities. Most importantly, its break-even load factor was down to 48 per cent—less than half the potential payload in passengers and freight had to be achieved—and anything above this was highly profitable.

Foreign airlines were providing increasing competition. Alitalia was stepping up its frequencies until it had three flights weekly to Australia by 1965. Lufthansa began flying into Sydney the same year and Qantas countered with two flights a week through Vienna to London. Japan Airlines in 1965 also announced its intention of flying to Sydney. While both TEAL and Qantas were flying Electras across the Tasman, Christchurch built a big new airport and Qantas started its jet services to that city. Qantas for its part was seeking routes which would not necessarily involve reciprocal rights. In November 1964 the Boeing 707 *City of Launceston* inaugurated the new Fiesta Route under the command of Captain Ron ('Torchy') Uren, who had flown for the RAAF in the Coral Sea battle in 1942. The new route was an imaginative and alternative round-the-world service, flying from Sydney to Nadi, Papeete, Acapulco, Mexico City, Nassau and Bermuda, then on to London. It did not live up to the Qantas hopes and was closed down a few years later.

The decade saw the retirement of Sir Hudson Fysh on 30 June 1966, a significant changing of the guard in Qantas. His replacement as chairman was Sir Roland Wilson, Secretary of the Treasury, who had been made a director a few years earlier. His appointment was seen as direct involvement by the Government and bureaucracy in the affairs of Qantas

and was reported in the media as clamping the hand of government on a prospering Australian institution. Wilson's deputy had been Fysh's vice-chairman, Sir Robert Law-Smith, who was also on the Board of TAA. Wilson, who liked all his reports and advice to be on paper, was clearly heading on a collision course with Turner. The latter was regarded as likely to want the chairmanship because his 60th birthday—due in 1967—was the Qantas retiring age.

But Turner never even made it to the Qantas Board. A strong leader, who inspired loyalty from his staff he retired on 30 June 1967 and was knighted in recognition of his work. His successor was Captain R J (Bert) Ritchie, whose aircraft evaluation skills were highly regarded in international aviation.

At that time, Qantas was studying the proposed new supersonic aircraft from Europe and the USA. The airline opened the new Wentworth Hotel in Sydney, announcing plans to redevelop the site of the old hotel as a big new headquarters complex. Boeing announced plans to launch a huge new airliner, the 747, which would be two and a half times bigger than the new Boeing 707-338Cs that Qantas was in the process of ordering. Qantas was in the middle of a searching evaluation of its equipment options for the future. It put the review on hold while it looked at the Boeing giant which was to transform the airline—and Australia—as much as the first jets had done.

The 707 City of Sydney *at San Francisco International Airport in early 1960.*

Chapter 11

Behind
the scenes

PURSUIT OF EXCELLENCE

Left: Qantas is renowned as the world's safest airline.

Qantas maintenance area at Sydney Airport, in August 1961.

The Qantas transition from the piston-engined Constellations to the Boeing jets brought about profound changes in engineering and support. As always, engineering planning had to take into account the fact that Qantas was on the other side of the world from the main support centres, such as Seattle for Boeing and Hartford for Pratt and Whitney engines. The advanced systems on the Boeings meant that the specialist shops—such as hydraulics—had to be completely refitted. And what were previously just 'instruments' were now electronic and became 'avionics'. To handle the work, new engine shops and hangars were necessary. It was a period of huge expansion which established what became known as the Qantas Jet Base at Mascot in Sydney.

Although jet power plants were new for Qantas, the Pratt and Whitney JT3D jet engines fitted to the Boeing 707-138s were 'mature', in that the US Air Force had been operating a military version for years. Qantas engineers programmed the jets for overhauls every 400 hours, as had been necessary with the temperamental reciprocating engines on all the aircraft up to this time. But the airline quickly learned that they could run 2200 hours—equivalent to about nine months in use—before they had to be disassembled and inspected.

With the first fan engines, the JT3D-1s on the -138Bs, the period between overhauls was even longer. However, apart from buying new engines for spares and to equip the later 707-138Bs, the new Qantas Jet Base developed a programme that was as ambitious as manufacturing the airline's own aircraft in Longreach 40 years before. With a kit from Pratt and Whitney, the engine shop completely rebuilt 25 of the existing engines and brought them up to the new standard.

Qantas engineers were improving their ability to service the new aircraft while the Constellations were being phased out. To complicate the task, four of the Lockheed Electras, with an Allison turbo-prop engine, were being introduced. The RAAF began depending on Qantas for Allison engine maintenance of its Hercules transports. The Mascot base developed its level of competency so it could carry out the block overhauls on the jets. In this major overhaul, the aircraft are stripped and every piece of the airframe and all the avionics are checked.

Maintaining and calibrating the avionics was a major undertaking in its own right. Qantas built a test rig for the automatic pilots, which was one of the first outside the USA. Later, with the RAAF, it built the first high-grade 'clean room' in Australia. In this shop, where delicate instruments such as gyros were stripped and rebuilt, the air was filtered to eliminate virtually all dust particles and workers dressed in enveloping nylon suits so they would not shed skin

The first Qantas 707 takes shape in Seattle.

RESERVATION SYSTEMS

Domestically and internationally airlines quickly found the old manual methods of controlling reservations inadequate as the volume of traffic grew and competition intensified. The US information management company Unisys was chosen by Trans Australia Airlines (TAA) to develop one of the most advanced reservation systems in the world. As deregulation approached, this system was constantly upgraded and expanded to provide ticketing, passenger boarding, load planning and cargo as well as other services such as hotel and car rental bookings.

Now, for Qantas, Unisys has provided a yield management system which analyses advance and past booking patterns. This information highlights business opportunities and also provides the optimum mix of fares to produce the best possible level of revenue from each flight.

A Boeing 747 rolls out of a new maintenance hangar built in the early 1970s at Mascot Airport, Sydney.

particles, hair or fluff from their clothes into the precision instruments. The first engine test cell, built for the early jets, had to be refurbished and recalibrated for the fan engines.

The shorter -138Bs were an excellent introduction to the jet era. But as traffic, particularly air cargo, built up, Qantas ordered the bigger version of the Boeing, the 707-338C Intercontinental series, with delivery from February 1965. These had more powerful JT3D engines, which also required training and other changes in the engine overhaul system. Eventually Qantas was to operate 21 of this type, phasing out the -138Bs, which—in excellent condition, thanks to the

Qantas reputation for high-grade maintenance—sold onto a strong market. For the 707s, Qantas acquired advanced simulators for pilot training, among the first ordered worldwide to have full movement and to provide simulated vision.

Another type of aircraft also came into service in 1966: the HS-125 executive jets, which Qantas used for command training. When the British engineers from Hawker Siddeley came to Sydney with the new aircraft, they brought with them elaborate plans for maintenance. In the words of a Qantas engineer at that time: *'They expected to find a bicycle-shop operation behind a hangar somewhere.'* What they discovered was

Maintenance manager Ern Aldis talks with some new apprentices in the early 1970s.

one of the world's leading maintenance and engineering complexes which, Boeing and Lockheed field engineers freely admitted, taught them *'a lot about airplanes we hadn't thought of before'*.

Up to the time the 707-338Cs started arriving in numbers, the basic principles of Qantas engineering had remained much the same, through biplanes, flying boats, converted bombers, the Constellations and Super Constellations. This had been a pragmatic, hands-on approach to aircraft maintenance, drawing on experience, with the work being organised on a time basis.

The Boeings were much bigger and more complex. They were also much more reliable than the Constellations. The round-the-world pattern of air services meant that individual aeroplanes were sent off for 10 days or more and, while there were strong

field service centres such as London and San Francisco, the base support was in Sydney. It soon became apparent that removing an engine from an aeroplane, stripping it down and inspecting it was leading to more problems than leaving it in place and carefully monitoring its performance. This approach led to developing systems to inspect engines and other components in situ. It also led to developing special traps in engine-oil systems to locate metal fragments, as well as analysing performance in flight. The new approach made engineering management more scientific, which led to profound changes in the

A long queue of people wait to inspect a Qantas 747SP at Coolangatta in the early 1980s.

The City of Gold Coast/Tweed *was the first SP (Special Performance) 747 to join the Qantas fleet in 1981. It is powered by four Rolls-Royce RB 211-B2 engines.*

way records were kept and analysed, and how work was assigned to engineers on the hangar floor.

At the same time, the training of apprentices was put on a more professional basis: the first female apprentices were hired, initially in the instrument overhaul shops, qualified engineers were recruited in greater numbers and engineering cadetships were established.

Qantas expertise in aircraft evaluation was respected internationally. The decisions to buy the Constellations and later the 707s were choices which could have ruined the airline if it had been wrong.

Throughout the 1960s and 1970s, aircraft evaluation was a constant process, involving much more than a head office cell. Qantas engineers had always worked at plants such as Lockheed and Boeing; their reports kept the head office team in touch with developments. At the same time, Qantas partners— such as BOAC—were to operate the Comet IV and Bristol Britannia to Australia, so engineers had to go to the manufacturers to acquire the hands-on experience that would enable them to service the aircraft on turnaround in Australia.

In the 1960s, Qantas paid for tentative production positions on six proposed supersonic aircraft from the USA and four of the Anglo-French Concordes. The thinking at that time was that the subsonic jets such as the 707 would be replaced in the 1970s by supersonic transports (SSTs). Qantas was one of the few non-US airlines which was asked to evaluate the two US SST proposals from Lockheed and Boeing. The Qantas study showed that neither looked like being a commercial success. The same conclusion was reached later on the Concorde.

The approach to the SSTs built on the experience of the introduction of the 104-passenger Boeing 707s, which had shown that, even if the aircraft were not much bigger than their predecessors, higher speeds resulted in a big increase in capacity. Throughout the 1960s traffic was growing rapidly and the need for a bigger aircraft was becoming apparent. Douglas at this stage was offering a 'stretched' DC8 capable of carrying up to 270 passengers, but this option did not attract Qantas.

In 1966 Boeing launched its huge 747, which at that stage was built to carry about 370 passengers or roughly two and a half times the capacity of the 707. The wide-bodied fuselage would obviously have greater passenger appeal. Pan American ordered 25 as a launch customer. The focus of the Qantas evaluation switched. Further analysis showed that, as traffic growth continued, Qantas could maintain frequency on its main routes with the 747. There were problems with range and payload. But Pratt and Whitney developed engines that provided what Qantas needed and in November 1967 Qantas ordered four 747s for delivery in May 1971.

The delay was to prove worthwhile. The Qantas delivery position allowed it to become the first airline to acquire the improved B version (the -200 series) with better use of space and more windows on the upper deck. This was an important passenger attraction which differentiated the Qantas 747B from the earlier -100 series which its competitors were flying.

The bigger 747 required a massive investment. Qantas bought an Australian aircraft tug to tow the jumbos at airports, big new mobile stairways, and built large new hangars. The more advanced systems and instrumentation also required new workshop support. Advanced simulators were required, along with special workshops to support them. A partner with Qantas from the early 1970s, Alasdair Macdonald Architects supervised construction of new buildings for Boeing 747 aircraft, workshops, passengers check-in and cargo facilities as well as passenger service centres in downtown locations around the world.

As with the 707 an opportunity arose to buy a bigger and more economical engine just after the 747s went into service and world fuel prices suddenly increased. Qantas became one of the first airlines to order the Pratt and Whitney JT9D-7 engine for its fifth aircraft, and rebuilt the earlier powerplants to the same standard.

The evaluation process continued even as the 747s went into service. In October 1977 Qantas decided to buy a Combi version, which could carry 28·8 tonnes of cargo on the main deck, with slightly reduced seating for 270 passengers. Another specialist version was ordered in 1981: the Boeing 747SP (Special Performance), a shorter aircraft offering longer range and much better field performance for the short Rongotai airfield in the New Zealand capital, Wellington.

Boeing was improving the 747, with a -300 series—the upper deck was extended to carry more passengers—which Qantas ordered as the Boeing 747-338. Rising fuel prices increased the competition between jet engine manufacturers. Seeking greater fuel economy, Qantas became a Rolls-Royce customer in 1979, the first time since just after the war. Since then all of its B747s have been delivered with Rolls-Royce engines. The first Rolls-Royce powered B747-238 aircraft was delivered to Qantas in 1980 with RB211-524C2 engines. These were upgraded to the more fuel efficient -524D4 version in 1982. These engines were 25 per cent more fuel efficient than the engines in the first Qantas B747s. The first B747-338 was delivered in September 1984, again with upgraded D4 engines. In 1989 the first 747-438 came with the even more efficient and powerful Rolls-Royce -524G engines. When the -338 arrived in Sydney, Qantas switched the upgraded engines to one of its 747SPs to improve that aircraft's capability on non-stop trans-Pacific flights. Qantas upgraded all of its earlier Rolls-Royce engines to the D4 standard. The first 747-438 was delivered in spectacular fashion: after making its debut at the Farnborough air show in the United Kingdom, it travelled non-stop from London to Sydney, the longest flight by a civil aircraft at that time.

For some years, Qantas was an all-747 carrier but it became apparent that there were routes better served by smaller aircraft operating more frequently. After an extensive evaluation of Douglas, Lockheed and Airbus types, Qantas chose Boeing's twin-engined 767 series. The first model was the -200ER (extended range), using Pratt and Whitney engines, delivered in 1985. Later the stretched 767-300ER was ordered, with General Electric CF6-80C engines, and delivered in August 1988. The attraction of this combination was that it had been certificated for twin-engine operation over water over extended ranges. Qantas used these aircraft from Cairns to Honolulu and Los Angeles for a period.

Above right: Mascot Airport in 1930. Note the Chinese market gardens next to the hangars.

Right: The Qantas Jet Base and headquarters complex at Mascot in Sydney.

Chapter 12

The Ritchie era

CHALLENGES OF GROWTH

Left: Detail of a poster celebrating 70 years of Qantas.

Qantas reached another plateau, operationally, in management, engineering and marketing when Captain R J (Bert) Ritchie, the wartime pilot and skilled aircraft evaluator took over as chief executive. This followed the retirement of Sir Cedric Turner at a time of profound change. Qantas was still bedding down the engineering and management problems generated by the complexity of the Boeing 707 for a relatively small airline.

Ritchie guided the airline from luxuriously servicing an elite clientele prepared to pay high prices for fast travel to competing in the mass market and bidding for the discretionary consumer dollar. He was also to hand over to a new, postwar generation of Qantas personnel as dedicated as himself. The new generation was international in outlook and very cost conscious. Australia had changed profoundly since the war days, when Ritchie, in an overloaded Catalina, had taken off from the Swan River to hold open an Empire link. 'Empire' had gone from the name of the airline and a new era was fast approaching.

Captain R J (Bert) Ritchie, CBE, general manager of Qantas from 1967 to July 1976.

Ritchie's reign was to see the end of the Commonwealth pool and the failure of the final attempt to buy an Anglo-French aeroplane, the Concorde. Unrelenting Qantas commonsense, which Ritchie had helped instil, was to burst the bubble of supersonic transport in favour of big aeroplanes chasing the lowest seat-kilometre cost and efficiencies in every aspect of the business.

Ritchie was to serve under three government-appointed chairmen. He took over at a time when an economic crisis in the world airline industry was developing. But he left Qantas to his successors in a state that ensured its survival in viable form when rivals like Pan American would eventually disappear.

The problems of the growth of the past began to emerge soon after Ritchie eased himself into the chief executive's chair. Expenses were soaring. Wages had grown to 35 per cent of Qantas expenditure. There was heavy spending on infrastructure, including computers to handle first message-switching, then reservations. War in the Middle East led to route diversions. The Electras came off the South African route to be replaced by 707s and were eventually to be sold off. And management was engaged in detailed negotiations with Boeing over the modifications that Qantas required to the 747. The Pacific route was causing concern, with competition from Air New Zealand and Pan American, and some revenue diversion to BOAC, which had picked up British Pacific rights. The fleet was mixed—three Electras, 12 B707-138Bs and eight B707-338Cs with another 13 on order. The productivity increases generated by the 707s had flattened out and would not be resumed until the 747s with their lower operating cost per seat came in through 1971.

Generally the late 1960s were troubled times for Qantas. Its pilots were restive, calling one-day stoppages in the union campaign for higher wages. They were awarded a 23.9 per cent increase in 1970. The USA was pressuring Australia to allow a second airline with daily flights into Australia. The US nominee was American Airlines, one of the most powerful in the world, which eventually came onto the route only to retire after severe losses. In 1970, Australia was to agree to capacity of 13 'Boeing 707 equivalents' for US carriers on the one hand and Qantas on the other. Shortly after this agreement was reached, Australia was pressed to give more and would do so. The Americans held the high ground on rights because Australia had had to give away so much to obtain the round-the-world service, when it was seen as strategically and commercially necessary.

Hijacking was an international problem and required much tighter (and more expensive) security. And the tourism lobby was pressing for lower fares into Australia through the licensing of charter carriers.

In March 1970 Qantas celebrated its 50th birthday. The Queen and Duke of Edinburgh began a tour of Australia which was to include a visit to a Qantas exhibition in Longreach. In June, Sir Roland Wilson was re-appointed chairman for a further three years, with Robert Law-Smith continuing as vice-chairman. Wilson was seriously concerned about the airline's

Top. Service with a smile 1970s style.
Above. Distinctive Qantas uniforms of the era.

financial position. Since 1967 he had argued for a capital injection of A$50 million to help finance the 747s; but while agreeing, the Government had not acted.

The pressing operational and financial problems, however, took second place in May 1971 when Qantas became victim of an extortion threat. The first move was when a 'Mr Brown' called airport police and told them there was a sample bomb in a locker at the airport. Police found it in a vinyl bag with three letters. One explained that the bomb was activated by the aircraft's altitude, a second that a similar bomb had been placed on a 707 bound for Hong Kong with 127 passengers and crew, and a third, addressed to Ritchie, demanded $500,000 in used notes before 4 p.m. When he received the money, 'Mr Brown' said, he would tell Qantas how to find the bomb and defuse it.

Calls to Qantas House started while the aircraft was returned to Sydney and told to fly above 6000 metres. It was systematically searched but nothing was found. The Qantas finance director Bill Harding went to the Reserve Bank and brought back 10 bundles of $20 notes. Meanwhile, tension was building because the aircraft would have to land by 7 p.m.

As arranged, the money was handed over by Ritchie personally to the driver of a yellow van at 5.30 p.m., while pursuing police got themselves trapped in a lift that stopped at every floor. 'Mr Brown' got away. He then phoned Qantas with the message there was no bomb after all and the aircraft landed safely. Later, a man was arrested and sentenced to 15 years' gaol. Half of the money was recovered.

At the beginning of the 1970s, the world economy was turning down, with serious consequences for the airline industry, because of the extra capacity provided by the wide-bodied jets. IATA control of air fares was breaking down. Charter operators, not burdened with scheduled overheads, were advertising lower fares, particularly out of Europe. There was strong pressure on the Australian Government to allow these operators to offer lower air fares to the Australian public.

Qantas had been dipping a toe into charter operations with migrant carriage on its own aircraft and on planes hired from British Caledonian. These carried some 71,000 passengers in 1971 (when the total number on all services was 790,000), about half of whom were migrants. Qantas believed that the only way to offer lower fares was to build up sound, scheduled services. At one stage it prepared to launch its own subsidiary carrier but 'Qantair' never took off because European and the British governments would not give it rights. The early charter experience, blended with capacity on scheduled flights, provided the basis on which Qantas launched its own low-fare holiday program with resounding success the following year.

While the charter issue blazed up in media controversy and simmered more quietly in debates within government departments and within Qantas itself, fundamental changes were taking place in the airline. After a report from US management consultants, a major change in the company

MASS TRAVEL

Changes in the distribution system of airline services that occurred in the 1960s required a more effective method of reaching potential customers. As a result, there was a significant increase in the number of travel agencies focused on selling into the mass market.

Concorde International Travel was one of the first in this area, working with Qantas to reach the then newest segment of the air travel market. In 1995 it is one of Australia's largest, integrated travel companies and maintains strong links with Qantas through the distribution of Qantas product and employing many former Qantas staff.

organisation took place in March 1971. For the first time a senior executive, Keith Hamilton, was appointed to run day-to-day operations. He was 40 and little known outside Qantas, but had a legendary reputation inside the airline industry. During the *konfrontasi* upheavals, he had been senior traffic officer in Jakarta when there had been Indonesian threats against Qantas flights. One story maintained that unless the captain of the incoming Qantas flight could see Hamilton make a private sign that it was safe to come into the terminal, he was under orders to turn and take off again. Later Hamilton was seconded to Malayan Airlines and became general manager of the merged but short-lived Malaysia–Singapore Airlines (MSA), helped found Malaysian Airlines and eventually became a chief executive of Qantas.

In September 1971 Qantas introduced its 747Bs on the Kangaroo Route, first to Singapore and then to London. It had hoped to start them on the Pacific, but the USA was using formalities to try to secure more capacity on the route. Qantas could not start the 747 Pacific services later in the year if Australia did not agree to the US request. This was the depth of the airline industry depression, with simply too many seats for the traffic available. Most airlines were chalking up huge losses by flying near-empty aeroplanes. Qantas had to trim staff, standing down air and cabin crew at first, because of the reduced number of flights, and later ground crew went as well.

Aware of the competition from charter operators, typically flying from Singapore to London, Qantas took a decision to attack the interlopers and to market its way out of the depression by cutting prices to chase volume. Working through IATA, Qantas obtained approval for an excursion fare of $700

A Boeing 747-400 with the Flying Kangaroo livery.

return between Sydney and London from early 1972. This was subject to conditions of stay at the destination that made the low fare unusable for business travellers. The airline conference would not agree to a one-way fare of $420 but Qantas argued that, as there was no fare agreement, an 'open-rate' situation prevailed which allowed it to act unilaterally. Qantas put both fares on sale. It was the start of the era of low fares and mass travel.

Within three months the steady decline of traffic had been reversed but not before Qantas had to report a loss of $6 million for 1971–1972. One reason, the chairman explained, was the diversion of 16,000 passengers carried to Singapore who then boarded cheap charters to fly on to Europe. The tide appeared to have turned following the new, low fares. The September 1972 schedules saw a planned increase in 747B flights from three to five a week and a reduction in stops, bringing the flight time to Europe down to less than 25 hours.

On the national scene, the Whitlam Labor Government was elected in 1972, ending the rule of conservative parties since 1949, bringing a deeper government involvement in the operation of the airline and Australian aviation policy.

Following the success of the low-fare initiatives to Europe, Qantas and Malaysia–Singapore Airlines launched a daring holiday programme to Asia in 1972. Inclusive tours on special 707 flights designated 'charters' offered a week in Singapore for under $300, with an additional week in Malaysia available for an extra $100. The original programme was designed to fill 6000 seats but was so successful that another 4000 were added and quickly sold. The annual report for the year ending 31 March 1973 was to reflect the increase in passenger numbers, albeit at lower fares. It reported a modest profit of $466,000, a sharp turnaround. In calendar year 1973, Qantas was to carry more than one million passengers for the first time, 1,113,131, a 28 per cent increase on the previous year. In the financial year, the profit rose to $11.1 million.

The success of the Asian holiday programme led to wider inclusive tour holiday marketing. The low-fare initiative to Britain and Europe resulted in a leap of almost 50 per cent in traffic on the route in the first year and 25 per cent in the second. In 1973 the planning was for continued growth of 20 per cent by 1975-76. Qantas decided to use only 747s on the Kangaroo Route, to take advantage of its lower costs, estimated at the time to be about 13 per cent below those of the 707.

In July 1973 the Government appointed Sir Donald Anderson, the Director-General of Civil Aviation, as a director. Sir Hudson Fysh, the co-founder of the airline and chairman until the mid-1960s, died in April 1974.

By the mid-1970s, Qantas was facing another serious challenge. The oil-producing countries lifted their prices progressively. The result for the airline was an immense rise in operating costs. This came in Australia with a burst of wage inflation, presenting Qantas with an immediate financial crisis. The budget for 1974-1975 had predicted a profit of $9.7 million. Within weeks, this estimate plummeted to a loss of $10 million.

While all airlines had to face the fuel increases, new carriers such as Singapore Airlines (SIA) were able to come from a cheaper labour base (SIA had been formed after the split-up of MSA in October 1972). SIA filed for a big increase in flights between Australia and Singapore, which Qantas resisted. There was also a rash of discounting from other international airlines with surplus capacity on routes into and out of Australia. One way for Qantas to compete was to establish its own inclusive tour subsidiary, Jetabout Ltd, in 1974.

The financial and commercial problems were set aside at Christmas 1974 when Cyclone Tracy struck Darwin, precipitating the biggest airlift in Australia's history. The Qantas fleet was enlisted and evacuated 5000 people from the city in six days, setting carrying records for both the 747 and 707. A single 747 flight on 29 December carried 673 people, including babies and children. Two days earlier, a 707 had carried 327.

The New Year saw Qantas surge into marketing low-cost travel. After agreements with six Asian airlines, Qantas offered excursion fares to major Asian cities at discounts of 30 to 40 per cent off normal economy fares. Jetabout launched package tours to Asia, Japan and New Zealand in the first part of the year and to Hawaii and North America in the second. In 1975 the full effects of fuel prices and resulting inflation worldwide hit international airlines. Qantas estimated that its wage bill had risen $40 million and its fuel bill $30 million. The answer lay partly in raising fares modestly, partly in increasing the seating on 747s to 10 abreast in economy class.

The year was also to see the resignation, due to ill health, of Sir Donald Anderson, who died in 1975. He was replaced by another senior career bureaucrat, Sir Lenox Hewitt, who was already on the Qantas Board. It was a year of crisis for Qantas. Estimates showed that revenue would fall well short of meeting costs. At the same time, Qantas's share of traffic into and out of Australia, traditionally about 50 per cent, was slipping. Mass, low-cost air travel had arrived in Australia at a time of inflationary pressures and political instability. On the Kangaroo Route to the United Kingdom/ Europe, Qantas had carried 40,000 passengers in 1971–1972. In the year ending 31 March 1975 the total was 255,000, but it was a profitless boom. In the year to 31 March 1976, Qantas reported a loss of $14.1 million, moderated by a profit on the sale of three Boeing 707 aircraft, which brought in $7 million.

The new chairman and the executive team faced the task of rebuilding Qantas. Management under Ritchie had begun this process. The expansionary dreams of Turner could not have survived in such an era. In March 1976 the Board unanimously decided to appoint Hamilton as general manager from July. Ritchie bequeathed his successor an airline that was completely different in outlook from the one he had inherited from Turner.

The Qantas International Centre in George Street, Sydney was the headquarters for the company between 1982 and 1992.

Chapter 13

The Hamilton era

A MODERN QANTAS EVOLVES

Left: Sporting a new image—the new livery and new uniforms.

In the period up to 1990, Australia went through the painful process of recognising that it could not continue to protect its industries with tariffs, that it had to become part of the world financial system. It also began looking for a closer economic and strategic relationship with Asia. These processes had started in Qantas almost 20 years before. The pragmatic Keith Hamilton, who had close personal links with Asian airlines and who was willing to switch from one course of action to another if necessary, began the process which led Qantas, Australian business, and eventually the Government, down the same path.

The fall of the Whitlam Labor Government in 1975 led to a conservative coalition government under Malcolm Fraser. When Keith Hamilton took over at Qantas, the new Minister, Peter Nixon, had made several new appointments to the Board which included business people. This leavened the appointments of the previous government, which had included trade union representatives and former public servants. Nixon was also less inclined to intervene than some of his predecessors.

Hamilton's first organisational task was to revitalise the management. Management consultants Booz, Allen and Hamilton, who several years before had recommended the new corporate structure, had also found that there was no executive development program within Qantas. The two deputy general manager positions were consolidated into one, also doubling as chief operating officer. Ron Yates, the engineer who had played a big part in choosing new types of aircraft and bringing them into service, was appointed to the post. The existing 14 senior executive positions were reduced to nine.

To trim costs and reduce staff numbers, Hamilton introduced a voluntary separation plan. The chairman, Sir Lenox Hewitt, reporting the 1976–1977 profit of $11.8 million—a dramatic turnaround from the previous year's loss of $14.2 million—pointed the finger at the burden of high wages in Australia. He wrote that in 1977 an average employee cost Qantas $15,569 per annum, British Airways $8782, Singapore Airlines $6841 and Air New Zealand $8620. Hewitt claimed that, if Qantas's cost structure had been comparable with that of Singapore's, the airline would have made $125 million.

Keith Hamilton

Hamilton also reduced the airline's commitment to the grand Qantas Centre plan, the whole city block including the site of the old Wentworth Hotel, Sydney, where the first of three proposed towers was slowly rising, with costly delays caused largely by industrial trouble. Part of the Centre was already being put to use: the big Qantas computer arm, Qantam—which the airline had been building up—occupied seven floors below ground level.

Hamilton quickly perceived that Qantas was under threat from competition by foreign carriers with cheaper cost structures. Some of the competition came from supplemental or charter airlines, which the United States had encouraged for its Vietnam airlift and which had grown in Europe to serve the dense, inclusive-tour holiday traffic market. Other competition came from foreign carriers with rights to Australia which were prepared to undercut the official prices or pay high commissions and other inducements to travel agents in their desire to fill empty seats. But the biggest threat came from the Asian airlines, from countries on the Kangaroo Route to Europe. Singapore Airlines was a classic example. In an airline world which had generally recognised the so-called 'third and fourth freedoms' of air traffic, these airlines had used their geographic location to build up what was now referred to as a 'sixth freedom'.

The 'freedoms' related to the postwar agreements which established the pattern of government-to-government negotiation of air service agreements. 'Third' and 'fourth' freedoms were an exchange between country A and B which recognised the right to carry passengers and cargo originating in these two countries to one another. The 'fifth' freedom was a completely open market in which non-nationals could operate between two points. 'Sixth' freedoms were created when, say, Singapore carried 'fourth-freedom' traffic from Australia to Singapore, then 'third-freedom' traffic on to London. Australia and the United Kingdom would regard that traffic as their entitlement under the third and fourth freedom rules.

At that time, much of Australian industry survived behind high tariff walls of protection. The airline inclination was to look for some form of defence that would protect Qantas from the attack by foreign carriers with lower labour costs. Hewitt's estimates were presumably right. Qantas, with young 747Bs and long-haul routes, was to prove capable of competitive efficiencies but only when the protectionist regime proved impossible to enforce.

Hamilton told the Board Qantas could survive only if the Government enforced the rules of the air service agreements, in fares, in agent overrides and commissions and in limiting access to third- and fourth-freedom traffic. He also proposed a pattern of terminating air services rather than serving the intermediate points by stops on the Australia–United Kingdom services. Singapore would become a hub for flights from individual Australian capitals, with the aircraft arriving at about the same time, then being bulked and distributed on to flights bound for individual European destinations.

The Board passed Hamilton's misgivings on to the Department of Transport. On a practical level, directors and management worked towards giving Qantas the most efficient fleet possible—all 747s. They were to succeed, in 1977–1978, in reporting the airline's highest profit up to that time: just under $16 million. By 1979 the last of the Boeing 707-338Cs would be retired.

Qantas was also fighting a battle on two fronts. Across the Pacific, it was resisting the huge amount of capacity that US carriers wanted to put on the Australian route. On the Kangaroo Route it needed to keep out charter-type competitors. Britain's Freddie Laker (who was later to go out of business in the face of fierce competition) was generating reams of publicity with claims that he could provide fares to Australia that were much cheaper than the lowest Qantas one - then $850. On behalf of Qantas, Hewitt argued that Australia's interests were best served by providing the cheapest possible fares on scheduled services. If charter flights were brought in, the number of Qantas scheduled flights, then 16 a week to Europe, would be reduced to nine.

The Department of Transport began its review of international air services and regulatory procedures, giving high priority to lower fares for Australian travellers and increased tourist traffic. The International Civil Aviation Policy review formed the acronym ICAP. The Nixon policy, announced in October 1978, generally adopted the Qantas plan to limit services between Australia and other destinations to third and fourth freedom air services agreements, while at the same time permitting special-purpose and freight charters.

The policy implied that Asian carriers such as Singapore would have to restrict the number of services they were providing to an amount that would serve only Australia–Singapore traffic entitlements. Singapore and its ASEAN allies strenuously objected and a war of words raged between the Singapore and Australian governments and their national airlines.

ICAP also meant changes in matters such as seating in the 747s, with more economy seats. Qantas used the occasion to introduce an intermediate Business Class. This was to be a notable success and within a short time every international airline imitated the Qantas lead. The more powerful Pratt and Whitney JT9D-7F engines had become available, allowing the gross weight of the 747 to be lifted, thus permitting it to carry more passengers, cargo and fuel—which in turn gave it a greater range and allowed it to overfly previous stops.

To implement ICAP, Australia served notice of termination of air agreements. But it had to climb down in the face of US opposition. The Americans designated Continental Airlines onto the route. Given the dominant American position, Australia had to agree, and the first hope of ICAP—capacity control

Push back. A Qantas 747-400 leaves the terminal.

on a key route—was shattered.

While Qantas management looked at soaring fuel prices and plummeting yields (because of the ICAP related excursion fares), the airline was pessimistic about the immediate future. But profits ran high, in 1978-1979 reaching $23 million on airline operations but cut back in the profit and loss account by exchange losses on earlier overseas borrowings to $773,000.

Fuel costs became of increasing concern as they continued to rise throughout the 1970s. For a while Qantas was helped by the lower cost of indigenous fuel (about 40 per cent of uplift) but a government parity pricing policy annulled this advantage. In the period to 1980 there was another savage round of price increases. Qantas moved to acquire the more economic Rolls-Royce engine and to buy more fuel-efficient, later-model 747s, trading in its original aircraft. The main concern for Qantas was that it had to seek permission for fare increases. These lagged behind the fuel and wage cost rises. In 1979–80, the airline made an operating loss of more than $10 million and an overall loss, counting extraordinaries such as exchange losses, of $21.2 million.

The pressure on Qantas from operators such as Laker, claiming he could provide much cheaper fares, and also from Ansett Transport Industries wanting to operate regional services continued into the 1980s. Hewitt retired on 30 June 1980. His successor was a businessman, Jim Leslie, a Board member since October 1979 and a former oil company executive.

The change brought a realisation in management that ICAP's regulatory regime was not going to work.

Asian countries condemned it as a move by a rich country to freeze out emerging Asian airlines. An attempt by the Australian Government to prosecute Singapore Airlines for offering discount fares failed. At the other end of the scale, the US Government presented competition rather than regulation as the way towards lower fares and better services.

These developments came at a time of deepening recession in Australia and in the airline industry worldwide. Aircraft were flying with thousands of empty seats and the industry was suffering big losses. Qantas carriage on the Kangaroo Route was down 10 per cent in the first four months of the 1980–1981 financial year. British Airways was predicting a loss equivalent to A$210 million and Pan American was heading towards a loss of US$115 million.

At home, Ralph Hunt—a less decisive man than Nixon—had taken over as Minister. Hunt was pressed hard to allow the Australian domestic airlines to operate some regional Qantas routes and the new Board, under Leslie, began a spirited defence. In January Leslie led the Qantas Board to Canberra for an unprecedented confrontation with the Fraser Government. Leslie warned that the government was well advanced on a path which would reduce Qantas to a shell and allow it to be taken over at a bargain price.

As the economic position of Qantas deteriorated during 1981. Leslie called on the Government urgently to subscribe $50 million in capital, which would still leave it a ratio of 83 per cent debt to 17 per cent equity. While not refusing, the Government said that it could not make a decision until later in the year.

The financial results for that year were a blow: a $19.5 million loss, including a loss on airline operations of $41 million. The Board blamed an industrial dispute over crewing levels on the 747SP for the extent of the disaster.

A new Qantas attitude was becoming apparent. The airline believed that financial recovery and the defeat of discounters lay in the maintenance of high standards and good value, together with 'realistic pricing'. Qantas was choosing a strong focus, the Australian traveller, the company said. Statements indicated that the airline was prepared 'to fly its way out' of the recession with a new and aggressive strategy to target competitors after the government conceded powers on fare-setting to the airline. In 1982 Qantas moved into the market with wholesale discounting, dropping some fares by up to $200. The airline also deployed capacity away from Europe to Asian routes and, with the lower fares, began to experience encouraging growth again. A new general manager for marketing, John Ward, declared that the future of Qantas lay in the Asia-Pacific region.

To restore some solidity to the balance sheet, Qantas announced plans to sell the new Qantas Centre, its property in San Francisco and its interest in Qantas Wentworth Holdings, the owner of the Wentworth Hotel in Sydney. Along with a belated $25 million equity injection, the moves greatly increased the cash position at a time when the airline was to report, for the financial year, an operating loss of $24 million. The profit reported was $63.5 million, including the asset sales. Finally, in what were to be the last days of the Fraser Government, Wal Fife was named Minister for Aviation. Sir Cedric Turner died in November 1982.

The Fraser Government was defeated in March 1983 and Kim Beazley became Minister for Aviation in the Labor Government. Qantas and the new Minister established an early rapport, which was to result in an overhaul of the old financial directive, freeing the airline to conduct its business in a more commercial manner. While aggressively pursing its new commercial policies, Qantas incurred a loss in 1982–1983 of $34.4 million, with the loss on airline operations at $47.6 million. One of the measures being taken was to reduce staff numbers by more than 1000, even though the total was the lowest since 1969–1970. Fuel costs had risen by $44 million, much of it in exchange rate variations. The rise in traffic brought about by aggressive marketing, and the lower costs achieved by smaller staff numbers and control of operations, resulted in a profit for 1983–1984 of just under $56 million from airline operations. Leslie reported that Qantas, was 'now a leaner, tougher and smarter airline'.

Qantas appeared to be firmly on a new path by the end of the year, which brought credit on both Leslie as chairman and Hamilton as managing director. But Hamilton was not to see the full fruits of his work. He died suddenly at his home in December 1984. In a tribute, Leslie called Hamilton 'the architect of the company's return to profitability and its continued ability to compete efficiently and successfully in the international market place'.

Chapter 14

The friendly way

AN AUSTRALIAN ADVENTURE

Left: Dawn breaks over the tails of Australian Airlines and Qantas aircraft.

A single-engine Otter aircraft used by TAA on its Papua New Guinea Sunbird service.

The other airline stream, which eventually joined Qantas, began at dawn on 9 September 1946 when 21 passengers boarded a DC3 at Laverton near Melbourne to fly to Sydney. This was the first flight of Trans-Australia Airlines (TAA) which was to be renamed Australian Airlines in 1986 and merged with Qantas in 1993.

Australian Airlines brought with it a considerable dowry of history and experience. One of Australia's two domestic airlines, it had been profitable for most of its 47 years, with a network that extended into all the main domestic markets.

As Australian Airlines, it also brought to the merger its own extensive marketing and computer reservation systems, industry know-how and access to terminals. Its assets included resorts at Lizard, Dunk, Bedarra, Brampton and Great Keppel islands in Queensland. Constrained by a limited share of regional and commuter airline business, Australian had only 41 per cent of total domestic traffic but more than half of the trunk route traffic.

TAA was born in political controversy after World War II. The Labor Government originally wanted to nationalise the airline industry. Before the war had ended, the Government passed the Australian National Airlines Bill. Operators of privately owned airlines challenged the legislation in the High Court, which ruled in December 1945 that the Commonwealth could not nationalise air services but that it could launch its own airline.

The Australian National Airlines Commission— which was in effect the TAA Board—was formed in February 1946. The Commission chose Trans-Australia Airlines as its trading name. TAA's first appointments provided the airline with a blend of commercial and aviation expertise. Arthur (later Sir Arthur) Coles, a founder of the retail chain G J Coles —now a part of the Coles–Myer group—became its first chairman. Captain Lester Brain was recruited from Qantas as the first general manager. The new airline attracted talented pilots, engineers, ground crew and administrators, many from the wartime RAAF, and acquired DC3s and DC4s. Brain applied to TAA the high standards he had set in Qantas. One of his earliest decisions was to establish a commercial pilot training school at Point Cook for both ex-RAAF and civil airline pilots. All pilots had to go through this initial check and training. Apart from checking all pilots and ridding them of any flaws in technique, the course provided a means of developing discipline and loyalty to the new airline.

One of the first goals was to establish an interstate network. Within a month of its first scheduled flight to Sydney, TAA began flying to Brisbane, adding Hobart in November. By the end of 1946, it had daily flights to all State capitals. The creation of the country's first viable national trunk airline network provided the social and economic justification for the airline being in the public sector. Initially TAA had permission only to operate interstate services. But in 1947 the Queensland and Tasmanian governments granted the new airline rights to fly within their States.

TAA then launched flights as far north as Cairns in Queensland.

During 1948 and 1949, TAA expanded its services in Queensland and took over the 5870 kilometres of internal routes served by Qantas. By then TAA had the biggest unduplicated route mileage of any domestic airline in the world. For its Outback routes, it replaced the ageing de Havilland aircraft, regarded as the workhorse of the Outback, with the Australian-designed and built tri-motor de Havilland Drover and extended its services to the Gulf of Carpentaria. By the end of 1951, its network comprised 35,070 unduplicated route kilometres.

TAA's network continued to expand into the 1960s. It became the first Australian airline to carry more than one million passengers, in 1959–1960. In July 1960 it took over Qantas operations in

The TAA DH84 John Flynn *in use by the Royal Flying Doctor Service.*

Brampton Island, one of Qantas' holiday resorts.

Papua New Guinea. The airline displayed its versatility with a mixture of services from jet flights every two hours in each direction between Sydney and Melbourne to weekly flights to cattle stations in the Outback. TAA dropped fodder to stricken cattle during floods and also flew and maintained the aircraft of the Royal Flying Doctor Service and the Northern Territory Aerial Medical Service. By the mid-1960s it served 140 ports on more than 64,000 kilometres of routes. But these were soon to be pruned by withdrawal from unprofitable routes and the eventual handover of Australia–Papua New Guinea services to Air Niugini.

From its early days, TAA showed a flair for marketing. In the booming postwar years it won market share by advertising 'One Fare for All—the Lowest'. The slogan attacked the rival Australian National Airways (ANA), then the biggest domestic airline, which discounted to individuals and organisations. About 60 per cent of its passengers got the discounts. The slogan won business for TAA which priced its fares on the lower rate. From its early years the airline also used a slogan which became one of Australia's best known: 'Fly TAA—The Friendly Way'.

Innovative fleet decisions consolidated TAA's place in the market. In 1948, it ordered Convair 240s, the first pressurised aircraft to enter service in Australia and one which captured the public's imagination. The Convair brought comfort to air travel and also introduced innovations such as thermal de-icing, hollow-steel reversible pitch propellers and electrically heated windshields. In its first demonstration flight after arriving in Melbourne, the new aircraft brought gasps from onlookers as it took off into a climb that would have meant a stall for any other airliner in use in Australia at the time.

TAA became the first Australian airline to operate turbine-powered aircraft when it introduced the prop-jet Vickers Viscount in 1954. Its rival, ANA, was more conservative and chose piston-engined aircraft. The decision was to lead to the demise of the old ANA. Equipment decisions were a central issue in the formation of the two-airline policy which regulated the Australian domestic airline industry for more than 30 years. Much of TAA's history was inextricably bound up in this policy.

TAA had made good progress with its finances. It lost more than $1 million in its first year of operations (1946–1947), $431,344 in 1947–1948, and in 1948–1949 $189,772, which later became a profit when the Government announced retrospective rebate of air route charges as part of its new airline policy.

TAA, 'The Nation's Jetline'. The Super Viscount was used by TAA on mainland services between 1954 and 1970.

After the 1949 election of a coalition government, the incoming administration inherited an energetic business which was about to announce its first profit. TAA had become a national asset and was popular with the travelling public.

The government decided to retain TAA but changed the rules to ensure that ANA received more Government business and also its share of air mail carriage. It substantially reduced air route charges for both airlines and offered to help them with finance for new aircraft. Routes, schedules, fares and freight were rationalised.

The terms of this—the first of Australia's two-airline policies—were set down in the *Civil Aviation Agreement Act 1952*, which was to last 15 years. The government also amended the *Australian National Airlines Act* (the legal foundation of TAA) to put TAA

on a basis similar to that of a public company. TAA was required, for the first time, to pay income and sales tax. Despite the 1952 moves, ANA failed to solve its financial problems and was sold to Ansett Transport Industries in 1957 for $6.6 million.

Following the ATI takeover of ANA, the Civil Aviation Agreement was amended in 1957. Operating rules were introduced which controlled seating capacity to achieve specified load factors. The rules set out to maintain balanced competition—to prevent either airline becoming dominant and jeopardising the existence of the other. At this time, TAA favoured buying the Caravelle jet. Ansett–ANA favoured the Electra prop-jet, which both airlines subsequently purchased.

The controls were strengthened by other legislation. The *Airlines Equipment Act 1958* specified

The 727, flagship of the TAA fleet from 1964.

that both airlines had to start flying new aircraft on the same day. It stipulated that the aircraft purchased be comparable in size and performance.

A cross-charter agreement in 1960 required TAA to hand over three Viscount 700s to ANA in exchange for two DC6Bs to achieve fleet parity. The policy acted as a brake on TAA. It had to take the outcasts of its rival's fleet and was not able to order jets for another seven years. The system also established controls over fares and service, restraining TAA from introducing special fares to foster the growth of holiday travel within Australia and overseas tourism to Australia. These controls were unpopular, but they achieved the objective of building a financially viable domestic airline industry.

TAA entered the jet age with Boeing 727s in November 1964. The 727s were an immediate success with the public. With their speed, comfort and mechanical reliability they stimulated amazing growth in the Australian airline industry. The 727 was followed by the introduction of the DC9 in 1967.

Highlighting the increased mechanical dependability of jet aircraft, TAA's first two DC9s set a world record for mechanical reliability by completing 495 separate revenue flights without a single delay for mechanical reasons. The record run was halted when a bird or a stone was sucked into an engine.

When the jets arrived, TAA had a fleet of 16 aircraft with 15 different engines. General manager John Ryland started Operation Streamline to reduce the number to four aircraft types and three engines. He also began withdrawing the airline from unprofitable routes. These decisions began to reshape the airline for the future.

TAA was prevented from engaging in activities other than air transport before 1973, when its Act was amended. It subsequently bought into non-aviation business, some with partners. These included Australian Accommodation and Tours (AAT), Hertz and resorts at Dunk Island, Bedarra Island, Great Keppel Island, Brampton Island, Lizard Island and Airlie Beach. AAT, Hertz and the Airlie Beach property were later sold.

Although the Ansett group had acquired strategic regionals back in the 1940s and 1950s, it was not until 1985 that TAA was allowed to buy its first regional operation, Air Queensland. But substantial operational, financial and contractual difficulties led to much of the Air Queensland operations being phased out by April 1988.

Lyndon McKenzie, who became general manager after Ryland's death, made the moves into island resorts and introduced creative fares aimed at broadening the airline's traffic base. TAA built alliances to help its business to grow, including arrangements with international carriers for the valuable on-carriage on international traffic within Australia. Recognising the potential of tourism, it used its marketing resources to assist local tourist industry bodies with destination promotions.

Control of ATI passed to News Corporation and TNT in 1979–80 when ATI diversified internationally into aviation and associated activities. News chief Rupert Murdoch and TNT's Sir Peter Abeles, soon after taking control, ordered an entirely new fleet of Boeing aircraft—including the wide-body 767, more 727s and a brand new fleet of Boeing 737-200s to replace DC9s. They also introduced free drinks in first class, greatly improved in-flight catering and started a frequent flyers club with its own airport lounges.

Before the Murdoch–Abeles takeover, TAA had ordered the A300, the first wide-bodied aircraft to be used domestically. In 1979, congestion at capital city airports, especially at Sydney, was becoming critical, and noise was an associated difficulty. Strong growth in air travel was the pattern and wide-body jets with bigger capacity, less noise and better reliability seemed to be the best available option. However, before the aircraft entered service, recession arising from a worldwide oil crisis led to high inflation and unemployment.

TAA, which carried a record 5.14 million passengers in 1980, saw market forecasts evaporate. It did not carry five million passengers again until 1986. TAA made a loss for two consecutive years (1981–1982 and 1982–1983), its first since 1951–1952.

The proud new face of Australian Airlines in 1986.

The next general manager, Frank Ball, a former captain who was the first Australian airline pilot licensed on turbine aircraft, set out to size TAA to the needs of the market. This meant slashing costs, reducing staff numbers by 1200, giving up loss-making routes and closing both the city terminals and the airport bus system.

In this period, TAA introduced Business Class—an initiative which helped the airline to claw back the vital business travel market share from Ansett. TAA was the first airline in the world to have three classes—first, business and economy—on wide-bodied and narrow-bodied aircraft on short-haul flights. Achieving this meant reorganising catering, seat configuration and seat allocation.

This task fell to James Strong who took over as general manager after Ball retired in November 1985. Deregulation of the domestic airline industry was on the horizon with widespread speculation about privatising the Government-owned airline. Strong's response was to transform the airline to allow it to compete more vigorously. He immediately set about changing the culture of the airline, motivating staff personally at all levels to bring about a complete change in the way they served their customers.

When the airline took delivery of new-generation Boeing 737-300s in mid-1986, Strong changed its name and its colours. As Australian Airlines, it shaped a new strategy of vigorous competition in the business and regular travel market. Strong reorganised its internal structure to make it more responsive to market needs. This development came at a time when the Government announced plans to move towards a greater degree of deregulation and competition. Australian Airlines under Strong, with enthusiastic support from his executive team, staff and customers, welcomed the challenge.

The airline improved skills in yield management to focus more sharply on route profitability as it dealt with the reality of carrying passengers with a mixture of first class, business, economy and discount fares. Australian also launched innovative marketing measures, greatly enhancing its Flight Deck Clubs to provide more adequately for the corporate travel needs of its business passengers and introduced a frequent flyer scheme to build passenger loyalty. These measures, combined with new service standards both on the ground and in the air, helped win customer loyalty.

On 30 April 1988, Australian Airlines became an incorporated public company. The provisions of the *Australian National Airlines Act*, which had controlled the carrier's activities since 1945, ceased to apply. A new board was appointed under chairman A E (Ted) Harris. The airline was given greater managerial freedom. After Strong left to become chief executive of a national law firm in 1989, Australian ran into a major crisis when its pilots, along with those of its rival Ansett went on strike over demands for a 29 per cent pay rise and other claims. With government assistance, both airlines chartered aircraft and crews from international operators and used Royal Australian Air Force and Navy aircraft to rebuild networks. After the pilots

resigned en masse on 24 August 1989, Australian recruited a new pilot force working on new contracts and by 1990 services had virtually returned to normal.

When deregulation arrived in 1990, Australian Airlines competed vigorously with Ansett and new entrant Compass in a period which saw heavy price discounting and fierce marketing activity aimed at securing market position. As the chairman, Ted Harris, observed in his report on the 1991–1992 financial year: *'Uncertainty surrounding the future of the group, together with extremely* *volatile economic conditions made it a difficult and challenging year'*.

Australian's general manager during that phase of its history was John Schaap, who like Lester Brain had come to the airline after long experience with Qantas. Schaap was at the controls when the Government facilitated the Qantas purchase of the domestic carrier in 1992.

Two great airlines merge in 1993.

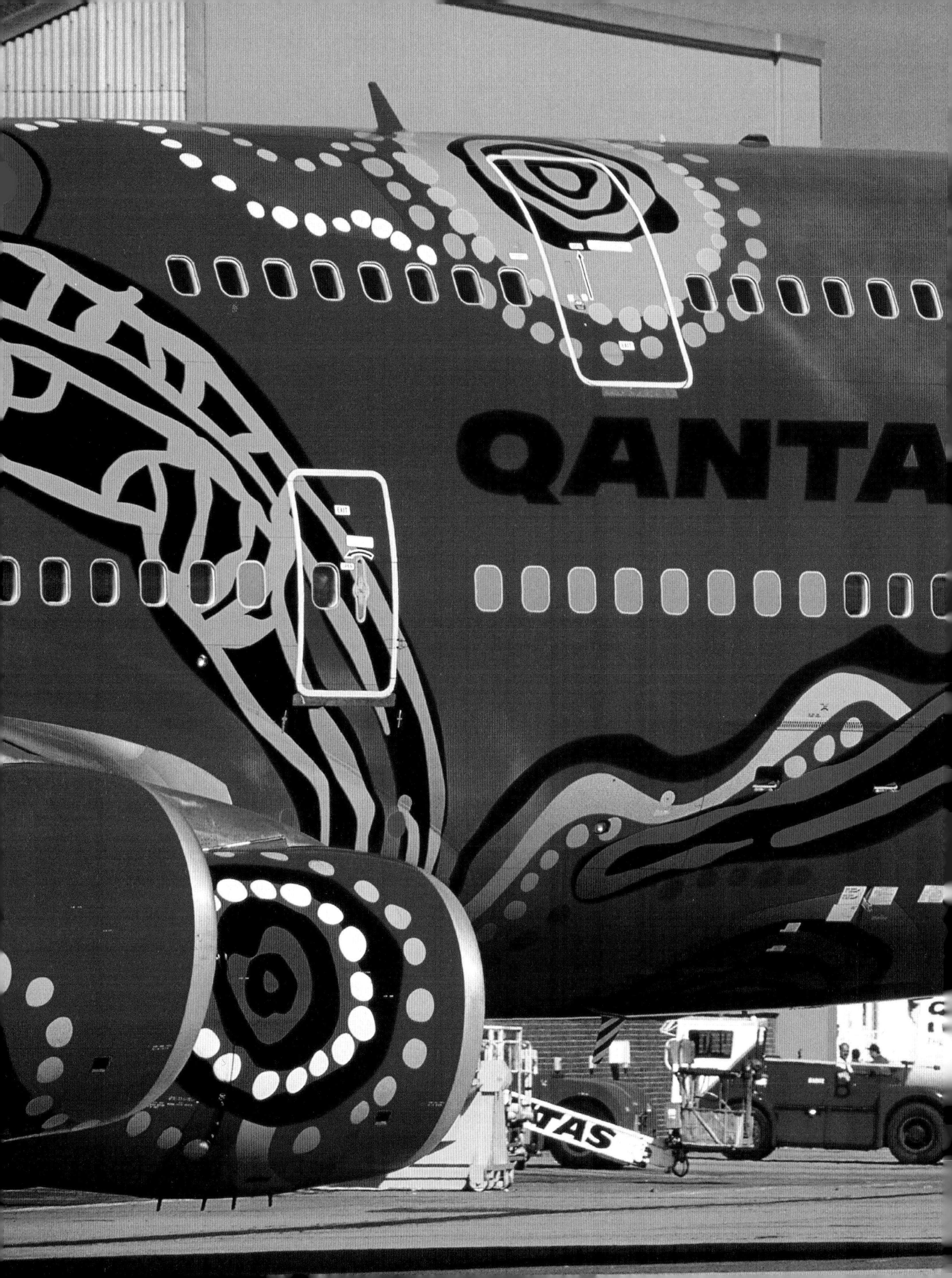
QANTA
TAS

Chapter 15

Towards privatisation

THE NEW ERA BEGINS

Ron Yates who had already passed retiring age when he became chief executive, appointed two men whom he described as 'young Turks', John Ward as deputy chief executive, and Peter Stainlay as general manager marketing. In Canberra, too, there were changes. Kim Beazley became Minister for Defence and Peter Morris, who had been Opposition Spokesman on Transport, became Minister for Transport with responsibility for aviation.

A new order for a 747-300 for March 1986 meant that within a year the Qantas fleet would total 21 747s and six 767s. The airline planned average utilisation of the 747s at about 11 hours a day. With the new -300s Qantas sought to increase their daily utilization, an indication that the economic cycle had again changed and the market was growing.

In February 1986, the Board decided to appoint John Menadue, a former Prime Ministerial Private Secretary (to Gough Whitlam), high level public servant, senior newspaper executive and Australian Ambassador to Japan. He was the first chief executive to come from outside the airline.

Menadue saw that he had inherited an organisation that was clearly excellent in operational terms but in his view lacking in some areas of management. He felt that management attitudes were contributing to continuing industrial problems at the Jet Base. Menadue believed that Qantas had to expand through promotions, by quality of market and by attacking individual markets, specifically Japan—although the whole of Asia offered potential

Previous page: Wunala (Kangaroo) Dreaming. The vibrant Aboriginal designs on this 747B are a tribute to the art of Aboriginal Australians.

A selection of Rolls-Royce engines on display.

*The Qantas Centre at Mascot in Sydney is only minutes
away from the domestic and international airport
terminals, the Jet Base and catering operations.*

for tourism to Australia. His prior involvement
with Japan as Australian Ambassador convinced him
that Qantas should drive into the Japanese market
which was to become a significant revenue earner for
the airline.

Another of his initiatives was to take Qantas out of
the high-rent area of central Sydney to a lower-cost
location on the outskirts, which was to lead eventually
to the shift of its corporate office to Mascot, close to
the airport.

By 1987 Boeing had committed to a new
generation of the Boeing 747, the -400 model with a
changed wing and improved avionics which would
allow two-pilot operation. The -400 had extremely
long range which would permit Qantas to operate its
Sydney to Los Angeles services with minimal payload
penalties and also one stop flights from Sydney to
London (via Bangkok or Singapore). Boeing planned

to stretch the Boeing 767 to produce the Boeing
767-300ER, which also appealed to Qantas.

Riding on the crest of the traffic revival and new
equipment during 1986, the airline reported a record
profit of $104.2 million in the year to 31 March 1987,
carrying more than three million passengers in the
year. With one-stop services to London and Europe
proving attractive to the business community, Qantas
plunged heavily into the new Boeing 747-400. It
ordered four, with options on another 15 in May 1987.
It also placed one firm order for the twin-engine
Boeing 767-300ER, with seven options. Later in the year,
the Board was to authorise three more 767 options.

In Canberra, Senator Gareth Evans replaced
Peter Morris as Transport Minister.

In mid-1987, the Australian travel market was
growing so rapidly that Qantas management had
to charter aircraft from outside companies to carry
the passengers. The travel industry was building up
strength in the Australian economy and with it came
pressure for more foreign carriers to be granted
Australian services.

With new aircraft on order, an expansion of the
Jet Base and other requirements, Qantas told the
government that it needed about $600 million in
funding to maintain a proper debt to equity ratio.
Senator Evans took the daring step in 1988 of
preparing a paper for the Labor caucus, which set
policy for the ruling party, canvassing privatisation for
the airline. He drew attention to factors such as the
need for capital, the fact that a government-owned
airline was seen as expressing foreign policy and also

Qantas chefs take great pride in their work.

Quality service is a hallmark of Qantas.

as being involved in migration policy. These were factors that could affect the airline's commercial performance. Privatisation was on the agenda and in 1989 management proposed a plan to float half the airline by 1990, with the Government retaining a 'golden share' that would give it control on questions of national interest. The call by the then Treasurer, Paul Keating, for limitations on borrowing by government-owned entities, which would have emasculated the Qantas equipment programme, meant that some new solution would have to be found.

Government relations with the company, which required ministerial approval for many actions, including industrial relations matters, were cumbersome and inhibited decision-making. The paper, although bitterly debated in both caucus and Labor Party conferences, was to lead eventually to privatisation.

New Zealand had already gone down the path of privatisation and had decided to divest itself of the national carrier, Air New Zealand. Qantas bid for 25 per cent of the airline in May 1988. The move was part of a growing perception in the airline community that giant airlines would dominate the industry in the 1990s and beyond. Smaller ones would either form alliances, operate in 'niche' roles or go under. A holding in Air New Zealand would strengthen Qantas and its alliances in the Pacific area. Qantas took a 19·9 per cent shareholding in Air New Zealand in 1988.

Meanwhile, the Australian Government, in a policy statement by the prime minister, said government enterprises would seek the highest level of operational

Attention to every last detail. The Qantas symbol receives some special attention.

efficiency with minimisation of government day-to-day controls, although they would be required to meet 'goals and targets' established through individual corporate plans. However, purely commercial imperatives would not necessarily apply as the government would have 'wider policy initiatives'. The boards would be required to work towards financial targets agreed with ministers in advance. The problem of inadequate equity remained.

The Qantas Board, still operating somewhat in the dark as far as policy was concerned, budgeted for a pre-tax profit of $258.4 million in 1988–1989, increasing capacity to Japan, the ASEAN countries and across the Tasman. However, growing staff

numbers, which had reached 16,000 while the indicator of productivity in terms of available tonne-kilometres had begun to level off, were a concern.

Menadue had worked to institute a staff bonus scheme, which would give most staff an extra week's pay. But in a time of government restraint the government ordered withdrawal of the plan. Airlines were running into a severe shortage of engineering staff as award rates lagged behind wages being paid in the Sydney area. In 12 months, Qantas lost 371 tradespeople, an attrition rate of 15 per cent. Shortages of staff were beginning to delay maintenance and hence aircraft. At this time, outside airlines and manufacturers sought to contract

WORLD CLASS QUALITY

For the first time in the 75 year history of Qantas its entire uniform requirements are supplied and manufactured by Australian fashion companies. The airline has never hesitated to search the fashion houses of the world for the most contemporary styles of apparel to match its image of quality. Qantas has always been uncompromising in the presentation of its personnel and the quality of its wardrobe.

That Australian fashion houses now provide Qantas with its wardrobe is recognition of the fact that the Australian fashion industry delivers world class quality in every aspect.

The key Qantas Wardrobe suppliers include Calcoup, knitwear; S. F. Corporate Clothing, uniforms; John Kaldor Fabricmaker, fabrics; Kolotex Australia, hosiery; Luigi & Anthony, trousers and tailored skirts; Macquarie Textiles, textiles; Moda Design, blazers and jackets; Oroton, handbags; Neoman, designer shirtmaker; Solution V, luggage and belts; Sydney Neckwear Company, ties and neckwear; Top Ryde Tailoring and Alterations, tailoring and alterations.

The new Qantas uniform is the first 'all Australia' uniform produced for the airline.

INNOVATIVE MARKETING

Over recent years the distinctive green card of American Express has become synonymous with the commercial relationship the company has developed with Qantas.

The rapid development of airline loyalty programmes during the 1980s has evolved to the point where American Express now links its own product with Qantas' Frequent Flyer Plan. This innovative arrangement affords benefits to both Qantas passengers and American Express customers by encouraging each company's customers to use the services of the other in exchange for significant additional benefits.

In Australia, American Express also operates a national travel agency network with over 200 offices making it one of Qantas' largest and most highly regarded retail distributors.

Together with its other products and services, American Express provides unrivalled services and access for Qantas travellers, both in Australia and around the world.

Worldwide American Express promotion involving five million postcards made available to the public to encourage Australian's friends and relatives to visit Australia.

Cleaning the windscreen of the 747-400, Longreach.

maintenance to the Qantas Jet Base but this work had to be sent elsewhere.

Qantas management at the end of 1988 was developing a business plan that called for an emphasis on quality and service, not necessarily on the lowest cost fares. It saw Qantas operating into fewer European ports in particular, but hubbing with local carriers around the world to carry passengers on to their eventual destinations. In 1989 Qantas management was also to propose the formation of an arms-length airline, Australia-Asia, to fly to Taiwan, a country of political sensitivity to China. By 1992, these Boeing 767 services were to build up to four a week to be subsequently replaced by 747SP services in 1994, increasing capacity by one third.

Significant changes were to take place at the top of the airline during 1989. John Menadue left the company in July and John Ward was appointed acting chief executive while the position was advertised. Ward, a former deputy chief executive and chief operating officer, had joined Qantas in 1969 and had broad management experience across the financial planning and commercial areas of the airline.

When Qantas was preparing for the anticipated march of profits, the domestic airlines were stopped by pilots who resigned in August 1989. The thriving tourism industry came to a virtual halt and Qantas revenues plunged with the uncertainty. It was during this period that Jim Leslie's term as chairman, from 1980 to 1989, ended. His last statement was a strong call for privatisation of Qantas to free it from government controls. His successor was W L (Bill) Dix, former president and chief executive of the Ford Motor Company in Australia. In December, John Ward was named chief executive on the eve of the celebrations of the 70th anniversary of the airline.

Financially, the deregulation of the 1980s had brought a ferment of takeovers, conglomerates and massive debt to companies throughout Australia. The burden of this debt was to bring the castles of several entrepreneurs crumbling into bankruptcy. Worldwide, the airline industry was in a similar state of turmoil. Much of it, including Qantas, was not competitive, in terms of the yield that was available in the severely competitive markets that had in many instances brought fares down below cost of production.

Many airlines were convinced growth would

continue and were placing orders for the new-technology aircraft from Boeing, Airbus and McDonnell Douglas which seemed, in their efficiencies, to promise lower operating costs. The result was much more capacity being placed on routes and still lower fares.

The nature of the industry appeared to be changing. The so-called 'mega-carriers' were emerging from a maze of airline alliances and there were predictions that the way the industry was shaping several big carriers in the USA and Europe would dominate the industry.

The dizzy days of the boom ended abruptly in 1989 when Australia's domestic airline pilots stopped work in an industrial dispute, then resigned en masse and brought the internal network virtually to a standstill. While Qantas pilots did not join in, the lack of domestic flights severely curtailed the overseas tourist inflow, which had driven growth strongly in the late 1980s. The government supported the airlines, both in the industrial relations field and with subsidies (it also authorised the use of military aircraft for civilian flights), but did not compensate Qantas for the heavy loss of business which resulted.

The sudden shock forced Qantas to rethink its strategy for the 1990s. The immediate crisis was to control costs and generate cash to keep the airline growing. Qantas management called in consultants Coopers & Lybrand from New York to advise on the changes that were needed and the recommendation was to cut staff numbers, which had grown so strongly in the preceding years.

In all there were to be 3300 redundancies, what seemed a savage toll. Management moved to reassure banks on the airline's viability while teams were set up to look at every aspect of the company to cut costs. Management benchmarked itself against British Airways, Air New Zealand, United Airlines, Singapore Airlines and Cathay Pacific. When the process started, Qantas costs were in the top rank.

In engineering and maintenance, management was able to negotiate changes in work practices that introduced efficiencies. One step was to reduce stockholdings, which resulted in considerable savings.

Looking at the way the product was marketed, the teams identified high selling costs, such as agent commissions, which had risen over the years as

Maintenance work on Wunala Dreaming.

James Strong, managing director of Qantas.

airlines competed to win business. Despite fears that if Qantas cut commissions, agents (who generated most of the airlines' sales revenues) would switch customers to other airlines, the cuts went ahead. Initially rival carriers did well, but with these airlines also facing their own costs pressures, the general level of commissions came down throughout the industry.

Qantas also moved to sell off its earlier Pratt and Whitney-powered Boeing 747-200s, which had been superseded by higher capacity -300s and during the period by the even longer range -400s, which achieved even greater levels of saving. The airline sold nine 747s at the peak of the used-aircraft market (because the crisis that had hit Qantas had not arrived in the wider airline community). It was able to realise a $350 million profit but more importantly to generate cash during the slump caused by the domestic airline stoppage.

Still benchmarking, Qantas found that its costs had dropped to well below Air New Zealand and British

Airways and were comparable with the giant, United (which had huge efficiencies of scale) and the Asians, which at that time had lower labour costs.

Late in 1990, two related disasters hit the world airline industry. Iraq invaded Kuwait, leading to the Gulf War. Suddenly, with fears of terrorist attack one of the causes, travel slumped across the world. Fuel prices quadrupled because of the turmoil in the Middle East. The airline industry was to lose US$15.6 billion between 1990 and 1993.

One effect of the dramatic pilots' strike was that it forced Qantas to restructure, taking it well along the efficiency path by the time other international airlines realised the extent of the trouble they faced.

Qantas had emerged with a clear, seven-point strategic direction. The first priority was to sustain profitability by continuing to attack costs and moving towards a costs structure that achieved best practice internationally. Another key priority was to maintain and where possible to improve service to customers and ensure the cuts did not affect the product features that gave Qantas is strengths in the market. There were continual reviews of service quality and customer expectations in an effort to prune features that were not needed and improve those that customers appreciated.

A third step was to restructure the network, providing capacity and services where they were needed most and where they presented emerging opportunities (notably in Asia), as well as modernising the fleet.

In a ground-breaking initiative, Australia had

The flight deck of the 747-400 series. Qantas has one of the youngest jet fleets of any airline in the world.

bartered new rights with Asian carriers, which wanted to add extra Australian services. The Australian negotiators sought rights for Qantas to go beyond cities such as Singapore, Bangkok and Hong Kong so that eventually a 'golden triangle' of intra-Asian services could be developed. Originally these were modest, operated by Boeing 767s and aimed at carrying Australian tourists on an Asian circuit. By 1995 Qantas was operating more than 140 flights a week linking Australia with 11 countries in North Asia and South East Asia.

The Asian services built on the Qantas concept of off-shore hubbing, which had been developed at Singapore (and also, for Pacific routes, at Honolulu). State governments, which wanted to encourage tourism, had always lobbied for direct international services from the smaller capitals. The use of the 767s with fewer seats allowed flights to be routed, for instance, from Adelaide to Singapore. Passengers bound for European destinations, such as London and Frankfurt, were then able to transfer to the 747s that had originated in Sydney or Melbourne.

Services also began between Australia and South Korea. The Seoul flights grew to four a week during the 1994 holiday season. Asian holiday traffic became an important source of Qantas revenue, with flights from five Japanese cities (after Osaka Airport opened in 1994) to new Australian destinations such as Cairns. Seoul and Taiwan flights were also to be routed to Cairns and Brisbane.

The welcoming face of Qantas.

On the financial side, the debt had to be attacked and with the government as shareholder unwilling to contribute more capital, privatisation offered the only way to continued viability. A public share issue also offered a chance to achieve widespread Australian ownership.

The Qantas Board and management set about trying to persuade the government to liberalise the aviation industry in Australia, notably seeking an end to the restrictions which prevented Qantas from operating within the country. Such a move would also clear the way for rationalisation by allowing Qantas to acquire one of the two domestic airlines.

Internationally, the strategy was to ensure Qantas joined one of the leading groups of carriers that would achieve strength through size and domination of selected markets.

When he took office, Prime Minister Paul Keating gave signs he wanted to break from the past and promote real change in Australia.

In early 1992, Prime Minister Keating said the Australian government would remove its previous barriers between domestic and international air

services. This would allow Qantas to offer domestic flights on its international aircraft transiting between Australian ports, while ending its previous monopoly on international flights. The statement cleared the way for Qantas to bid for Australian Airlines, which it eventually was to buy for $400 million. In approving the Qantas offer, the government announced a change of course: it would sell off all the airline instead of limiting the sale to the 49 per cent which was previously proposed.

The Qantas purchase of Australian Airlines was completed in September 1992 and the combined airline moved quickly towards privatisation. The Board decided to clean up the balance sheet and wrote off substantial intangibles, the biggest of which was a result of the Australian Airlines purchase. Also included in the clean-up were write-downs of the Boeing 747SPs to reflect their residual value (they were to be chartered to Australia–Asia Airlines and put on the Taiwan route) and also write-offs of obligations still remaining on long-term rental costs at the former Sydney headquarters. These measures were reflected in the accounts for 1992–1993.

As a first step in privatisation, the government sought a 'trade' investor to buy into Qantas, to ensure it joined one of the major alliances that were forming among world airlines. The trade sale offer produced two possibilities. Singapore Airlines saw an opportunity to take equity in Qantas and for Qantas later to take equity in Singapore, which, when linked with other Asian carriers, would produce a strong competitor in the Asia–Pacific areas to the mega-carriers.

British Airways, already one of the mega-carriers, had developed a strategy which saw strengths in having an alliance at both ends of the world's longest air route. This would give Qantas access to Europe and North America and British Airways the entry into the Pacific. The alliance would also produce a number of synergies that would produce cost efficiencies. The government accepted the higher British Airways offer of $665 million for a 25 per cent share in Qantas, with conditions that gave it three seats on the board.

In February 1993 the long battle by successive Qantas boards for adequate capitalisation was finally recognised. The government injected $1.35 billion in capital into the airline as British Airways completed its purchase.

March brought another significant change. Gary Pemberton, who had been chairman of Brambles as well as a Qantas director, succeeded Bill Dix. The directors decided that the merged Qantas and Australian Airlines would trade under the single name 'Qantas The Australian Airline'. In mid-1993, John Ward stepped down as chief executive of Qantas and the chairman took over in an acting role until the board appointed James Strong as managing director.

Strong, a director of Qantas and a former managing director of Australian Airlines, restructured the Qantas management, in part to reflect the operation of both domestic and international services. There were a number of new appointments, many of whom were executives with extensive experience in airlines and other industries.

Because of the state of the Australian stock market and the need for Qantas to prepare for a float, the government announced that the sale of the remainder of the shares would take place in the financial year 1994-1995. The offer was eventually made slightly later, in July 1995.

With the new structure bedded down and a single 'brand name' airline, Pemberton announced a group profit on operations of $32.9 million for 1992–1993 on revenue of $5.8 billion. In the following financial year Qantas announced an operating profit of $301.8 million. The profit rose further to $320.4 million for 1994-1995.

Relaxing in one of the newly-designed Qantas Club lounges.

The alliance between British Airways and Qantas was given expression in August 1994 when the two airlines announced plans to cooperate on the Kangaroo Route between Australia and Britain. The plan was for mutual marketing and rationalisation of services. The plan had to be referred to the Trade Practices Commission in Australia. After extensive examination, the commission allowed the cooperation to go through, providing a firm basis for global planning by the alliance.

The new management was also able to concentrate on affairs at home. The merger of domestic and overseas operations, from the small regional aircraft to the biggest 747s, had been a difficult task. The domestic rival had taken advantage of the situation to increase market share. When restructuring was complete, Qantas was able to concentrate aggressively on the home market and had extended market share to 50.9 per cent by February 1995 and more than 53 per cent by the end of the following June.

After extensive preparation the Government launched the float of the remaining 75 per cent of the company in June 1995. Hundreds of thousands of copies of the Qantas Public Share Offer Prospectus were mailed to potential investors. The float closed in late July with an overwhelming demand for shares. Small investors were allocated shares for $1.90 each—a 10 cent discount from the institutional price. Local institutional investors were allocated 27·5 per cent and foreign institutions 20 per cent of Qantas at $2.00 a share.

From the time the shares began trading on the Australian Stock Exchange on 31 July 1995, they sold at a premium, settling down in early days to about $2.15 but strengthening in line with factors such as the airline's growing domestic market share.

The float was the culmination of the government's long campaign to sell the airline to domestic and international investors. The issue was fully subscribed, with particular enthusiasm from overseas institutions. And most importantly Qantas went from having a single owner—the Australian government—to two when British Airways came aboard, then suddenly to about 117,000, achieving the objective of private, widely spread ownership which the management had sought in its plans for the 1990s.

THE QANTAS FLEET*

AIRCRAFT TYPE	NUMBER
Boeing 747-400	18
Boeing 747-300	6
Boeing 747-200B	5
Boeing 747SP	2
Boeing 767-300ER	15
Boeing 767-200ER	7
Airbus A300-B4	4
Boeing 737-400	19
Boeing 737-300	16
Total	**92**

Regional airlines in the Qantas Group, Airlink, Eastern Australia Airlines, Southern Australia Airlines and Sunstate Airlines, currently operate 45 aircraft.

AIRCRAFT TYPE	NUMBER
British Aerospace BAe146	9
de Havilland Canada Dash 8-100	13
de Havilland Canada Twin Otter	5
British Aerospace Jetstream 31/32	4
Shorts SD360	6
Cessna 404 Titan	8
Total	**45**

* Current at 16 November 1995.

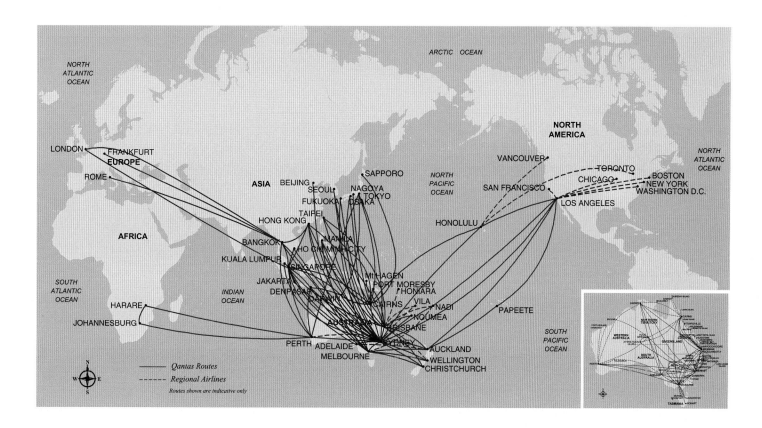

QANTAS ROUTE NETWORK
Countries served—total 26

Asia and Pacific Australia, China, Fiji, Hong Kong, Indonesia, Japan, Malaysia, New Caledonia, New Zealand, Papua New Guinea, Republic of Korea, Singapore, Solomon Islands*, Tahiti, Taiwan**, Thailand, The Philippines, Vanuatu*, Vietnam.

Europe Britain, Germany, Italy   **North America** Canada*, USA   **Africa** South Africa, Zimbabwe

DESTINATIONS SERVED—TOTAL 92

Adelaide, Alice Springs, Armidale, Auckland, Ayers Rock, Bamaga, Bangkok, Beijing, Blackwater, Boston, Brampton Island, Brisbane, Broken Hill, Broome, Bundaberg, Burnie, Cairns, Canberra, Chicago*, Christchurch, Coffs Harbour, Coolangatta, Cooma, Darwin, Denpasar, Devonport, Dubbo, Dunk Island, Emerald, Frankfurt, Fukuoka, Gladstone, Gove, Grafton, Great Keppel Island, Harare, Hervey Bay, Ho Chi Minh City, Hobart, Hong Kong, Honiara*, Honolulu, Jakarta, Johannesburg, Kalgoorlie, Karratha, Kuala Lumpur, Launceston, Lizard Island, London, Lord Howe Island, Los Angeles, Mackay, Manila, Maroochydore, Maryborough, Melbourne, Mildura, Moree, Mount Hagen*, Nadi, Nagoya, Narrabri, New York*, Newcastle, Noumea, Osaka, Papeete, Perth, Port Hedland, Port Macquarie, Port Moresby, Port Vila*, Proserpine, Renmark, Rockhampton, Rome, San Francisco*, Sapporo, Seoul, Singapore, Sydney, Taipei**, Tamworth, Taree, Thursday Island, Tokyo, Toronto*, Townsville, Vancouver*, Washington DC*, Wellington.

REGIONAL BREAKDOWN OF SCHEDULED DESTINATIONS

Australia	52	UK	1	USA	7	South Africa	1
New Zealand	3	Other Europe	2	Canada	2	Zimbabwe	1
Other Pacific/Asia	23	**Total**	3	**Total**	9	**Total**	2
Total	78						

* Indicates codeshare services operated by other airlines on behalf of Qantas.   ** Taiwan is served by Australia–Asia Airlines.
Scheduled services. Information correct at September 1995.

Roll of honour

PARTNERS LIST

Roll of honour

LEAD PARTNERS	MAJOR PARTNERS	CONTRIBUTING PARTNERS
American Express International Inc.	Barnwell Cambridge	Alasdair Macdonald Architects
The Boeing Company	Cathay Pacific Catering Services (HK) Ltd.	Air BP
Concorde International Travel	Commercial Computer Centre / Key People	Broadlex Cleaning Australia
The Shell Company	Commonwealth Bank of Australia	Cabcharge Australia
Unisys Australia		Caterair Airport Services
	Federal Airports Corporation	Clintons Toyota
QANTAS WARDROBE SUPPLIERS	Guntar Graphics	Compaq Computer Australia
Calcoup Inc	Hertz Australia	Connat Flight Services
John Kaldor Fabricmaker	Kraft Foods Limited	Feltex Carpets and Wool Group
Kolotex Australia	Lend Lease Property Services	Hilton International
Luigi & Anthony	Lucas Aerospace	ITT Sheraton Hotels
Macquarie Textiles Group	Rolls Royce	Itochu Aviation Co. Ltd / Jamco Corporation
Moda Designs	Telstra	Jardine Airport Services
Neoman	United Travel Agents Group	KPMG
Oroton International		Memorex Telex
S. F. Corporate Clothing		Noritake
Solution V	Berrivale Orchards	Rawlinsons NSW
Sydney Neckwear Company	F T Cleary & Sons	SBC Warburg / McIntosh
	Phillip Lipman Pty. Ltd.	TFK Corporation
Top Ryde Tailoring	SNP Security	Unistat
		Woods Bagot

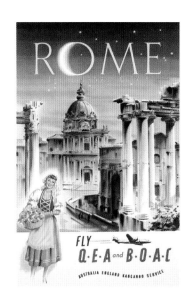

An American Express company

AMERICAN EXPRESS INTERNATIONAL INC

ARBN 000 618 208

ALBERTO MODOLO AO *Chairman* JOHN SCHAAP *Chief Operating Officer*

101 Waterloo Road, North Ryde NSW 2113. Telephone (02) 886 1111 Facsimile (02) 886 1860

American Express has a network of over 1700 offices in over 120 countries around the world. Within Australia, American Express is one of the largest travel agencies, with offices in every city, and many regional centres.

American Express travel-related services include:
American Express Travel, American Express Travellers Cheques, American Express Card, American Express Corporate Card

American Express aims to become the most respected service brand in the world, within the travel and financial services industries. With Qantas we share a commitment to customer service, to quality, and to teamwork, from the smallest business unit of our company to international relationships with business partners.

AMERICAN EXPRESS INTERNATIONAL INC
TRADITIONS OF SERVICE EXCELLENCE

Within the travel and tourism industry, Qantas and American Express share more than a close business relationship. They share a history of service excellence to clients around the globe, and they also share an aim—to extend that history into a future in which both companies continue to lead their fields as world-class service providers.

This philosophy, and intrinsic commitment to quality, motivates staff at both companies to constantly seek to improve their services to customers. It sets both Qantas and American Express apart from their competitors within the industry.

American Express has been operating in Australia since 1954, when a travel office was opened in Sydney to assist American Express travellers and Cardmembers in Australia. Not long afterwards, American Express began providing travel to Australians travelling overseas, and a close bond was formed with Qantas.

Since then, Qantas and American Express have worked closely together to promote tourism through projects such as the highly awarded *Come Walkabout* campaign which focused attention on the potential of Australia as a tourist destination. The close relationship between the two organisations saw the introduction of American Express' Membership Miles (now known as Membership Rewards) in December 1992, which allows points earned for spending on the American Express Card to be redeemed as Qantas Frequent Flyer points.

In 1994 American Express purchased Westpac Travel from Qantas, further cementing the relationship between the two companies. Both Qantas and American Express spend considerable time and effort on developing the travel and tourism industry, sharing sponsorships for tourism awards, and generally fostering excellence.

American Express congratulates Qantas on its 75th anniversary, and looks forward to a fruitful relationship during the years to come, as both companies face up to the challenges ahead in this dynamic industry.

THE BOEING COMPANY

FRANK A SHRONTZ *Chairman & Chief Executive Officer* PHILIP M CONDIT *President*

7755 East Marginal Way S, Seattle, WA 98108, USA. Telephone (206) 665 2121 Facsimile (206) 237 1240

BOEING INTERNATIONAL CORPORATION

Sydney Airport Centre, 15 Bourke Road, Mascot NSW 2020 Australia. Telephone (02) 317 4767 Facsimile (02) 667 0365

*Delivering value is the key to customer satisfaction and industry leadership. This is the basis of Boeing's relationship
with Qantas, dating from 1956 when it was amongst the first of the world's great airlines to order the 707.*

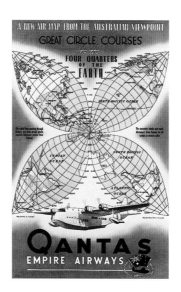

CONCORDE INTERNATIONAL TRAVEL PTY LTD

ACN 003 237 189

AGOSTINO PISTORINO *Chairman*   LESLIE A CASSAR *Group Managing Director*

EDDY BALDACCHINO *Managing Director*

AUSTRALIA

403 George Street

Sydney NSW 2000

Telephone (02) 321 9222

Facsimile (02) 290 3641

NEW ZEALAND

World Aviation Systems

Trustbank Building

Level 6

229 Queen Street

Auckland, NZ

Telephone (649) 379 4455

Facsimile (649) 377 5648

UNITED STATES

Air Tickets Inc

Suite 1908

205 East 42nd Street

New York NY 10017, USA

Telephone (1212) 557 3270

Facsimile (1212) 557 3282

MALTA

World Aviation Systems

20 Republic Street

Valletta Malta

Telephone (356) 242 233

Facsimile (356) 223 887

ITALY

World Aviation Systems

Corso Monforte 45

20122 Milano, Italy

Telephone (392) 796 475

Facsimile (392) 7600 1975

VIETNAM

Indochina Marketing

157 Huynh Van Banh Street

Phu Nhuan District

Ho Chi Minh City, Vietnam

Telephone (848) 442 022

Facsimile (848) 455 099

TRADE NAMES

Air Tickets, Concorde Holidays, World Aviation Systems,

Indochina Marketing, Ski Max, World Aviation Systems Cargo

The principal aim of the Concorde Group is to provide a global, automated ticket and product distribution

service for the airline and travel industries, and to do so in the most professional and profitable way.

CONCORDE INTERNATIONAL TRAVEL
A SUPERSONIC PARTNER FOR QANTAS

Concorde International Travel is Australia's largest integrated travel company, and a major supporter of Qantas Airways Ltd.

Concorde is one of the most dynamic participants in the travel industry, having established a presence not just throughout Australia, but in the USA, New Zealand, Europe and Asia through a programme of focused strategic growth. Significantly, the latest developments have occurred in 1995—the 75th anniversary year for Qantas—with Concorde expanding its activities into the world's largest market, the USA, and into the burgeoning market of Vietnam, which is fast becoming both the next tourism tiger of Asia and a booming centre of business as its programme of economic revitalisation progresses at a pace.

Concorde is a 'household name' to the Australian travel industry as a service company whose partners are travel agents and airlines in major markets around the world. Through its core activity as an air ticket wholesaler to travel agents, Concorde is responsible for issuing a major share of international and domestic airline tickets sold in Australia by travel agents. Its ticket wholesaling division—which trades under the simple but highly effective name 'Air Tickets'—currently accounts for some 70 per cent of the group's revenues.

Concorde's airline representation company, World Aviation Systems, acts as General Sales Agent in Australia, New Zealand, Europe and Asia for more than 40 passenger and freight carriers from the USA, Europe, Asia, the Middle East, the South Pacific and Australasia.

The group's wholesaling divisions—Concorde Holidays, Travel Indochina and Ski Max—give Concorde a solid and growing presence in key leisure travel markets. Concorde Holidays develops package holiday programmes in Asia, Europe and the USA in conjunction with major suppliers including Qantas. Travel Indochina is a specialist offshoot, whose core activity is to develop and wholesale holiday programmes in the emerging markets of Indochina (Vietnam, Cambodia and Laos), plus surrounding markets including Thailand and Burma (Myanmar). In Vietnam, the Concorde Group is the inbound operator for Qantas. And Ski Max is the newest leisure division, focused solely on the fast-growing snow holiday markets of New Zealand, the USA, Canada, Europe and domestically at Kosciusko Thredbo in the Australian Alps.

Like Qantas, Concorde is a company with a proud Australian heritage. As the airline had understated beginnings as a small operator in outback Queensland, so Concorde started small as a retail travel agent in Melbourne. That was back in 1949, when the company's founder, Mr Agostino Pistorino, (now Concorde group chairman) first opened his agency's doors to the public, with a vision to create a formal market segment from the large number of people travelling internationally to visit friends and relatives. He was joined in later years by a former competitor, Mr Henri Crusi, a specialist in travel by sea and one of the first in Australia to recognise the future potential of air transport as a means of moving large numbers of travellers internationally. Messrs Pistorino and Crusi signed a 'Concordat', or agreement to merge their businesses—hence the name Concorde.

In 1967, a third partner—Mr Eddy Baldacchino—joined Concorde after a distinguished career in the banking and financial services industry in Australia and the UK. Then in 1978, Mr Leslie Cassar—a Qantas veteran—became the group's fourth partner, helping to expand the business still further with the creation of the airline representation arm, World Aviation Systems. This elevated Concorde to a national, and later, international enterprise. Concorde grew rapidly, and in 1987 gained British Airways as a 50 per cent shareholder with the four existing partners. In that year, turnover for the Concorde Group reached $100 million; in 1994-1995, just eight years later, that figure had climbed to $800 million, reflecting the group's diversity, growth, sound commercial judgment and, most importantly, staff commitment.

Where Concorde started out with just two staff in those early days, it now boasts more than 400 around the world, many of them previous employees of Qantas or the former domestic carrier Australian Airlines/TAA. Concorde's phenomenal growth is set to continue, as the group consolidates and expands its presence overseas, and continues to secure business in the expanding Australian market. Qantas will be a major beneficiary of Concorde's success.

THE SHELL COMPANY OF AUSTRALIA LIMITED
ACN 004 610 459

DR J ROLAND WILLIAMS *Chairman and Chief Executive Officer*
RUSSELL R CAPLAN *Executive Director, Downstream Oil & Chemicals*

THE SHELL COMPANY OF AUSTRALIA LIMITED
1 Spring Street, Melbourne VIC 3001. Telephone (03) 9666 5444 Facsimile (03) 9666 5008

SHELL INTERNATIONAL TRADING AND SHIPPING COMPANY LIMITED
Shell Centre, London, United Kingdom

TRADE NAMES
Jet A–1, Avgas, Aeroshell Lubes & Greases

Shell Australia's objectives are to engage safely, efficiently, profitably and responsibly in the oil, gas, chemicals and coal businesses.

Our relationship with Qantas began in 1926 and together we pioneered the first Australia–UK air mail route, established the world's longest non-stop air route, and played an integral role in the inaugural Australia–Johannesburg air service.

In modern times, this tradition of excellence continues and together the two companies have been responsible for setting a new non-stop distance record and recently supported the historic re-enactment of the first flight from England to Australia.

Gallery of excellence

THE SPIRIT OF CO-OPERATION—QANTAS & SHELL

There is perhaps only one other organisation in Australia which can match the long and distinguished record of Qantas in commercial aviation. The Shell Company of Australia.

When Qantas first registered as a company in 1920, Shell had already made aviation history with its participation in an impressive list of firsts. First cross English Channel flight ...first flight England to Australia ...first trans-Atlantic flight by airship to name but a few. By 1926, when the two companies signed their first fuel pump agreement, Qantas had already chalked up a few firsts of its own.

That original partnership proved to be an enduring one, and together, the two companies remained at the leading edge of the aviation industry. While Qantas opened up new routes with ever more advanced aircraft, Shell was busy with the development of the fuels and refuelling systems which help make safe, reliable and economical commercial aviation possible.

With Shell's help, Qantas pioneered the first UK–Australia airmail route in 1934. During the war years, Qantas, using Shell fuels, established the world's longest non-stop air route—3,513 miles from Perth to Ceylon. In 1953, Qantas and Shell personnel were living side-by-side on the Cocos Islands, the re-fuelling point on the inaugural Australia-Johannesburg air service.

In modern times, that tradition of partnership continues. In 1989, Shell developed and supplied fuel for the Qantas Boeing 747-400 which set a new non-stop distance record—17,850 kilometres from London to Sydney. Last year, Shell played an integral role in the re-enactment of the first flight from England to Australia, which was pioneered by brothers Ross and Keith Smith 75 years prior. The Smith brothers answered the call of 'Billy' Hughes, the Prime Minister of the day, who offered a £10,000 prize to the first Australian aviators to successfully complete the trip within 30 days. Sir Hudson Fysh, founder of Qantas, was contracted by the Australian Government to prepare landing fields for the Smith brothers in outback Australia. The commemorative re-enactment of this historic event, which took place in the Shell Spirit of Brooklands Vimy, was supported by Shell and Qantas.

Today Shell continues to be a market leader for the supply of aviation fuel, covering more than 800 airports spanning 80 countries. All at Shell congratulate Qantas on 75 years of outstanding services and achievement, and look forward to continuing with the tradition of excellence our companies began 69 years ago.

UNISYS

UNISYS AUSTRALIA LIMITED

ARBN 000 002 086

WORLD HEADQUARTERS

Unisys Corporation, Township Line and Union Meeting Roads, Blue Bell, Pennsylvania 19424, USA
Telephone (215) 986 4011 Facsimile (215) 986 6004

HEAD OFFICE AUSTRALIA

Unisys Australia Limited, 213 Miller Street, North Sydney, NSW 2060 Australia. Telephone (02) 9931 6666 Facsimile (02) 9957 3370

574 St Kilda Road, Melbourne, VIC 3004, Australia. Telephone (03) 9522 3666 Facsimile (03) 9522 3674
91 Northbourne Avenue, Turner , ACT 2601 Australia. Telephone (06) 274 3555 Facsimile (06) 274 3533
147 Coronation Drive, Milton, QLD 4064 Australia. Telephone (03) 361 1888 Facsimile (03) 361 1866

TRADE NAMES

2200 Mainframes, USAS Airline Applications, Mapper, Linc, Unisys Communication Processors

Unisys is an information management company—we help our clients transform their businesses by creating innovative solutions
that change the way they use information. Qantas uses USAS to facilitate activities such as passenger bookings, seat reservations,
ticketing, passenger flight boarding activities, hotel bookings, load planning and cargo processing.

UNISYS AND QANTAS

Unisys is an information management company—we help our clients transform their business by creating innovative solutions that change the way they use information. Our clients include many of the world's largest financial services companies, leading communications companies, major airlines and transportation companies and government agencies.

Our relationship with Qantas spans almost a quarter of a century. In the 1970s we worked closely with Australian Airlines and a number of international airlines to develop a Reservation System which became the basis of our USAS airlines application suite.

During the following decade, we developed departure control, maintenance, engineering and flight operations systems with Australian Airlines and the USAS Freight Management applications with Qantas. More recently, we have developed and delivered advanced revenue management and airport processing systems in partnership with the now merged Qantas Airways.

Our association with Australian Airlines and Qantas has substantially contributed to the development of a comprehensive suite of airline and travel application systems now employed by over 150 of the world's airlines.

In addition, we have provided Qantas with the advanced technology to run these applications. From the first Univac 494 Dual Processor in 1971 to the Unisys 2200/900 in 1995, Qantas has, and continues to, employ our most advanced and powerful computing technology.

Qantas is an important Unisys customer. We have greatly enjoyed working with Qantas delivering information systems to enhance its position as one of the world's leading airlines.

We congratulate Qantas on 75 years of service.

QANTAS WARDROBE SUPPLIERS

CALCOUP INC PTY LTD
ACN 003 449 269

NEIL COUPER *Joint Managing Director*
PETER CALLAGHAN *Joint Managing Director*
11-15 Harp Street, Belmore NSW 2192
Telephone (02) 718 7377 Facsimile (02) 718 7482

TRADE NAME *Calcoup Knitwear.*

*Calcoup set up business seven years ago and has been the
knitwear supplier to Qantas for the past four years. Calcoup
employs 45 people at their Belmore factory and uses raw materials
supplied by Australian companies. Specialising in knitwear,
Calcoup has continually upgraded its plant, one of the most
modern in Australia, and is equal to world standards.*

JOHN KALDOR
FABRICMAKER PTY LIMITED
ACN 000 742 307

JOHN KALDOR AM *Chief Executive*
110 McEvoy Street, Alexandria NSW 2015
Telephone (02) 698 7700 Facsimile (02) 698 1375

*John Kaldor sells apparel, decorative products, menswear and
craft fabric. John Kaldor is proud to supply the Qantas uniform
with the 'Cosmic Blue' corporate print and the 'Cosmic Blue'
plain chambray as well as the pilots' white shirting fabric.*

KOLOTEX AUSTRALIA PTY LTD
ACN 002 716 716

RAY MUNDY *Chief Executive Officer*
22 George Street, Leichhardt NSW 2040
Telephone (02) 560 7622 Facsimile (02) 550 9115

TRADE NAMES
Kolotex, Sheer Relief, Leon Worth Voodoo, Kicks, Shout.

*Kolotex, proudly Australian-owned, has been
in association with Qantas since 1972, supplying
the uniform with Australian-made hosiery.*

LUIGI & ANTHONY PTY LTD
ACN 001 117 942

LUIGI ALIBRANDI *Managing Director*
117 Constitution Road, Dulwich Hill NSW 2203
Telephone (02) 550 9255 Facsimile (02) 550 9343

TRADE NAMES
*Dowd Corporation Pty Ltd, Peter Weiss Pty Ltd, S F Corporate
Clothing Pty Ltd, Rainier Pty Ltd, Peter Metchev Pty Ltd.*

*Since its inception in 1964, Luigi and Anthony Pty Ltd
has represented a synergy of Italian craftsmanship and
Australian ingenuity. We are proud to have been associated
with Qantas for the last ten years promoting the quality of
Australian manufacturing and services to the world.*

MACQUARIE TEXTILES GROUP LTD
ACN 000 012 877

DEREK HODGE *Chief Executive Officer*
Bridge Street, Albury NSW 2640
Telephone (060) 430 200 Facsimile (060) 411 321

TRADE NAMES *Macquarie Fabrics, Onkaparinga.*

*The Macquarie Group is Australia's largest woollen and
worsted textile company, with over 100 years experience in
manufacturing. Macquarie produces an impressive range
of woollen and worsted fabrics for apparel, furnishing and
domestic blanket and rug markets. With a clear focus on
producing competitively priced world-class textiles, Macquarie's
new A$60 million facility located at Albury, New South Wales,
is designed to provide the high speed, high capacity, highly
flexible mill demanded by today's customers. Quality assurance
is integrated into each step of the process, starting with the
selection of raw materials, through to the inspection of finished
pieces. Matching this commitment to producing outstanding
products is the provision of excellence in customer service.*

MODA DESIGNS PTY LIMITED
ACN 056 612 287

212-220 Parramatta Road, Camperdown NSW 2050
Telephone (02) 516 2811 Facsimile (02) 550 5117

TRADE NAMES
Weiss, Marcs, SF Corporate, Oxford Shops, Skin Deep.

*Moda Designs manufacture mens' and ladies' blazers
for the new elegant Qantas uniform with traditional
tailoring expertise. Moda also aims to provide caring
and personal attention to the made to measure service.*

Gallery of excellence

QANTAS WARDROBE SUPPLIERS

OROTON INTERNATIONAL LIMITED
ACN 000 038 675

ROBERT LANE *Executive Chairman*
52-54 Balgowlah Road, Balgowlah NSW 2093
Telephone (02) 9951 0500 Facsimile (02) 9951 0506

TRADE NAMES
Oroton, Fiorelli, Ken Done, Anne Klein, Carlo.

Oroton, proudly Australian owned, designs and manufactures staff handbags to Qantas specifications.

NEOMAN
ACN 001 666 217

GUNTER ZECHNER *Managing Director*
172–182 Princes Highway, Arncliff NSW 2205
Telephone (02) 567 7700 Facsimile (02) 567 2555

TRADE NAMES
Country Road Clothing, Ranier—Darling Harbour Casino, Messini Dissimore—winner of 3 FIA Awards, Oxford Shop, Rarity Shirts.

Quality counts at Neoman Pty Ltd, the premier supplier of Australian-made corporate and high fashion shirts. The reputation and success of Neoman has been built over many years of providing a level of quality and reliability that is unsurpassed in the industry.

S F CORPORATE CLOTHING PTY LTD
ACN 054 692 901

DAVID GRUNDY *Managing Director*
76-82 Botany Road, Alexandria NSW 2015
Telephone (02) 310 7000 Facsimile (02) 310 7111

S F Corporate Clothing is 100% Australian owned with a manufacturing base in Sydney. S F Corporate Clothing designs, manufactures and distributes uniforms. We are totally focused on the uniform market, establishing systems and procedures that ensure our customers' needs are catered for according to their structure. Our involvement with the Qantas uniform started in 1990 and we currently manufacture blouses and printed skirts for the new uniform. We are also manufacturing and distributing the entire uniform for Qantas Flight Catering.

SOLUTION V PTY LIMITED
ACN 003 770 910

SATIS PATEL *Managing Director*
PANKAJ PATEL *General Manager*
Unit 3, 372 Eastern Valley Way, Chatswood NSW 2067
Telephone (02) 417 6644 Facsimile (02) 417 5787

TRADE NAMES
Solution V, On The Go Luggage.

Solution V supplies luggage, leather belts and accessories for the Qantas uniform in addition to Qantas Frequent Flyer cabin bags and small leathergoods.

SYDNEY NECKWEAR CO PTY LTD
ACN 003 876 819

PHILIP ZYLSTRA *Managing Director*
221-229 Sydney Park Road, Erskineville NSW 2043
Telephone (02) 565 1811 Facsimile (02) 565 1075

TRADE NAMES
John & Lois Ties, Sydney 2000 Ties.

The Sydney Neckwear Company has supplied the Qantas Uniform with quality Australian-made neckwear for the last ten years. Through close liaison with designers on product development, we have become a leading supplier of corporate neckwear throughout Australia.

TOP RYDE TAILORING AND ALTERATIONS CENTRE
ACN 002 672 737

SALVATORE OLIVIERI *Director*
95 Blaxland Road (corner of Tucker Street), Ryde NSW 2112
Telephone (02) 809 2642 Facsimile (02) 809 7935

TRADE NAMES
NSW Fire Brigade, Myer/Grace Bros, David Jones, Ericsson Australia, Ryde RSL Club.

Top Ryde Tailoring and Alterations Centre, established in 1960 has a staff of 14 fully qualified tailors and machinists. Every article of clothing issued to Qantas staff (blouses, jackets, overcoats, shirts, skirts, trousers, etc.) is altered by Top Ryde Tailors. Our aim is to provide fast, efficient service and attention to detail.

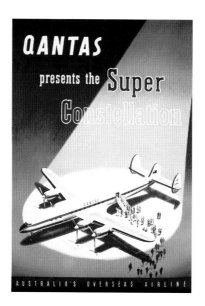

BARNWELL CAMBRIDGE PTY LTD

JOHN CAMBRIDGE *Chairman* ROBERT BARNWELL *Director*

633 Princes Highway, Kogarah NSW 2217. Telephone (02) 556 1666 Facsimile (02) 556 1566

Barnwell Cambridge Pty Ltd is an electrical contracting and engineering company engaged in all facets of maintenance, commercial, industrial and refurbishment installation work. The Company has earned a reputation for quality workmanship having successfully undertaken numerous complex installations requiring expertise in co-ordination and programming of services. Directors maintain a hands-on approach to the day to day operations.

Our company has maintained a continuous presence on the Sydney Jet Base and peripheral centres, assisting Qantas maintenance staff in the installation and servicing of electrical services to the administration, aircraft maintenance and flight service facilities to meet the stringent procedures required by Qantas, and to ensure, in part, the maintenance of their enviable safety record.

Congratulations Qantas.

CATHAY PACIFIC
CATERING SERVICES

CATHAY PACIFIC CATERING SERVICES (HK) LIMITED

PATRICK TSAI *Chairman* ANTHONY WONG *Chief Executive*

9/F CPA Building Block D, Hong Kong International Airport, Hong Kong. Telephone (852) 2747 3188 Facsimile (852) 2765 7355

COMMERCIAL COMPUTER CENTRE

ACN 001 896 144

ROBERT D ROSENGREEN *Chairman*

HEAD OFFICE	MELBOURNE	ADELAIDE
Suite 40, 70-74 Phillip Street,	*Level 3, 99 King Street*	*Level 1, 146 Fullarton Road*
Parramatta NSW 2150	*Melbourne VIC 3000*	*Rose Park SA 5067*
Telephone (02) 635 4544	*Telephone (03) 9615 8888*	*Telephone (08) 332 5322*
Facsimile (02) 891 1969	*Facsimile (03) 9614 2347*	*Facsimile (08) 31 6812*

SYDNEY	BRISBANE	PERTH
Suite 903	*Ground Level*	*Ground Level*
Level 9, Gold Fields House	*221 Logan Road*	*47 Colin Street*
1 Alfred Street, Sydney NSW 2000	*Buranda QLD 4102*	*West Perth WA 6005*
Telephone (02) 251 2566	*Telephone (07) 3391 4588*	*Telephone (09) 324 1275*
Facsimile (02) 252 1606	*Facsimile (07) 3891 6902*	*Facsimile (09) 481 5201*

PRODUCT NAMES

CCC Data Management, Key People, Australia on Disk, Green Pages, Imaging Technology

Keeping a first-class airline flying requires exacting performance standards. This includes the management of data which is a critical resource.
CCC has supported Qantas through its Data Management, Key People and Imaging Technology divisions over the years in achieving 'data integrity'.

COMMONWEALTH BANK OF AUSTRALIA

ACN 123 123 124

TIM BESLEY AO *Chairman*   DAVID MURRAY *Managing Director*

HEAD OFFICE	INSTITUTIONAL BANKING VIC	INSTITUTIONAL BANKING SA
48 Martin Place, Sydney NSW 2000	*385 Bourke Street, Melbourne VIC 3000*	*96 King William Street, Adelaide SA 5000*
Telephone (02) 378 2000	*Telephone (03) 9675 7115*	*Telephone (08) 206 4582*
Facsimile (02) 378 5081	*Facsimile (03) 9670 1082*	*Facsimile (08) 206 4145*
INSTITUTIONAL BANKING NSW	INSTITUTIONAL BANKING QLD	INSTITUTIONAL BANKING WA
48 Martin Place, Sydney NSW 2000	*240 Queen Street, Brisbane QLD 4000*	*150 St George's Terrace, Perth WA 6000*
Telephone (02) 378 3604	*Telephone (07) 3237 3434*	*Telephone (09) 482 6994*
Facsimile (02) 378 5081	*Facsimile (07) 3237 3633*	*Facsimile (09) 482 6099*

The Commonwealth Bank and Qantas have shared a longstanding and highly valued association
spanning over 60 years. This strong association has grown with the Bank being instrumental in
the leasing of aircraft and playing an active role in the Qantas Public Share Offer.

FEDERAL AIRPORTS CORPORATION

IAN D. FERRIER *Chairman*   JACK F. MOFFATT *Acting Chief Executive*

HEAD OFFICE

2A, Lord Street, Botany NSW 2019. Telephone (02) 207 7777   Facsimile (02) 316 5606

*Sydney, Melbourne, Brisbane, Adelaide, Perth, Hobart, Essendon, Moorabbin, Parafield,
Coolangatta, Canberra, Darwin, Townsville and Mount Isa, Alice Springs and Tennant Creek,
Launceston, Bankstown, Camden and Hoxton Park, Archerfield, Jandakot*

*The FAC is an autonomous, self-funding government business enterprise responsible for the
development, operation and management of Australia's primary and major secondary airports.*

GUNTAR GRAPHICS

ACN 006 342 203

GUNTER TARESCH *Managing Director*   HERMINE TARESCH *Director*

79 Curzon Street, North Melbourne VIC 3051. Telephone (03) 9329 0129 Facsimile (03) 9329 0152

Guntar Graphics' renowned personalised service has been valued by the airline since 1970, through TAA, Australian Airlines, Australian air Express and now as a close service provider of Qantas. Producing timetables, brochures and a vast range of literature, we have also proudly been involved with most of the airlines's major promotions. We offer typesetting, colour reproduction, print supervision, extensive warehousing and a comprehensive distribution service.

HERTZ AUSTRALIA PTY LTD

ACN 004 407 087

DAVID J SCHULTE *Managing Director*

HEAD OFFICE
10 Dorcas Street
South Melbourne VIC 3205
Telephone (03) 9698 2444
Facsimile (03) 9698 2408

QUEENSLAND
110 Albert Street
Brisbane QLD 4000
Telephone (07) 3221 6665
Facsimile (07) 3210 0572

WESTERN AUSTRALIA
Suite 4B, 20 Teddington Street
Victoria Park WA 6100
Telephone (09) 470 6233
Facsimile (09) 470 3374

NEW SOUTH WALES
Unit 5 Harcourt Estate
809-821 Botany Road
Rosebery NSW 2018
Telephone (02) 667 8700
Facsimile (02) 669 5142

SOUTH AUSTRALIA
Vimy Court
Adelaide Airport
Adelaide SA 5950
Telephone (08) 234 4774
Facsimile (08) 234 4808

USA
The Hertz Corporation
225 Brae Boulevard, Park Ridge
New Jersey USA 07656-0713
Telephone (201) 307 2000
Facsimile (201) 307 2652

Hertz is proud to be the preferred car rental company of Qantas.

As the original inventor of the car rental concept some 77 years ago in Chicago in 1918,
Hertz is today the world's number one car rental company, operating in over 150 countries from 5,400 locations.

Hertz is committed to continuing to be the industry innovator, and to providing the very best of service, at competitive rates,
to both business and leisure renters alike, who appreciate the convenience and flexibility that only car rental offers.

KRAFT FOODS LIMITED

ACN 004 125 071

TOM PARK *Managing Director*

HEAD OFFICE

850 Lorimer Street

Port Melbourne VIC 3207

Telephone (03) 9676 5555

Facsimile (03) 9676 5340

ADELAIDE

170 Greenhill Road

Unley SA 5061

Telephone (08) 272 7444

Facsimile (08) 373 1193

BRISBANE

303 Coronation Drive

Milton QLD 4066

Telephone (07) 3369 9288

Facsimile (07) 3369 2090

SYDNEY

28 Burwood Road

Burwood NSW 2134

Telephone (02) 715 0550

Facsimile (02) 715 0555

PERTH

172 Burswood Drive

Victoria Park WA 6100

Telephone (09) 361 8111

Facsimile (09) 470 2321

MELBOURNE

Suite 4, 1st Floor 606 Hawthorn Road

East Brighton VIC 3186

Telephone (03) 9276 5141

Facsimile (03) 9276 5138

TRADE NAMES

Vegemite, Kraft Peanut Butter, Coon, Kraft Cheddar Cheese, Kraft Philadelphia

LEND LEASE PROPERTY SERVICES

DAVID HIGGINS *Chief Executive Officer, Lend Lease Corporation*
PETER SCOTT *Managing Director, Civil & Civic*

Tower Building, Australia Square, George Street, Sydney NSW 2000. Telephone (02) 236 6111 Facsimile (02) 232 8086

MELBOURNE
Level 3, 601 St Kilda Road
Melbourne VIC 3000
Telephone (03) 522 6222 Facsimile (03) 522 6290

BRISBANE
Level 38, Riverside Centre
123 Eagle Street, Brisbane QLD 4000
Telephone (07) 833 2333 Facsimile (07) 833 2351

SINGAPORE
Lend Lease Asia
510 Thomson Road,
06-01 SLF Building, Singapore 1129
Telephone (65) 258 7116 Facsimile (65) 259 9077

BANGKOK
Lend Lease (Thailand) Ltd
7th Floor, Alma Link Building
Lumpini Patumwan, Bangkok 10330, Thailand
Telephone (662) 253 9124 Facsimile (662) 253 9165

LEND LEASE PROPERTY SERVICES IS A GROUP
OF SIX REGISTERED AUSTRALIAN COMPANIES
Lend Lease Development ACN 000 311 277, Lend Lease Residential ACN 000 375 897,
Lend Lease Retail Projects ACN 002 909 908, Lend Lease Interiors ACN 002 928 510,
Lend Lease Design Group ACN 003 977 071, Civil & Civic ACN 000 098 162.

Lend Lease Property Services is an integral part of the Lend Lease Group and aims to be the premier Project Management group
in Asia and Australia; is an international Property Developer, and the leading manager of institutional property around the world.

LUCAS AEROSPACE LTD

ACN 004 154 125

SIR BRIAN PEARSE *Chairman*   FRANK TURNER *Managing Director*

HEAD OFFICE
Brueton House, New Road, Solihull
West Midlands B91 3TX, UK
Telephone (0121) 704 5171
Facsimile (0121) 711 2736

AUSTRALIA
Lucas Aerospace Limited
84-92 Epsom Road, Zetland
NSW 2017, Australia
Telephone (02) 313 4480
Facsimile (02) 313 4489

USA
Lucas Aerospace Inc
11180 Sunrise Valley Drive
Reston VA 22091-4399, USA
Telephone (703) 264 1704
Facsimile (703) 620 8905

FRANCE
Lucas Aerospace (France)
11 Rue Lord Byron, Paris 75008, France
Telephone (145) 619 525
Facsimile (145) 611 097

TRADE NAME
Lucol

Lucas Aerospace is a global leader in the provision and support of high-integrity
control systems and equipment. It has a long association with Qantas as a supply partner
and continues to supply and support Qantas on the latest generation aircraft.

ROLLS-ROYCE plc

SIR RALPH ROBINS *Chairman*   SIR TERENCE HARRISON *Chief Executive*

65 Buckingham Gate, London SW1E 6AT, UK.
Telephone (0171) 222 9020 Facsimile (0171) 227 9170

Rolls-Royce and Qantas continue to celebrate one of the most enduring relationships in aviation history.

Hudson Fysh, co-founder of Qantas in 1920 and its Chairman until he retired in 1966, was in Darwin on
10 December 1919 to greet the Vickers Vimy as it completed the first-ever flight from England to Australia.
The Vimy was powered by two Rolls-Royce Eagle engines.

Today, all Qantas' flights between England and Australia are powered by Rolls-Royce RB211 engines which
are installed throughout the entire Qantas B747 fleet.

Qantas and Rolls-Royce together have set world-leading standards for engine reliability—a tribute not only to
Rolls-Royce engineering but also to the excellence of the Qantas engineering and maintenance organisation.

TELSTRA CORPORATION LIMITED
ACN 051 775 556

DAVID M HOARE *Chairman*   W FRANK BLOUNT *Chief Executive Officer*

AUSTRALIA
242 Exhibition Street

Melbourne VIC 3000

Telephone (03) 9634 1111

CHINA
Unit 26, Level 23, China World Tower,

China World Trade Centre, 1 Jian Guo Men

Wai Avenue, Beijing 100004, China

Telephone (10) 505 5635

Facsimile (10) 505 0345

INDIA
506-507 Tolstoy House

Tolstoy Marg

New Delhi 110001, India

Telephone (11) 335 5985/86

Facsimile (11) 335 5987

UNITED KINGDOM
1st Floor, 14 Buckingham Gate

London SW1E 6LB

United Kingdom

Telephone (171) 828 2328

Facsimile (171) 828 7938

INDONESIA
12th Floor, World Trade Centre, JL Jendral

Sudirman, Kav29, Jakarta 12920, Indonesia

Telephone (21) 521 1534

Facsimile (21) 521 1532

VIETNAM
18 Nguyen Du Street

Hanoi, S R Vietnam

Telephone (4) 265 936

Facsimile (4) 265 949

TRADE NAMES
Freecall™ 1800, DDS™ Flexnet®, MobileNet™, ISDN Macrolink™, Lightstream™

Telstra is Australia's leading telecommunications company.

*As an Asian-focused Australian, Telstra combines Western technologies and management style with
a responsive understanding of national objectives and cultural needs throughout the Asia-Pacific region.*

Like Qantas, Telstra's business is connecting worlds, and bringing people together.

UNITED TRAVEL AGENTS GROUP LTD
ACN 001 763 819

ROBERT STEEL *Managing Director*

122 Walker Street, North Sydney NSW 2060. Telephone (02) 9956 8399 Facsimile (02) 9956 8540

UTAG's 300-plus member agencies are located Australia-wide, and your closest office can be contacted on 13 13 98. Further, UTAG members are part of the global Woodside Travel Trust, ensuring that you have a local contact point at any of the 3,000 worldwide offices.

TRADE NAMES
UTAG Ltd—Travel Automation Products
UTAG Services—Management
UTAG Ticket Centre—Airticket consolidation for QF
UTAG Training Academy—Training Agency Personnel
UTAG Insurance—Specialised Insurance Product

UTAG is a multi-tiered distribution system of 300-plus independently owned retail travel agencies located in every state of Australia. Members are representative of all sized agencies from small country towns to large corporate travel management companies.

BERRIVALE ORCHARDS LTD
ACN 008 077 889

ROBERT V LOXTON *Chairman*   PETER N WOOD *Managing Director*

39-41 Dequetteville Terrace, Kent Town SA 5067. Telephone (08) 364 3060 Facsimile (08) 364 3336

Berrivale Orchards is Australia's leading manufacturer and marketer of fruit-based beverage products.
Berri Foodservice are the major supplier to Qantas of fresh fruit juices for both overseas and domestic flights.

F T CLEARY & SONS PTY LTD
ACN 000 275 132

MICHAEL CLEARY *Director* CHRISTOPHER CLEARY *Director*   HELEN MILLETT *Director*

201 King Street, Mascot NSW 2020. Telephone (02) 667 2722 Facsimile (02) 317 5607

Cleary's News Mascot began supply of newspapers and magazines for inflight and outstation use to Qantas Airways on their
Kangaroo Route in the early 1950s. We are proud to have been associated with the growth of Qantas Airways through the years.

PHILLIP LIPMAN PTY LIMITED
ACN 001 548 830

COLIN GING *Chairman*   ANTHONY WOOD *Managing Director*

Level 6, 66 Berry Street, North Sydney, NSW 2060. Telephone (02) 9955 7000 Facsimile (02) 9955 3166

Phillip Lipman Pty Limited is proud to have provided professional building and construction management services to Qantas over the last
10 years. We are committed to achieving excellence, through people, for people. Our customer's satisfaction is a measure of our success.

SNP SECURITY PTY LTD
ACN 000 013 098

KEVIN ROCHE OAM *Managing Director*   PETER ROCHE *Director*   TOM ROCHE *Director*

4-6 Elva Street, Strathfield NSW 2135. Telephone (02) 746 0444 Facsimile (02) 746 1479

SNP provides all aspects of commercial and industrial security from on-site guards to high security electronic systems to aviation security. SNP
has proudly been a service provider to Qantas since the commencement of passenger screening at Sydney International Airport in the early 1970s.

Alasdair Macdonald Architects

ATMAC PTY LIMITED

ACN 002 067 281

ALASDAIR MACDONALD *Director* SIMON BATHGATE *Director*

11 Randle Street, Surry Hills NSW 2010. Telephone (02) 211 2922 Facsimile (02) 281 4604

The firm provides design expertise and planning disciplines in advanced technology, combining engineering skills and total cost management in the delivery of modern architecture. The company has been designing aircraft ground support buildings and passenger travel facilities for Qantas since 1970.

AIR BP

ACN 004 085 616

CHRIS MOORHOUSE *CEO Air BP International* IAN PALLISER *Regional Manager Australasia*

Melbourne Central Tower, 360 Elizabeth Street, Melbourne VIC 3000. Telephone (03) 9268 4111 Facsimile (03) 9268 4478

To globally market aviation fuels and related services safely and to our customers' satisfaction.

BROADLEX CLEANING AUSTRALIA PTY LIMITED

ACN 060 581 526

ANGELA SAKELLIS *Director* GEORGE TSIVIS *Director*

16–18 Waltham Street, Artarmon NSW 2064. Telephone (02) 437 4000 Facsimile (02) 9906 5500

Broadlex is one of the major commercial and industrial cleaning contractors, providing services in Sydney, Melbourne and Canberra. Broadlex and Qantas have been working together for over ten years. This association extends to all three of the above cities. Broadlex looks forward to a growing business relationship with Qantas, benefiting both Qantas and Broadlex.

CABCHARGE AUSTRALIA PTY LIMITED
ACN 001 958 390

REGINALD L KERMODE *Chairman and Managing Director*

152 Riley Street, East Sydney NSW 2010. Telephone (02) 332 9222 Facsimile (02) 332 9270

Cabcharge was launched by Taxis Combined Services Pty Ltd (Sydney) in partnership with the Yellow Cabs Group in 1976, providing a national charge account facility for taxis. Growth was rapid with some 280 taxi and hire care companies throughout Australia now offering the Cabcharge facility to more than 45,000 account holders. Qantas have been associated with Cabcharge since inception and continue to be a major trading partner.

CATERAIR AIRPORT SERVICES PTY LIMITED
ACN 008 646 302

ROBERT M HELD *Managing Director* JILL E ANDERSON *Chief Financial Officer*

300 Coward Street, Mascot NSW 2020. Telephone (02) 667 8013 Facsimile (02) 313 4129

Caterair supplies Qantas and a host of international airlines from Brisbane, Cairns and Sydney. Caterair's 1,300 highly motivated associates in Australia will combine their skills to prepare over 6 million meals, clean 60,000 aircraft and produce over A$100 million in revenues in 1995.

CLINTONS MOTORS PTY LTD
ACN 008 444 844

BARRY W CLINTON *Chairman* JEREMY W CLINTON *Co-Managing Director*

MARIO KORDOVOLOS *Co-Managing Director*

3-17 Queen Street, Campbelltown NSW 2560. Telephone (046) 281 8888 Facsimile (046) 27 1396

The Clinton Motor Group, currently celebrating its 50th Anniversary, is a family-run, customer service-oriented operation with car dealerships across Sydney at Campbelltown, Camden, Lakemba and Haberfield. The Group carries vehicle ranges from Toyota, Daihatsu, Mercedes-Benz and Aston Martin Lagonda.

COMPAQ COMPUTER AUSTRALIA
ACN 002 955 722

IAN PENMAN *Managing Director*

18-20 Orion Road, Lane Cove NSW 2066. Telephone (02) 9911 1999 Facsimile (02) 9911 1800

Compaq is the world's largest supplier of personal computers, offering desktop PCs, notebook PCs and servers. Compaq began working with Qantas back in 1989 and one of the first projects was the development of the highly successful QIK-RES reservation system. Since then Compaq and Qantas have continued to work together and today Compaq is a preferred supplier of personal computing products to Qantas.

CONNAT FLIGHT SERVICES PTY LTD
ACN 064 142 418

PETER SMITH *Managing Director* **YVONNE SMITH** *Director*

Level 2-16 Queensland Avenue, Broadbeach QLD 4218. Telephone (07) 559 25545 Facsimile (07) 559 26632

Connat's principal business is Inflight Catering and we have been associated with Qantas since 1989 when we began catering for Australian Airlines in Hobart and for Qantas on the Hobart to Auckland flight.

FELTEX CARPETS & WOOLS GROUP

CJ (CHRIS) DAVIS *Group General Manager* **BJ (BRUCE) McCLINTOCK** *Group Financial Controller*

Feltex Centre, 145 Symonds Street, Auckland 1, New Zealand. Telephone (09) 379 1910 Facsimile (09) 379 1911

The Feltex Carpets Group manufacture and market globally Woven, Tufted and Modular carpet to all sectors of industry. Their diversity of production technologies and design capabilities has seen Qantas select custom-designed carpets for use in their aircraft, airport terminals and commercial properties.

HILTON INTERNATIONAL AUSTRALIA
ACN 008 419 485

WALTER ANNEN *Divisional Director, Hilton International Australia*

259 Pitt Street, Sydney NSW 2000. Telephone (02) 266 0610 Facsimile (02) 265 6065

Hilton International Australia is proud to be linked with Qantas and to hold the honoured position of preferred supplier for the Qantas Getaway Program. Operating seven first-class hotels in Australia, our principal area of business is the Australian corporate and leisure traveller.

SHERATON PACIFIC HOTELS PTY LIMITED
ACN 000 575 048

PETER THOMPSON *Director of Operations, Australia*   **PAUL SERGEANT** *Director of Sales & Marketing, Pacific*

161 Elizabeth Street, Sydney NSW 2000. Telephone (02) 286 6000 Facsimile (02) 286 6686

ITT Sheraton Corporation is a global hospitality network focused on quality, with a portfolio of more than 450 properties catering for the personalised needs of leisure and business travellers. ITT Sheraton has enjoyed a very long and successful partnership with Qantas through various joint marketing initiatives, including the Qantas Frequent Flyer programme.

ITOCHU AVIATION CO., LTD.
AKIRA SATO *President*

AKIO MIYAGAWA *Director & Division General Manager, Aerospace Project Division*

5-8, Kita-Aoyama 2-Chome, Minato-ku, Tokyo 107 Japan.

Telephone (81) 3 3497 8288 Facsimile (81) 3 3497 8300

Itochu Aviation Co Ltd, 100% owned by Itochu Corporation, one of the largest trading companies in the world, has been sharing vital roles in aerospace industries for more than 30 years. Itochu Aviation continues to commit to the global good.

JAMCO CORPORATION
YOSHIRO MATSUO *President*

MASATO KAWATA *General Manager Marketing Dept*

6-11-25, Osawa Mitaka, Tokyo 181 Japan.

Telephone (81) 425 28 6111 Facsimile (81) 425 28 6161

Jamco Corporation have served the airline market as one of the leading manufacturers of cabin equipment, sharing 30% of aircraft galley and 60% of the aircraft lavatory market. Jamco is committed to the continuous supply of the best quality products to the airline market.

JARDINE AIRPORT SERVICES LIMITED

K C STANLEY KO *Chairman*   JAMES CAREY *Director & General Manager*

Jardine Pacific Limited, 25/F Devon House, 979 King's Road, Quarry Bay, Hong Kong. Telephone (852) 257 92888 Facsimile (852) 285 69868

Jardine Airport Services have 50 years experience as a ground handling service supplier at Hong Kong International Airport, handling 19 international and mainland China airlines. They are proud to be associated with Qantas as their service partner and share the same goal in the partnership in satisfying all Qantas customers with unparalleled service standards.

KPMG

JOHN HARKNESS *Chairman*   ANTHONY CLARK AM *Managing Partner*

The KPMG Centre, 45 Clarence Street, Sydney NSW 2000. Telephone (02) 335 7000 Facsimile (02) 299 7077

KPMG has major accounting and management consulting practices in Australia and around the world. Partners and staff service clients across all industries and a wide range of services is available. KPMG acts as auditors, taxation, corporate and accountancy advisers to Qantas.

SBC Warburg

SBC WARBURG AUSTRALIA LIMITED
ACN 008 582 705

DAVID ADAM *Chairman*
CLIVE STANDISH *Managing Director & Chief Executive Officer*
Level 25, Governor Phillip Tower, 1 Farrer Place, Sydney NSW 2000
Telephone (02) 375 6868 Facsimile (02) 247 7771

McIntosh

McINTOSH CORPORATE LIMITED
ACN 006 995 900

WILLIAM J CONN *Chairman*
R JOHN MAGOWAN *Managing Director*
Level 39, 120 Collins Street, Melbourne VIC 3000
Telephone (03) 9659 2211 Facsimile (03) 9659 2699

Joint lead managers and bookrunners to the highly successful Qantas public share offer.

MEMOREX TELEX PTY LTD
ACN 000 835 487

PETER THOMPSON *Vice President, Asia Pacific*   MARK NICKLIN *Finance Director, Asia Pacific*

3 Thomas Holt Drive, North Ryde NSW 2113. Telephone (02) 805 5805 Facsimile (02) 805 0420

Memorex Telex is a leading network integrator. We build on strong relationships with market and technology leaders to integrate superior products and services into networking and storage solutions, supported, as Qantas is, internationally.

Noritake

NORITAKE (AUSTRALIA) PTY LTD
ACN 000 243 925

SHUNZO KAWABATA *Managing Director*   RAY SAYCE *Director*

Unit 4, 153 Beauchamp Road, Matraville NSW 2036. Telephone (02) 316 7123 Facsimile (02) 316 7085

Noritake was established in 1904 as a manufacturer of high-quality tableware for the international market and now serves Qantas Airways Limited with bone china, fine china and cutlery in inflight/lounge service.

Rawlinsons.

RAWLINSONS (NSW) PTY LTD
ACN 003 093 954

GRAHAM MOULT *Managing Director*

Level 10, 153 Walker Street, North Sydney NSW 2060. Telephone (02) 9929 5922 Facsimile (02) 9959 5297

Rawlinsons are construction cost managers to Qantas, providing the airline with quantity surveying, cost-planning and cost-control services in the construction of its on-ground physical facilities.

TFK CORPORATION

SUSUMU ASHINO *Chairman* TSUTOMU NOMAGUCHI *President*
PO Box 126, New Tokyo International Airport, Narita City, Chiba Pref, Japan 282.
Telephone (81) (476) 32 5558 Facsimile (81) (476) 32 5586

Dedicated to serving the airlines of the world, the name of TFK has been linked to Qantas for the past 33 years.
Building on inflight catering experience, TFK also operates two hotels and two restaurants in the Narita Airport vicinity.

UNISTAT PTY LIMITED
ACN 000 065 065

WILLIAM B MOORE *Chairman* MARTIN J MCMURRAY *Chief Executive*

11 Carrington Road, Castle Hill NSW 2154. Telephone (02) 843 0777 Facsimile (02) 634 7018

WOODS BAGOT
ACN 007 762 174

DR ANDREW HOLSMAN *Chairman* DAVID TREGONING *Group Managing Partner*
Level 4, 146 Arthur Street, North Sydney NSW 2060. Telephone (02) 9957 5919 Facsimile (02) 9929 5749

Woods Bagot and Qantas have a long association through planning and designing international and
national airport facilities. Woods Bagot takes pride in their 125 year history and reputation for innovative,
long-term solutions in architecture, interior design landscape and urban design, and strategic planning.

AMERICAN GRAND PRIX RACING

RACING

A Century of Drivers & Cars

Tim Considine
Foreword by Phil Hill

MBI Publishing Company

First published in 1997 by MBI Publishing Company, 729 Prospect Avenue, PO Box 1, Osceola, WI 54020-0001 USA

MBI Publishing Company books are also available at discounts in bulk quantity for industrial or sales-promotional use. For details write to Special Sales Manager at Motorbooks International Wholesalers & Distributors, 729 Prospect Avenue, PO Box 1, Osceola, WI 54020-0001 USA.

Library of Congress Cataloging-in-Publication Data
    American Grand Prix racing : a century of drivers & cars / Tim Considine.
       p.   cm.
    Includes index.
    ISBN 0-7603-0210-3 (hardbound : alk. paper)
    1. Grand Prix racing—History.   2. Automobile racing drivers—United States—Biography.   3. Formula One automobiles—History.
    I. Title.
    GV1029.15.C66   1997
    796.72'0973--dc21   97-27507

On the front cover: Dan Gurney on his way to fifth place in the Eagle-Climax at the 1966 Mexican Grand Prix. After two DNFs with the faster but undeveloped 12-cylinder Weslake, Gurney opted for his four-cylinder Eagle. *Pete Biro*

On the frontispiece: David Bruce-Brown at the wheel of the imposing 14-liter Fiat powers his way to victory in the 1911 American Grand Prize. Brown was just twenty-one years old. The face masks worn by Brown and his mechanic provided a modicum of protection from rocks and other debris. *Lew Balderson collection*

On the title page: Phil Hill's 60-degree V-6 Ferrari 156 Dino in second place ahead of Joakim Bonnier's #2 Porsche at Monaco in 1961. Ultimately, Hill waved Richie Ginther's faster 120-degree Ferrari by, settling for third place. *Dave Friedman photo collection*

On the back cover: Top: Mario Andretti managed to score his first World Championship victory in his first works Ferrari ride, at the 1971 South African Grand Prix. *Dave Friedman photo collection* Bottom: Lance Reventlow ponders the heart of his Scarab Grand Prix car, the only all-American-made engine ever to run in a World Championship Formula One race. Designed by Leo Goossen and built at Meyer & Drake, the Scarab motor was a conventional 2,490-cc four-cylinder, two-valve design. It's one distinctive feature, desmodromic valves copied from the Mercedes W196 and 300SLR valve train, turned out to be a bust. *Cheryl Reventlow Post collection*

Edited by Zack Miller
Designed by Katie Finney

Printed in Hong Kong through World Print, Ltd.

CONTENTS

FOREWORD

My interest in motor racing began more as a curiosity than anything else. The period in time was the early 1930s, and I remember well the anecdotal banter of the adults in our neighborhood concerning our "Santa Monica Road Races." These discussions were always intense, and they were most intriguing to a young boy's imagination. I never could get enough of it. We lived (and still do) just a few hundred yards from San Vicente Boulevard, which had been one of the fastest parts of the circuit. The last race was in 1919, 10 years before my family's arrival.

I'm certain beyond a doubt that my attraction to road-racing was due to living next to the old Santa Monica circuit. My fascination with the idea of tearing through "Death Curve" at Ocean Avenue and Wilshire Boulevard (then called Nevada Avenue) had much to do with my ending up at places like Sebring, Spa-Francorchamps, Monza, and countless other road-racing venues. Granted, there was a period in my late teens that I was wrapped up in midget racing, but with the postwar revival of interest in sports cars, road-racing, etc., I was ready to become a part of it.

To digress . . . simply hearing about the early races was never enough for me. Something was missing. Well, Tim Considine's wonderful book filled in all the missing bits and then some. *American Grand Prix Racing; A Century of Drivers & Cars* begins before the turn of the century and marches right up to the most recent involvement by an American in Formula One. The entire story is presented in a most interesting and exciting way, and once the reader has started, the book is hard to put down.

I had been aware of the driver, George Heath, for example, and knew that he had won the first Vanderbilt Cup on Long Island in 1904 in a Panhard. But I had no idea that he was an American. Tim calls him "our first American star." He was the first Yank to race in a European event, and by 1904, was number one on the Panhard team. He had won against the best and returned home to win the Vanderbilt Cup on his native Long Island. By 1906, he had finished sixth in the first and original Grand Prix at Le Mans and thereby became the first American GP driver. This is just one little biographical gem of many found in this work.

I particularly enjoyed the years 1948–1968, because those were "my" years, and Considine has covered them with great accuracy. His interviews with living drivers are wonderfully revealing in that there is so much new material. The last subject is Michael Andretti's 1993 season in Formula One and the enormous pressure and frustration he had to endure.

It's a wonderful book and a wonderful read. Be assured also that there is no other like it. For Tim Considine to have undertaken this project and end up with such an outstanding record for posterity on over 144 Yanks that fought at motor sport's top level is indeed worthy of praise.
Phil Hill

PREFACE

Grand Prix has always been to motor racing what the World Series is to baseball or the World Cup to soccer. It remains so today, as the Formula One World Championship. The Indianapolis 500 may be the biggest and most famous single automobile competition, but Formula One is certainly the world's most prestigious and technically advanced motor racing series. It is ironic that America, the most technologically advanced country in the world, where more cars are produced, driven, and raced than anywhere, has never been a power in Grand Prix competition.

With the exception of the brief period between 1908 and 1916, when the major European racing drivers and teams traveled to the United States for American Grand Prize events, distance and circumstance have kept American participation to a minimum—with predictable results. In nearly 800 international Grands Prix over 90 years, only five have been won by American cars (Pullen's Mercer in 1912, Murphy's Duesenberg in 1921, Gurney's Eagle in 1967, Watson's Penske in 1976, and Jones' Shadow in 1977—the latter two, admittedly, English-made) and just 36 (including Aitken, who relieved Wilcox in the final American Grand Prize in 1916) by American drivers. Andretti was the last in 1978. With 22 wins between them, the names Phil Hill, Dan Gurney, and Mario Andretti, of course, are chapter heads in the annals of Formula One. These three proved that, given equal equipment, American drivers can compete with anyone. Also, it must be said that much of the technology employed in Grand Prix racing was invented, developed, or first used in competition in the United States.

Monocoque construction, perfected in Colin Chapman's brilliant 1962 Lotus 25, first appeared at Indy in 1915 in the one-off Cornelian driven by Louis Chevrolet. So did four-wheel independent suspension—19 years before Mercedes and Auto Union used it in Grand Prix competition. Modern disc or "spot" brakes were used on midgets and other U.S. oval track cars in the late 1940s. In fact, but for a steering pin failure just nine laps from the finish, Bill Vukovich would have won the 1952 500 (as he did the following year) with a disc brake-equipped racer, just as BRM and the Thinwall Special were introducing that technology to Formula One.

The world's first supercharged Grand Prix car wasn't, as widely published, Fiat's 805 at the 1923 French Grand Prix. Rather, it was a Pottstown, Pennsylvania-made Chadwick in the 1908 American Grand Prize at Savannah. The first turbocharged race car sat on the pole in 1952 at Indy, when that race counted in the Formula One world championship. The first and only turbine engine to run in Grands Prix was produced by an American company. Wide, slick tires, wings, efficient intercoolers, ground effects, all were developed first in America. So, too, were car-to-pit radio links, telemetry; carbon fiber chassis, brakes, and clutches; safety harnesses; crash-resistant fuel bladders; fire suits; and full-coverage helmets.

No, America has not yet been a Grand Prix power, but Yank drivers have been competitive more often than is commonly thought. And American cars, even when not specifically designed for "road racing," have often introduced innovative and advanced technologies. What follows is a blatantly chauvinistic account of the American men and machines that have taken part in Grand Prix competition, from its origins to the present. It is a tale of what was—and sometimes, what might have been.

Tim Considine

ACKNOWLEDGMENTS

First and foremost, this work could never have been completed without the cooperation of the drivers quoted herein. From the very beginning, when the story was to be a single magazine article, then a series of articles, and finally, to a full-blown book, their enthusiasm and encouragement was absolutely inspiring. But I am also deeply grateful for the generous help, advice, information, and materials provided along the way by the following individuals and institutions: Tyler Alexander; Lew Balderson; Pat Batchelor; Pete Biro; Griff Borgeson; Ognan Borrisov, Interfoto; Ken Breslauer; Gregg Buttermore, Auburn Cord Duesenberg Museum; Bernard Cahier; Paul-Henri Cahier; Dick Carlson; Mark Dees; John B. Dodge; Suzanne Dreyfus; Steve Ellis, IMS Photos; Bob Estes; Dave Friedman; Peter Giddings; Brad Gray; Terry Griffin; Chuck Groninga; Phil Harms; Mike Hollander; Pat Jones, IMS Photos; Beverly Rae Kimes; Dale LaFollette; Steve Lehmer; Mike Martin; Teddy Mayer; Dorothy Mays; Rex Mays, Jr.; Denise McCluggage; Rick Miller; Robert Newman; Patrick O'Brien; Harold Osmer; Mark Patrick, Detroit Public Library, National Automotive History Collection; Fred Roe; Carmen Schroeder; Ken Stewart; Bob Tronolone; Frederick Usher; Dale Von Trebra; Ed Watson; Gordon White; Janos Wimpffen; and Robert Young.

And finally, special thanks to Phil Hill, David Woodhouse, Bob Schilling, and Jim Sitz, who were kind enough to check the manuscript for errors. Any that remain are the author's alone.

Jimmy Murphy and co-driver Ernie Olsen after dominating the 1921 A.C.F. Grand Prix with their Duesenberg. Murphy and others proved that given a good horse, Americans could race with anyone, anywhere. *Indianapolis Motor Speedway*

The Beginnings, America's Pioneers

1906–1921

Amerca's involvement in "European" motor racing dates back to 1895 and what is considered the first legitimate automobile race, 732 miles from Paris to Bordeaux and back. Two prominent Americans contributed to the prize money for that premier competition, teenage motor car enthusiast "Willie K." Vanderbilt, who would later set two Land Speed Records and found America's first international race series, and flamboyant expatriate James Gordon Bennett, the Paris-based owner and publisher of the *New York Herald*. In 1889, inspired by a challenge from feisty American car builder Alexander Winton to Fernand Charron, France's most famous driver, Bennett commissioned the creation of a permanent trophy, the Gordon Bennett Cup. It was to be awarded to the winner of a race contested annually by three-car teams representing different nations.

Though never as successful as its founder had hoped, the Gordon Bennett Cup races, contested from 1900 to 1905, were the first truly international racing series and importantly, they introduced the first motor racing formula (strict weight limitations) to even the competition.

The first Grand Prix, the 1906 Grand Prix de l'Automobile Club de France (ACF), was in essence a reaction to and direct outgrowth of Bennett's pioneer series between national teams. With an abundance of automobile manufacturers eager to compete, France had chafed under Gordon Bennett Cup rules limiting each country's representation to a single three-car team. Needless to say, the sponsoring ACF quickly dropped that provision. No less than 23 French cars were entered in the first event, to be run June 26 and 27 over a roughly triangular 64.12-mile course on the outskirts of Le Mans. To emphasize the importance of this first Grand Prix, and re-establish the pre-eminence of France's ACF, the total distance was set at 769 miles, about twice that of successful races held the same year in Italy, Belgium, and America.

Italy was represented by six cars, Germany, three. There were no American or British cars, but two American drivers then living in France did take part. One, George Heath, was a seasoned veteran. In 1898, he had become the first American to compete in a European race, finishing 13th out of 22 in the Paris-Amsterdam. Now considered the number one driver for Panhard's team at Le Mans, in 1904 Heath had driven a Panhard to win against the best European drivers, both at Belgium's Circuit des Ardennes and in the premier Vanderbilt Cup race on his native Long Island.

The other American in the first Grand Prix was Elliott Shepard, a cousin of Willie K. Vanderbilt, who had never raced in a major competition. Shepard, however, proved to be the surprise of the first half of the race. The newcomer had his French Hotchkiss up to third by the fourth lap

1

left top: Barney Oldfield in J. Walter Christie's 1907 WC-5. Fittingly, America's first Grand Prix car was a big-banger. Christie had gone to the radical 30-degree V 4 configuration specifically to permit larger-bore pistons than his in-line designs would allow. Both bore and stroke measured a whopping 7.3 inches, meaning the displacement of *each* of the four cylinders was not much less than that of a modern Chevrolet Corvette engine. The WC-5 must have thumped like an artillery barrage! *John B. Dodge collection*

bottom left: America's pioneer international motor racing star, George Heath, shown here when he returned from Europe to drive a works Panhard to victory in America's first international race, the 1904 Vanderbilt Cup. *Phil Harms collection*

bottom right: Joe Tracy and mechanician Al Poole ran this A.L. Riker-designed Locomobile in France in the last Gordon-Bennet Cup race, in 1905. The car performed poorly, but in October of the same year, in the second Vanderbilt Cup, Tracy and Poole brought the car home third, the best performance yet by an American-made car in international competition. Encouraged, Riker designed another Locomobile, "Old 16," with which George Robertson would win the 1908 Vanderbilt Cup for America's first international victory. *Phil Harms collection*

George Heath, a native New Yorker, was a resident of Paris, the hub of city-to-city road racing in the late 1800s. For his first try, in 1898, the tall American chose an 889-mile race from Paris to Amsterdam and back to Paris. Just to finish this grueling six-day event was an accomplishment. Heath showed grit and real potential, arriving home ahead of nine others with his 6-horsepower Panhard, the only make he would ever race. A year later, in the original Tour de France, a 1,350-mile loop around the country, Heath finished sixth.

George Heath

If he hadn't gotten the attention of Panhard yet, he certainly must have six days later with an impressive fourth-place finish in the Paris-St. Malo race. By 1904, Heath was a full "works" driver for Panhard. That year, at Circuit des Ardennes, he overcame a slow penultimate lap to defeat teammate George Teste by less than one minute.

Fittingly, it was Heath, America's first international star (and soon, America's first Grand Prix driver), who returned to Long Island and held off 19-year-old Albert Clément, in the Clément-Bayard, to win America's first international motor race, the 1904 Vanderbilt Cup. Heath was second in the 1905 Vanderbilt Cup and managed to hold on for sixth at Le Mans for the 1906 Grand Prix, but Panhard's domination had ended. So had the American's luck. Mechanical problems would put him out of the 1907 Grand Prix, and though he would race until 1909, there would be no more impressive results for the pioneering George Heath.

George Heath. *Detroit Public Library, National Automotive History Collection*

William Kissam "Willy K" Vanderbilt II (1878–1944), great grandson of shipping and railroad magnate "Commodore" Cornelius Vanderbilt, was a racing pioneer and patron of international motor competition in the United States. He was also a skilled driver himself, finishing third with his French 60-horsepower Mors in the world's first closed-circuit race, at Belgium's Circuit des Ardennes. Vanderbilt was a two-time (and America's first) Land Speed Record holder, first with the Mors in France (76.08 miles per hour), then in a Mercedes at Ormond Beach near Daytona (92.30 miles per hour) in 1904, the year he sponsored the first Vanderbilt Cup race. Detroit Public Library, National Automotive *History Collection*

and finished the first day in a solid fourth place, three positions ahead of Heath. On the second day, however, Shepard's car refused to fire and he lost a half hour before getting under way. It was an omen of what was to follow, for on the eighth lap, a wire wheel collapsed and forced Shepard to retire.

Heath, slowed by multiple tire punctures and, importantly, the lack of detachable rims, nevertheless went on to finish sixth behind Szisz's winning Renault, a point by today's scoring system!

Both Heath and Shepard competed in the 1907 ACF Grand Prix. Heath was out on the first lap and Shepard, this time driving a French Clément-Bayard, finished ninth. The first and sole American-made entry was, if not the fastest, certainly one of the most technically interesting and innovative. Walter Christie's car, lightest of the 37 entered, was a front-wheel drive, powered by a transversely mounted V-4 displacing just under 20 liters, the largest engine ever to contest a Grand Prix. The powerful, albeit ill-handling, Christie proved, in spite of its performances in the States, surprisingly slow and unreliable, retiring on only the fifth lap. To his dying day, Walker Christie suspected foul play. The driver who led more than half the 1907 Grand Prix and appeared to be uncatchable until transmission problems struck was

New Yorker Lewis Strang was a bust at the 1908 ACF Grand Prix in the Thomas, but was declared National Champion the same year for his success in Italian Isottas. In 1909, Strang joined the hard-charging Buick team, winning several events that year, among them, the 100-mile G. & J. Trophy at the inaugural races at Indianapolis. He started from the pole in a Case at the first 500, but DNF'd. Ironically, two months later, Strang was killed—at about 10 miles per hour—when a muddy section of road gave way and his Case rolled over and crushed him at the Wisconsin Reliability Run. *Indianapolis Motor Speedway*

American-born Lorraine-Dietrich driver Arthur Duray. Though born in New York in 1881 to Belgian parents, Duray later became a French citizen.

In that second-ever Grand Prix, weight limitations were relaxed in favor of a 9.41-mile-per-gallon fuel consumption formula, but national colors, first used in the Gordon Bennett Cup series, were once again adopted. This custom would be followed until 1968, when Colin Chapman's Lotus cars eschewed British Racing Green for the livery of Gold Leaf cigarettes. (As usual, Chapman was ahead of his time. In today's Formula One, only Ferrari retains its traditional national color, blood red. That color had originally been given to the United States and was assigned to Italy—and Nazzaro's winning Fiat—for the 1907 Grand Prix.)

For 1908, the ACF instituted a new formula calling for a minimum weight of 2,425 pounds and a maximum bore of 155 mm for four-cylinder engines and 127 mm for six-cylinders. Also new, to clear the view for ground-level spectators when competitors stopped for service, was a 5-foot deep trench along the front straight to house spare parts and supporting crews, thereafter known as the "pits."

Heath returned in the Panhard-Levassor and a new American entry, the Thomas, was to be driven by Lewis Strang, Walter Christie's nephew who had ridden as Christie's mechanic the previous year. Strang could drive. Sports writers would declare him National Champion in 1908, but his biggest wins that year came at the wheel of an Italian Isotta-Fraschini, not a Thomas.

While Thomas cars had won several endurance races in the United States and another was at the moment just weeks away from victory in the around-the-world New York-to-Paris marathon, Strang's entry in the third Grand Prix proved, once again, how far America's cars lagged in mechanical sophistication. Little more than a stripped-down stock model, the Thomas lost first and second gear immediately and retired on the fourth lap.

In truth, on a road course, no American car was a match for Lautenschlager's 1908 Grand Prix-winning Mercedes or the fastest cars from Italy and France. Not yet. Centuries of civilization, commerce, and war had left Europe's cities linked with a network of well-kept, often paved roads—a circumstance that greatly accelerated the development of the automobile. In America, a vast, relatively new state with only primitive roads connecting distant population centers, it was just

*J*ohn Walter Christie
1867 to 1/11/44

J. Walter Christie was born on a farm in River Edge, New Jersey, in 1867. By 16, he was working in New York in the machine shop of the huge De Lamater plant, where he would help build the world's first submarine. Studying engineering at night, Christie honed his skills as a shipbuilder, then became a freelance engineer and consultant. In 1899, he was rehired by a former employer, William Cramp & Sons in Philadelphia, to design the turret-turning assembly for a new big-gunned battleship, the U.S.S. Maine. That technology was later adopted by the British Navy.

In 1901, Christie realized a longtime personal ambition, designing and constructing his first car, the transverse-engine, front-drive WC-1. Among his other radical experiments were a twin-engine, four-wheel-drive racer and, of course, the behemoth transverse Grand Prix V-4. Christie was a tireless advocate of front-wheel drive, a technology prevalent today.

Unlike most carmakers of his time, Christie raced his creations and did so with some success from 1904 through 1910. He competed in the 1905 Vanderbilt Cup race, but was out after a collision with the leading Fiat, driven by Vincenzo Lancia. Christie never drove in a major event after the 1907 French Grand Prix, but did barnstorming tours, match races, and record attempts across the United States. Barney Oldfield also toured with Christie's cars. Not long after attaining nearly 120 miles per hour in one of his massive front-drivers at Ormond-Daytona in 1910, Walter Christie quit competing.

Christie created innovative designs for airplanes, fire engines, and from the 1920s on, high-speed armored cars and tanks. Though his prototypes always tested well, Christie's efforts to get the U.S. government to properly fund or even reimburse his work were frustrated year after year, to the point of financial ruin. Ironically, in the end, his tank designs were appreciated more abroad than at home. In World War II, Christie tanks helped the British to defeat Rommel in Africa and the Russians to defend Moscow.

Sadly, Walter Christie died virtually penniless, a broken man, on January 11, 1944. More than 30 years later, he was inducted into the Ordnance Hall of Fame of the U.S. Army in sincere, if belated, recognition of his genius.

Walter Christie. *Detroit Public Library, National Automotive History Collection*

Len Zengle and his mechanician, Frieberg, in the Acme wait for the start of Savannah's 1908 American Grand Prize. Though it had a motor designed by ex-Daimler engineer Victor Jakob, the Reading, Pennsylvania-made Acme was no match in power, speed, or toughness for the European cars. By the end of lap one, Zengle had already lost five minutes to DePalma's leading Fiat. Five laps later, after attempting to fix a broken front spring on the third tour, Zengle went out for good, more than an hour and a quarter behind the leader. *Detroit Public Library, National Automotive History Collection*

the opposite: the automobile accelerated the building of roads. Indeed, America's first international motor race, the premier Vanderbilt Cup event in 1904, came only a year after a Vermont doctor and his chauffeur made the first successful coast-to-coast crossing of the United States in a motor car. It took 64 days.

While Europeans were testing their machines in marathon city-to-city races or on high-speed closed road courses on the continent, pioneer American car builders and drivers usually made their reputations in all-out speed attempts, solo runs across the country, or increasingly, careening around dirt ovals originally meant for horse racing. Born

because of a lack of good roads, this fascination with oval tracks was to have far-reaching consequences in American motor sport.

After suffering the embarrassment of being beaten by both Italian (Fiat) and German (Mercedes) cars in 1907 and 1908, French automobile manufacturers withdrew all support for Grand Prix racing. Soon, other European carmakers, eyeing huge budgetary savings, followed suit and entered into a pact renouncing direct factory involvement. The ACF held no Grand Prix for three years. Except for Italy's Targa Florio, international events were limited to smaller *voiturette* cars. Except, ironically, in America.

Catching On and Catching Up

It started with the Vanderbilt Cup, a Tiffany silver trophy offered by Willie K. Vanderbilt for a series of international Gordon Bennett Cup-type events sanctioned by the American Automobile Association (AAA). From the outset in 1904, pact or no, European teams were well represented and most often prevailed. At least, their cars did. Fittingly, an American, George Heath, won the first Vanderbilt Cup race, but it was in a French Panhard.

Mulford and the Lozier, often a winning combination in American racing, got nowhere in the 1908 Grand Prize. After a troubled and slow run, the Lozier finally went out on lap 11. *Detroit Public Library, National Automotive History Collection*

American cars, a Pope-Toledo and a Packard, finished a distant third and fourth. In fact, technically, they didn't finish, as the race was called off after the first two cars were flagged in due to spectators flooding the course, a serious problem that would continue to plague the Vanderbilt Cup races.

European cars again dominated in the 1905 and 1906 Vanderbilt Cups, though Joe Tracy's third place in a Locomobile gave some hope to American enthusiasts in 1905. The following year, Tracy had a new 16.8-liter, 90-horsepower Locomobile that set the fastest time for a single lap. But tires were a problem and neither Tracy's Locomobile nor any of the other American entries were even close to the five leading European cars when the race was stopped, again due to unruly crowds. In Peter Helck's book, *The Checkered Flag*, the winner, Darracq driver Louis Wagner, was quoted as saying,

"The miracle was not my winning but that hundreds were not killed in my doing so." Indeed, so great were concerns for the safety of drivers and spectators alike that the 1907 event was canceled.

In 1908, the Vanderbilt Cup race was resumed and run over a revised 23.46-mile Long Island circuit that included 10 miles of new concrete roads, much of it bordered with protective wire fencing. Only one foreigner, Mercedes driver Emil Stricker, contested the 1908 Cup race. George Robertson, driving the ex-Tracy "Old 16" Locomobile, finished ahead of six European cars to claim America's first major motor racing victory. Europe's best drivers came in force a month later for the 1908 American Grand Prize in Savannah, Georgia, the first race in a new series that would soon eclipse the Vanderbilt Cup.

Organized by the Automobile Club of America (ACA), the American Grand Prize would give American drivers their best opportunity to race against or, in many cases, drive some of the best overseas machinery. Apparently, ACA and Savannah officials considered calling their race a Grand Prix, but in the end, decided that was too "Frenchified." However, with a purse of $4,000, twice that offered by the Vanderbilt Cup, and the promise of a first-

David Bruce-Brown's No. 15 Benz thunders down the main straightaway on the way to victory in the 1910 American Grand Prize, in Savannah. *Lew Balderson collection*

class course with good crowd control, the Savannah races easily lured European teams that had abandoned the Long Island races to the South.

The Savannah Automobile Club had been rejected as host for the 1908 Vanderbilt Cup, and when granted the opportunity to stage the ACA Grand Prize, was determined to put on an impressive, trouble-free event. Meticulous planning and the full cooperation of city and state authorities ensured they would accomplish their goal. Convict labor cut a beautiful 25.13-mile course through the forest. A smaller 9.8-mile loop, using only one section of the main course, was prepared for a supporting "light" car race. The 30- to 60- foot-wide road was oiled gravel, virtually dust-free, with properly banked turns.

Teams were headquartered in separate camps close to the race course. Some were temporary while others were specially erected structures. Road access to Savannah was limited, so teams, cars, and more than 100,000 spectators arrived mainly by boat or train. Some had been chartered from cities as far north as New York. With a reported 16,000 Georgia militia troops deployed around the course, there would be no crowd control problems. On Thanksgiving Day, November 26, 1908, six American cars faced off against 14 of the best European makes in the first American Grand Prize.

None of the American cars—really just hot-rodded production cars— had much of a chance against the sophisticated racers fielded by the Euro-

pean manufacturers. Probably the fastest American entry, and certainly the most interesting historically, was the Chadwick Six driven by Willie Haupt. A successful hill-climber, it was the first supercharged car ever to run in a Grand Prix. Haupt had the Chadwick seventh at the end of the first lap, but was out by lap five with bearing trouble.

In the Light Car race run the previous day, the Buick team's "Wild" Bob Burman had lived up to his nickname, electrifying the crowd with spectacular driving. His 18-horsepower "underslung" Buick led until an extended pit stop put him far back, but Burman clawed his way back and salvaged second place. No such luck in the Grand Prize. The larger 50-horsepower Buick "underslung" racer lasted only two laps, and one of America's most exciting young drivers was the first out of the race.

One by one, American entries dropped from the field. Len Zengle, in the Acme, was out after only six laps with a broken front spring. Ralph Mulford had a troubled run in the Lozier, a car usually known as much for durability as speed. On this day, however, it had neither. Never better than 15th, Mulford's Lozier retired after 10 laps. Hugh Harding completed only one more lap in the National before a camshaft failure. Of the six American cars that started, only Joe Seymour's Simplex was running at the finish, albeit a full lap behind winner Louis Wagner's powerful Fiat.

If America's cars weren't competitive, better things were expected from Lewis Strang. He had already won three races back-to-back in an Italian Isotta, beginning with the Savannah Challenge Cup race in March 1908. For the Grand Prize, Strang drove a Renault

Burman and mechanic Hall struggle with one of 15 tire changes on the Marquette-Buick. Tires were always a problem for the hard-charging Burman, but he was fast, wrestling his 40-horsepower Buick to third place, the highest Grand Prix finish yet for an American car. *Lew Balderson collection*

to sixth, the highest of any American, and was still on the same lap as the winner after 402 miles.

But it was another American driver, Italian immigrant Ralph DePalma, who proved to be the surprise of the 1908 Savannah race. Given Vincenzo Lancia's seat on the Fiat team, the soon-to-be superstar DePalma

charged to the front—setting a lap record in the process—to become the first American to lead a Grand Prix. Unfortunately, mechanical woes and multiple stops relegated him to ninth.

U.S. drivers had indeed been impressive on the occasion of the first American Grand Prix. The same could not be said for American cars. No surprise Fiat, Benz, and Mercedes cars driven by Americans began to win regularly on home oval tracks as well. In fact, a Benz driven by Barney Oldfield was fastest in a 1-mile speed test at the August 1909 opening of a new 2 1/2-mile track in Indiana, the future home of the Indianapolis 500.

Willie Haupt could be considered the father of automobile supercharging. In 1906, he persuaded his employer, Lee Chadwick, to put a centrifugal compressor on the car that would be called the Great Chadwick Six. Haupt was also the factory driver for Chadwick and was particularly adept at hill climb competitions. When Haupt fitted a three-stage version of the supercharger in 1907, his Chadwick became very difficult to beat in any contest that called for short bursts of acceleration. Haupt's Chadwick won the 1-1/2-mile Giant's Despair Hill Climb in Wilkes-Barre, Pennsylvania, two years in a row and briefly led the 1908 Vanderbilt Cup before falling back to 10th with ignition trouble. He lasted only three laps that year in the American Grand Prize at Savannah.

Though Willie Haupt would lead the 1910 American Grand Prize and set the lap record in his Benz, he pushed too hard just a lap later and left the road.

The last significant drives for Haupt came at Indianapolis. In 1913, Haupt finished ninth in the Duesenberg-made Mason. The following year, with the Mason renamed Duesenberg, Haupt finished 12th. He was 11th in 1915 in an Emden. In his final appearance at the Speedway, Haupt's Meteor (nee Duesenberg) was classified 16th, having gone out on the 147th lap.

Willie Haupt
1885 to
4/20/1966

Willie Haupt. *Indianapolis Motor Speedway*

Ralph Mulford's No. 4 Lozier hangs on to Louis Wagner in the big Fiat as onlookers behind a barbed wire fence cheer them on. Only Mulford would finish—fourth—about 18 minutes behind Bruce-Brown's Benz. *Lew Balderson collection*

In spite of Savannah's success in 1908, there would be no Grand Prize in 1909. Temporarily reconciled with the rival AAA, the ACA agreed that future Grand Prize races would be held on Long Island, where the fifth Vanderbilt Cup would be staged, albeit under new rules that would diminish its stature. As of 1909, the Vanderbilt Cup was no longer open to full-out racing cars. Rather, it was to be limited to stripped down stock models with engines from 301 to 600 cubic inches. Harry Grant's Alco won the 1909 Vanderbilt Cup, but against only a few European cars, none of them piloted by foreign drivers. Grant and the Alco won again in 1910 in a Vanderbilt Cup marred by the death of one spectator and serious injuries to a number of others. Though a Grand Prize was supposed to be run that year on Long Island, fears of more carnage forced the ACA to cancel it.

David Bruce-Brown, America's first Grand Prix winner, is hoisted onto his teammates' shoulders after the 1910 American Grand Prize in Savannah. *Lew Balderson collection*

Fortunately, the Savannah Auto Club was prepared to act. Their bid was quickly accepted and within a month, the 1908 course, cut back to 17 miles, was smoothed and made ready. This time, however, only six European cars would compete, none of them from the still-reluctant French manufacturers. Three Benzes were to be driven by French ace Victor Hémery, former Chadwick driver Willie Haupt, and a young amateur from New York, David Bruce-Brown. The Fiat team remained unchanged from 1908, with the winner of that race, Wagner, third-place Nazarro, and the impressive Ralph DePalma.

Initially, 17 American cars entered, but by race day, that number had diminished considerably. Louis Chevrolet, who had talked of making the Grand Prize his final competition as a driver, withdrew after crashing his Marquette-Buick in the October Vanderbilt Cup. A Simplex to be driven by Georgia racer Joe Matson never made it through practice due to mechanical problems. One fast special, the Sharpe-Arrow, crashed on the last practice day, killing the riding mechanic immediately and, later, driver W. H. Sharpe. Another one-off, Washington Roebling's Roebling-Planche, blew

up during practice. The Stoddard-Dayton and American were withdrawn, and the two Nationals never arrived.

Of nine remaining American entries, the two Marquette-Buicks were the most interesting. True race cars, the light Louis Chevrolet-designed chassis had been successful in the months preceding Savannah and now carried 9.7-liter four-cylinder engines, quite large by American production car standards. The trouble was they were almost tiny compared to the behemoth Benz motors, two of which (Hémery's and Bruce-Brown's) had been enlarged to 15 liters, the other (Haupt's car) at 12 liters. Even the Fiats had new 10-liter motors. Nevertheless, much was expected from the always dynamic Buick team drivers, Louis' brother, Arthur Chevrolet, and the daredevil Bob Burman.

Marmon drivers Ray Harroun and Joe Dawson had been winning races all year long. Indeed, between them, they would notch over 25 victories and be designated one-two in the 1910 AAA national championship. (Harroun

Bob Burman, a farm boy born in Imlay City, Michigan, was among the fledgling Buick company's first employees and tested the first Buick made. Later, he worked as chief tester for the Jackson Automobile Company. It was in a Jackson that Burman won his first race, in Detroit in 1906. The following year, Burman's Jackson won a 24-hour race on the 1-mile dirt track in St. Louis by a margin of 82 miles. Remarkably, on that occasion, Burman's co-driver was behind the wheel for only two hours. Buick headman Will Durant persuaded the obviously skilled 23-year-old daredevil to join Buick's factory racing team that year, alongside, among others, Louis and Arthur Chevrolet. Burman's exciting all-or-nothing driving style earned him the nickname "Wild Bob" and the distinction of being even better known than his frequent adversary, Barney Oldfield.

Bob Burman
4/23/1884 to 4/8/1916

In the preliminary International Light Car Race at Savannah in 1908, Burman's Buick overtook and pulled away from the heavily favored Lancia of Hilliard, before being held in the pits for eight minutes due to a misplaced part. Driving like a madman, Burman still managed to finish second, just six minutes behind Hilliard. He also took one of the inaugural automobile races at Indianapolis Motor Speedway in 1909. The following year, Burman won both the 50- and 100-mile events and the 1-mile Speed Trial at Indianapolis in the Marquette-Buick. In 1911, on his 27th birthday, Bob Burman set a new Land Speed Record with the famous ex-Oldfield "Blitzen Benz" at Ormond-Daytona, driving 141.732 miles per hour—twice the speed any airplane had flown. As a publicity stunt, Burman broke the 1-mile track record at Indianapolis with the Benz the day before the first Indianapolis 500. Crowned "World's Speed King" by Harvey Firestone in a prerace ceremony, Burman drove a smaller Benz to 19th in that inaugural event. On the dirt that year, Burman was indomitable, winning no less than 33 of the 43 races he entered, with eight second-place finishes.

In 1914 and 1915, Burman successfully campaigned a Peugeot. He posted his best finish in the 500, sixth place, with that car in 1915. At the 1916 Corona road races, Burman was closing fast on eventual winner Eddie O'Donnell's Duesenberg, when a rear wheel collapsed, sending his No. 7 Peugeot slamming into a pole. The colorful and popular Wild Bob Burman, one of America's fastest and most exciting drivers, and his riding mechanic both died that day.

Bob Burman. *Indianapolis Motor Speedway*

The formidable Benz team, Hémery, widely regarded as the favorite, and Americans Bergdol, and Hearne, pose at Savannah before race numbers are assigned for the 1911 American Grand Prize. *Lew Balderson collection*

would enter history books the following year by winning the inaugural Indianapolis 500. Teammate Dawson would follow suit in 1912.) But at Savannah, their relatively puny 5.2- and 6.2-liter Marmons looked overmatched.

The month before, Harry Grant had won his second consecutive Vanderbilt Cup race in the Alco, and there were high hopes for this American combination at Savannah. Ralph Mulford was back, in the Lozier, with teammate Joe Horan in another. Two Pope-Hartfords, driven by popular barnstormer Lou Disbrow and Charlie Basle, were the final American entries to make the race.

The second American Grand Prize got under way on the morning of November 12, 1910. Arthur Chevrolet was flagged away first, followed at 30-second intervals by the rest of the field. At the end of the first of 24 laps (415.2 miles), electronic timing, in use for the first time, showed Hémery (Benz) to be leading Chevrolet's Marquette-Buick by a second. Then came Wagner, in the first Fiat, and Hémery's Benz teammates, Bruce-Brown and Haupt. Surprisingly, it was Arthur Chevrolet's Buick rather than Burman's that dueled furiously with Wagner's Fiat for second place. But on lap three, Chevrolet paid for his early speed, making the first of many tire stops that would plague both Marquette-Buicks all day.

The first car out was Dawson's Marmon, its crankshaft broken on the fifth lap. Disbrow's Pope-Hartford (cracked cylinder block) and Chevrolet's Buick (broken crank) made it only to lap nine. The Alco's gearbox packed up two laps

Ralph DePalma was America's first true superstar driver, and with his short-lived contemporary, David Bruce-Brown, the first to be respected in Europe. Much like another famous Italian-American driver who would reach world prominence nearly half a century later, DePalma could drive virtually anything, anywhere. He was equally good on road courses, dirt tracks, board tracks, at the Brickyard, or on the beaches of Daytona.

Born in Troia, Italy, in 1883, Ralph DePalma immigrated to New York with his parents at the age of 10. Young DePalma was athletic, making his mark first as a track star, then a bicycle racer. It was a natural step to motorcycles, which he raced with some success at dirt tracks in and around New York. DePalma was 21 when he saw his first automobile race, the Vanderbilt Cup. From that day forward he was determined to race cars. His first attempt was an embarrassing failure.

In May 1907, DePalma was given the chance to drive an Allen-Kingston in a climb up Ft. George Hill in New York. Trouble was, pulling up to start, he rolled a few inches over the line, drawing a warning to back up or be disqualified. DePalma was still going backwards when the starting gun went off and the other cars charged ahead. At the Briarcliff Trophy Race in 1908, DePalma was assigned to ride as a mechanic with Allen-Kingston driver Al Campbell. But Campbell was injured in a practice crash and DePalma took over. Not that he did much better, ending up in a ditch soon after the race started. DePalma learned fast, however. He won his next race two months later at Readville, Massachusetts, beating, among others, one very angry veteran, Barney Oldfield. It was the beginning of a long and particularly bitter rivalry between Oldfield and the handsome, always impeccably turned-out Italian-American.

DePalma's stunning heroics at Savannah in 1908 marked the beginning of an amazing racing career that would span three decades. Counting the match races and short sprint races that often preceded feature events, DePalma is believed to have won over 2,000 races. He was the first two-time AAA national champion (1912 and 1914) and his record of 24 Championship victories keeps DePalma in the top 10 for Indy car wins even today. DePalma's last championship, in Canada, was won in 1929 when he was 46 years old.

DePalma's fame was fueled as much by the races he didn't win and the sportsmanship he showed in the face of what was often cruel luck. The most famous example of this, of course, was what happened to DePalma in the 1912 Indianapolis 500. With a commanding lead of several laps, DePalma's Mercedes began to falter 7 miles from the checkered flag. Then, just a lap and a half from the finish, a connecting rod let go and the Mercedes stopped cold. As eventual winner Joe Dawson pulled back lap after lap, an exhausted DePalma and mechanic Jeffkins won the crowd's heart by pushing the car all the way around to the pits. DePalma's courage and grace in defeat that day probably brought him more fame than his popular victory at the Speedway in 1915.

Even after retiring as a driver in the 1930s, DePalma stayed close to the automobile industry, working as a consulting engineer for Mobil Oil. America's first great racer died in 1956 at the age of 73.

Ralph DePalma. *Lew Balderson collection*

---

later, about the time Willie Haupt took the lead. On the 12th lap, Haupt scorched the track with what would be the fastest lap of the day, 13 minutes, 32 seconds. The glory was all too brief for the hill-climbing champion. He pushed too hard on lap 13, left the road, his Benz overturning and pitching both Haupt and his mechanic out of the car, and fortunately, into some bushes.

By lap 17, American drivers were running one-two, DePalma and the amazing young New Yorker David Bruce-Brown. DePalma looked unbeatable until the penultimate lap, when a stone pierced his radiator, causing the engine to overheat and crack one cylinder. Bruce-Brown withstood a desperate last-lap charge by Hémery to become the first American ever to win a Grand Prix. After 415 miles and just short of six hours, he beat Hémery by the scant margin of 1.42 seconds. David Bruce-Brown had burst upon the international racing scene with the closest finish in motor racing history. French champion Victor Hémery pronounced his teammate a "young master," then emptied a foaming bottle of champagne over his head in celebration, a victory ritual that survives today.

Not to be overlooked was Bob Burman's gritty performance in the Marquette-Buick. His third-place finish, in spite of no less than 15 tire stops, was the highest an American car had ever achieved in a Grand Prix. Adopting a more conservative pace, Mulford and Horan brought the Loziers home in fourth and fifth. Harroun and Dawson, who relieved his teammate on lap 14, were sixth in the Marmon. Again, though the Marquette-Buicks in particular had shown competitive speed, America's drivers were more impressive than the cars, particularly Bruce-Brown and DePalma. One can only wonder what impact Buick's powerhouse team captain, Louis Chevrolet, might have had on the race, had he run.

(who some claim was incorrectly scored and actually won). DePalma, near the front all day, ended up sixth in the 90-horsepower Simplex.

Hémery and Wagner were the only two European drivers to compete in the 1911 Grand Prize at Savannah, but there was no shortage of foreign cars. By then, Bruce-Brown had joined the Fiat team, along with wealthy California amateur Caleb Bragg. They, along with Wagner, would drive the giant, new Type S74s, built in anticipation of a possible resumption of Grand Prix racing in Europe. Under shoulder-high hoods, these behemoths packed 14-liter fours pumping out 190 horsepower at 1,600 rpm.

Against the Fiats was the Benz team of Hémery and two wealthy American sportsmen, Erwin Bergdoll, son of a prominent Philadelphia brewer, and Eddie Hearne, who had purchased Hémery's 1908 second-place Benz, then lent it back to him for the 1910 Grand Prize. For 1911, the huge Benz motors had been further enlarged to 15.2 liters. Ralph DePalma and another wealthy amateur, 21-year old Spencer Wishart, were in specially modified Mercedes Grand Prix cars, now carrying 140-horsepower motors and sleek, swept-back V radiators. Wishart had driven his to fourth at Indianapolis, while DePalma first tested his Mercedes three days before the Grand Prize, when both he and Wishart contested the Vanderbilt Cup race, run that year at Savannah. Driving the by-now almost bulletproof Lozier, Mulford had stunned everyone, winning in front of DePalma's and Wishart's GP cars.

If there was hope for an American car in the Grand Prize, it was thought to be Ralph Mulford's white Lozier. The 26-year-old had

Seven months later in the first Indianapolis 500, it took only 12 laps for Bruce-Brown to get from his 25th starting place to the front. After that, his Fiat led most of the first half of the race, at one point pulling out to a lead of more than seven minutes. But in the end, it was clever strategy and American ingenuity that won the day. With some relief from Cyrus Patschke, Ray Harroun came from even farther back (29th) to win in a most unusual car of his own design. Harroun's 7.8-liter six-cylinder Marmon was a true single-seater and, actually, the first "monoposto" racer. The conventional riding mechanic's space—and weight—was eliminated, allowing a narrower, more aerodynamic race car. To assuage his competitors' safety concerns in passing situations, Harroun had fitted another novelty, a rear-view mirror. Slowed somewhat by a broken spark lever at the very end, Bruce-Brown finished third, also being passed by the Lozier of Mulford

been nearly unbeatable that year and was on his way to the 1911 AAA national championship. Nor could the Marmons be counted out with the always hard-charging Burman and teammate Cyrus Patschke at the wheel. The latter had driven in relief for both the winning and fifth-place Marmons in the 500 and had taken Harroun's "Wasp" from fifth to second before handing it back to him. Buick's superteam had broken up, so expectations for the Marquette-Buick 100s of Basle and Harry Cobe weren't as high as before. Less threatening were Disbrow's Pope-Hartford and the two almost bone-stock Abbot-Detroits driven by Carl Limberg and Al Mitchell, certainly the lowest powered cars in the race.

Although the margin was smaller, America's cars were still outclassed, at least in terms of power. To no one's great surprise, it was the brute Fiats that thundered into the lead in the third American Grand Prize. But it was the American amateurs Bragg and Bruce-Brown at the front, not the European pros. In fact, neither Wagner nor Hémery would lead a lap, though the Frenchman, resigned to the fact that his failing motor could not last the distance, did accomplish the fastest tour of the day, at the amazing average of 81.6 miles per hour.

Up front, the Yankees were putting on a show. First it was Bragg, then DePalma, then Hearne that pushed forward to lead. Then, on the seventh lap, amazingly, Patschke, in the Marmon. It was the first time an American car had ever led a Grand Prix. Appropriately, perhaps, the same make had won the first Indianapolis 500, an effort to which Patschke had also contributed. His glory was short-lived, however, as the Marmon's engine mounts failed. With the motor flailing about in the chassis, Patschke pulled off, ending a brilliant effort on lap 10. Wishart's Mercedes cracked a cylinder and was finished on the same lap, and Basle's Buick blew on the next tour. Hearne, in the Benz, now led.

Cobe's Buick and Burman in the other Marmon had gone out earlier, as had Hémery and Bergdoll on the eighth lap. On lap 15, trying desperately to catch the flying Hearne, Wagner failed to make a corner and shot off the road. His race was run. Then fatigue began to wear at Hearne, and by lap 20 he'd been overtaken by Bruce-Brown and Mulford in the Lozier. It was almost over and three Americans were fighting for the lead. Even more amazing, an American car was in second, just 12 seconds behind the leader.

Two laps later, all three careened into the pits for tires and fuel. The crowd jumped to their feet, screaming, as drivers and mechanics feverishly struggled to attend to their cars. There were just 35 miles to go. Who would be first to return to battle? It was Mulford! A wild cheer went up as the white Lozier rumbled away, followed moments later by Bruce-Brown's Fiat, then Hearne in the Benz. Could it be possible? Could an American made-in-Detroit racer go head-to-head with the best from Italy and Germany and win?

Mulford knew the answer. He knew his Lozier could do it. He was inspired, driven, and, alas, momentarily blinded by the vision. It was an uncharacteristic lapse. Approaching a dangerous track crossing he'd passed safely 22 times before, Mulford this time stayed on the gas. The white Lozier took flight for 50 feet before slamming to the ground, snapping the driveshaft. Mulford slumped as the white car ground to a halt. No American car would win that day.

David Bruce-Brown
1890 to 10/1/1912

Early in the 20th century, the automobile was a rich man's toy. Enthusiasts, those who could afford to actually buy and drive motor cars, almost always came from wealthy families. David Bruce-Brown was from just such a family on New York's fashionable East Side. At 18, while he was still in prep school, Bruce-Brown was interested not only in driving cars, but racing them. Tall, good-looking, and well-mannered, the youngster, over objections from his family, talked his way into accompanying the Fiat team to Daytona in 1908 as an apprentice mechanic.

By the end of Speedweeks, Bruce-Brown even managed to ride with Fiat driver Emanuele Cedrino, who would become a mentor to the young enthusiast. After the professional races, "Cedrino's millionaire mechanic" was allowed to drive one of the Fiats in the amateur mile event, which he promptly won at record speed. This first taste of competition was followed by another amateur class victory at the Yale University-sponsored Shingle Hill Climb. Family approval or not, young Mr. Bruce-Brown was hooked on racing and bought himself a proper racecar, the 120-horsepower Benz in which Hanriot had finished fourth at Savannah. With this car, Bruce-Brown again won the Shingle Hill Climb amateur class in 1909 and set new amateur records at Daytona the same year.

After setting yet another record in the 1910 Giant's Despair Hill Climb, Bruce-Brown was invited to race with the Benz team in the Vanderbilt Cup in Savannah, a month before the Grand Prize. In practice before the race, Benz teammate George Robertson was asked to take a journalist for a demonstration ride. At some point on the course, the journalist panicked and grabbed Robertson, who lost control and suffered career-ending injuries in the resulting crash. Totally unnerved by this, the Benz team performed poorly in the race itself. Of course, news of Robertson's fate increased family pressure on Bruce-Brown, and when he traveled to Savannah several weeks later for the Grand Prize, his mother followed, vowing to disown Bruce-Brown if he took part. She stayed and watched, and toward the exciting conclusion of the race, gave in to the moment, inadvertently striking people around her with her umbrella as she wildly cheered her son on to victory.

Mrs. Bruce-Brown remained fearful of her son's passion for racing, but she did see him win again the following year and took pride in his obvious skill. A mother's worst nightmare came true one year later, when a practice crash before the 1912 Grand Prize at Milwaukee ended the all-too-brief life of one of America's most brilliant natural driving talents.

David Bruce-Brown. *Lew Balderson collection*

Did Ray Harroun win the first Indianapolis 500 or did Ralph Mulford? It is a question still asked by many but one that, unfortunately, will never be answered. It was, in fact, Mulford who was given the checkered flag. Thinking he'd won, Mulford completed three "insurance" laps before coming in, according to his pit instructions, only to find Harroun's Marmon already parked in the victory circle. Confusion reigned amongst the timers, and three different results were announced. Ultimately, Harroun was declared winner, though to many Mulford seemed in control. Although Mulford would race in 10 more 500s and finish in the top 10 on five other occasions, he would never better his "second place" in 1911.

Ralph Mulford
1885 to 10/23/1973

Ralph Mulford was born in 1885, in New Jersey. By the age of 16, he was employed as a marine engineer at the Lozier Motor Company, a maker of boat engines, in Plattsburgh, New York. No one was happier than aspiring automaker Mulford when Lozier began to manufacture in cars in 1905. Fittingly, it was in a Lozier that Mulford won his first 24-hour race, in July 1907. Several more 24-hour victories followed through 1908, when Mulford tried, with little success, to run his virtually stock Lozier against the big European Renaults, Fiats, and Benzes at Savannah.

What set Mulford apart from his more flashy contemporaries was a combination of meticulous preparation, pace, and exceptional smoothness, whether on the dirt, on the bricks, or on the high-banked board tracks. In the 1910 American Grand Prize at Savannah, the hard-charging Bob Burman changed 15 Michelin tires on his third-place Buick. Mulford, fourth in the Lozier, finished on his original set. In 1913, he became the first driver to go 500 miles at Indianapolis without changing tires, finishing seventh in a Mercedes. Mulford was designated AAA national champion in 1911 and 1918, a remarkable feat, considering the number of Sunday races he missed throughout both seasons because of religious beliefs.

The popular Mulford, called "Smiling Ralph" for his ready smile and congenial personality, was always recognizable in pure white coveralls and a white cloth helmet. He won many races for Lozier, but after that team dissolved late in 1911, drove Knox, Duesenberg, Hudson, Mercedes, Peugeot, and Frontenac cars, as well as Paige, Cleveland, and Chandler racers in which he often had an engineering hand. With the latter two, Mulford held many hill-climbing records, including Pikes Peak and Mount Washington. In 1920, Mulford finished ninth at Indianapolis in a car bearing his own name. Except for a couple of financially unsuccessful attempts, this was as close as he would get to his longtime ambition of manufacturing his own passenger car. Ralph Mulford's last race was at Des Moines for Duesenberg in 1927.

Ralph Mulford.
Indianapolis Motor Speedway

Ralph Mulford moves away at the start. By the end of 17 laps, the relentless and steady Mulford had moved his American Lozier into second place and had begun a thrilling duel for the lead that ended only one lap from the finish with a broken driveshaft. *Lew Balderson collection*

Cheered on by a wildly appreciative audience, the popular David Bruce-Brown won his second consecutive Grand Prize. Hearne, in the Benz, was second, then DePalma's Mercedes, and Bragg's Fiat. Behind them, four nearly stock American cars had shown remarkable durability, running not only the 411-mile Grand Prize, but, three days earlier, the Vanderbilt Cup, as well. Disbrow's Pope-Hartford was flagged in fifth, followed by Mitchell's Abbot-Detroit, Mulford's Lozier (far enough along to be classified seventh), and Limberg in the other Abbot-Detroit. If there had been any questions about American driving skill, there were no more. At Savannah, American drivers had proved they could run with anyone. Soon, two of the best would have a chance to prove it overseas.

Eddie Hearne
? to
2/10/1955

Chicago native "Grandpa" Eddie Hearne came by his nickname honestly. The popular heir to a gold-mining fortune raced for nearly 20 years. It's no surprise that Hearne was second in the only Grand Prize he finished. Road courses, dirt tracks, Indianapolis, and the board tracks, Hearne did them all. Amazingly, in 1923, 14 years after he began racing cars, Hearne won the AAA national championship in a Cliff Durant-owned Miller. One of his 1923 victories was at the inaugural race at Altoona, where his friend Howdy Wilcox was killed. From his winnings that day, Hearne donated $1,000 to each of Wilcox's children. (Four months before, Wilcox had driven in relief for Indianapolis 500 winner Tommy Milton.)

Hearne had finished fourth at Indy in 1923, one of his 15 appearances at the Speedway as a starter or relief driver. In that time, Hearne also had a second, a third, a sixth in the 500, and in his last start, in 1927, a seventh place. His record over the years in big-time board track racing was no less impressive: 40 top-five finishes in 62 starts, with wins at five different speedways.

There were a couple of years, however, when Hearne plied his skills on another kind of board. After his 1923 championship, Grandpa Eddie toured as a tapdancer in vaudeville. No kidding.

Eddie Hearne. *Indianapolis Motor Speedway*

The Next Step

The 1912 ACF Grand Prix signaled not only the resumption of international Grand Prix racing in Europe, but a revolution in the technology of race cars. Until then, thundering chain-drive behemoths like the 14-liter Fiats entered for Bruce-Brown, De Palma, and Wagner and the 15-liter Lorraine-Dietrichs of Hémery and Hanriot ruled the world's racetracks. At Dieppe, Peugeot introduced the L-76, a new lighter, smaller shaft-driven race car powered by what is still considered the prototype for the modern racing engine, a 7.6-liter four-cylinder with four valves per cylinder and double overhead cams. Three appeared at the Grand Prix, and in practice, Georges Boillot proved their speed by scorching the 48-mile circuit with a quick lap of just under 36 minutes. The Peugeots possessed two other important advantages. Tire-changing was facilitated by detachable wheels rather than the clumsy and time-consuming detachable rims of the Fiats. And while fuel had to be churned into the Fiat tanks by hand, the Peugeots were fed by a new pressurized

Charlie Basle's Marquette-Buick goes wide as Patschke in the Marmon comes through on the inside. Neither would finish, but Patschke was on his way to doing what no other American had: lead a Grand Prix with an American car. After 120 miles, Patschke's Marmon overtook Hearne in the Benz. Alas, Patschke's charge to the front was too much for the Marmon, and he was out of the race before another 17-mile lap could be completed. *Lew Balderson collection*

Bruce-Brown in the 14-liter Fiat thunders down the main straight past Carl Limberg's Abbott-Detroit fueling in the pits. Limberg would end up eighth, the last car to finish. His Abbott-Detroit teammate, Bill Mitchell, finished sixth on distance, just behind the snakebit Mulford. *Lew Balderson collection*

Bruce-Brown on his way to victory number two, this time in a giant 14-liter Fiat. After five hours, 31 minutes, and 29 seconds, the 21-year-old New York phenom was flagged in as winner of the 1911 American Grand Prize. Note the face masks Bruce-Brown and many American drivers wore for protection from rocks, a practice that became popular on U.S. dirt ovals. *Lew Balderson collection*

refueling system. Clearly, Bruce-Brown and DePalma had their work cut out for them.

Had an American car started the 1912 ACF Grand Prix (a Ford was entered but did not run in the concurrently held *voiturette* race), it would have been painted in the newly assigned national colors of white and blue. But it was Italy's national color, blood red, on the Fiat of Bruce-Brown that led the first lap ahead of Boillot (Peugeot) and Hémery (Lorraine-Dietrich). Easily recognized because of the dirt-track style face mask he and his mechanic wore, the American continued to lead throughout the first day, ending up with a two-minute lead on Boillot in the new Peugeot. DePalma had been up to fifth before a broken fuel line necessitated adding fuel out on the course, cause for disqualification.

Day two saw the road surface break up on some of the curves, and much of the course was slick from rain. Boillot in the lighter, more agile Peugeot now mounted a furious charge. For 150 thrilling miles, Bruce-Brown held the advantage in what was often a neck-and-neck duel with the determined Frenchman.

Two of America's premier drivers, Ralph Mulford and winner David Bruce-Brown, after their desperate struggle in the 1911 American Grand Prize. *Lew Balderson collection*

27

Barney Oldfield, one of America's first motor racing heroes, made his road-racing—not to mention Grand Prix—debut at the 1912 American Grand Prize, at Milwaukee. Sadly, it was in the repaired Fiat in which David Bruce-Brown was fatally injured practicing for the same event. Oldfield would finish a respectable fourth in his first Grand Prix, albeit 20 minutes behind the winner, Bragg. *Phil Harms collection*

George Clark, nowhere near as well-known as his teammates DePalma and Wishart, was the only Mercedes driver to actually finish the Grand Prize at Milwaukee, although on distance covered he was still classified in sixth, one position behind the crashed DePalma. *Phil Harms collection*

Indeed, it appeared that America might soon have its first European Grand Prix winner. Alas, it was not to be. Suddenly, on lap 14 (of 20), the big Fiat slowed. A fuel line had broken as it had in DePalma's car. The young amateur was able to make hurried repairs out on the course, but some fuel had to be taken on to get back to the pits. Bruce-Brown knew this meant disqualification, but was persuaded to soldier on to finish an unofficial third, behind Boillot's Peugeot and Wagner. Official finish or not, the point was made. Bruce-Brown's two Grand Prize wins in Savannah were no fluke. The Americans could drive.

Sadly, the immensely popular David Bruce-Brown would lose his life only nine weeks later. Granted extra practice time for the fourth American Grand Prize, this time held over a 7.88-mile road course in a Milwaukee suburb, Bruce-Brown and his mechanic were fatally injured when a tire failed, causing his big Fiat to flip. Several drivers were so upset that they withdrew from the Grand Prize. But in the end, all of them started, except for Ralph Mulford, whose Knox developed ignition problems. Without the Knox, there were only three American cars at Milwaukee, Fountain's Lozier, a Mercer driven by Hughie Hughes, originally from England, and Norwegian-born Gil Anderson's works Stutz. Against them there were nine formidable European cars, all to be driven by Americans. DePalma's and Wishart's Mercedes were joined by another from George Clark. The spectacular Burman was entered in a Benz, as were Bergdoll and Joe Horan. In Fiat S74s were Teddy Tetzlaff, Caleb Bragg, and Barney Oldfield. The amazing barnstormer, now 34 years old, was driving in his first major road race.

Tetzlaff, known as "Terrible Teddy" for his contentious personality and aggressiveness, had been battling with DePalma the whole year. The two were neck and neck for top point-getter in AAA championship races. With Tetzlaff, it was all or nothing, and at Milwaukee he took the lead immediately, wrestling his big Fiat around the narrow course like a madman. Teammate Bragg, never far behind, took over the point when Tetzlaff stopped for tires at 80 miles. When Bragg pitted for tires, DePalma pushed his Mercedes into the lead, only to be passed again by Tetzlaff when he was forced to stop. Of the 12 starters, only eight were still running. Burman's Benz went out after only three laps with piston trouble. Wishart's Mercedes lasted only one more lap before throwing a rod. Hughes, in the Mercer, made it to lap 18 before a fuel line broke, stranding him. When Fountain lost the steering on his Lozier on lap 23, Anderson's Stutz was the only remaining American car.

Finally, Tetzlaff's hell-for-leather driving style took its toll. His Mercedes ground to a halt on lap 32, its rear axle adrift. Bragg led now, but DePalma was on the charge. Though still behind on time, DePalma managed to catch Bragg on the last lap. But in trying to pass, their cars touched, sending DePalma's Mercedes careening off the road and in a series of flips. After already losing one friend, Bragg feared another tragedy and barely managed to make it to the finish. America's second Grand Prix winner was anything but joyous. Luckily, DePalma suffered only a broken leg and abdominal wounds and, typically, was quick to exonerate Bragg of any blame. Bergdoll brought his Benz in second, followed by Anderson's Stutz. Behind them came Oldfield, DePalma (on distance), George Clark, and Burman, who had taken over Horan's Benz at 32 laps.

Even as he recovered from his Milwaukee injuries, DePalma was declared 1912 AAA champion, edging out Tetzlaff by just 100 points. He missed the 1913 ACF Grand Prix, as did all his American colleagues. At home, road racing was on the decline. America had entered the board track era, and in fact, there were few suitable road courses left in the country. When Savannah demanded unacceptable terms to stage the 1913 Vanderbilt Cup and Grand Prize, both were canceled. Ironically, it would be in the board tracks' birthplace, southern California, that the 1914 Vanderbilt Cup and Grand Prize would be held on a high-speed, 8.4-mile course on the shores of Santa Monica.

The ACF Grands Prix in 1912 and 1913 were won by Peugeot, then at the forefront of racing technology. Equipped with double overhead cams, integral

Caleb Smith Bragg
1888 to ?

Caleb Bragg looked like anything but a race car driver. The son of a wealthy publisher in Cincinnati, Bragg was slight if handsome, always attired in expensive tailored suits and fine leather gloves (which earned him the nickname, "Chesterfield of the racing crowd"), and he was a Yale graduate. He just happened to have a passion for fast cars. He could afford the best, and he could drive with the best.

Bragg plunged into motor racing in April 1910 by choosing as his first opponent someone who was totally opposite in manner and appearance—and very famous. The occasion was the inaugural races at the world's first board track, Playa Del Rey, a perfectly round, steeply banked 1-mile bowl near the beach in Los Angeles. When Ralph DePalma was unable to get his temperamental 200-horsepower *Mephistopheles* Fiat to the grid for a match race against perennial rival Barney Oldfield as advertised, it was 22-year-old Bragg who stepped forward with a challenge. He would take DePalma's place in his own hotted up Fiat 90 against Oldfield's Blitzen Benz. What's more, he'd put up the prize money, $2,000 cash to the winner of two out of three two-lap sprints.

It was an offer the cigar-chomping showman couldn't refuse. Maybe this unknown amateur had beaten a few locals over the past couple of days, but no way could he measure up against a seasoned and crafty professional in the famous Blitzen Benz—or so thought Oldfield. Wrong. Beat him twice in a row. Young Caleb Bragg had arrived.

Bragg's debut at the inaugural Indianapolis 500 the next year was less successful. His Fiat was parked in the pits when another car plowed into it. End of story. But at Savannah, "Caley," as he was called, showed real skill, finishing fourth in his first big-time road race. Then in 1912, at the Santa Monica road race, Bragg finished second to "Terrible Teddy" Tetzlaff. The very next day, Bragg won a 5-mile match race at Playa Del Rey, setting U.S. closed circuit records for 2, 3, 4, and 5 miles. Among those who were impressed was Tetzlaff, who asked the young charger to relieve him in the 500 later in the month. Bragg's second drive at the Speedway was spectacular if short. At 220 miles, Tetzlaff pulled into the pits and signaled for relief. Bragg pulled out of the pits in third place, quickly gained a lap back on the leader and advanced to second before having to return to the pits to replace his abused tires. Tetzlaff jumped back in and finished second.

Seven months after his bittersweet victory in the Grand Prize at Milwaukee—where close friend David Bruce-Brown was killed—Bragg was the fastest qualifier for the 1913 Indianapolis 500, driving an American-made Mercer. In the race itself, he was not a threat, finally going out on lap 129 with a broken pump shaft. The next year at Indy, Bragg qualified the Mercer sixth-fastest and twice led the race for short periods, but then fell back and eventually went out with a broken crank, the same problem that would force his "Californian" Mercer out of the 1915 Grand Prize.

Caleb Bragg. *Indianapolis Motor Speedway*

Californian Teddy Tetzlaff's reputation was greater than his record would suggest. But Tetzlaff was fast. A hell-for-leather charger in the mold of Bob Burman, Tetzlaff would usually jump out to lead, as in the 1912 Grand Prize. Most often, however, the car couldn't withstand his furious pace. But in 1912, Tetzlaff won enough to finish second behind DePalma in AAA national championship points. Nicknamed "Terrible Teddy" for his tough, sometimes defiant character, Tetzlaff lived through his wildness and died of natural causes in 1929. His son and namesake became a famous Hollywood cinematographer and motion picture director. *Indianapolis Motor Speedway*

heads, shaft drive, quick-change wire wheels, and adjustable shocks, they were years ahead of any car made in America. Indeed, in 1913, Jules Goux's Peugeot easily won the third Indianapolis 500, and later, another Peugeot with an even smaller, more efficient version of the revolutionary DOHC engine, would win the 500 again in 1916. But American carmakers were learning. Stutz and Mercer, in particular, had both fielded new ground-up designs, which if not as technically advanced or powerful as the Peugeots, were now competitive with the big-engine powerhouses from Italy and Germany.

Stutz, in the hands of Tetzlaff and Charlie Merz, had won big races in 1912, as had Mercers driven by DePalma, Eddie Pullen, Wishart, and Hughes. And at the 1912 Vanderbilt Cup, Hughes' Mercer, with the smallest engine in the field, had finished only 43 seconds behind DePalma's winning Mercedes. There were even more American successes the following year. Interestingly, while a Peugeot won the 500 and one other race at

Galveston, Texas, and a Fiat and a Benz won the two San Diego races, the remaining 10 AAA championship races in 1913 were won by American cars. In 1913, Stutz driver Earl Cooper was the top point man in AAA racing.

Finally, a Winner

For the February 1914 Vanderbilt Cup and Grand Prize at Santa Monica, the first AAA championship races of the year, Mercer had built a special new car, with a larger, more powerful 7.4-liter motor. Ralph DePalma, now Mercer team captain, was rated as one of the favorites for the Santa Monica races in the new machine. That is, until a few days before the Vanderbilt Cup. Without DePalma's knowledge, Mercer management hired Barney Oldfield as a team driver. It was common for rivalries to be hyped before a race, but the one between DePalma and Oldfield was real—and bitter. DePalma abruptly resigned from the Mercer team and, with little time to make other arrangements, agreed to drive his trusty old 1911 chain-drive "Grey Ghost" Mercedes at the Santa Monica events.

DePalma won the Vanderbilt Cup race, beating Oldfield's faster Mercer with brilliant tactics, and, according to a story popularized later, a ruse. Near the end of the race, with Oldfield about to overtake for the lead, DePalma signaled the pits that he'd be in on the next lap, or so the story goes. Oldfield saw this, stormed by, and ducked into the pits the next time around. DePalma never stopped—and won by 80 seconds. In his postrace comments quoted in the *Los Angeles Times*, DePalma mentioned nothing about a "fake" signal to the pits, claiming, in fact, that he had earlier considered stopping for oil, but at the end, signaled the pits that he *wasn't* coming in. Deceived or not, rival Oldfield lost the race when he made his stop—and the stage seemed set for an epic rematch in the fifth American Grand Prize.

For the first time, American cars outnumbered European cars. Of critical importance, there were no Peugeots. DePalma's Mercedes and the three big Fiats of 1910 and 1912 Santa Monica-winner Tetzlaff, Dave Lewis, and Frank

As a competitor passes, Mercer driver Hughie Hughes struggles vainly to repair his broken fuel line after 142 miles. Fountain's Lozier went out four laps later and third-place Anderson's Stutz would be the only American car to finish the Grand Prize at Milwaukee. *Phil Harms collection*

Free from DePalma's challenge, Bragg's Fiat rumbles down the back straightaway on the way to victory in the 1912 American Grand Prize. *Phil Harms collection*

The Mercers of Gordon, Oldfield, Wishart, and Pullen inside the Mercer garage prior to the running of Santa Monica's 1914 American Grand Prize. Note the posters trumpeting Mercer's recent competition successes, including DePalma's win on the same course at Santa Monica in the previous May's "Open Stock Car" race. *Phil Harms Photo collection*

Verbeck, and the British Sunbeam driven by John Marquis were the only foreign makes entered. Against them, 12 American racers lined up. Among them, the new, more compact shaft-drive cars were favored; the four Mercers of Eddie Pullen, Oldfield, Wishart, and Huntley Gordon (his with the normal 300-cubic-inch engine), the Stutz team, Gil Anderson and Earl Cooper, who'd won at Santa Monica in 1913, and the new Duesenberg-built 5.7-liter Mason of Eddie Rickenbacker. Two six-cylinder Marmons driven by Guy Ball and first-timer Charlie Muth were given less of a chance, as were the chain-drive Alcos of Tony Janette and Billy Taylor (the former in Grant's two-time Vanderbilt Cup winning car, the latter in the rebuilt wreck of one of the last two Alcos to be manufactured) and the Apperson of Frank Goode, rebuilt from a stock car.

Predictably, Tetzlaff, in his 1912 Santa Monica record-setting Fiat, charged into the lead, but was passed by Wishart's Mercer on lap two.

Verbeck's Fiat was out after only one lap with a broken valve. By lap five, behind Wishart were Oldfield and Pullen in the other Mercers, followed by Anderson and DePalma. Marquis was a surprise sixth, as his Sunbeam's engine, the smallest in the field, displaced only 299 cubic inches. Cooper's Stutz retired on lap six with a broken valve. Tetzlaff would alternately slip, fall back, then blast his way forward into this group again. On the 12th tour, he turned the fastest lap of the race for an average of 86.6 miles per hour. Six laps later, while running second, his Fiat threw a rod. The "Terrible" one was finished. So, too, was Goode, whose Apperson blew on the same lap.

Steady DePalma then made his move and when Wishart's Mercer fell out on lap 23, it was the Mercedes that led, followed by Pullen, Anderson, and Oldfield. Then it was Marquis pushing forward in the little Sunbeam, passing DePalma into the lead on lap 31, albeit a short-lived lead. Two laps later, Marquis lost it going into the first turn, Santa Monica's ominously named "Death Curve." The Sunbeam overturned injuring both driver and mechanic. Now Pullen led over Anderson's Stutz, Oldfield, DePalma, and Rickenbacker's Mason, which would last only one more lap before the crankshaft broke. By this time, Lewis in the third Fiat had gone out, Janette's

Alco had cracked a cylinder, and Muth was stranded on the course without fuel. Only seven cars still ran. The hoped-for rematch of Santa Monica's late-race shootout between Oldfield and DePalma fizzled when Oldfield's Mercer went out with bearing failure on lap 37. Then, after closing on the leading Mercer, Gil Anderson's Stutz lost a piston with just three laps to go.

Pullen eased up after the Stutz fell out, but still won with the highest average speed to date in a road race, 77.2 miles per hour. His Mercer became the first American car to win a Grand Prix. Second, almost 40 minutes back, was Ball in the Marmon. Taylor's Alco-6 was third and DePalma, slowed by a next-to-last lap pit stop, finished fourth, his venerable Mercedes the only European car to make it to the end. Anderson, on distance, placed fifth, followed by Gordon's Mercer.

There had certainly been progress, but against what competition? Any notions of parity American carmakers might have entertained after Santa Monica were destroyed at Indianapolis three months later. There, René Thomas simply dominated in the Delage and Oldfield's fifth-place finish in the Stutz was the best America could do against the newest French Grand Prix racers. The mechanical gap yawned as wide as ever.

DePalma ran the 1914 ACF Grand Prix a couple of months after the 500. There was little chance to shine, though. His mount, a British Vauxhall,

---

Long before there was DePalma or Bruce-Brown or Harroun, there was Barney Oldfield. Known from coast to coast, cigar-chomping Barney Oldfield was the first American motor racing hero. He was part racer, part showman, and part hustler, but he could drive anything with wheels.

Berna Eli "Barney" Oldfield
6/3/1878 to 10/6/1946

Born in Wauseon, Ohio, in 1878, Oldfield left school at 12 to work. By the age of 17, he was a skilled bicycle racer. In 1901, Oldfield took part in an exhibition bicycle race at a mile dirt track in Grosse Pointe, Michigan, on the same day that a mechanic-turned-builder named Henry Ford drove his first racing car to a win over the highly favored car of Alexander Winton. Ford and Oldfield met that day and within a year, Oldfield was given the chance to drive Ford's newest racer, called 999 after a record-setting train.

Though he'd never driven a motor car before, Oldfield immediately took to 999, easily winning his first race at Grosse Pointe, on October 25, 1902, again against Winton. He set a record that day for a 5-mile race on a mile track, the first of many that would be set on tour in 999 and its twin, "The Arrow" or alternatively, "The Red Devil." In 999, Oldfield became the first to cover a mile on a closed track in less than one minute. Soon, the name Barney Oldfield became synonymous with speed and speed records all across the country. Subsequent barnstorming tours, in which he would courageously come from behind on the last lap for a dramatic victory, spread Oldfield's fame and the popularity of motor racing. Never mind that the "opponents" and the timekeepers were part of the traveling show. America was thrilled and entertained.

When the new 2.5-mile Indianapolis Motor Speedway opened in 1909, Oldfield set a 1-mile record of 83.1 miles per hour on the first day, driving a Benz. The following year at Daytona-Ormonde Beach, Oldfield set records at 5 miles (128.88 miles per hour) and 1 mile (131.724 miles per hour), the latter the Land Speed Record to that date, in the famous 200-horsepower "Blitzen Benz."

When the first Indianapolis 500 was run in 1911, Oldfield couldn't enter, as he was under one of six "lifetime" AAA suspensions that would dog his career. This one occurred in 1910, when, in spite of warnings from the AAA, Oldfield took part in an unsanctioned two-heat, 5-mile match race at Sheepshead Bay, New York. His opponent? Heavyweight boxing champion Jack Johnson. Never one to bow to authority, Oldfield risked suspension on many occasions, as at San Francisco, when during a rain delay, he challenged an AAA official to a fistfight. Oldfield was also known for his match races and real-life feud with Ralph DePalma, whom he derisively referred to as "the barber."

Some in motor racing criticized Oldfield's theatrics, but the fact is, he could drive. In 1912, in his first big-time road race, Oldfield took over the repaired Fiat in which David Bruce-Brown had been killed several days before and finished second at Milwaukee in the Grand Prize. When he finally did get to drive at Indianapolis, in 1914, Oldfield finished fifth in a Stutz, the highest placed American car that year. He was also the highest placed American driver in what otherwise seemed an all-European 500. In his only other race at Indy, in 1916, Oldfield finished fifth again. The same year, in a special one-lap demonstration, Oldfield ran the first 100-plus-mile-per-hour lap at Indianapolis in the diabolical handling front-drive Christie.

Barney Oldfield. *Indianapolis Motor Speedway*

Also in 1916, Oldfield and several other name drivers organized the first successful driver's union, which then lobbied for and won safety and minimum purse regulations from the AAA, as well as an insurance program for drivers.

In 1918, though he'd retired and unretired before, Oldfield retired for good to form the Oldfield Tire and Rubber Company (Firestone made his tires). It was on Oldfield tires that Jimmy Murphy's Duesenberg won the 1921 ACF Grand Prix at Le Mans. The following year, Firestone bought out Oldfield's company, which became its racing division. Oldfield lost his fortune in the crash of 1929, but later became a consultant to automotive companies.

Motor racing pioneer Barney Oldfield died in 1946 at the age of 69 in Beverly Hills, California, just a few months after being honored by the automobile industry and the city of Detroit.

was out early with a broken gearbox. That epic struggle at Lyons, in which new Mercedes racers finished 1-2-3 over the best from France, was, as it turned out, the last European Grand Prix before World War I. Few of the newest European cars would make it to America before the end of the war. Even fewer European drivers. One who did was Dario Resta, an Italian-born resident of England. He and one of the advanced Peugeot Grand Prix cars arrived early in 1915, just in time for the sixth American Grand Prize, this time, to be held on a strange, 3.84-mile road circuit on the grounds of the Panama-Pacific Exposition in San Francisco. The last section of the circuit was laid out over a horsetrack, paved over with boards for the race. The problem was that because of wet weather, the boards would sink as the cars thundered over, often squirting spouts of mud and horse manure straight up onto the racers.

Aside from Resta's Peugeot, there were only three other European cars in the field; a Delage driven by Claude Newhouse, the Bugatti of John Marquis, now recovered from his Santa Monica spill, and DePalma's Mercedes. This was not his new Elgin-winning four-cylinder, one of the dominating works entries at Lyons. Destined to carry DePalma to victory in the 1915 Indianapolis 500, that car and in particular, its aero-inspired motor, was being studied and measured by its new owners, the Packard Motor Company, for their own aero engine program. Instead, DePalma was to drive one of the much less successful 1913 six-cylinder Grand Prix Mercedes. Against the four foreign cars, no less than 27 American racers would contest the 1915 Grand Prize.

Once again, it was the Stutz team of Anderson, Cooper, and Howdy Wilcox, and the Mercer crew of Pullen, Glover Ruckstell, and Louis Nikrent, that seemed to be the biggest threats, along with works teams from Duesenberg consisting of Eddie O'Donnell and Tom Alley, and Maxwells driven by Oldfield, Rickenbacker, and Billy Carlson. For the first time, Chevrolet fielded two cars, for Cliff Durant and Jack LeCain, as did Case, for Hearne and Harry Grant. And there were single entries from Simplex, for Disbrow, Californian for Bragg (in fact, the car was a Mercer), King for Arthur Klein, Overland for McKelvy, and Alco for Taylor.

There were also, for the first time, a number of "specials" entered in the Grand Prize, usually a mix of chassis and engines, occasionally with some special bodywork, like Hughes' Ono. Actually, the Ono was Tetzlaff's old Fiat mated to a 389-cubic-inch Pope-Hartford engine and radiator. Rounding out the field were Jim Parsons' Parsons Special, the two Edwards Specials driven by Gandy and "Cap" Kennedy, Huntley Gordon's Gordon Special (another Mercer), and Jack Gable's Tahis Special.

Ruckstell led off in the Mercer, but within 10 laps Resta had moved the Peugeot to the front. One of the prerace favorites, Cooper's Stutz, was out after only three laps with a broken crankcase. Poor Marquis lasted only three more laps, his Bugatti's ignition shot. By lap 15, it was Resta, Ruckstell, Alley in the Duesenberg, Carlson's Maxwell, Anderson, and DePalma. Eddie O'Donnell, whose Stutz had won two of the first three 1915 races, and other favorites Oldfield, Pullen, and Bragg, in the Californian (nee Mercer), were locked in a struggle—not for the lead, but for 12th through 15th. Up front, newcomer Resta just slowly pulled away.

By lap 31, the wind picked up and rain began to fall from a darkening sky. Resta pulled in for "nonskid" tires, letting Carlson's Maxwell

Ed Pullen. *Indianapolis Motor Speedway*

into the lead—for a few laps, until Resta caught up and passed again. Inevitably, bitter rivals DePalma and Oldfield found themselves running together on the track, if not the scoring sheets. As DePalma's Mercedes began to pass going into a turn, Oldfield spit a huge wad of tobacco juice into the faces of DePalma and his brother, along as riding mechanic. Not long after, DePalma struck back, slamming his front wheel into the right side of Oldfield's Maxwell, virtually collapsing his rival's exhaust pipe. Oldfield's race was almost over.

Wind and rain pounded the combatants. Parts of the course flooded, including much of the board track front straight. Boards began to buckle

Spencer Wishart was a wealthy and talented amateur who began racing as a teenager. At 19, he came in fourth in a Mercedes in the accident-plagued 1909 Vanderbilt Cup. Wishart led the opening laps and finished fourth in the inaugural Indianapolis 500, also placing third in that year's Vanderbilt. He joined the Mercer team with his friend DePalma, finishing third in the 1913 500. Wishart led often, but rarely finished, as was the case at Santa Monica in 1914. Later the same year, Wishart was leading at Elgin when he hit a lapped car, lost control, and was thrown to his death. He was 24. *Indianapolis Motor Speedway*

Stutz specialist Gil Anderson and mechanic Tom Rooney at speed in the 1914 American Grand Prize at Santa Monica. Anderson would make his way up to second place only to be foiled by a broken piston with just a few laps remaining. He still finished fifth. *Phil Harms photo collection*

After taking the lead from DePalma, John Marquis loses control of his Sunbeam and turns over in "Dead Man's Curve." Mechanic Harry Hough, seen with his arm extended, was thrown clear, but Marquis had to be pulled from under the Sunbeam. Upon seeing the bloodied and unconscious driver, Hough buried his face in his hands and ran away until he was stopped and brought back to the ambulance. Fortunately, Marquis' head injuries were not as serious as they appeared, and he recovered. *LaFollette Archives Vintage Motorphoto*

Pullen's winning Mercer pulls out of the pits. Tough, compact, shaft-driven, and powered by a modified 453-cubic-inch four-cylinder, the 1914 Mercer, while not as advanced or sophisticated as its European counterparts, was an example of a new generation of American racecars. Fittingly, it would be the first American car to win a Grand Prix. *Phil Harms collection*

and pull away. By halfway, Resta would pull in again, then recover the lead for good. Gandy's Edwards Special had crashed at 80 miles. Oldfield, lap 31, Bragg, lap 35, Rickenbacker, lap 41, and Klein, in the King, lap 51, all fell out with engine failures, as would O'Donnell. They were lucky. Driving conditions became so dangerous that one by one, cars were withdrawn. Parsons, in the Parsons Special, Gordon, Hearne, Ruckstell, Pullen, LeCain, Alley, and Carlson all were forced to give up. DePalma simply abandoned the Mercedes near the railroad tracks and took a streetcar home.

In the end, it was Resta, having taken 7 hours, 7 minutes, and 54 seconds to go just over 400 miles, or 104 laps for an average of 56.13 miles per hour. He was followed by Wilcox's Stutz seven minutes later, then Hughes in the Ono, Anderson's Stutz, and Disbrow's barnstorming Simplex "Zip." Also flagged were Nikrent in the Mercer and Grant's Case on lap 102, McKelvy in the Overland and Carlson's Maxwell on lap 99, Newhouse' Delage and Gable in the Tahis Special on lap 92, Durant's Chevrolet on lap 91, Alley's Duesenberg on lap 89, Kennedy's Edwards Special on lap 84, and finally, Taylor's Alco-6.

In truth, the 1915 American Grand Prize was more ordeal than race, except for Resta in the Peugeot. He went on to win the Vanderbilt Cup race one week later, place second in the 1915 Indianapolis 500 behind DePalma's Mercedes, and finish just 460 points shy of designated AAA national champion Earl Cooper at the end of the year. In two years, Resta and the Peugeot would win nine of 19 championship races entered, among them, the shortened 1916 Indianapolis 500. He was declared AAA national champion that year.

For 1916, the Vanderbilt Cup and Grand Prize were moved back to Santa Monica and the month of November. Unfortunately, the races were only two days apart and, for the first time, both were contested by engines limited to 300 cubic inches. In fact, 450 cubic inches was the limit for the Grand Prize, but no AAA championship points were to be given for engines over 300 cubic inches, so no one ran them. And, of course, with a full-blown war raging in Europe, there was little international competition in the 1916 Grand Prize. Exceptions were Resta and the two other Peugeots, owned by Indianapolis Motor Speedway and driven by Howdy Wilcox and Johnny Aitken, the latter in a desperate struggle with Resta for the 1916 AAA

The "White Squadron" Stutz team of Wilcox, Cooper, and Anderson pose on the grounds of the Pan-Pacific Exposition before the 1915 American Grand Prize. At this point, only No. 5, Anderson, had the new, more compact and streamlined body, but all carried Stutz's patented transaxle and the latest four-cylinder motors made by the Wisconsin Engine Company. Borrowing heavily from the 1914 Mercedes GP design, these were single overhead cam, four-valve engines made for the new U.S. 300-cubic-inch displacement limit. Anderson would end up fifth, but Wilcox would finish second, about seven minutes behind Resta's Peugeot. *Bruce Craig collection*

Ralph DePalma works on his Mercedes during practice for the 1915 American Grand Prize. On lap 66, DePalma would be one of many to withdraw after heavy rains flooded parts of the course in San Francisco. *Bruce Craig collection*

36

Trademark cigar stuck in his mouth, Barney Oldfield puts on his best race-face in the No. 1 Maxwell. In fact, Oldfield bit down on the stogies to keep from breaking teeth while he was racing. At San Francisco, he needn't have worried after 31 laps. *Bruce Craig collection*

championship. With only the 150-miler left afterwards, the Seventh American Grand Prize would be the final chance to score big points.

Works teams from Stutz, drivers Cooper and Durant; Mercer, drivers Pullen and Ruckstell; and Duesenberg, drivers Rickenbacker, Virginia millionaire William Weightman, Mike Moosie, and George Buzane, were joined by a new team from Hudson, with A. H. Patterson, Clyde Roads, and Ira Vail driving "Super-Sixes." There were also factory entries from Marmon, driven by Lewis Jackson; Hercules, with Agraz at the wheel; National, driven by Bill Cody; and Kissell, with Dave Anderson driving. The field was rounded out by Sterling Price's Gandy Special, William Carleton's Owl Special, and the Duesenberg-powered Omar Special of Omar Toft.

It all went wrong for Johnny Aitken on lap one when his Peugeot broke a piston. Immediately, the would-be AAA champion began to signal Wilcox to take over his Peugeot—to no avail. Aitken's nemesis, Resta, went straight to the front. What's more, he stayed there for 18 laps, until the Peugeot began to misfire and headed for the pits. There Resta tried to repair the stuttering engine, repeatedly changing spark plugs, but to no avail. Years later, stories were written that Resta tried desparately to buy another car, but contemporary eye-witness accounts don't mention it. At that point, Earl Cooper's famous No. 8 Stutz was third behind Wilcox, in the one remaining Peugeot, and Rickenbacker's Duesenberg. Behind them, Buzane's Duesenberg, Patterson in the Hudson, Ruckstell's Mercer, and Roads in the other Hudson followed.

Already, more than half the field was out. The Hercules retired after only two laps with a broken rod; the Kissell and Moosie's Duesenberg three laps later, with a dropped valve and clutch; the Owl Special, a broken pump

37

Earl Cooper leads briefly over a street section of the course, but his Stutz will be out in three laps. *Bruce Craig collection*

Trouble in the Maxwell pits, as Rickenbacker tries vainly to fix the ignition problem that will sideline him on lap 42. Bruce *Craig collection*

on lap six; Pullen's Mercer, a fire on lap eight; Vail's Hudson, bearings on lap nine; Toft and Price, clutches on laps 10 and 12; and Durant's Stutz, sidelined with a broken valve on lap 17. Four laps before, a tragedy had occurred directly in front of the shaken Durant. Trying to make up time lost when his car jumped a curb and broke a wheel, Lewis Jackson lost control of his Marmon at an estimated 110 miles per hour and hit a concession stand, instantly killing its occupant. The careening Marmon then hit and killed a photographer before literally wrapping itself around a tree, where Jackson himself lost his life. Shrapnel from the crash fatally injured a fourth person. On the 13th lap of his first major race as a driver, Lewis Jackson became the first American to lose his life in a Grand Prix.

Much to the displeasure of Dario Resta, on lap 21, Wilcox relented and gave the leading Peugeot to Johnny Aitken, who went on to win. At first, it was thought he'd be given the points from Santa Monica, enough to sew up the championship, but the AAA later reversed itself, giving Resta the 1916 title. Only five cars were running at the finish, Aitken, Cooper, the two Hudsons of Patterson, who went nonstop, and Roads, and Rickenbacker, who took over for patron Weightman three laps after his own Duesenberg suffered stripped gears on lap 27. Teammate Buzane's car broke a piston on the same tour. Cody's National and the Ruckstell Mercer were the last mechanical casualties on laps 33 and 39.

From its lofty beginnings in Savannah in 1908, the American Grand Prize had, because of diminished European competition, lost much of its stature. The 1916 event was the low point in that respect, and sadly, it would be the last of the series. By mid-1917, the United States was at war and racing at Indianapolis had been suspended, ending an embarrassing four-year sweep of America's greatest race by European Grand Prix cars.

Racing did continue in the United States, throughout the war, but not on road courses. More and more, America's racing needs were satisfied on closed dirt and high-banked board tracks. The cut-and-thrust, wheel-to-wheel jockeying for position and high-speed maneuvering of "circle-track"

Resta overtakes Carlson's Maxwell for the lead as both struggle to stay inside their cars over the treacherously uneven boards. *Bruce Craig collection*

Johnny Aitken
? to 12/1918

Johnny Aitken scored important victories in 1910 at Atlanta and Indianapolis (where he won 10- and 200-mile races) in a National. In 1915, driving one of the Indianapolis Motor Speedway-owned Peugeots (bought to ensure full fields as war threatened), Aitken led the closely fought inaugural race at Sheepshead Bay on Coney Island until a rod let go. But Aitken's most memorable year was 1916, when he came out of "retirement" to make a thrilling run for the AAA national championship in the Peugeot.

After a string of victories and world-record performances, it all came down to the 1916 Vanderbilt Cup and Grand Prize at Santa Monica, the last two big points-paying races of the season. Only Dario Resta could keep him from the title. Aitken took charge of the Vanderbilt Cup, leading most of the first half, but his Peugeot engine faltered and Resta won. The Grand Prize was Aitken's one remaining chance to take back the points lead. When both dropped out and only Aitken got a relief drive—in the winning car—he was proclaimed AAA champion. But AAA officials were reminded that Resta had not been given points for a relief drive earlier in the season. In fairness, the Contest Board reversed their decision, giving points for the Grand Prize back to Howdy Wilcox alone, and the 1916 championship to Resta. It was Johnny Aitken's last chance for motor racing glory. He is believed to have died in the influenza epidemic of December 1918.

Johnny Aitken.
*Indianapolis
Motor Speedway*

Cooper's No. 8 Stutz, Ruckstell in the No. 6 Mercer, and Newhouse's No. 15 Delage head the field just before the start of the 1915 American Grand Prize. Resta's winning No. 9 white Peugeot is on the outside of row five. Note how the wood surface has been laid directly over dirt on the already muddy horse track. After hours of pounding rain, boards would begin to separate and lift. *Chuck Groninga collection*

below: Millionaire William Weightman and mechanic Pete Henderson pose in their Duesenberg on the palm tree-lined start-finish straightaway at Santa Monica before the 1916 American Grand Prize. Two days earlier, in the Vanderbilt Cup, Weightman finished a creditable third in his first big race. Riding with him that day was future American driving prodigy Jimmy Murphy. In the Grand Prize, Weightman allowed Eddie Rickenbacker to relieve him on lap 30. Their Duesenberg would finish fifth, the last car running, albeit two laps down. *Phil Harms collection*

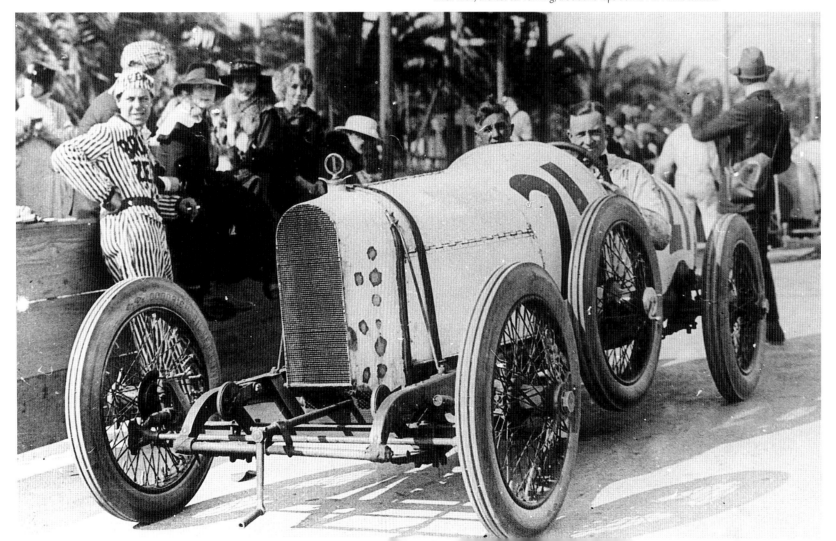

racing certainly sharpened the skills of American drivers. It also introduced new techniques that would later be used in all forms of racing, like the whole science of "drafting" and the "slingshot" pass. These old velodrome motorcycle racing tricks were first applied to car racing on the 2-mile board track at Sheepshead Bay by ex-motorcycle racer Ira Vail, just six months before he ran, albeit briefly, in the last Grand Prize, at Santa Monica.

Oval racing would prove to be a double-edge sword for American car-builders. On the one hand, without the need of constant gearshifting and braking as on a road course, those systems, that is the transmission, clutch, and brakes, advanced little. However, the high-speed board tracks provided valuable experience in the areas of weight placement and weight and frontal area reduction on track racers. Similarly, innovations in lightening and balancing the innards of an engine and the perfection of new fuels as well as fuel delivery systems also came from the constant high revs necessary on oval speedways. American car-builders had just begun to learn some of these lessons when the first postwar Indianapolis 500 was run in 1919, and they were eager to compete with the Europeans again.

Frenchman Réne Thomas qualified a new eight-cylinder Ballot on the pole at an astonishing 104.70 miles per hour and two Peugeots completed the first row, but American Frontenacs (first to use aluminum blocks and pistons in 1915) posted the second, third, and fourth fastest qualifying speeds. In an accident-plagued race, DePalma led the first 65

As the main grandstands begin to fill, the field of 21 assembles on Ocean Avenue for the start of the 1916 American Grand Prize. *Chuck Groninga collection*

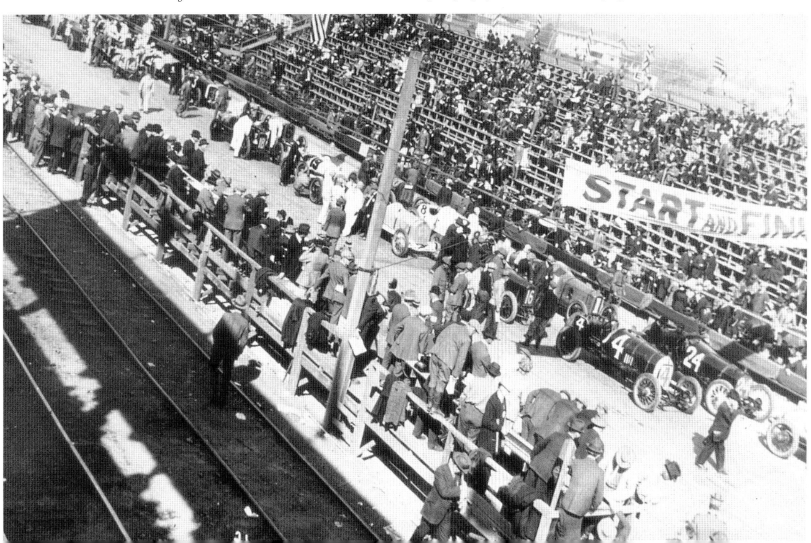

Howard "Howdy" Wilcox

1889 to 9/4/1923

Indianapolis resident Howdy Wilcox started as a riding mechanic for Johnny Aitken. During his racing career, Wilcox drove Indianapolis-made or sponsored cars almost exclusively, except for the Speedway-owned Peugeots. His first AAA points-paying victory was at Indianapolis in September 1910, in a National. His next wouldn't come until 1916 at Santa Monica, when he became the fourth American (not counting relief driver Aitken) to win a Grand Prix, in this case in the Peugeot.

In Dick Wallen's book BOARD TRACK, Robin Miller recounts a story about Wilcox and his bride leaving Indianapolis on their honeymoon in 1917, only to be stopped for speeding and arrested in Anderson, Indiana. Wilcox was actually thrown in jail until summoned before the mayor about an hour later. It turned out to be a gag perpetrated by the popular Wilcox's friends, who joined the newlyweds and, presumably, the mayor, in a party that night.

Ironically, the only other occasion on which Wilcox would win a "national" was his Indianapolis 500 victory in 1919. On the strength of that one win and several other good finishes that year, Wilcox was the 1919 AAA champion.

Wilcox had the unique distinction of driving in each of the first 11 Indianapolis 500s and in his last appearance there, in 1923, took over winner Tommy Milton's HCS Miller for 115 miles while Milton's blistered hands were being taped. Four months later, at the inaugural race on the 1.25-mile board track at Altoona, Pennsylvania, Howdy Wilcox suffered a fatal accident when his Duesenberg blew a tire.

Howdy Wilcox. *Indianapolis Motor Speedway*

Earl Cooper looks back as he exits "Dead Man's Curve." His famous No. 8 Stutz would finish second, just over six minutes behind the Aitken/Wilcox Peugeot. *Phil Harms collection*

In the No. 24 Marmon, Lewis Jackson awaits the start. After riding as a mechanic in Eastern races, his lifelong ambition, to drive his own racer, was finally being realized at Santa Monica. Thirteen laps into the race, at an estimated speed of 110 miles per hour, Jackson lost control in a fast bend on the San Vicente backstretch. His red Marmon shot off the road into a line of trees, instantly killing the 24-year-old driver and two others and fatally injuring a third onlooker. *Chuck Groninga collection*

laps in a Packard V-12 (the first V-12 in motor racing) before he was forced into the pits for a long stop to replace an exhaust valve. Louis Chevrolet's own Frontenac took over the lead until lap 75, but tire and wheel problems also caused him to pit. Though DePalma's Packard led convincingly again through lap 102, another agonizingly long pit stop to replace a wheel bearing dropped him back, eventually to finish sixth. The American cars had shown good speed, but did not yet possess the reliability to win. Howdy Wilcox inherited the lead in the Speedway's own Peugeot, one fed by an American track-developed Miller carburetor, and went on to notch yet another important victory for the French automaker. A Peugeot also won the Targa Florio that year, Europe's first important postwar race.

In 1920 there was no ACF Grand Prix organized, so the focus of international motor racing again shifted to the Indianapolis 500, now using the same 3-liter displacement formula mandated by the Europeans. The stage was set for a new round of head-to-head competition.

DePalma took the pole in qualifying, but Boyer's Frontenac, starting in the middle of the first row, led for 39 laps before the Ballot could get by. DePalma then proceeded to build up a two-lap lead over Gaston Chevrolet's Monroe (Frontenac) until a magneto broke with a little over 30 miles to go. Chevrolet hung on, in spite of a last-moment stop for gas, to beat Thomas in the Ballot. The five-year European victory streak was broken and America had regained some pride.

In 1921, DePalma led once again in the Ballot until a rod let go on the 112th lap. Milton's Frontenac won and for the first time in the history of the 500, no European car finished in the top three. America's drivers had proved themselves the equal of any and now, with uniformity in the AAA and European engine formulae, the technical gap had closed. If, as some claimed, the Frontenacs were only "track specials," unfit for international road racing competition, certainly the eight-cylinder, single overhead cam Duesenbergs that finished third, fourth, and sixth at Indy (and scored victories on board, dirt, and road courses throughout the United States) were in the same league as anything made in Europe.

Peugeot sent new cars for Goux, André Boillot, and 1919 winner, Wilcox. DePalma joined Thomas and Chassagne in the powerful Ballots. America's hopes lay with the cars that had been winning races on the country's dirt and board tracks, the Duesenbergs, all but one with the eight-cylinder motor, and DOHC four-cylinder Frontenacs, four of which were called Monroes, after their patron.

After taking over Wilcox's No. 26 Peugeot, Aitken overtakes Ruckstell's Mercer on his way to win the 1916 American Grand Prize. Ruckstell would go out on lap 39. *Phil Harms collection*

HERE COME THE YANKS
1921–1937

The ACF Grand Prix was revived in 1921, fittingly, at Le Mans, though not on the original 1906 course. This historic meeting would, much to the surprise and dismay of the French, be the high point of the American experience in Grand Prix racing until the 1960s. DePalma was to drive for the favored Ballot team and for once, an American manufacturer, Duesenberg, had mounted a credible challenge, albeit a late one that AAA Paris representative, journalist W. F. Bradley, had to negotiate with French authorities. (An entry fee double that paid by everyone else was the solution.) Headed by veteran driver Joe Boyer and California phenom Jimmy Murphy, the four-car Duesenberg team was well prepared, bringing not only a fast, proven engine-chassis combination, but innovation as well: the first detachable cylinder heads and four-wheel hydraulic brakes ever used in a Grand Prix.

Duesenberg's third and fourth entries were to be driven by two Frenchmen, the noted Albert Guyot, sixth in the 500 in a Duesenberg just five weeks before, and a wealthy, young friend of his, Louis Inghibert. An amateur, Inghibert asked Murphy to take him around the course for a few laps and some tips. During the lesson, disaster struck. Before the brakes had been properly balanced, Murphy locked up the front set approaching one corner, sending the Duesenberg somersaulting off the road. Both men had to be taken to the hospital, Murphy with painful rib and internal injuries. Inghibert withdrew on the spot (French wine magnate André Dubonnet would take over his car), and it appeared unlikely that Murphy would recover in time to drive.

Oddly, in the week before the race, another Yank's effort had begun to unravel. DePalma had a different sort of problem, though. In practice, he'd been able to lap significantly faster than the other Ballots. This puzzled not only his well-known French teammates, Wagner, Goux, and Chassagne, but the boss, Ernest Ballot, as well, because the cars were all the same, but for one seemingly insignificant change. DePalma had requested that the shifter for his right-hand drive Ballot be moved from the outside to the center, ostensibly so that he could shift with his left hand. In fact, the wily Italian-American had found that precious seconds could be saved entering and exiting the turns if he let his riding mechanic, nephew Peter DePaolo, do the shifting! DePalma figured this racer's edge would add up to six minutes over the 300-mile distance of the Grand Prix.

On the last day of practice, the plan came a cropper. M. Ballot and his head engineer were observing at a particular corner when DePalma approached. Perhaps momentarily unnerved by seeing them, young DePaolo missed his shift, grinding noisily against reverse and causing the engine to over-rev. Over DePalma's heated objections, Ballot ordered the shifter moved back for the race. Was this to ensure that DePalma had no advantage over his French teammates, as DePaolo later maintained (also claiming his uncle was deliberately given the weakest engine)? Whatever the reason, DePalma was irate, then dispirited. By race time, it was feared he'd merely go through the motions and retire at the first opportunity.

Murphy, on the other hand, was not to be denied, cracked ribs or no. Taped from shoulders to waist, the gutsy little California racer left a hospital bed to be hoisted into the white No. 12 Duesenberg and take his place on the starting grid alongside riding mechanic Ernie Olsen. Grand Prix starts

As both cars thunder out of the esses at Le Tertre and uphill toward the grandstands, riding mechanic Ernie Olsen motions to DePalma in the No. 1 Ballot that Murphy's Duesenberg is coming through. *Indianapolis Motor Speedway*

The field (DePalma and Mathis are out of frame in the front row) just before the start of the 1921 ACF Grand Prix at Le Mans. Guyot's Duesenberg, No. 6, is in row three, Murphy's No. 12, one row back, and Boyer, No. 16, and Dubonnet, No. 18, in row six. *Indianapolis Motor Speedway*

below: Segrave, No. 10 Sunbeam, and Murphy await the timer's signal to go, exactly 30 seconds after Guyot's Duesenberg and Chassagne in one of the fast Ballots are sent off from the row ahead. Wagner's No. 14 Ballot is behind in row five. *Indianapolis Motor Speedway*

With the Stars and Stripes emblazoned on its tail, Murphy's Duesenberg rounds the Pontlieue Hairpin, where four-wheel brakes would serve the Americans well all day long. *Indianapolis Motor Speedway*

were made two-by-two at 30-second intervals and at the end of the first lap, Boyer's Duesenberg and DePalma had posted equal times to share the lead. Seven seconds back were Murphy and in the second Ballot, Chassagne. By lap two, Murphy had pushed ahead, but not by far. Boyer was just six seconds back. Chassagne had passed DePalma for third and was now closing on Boyer.

The three leaders pulled away slowly, their order unchanged until the end of the fifth lap, when Boyer skidded to a stop in his pit. The Duesenberg's handling felt strange. Both front wheels were shaken and with nothing found amiss, Boyer took off again, now in third. By lap 10, Murphy had pulled out a two-minute lead over Chassagne, who was now only 35 seconds ahead of Boyer. Guyot and Dubonnet bracketed DePalma to place Duesenbergs first, third, fourth, and sixth. American cars and American drivers, in first, third, and fifth, were dominating the Grand Prix.

On lap 12, Murphy pulled in to change two tires and take on fuel, letting Chassagne through to first. At last, the French crowd had something to cheer for, but five laps later, Chassagne rolled into his pit, fuel pouring from his car. The Ballot was finished. A lap later, Boyer was out, a connecting rod broken. Murphy was never headed again, though he was forced to stop and top off his boiling radiator after a stone had pierced it.

The Duesenbergs had proved every bit as fast as Ballot's racers and, thanks to hydraulic brakes, stopped better, particularly when the road surface began to break up. Bruised and bloodied by flying stones and limping in on two flat tires, Murphy crossed the finish line 4 hours and 7 minutes after starting, 15 minutes ahead of DePalma in second place. An American driver had won a European Grand Prix—convincingly—in an American car.

For the once invincible French, it was a stunning and humbling defeat. There were even a few boos from the mostly silent spectators on Murphy's last lap. Ernest Ballot added to the disgrace. In an emotional speech to the crowd, he decried the American effort, labeling the Duesenbergs as "junk" and his cars the real winners if the race were to begin rather than end now. Fittingly, it was popular French driver Albert Guyot (sixth in a Duesenberg) who salvaged his nation's honor, silencing the ranting M. Ballot and evoking great laughter with the remark, "There's only one winner in any race: the man who gets home first."

Jimmy Murphy
1895 to 5/5/1924

James Anthony Murphy was born in San Francisco in 1895. His mother died when he was two and Murphy was orphaned at 11 when his father died in the 1906 San Francisco earthquake. He was adopted by relatives and raised in Vernon, California. Small in stature and shy, Murphy quit high school one year before graduating to work on cars in a garage. He was already enamored of motor racing and spent time hanging around the Beverly Hills board track. Murphy's first break came when Duesenberg driver Eddie O'Donnell's riding mechanic became ill at the 1916 Corona road race. Murphy filled in and O'Donnell won.

After serving in the Air Service (later the Army Air Corps) during World War I, Murphy returned to the Duesenberg team, where he came under the wing of Tommy Milton. Murphy became his protégé, and when Milton won the 1919 Elgin Road Race, Murphy was riding with him. The same year, Milton was responsible for getting Murphy his first ride. He crashed that day and it took Milton's threats of quitting Duesenberg to get him another chance. Within a few months, Murphy had won his first race. He finished fourth, right behind Milton, in the 1920 Indianapolis 500 and by the end of the year, was second only to his mentor in AAA championship points. There was, however, a rift between the two. Milton had been injured in 1919. While he was hospitalized, Duesenberg asked Murphy to drive Milton's twin-engine Land Speed Record car. He did, to a new record. Though Milton would soon exceed Murphy's mark in the same car, by 1921 he had left Duesenberg.

Driving for Duesenberg, Murphy continued to win. His victories included four 1921 championship events and, of course, the ACF Grand Prix. But he crashed at Indianapolis and finished no better than fourth in AAA points for the year. Milton won at the Speedway and was point champion that year as well. Murphy turned the tables in 1922, winning both the 500—with a Miller-8 now in his Duesenberg— and the AAA national championship. Second to AAA points champion Eddie Hearne in 1923, Murphy had already clinched the following year's points title when he was killed in a 100-mile race in Syracuse in May while challenging for the lead, naturally. He was awarded the 1924 AAA national championship posthumously.

Jimmy Murphy's exciting, if brief, racing career lasted only six years, but in that time, he won the Indianapolis 500, two national championships, more board track races than anyone else, and, of course, became the first American to win a European Grand Prix with an American car.

Jimmy Murphy. *Indianapolis Motor Speedway*

Duesenberg pit stop on lap 12. While Olsen fuels, Murphy changes the left rear. Much to the joy of French spectators, Chassagne's Ballot once again leads. But not for long. *Indianapolis Motor Speedway*

Faces blackened by oil and dirt, Murphy and Olsen head for the finish. They'll have to make one more stop to take on water due to a stone-holed radiator and suffer two flat tires, but regardless, no one will be able to keep up. *Indianapolis Motor Speedway*

It had been the Americans' day. U.S. car-builders had been forced to play catch-up from the beginning, but by 1921, the eight-cylinder Duesenberg was equal to or better than any car in Grand Prix racing. American drivers had finished one-two and if Boyer's car hadn't blown due to an improperly fitted connecting rod, it probably would've been one-two-three. If Le Mans had been a triumph for the Yanks, it would unfortunately be their last for many, many years. Murphy and the Duesenberg team had commitments at home and had to leave before the first Italian Grand Prix (DePalma's Ballot was a DNF). This proved to be the last race run under the three-liter formula, two-liter engines being mandated thereafter for several years.

Jimmy Murphy bought his Le Mans-winning Duesy, installed a Miller engine, and won the Indianapolis 500 with it in 1922. At Strasbourg that year, a mass start, common practice in the United States, was used in a Grand Prix for the first time. Three months later, an Italian amateur named Franco Caiselli drove his Packard "Indy" to ninth place in the Formula Libre Autumn Grand Prix at Monza.

Different Paths

Rule changes at Indianapolis allowed single-seat racers in 1923, but three of the two-seat Miller 122s were entered that year in the Italian Grand Prix at Monza. The drivers were two wealthy sportsmen who had driven Bugattis in the 500, Count Louis Zborowski (of the fabled "Chitty-Bang-Bang" aero-engined race cars) and Argentine amateur Martin de Alzaga, and in the third Miller, in his only other European appearance, Jimmy Murphy. At Monza, Murphy managed to finish third, but clearly, the 2-liter unblown Miller eight, capable of dominating at Indy and other American oval tracks, was no match on a road course for the latest supercharged Fiats. De Alzaga, recovering from a crash in practice, finished far enough back not to be classified. But his car,

the only one to have effectively one carburetor throat and a ram intake for each of the Miller's eight cylinders, apparently caught the eye of Eduardo Weber, who would employ these concepts to good use in the future.

Zborowski was a DNF at Monza with a broken rod, but in Spain two weeks later at the new banked Autodrome at Sitges, a track better suited to the Miller, he was leading the first Spanish Grand Prix when a tire blew in the closing laps, forcing a pit stop. Zborowski still finished second. America's second European Grand Prix victory was almost won by an English-born Polish Count with an American mother.

Zborowski had less luck the following year in his third—and last—Grand Prix with the Miller 122. The first-ever private entry in the ACF Grand Prix, Zborowski's Miller was overmatched against purpose-built, supercharged GP cars, and retired with steering problems less than halfway to the finish. Oddly, the previous year, in the ACF Grand Prix at Tours, an American-born driver won. Driving a Sunbeam, Henry Segrave (Henry O'Neal de Hane Segrave), regarded in history as Britain's first Grand Prix winner, was actually born in Baltimore, Maryland, in 1896, to an American mother and an Irish father.

After 1923, development of the supercharger—centrifugal in America, for the mid- and top-end power necessary at Indy, and low-end and mid-range Roots-type blowers for European road racing—would further emphasize a growing incompatibility of cars built for the two kinds of racing. No European Grand Prix car would finish in the top three at Indy before 1939 and it would be 28 more years before an American car would win a Grand Prix. Naturally, America's racers found fewer and fewer opportunities to drive against their European counterparts, too. There were, however, some interesting exceptions in the 1920s and '30s.

Former riding mechanic Peter DePaolo followed successfully in his uncle's footsteps. In 1925, he won the Indianapolis 500 and would go on to be AAA national champion. Following the 500, arrangements were made for DePaolo to take the number-three seat on the vaunted Alfa Romeo team for the Italian Grand Prix at Monza. In fact, though he'd ridden as mechanic with DePalma in the 1921 ACF Grand Prix and at Strasbourg with Count Masetti the following year, it would be DePaolo's first road race as a driver. Of equal interest at Monza was a two-car entry from Duesenberg, with Peter Kreis, eighth at Indianapolis that year, and Tommy Milton, the first two-time 500-winner and AAA national champion in 1920 and 1921. (Milton's racing feats were made more amazing because he had sight only in one eye.) One of America's finest racers ever, Milton could drive anything anywhere. Like DePalma, he won on the dirt, on bricks, on board tracks, and on road courses.

Surprisingly, it was Peter Kreis who was fastest in practice and, in spite of his speedway-type gearbox, made a brilliant start from the second row to lead the Grand Prix on lap one, with the Alfas of Campari, Brilli-Peri, and DePaolo in hot pursuit. Milton, however, had stalled his Duesenberg on the start and was now picking his way through the field. On the second tour, Kreis increased his lead, turning what would be the fastest lap of the day—all to no avail. Perhaps trying too hard, Kreis left the road at the Lesmo curve and was finished for the day. By lap 10, Milton had caught up and overtaken DePaolo for third. By delaying his fuel stop, Milton actually led for several laps when the Alfas pulled in to fill up. His own stop was a slow one, but Milton fought his way back up to third again, before a split oil pipe forced another stop. The repair took all of 20 minutes. Transmission prob-

lems couldn't be remedied, though, and Milton had no choice but to soldier on with just top gear. Regardless, he still managed to finish fourth, one position in front of DePaolo, who had been up to second when a carburetor casting broke. Reportedly, afterwards, DePaolo confided to Alfa mechanic Giulio Ramponi, "Pity I didn't have my Duesy. It handles better."

Contemporary Italian press accounts referred to the superior streamlining of the narrow "monoposto" Duesenbergs, even though their bodywork had to be clumsily modified at the Isotta-Fraschini factory to hold a mechanic's seat. Ironically, it was because of that last-minute bodywork modification, enforced only after Kreis's quick practice laps, that Milton didn't have time to fit his Duesy with the more robust "roadracing" gearbox he'd brought with him. The only other American car to run in a Grand Prix in 1926 was the Montier-Ford, a Model-T Ford-powered special built and raced by a Paris Ford dealer. Several members of the Montier family would race their Ford-powered specials, one with two four-cylinder Model-T blocks joined to make an eight-cylinder motor, in various smaller Grands Prix through the mid-1930s.

If DePaolo and Milton and Kreis seemed like logical choices to try their hand at European Grand Prix racing, the next American to do so might have raised a few eyebrows at home. It was a woman.

Lucy O'Reilly was the daughter of a prominent New York family. She and her husband, Laury Schell, were American expatriates living in Paris with their two young sons. In August 1927, Lucy O'Reilly Schell made history by driving a 1.5-liter Bugatti in the Marne Grand Prix, becoming the first—and to date, only—American woman to take part in a Grand Prix. While her 12th-place finish there and a 14th in the 1928 Marne GP were less than spectacular, Mrs. Schell's third attempt, at the Baule Grand Prix a month later, yielded a respectable eighth overall—six seconds ahead of

Merde! Victoire pour les Americains! Ernie Olsen raises his hand in triumph as Jimmy Murphy is flagged for the most important American Grand Prix win yet. It is a personal, technological, and national victory for the Yanks. *Indianapolis Motor Speedway*

Murphy and riding mechanic Ernie Olsen trail Albert Guyot's No. 4 Rolland-Pilain and the smoke-belching No. 3 Voisin Laboratoire of Eugenio Silvani at the start of the 1923 Italian Grand Prix. Of the three Miller 122 track racers entered, Murphy's was fastest but overmatched on Monza's road course against the new supercharged Fiat Grand Prix cars. Murphy did well to finish third, Zborowski threw a rod, and De Alzaga was too far back to be classified. *Mark Dees collection*

Frenchman Eduard Brisson's 4.9-liter Stutz, the runner-up at Le Mans earlier in the year.

The Schells were an extraordinary family, and decidedly racy. Both continued to compete, with some success, in European events through the 1930s, in addition to sponsoring the Ecurie Bleue racing team.

In 1927 at Monza, Europeans got their first look at real monopostos in a Grand Prix. George Souders' Indy-winning Duesenberg and two Cooper Specials (front-drive Miller 91 copies) driven by Kreis and 41-year-old builder-driver Earl Cooper. An extremely talented race car driver in earlier years, Cooper had won AAA national championships in 1913, 1915, and 1917, and barely missed his fourth AAA crown in 1924.

The Duesenberg and Cooper Specials at Monza were typical speedway racers. That is, they featured a central rather than offset single seat, as would all GP cars after Alfa Romeo brought out the P3 Monoposto in 1932. Souders was the fastest, holding second on a rain-slick track until water found its way into the Duesenberg's carburetor and magneto, sidelining him on lap 12. Kreis, who blew his own front-driver on the first lap, took over Cooper's to finish third among the four remaining cars. Only six had started this last Grand Prix of the 1.5-liter formula. One more American driver, phenomenal 1926 Indy-winner Frank Lockhart, had also been slated to drive at Monza, but chose instead to stay at home and work on the Stutz-Blackhawk record car in which, tragically, he'd lose his life the next year.

In 1929, Leon Duray made a spectacular, if ultimately unsuccessful, trip to Monza for a "Free-Formula" Grand Prix, with separate heats for 1.5-liter,

On the high banks of the Sitges Autodrome, Zborowski's Miller 122 leads Resta's No. 4 Sunbeam in the 1923 Spanish Grand Prix. Zborowski, who made the fastest lap of the race, finished second, a minute behind Divo's Sunbeam. A blown tire late in the race dropped Zborowski from the lead, ending his chance for a victory. *Mark Dees collection*

50

3.0-liter, and Formula Libre cars, and a final for the heat winners. After only two laps of practice, broad-sliding around Monza's oval and road course, Duray stunned the Europeans by shattering the track record in his front-drive "Packard Cable Special" Miller 91. Slow off the starting line in heat one (the effects of a speedway-type gearbox and centrifugal blower), Duray knifed his way to the front and was easily leading the Talbots of Luigi Arcangeli and Tazio Nuvolari when the Miller lost oil pressure on lap 12. No problem for the colorful Duray, who talked his way into the 3.0-liter heat with a second team car, claiming it was an oversize 1,505 cc. Here, once again, Duray was able to dice with larger Alfa Romeos and Maseratis at the front, but broke his circle-track gearbox attempting to downshift for Monza's road sections. Ettore Bugatti was impressed enough to buy both Millers on the spot (actually, trading Duray three Bugatti sports cars and some cash) and later, meticulously copy their double overhead cam heads on his Type 51.

There were, of course, lesser European races, often contested by more than one class, that carried the title Grand Prix, and occasionally an American car would turn up in these lesser events. One such was the 1930 Grand Prix de Picardie in France. Along with Ferdinand Montier's Ford-powered special, a driver named Pesato entered, of all things, a De Soto in the 5.0-liter Sports Car class. Let the record show that in 1930, a De Soto finished ninth overall (and third in class) in a Grand Prix, one place ahead of the Montier-Ford.

Four months later, at Monza, in a proper Grand Prix, American journeyman Babe Stapp drove a Duesenberg Model A to third place in his heat and, after being slowed by mechanical difficulties, eighth in the final. This in contention with such names as Nuvolari, Caracciola, Maserati, Varzi, Campari, Borzacchini, and Fagioli.

In what surely must rank as the most unlikely appearance made in a true Grand Prix by an American car, Indianapolis driver Phil "Red" Shafer brought his pushrod Buick-powered Shafer-8 Special to the Nürburgring in 1931 for the German Grand Prix. About the only thing that impressed the Europeans was Shafer's portable electric starter. Built to Indy's early-1930s semi-stock "junk formula" specs, the roadster was out of its element at the Ring, particularly in the rain, and retired two-thirds of the way through the race.

A New American Challenger

By the early 1930s, motor racing had bloomed throughout Europe. Smaller "Grands Prix" were held in many countries. To guarantee full fields, some, like the Swedish Summer and Winter Grands Prix, allowed many classes to run simultaneously. American cars—Buicks, De Sotos, Chryslers, Chevrolets, and Fords—would frequently run in the same race with whatever sports cars and open-wheel cars showed up at these events.

Such was the case in the Swedish Winter Grand Prix early in 1932. That race, eight laps around a 30-mile circuit of frozen roads near Lake Ramen, also marked the "Grand Prix" debut of millionaire American expatriate Whitney Straight in his recently purchased 2.5-liter Maserati GP car. A 19-year-old Cambridge student, Straight was out after only two laps. But he'd diced for second place and clearly enjoyed himself. By the end of the year, young Straight would be marked in British racing circles as not only a talented amateur, but a real prospect.

Leon Duray returned to Monza in 1932, in the company of Wilbur Shaw. This time, Duray attempted to run a rear-drive Miller 91, still fast in a

Leon Duray
4/30/1894 to 5/12/1956

Leon Duray, whose real name was George Stewart, was one of the most colorful and exciting drivers of the 1920s. A showman through and through, Duray was tall, dark, and leading-man handsome. Legend says that then-taxi driver Stewart brought his fare, barnstorming tour promoter Alex Sloan, to a West Coast track and was hired on the spot to drive in his shows. It was Sloan who made Stewart change his name to Leon Duray, after popular French driver Arthur Duray, then "cast" him as a former French aviator war hero turned racer. Reporters were told that Duray spoke no English. The ruse was soon discovered, but nobody cared, because Duray was such an interesting character, and incredibly fast on "outlaw" dirt tracks or high-bank boards, or at Indy.

Duray didn't win a lot of races. He didn't finish many. But while his car was running, Duray was always spectacular and always a threat. From 1922 through 1928, on board tracks, the crowd-pleasing Duray won only four races in 42 tries, but he often set records and led, only to blow up or break down during the race. It was the same at Indy. In eight races, Duray finished in the top 10 only once, in 1925, when he finished sixth. But in 1928, in one of the front-drive Millers he would take to Europe, Duray set a four-lap qualifying record (122.391 miles per hour) that was unbroken for nine years—the longest any qualifying record has stood at Indianapolis. Two weeks later he drove the same car to a closed-course record at the new 2.5-mile oval at the Packard Proving Grounds, blazing a lap at 148.7 miles per hour. That one stood until 1934.

Before going to Monza in 1929, Duray drove the sister car to his record Miller to world and class records on the banked Montlhéry track in France. Europeans were astonished at the speeds the 1.5-liter cars could achieve. Duray's Millers were rated at over 200 horsepower, some of which came from special modifications made by master mechanic Jean Marcenac, later of Novi fame, and the innovative Duray himself. His cars were the first to successfully use methanol as a fuel at Indianapolis. Building on Frank Lockhart's pioneer work with intercoolers, Duray set new standards. And then, of course, there was the blown 16-cylinder

Leon Duray.
Indianapolis Motor Speedway

two-stroke engine he ran at Indy in 1931, said to be the loudest engine ever to run there. Lacking full development, it failed, but two-stroke mavens still marvel at the boldness of its design.

There was never anything conservative about Leon Duray. Known as "The Black Devil," he even dressed the part: jet-black coveralls trimmed with a white cap, belt, and gloves. Above all, he never held back. Anyone who ever saw Duray on the high banks of Fulford-by-the-Sea, Salem, Altoona or Culver City, or at Indy or Monza, will never forget him. Those of us who didn't have the pleasure might catch a glimpse in the old MGM silent film Speedway, in which the Black Devil appears, appropriately, as the villain, in one of his magnificent Miller front-drives.

America's first female Grand Prix driver, Lucy O'Reilly Schell, and noted French driver (and later, American restaurateur) René Dreyfus, who drove for the Schells' Ecurie Bleue team. Mme. Schell was a vivacious, strong-willed New Yorker whose passion for racing was financed by her wealthy father. Her final Grand Prix was the 1932 Baule Grand Prix (10th in an Alfa Romeo), but she continued to compete in sports car events and rallies until 1939, when her husband, Laury Schell, died in a road accident. *Suzanne Dreyfus collection*

Peter DePaolo in the two-liter Alfa Romeo P2 at Monza before the start of the 1925 Italian Grand Prix. The tail of Tommy Milton's No. 7 Duesenberg can be seen. DePaolo was running second when forced to pit to repair a broken carburetor casting. He finished fifth. Milton would overcome a terrible start (he stalled), gearbox problems, and very slow pit stops to finish fourth. *LaFallette Archives, Vintage Motorphoto*

straight line, but totally unsuitable for road racing. The whole trip was a bust. After an embarrassing spin in front of the main grandstand, Duray was later defrauded out of his starting money by the promoter. As a result, he and Shaw ran out of funds and had to sail home as wards of the U.S. government.

Interestingly, the next American car to run in a Grand Prix was entered by Scuderia Ferrari, the racing team run by Enzo Ferrari. Supplementing his works Alfa Romeos, Ferrari entered a blood-red 4.3-liter Duesenberg racer for Count Trossi to drive at Monza in 1933. It may have figured indirectly in the deaths that day of three popular drivers. Leading briefly in the first heat race of the Monza Grand Prix, on lap seven, Trossi's Duesy lost its oil through the notorious south curve on Monza's high-speed oval. In the two subsequent heats, Baconin Borzacchini (Maserati) and Giuseppe Campari (Scuderia Ferrari-Alfa), and then, Stanislas Czaikowski (Bugatti) lost control there, most likely in

the oil, and crashed fatally. Whitney Straight bought the Trossi Duesenberg, his first American race car, which would be used in record attempts at Brooklands.

Straight had raced earlier in the day in the Italian Grand Prix, finishing a creditable if not spectacular 11th. Two months before, his first real European Grand Prix, Straight had ignored scorched feet from an overheated transmission to finish fourth at Reims in the Marne GP. He had then DNF'd at Comminges and finished second in the lightly contested Albi GP. In comparison to those events, Monza was the big time. In the Italian Grand Prix, all the "name" drivers took part, most driving the latest factory racers. Among the cars gridded were six newer 3-liter Maseratis, considerably faster than Straight's venerable 26M. It was no doubt a reality check for the young American, but in no way did it dim his enthusiasm.

Within a month, Straight had made a momentous decision. He would forsake his Cambridge education and pursue motor racing as a business venture. For the 1934 season, the Whitney Straight Ltd. team would campaign 3-liter Maserati 8C-3000s to be driven by himself and, on occasion, two other drivers. Straight, his personal valet, Dewdeney,

Earl Cooper's No. 10 Cooper Special at Monza for the 1927 European Grand Prix. Rain was not an advantage for the two front-drive Miller 91-inspired Coopers at Monza, but Earl Cooper and Kreis, whose No. 2 car blew an engine on lap one, hung on to finish third—some 36 minutes behind Benoist's winning Delage—among the four who made it to the end. *Mark Dees collection*

and team drivers would fly to races by private plane, while the cars would be transported in team vans under the direction of head mechanic Giulio Ramponi, himself a capable former Alfa driver and works mechanic.

A practice crash nearly spoiled Straight's first Grand Prix, in 1934 at Monaco, but spare parts were flown from his team headquarters in Milan in time to qualify, albeit two seconds off the front runners. After 3 1/2 hours, Straight finished seventh, four laps behind winner Guy Moll's "works" Scuderia Ferrari Alfa. Considering the quality of the competition, it was a good first result for the new team.

A month later, Straight flew to North Africa for the Grand Prix of Tripoli. There, an American Miller would make history as the first four wheel drive car to take part in a Grand Prix (a Bugatti four-wheel drive practiced at Monaco in 1932, but didn't race). Peter DePaolo came out of retirement to drive one of the

two special four-cam V-8-powered Millers in the Tripoli race. The Italian-speaking DePaolo struck up a friendship with Libya's speed-crazy Governor Balbo, whom he took for a ride around the high-speed 8-mile course. Afterwards, DePaolo accepted Balbo's challenge to race his plane for one lap—and lost.

In the race, DePaolo and Lou Moore, who was entered in the two-place Miller-powered Duesenberg he had driven to third at Indy the previous year, found their horses overmatched. The American cars were very fast on the straights, but hopelessly outclassed in braking and in the turns. Regardless, Moore, in the lighter Duesy, and DePaolo finished a creditable sixth and seventh. Whitney Straight was out after only 10 laps, but Hugh Hamilton in the other Straight Maserati was an amazing fourth at the three-quarter distance, when he, too, fell out with engine trouble. Lou Moore headed home, but DePaolo went on to Berlin, where he hoped the long straights of the high-speed Avus track would be better suited to his Miller.

In terms of horsepower, DePaolo's Miller V-8 was equal to even the revolutionary new V-16 rear-engine Auto Unions. Weight and the slow-shifting three-speed gearbox were still a problem, but rain on race day evened things somewhat. DePaolo was running third behind Stuck's Auto Union and eventual race-winner Moll in the Alfa when two rods let go in the 308-cubic-inch V-8 on the main straightaway. According to a DePaolo letter quoted in Mark Dees' landmark book, *The Miller Dynasty*, shrapnel from this cataclysmic blow-up "just missed 'Heil Hitler' in his box." It was the last time an American driver in an American car took part in a European Grand Prix before World War II. DePaolo did go to Barcelona, where he was to drive a Maserati in the Pena Rhin Grand Prix. But in practice, he crashed to avoid some Spanish kids who ran out onto the course. DePaolo recovered from head injuries, but never raced again.

Straight continued racing through 1934. Two weeks after Tripoli, he finished an impressive fourth in the Moroccan Grand Prix. At Le Marne, he retired early with engine problems, but again, Hamilton finished fourth in the second team car. A week later, Straight won his heat in the Vichy Grand Prix and seriously challenged winner Trossi's Ferrari team Alfa in the closing laps, finally finishing just five seconds back. It was the young American's best "international" effort so far, though he'd been scoring impressively in hill climbs and other British events between Grands Prix throughout the season.

At Montreux, Straight finished fourth. He was up to fourth again at Nice before a miscue and his first crash. A week later, Straight rebounded at the Comminges Grand Prix with a solid third, in spite of slow pit work and an unplanned stop to change a tire late in the race. Tragically, the same day, at the Swiss Grand Prix, Hugh Hamilton, running Straight's other car, lost control on the last lap and flew off the road. The Maserati slammed into a tree, killing Hamilton instantly.

Straight next ran at Monza in the Italian Grand Prix, facing for the first time the full might of the new Mercedes-Benz and Auto Union teams, not to mention more powerful entries from Scuderia Ferrari and the Maserati works.

One of only four drivers to finish without relief, Straight ended up eighth.

In the absence of the German and Italian works teams, Straight would win a month later at Donington Park and finish third in the Algerian Grand Prix, but it was obvious that his Maserati was no longer competitive. If he wished to race at the highest level, and he did, a stronger horse would be needed for 1935. Straight aimed high and tried to buy one of the awesome 16-cylinder Auto Unions. While that was not possible, Auto Union team manager Willi Walb, who had been duly impressed by the American, reportedly offered Straight a works ride for 1935. In any case, love won out over speed (on the ground, anyway) and Straight honored a promise made to his intended wife and retired as a driver to concentrate more on his other passion, flying.

Whitney Straight, arguably the most successful independent Grand Prix driver of the mid-1930s, raced only once more, accepting an

A truly fascinating character, Whitney Straight raced in more Grands Prix than any American before World War II. Though he was widely reported in the British press, little is known about him in the United States. Straight, the eldest of three children, was born in Old Westbury, New York, in 1912 to wealthy parents. Willard Straight was a distinguished government officer who with his wife, Dorothy Whitney, an early feminist and political activist, founded The New Republic magazine in 1914.

Whitney Straight
11/6/1912 to 4/5/1979

Widowed in 1919, Straight's mother married an Englishman in 1925 and moved the family to England the following year. Within a few years, Straight's two great passions, fast motoring and flying, had begun to flower. At the age of 16, he was reportedly the youngest licensed pilot in England. Straight's first taste of automobile competition came in 1931, when he was 19 and a student at Cambridge. At the famed Shelsley Walsh Hill Climb, Straight won the 1,100-cc amateur class in his Riley sports car. Second, in an identical machine, was Straight's new Cambridge friend and future British driving star Dick Seaman. Within weeks, Straight had purchased a Grand Prix Maserati from British independent Sir Henry "Tim" Birken. One can imagine how delighted and surprised the promoters of Sweden's rather ambitiously named "Winter Grand Prix" were in 1932 when the young American flew in and gridded a genuine race car amongst the usual Fords, Chryslers, Buicks, and the odd "sports car" in their event. For Straight, it was a low-pressure, out-of-town tryout of his new toy.

Cambridge professors did their best to keep Straight from racing in 1932, but the young American easily got around the restriction on students' personal cars by bicycling to a nearby airport, where his private plane was kept. While he and Dick Seaman could do little more than talk about Grand Prix racing in 1932, records show that Straight did manage to finish second with the Maserati at one Brooklands meet and to set a record at another. The following year, though, Straight applied himself more to racing than school, and almost immediately got the attention of the British press. After a win at Brooklands, the British monthly magazine Motor Sport praised his "magnificent handling of the 2.5 Maserati," adding that the young American "always looked safe." With two wins under his belt in a Bentley 8-liter and a second place in the Maserati at the Kesselberg Hill Climb, Straight's star was on the rise in Britain.

By the end of 1933, Straight's exploits in Grand Prix racing "on the Continent" as well as in speed trials and hill climbs (where his times beat records set by Caracciola and Stuck) had made him a genuine celebrity. Having spent the greater part of his life in England, Straight had become, as his brother would note years later, more British than the British. Two years after withdrawing from motor racing, Whitney Straight made it official and became a British subject. During the war, he served with great distinction in the Royal Air Force and was credited with shooting down a number of German fighters. In 1941, he was shot down by ground fire over occupied French territory and captured. Remarkably, Straight escaped a year later and with the help of the French Underground, made his way

Whitney Straight.
Ken Stewart collection

back to fight again. By the end of the war, Straight was an RAF Group Captain with decorations from several countries, including the United States, which awarded him the Legion of Merit.

Straight maintained his interest in aviation after the war. He owned several airfields in England, became a managing director of BOAC, and served on the board of Rolls Royce. Whitney Straight was an extraordinary individual from an extraordinary family. His brother and one-time-only Grand Prix racer Michael is a noted author and their sister, Beatrice, is an Academy Award-winning actress.

Straight died in England in 1979 at the age of 66.

As Tripoli's Governor Italo Balbo approaches, Peter DePaolo stands by his four-wheel-drive Miller V-8 before the start of the 1934 Tripoli Grand Prix. Note the crossed American and Italian flags on the cowl—and oddly, the Firestone "knobbies" fitted to run on a high-speed road course! The Miller showed good speed on the straights, but was lacking in brakes and handling. DePaolo finished eighth. *Mark Dees collection*

invitation to drive in the first South African Grand Prix in late December 1934. Ever the businessman, Straight agreed only after assurances that all expenses would be paid.

In 1934, traveling to Africa from England was no small feat. Ramponi was sent ahead by ship with the machinery, but Straight, accompanied by valet Dewdeney, Dick Seaman, and younger brother Michael Straight, was determined to fly his own plane to East London, South Africa. In his 1983 autobiography, *After Long Silence*, Michael Straight noted that instrumentation in their twin-engine De Havilland Dragon was spare—an altimeter, a tachometer, a compass, a faulty airspeed indicator, and no radio. On Christmas vacation from his first year at Cambridge, the younger Straight had been "persuaded" by Whitney to come along and race his Railton-modified Hudson-Terraplane.

"He sort of put it up to me," Michael Straight remembered at 80, "and I couldn't very well turn him down. It was like a dare or a challenge. My mother, I'm sure, was horrified. She sort of bit her lip and

kept quiet about it all, but I'm sure she was appalled. So, it was just his way of appropriating me, you know, challenging me to do it, which, of course, I accepted. But I was basically scared. You know, racing wasn't my line."

The journey was certainly as dangerous as the race. Taking off and landing in darkness, their twin-engine biplane pushed its way through headwinds to average a paltry 60 miles per hour to Marseilles, the first of a series of overnight stops. Cairo was next; then, on the morning of the third day, they reached Salisbury, Rhodesia, with the intention of leaving immediately for Johannesburg. But there was a problem. In Salisbury's thin air, Whitney Straight was unable to lift the Dragon off the runway. The biplane jumped an irrigation ditch, tore through a wire fence, finally coming to a crashing halt on the plain. Luckily, no one was hurt, but there was considerable damage to the lower wing. After two days of shoring up and patching, Straight *just* managed to get the Dragon airborne and after another day-long flight, landed at East London, the site of the race, where hundreds of South Africans greeted them with welcoming banners.

"It was wonderful," said Michael Straight. "They were very enthusiastic." Nevertheless, Whitney worried about possible anti-outsider tactics during the race. On the handicap system, Michael's Railton-Terraplane, Dick Seaman's blown MG, and Whitney's Maserati were the fastest cars. They would start at the back and would have to work their way through the entire field.

"The main concern was that they'd . . . that a couple of them would jam us. Whitney insisted on having guys posted around with flags to wave them to the side if they did try to block us. But, of course, they didn't."

Barely 18 years old, in a foreign country, and on the brink of his first race, Michael Straight was understandibly nervous. Because of their delayed arrival and hours lost the next day waiting for a swarm of locusts to move on, there was little time for practice. The course itself was daunting, 15 miles around, part tarmac, part dirt, with particularly dangerous sections winding along the face of rocky cliffs. To spare both driver and car, Ramponi wouldn't let Michael start the engine until *just* before he was flagged away. By that time, 15 other cars had started.

In *After Long Silence*, Michael Straight humourously recalled his first racing moments. "'Now!' Ramponi shouted. I heard him from a great distance. The Railton seemed to start up on its own. I lost my sense of limits when the flag fell. As we rounded the first corner, I felt the inside wheels of the Railton lift off the road. That brought me to my senses. 'Easy,' I said to myself. 'Easy!' I passed one car on my first lap—smashed flat into a rock face."

In fact, young Straight passed many cars, some of them evidenced only by skid marks leading over a cliff. On the sixth and final lap, he was running second, behind local James Herbert Case in a hot open-wheel Ford V-8 special, when Whitney drew up, passed with a wave, then proceeded to reel in Case and pull away to win at the amazing average of 95.43 miles per hour. Michael caught up to Case, too, but at the wrong place. "The scariest thing was going from tarmac to dirt. I followed his Ford into a dirt stretch for about a quarter-mile and I couldn't see anything at all except his rear. I couldn't pass him before we got to the end." Case held on to finish second. Straight just held on. "I could've been thrown out at any point. I had no seat belts, no helmet. I just wore a little cloth helmet. That was all. We

February 15, 1934: Whitney Straight in his brand new 3-liter Maserati 8CM at Brooklands. Personal chauffeur/butler Dewdeney is pushing Straight to start Maserati No. 3011, perhaps for the first time. Note that it is painted U.S. colors, white with blue trim, and that as yet, the grille is standard Maserati. Straight would soon order special bodywork by J. Gurney Nutting and mechanical alterations by master tuner Reid Railton and Thomson & Taylor Ltd., including larger tanks, new springs, a larger radiator, frame-strengthening, and the installation of a Wilson/ENV "preselector" gearbox. *Giddings collection*

had no protection at all." Regardless, Michael Straight brought his Hudson-8-powered Railton-Terraplane home third—a podium finish in his first motor race. And last. Asked if he had ever thought of racing again, Straight was unequivical, "Absolutely not!"

Another Ford V-8 special (DNF) and two modified Hudson-Terraplanes also took part in that final Grand Prix of 1934, one finishing fourth, the other, crashing. As it happened, only one other American driver would take part in a Grand Prix again before World War II, Lucy O'Reilly Schell's husband, Laury.

Lucy O'Reilly and Laury Schell were patrons of the French Delahaye racing efforts. Both ran the Monte Carlo Rally in Delahayes, Lucy finishing third in 1935 and runner-up the following year. Laury drove a six-cylinder Delahaye 135 in the 24-hour race at Spa in 1936. Later the same year, he ran one in the second Donington Grand Prix, along with co-driver "Alan Sel-

bourne." They finished 12th in that 4-1/2-hour race, albeit six laps behind the winning Alfa Romeo of Hans Ruesch and Dick Seaman. The following year, Schell finished third in the Mille Miglia with a 135.

In April 1938, the Schells' Ecurie Bleue team fielded a 4.5-liter pushrod V-12 Delahaye 145 that René Dreyfus drove to a stunning—and historic—victory over Mercedes works drivers Caracciola and Lang at the Pau Grand Prix, thereby spoiling the debut of the legendary Mercedes-Benz W154. A month later, in the Tripoli Grand Prix, Ecurie Bleue entered 145s for Dreyfus and Gianfranco Comotti, and a third to be driven by Laury Schell himself. This time, there would be no victory over the German Silver Arrows, which finished a more characteristic one-two-three. Dreyfus could only manage a seventh place and neither Comotti nor Schell finished.

Tripoli was the last Grand Prix in which an American driver would take part until after World War II. Neither of the colorful Schells would drive competitively again (Laury was fatally injured in a road crash in 1939), but their son, Henry O'Reilly "Harry" Schell, was destined to make his own indelible mark in Formula One nearly a decade later.

What Might Have Been

Whatever the reasons and excuses, the incontrovertible truth is that in the first 34 years of Grand Prix competition, even counting Whitney Straight's victories at Donington Park, Vichy, and in the relatively minor South African race, only six Americans (seven, counting Aitken's 1916 relief stint) had managed to win a Grand Prix, and only Bruce-Brown and Straight had won more than once. Worse, just two American cars had accomplished the feat, Pullen's Mercer and Murphy's Duesenberg. Still, one can only wonder how different it might have been if American designers and builders like Miller, Duesenberg, Goossen, Van Ranst, Winfield, and Offenhauser or drivers like Murphy, Milton, Lockhart, Meyer, Shaw, or Mays had turned their interest and talents toward road racing. California's "Riverside Rocket," Rex Mays, in fact, came closer to doing just that than most people realize.

In 1937, at a time when state-supported German superteams fielded by Mercedes and Auto Union had achieved virtual Grand Prix invincibility, Mays accomplished something that no other driver did the whole season. The Vanderbilt Cup had been revived in 1936 under the name of a distant cousin of Willie K., George Vanderbilt, after a 20-year hiatus. That race, run over a twisty, slow course at Roosevelt Park on Long Island, was won by the great Tazio Nuvolari. The following year, the course was modified to allow greater speeds and all the leading European teams were represented. Though it was never called such, the 1937 Vanderbilt Cup is regarded as the first "modern" Grand Prix held in the United States.

In qualifying for the 1937 race, Rex Mays, much to the astonishment of the Europeans, managed to put his two-year-old eight-cylinder Alfa Romeo (actually the Ferrari team practice "mule" from 1936) on the front row. This put Mays ahead of two of the vaunted 600-horsepower German cars, Dick Seaman's Mercedes and the Auto Union driven by von Delius, as well as the V-12 Scuderia Ferrari Alfas of Nuvolari and Farina. Mays' performance in the race itself was no less brilliant. In spite of an agonizingly long pit stop, he finished third, behind Rosemeyer and Seaman. Though eventually, Seaman had gotten his much-faster Mercedes out of range, during the race Mays had delighted the 80,000 spectators by sliding dirt-track style around the outside of the young Brit to pass in the high-speed horseshoe turn.

It would be the only time in 1937 that any non-German car finished in the top three of an international race. Within weeks of the Vanderbilt Cup, Mays was invited to Europe to compete in the Grand Prix of Monaco, a course that favored drivers rather than horsepower. Accompanied by his wife, Dorothy, Mays got as far as the dock, where he presented State Department officials documentation for the Bill White-owned Alfa.

Dorothy Mays was less than pleased with White, feeling he'd taken advantage of her husband, who'd been persuaded to front travel money out of his own pocket. When a State Department official talked of the costs involved and told Mays, "It's great that Bill White is paying for this European trip," Mrs. Mays shot back, "He is not!" and stepped outside for further consultation with Rex. "Forget it," she told him, stuffing the paperwork in a nearby mailchute.

Needless to say, Monaco had to do without Rex Mays in 1937, but a more tempting offer came before the end of the year. Maserati made contact with Mays through a letter sent to officials in the AAA offices. Their proposal called for Mays to drive the newest Maserati in the 1938 Indianapolis 500, then contest the full Grand Prix season in Europe. Though certainly not on the same level as the German teams, Maserati aspired to be a player at the highest level of racing. Whether or not Maserati was up to that task, if Rex Mays had accepted the offer and displayed his truly prodigious skills in Europe over a full season, at the very least, would he not have been "noticed" and sought out by the best teams? And if so, wouldn't the American public—and, important, his country's architects of speed—have taken pride and a new interest in the kind of racing the fair-haired Yankee hero was doing? If they had, the history of Grand Prix might well have been quite different. For one thing, America might not have had to wait 24 years for its first World Champion.

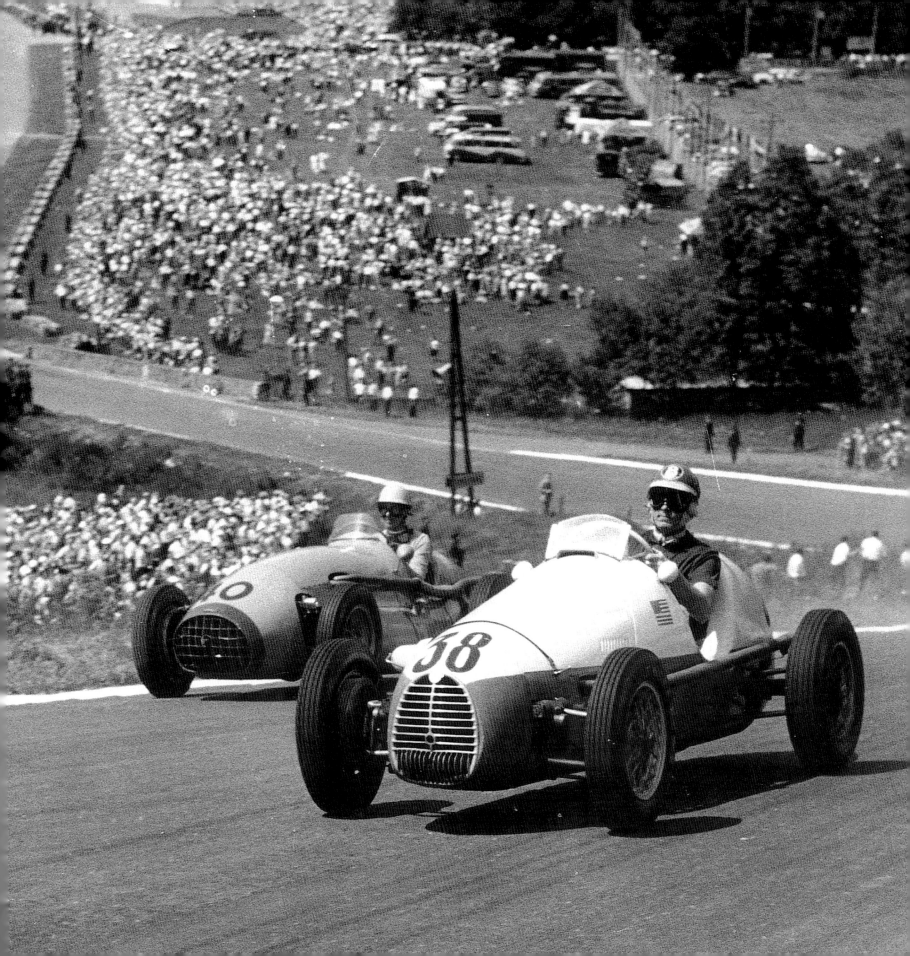

Gearing Up

1945–1955

It didn't take long for motor racing to resume in Europe after World War II. The first postwar race was held in the Bois de Boulogne circuit in Paris on September 9, 1945. This and other Grand Prix-type events held the following year, most on improvised street circuits, were contested primarily by prewar Grand Prix machines and converted sports cars. One interested spectator at these postwar Grands Prix was an American circle track racer who had served in France during the war as a civilian attached to the Army Air Force. When he returned home, Duane Carter, who would be USAC director of competition in the 1950s, immediately set about building a car to campaign in Europe—a lengthened Offenhauser midget, with independent front suspension, a clutch, and a two-speed transmission.

"I figured a stretched midget could whip those guys over there, because right after the war, they didn't have any good equipment," said Carter. "The only place it would've been at a disadvantage was on a big long straightaway, but on the road courses through towns and everything, it would've been ideal, I think." Indeed it might have been, and thereby changed the course of American automobile racing history—that is, had Carter finished the project. Limited in time and money during the next two midget racing seasons, Carter finally gave up, reconverting the car to its original configuration in 1948. Ironically, 11 years later, when an American-made car finally did appear in a postwar Grand Prix, it was a midget, at the first U.S. Grand Prix. It would be two more years before an American Grand Prix car raced in Europe. Fortunately, America would not wait so long to see one of its own drivers competing on a GP circuit.

As had been the case with the first Americans to drive in a Grand Prix—George Heath and Elliot Shepard in 1906—America's first postwar Grand Prix representative was an expatriate living in Paris, Harry Schell. In fact, Schell never even saw the United States until 1940. At 19, he had come to Indy with his mother Lucy O' Reilly Schell's two-car team of Maserati 8CTF GP cars, one of which was driven to tenth place by her prewar Ecurie Bleue drivers, René Le Begue and René Dreyfus.

The proprietor of a popular Franco-American bar in Paris and one of the most colorful drivers of the next decade, Schell made his Grand Prix debut at Nice in a Maserati 6CM for the first race of the 1946 season. Not surprisingly, he qualified dead last in a field that included Louis Chiron, Philipe Etancelin, Raymond Sommer, Luigi Villoresi, and Maurice Trintignant, among others, and crashed out of the race. Similar results in several races that year and the fact that he didn't qualify at the Valentino GP, the first to be run according to the new rules of Formula One (called Formula A at the time), may have convinced young Schell that he needed a bit more experience with something smaller than the Maserati. For the next two years, Schell's mount was an 1,100-cc, Fiat-powered Cisitalia single-seater.

By 1949, the irrepressible Schell was confident enough to enter some races with a real Grand Prix car again, a dusted-off prewar Talbot-Lago. In the last race of the season, at Montlhéry, Schell managed to finish second behind Sommer, also in a Talbot. Sixth, incidentally, was a French motorcycle champion being touted as a car-racing prospect, Jean Behra.

When the Formula One World Championship began in 1950, Harry Schell missed the inaugural round at Silverstone, but he did take part in the second event, the Monaco Grand Prix—at

With the American flag painted on his blue-and-white #58 Gordini, Fred Wacker and André Pilette in the #10 Connaught chase Villoresi's Ferrari out of Eau Rouge and up the hill at Spa. Wacker would soldier on in his first World Championship Grand Prix to finish a creditable 10th. *Bernard Cahier*

least, for a short time. His Cooper-JAP was one of 10 cars eliminated in a huge first-lap pileup when sea water was unexpectedly blown up onto a portion of an otherwise dry track. Schell's short drive was historic, however, as the first mid-engine car in a Formula One World Championship round.

During the course of his career, Harry Schell would race more different makes and for more teams than any other American Grand Prix driver. His rides were not always the most competitive. In the early 1950s, Schell had to struggle just to keep the works Alfa Romeos and Ferraris in sight while driving unreliable and usually underpowered private Maseratis or, in the Formula Two races of 1952 and 1953, French Gordinis. His best finish with the Gordinis was a second place in 1953 at the non-championship Circuit De Cadours GP, where Schell actually led Rosier's winning Ferrari until a valve started to go.

For the first few years of postwar racing, other than Italian-born but naturalized U.S. citizen Luigi Chinetti (who DNF'd in the 1950 Penya Rhin GP), Harry Schell, a European in sensibilities despite his U.S. passport, was the only "American" in Grand Prix competition. That is, unless one counts the Indianapolis 500 as a GP. From 1950 through 1960, though run under a vastly different engine formula, the 500 was included in the World Championship. As a result, 1950 Indy-winner Johnnie Parsons became the first American driver to score points in the Grand Prix World Championship.

Henry O'Reilly "Harry" Schell was one of the most charismatic and colorful characters in postwar Grand Prix racing. He came by it naturally, as the eldest of two sons of Laury and Lucy O'Reilly Schell, popular American expatriates who were themselves heavily involved with motor racing before the war. Schell was handsome and charming, a notorious practical joker, and he always had an eye for women. If a stunningly beautiful woman was in attendance, said his friends, she was most often with Schell, or soon would be. Harry Schell had style. He was the sort who would strut into a restaurant, demand to meet the chef, and tour the kitchen. After a few compliments, of course, Schell and his guests would be treated like royalty.

Harry Schell
6/21/1921 to 5/13/1960

Like his father, Laury, Schell was often described as more French than American. In fact, when he first saw the country whose passport he carried, Schell spoke barely a few words of English. That hardly stopped him from charming the ladies, according to René Dreyfus in his book co-written with Beverly Rae Kimes, My Two Lives. The year was 1940. Schell, 19, was sent to the United States, along with Ecurie Bleue drivers Dreyfus and René LeBegue and team manager Luigi Chinetti, to take part in the Indianapolis 500. Harry stayed on after the race, as did Dreyfus and Chinetti, all three taking up residence in America. Typically, Schell just wanted to have some fun.

Schell joined the U.S. Army during World War II, reportedly stationed in Monaco for a good portion of his service. He came to Indianapolis again in 1946, this time as a driver, although the sum total of his driving experience was at that time two Grands Prix. In the first, he'd crashed; in the second, he did not qualify for the final. Schell had arrived at Indy little more than a week before the race, and, not surprisingly, never even completed his driving test.

After that, it was back to Europe for the rest of a difficult first Grand Prix season. In the three remaining races, Schell suffered a mechanical failure, crashed, and failed to qualify. It was much the same in 1947, except he did manage to finish once, 12th at Comminges. In 1948, Schell raced only in Formula Two events and made some progress, with a second-and a third-place finish. The following season, it was back to the big time. At the 1949 British Grand Prix, where Schell's car never arrived, his alternate driver was listed as Zora Arkus-Duntov, later known as the godfather of the Corvette.

By the mid-1950s, Schell's reputation as a driver had grown with some good performances in 2.5-liter Maseratis and Vanwalls. In these years of the awesome Mercedes Benz W196, his best results were, understandably, at some of the smaller, non-Championship Grands Prix. In 1954, after Schell scored his first World Championship points at Argentina, he finished second in the Rome GP, and third at Pescara and Aintree. The following year, in addition to a pair of sixth-place Championship finishes, in the new Vanwall, Schell scored wins in the Redex and Avon Trophy Grands Prix at Snetterton and Castle Combe. He also won the non-points Caen Grand Prix in 1956 in a Maserati. A DNF that year brought Schell the most attention. At the high-speed Reims circuit, Schell, relieving Mike Hawthorn, stunned everyone by coming from eighth place to catch and

Harry Schell.
Indianapolis Motor Speedway

dice with the leading Lancia/Ferraris before a fuel-injection problem took him out.

In truth, Schell was rarely in a front-line car. But on occasion, he showed he could be as fast as anyone—early on, at least. In the modern world of professional motor racing, his sense of humor, style, and buoyant enjoyment of life's pleasures might seem out of place, but in his time, Harry Schell was a bright light and much beloved.

Harry Schell (seated) and Fred Wacker (right) with fellow Gordini drivers Jean Behra (left) and Maurice Trintignant in the pits at Spa for the 1953 Belgian Grand Prix. "Schell was a nice guy, a really colorful free spirit," recalled Fred Wacker. "Trintignant was the best driver on the team. Behra was probably the most daredevil. He let it all hang out. Trintignant was the only one that helped me at all. I was a neophyte. What the hell, I didn't know anything. Trintignant was a nice man. Now, Behra, he would purposely give me bad information. You know, like I was a competitor or something. A couple of times I tried doing the things he suggested and damn near killed myself. I didn't listen to him after that." *Bernard Cahier*

Parsons actually came closer than most people realized to a proper Grand Prix ride—with Ferrari in 1952. The popular Yank traveled to Italy to work out the terms of his contract, and the plan was that he would start driving in early-season non-points events. An entry list for the Valentino Grand Prix on April 6, 1952, shows Parsons as the driver of Scuderia Ferrari's number-two car. The deal went sour when Parsons was informed that in the Championship rounds, he'd have to run behind Ferrari team drivers Alberto Ascari and Gigi Villoresi.

World Champion in 1952, Ascari tried his luck that year at the Speedway with a 4.5-liter Ferrari GP car. While the personable Italian qualified and impressed all with his skill, the Grand Prix car was not competitive, retiring from ninth place at 40 laps with a broken wheel. Parsons had also been offered a Ferrari for the 500, but after some test laps, passed in favor of a conventional roadster.

In 1952, amateur sports car driver Robert O'Brien co-drove a Ferrari 166MM to fourth place in America's first international sports car race, the inaugural 12-Hours of Sebring. To broaden his racing experience, O'Brien toured Europe that season, towing his Frazer Nash behind a Cadillac. In June of that year, O'Brien borrowed a Simca-Gordini from Belgian driver Johnny Claes and somehow managed to get an entry in the Belgian Grand Prix. He qualified next to last, 1 minute, 23 seconds slower than Ascari's Ferrari and finished far enough back, 14th, not to be classified. Still, O'Brien's little-known adventure marked the first appearance of an American-born driver in a World

Championship Grand Prix. The next American to get a ride in a European GP was a wealthy businessman and amateur sports car driver from Chicago.

Fred Wacker was an SCCA pioneer. He had founded the Chicago Region in the late 1940s and was SCCA national president when he made arrangements to buy a factory-supported Gordini to race in Europe in 1953. Wacker's Cadillac-Allard was a front-runner in Midwest SCCA events. He had raced at Le Mans on the Cunningham team in 1951, but when Wacker was taken out to Montlhéry to test his new Gordini, painted white and blue, with a small American flag on the sides, it was the first time he'd ever sat in a single-seat open-wheel race car. Wacker's friend, veteran Midwest circle-track racer Wally Mitchell, gave the amateur a pep talk to convince him his ability was sufficient for Grand Prix racing. But at Montlhéry, in a strange car (and about as far from a V-8-powered Allard or Cunningham as one could get) on a race course he'd never seen and under the scrutiny of a French crew with whom communication was scant, Wacker was understandably nervous. Decades later, the self-effacing Wacker recalled that day with amusement.

"I got in the car and nobody told me anything. I think they told me the shift pattern and that was about it. And I remember I just started to go around this track at Montlhéry, which I'd never seen before. And of course, I didn't have many brains in those days. I didn't have sense enough to go slow. I wanted to win on the first lap. Well, I went over this bump. I didn't see it. I was probably doing, I don't know, maybe 130 miles per hour. And I almost came out of the car. We didn't wear seat belts then. I was like W. C. Fields coming down the side of the mountain in *The Bank Dick*, you know, with the steering wheel in my hands. So I came in and told them that I had some trouble staying in the car and they said, 'Oh, well, you have to keep your left foot pressed up against the firewall and push your back against the seat. That's the way you stay in.' See, nobody told me that, and I could have loused myself up pretty good."

No doubt pressed *firmly* against the Gordini's seat back, Wacker wound up third in his first Grand Prix, a crash-plagued non-points race called the Frontieres GP, at Chimay, Belgium. While it was not a major Grand Prix, Wacker's third place, within 2 1/2 seconds of the winner, Gordini number-one works driver Trintignant, was the first postwar podium finish for an American-born driver.

A month later at the daunting Nürburgring, Wacker survived a scary high-speed "off" in practice and rain during the race to finish ninth in the Eifelrennen, another non-points Grand Prix. Wacker was to drive his first World Championship round at Zandvoort in the Dutch Grand Prix, but in practice at the notoriusly sandy seaside course, the American found his Gordini to be disturbingly twitchy.

"I had a hell of a time controlling the car," he remembered, "I just didn't feel comfortable at all." Wacker's friend Mitchell, who built as well as drove race cars, assured him that evening that the problem wasn't his driving, but that the car wasn't properly set up. He'd already made notes of changes to be made to the steering geometry, suspension, and chassis that would significantly improve the car's handling.

Harry Schell was also having Gordini problems. He'd blown his engine, and at the hotel he approached Wacker about using his motor for the race.

"He said, 'I get more starting money than you do,'" which was true, 'and it's important for Mr. Gordini to have the money,' and this whole big story.

Gentleman racer and World War II hero John Fitch was one of America's postwar pioneer Grand Prix drivers. His dream had been to get paid for racing cars. "Racing was an amateur sport in the United States. And I was a square who played the game," explained Fitch. "I went to Europe so I could race professionally. That $228 I was paid was a lot more money back then than it would be today. And I didn't buy rides. I was supposed to earn them. It was just racing, though. I did enjoy it, but it wasn't my venue." *Indianapolis Motor Speedway*

So, I said, 'Well, Harry, I don't know about that. I came all the way over from the United States to race here, so I'll have to think about it.' And we agreed to meet in an hour."

Immediately after Schell left, Wacker was on the phone to Amédée Gordini with a business proposition. He would loan his motor to Schell if Gordini would have Wacker's car modified to Mitchell's specs. Gordini was struggling to keep his tiny race car-building enterprise afloat and readily agreed. Within an hour, Schell was back and Wacker "reluctantly" agreed to let him use his motor.

"Of course, I was tickled pink," laughed Wacker, "because I didn't want to drive. You know, the car just wasn't right and I didn't want to kill myself." As it turned out, Wacker's engine did Schell little good at Zandvoort. Gearbox problems kept him out of the running and the Ferraris, as they would all season, ran away from everyone. Gordini only partially lived up to his part of the deal, modifying the steering as per track-racer Mitchell's suggestions. "Mr. Gordini suffered from the 'not-invented-here' syndrome. His ego just wouldn't let him make the other changes." After a few laps in Wacker's car at Montlhéry, works drivers Trintignant and Behra asked that the steering be changed on their cars, as well.

Wacker ran his first World Championship Grand Prix two weeks later, at Spa in the Belgian GP, qualifying his anemic Gordini 15th, just behind teammate Behra, but over half-a-minute slower than the front-row works Maseratis and Ferrari of Juan Manuel Fangio, Froilan Gonzalez, and Ascari. Wacker finished 10th, two places behind Schell in the first postwar Grand Prix to have two Americans competing.

Wacker was next scheduled to run in the Swiss Grand Prix but labor problems at his Chicago plant forced a flight home the week before the race. By the time he returned to Switzerland, exhausted from his marathon flights, there was only one qualifying session left—on a racetrack Wacker had never seen.

"There was one hour left to qualify. I didn't even have time to put a driving suit on. I just got in the car, put my helmet on and started going around. And every time I'd come around, they'd give me the 'kick it' signal. I wasn't going fast enough. And finally, I made a real good lap. I think it was sixth fastest of the day or something, and they waved me to come in."

But while he was still at speed, Wacker lost it and went off course. The Gordini flipped, pitching the American out. Wacker was hospitalized with a fractured skull, broken ribs, and friction burns over much of his body. There would be no more racing in 1953 for Fred Wacker. Indicative of a more innocent time in motor racing, when true sportsmanship reigned, many of the current drivers came to see Wacker in the hospital, among them Stirling Moss, Mike Hawthorn, and Trintignant. But it was the Argentine phenom, Fangio, who impressed the American the most.

"I was really out of it when Fangio came in," Wacker remembered, "but somehow I admired a little pin he had in his coat button hole, a little checkered flag. Well, he took it off and gave it to me. His name was inscribed on the back of it. It's something he'd won for something or other. But I have that to this day. It's one of those things that I really prize. It was a nice human thing to do."

SCCA's first national champion (1951), John Fitch, also raced in Europe in 1953. Fresh from winning the first-ever Sports Car World Championship round at Sebring and a third-place finish at Le Mans in Cunninghams, the tall, lanky Fitch was paid $228 (80,000 Francs) to drive a Cooper-Bristol in a non-championship Grand Prix at Aix-les-Bain, France. In the heat race, Fitch finished eighth, 20 seconds behind Schell, who had been fastest in practice and led until forced to stop after being bumped from behind. As was all too often the case, Schell's Gordini retired in the final, but Fitch, in spite of some mechanical problems, finished a very respectable fourth. At Monza, the same year, Fitch drove an underpowered HWM in the Italian Grand Prix, retiring with a blown engine, perhaps mercifully, after only 14 laps.

After two years during which all World Championship rounds were Formula Two events, Grand Prix racing returned to Formula One in 1954. Now Maserati-mounted, Harry Schell began the season with a solid sixth-place finish at Argentina, the best result yet for an American in a World Championship Grand Prix.

Fred Wacker was back in Europe late in the 1954 season, fully recovered and once again driving a Gordini—this one in the team's French colors rather than America's. If the 2-liter Gordinis were underpowered in 1952 and 1953, they were even less competitive when the World Championship reverted to Formula One in 1954. That year Mercedes re-entered the Grand Prix world, with the incomparable Fangio leading the team. Wacker chose Bremgarten, the scene of his serious accident the previous year, to make his F1 return in the Swiss Grand Prix, now a World Championship round. He qualified the Gordini, albeit amost a minute and 20 seconds behind front row starters Gonzalez in the Ferrari, Fangio, the eventual winner, in a Mercedes W196, and Moss in a Maserati 250F. The Gordini's transmission broke on lap 10.

Two weeks later, at Monza, aside from the three awesome silver W196 cars, there were no less than five works Ferraris (one of them for Trintignant) and six factory Maseratis. Regardless, Wacker put his anemic Gordini in the race and hung on to finish a very respectable sixth, a World Championship point today, but not in 1954. In non-points races in the next couple of weeks, Wacker had a fourth and another sixth, but it had become clear to him that he wasn't going to do anything in Formula One with the Gordini. "I couldn't get a ride with any of the major teams, but in the end I just had to choose between motor racing and my manufacturing business, and I chose the latter."

In the final Grand Prix of 1954, in Spain, Harry Schell began to show some real speed, putting his factory-entered Maserati 250F on the front row with the likes of Ascari, Fangio, and Hawthorn. Aided somewhat by half-full fuel tanks, Schell jumped out in front and, except for seven laps,

Mismatch. Fred Wacker, in his first 2-1/2-liter Formula One race, the 1954 Swiss Grand Prix, gets a taste of reality as Fangio's winning W196 Mercedes roars by his puny works Gordini. Though he would finish an impressive sixth two weeks later at Monza in the 1954 Italian Grand Prix, the handwriting was on the wall for Wacker. *Fred Wacker collection*

when Ascari passed him and began to pull away from everyone with his fast, if short-lived, new Lancia, it was Schell who most often led the pack—until he overdid it and spun, retiring shortly thereafter with gearbox problems. This startling display of early speed and the failure to finish was a pattern that would mark Harry Schell's career.

America's first Formula One superstar might have been Phil Walters, had it not been for a disaster at Le Mans in 1955. The week before the French classic, Walters, a two-time winner at Sebring and a dominant force in U.S. sports car racing, had met with Ferrari and team officials in Maranello. Ferrari was in trouble. Between the Mercedes team and Lancia's new cars, Ferrari had managed to win only one Grand Prix. And that one, Trintignant's victory at Monaco, had been due to attrition. Harry Schell, announced as a new team driver in March, had been unable to find enough speed. Something had to be done. Perhaps the American sports car driver could help? Decades later, at 80, Walters, remembered the occasion quite clearly. "Ferrari had wanted an American to be on their team for long distance races, and Chinetti

recommended me. So I went to the factory, and we made an agreement." But then, il Commendatore raised the subject of Grand Prix racing.

"Ferrari wanted me to do a test drive on some little track near the factory, but the team manager, Ugolini, had seen me race at Sebring and Le Mans and said, 'Why test? I'm sure he can do it.' So I didn't test. I did sit in a car at the factory and Ferrari was right there. I asked if it was Trintignant's car. He said, 'It is Trintignant's *seat.*'"

So the deal was done. Walters was to begin with the first Grand Prix after Le Mans. But everything changed on the night of June 11. In five fateful seconds, there was horror and carnage as motor racing had never before seen when Levegh's 300 SLR careened off another car and plunged into the spectators. When the wreckage cleared and the smoke lifted, 84 people had lost their lives. The searing images of that night at Le Mans never left Walters. "It had a profound effect on me, the fact that innocent women and children were killed. You know, I always thought if a driver got killed, he killed himself. But so many women and children were killed there. I just couldn't justify having anything to do with even the possibility of something like that happening. I called up Ferrari and spoke to him through the lady who worked in his office. She interpreted. I just told him that I couldn't see myself driving again at that point, but that if I ever did, I'd call him first. And that was that."

Phil Walters never raced again. Other Americans, however, were on the way.

THE SECOND WAVE
1955–1959

By the mid-1950s, an enterprising Texan named Carroll Shelby had emerged as one of America's finest sports car drivers. And as it turned out, the affable and able Shelby was the next American to test the waters of Formula One. In Sicily, in a non-points Grand Prix at Syracuse ("Seerah-cooosah," in the Texan's wonderful drawl), Shelby got his first open-wheel ride, driving a factory Maserati 250F to sixth, just behind Harry Schell in a special streamlined 250F. Schell and Shelby, two free spirits with seemingly little in common but fast cars and a love of life, would later become close friends.

"Oh, Harry was a hell of a guy," said Shelby almost four decades later. "He could go fast, too. Harry would lead a lot of races, but he was old. He was about 10 years older than people thought he was. He didn't have any stamina, but he would go fast. Harry was a character. He had a French father [sic] and an American mother. She had some money, but I think Harry and his brother Phillip managed to squander it early in life. Like I said, Harry was a real character."

After Shelby's one-off ride at Syracuse, Harry Schell was soon the only American driving in Grand Prix competition. John Fitch drove in one more GP, again at Monza, in 1955, nursing Stirling Moss' own by-now tired and practically shockless Maserati 250F home to ninth place. Moss, with whom Fitch teamed to win the Tourist Trophy in a Mercedes-Benz 300 SLR the same year, was in one of the all-conquering Mercedes W196 GP cars at Monza. Actually, Fitch ended up doing better than his "owner," Moss, whose engine blew after he had set the fastest lap of the day. It was to be the last appearance of the Silver Arrows, as Mercedes had announced its intention to withdraw from racing in the wake of the horrible tragedy at Le Mans.

At the time of the Le Mans accident, the driver ready to take over Umberto Magliol's fourth-place 4.4 Ferrari in that race was an American with a great future in Formula One. Due in part, no doubt, to a gritty second-place finish behind Magliol's works car in the 1954 Pan American Road Race and another second in a Ferrari at Sebring four months later, 28-year-old Phil Hill was driving his first race for Ferrari. Hardly calm under normal racing circumstances, Hill must have needed to summon all his powers of self-control after witnessing the horrors of that night. One of the last images in his mind as he jumped into the Ferrari was that of a nearby *gendarme* who had had his leg severed by shrapnel from the horrific crash.

The Magliol/Hill Ferrari moved up as far as third before a rock-pierced radiator put them out. Hill would have other successes in 1956 for the Italian marque, particularly his victory in the Swedish Grand Prix (for sports cars), which clinched the World Manufacturers' Championship for Ferrari. But other than once being asked if he'd like to drive in the 1956 German Grand Prix—Hill hesitated because Mike Hawthorn had strongly advised against driving his first Formula One race at the Nürburgring—and a very short practice run at Reims in 1957, there were no offers of a Ferrari Grand Prix seat for the next two years.

Phil Hill was not to be the next American in Formula One. He wouldn't even be the next American to drive a Ferrari in Formula One. That honor would fall to Masten Gregory, taking over for a heat-exhausted Peter Collins in the first heat of the non-points Buenos Aires Grand Prix in early 1957. Gregory, or "Mastoid" as his American compatriots called him in fun, was in the first wave of American drivers to attempt to make a name for themselves abroad. A slight, bespectacled man with a distinctive

Ferrari team mechanics push Dan Gurney out to practice at Reims for his first Formula One race, the 1959 French Grand Prix— heady stuff for a 28-year-old rookie with no more than 20 race starts. *Dave Friedman photo collection*

basso voice, Gregory was a tenacious and courageous competitor. Sometimes too courageous. His career would be marked by a series of spectacular crashes, all of which he miraculously survived. Though he was well-liked, Stirling Moss warned Gregory early on that he was surely going to kill himself.

"Mastoid?" recalled Dan Gurney, with a smile, "I think Masten had a certain gift. He was one of those guys who had some money, you know, inherited some fortune and loved the environment of racing. He had sort of a cavalier attitude. He had the gift to drive fast, also. I'm not so sure he knew how to do it so well, but he was quick and he was brave and he was a great character."

Gregory's trademark was the high-speed bailout. When faced with a sure crash, he'd stand up on the seat of his moving race car and launch himself in the air before the impact. Shelby remembered it well. "Masten and I were roommates in London for a while," said the famous Texan, "Hell, I nursed him back to health a couple of the times he jumped out of a car doin' about

"He was the fastest American that ever went over to drive a Grand Prix car," says Carroll Shelby of Masten Gregory, "Hell, he scored more points than anybody did in their first year." That much is beyond argument, and he was driving for the independent Centro Sud team in Maseratis that were at least one year behind the latest factory 250Fs. Gregory qualified his mount on the front row twice, the first time, in his first full Grand Prix. He finished every race he entered, scored points in six of eight Grands Prix, and in his first-ever World Championship round, got a podium finish—America's first. All this against the full might of works teams from Ferrari, Maserati, Vanwall, and BRM. "And he couldn't see shit," adds Shelby. "His glasses were as thick as Coke bottles."

Masten Gregory

2/29/1932 to 11/8/1985

Masten Gregory, the youngest of three children born to parents in the insurance business in Kansas City in 1932, did indeed have weak eyes. He was also short, slight of build, and as a child, spoke with a startlingly low voice and a lisp. The latter disappeared but was no doubt responsible for Gregory's deliberate and emphatic speech, softened only slightly by his midwestern twang. Gregory's father died when he was three, and when the family's insurance holdings were liquidated by his mother later, a considerable inheritance was made available to the children on their 21st birthdays. Married at 17, and thus, in Kansas, an adult at 18, Masten Gregory didn't wait. He quickly shelled out enough of his newfound funds to buy a sports car, and then another. Soon, he bought a Mercury-powered Allard to race like his brother-in-law, Dale Duncan.

Gregory's first race was a wash, literally. In November 1952, Gregory slid around wildly on a wet track at Caddo Mills, Texas, until the Mercury blew a head gasket. With a new Clay Smith–built Chrysler installed, Gregory next raced at Sebring, where he lasted little of the 12 hours. But at Sebring, Gregory did something he would soon be known for almost as much as for his prodigious speed. He bought someone else's race car, a C-Type Jaguar, on the spot.

Gregory's first win came in his third race, with brother-in-law Duncan finishing second in the Jag. There were more victories in 1953. When Gregory finished, he finished well. If his car failed or was slower than the winner, he simply bought the faster car. Such was the case at the 1954 Argentine 1,000 Kilometers, where Gregory's Jag retired and he ended up the owner of the winning 4.5 Ferrari. This was the car, rebuilt after a huge crash at Pebble Beach, that Gregory first raced in Europe. On both sides of the Atlantic, people were taking notice of the deep-voiced Kansan.

His big break came a week before the preseason 1957 Buenos Aires Grand Prix, when Gregory, Luigi Musso, Eugenio Castelloti, and Cesare Perdisa, shared the winning car in the Argentine 1000 sportscar race, in front of all the bigshots of international racing. That's how he got the chance to relieve Collins in the Grand Prix, and to impress, among others, Centro Sud's headman, Mimo Dei. Unfortunately, due to lingering injuries from one of his patented high-speed launches from an out-of-control Lister-Jaguar at Silverstone early in 1958, Gregory was unable to capitalize on his brilliant first season. Although he was passed over for a works team ride for 1958, in Temple Buell's uncompetitive Maserati 250F he still managed two World Championship Grand Prix finishes, fourth (with Shelby) at Monza and sixth at Morocco.

Cooper tapped Gregory for 1959 and once again, the rapid Kansan's fortunes seemed to rise. But there was another huge sports car crash, another launch, and more injuries. Gregory missed one non-points Grand Prix, finished third at Zandvoort, but was forced out from exhaustion at Reims when running second. After Portugal, where Gregory finished second, relations with Cooper soured and his seat was given to young Bruce McLaren. Shelby has his

Masten Gregory.
Road & Track

own opinion about why, "He was faster than Brabham, so Brabham had Cooper fire him." More often than not, when Gregory and McLaren went head to head (both drove Cooper Formula Two cars, as well), the American was quicker.

Had Masten Gregory been able to stay with Cooper, he might well have been the first American to win a Formula One race. As it turned out, his chances as a contender in Grand Prix racing were over. Able only to secure independent rides from that point on, Gregory would score points in a Championship round only one more time in his career, a sixth at the 1962 U.S. Grand Prix. But he was still fast. In 1961, in the Nurburgring 1000, Gregory and Lucky Casner beat all the works teams in a "birdcage" Maserati. And in 1965, at Indianapolis, starting from the last row, Gregory had passed 14 cars before turn one and was all the way up to fifth before engine problems put him out. A month later, driving a Chinetti-entered Ferrari, Gregory and Jochen Rindt won at Le Mans.

Masten Gregory drove until 1972, when his friend Joakim Bonnier was killed at Le Mans. Gregory had survived seven major crashes himself, any one of which could have had the same result. He had grown to enjoy the European lifestyle and was in his apartment in Porto Ercole, Italy, when he died in his sleep of a heart attack in 1985.

120 mile an hour. Oh, he was a character, but ol' Masten really loved to drive automobiles and he could be as fast as anybody on a given day."

Gregory's first year in Formula One, 1957, was an eye-opener. Driving a privately entered Maserati, he finished fourth at Pau, a non-points race, third at Monte Carlo, in his first Championship race, eighth at the Nürburgring, and fourth at Pescara and Monza. Incredibly, Gregory finished every race he started in 1957, ending up sixth in the standings with 10 Championship points, the most yet scored by an American.

At the French Grand Prix at Rouen that year, one of the three races Gregory did not contest, another young American made his Formula One debut, Herbert Mackay-Fraser. "Mac" Fraser was from a well-to-do eastern family that all but disowned him when he began to race. Phil Hill had known him well when he moved to Los Angeles. At Rouen, Fraser drove for the struggling

Carroll Shelby is an American original—"aw-shucks" on the surface, but much more fox than hound dog. Born in Leesburg, Texas, the son of a mail clerk, Shelby drove in his first race in 1952. Behind the wheel of a friend's MG TC, Shelby not only won his class, but beat the Jaguar XK120s, as well. In the next year, Shelby tore up the whole southwestern region of SCCA in Cadillac-Allards, establishing along the way a certain sartorial style that would always be identified with him. Due to compete after working on a farm one day, Shelby neglected to change out of his striped bib overalls. He won that hot, humid day in Fort Worth, Texas, and was comfortable doing it. People seemed to be amused by his racing suit, so a tradition was born.

Carroll Shelby
1/11/1923 to

A 1954 race in Argentina proved to be a turning point in Shelby's career. Once again in a Cad-Allard, Shelby won the SCCA Kimberly Cup as the highest-finishing amateur in a race of international professionals. As with many stories concerning Shelby, the Argentine episode is also remembered for a rather humorous incident. During a pitstop, the Allard's carburetors burst into flames. In the absence of a fire extinguisher, quick-thinking Dale Duncan, Masten Gregory's brother-in-law, doused the fire by urinating on the engine. Shelby's spirited drive impressed Aston Martin's John Wyer, who offered a works ride to the Texan at Sebring. Mechanical ills would sideline that effort after only 77 laps.

A month later in England, Shelby finished second in a private Aston Martin to Duncan Hamilton's C-Type Jaguar. There were several more races on this first European trip, one of which netted Shelby $2,000, his first professional winnings. At home, Shelby joined Donald Healey, whom he'd met in England, Captain George Eyston, and Roy Jackson-Moore at Bonneville to set more than 70 Class D speed records in Austin Healeys. He was to drive a Healey with Jackson-Moore in the Pan American Road Race but crashed in practice, breaking his arm. With his arm still in a cast, Shelby teamed with America's other premier racer, Phil Hill, at Sebring to finish a very close—and controversial—second in Allen Guiberson's Monza Ferrari to the D-Type Jaguar of Mike Hawthorn and Phil Walters.

Shelby scored a number of wins at home in 1955, most often in one of the Ferraris owned by West Coast construction tycoon Tony Parravano. It was during a car-buying tour of Italy for Parravano that Shelby got his first ride in a Grand Prix car. "It was him that got Maserati to give me a Formula One," said Shelby. "I could've driven for the factory, Maserati, in '56 if I wanted to, but I couldn't stay over there. You know, I had the kids back in Texas and I couldn't stay for the whole season."

Driving for millionaire John Edgar, Shelby had wins in cars of various engine size, which probably worked against him winning an SCCA national championship in any particular class. In September 1957, he suffered a terrible crash at Riverside, requiring three vertebrae to be fused and plastic surgery for his face. Nevertheless, Shelby was back at Riverside two months later and despite a first-lap spin, won a classic victory over Masten Gregory, Walt Hansgen, and Dan Gurney.

Shelby had several more rides for Wyer and Aston Martin in 1958 and an abortive attempt at Indianapolis, where he was to drive a car entered by SCCA racer Jack Ensley. Trouble was, Ensley took a driver's test in the car and when Shelby went to do his, USAC officials stepped in. "That ol' goofball, Harlan Fengler, made up a rule that two people couldn't test in the same car. Fengler says, 'No, you can't.' And I says, 'I'm going to Belgium.'"

At Spa, once again driving for John Wyer, Shelby finished third in a works Aston Martin. On this trip to Europe, he also agreed to drive in three Grands Prix for an inde-

Carroll Shelby.
Indianapolis Motor Speedway

pendent team. In truth, Shelby knew Scuderia Centro Sud's Maserati 250Fs were far from competitive. There was hope for 1959, however, when in addition to Aston Martin's thriving sports prototypes, there would be a new Formula One car.

In 1959, an eventful year for Shelby, he and Roy Salvadori won Le Mans, although the Aston Martin GP car was a complete flop. What's more, early in the year, Shelby had had the first hint of heart pains. These got more serious in 1960, and before he quit driving at the end of that season, Shelby had raced more than once with nitroglycerine pills under his tongue.

Within a year, Carroll Shelby had embarked on a course that would see the creation of the Cobra, a world-class sports car that would in 1965 win America's first World Championship; formation of All-American Racers, a Goodyear-funded partnership with Dan Gurney that would field three Indy 500 winners and America's first Grand Prix-winning car in 46 years; and development of a program that would turn around Ford's GT40 effort and produce the first all-American win at Le Mans. Carroll Shelby: racer, snake-charmer, entrepreneur, winner.

Harry Schell in his Maserati 250F at the first Grand Prix of 1955, in Argentina. Schell qualified seventh and finished sixth. But like every other finisher—except winner Fangio, in the Mercedes W196, and fellow Argentine, Roberto Mieres—Buenos Aires' extreme heat demanded Schell get relief to get to the end. Jean Behra took over for him just past the halfway mark. It would prove to be an exciting year for Harry Schell, who would drive two races for Ferrari, win two non-championship Grands Prix for Vanwall, then notch another sixth with a Maserati at Syracuse, where Carroll Shelby made his Grand Prix debut. *Road & Track*

In his third World Championship Grand Prix, Masten Gregory is on the way to his second points finish in the independent Centro Sud Maserati at Pescara. *Bernard Cahier*

BRM team. Surprisingly, he managed to hold sixth position from Hawthorn's Lancia-Ferrari for 25 laps until transmission problems sidelined the BRM. Fraser was to drive the BRM in the Reims Grand Prix a week later, but neither of the two BRMs was ready and entries were withdrawn. A perhaps more competitive Maserati 250F was then made available for the young American, but tragically, Fraser was one of two drivers killed in a Formula Two race on that high-speed track earlier in the day.

"I think Mac was sort of blinded by the whole thing," Hill remembered, "He was so carried away with being involved at all, I mean, that all the inhibitions were off." Hill shook his head, still uncomfortable with the memory of a particularly cruel time when he was burying friends with increasing frequency. "I don't know," he finally shrugged, "Mac showed that he certainly had skill, but you've got to stay alive first."

In 1958, Ferrari again won the Manufacturers' Championship for sports cars. And, as before, Phil Hill was largely responsible. He had scored wins at Buenos Aires, Sebring, and Le Mans, clinching the title there, as he became the first American ever to win the famous 24-hour event. Hill had come a long way since his first European race at Le Mans in 1953, where his and Fred Wacker's privately entered OSCA ran first in class until the differential broke in the ninth hour. Still, there seemed to be a cost to Hill's progression. With each bit of experience gained, with each step toward success, Hill had to endure the loss of another friend, teammate, or competitor—young Tom Cole in that first Le Mans, Ernie McAfee at Pebble Beach in 1956, and Castellotti, Mac Fraser, and De Portago in 1957. This, of course, was a dilemma for every driver of the time, but for a man of Hill's

uncommon intelligence and sensitivity, it was far worse. Such a man can torture himself with unanswerable questions, "Is it all worth it? Is this so important?" Such a man can also expertly inflict the sharpest cut of all, self-doubt "Am I really any good at this?" Away from the cockpit of a race car, where skill and determination ruled, where there was no time to think, just to be, Phil Hill stood squarely between himself and greatness. He was regarded as one of the world's best in a racing sports car, yet he had never been offered—nor demanded—what he wanted and deserved, a Formula One ride.

Dan Gurney was a young and very fast California charger who was just breaking into the European racing scene—with help from Phil Hill. "It was something about Phil I never understood," said Gurney, "He had sort of an inferiority complex which wasn't warranted. I mean, the guy was damn good. Phil was brave, he was competent, he was driven, you know. I thought he was a hell of a driver. He was smart and he had experience. But it's funny, I always knew I rated Phil higher than he did."

Other friends in racing agreed and were outraged that Ferrari had given drivers less talented than Hill a Formula One seat before him. Finally, egged on by all those around him, Hill took matters in his own hands in 1958. He accepted Joakim Bonnier's offer of his older 250F Maserati for the French Grand Prix. There were objections, even threats, from Ferrari, but after a stirring performance at the Monza "Race of Two Worlds," in which he relieved a less than enthusiastic Mike Hawthorn, to drive Ferrari's ill-suited hot rod to third with Musso, Hill remained adamant. He would drive the Maserati at Reims.

Harry Schell at Spa in the BRM on the way to a fifth-place finish in the 1958 Belgian Grand Prix. It was Schell's best year yet; every time he made it to the end of a Grand Prix, he would finish in the points. *Road & Track*

The 1958 French Grand Prix will be remembered for many reasons. It was Phil Hill's first, of course. Troy Ruttman, 1952 Indy winner, made his GP debut, also in a Maserati. Ruttman had come over for the Monza "500" race and was now hanging out with Gurney. Shelby was back, this time in the Centro Sud Maserati, and Schell in a BRM. So, for the first time, four Americans took part in a Formula One race and one, Schell in the BRM, was in the front row. Dan Gurney watched in the wings. Hill drove well, finishing 7th in the ancient 250F, first among the privateers—and ahead of "owner" Bonnier's newer Maserati. Ruttman was 10th, and both Shelby and Schell DNF'd. It was the last Grand Prix for Fangio, who retired afterwards, and the last for the brave Italian, Luigi Musso, who died in the hospital after a horrific end-over-end crash. Yet another bittersweet step up the ladder for Phil Hill.

In spite of its threats, Ferrari nominated Hill to drive a Formula Two car (with the future 1,500-cc GP engine) at the Nürburgring. Ruttman and Gurney were there, though only the Indy winner had a ride in the Grand Prix. Unfortunately, Ruttman made more laps around the difficult 14-mile course with Gurney in a Renault Dauphine than in his race car. After only a few laps of practice, a piston seized in the ancient Centro Sud Maserati, stranding the tall American deep in the Eifel forest. Ruttman ended his short Grand Prix career hitching a ride back to the pits on the tail of Bonnier's Maserati.

"Oh, I enjoyed it," said Ruttman, "but the way it appeared to me back then was that any equipment that one of us guys were gonna get, including Phil Hill and Dan Gurney, would be a hand-me-down from someone else. Something that the factory'd used and then said, 'Well, take this one. We have a new model.' Also, I was havin' some personal problems right then and, you

Rutt's European Adventure

Due to the passage of time and, Troy Ruttman was quick to admit, his lifestyle at the time, many details of his month-long stay in Europe had long since faded away. One memory that remained, though, was of Luigi Musso, the brave Italian who outqualified all the Indy drivers at Monza in 1958 in the hybrid Ferrari. "Musso and his wife and my wife and I rode the train together to go to Reims. And he was killed there. It happened about a hundred yards in front of me. It was a long sweeper and the Ferraris had just passed me. And he, I still don't know what happened, but, Jesus Christ, he started flipping. There was still smoke there the next time I went by."

Ruttman was supposed to drive at Silverstone after Reims, and was still not sure why he didn't. "They told me there was no car or no entry. I never did understand why, 'cause those guys could double-talk me somethin' fierce, 'cause I couldn't understand." He did, however, clearly remember the trip from Silverstone to the Nürburgring, made with Gurney and Ruttman's wife crammed into a tiny Renault Dauphine provided to him by the factory.

Gurney was at the wheel, Ruttman riding shotgun, and his wife, stuffed in the back seat with their luggage, when Gurney suddenly spied the cars of Hawthorn, Collins, and Moss parked by a roadside restaurant. "Well, Ol' Gurn says, 'Let's go back and see 'em,' and just yanked on the emergency brake to spin that little Renault around and go back. But a wheel rim must've dug in and that little thing just flopped right over on its side. Well, all our luggage was all over my wife and his feet were hangin' down and we're just sliding down the road. And it finally stopped and we climbed up out of it and here's some guys workin' down in a ditch. They were laughin' like hell. I think they thought we was nuts. Anyway, we set it back up, uncovered my wife, got the spare tire on it, and drove over to the restaurant. God, that was fun." So, too, apparently, was a certain evening spent with the two dashing young British Ferrari drivers. "You know, Peter Collins and Mike Hawthorn, I went with them to a little party those suckers had," laughed Ruttman, "and you talk about some playboys! Oh, man, took some broads, I'll never forget it as long as I live!"

But Collins, Hawthorn and Gurney were absolutely serious about racing in Formula One. Ruttman, at the time, wasn't. "I liked that type of racing. Probably, my favorite was road racing. I always liked to run Riverside and Paramount Ranch. But, you know, I was married and having some problems right then. And I could see that staying over there would really put some fly in the ointment."

In the years that followed, Ruttman did some stock car racing in the United States, and from 1960 to 1964, showed up at Indy, but never again finished in the top 10. He withdrew from competition in 1964. In his day, Troy Ruttman was a prodigy, an exceptional natural talent, as Phil Hill, Dan Gurney, and anyone else who ever saw him then will attest. In truth, the opportunity to drive in Formula One came to Ruttman too late. Had it not, who knows?

Troy Ruttman. *Indianapolis Motor Speedway*

Centro Sud director Mimo Dei (right-center in the white open shirt) holds court with team members and three of the four Americans at Reims for the 1958 French Grand Prix: Carroll Shelby, Phil Hill, and Troy Ruttman. Hill, making his Grand Prix debut in Joakim Bonnier's old Maserati 250F, would finish 7th, the highest placed nonworks car. Ruttman, also in his first—and as it turned out, only—Formula One race, would finish a creditable 10th in an even older Centro Sud Maserati. Shelby's Centro Sud Maserati DNF'd at Reims, as did Harry Schell's BRM. *Bernard Cahier*

know, it just didn't work out. So, a while later, I just decided that was it and came home."

Would he have succeeded if he'd stayed—and come to grips with his personal demons? Dan Gurney thought so. "I mean, Troy Ruttman, had he wanted to, had he been fit and so forth, would've done well. He was a very, very gifted driver, in a class by himself, in my mind. And one of the few who seemed to be able to do roadracing, even though he wasn't a roadracing specialist. He just had a natural gift."

In the German Grand Prix, Hill easily led the Formula Two class before spinning in another car's oil. Brake problems followed and eventually, he finished fifth in class and ahead of a number of Formula One cars. But tragedy struck again, this time even closer. Ferrari teammate Peter Collins, with whom Hill had often been paired in sports cars for two seasons, left the road, flipped, was thrown from his car against a tree—never to regain consciousness. Hill was devastated.

"Oh, that was terrible," he remembered, "I had been living on Collins' boat in Monte Carlo. I was really upset. And, you know, it was getting awful close to home. You're constantly rewriting this script as to why it's not you." Hill had been through this many more times than the young hotshoe from California. "With Gurney, it might just as well have been some stranger because he didn't have the same connection to Collins. I was sort of appalled that he didn't seem to be bothered by it. You know, this was a great tragedy! Peter Collins was killed—Mike Hawthorn's best friend—and Musso before and it was all falling apart! All these guys going off and hitting trees, and each time I was moving forward. And, at the same time, I knew where Gurney was

at because I had been there a few years earlier, you know what I mean, where nothing mattered."

Hill was right. He did move forward—into the seat left vacant by his friend Collins. Finally, after three years of loyal and productive service to the "prancing horse" of Maranello, Phil Hill drove his first Formula One race for the Ferrari team at Monza. Despite an unplanned stop to replace a thrown tire tread and a midrace spin (his foot slipped off the brake pedal), Hill set the fastest time of the race and charged back to third, where he slowed behind Hawthorn's crippled Ferrari, allowing his English teammate to finish second and gain vital points toward the World Championship.

The 1958 championship came down to the final Grand Prix of the season, on the Ain-Diab circuit in Casablanca, Morocco. Again, Hill played a critical role, moving over near the end of the race to let Hawthorn move into second-clinching the title, by a single point. Phil Hill had arrived in Formula One.

But the casualties continued. Stuart Lewis-Evans died as a result of a fiery crash at that final round. And the cruelest twist of all, Mike Hawthorn, who announced his retirement after Morocco, was killed in a road accident just three months later.

The American invasion of Formula One was in full swing in 1959. With Schell at BRM, Gregory with Cooper, Shelby with Aston Martin, and Hill with Ferrari, joined at midseason by the newest member of the club, Dan Gurney, five Yanks were on factory teams. Six if you count Pete Lovely, America's unknown soldier with Team Lotus. Lovely was a talented amateur sports car driver, best known on the West Coast in the mid-1950s for his successful 1,500-cc "Pooper," a Porsche-Cooper special. He was SCCA national champion with the Pooper in 1955 and co-drove a works Lotus Elite at Sebring with Colin Chapman in 1958. There, and in California several days later, Chapman went to great efforts to persuade Lovely to come to Europe to be number-two to Graham Hill on the Lotus Formula One team.

"I said, 'Are you kidding?'" remembered Lovely, "I said, 'This just doesn't make any sense. I've got a business and a wife and four kids and, okay, so I drive a race car a little bit, but, uh. . . .' And Chapman says, 'No, no, I want you. You're going to be the one.' And finally, after this great discussion went on for about, you know, between Sebring and Los Angeles, about four days, he finally dropped the clangor. He said, 'Well, I can get more starting money for an American.' So, *that's* how I got to go and do Formula One for Team Lotus."

Armed with his racing gear and $200 worth of travelers checks, Lovely set off to Europe. It was, as it turned out, a short tour. Lotus was not yet an F1 power and Lovely's car wasn't even ready for the first two non-points Grands Prix at Goodwood and Aintree. At the latter race, however, another American made his one and only Formula One start, in the BARC 200. Masten Gregory had arranged a ride for his brother-in-law, Dale Duncan, in a tired Centro Sud Maserati. Only Graham Hill's Lotus 16 and one Formula Two car qualified behind Duncan, who finished 15th, far enough back not to be classified.

Lotus did manage to field two of the fragile 16s for Hill and Lovely for the International Trophy at Silverstone, another non-points GP, but one important enough to draw entries from the major factory teams, including Ferrari. There, in his first Grand Prix, Pete Lovely qualified an impressive seventh, just behind Carroll Shelby in the new Aston Martin, but ahead of teammate Graham Hill (who qualified Lovely's car renumbered), and ahead of Phil Hill's Ferrari. It was all downhill from there. There were problems, not with

Troy Ruttman in the Centro Sud Maserati at Reims in 1958. Note the Indy roadster-type windscreen extension tacked onto the 250F to accomodate the six-foot-plus American. Starting 18th, at the back of the grid, Ruttman drove steadily to bring the old Maser home 10th. *Bernard Cahier*

Reims, the 1958 French Grand Prix. Phil Hill on the way to seventh place in his first Formula One race, a lap ahead of his car-owner, Bonnier, in a newer Maserati. *Bernhard Cahier*

the smaller engine he ran in the race, but with the infamous Lotus "queerbox" gearbox mounts. They failed during the race, causing the driveshaft, angled across the chassis under the driver's legs, to flex. "It bent, you know," said Lovely, shaking his head, "sort of like the old Pontiac "rope" driveshaft. And I'm thinking, 'I don't know if I want to do this.'" Teammate Graham Hill's car broke and Lovely barely made it to the end, finishing 15th, not classified. It would be Pete Lovely's only race for Team Lotus. At Monaco a week later, Lotus was unable to keep the American's car on the track for the required minimum 20 laps of practice and Lovely went home.

At Silverstone, Phil Hill was the highest-placed American, ending up fourth in the only Ferrari to finish. Poor Masten Gregory, for whom 1959 would eventually be a good year in the now full 2-1/2-liter Cooper-Climax, didn't even start. Earlier that day in a sports car race he'd had a bad crash featuring one of his patented "launches." Shelby, in the new Aston Martin, had run with the leaders until the engine blew, finishing sixth. From then on, though, things got worse for the Aston Martin team—and for Shelby.

"That season wasn't worth a shit," Shelby recalled, "At Silverstone, we were competitive with everything. We kept going down on horsepower all year. It seemed the more they worked on the motor, the worse it got. I don't

Pete Lovely in the flawed Lotus 16 at Silverstone's non-championship 1959 International Trophy race. It would be Lovely's only Grand Prix appearance as a works driver for the then fledgling Team Lotus. The peeling stick-on numbers allowed Lovely to qualify (seventh) then have his car renumbered for Graham Hill (whose Climax engine had blown up) to qualify the same car ninth, a full second slower. For the race, Hill was given Lovely's motor and the American, a tired 2.2-liter Climax. No matter, a gearbox mount failed and Lovely finished 15th. Two weeks later at Monaco, when for the third time in four races his car was not ready, Lovely quit and went home. *Pete Lovely collection*

know what the hell happened. I still don't know—unless we ran three liters at Silverstone!"

After four more races in 1959, Aston Martin and Shelby threw in the towel. "Yeah, any time I was ever in Formula One that I had an equal car, I didn't think there was anybody that could really outrun me very badly, but I was older than most of them. What I really wanted to

Clad in his trademark overalls and trend-setting full-coverage helmet, Carroll Shelby drives the classically beautiful, if stillborn, Aston Martin GP car for the second time, at Zandvoort in the 1959 Dutch Grand Prix. With no chance against the light and nimble midengine cars, Shelby could qualify no better than 10th, though he was more than a second faster than his teammate Salvadori. In a race that Masten Gregory's Cooper led easily until gear-selector problems slowed him on lap 11 (he finished 3rd), Shelby was never higher than 11th, going out with a blown engine on the 25th lap. Phil Hill hung on to finish 6th in his front-engine Ferrari. *Dave Friedman photo collection*

do was build my own car. I enjoyed driving race cars, but I knew I started too late."

Ferrari had a poor season against the pesky rear-engine Coopers, Tony Brooks scoring the only two victories. One of them was at the French Grand Prix at Reims. Driving in a Formula One race for the first time was the young Californian, Dan Gurney. Phil Hill, who knew better than anyone what a threat Gurney would be, recommended him to Ferrari.

"Yeah, I did. I don't know why," Hill laughed later, "If I had any sense, I would have said, 'No, I don't think Gurney should be here.' Because, I mean, why would anybody possibly want the guy that stood to show him up the worst on the same team? Did Prost want Senna to come and be a part of the team?"

Gurney had almost given up and gone home like Ruttman. "Phil helped a lot. A fellow American looked mighty nice to see when you're over there feeling pretty alone and not really speaking the language very well. I felt as though I was never going to get anywhere, but when it finally did happen, it came with a giant rush and I was thankful for every tiny bit of experience that I had managed to gain. I probably hadn't driven more than 20 races at that time." Twenty races and starting for Ferrari in Formula One!

Gurney's first Grand Prix ended after only 20 laps when a stone holed the radiator of his test-engine Ferrari, as he ran comfortably in seventh. Hill finished

Gurney's Ferrari Dino 246 on the high-speed circuit at Reims. Starting 12th, Gurney climbed to 6th in nine laps before being passed by teammate Behra. Ten laps later, Gurney was out with a pierced radiator, but it was an impressive debut by the Californian. Phil Hill would go on to finish 2nd, Schell, in the BRM, 7th. Early in the race, Masten Gregory had led all the Americans, briefly pushing his Cooper up to 2nd before retiring from heat exhaustion. *Dave Friedman photo collection*

Gurney on the north banking at Avus in the 1959 German Grand Prix. Making the best of his particularly strong Ferrari, Gurney parlayed a front-row start to finish second in the first heat, ahead of Hill, and third in the second heat—close enough to second-place Hill to pip his fellow Californian on aggregate time for the runner-up spot. This in only his second Grand Prix. *Road & Track*

a strong second behind teammate Brooks. Because of a strike in Italy, Ferrari missed the British Grand Prix, but four cars were prepared for the Grand Prix of Germany, held at Avus in Berlin in 1959. Basically, a 5-mile straight stretch of the Autobahn with a hairpin at one end and a high-speed banked turn at the other, Avus was a horsepower circuit, to say the least, and ideal for the Ferraris.

Tragically, in the sports car race preceding Sunday's Grand Prix, Jean Behra, who had been Gurney's and Hill's teammate at Reims, lost control of his Porsche and slid up and over the top of the rain-slick north banking to his death. On the starting grid, the drivers were informed that the Grand Prix would go on, but in case of rain, Avus' north curve would be considered a "neutral zone," with no passing permitted. As luck would have it, Gurney's Ferrari had proved to be a rocketship in practice, Hill's, a sled. So, in only his second Grand Prix, Gurney found himself starting on the front row in the company of Stirling Moss, Jack Brabham, and pole-sitter Tony Brooks. After Gregory's engine blew, no doubt from over-revving to dice with the leaders in the first heat, the race itself was a Ferrari parade. Brooks won both ends. Gurney and Hill traded second and third in heats one and two, with Gurney prevailing on aggregate time.

Gurney outqualified Hill, if just barely, in the next two Grands Prix. At Portugal, Hill's race ended when he hit the spun-out Lotus of Graham Hill. Gurney brought the first Ferrari home in third, behind Moss and Gregory in the Coopers. After landing 60 feet away from his mangled Tojeiro-Jaguar at Goodwood, Gregory was hospitalized once again and absent from Monza. There, Hill set the fastest lap of the race and might have had a chance to win had it not been for poor tactics by the Ferrari team—everyone in for a change of tires at nearly the same time, leaving Moss unharried

Ferrari drivers Tony Brooks and Phil Hill in the pits at Sebring for the 1959 U.S. Grand Prix. Note the new Bell "Shorty" Hill wore in 1959 instead of his familiar cork Herbert Johnson polo helmet, as worn by Brooks. Hill made the change after Peter Collins' fatal accident in the 1958 German Grand Prix. "Gurney'd been trying to get me to switch," explained Hill. "He said the old corker wouldn't pass the armpit test. You know, you put the helmet under your armpit and drop it. It breaks. Then, at the Nürburgring, Mike Hawthorn brought Peter's helmet up to the room. I don't think I ever used the corker after that." *Dave Friedman photo collection*

and able to conserve his tires. Ultimately, Hill finished second, Gurney fourth. Monza would prove to be Gurney's last race in a Formula One Ferrari. It was also Carroll Shelby's swan song in Formula One. While his famous bib-overalls and boots never caught on, the affable Texan did start one important trend in Grand Prix racing, as the first Formula One driver to wear what was then called a "full-coverage" helmet, one that extended down to protect the temples and back of the head.

From Santa Monica to Sebring—The U.S. Grand Prix

In 1959, after a gap of 43 years, Grand Prix racing finally returned to America. Appropriately, Alec Ulmann, who in 1952 had brought international sports car racing to the United States with his 12-hour Sebring endurance race, was once again the prime mover. The same famous airport course at Sebring, Florida, host to America's only international road race for seven years, was now to be the site of the first U.S.

Dominant. That's the only word for Rodger Ward's performance in 1959—everywhere but at the U.S. Grand Prix. He won the Indianapolis 500 that year, and scored four other championship wins, finishing third or better in eight of the 12 championship races he entered (the other three were DNFs) to win the USAC national championship going away. He also finished fifth in the Stock Car championship, with one win and three second-place finishes. And then there was Ward's first attempt at road racing, at the USAC Formula Libre race at Lime Rock. He had tried and failed to get a legitimate sports car ride for that race. Rebuffed as merely a "roundy-round" racer, Ward ended up in a 10-year old Offy-powered midget—and proceeded to take two out of three heats, shatter the lap record, and win easily over some of this country's best sports car drivers. It was a stunning performance.

R odger Ward

1/10/1921 to

At Sebring, however, it was no contest. Unlike Lime Rock, Sebring's airport course favored straightaway speed and strong brakes, neither of which the midget had. And, Ward's Offy had to be converted to run gas rather than alcohol and, as a result, was down on power. Nor had there had been any new Formula One cars at Lime Rock. In a USAC Formula Libre race at Watkins Glen three months after Lime Rock, Stirling Moss had won convincingly in his Cooper F1 car over a field that included several Offy midgets. Obviously, Ward knew at the outset that he had no chance in the Grand Prix. Why then would a champion risk embarrassment in such a no-win situation? It is an insight to both the depth of Rodger Ward's desire to compete and to the confidence he had in his ability that he would even try. Rodger Ward was a racer, as anyone who saw him at Sebring will attest. Contemporary accounts speak of Ward madly rowing the awkward shifters (one each for the two-speed gearbox and differential), yanking back on the outboard hand-operated brake lever to slow down, and most of all, sliding sideways, dirt-track style, around Sebring's bumpy corners. They outbraked him into the turns and powered by him down the straightaways, but nobody went through the corners like Ward in the midget.

Rodger Ward was born in Beloit, Kansas, in 1921. His family moved to Los Angeles, where Ward left high school in his junior year to concentrate on his Ford-engined hot rod and late-night street races. World War II made a flier out of Ward and by the war's end, he'd graduated from P-38 fighters to B-17 bombers, ultimately serving as an instructor for instrument flying. By then, he was stationed at Wichita Falls, Texas, and wrenching on Ford-engined midgets on the side. It was there that Rodger Ward got his first chance to drive in a race, filling out a short field in a midget.

Discharged in 1946, Ward spent the next two years racing midgets in California, linking up with legendary master mechanic Clay Smith in 1948. In Smith's midgets, he began to win regularly—and spectacularly. One night at Gilmore Stadium in 1950, Ward did what was thought to be impossible, he beat the Offys with a Ford V-8-60-powered midget. He began racing stockers and in 1951 won the AAA Stock Car championship. The same year, Ward ran at Indy for the first time.

From 1951 through 1958, Ward finished only once at the Speedway, an eighth place in 1956, but he had begun to attract national attention with other championship victories. Tragically, in the mid-1950s, Ward was indirectly involved in the deaths of two of the people in motor racing he respected the most. In a freak accident at DeQuoin, Illinois, when another racer lost control and hit him, Ward's brakeless car was knocked into the pit area, striking and killing Clay Smith. The following year, in the 1955 Indy 500, Ward's car broke an axle on the back straightaway, flipping end-over-end triggering the

Rodger Ward.
Indianapolis Motor Speedway

accident in which Bill Vukovich died. Ward was deeply troubled by these events and it took time to put his life together.

In 1957, he led more championship races than he finished, winning three (more than national champ Jimmy Bryan that year) and ended up 11th in the national championship race. He was fifth in 1958 and, of course, the following year, was both Indy and national champ, the first to accomplish this double since 1939. It was the beginning of an amazing six-year run at Indianapolis in which he would win twice, finish second twice, third once, and fourth once.

Ward continued to race and win, whether in champ cars or stock cars, until 1966, his last year at the Speedway. He was a perfect example of an American circle-track driving star who well might have been able to succeed in Grand Prix racing, had the opportunity presented itself at the right time. Like DePalma and Murphy before him and a few others like Andretti and Foyt and Parnelli Jones, if it had wheels, Rodger Ward could drive it.

Americans Bob Said and Masten Gregory at the U.S. Grand Prix at Sebring. Still hurting from his latest "bailout" at Goodwood's Tourist Trophy sports car race, Gregory missed Monza and the U.S. Grand Prix, where Bruce McLaren was given his Cooper. Ironically, McLaren won at Sebring. In spite of some truly impressive drives in 1959, Gregory would lose the only competitive Formula One ride he ever had when his contract with Cooper was not renewed for 1960. *Dave Friedman photo collection*

Rodger Ward in America's first Formula One car, an Offenhauser-powered Kurtis midget. Powered by a gasoline-fed 1.7-liter Offenhauser engine (meant to run on alcohol) through a two-speed gearbox and two-speed rear end (each with its own shifter) and slowed—to an extent—by hand-operated brakes, the midget was clearly out of its element on the long straightaways of Sebring's airport course. On the corners, though, Ward's high-speed dirt-track slides were spectacular—until the midget's clutch failed on lap 22. *Dave Friedman photo collection*

Grand Prix. And history would be made in this last F1 event of 1959. Twenty-two-year-old Bruce McLaren would become the youngest driver ever to win a World Championship race and Jack Brabham would clinch the first of his three World Drivers Championships.

Unfortunately, two of America's best drivers, Masten Gregory and Dan Gurney, were left without rides and Phil Hill's Ferrari, painted in the white and blue colors of America, was out by the ninth lap with clutch problems.

But the 1959 Sebring race will also be remembered for the antics of another American. It was there that notorious practical joker Harry Schell, a Sebring veteran with two seconds and a third-place finish in 12-hour races, pulled off his greatest scam. At the last possible moment, Schell was able to persuade officials to allow a suspiciously fast practice time, thereby promoting his Cooper-Climax from 10th position to the front-row. In fact, Schell had taken a shortcut across the infield on a remote part of the course.

"Yeah, he cheated!" laughed Hill, "We're all on the starting grid when they're wheeling him up and moving some of us back. You know, we thought, 'What the hell is going on?' He cut a whole *corner* off!" Schell gained little but a good laugh from his stunt, retiring with clutch problems after only six laps. Hill's Ferrari lasted only three laps more. Two other early outs were Americans making their only Formula One start, sports car aces Bob Said in a two-year-old Connaught, that make's last Formula One car, completed only after the company withdrew from racing in 1957, and George Constantine in a Cooper-Climax. Said never made a lap.

"What happened," Said recalled, "was the first time I hit the brakes with any degree of seriousness, they locked up. They never unlocked and I crashed." After barely running in practice and qualifying, the Connaught was moving pretty well. "It ran like a son of a bitch! I mean, I don't think it ever would've been competitive, but I was in front of Harry Schell when

it crashed. There was a big tangle on the first lap and a bunch of cars spun. I think I was in fifth or sixth place when I got to the end of the straightaway. I hit the brakes and that was it." George Constantine lasted only five laps before his Cooper blew a head gasket.

Another well-known American driver was making his Grand Prix debut in what was certainly a unique entry, if not the swiftest, at Sebring, the first all-American race car to contest a modern Grand Prix. The 1959 Indianapolis 500-winner, Rodger Ward, qualified last in a field of 18 starters, in a Kurtis midget, a dirt-tracker powered by a 1.7-liter Offenhauser modified to run on gas. A dozen years before, when Duane Carter had first thought of competing in Grand Prix racing with a midget, the results might well have been quite different, but in 1959, it was hopeless.

"Well, I obviously knew that taking a midget to Sebring was a waste of time in terms of winning the race or anything like that," Ward admitted, "But we'd won at Lime Rock in a midget against a bunch of sports cars, and I wanted desperately to get into roadracing. I called anybody and everybody who would talk to me about, you know, how do I get a Formula One car to drive, how could I get into this race, and nobody would talk to me. As a kind of last resort, we decided to take the midget down."

With its undersize and underpowered engine, two gear levers (one each for the two-speed gearbox and rear end), and outside handbrake, Ward's mount was clearly no match for Grand Prix cars, especially on Sebring's long

The start of the first U.S. Grand Prix, at Sebring, December 12, 1959. Even with Gurney and Gregory missing, no less than six Americans were in the field. From left to right, they are Bob Said in the No. 18 Connaught, already making up ground on the pack, Schell in the No. 19 Cooper, just behind Phil Hill's No. 5 Ferrari, and toward the back, George Constantine in the No. 16 Cooper, Rodger Ward's No. 1 Kurtis midget, and Harry Blanchard's No. 17 full-bodied Formula Two Porsche. Of them all, only Blanchard would finish, hanging on for seventh place in his only Grand Prix start. *Dave Friedman photo collection*

straights. Only in the slower corners did the midget reveal flashes of its prodigious cornering power—until lap 22, when the clutch failed. Ward's first odd brush with Formula One was over.

"I really did enjoy it. I got to meet some people that I later became very fond of, Stirling Moss, and, of course, Jack Brabham, and some of the others. And I really wanted to do roadracing. I would've done anything for an opportunity to go to Europe, but the opportunities just didn't present themselves and so, you know. . . ."

Both Phil Hill and Mario Andretti commented later that, among the circle-track racers of that era, Rodger Ward in particular might indeed have been successful had he been given the chance to campaign a Grand Prix car over a whole season. That was not to be. Ward would drive in Formula One only one more time, four years later. Long before that, America would have its first Grand Prix World Champion.

To the Front

1960–1967

If, in any way, the 1958 victories of Stirling Moss (Argentina) and Maurice Trintignant (Monaco) in tiny rear-engine Cooper-Climax cars were regarded as a fluke, Jack Brabham's virtual domination of the 1959 World Championship in a Cooper served notice that the rear-engine revolution had begun in Formula One. In 1960, there were promising new examples from BRM and Lotus. Dan Gurney left Ferrari to drive for BRM. "Probably bad judgment on my part," Gurney admitted later. "Enzo and I had a pretty good relationship, although it was a very distant one. I didn't really one-on-one with Enzo, but I think he liked the fact that I could run pretty good. I know there were times when I ended up with one of the quicker cars. But Ferrari was a little slow to go to a rear-engine car and I could see the handwriting on the wall. BRM offered me much more money than I made the whole year just to sign up. And I was thinking that the BRM car would be as tough and reliable as the Ferrari car was. Well, I was mistaken!"

Indeed, Gurney soon realized he'd picked the wrong horse. At best, his move was ill-timed, a circumstance that would unfortunately, occur more than once in his F1 career. While Gurney managed to put the BRM on the front row twice and led for 10 laps at the Grand Prix of Portugal, he actually finished only once in 1960, a poor 10th at the British Grand Prix. Worse, at Zandvoort, Gurney's brakes failed and the BRM shot off course, resulting in the death of a spectator.

One More American . . . and One Less

At Ferrari, Phil Hill had recommended another Californian to replace Gurney and, importantly, to accelerate the development of a rear-engine car between seasons. Richie Ginther was the younger brother of a schoolmate of Hill's and had followed Hill into the West Coast sports car racing scene, first as a mechanic and then as a driver. Ginther jumped at the opportunity. "That was Richie's thing," Hill explained. "For him it was a real high to stay there and grind around all winter long and to fiddle with this, that, and the other to develop those cars." Testing was also a way for Ginther to hone his skills and to gain valuable experience in the next generation of Ferrari Grand Prix cars.

The 1960 season began at Argentina and, an omen of things to come, two BRMs, a Lotus, and a Cooper qualified faster than the front-engine Ferraris. Forced to stop to repair a split water hose, Hill struggled to finish eighth.

Unfortunately, Argentina would prove to be the last World Championship Grand Prix Harry Schell would contest. Practicing a Cooper-Climax for a non-points race at Silverstone three months later, the popular and colorful Schell, America's pioneer F1 driver, lost control on a wet track and spun into a barrier. Without seat belts, he was thrown from the car, becoming the first American to die in Formula One. The world of motor racing had lost one of its great characters.

"It was a very sad day when Harry got killed," remembered Carroll Shelby. "We'd just finished going to New Zealand and Australia for that Tasman Championship series. We'd race and take all that ol' phony money we'd get down there, when you couldn't do anything with it. And we'd wear our overcoats down there in the summertime, 'cause it was wintertime here when we'd leave, and we'd wear long stockings up to our hips and we'd stuff those ol' 5-pound notes in 'em and the

Lance Reventlow exits Station Hairpin, harried by Brian Naylor's JBW-Maserati. Neither would qualify for the race. Even the amazing Stirling Moss, pole-sitter and the eventual winner at Monaco, couldn't find enough speed in Reventlow's Scarab to have made the grid. *Dean Batchelor*

Harry Schell and his Cooper-Climax. The popular expatriate Schell would lose his life practicing in the Cooper at Silverstone in May 1960. *Road & Track*

Months behind schedule, America's first Formula One car, the Scarab, emerges from Reventlow's Culver City, California, shop, Chuck Daigh at the wheel. A laid-over Offenhauser has been fitted for testing until the Scarab motor is finished. With body panels removed, the car's beautiful workmanship is plainly evident, as is a front-engine design that will be almost two years out of date by the time the car runs in a Grand Prix. *Cheryl Reventlow Post collection*

overcoats and go to Hong Kong and get us a suite in the Peninsula Hotel and we'd have, uh, we'd do about everything you could. Well, we had 50, 60,000 of that phony money to spend. It took about three weeks to blow the whole thing. Ol' Harry was a hell of a guy."

The Scarab—Too Little Too Late

The 1960 Grand Prix of Monaco marked the beginning of another short, but interesting chapter in American Grand Prix history. It was there that Woolworth heir Lance Reventlow's long-awaited all-American Grand Prix Scarabs finally made their first appearance, one for Reventlow and one for Chuck Daigh. While beautifully turned out with front-mounted Leo Goossen-designed desmodromic-valve four-cylinder engines laid on their sides, the cars were obviously at least a year out of date. And slow. Daigh and Reventlow were stunned at how much faster the other cars were. For Daigh, the revelation came on the way down to the Monaco's famous tunnel. "Gurney came by me in the BRM and, you know, I looked down to see if I had my

foot on the right pedal! I thought, 'Hell, he doesn't have a little more power. He has *twice* as much power as me. I never felt so damned hopeless in my life.'"

With zero development time, the Scarabs had neither the horsepower nor handling to compete with the new generation of lightweight mid-engine race cars. What's more, there was a troubling intermittent brake problem. Even the gear ratios were wrong—due, claimed Daigh, to deliberately false information passed on by Jack Brabham. "We were so damn far off, if the quick-change gears had been turned upside-down, we *still* wouldn't have been close. I don't know why in the world he thought we were a threat. But when they say Black Jack, that's no joke." It was a disaster. Not even Stirling Moss could get a competitive lap time from the Scarab in a practice run. Reventlow's pretty blue and white cars would not run at Monaco.

The Ferraris of Phil Hill and Wolfgang von Trips were the only front-engine cars to make Monaco's limited starting field. An experimental mid-engine Ferrari also lined up, with Richie Ginther at the wheel in his first Grand Prix start. Ginther's extensive testing paid off and he managed to equal Hill's qualifying time in the new car, but Hill would carry Maranello's colors in the race. One of several drivers caught out by a midrace rain, Hill spun, but rallied to haul his clumsy front-engine Ferrari back up to third after a grueling battle with the more nimble mounts of Bruce McLaren, Brooks, and Graham Hill. Ginther had transmission trouble in the new Ferrari but pushed it over the line to be classified sixth in his Formula One debut.

At Zandvoort, Ginther pipped Hill to qualify first among the three front-engine Ferraris, but there were no less than 11 midengine cars ahead of him on the grid. Hill shot up to fifth on the start, but did not finish. Again, Ginther ended up sixth, just behind von Trips. Daigh and Reventlow were back with the Scarabs, no faster, but seemingly more stable on Zandvoort's medium-speed corners than on Monaco's twisty streets. Daigh was in great form. He simply ignored the car's handling faults and posted a heroic full-lock, crossed-up, wheel-lifting qualifying lap to make the sixth row, actually, ahead of von Trips in the Ferrari. But there was a problem. Someone questioned Reventlow's qualifying time—apparently, not without reason. "They'd given him a time," said Daigh, "because they wanted the American cars in the race. And when this independent said something to him about it, Lance got up on his high horse." The hot-tempered Reventlow withdrew both cars in a huff, leaving Daigh furious and the Scarabs oh-for-two. Even so, Daigh had impressed the Grand Prix drivers with his spectacular cornering style, though Brabham needled, "We're goin' to Spa next. Let's see you dirt-track it there."

"Spa was an awakening," Daigh admitted. "It was frightening, that course. A couple of guys got killed that weekend. You went down this downhill straight into

Phil Hill could qualify the front-engine Ferrari no better than 10th among the lighter and more agile midengine cars. Despite a spin in the rain, he pushed his way forward to finish a very respectable third. *Dave Friedman photo collection*

an off-camber decreasing-radius corner, very high speed. And if you got in there too hot, you went right into a guy's horse corral." The corner was Burnenville. Daigh was behind Moss there when the latter's Lotus broke in practice. "It just come apart and pitched Moss out like a ragdoll." On race day, Reventlow's friend, Cooper driver Chris Bristow, would lose his life in Burnenville. "That's about the only place we could get going fast," shrugged Daigh, who would simply pitch the Scarab sideways at 130 miles per hour and slide through Burnenville, with the inside front wheel lifted 3 or 4 inches off the ground over the inside edge of the track. One turn marshal there became so unnerved he started waving the yellow flag as soon as he saw Daigh *approaching*."

Masten Gregory in the No. 40 Cooper-Maserati overhauls Daigh's Scarab in practice at Monaco. Though he lapped five and one-half seconds faster than Daigh (and seven seconds faster than Reventlow), Gregory was unable to qualify his Centro-Sud Cooper. The rest of his year wasn't much better. *Cheryl Reventlow Post collection*

Both Scarabs qualified for the Belgian Grand Prix and officially, Reventlow was faster than Daigh by nine seconds. In fact, it was Daigh who was in Reventlow's car when that time was posted, having taken the boss' out while his own was being worked on. "I don't know how we got into that race," said Daigh. "I think they were short of cars." Reventlow was clearly over his head and uncomfortable at Spa. It was no surprise when he went out on lap two with a blown engine. Daigh was convinced Reventlow simply "clutched" it—pushed in the clutch and revved the motor until a rod let go.

Even Daigh's heroic opposite-lock cornering couldn't make up for the Scarab's huge horsepower deficit, which, according to him, pitted the California car's approximately 200 horsepower against 245 horsepower for the Climax-powered cars and 300 horsepower for the Ferraris. Daigh stopped once for an oil leak, finally retiring for good after 16 laps. He did, however, stay running long enough to watch Phil Hill mount a determined challenge to Brabham in the agile Cooper.

"I had raced Phil several times in sports cars, but I never saw him drive as aggressively as he did in Europe. I mean, he drove the balls off that front-engine car." Indeed, at Spa, where Hill could make use of the Ferrari's power, somewhat offsetting its handling deficiencies, he had put it on the front row and was actually cutting into Brabham's narrow lead when a cockpit

Von Trips leads Hill into the Tarzan bend at Zandvoort in the 1960 Dutch Grand Prix. The black tire marks are from the locked front wheels of Dan Gurney's BRM when the brake line to the rear brakes failed. Gurney's car shot straight off the course at well over 100 miles per hour, killing one spectator and injuring several others before overturning. *Bernard Cahier*

Roy Salvadori (right) and others help a dazed Dan Gurney from his overturned BRM at the 1960 Dutch Grand Prix. Gurney had been running in fifth on lap 11 when his rear brakes failed at the end of the straightaway before the Tarzan bend. Ginther, in the sixth-place Ferrari, would be the only American to finish. *Bernard Cahier*

fire forced him to stop. Regardless, Hill managed to climb back to fourth at the finish. It was a remarkable performance that brought America's most prominent Formula One driver new respect. But any satisfaction Hill might have was surely limited because of fatal accidents that had taken the lives of two more of his competitors, Chris Bristow and Alan Stacey, and the wreck in which Stirling Moss was seriously injured.

At Reims, Ginther subbed for Reventlow in the Scarab, the story being that to get further support money from his mother, the young heir had to promise he'd personally race in no more Grands Prix. Regardless, neither Ginther nor Daigh could wrench anymore speed out of the cars. Daigh laughed about it later. "We're out on the circuit and I'm going, I mean, it was just practically a triangle, you know, with a bunch of long straightaways. McLaren come flyin' by me and I got a whiff of that death smoke, you know. I looked right at that gauge and it died. And sure enough, it smoked the bearings. But anyhow, we come back in the pits and Bruce says, 'Were you going flat out on the straights?' And I said, 'Fast as it'll go.' And he says, 'My, you must go around the corners fast!' You know, the guys'd go past you 20 miles per hour faster, the engine was just so far off."

In the end it didn't matter. By race day, all the engines had suffered terminal oiling problems. It was hopeless, and Reventlow sent the cars home. The ill-fated Scarab would only run one more Formula One race, when Daigh would finish 10th, five laps behind Moss' winning Lotus-Climax at the U.S. Grand Prix at Riverside.

Hill made the front row again at Reims and even managed to lead, but transmission failures sidelined the Ferraris. At Silverstone, they were out of the running, Hill finishing seventh behind teammate von Trips. Gurney and Gregory were an indifferent 10th and 14th. Chuck Daigh had been

given a ride in a third works Cooper entry, with the proviso that starting moneys belonged to the team. While the year-old Cooper was clocked faster than it had gone before, the Climax engine ran hot and Daigh qualified almost eight seconds off Brabham's pole time. Nevertheless, Daigh thought he could achieve a respectable finish if the heating problem was fixed and a few chassis changes made. No problem, he was told, his car would be race-ready the next morning, just the way he wanted it.

"They didn't change one damn thing," said Daigh, "it was just a third car. It meant nothing to them, except for the starting money." In the race, Daigh moved up five positions before the car started to overheat again. "And John Cooper came out with his little signs and I thought, 'Screw you.' I knew they had an engine contract so I just ran it until it stopped. That's the God's truth. I'm goin' down the back straight at Silverstone and all of a sudden I can feel cold air on my feet. And I just kind of giggled. No way could I be feeling cold air unless there wasn't *any* water in the radiator." Needless to say, Daigh didn't finish. In all, it was a miserable day for American drivers.

Ferrari ran two cars in the non-points Silver City Trophy Grand Prix at Brands Hatch, with Ginther again outqualifying Hill. Gurney, in a one-off ride in a Cooper, was faster yet, but in the race, Hill finished fourth, behind Brabham, Graham Hill, and McLaren in their fleet British mid-engine cars. Gurney was seventh, Ginther, six seconds back in ninth.

At Portugal, Gurney put the new BRM on the front row and led convincingly for 10 laps until engine oil sprayed on his tires and caused a spin. He recovered, but retired later with engine problems. In an excellent effort, Hill kept his Ferrari in second behind John Surtees until clutch problems caused a missed shift and Hill flew off the road, eventually to retire.

British teams boycotted the Italian Grand Prix, refusing, probably wisely, to subject their delicate cars to Monza's bumpy and dangerous

At Reims in the 1960 French Grand Prix, Gregory's Cooper-Maserati crossed up in front of Ron Flockhart in a works Lotus. While Phil Hill qualified second and diced furiously with Brabham for the lead, Gregory would be the first, and only, American to finish—ninth, his best result in a World Championship round that year. *Road & Track*

banking. Ferrari's only competition would come from a few privateer Coopers, one driven by American Fiat-Abarth specialist Alfonso Thiele (out with gearbox problems at 33 laps) and several Formula Two cars. Another American, Fred Gamble, would drive one of these, an ex-Behra Porsche entered by Camoradi USA, to 10th place. Hill took the pole, almost two seconds faster than Ginther, in second. Ginther got away first and maintained his lead over Hill until the first round of tire stops. Slowed by a botched pit stop, Hill had to press to catch his teammate, but took over the lead for good just past the halfway mark, setting the fastest lap in the process. Hill and Ginther finished one-two. With this victory, Phil Hill became only the second American ever to win a European Grand Prix, 39 years, one month, and ten days after Jimmy Murphy won the ACF Grand Prix at Le Mans. Monza was also to be the last World Championship Grand Prix ever won by a front-engine car.

With the Championships decided—Brabham and Cooper-Climax again—Ferrari sent no cars for the season-ending U.S. Grand Prix at Riverside. Once again, Gurney put the BRM on the front row and, once again, failed to finish after a strong run. Hill, driving a Cooper-Climax, stalled at the start, survived a midrace spin, and worked his way up through the field, finishing a quite respectable sixth, one place in front of Jim Hall (later, of Chaparral fame), in his Formula One debut. Hall, in a Lotus-Climax, had run as high as fifth before a broken transmission forced the unlucky Texan to push his car across the line. Hall's effort was no one-time lark, nor did it come easy.

"At that time of my life," Hall remembered, "I just wanted to keep on going as a driver, and Formula One was the pinnacle as far as I was concerned." The trouble was, Colin Chapman had promised Hall a Formula One Lotus, but what was delivered was a Lotus 18 with a 2.0-liter engine. Hall had to scramble to find a proper 2 1/2-liter motor. Finally, he was able to lift one out of a Cooper Monaco sports car. "Riverside was the first time

I'd ever driven the car as a Formula One." Had not the infamous Lotus "queerbox" transmission failed, Jim Hall would've had a points finish his first time out.

Chuck Daigh was back with the Scarab at Riverside, determined to at least give it one good long ride on its home track now that the oiling problems had been addressed. Shortened and lightened, the Scarab didn't handle or go much better, but Daigh was on home ground and there was enough speed to duel with von Trips' Cooper-Maserati throughout the race, in spite a persistent vapor lock.

"Yeah," laughed Daigh, "that's the only reason we finished. When we came back, I'd decided to take everything off the car that didn't actually do something, including half of the body, over the fuel tanks. The one mistake I made was that I took off the fuel cooler, too. Probably saved about 8 ounces. Well, I should've known, with Hillborn injection on gas, you blow your hot breath on the pump it'll vapor lock. So, I had to shift it according to fuel pressure, which wasn't very high. So, it ran all day. I couldn't break anything."

Daigh ended up 10th, just behind von Trips, to record the ill-fated Formula One Scarab's only finish. Behind him were two other West Coast drivers, Pete Lovely, 11th in a Cooper-Ferrari (one of the old four-cylinder Type 625 engines), and Bob Drake, appropriately, co-owner of the popular "Grand Prix" restaurant in Los Angeles, 13th in an ancient Maserati 250F. It was the colorful and underrated Drake's first and only brush with Formula One, but Pete Lovely, who'd made his inauspicious if humorous debut with Team Lotus the year before, would be back for another Grand Prix adventure almost a decade later.

Hill, America's Champion

Ferrari turned the tables on British manufacturers in 1961, having built and tested new engines for the 1.5-liter formula. What's more, they were in a modern rear-engine configuration. It looked to be a good year for Hill, whose major competition would come from co-number-one teammate von Trips and Ginther. Eager to put his frustrating BRM experience behind him, Gurney joined Porsche in its first year in Formula One and found reliability if not speed.

"Finished every race except the very first one," said Gurney, referring to the non-championship Brussels Grand Prix, where he only went two laps before the gearbox broke. But at his second race for the German team, another non-points GP, at Syracuse, Gurney's Porsche finished second and ran like a train, as it would all season.

"And that was a big, big, help for me. That's when I learned how to drive, really. It's difficult to learn anything if your car keeps breaking down all the time. And that's what happened the year before. I only ran three races, really. I mean, that's not enough to establish a style and approach and everything. I just drove my buns off the whole time. And, you know, that's all well and good, but you need more time to really get a feeling for what's going to happen so you don't make the sort of silly mistakes that a young charger wants to make. So, with Porsche, here was a platform that just would hang in there. Wasn't terribly quick, but it was quick enough to always be a threat."

As expected, the Ferraris were fast at Monaco and only a superb performance by Moss in the Lotus-Climax prevented a win. It was Ginther, in

Victory in sight at the Italian Grand Prix. Ferrari mechanics furiously change two wheels on race leader Phil Hill's final pit stop. Hill would accelerate away moments later, without losing the lead he'd taken for good from teammate Richie Ginther on lap 26. *Dave Friedman photo collection*

an obviously faster experimental 120-degree V-6, who shot out into the lead, only to be passed on lap 13 by Moss, then Bonnier. Twelve laps later, Hill got by Ginther and Bonnier and made a valiant if vain effort to catch the flying Moss. Finally, on lap 74, Hill waved the now third place Ginther through to go after Moss. Too late. Though he was able to cut into the Englishman's lead, Ginther couldn't quite catch the Lotus. The finishing order was Moss, Ginther, Hill and Trips in 60-degree V-6 Ferraris, and Gurney, limping home with the Porsche.

At Zandvoort, Ferraris (now all with the new 120-degree engines) made up the front row, with Hill on the pole, von Trips next with an identical time, and Ginther 0.2 seconds back. On raceday, however, Hill had to contend with every driver's nightmare, a suddenly evil-handling car. So it was Trips who jumped out to a lead he would never give up.

"Trips' car was clearly a better handler," said Hill, "I was going around oversteering all over the place, which I never had in practice. And Trips, you know, you look at all the pictures, and he's got this nice Zandvoort moderate understeer on. You know, you can just oversteer your way around that course so long and you've done in the tires—and run out of adrenaline."

As Trips motored on, Hill literally wrestled his car around the bleak, sand-bordered course. Finally, after a stirring race-long duel with Clark's

Lotus, Hill began to gain ground on his teammate. Too late, as team-manager Romolo Tavoni hung out a pit board saying, "Trips-Hill," thereby setting the finishing order. Was this team order a show of favoritism for the young German Count? "No, no, that's been overplayed tremendously." said Hill. "They just didn't want us ripping each other up once the thing was sort of stabilized. You know, in the last third of the race, when you've left the rest of the field in the dust, the implication was that once the damn thing is there, you know, if you're out in front, we're going to leave it that way."

Before the Belgian Grand Prix, Hill and Olivier Gendebien once again clinched the World Manufacturers Championship for Ferrari with their Le Mans victory. In the battle for the World Drivers Championship, Hill trailed teammate von Trips by two points going into Spa. Hill took the pole again and dueled with Gendebien first (Ferrari-mounted for his home Grand Prix), then von Trips until he led long enough for Tavoni to "freeze" the positions—

Phil Hill was one of the greatest long-distance racers of all time. In 1958, Hill won the 12 Hours of Sebring and became the first American winner at Le Mans. He would win both races two more times and, along the way, help Ferrari win several World Sports Car Championships. With Masten Gregory, Hill led the first wave of American drivers to compete regularly in Grand Prix racing, scoring America's first Formula One victory in 1960 (also the last front-engine Grand Prix win) and, of course, becoming America's first Formula One World Champion the following year.

Phil Hill
4/20/1927 to

Philip Toll Hill was born in Miami, but was raised in Santa Monica, California, where his father was postmaster. Even as a youth, Hill was drawn to cars, and in particular, to speed. "I don't have any memory of when it began, but it just seemed like I always had it. To go faster was always a big deal. If somebody else was driving, I would egg them on to see how fast they would go. I remember once my father—I would've been about two and a half or three when we first came out—had a 1928 Packard. The coast highway had just opened up and we drove to Oxnard on a picnic. I remember going down one of those hills seeing 80 on the speedometer. And stuff was blowing out of the car and my mother was screaming bloody murder—and I loved it."

By the age of 11, Phil Hill was bouncing his way around a neighbor's horse track in his own Model T Ford, a gift from his aunt. Soon, another lifetime interest began to bloom, a fascination with classic cars. His first project was a 1918 Packard the family had stored away. As a teenager, Hill would bicycle across town to hear his first racing hero, Ralph DePalma, reminisce at Horseless Carriage Club meetings.

Ironically, it was midgets and circle-track racing that first got Hill's attention. Before long, his analytical mind and burgeoning mechanical skills gained him access, and he became a valued helper in the pits. It was at a San Bernardino dirt track that Phil Hill got his first ride in a race car, an Offy midget. "Our regular driver got hurt and I was just supposed to qualify the car. You know, get it into the race." His first victory would come at Gardena's half-mile Carrell Speedway, but not in a midget. On the night of July 24, 1949, against a mixed field of modified and stock foreign cars, Hill drove his supercharged MG TC, his first sports car, to win his heat, the Trophy Dash, and the main event—and he got paid for it.

Hill continued to race—and win—at night, working as a skilled mechanic by day at International Motors, from whom he'd bought the MG. With their help, he went to England to pick up one of the new Jaguar XK120s and to take advanced training courses at Lucas, S.U., Rolls Royce, Jaguar, and MG. Hill successfully campaigned the Jaguar in West Coast racing, ending the 1950 season with a gutsy overall victory, without a clutch and, ultimately, without brakes at the first Pebble Beach road race. "That was sort of my breakthrough race. You know, with everything going wrong, I still won." It was at Pebble Beach that people began to take note of Phil Hill's special talents.

There would be other wins in the next few years in Jaguars, Alfa Romeos, a special or two, and beginning at Torrey Pines in 1952, in his own Ferrari. It was sold to Hill at half-price by U.S. Ferrari distributor Luigi Chinetti, who already had his eye on the Californian. A succession of strong performances at home, at Le Mans, and at the Pan American Road Race, brought more success and more attention. Inevitably, the success brought more stress to the high-strung Hill; he was diagnosed with ulcers and forced to lay off racing for several months in 1954. Hill would return later that year to drive Allen Guiberson's 4.5-liter Ferrari, broken and rebuilt along the way, to an impressive second in the final Pan American, beaten only by Umberto Maglioli's faster works 4.9.

In 1955, Phil Hill had an outstanding year. At Sebring in a Monza Ferrari, he and Carroll Shelby finished a scant 10 seconds behind Hawthorn and Walters' winning D-Type Jaguar.

Phil Hill. *Jim Sitz*

Then, there was Le Mans, where he DNF'd but impressed in his first works Ferrari drive. At Pebble Beach, Hill scored a unique double win, on the treacherous rainswept road course in his Sebring Monza, and at the prestigious Pebble Beach Concours, where the family Pierce Arrow Hill and his brother had restored won Best of Show. At the 1955 Bahamas Speed Weeks, Hill defeated Ferrari's new young ace, Alsonso De Portago, to score his first international victory. He won at home often enough that year to be crowned SCCA national champion. In 1956, Ferrari was convinced and took Hill onto the works team. In spite of typical intrigue and politics at Ferrari, over the next five seasons, Phil Hill would take his considerable skills to the highest level and make motor racing history.

After Formula One, Hill contributed to the early development of Ford's GT40 and MK II efforts. He also scored several important wins in Jim Hall's Chaparrals, one of them being that make's first international victory at the Nürburgring, in 1966. Another, a year later at Brands Hatch, was his final race. Almost.

While officially retired, Hill does compete in vintage races, often in cars he has restored. And though Hill & Vaughn, the noted classic car restoring concern he partnered in, has closed its doors, when he's not writing magazine articles, listening to fine music, fiddling with player pianos, or watching son Derek race, Phil Hill still finds time to work on favorite classic cars and occasionally, to thrill groups of enthusiasts with wonderful stories from the old days—much like his own American racing hero, Ralph DePalma, did at the Horseless Carriage Club.

Hill, Trips, Ginther, Gendebien. Hill had won his second Grand Prix. More important, he now led Trips by a point. Reims would be critical to both.

Sometimes you get a good car, sometimes a bad one. At Reims, Hill got a good one. "God, my car was clearly superior to Trips'," Hill admitted. "I mean, my car was a full half-second, three-quarters of a second faster. Now, Trips, he's getting really. . . he's all tweaked up, you know."

Seeing his chance for the Championship slipping away, the young German insisted that Tavoni make Hill drive his car to prove how slow it was. Normally, the Ferrari team didn't allow this. "They were sure we'd actually sabotage our teammate's car, one way or another, over rev it or do something. Anyway, Trips was begging Tavoni to let me take his car around and Tavoni was starting to back down a little bit. Just then, I hear somebody come in right in the next pit and they're saying, 'Oh, god, somebody's dumped oil all over the course.' I thought, 'Here's my chance.' Sure enough, Tavoni gives in and says, 'Okay, take it around.' So I jump in the car and I went as fast as I dared to see how the car was. It *wasn't* as good as mine! Then, I hung it all out on the next lap and managed to beat Trips' time by

America's first Formula One winner. A tired but jubilant Phil Hill celebrates after the Italian Grand Prix at Monza. Hill dominated, qualifying on the pole, leading the most laps, and setting lap (136.64 miles per hour) and race (132.07 miles per hour) records in the process. Hill's Ferrari Dino 246 would be the last front-engine car ever to win a World Championship Grand Prix. *Dave Friedman photo collection*

Dan Gurney at his home track, Riverside Raceway, in the 1960 U.S. Grand Prix. Gurney qualified his BRM third and was running second to Moss when a core plug blew on lap 18. It was the end of a frustrating sophomore Grand Prix season for the young Californian, who had again shown speed, but rarely had been able to finish in the BRM. *Dave Friedman photo collection*

half a second!" More than three decades later, Hill still laughed about what happened next. "I came into the pits, and I said, 'Well, I don't think it's really all that bad, but, of course, I really couldn't do too much because there's oil all over the place.' And Trips' face just dropped!"

Ironically, neither Hill nor von Trips would score any points at the French Grand Prix. Hill, with his admittedly faster car, qualified almost a second and a half ahead of his teammate and led easily for 10 laps. Then, mindful of the heat, he eased the pace to save his engine. When Trips closed up, Hill let him by, content to follow that early in the race—at a safe distance, as rocks and bits of melting pavement were a danger. Sure enough, a stone holed Trips' radiator and the Ferrari blew after 18 laps. Hill seemed to be home free and slowed to finish the race—slowed too much, apparently, as his concentration lapsed for one critical moment. Cruising down the straightaway toward Thillois hairpin, Hill was surprised to find Moss'

Making up for his bad start and a subsequent spin, Phil Hill overtakes Daigh's Scarab in turn six. Finding the handling of his midengine Cooper a pleasant surprise in comparison to the heavy Ferraris, Hill charged all the way back up through the field to finish sixth. Daigh drove as aggressively as his vapor lock problem would allow, finishing 10th in the only race in which the Scarab ever made it to the end. It would be the last opportunity for Lance Reventlow's ill-conceived if noble all-American effort, as the 1960 U.S. Grand Prix was the final race of the 2-1/2-liter formula. *Jim Sitz*

Lotus, two laps down, going past. Needlessly, Hill tried to outbrake the Englishman and both lost traction and slid off. Normally, that wouldn't have been a problem.

"I was a master at spinning at Thillois," said Hill. "There was nothing to hit there, so you could spin and just whip it around and get back and nobody'd even know you spun. I'd even practiced it. The trouble was that when I spun, Moss T-boned me and my engine stalled. Then, I couldn't get the damn thing started. I was finished."

Two laps—and the race—were lost before Hill could push-start his car to life. Ginther then stopped with an overheated engine, leaving Giancarlo Baghetti, in the last Ferrari, and the Porsches of Gurney and Bonnier. Then Bonnier slowed, and it was Gurney's Porsche against the appreciably faster Ferrari, both men vying for their first World Championship win.

"I tried maybe half a dozen times trying to find out what was the best of the compromises, the options I had," Gurney recalled. "I could either come out of the last turn behind him and draft by—but not before the start-finish line—or come out ahead of him, and he could get by me before the start-finish line. And that's the way it happened." Baghetti won by less than a car length. Might, as some in the European press asked, the young American have "made his car wider" or tried to block the Ferrari?

Pete Lovely hugs the inside line in a Cooper-Ferrari as race leader Moss overtakes in Riverside's turn six. Undeterred by his star-crossed Team Lotus adventure the year before, Lovely tried again in the U.S. Grand Prix. Despite a four-minute pit stop to fill his car's gearbox with oil, Lovely hung on to finish 11th at Riverside. *Jim Sitz*

Texan Jim Hall in his "kit car" Formula One Lotus leads Phil Hill's Cooper over the brow of Riverside Raceway's turn seven. Hall, whose Chaparral sports prototypes would later make history, drove impressively in his Grand Prix debut, running fifth, ahead of Hill, until transmission problems put him out on the final lap. *Pete Biro*

90

"Sure," answered Gurney, "but we just didn't do that. In those days, guys were getting killed all the time doing those things. And it wasn't that I couldn't do it with the best of them, but in those days, we were sitting in a car without a seatbelt, in a car that had conformal fuel tanks all the way around it. You were . . . gasoline was at least about 300 degrees around you, front, sides, and back. You know, the seat was part of the fuel tank. And it was just aluminum. It wasn't a fuel cell or anything. Those things would

catch on fire quicker than a Ronson. And we were in places that guys would no way think of racing today, the sort of circuits we were running on. It generated a different style. I mean, it wasn't that that sort of thing didn't cross your mind, but you felt almost honor-bound not to do it."

Next up was the British Grand Prix. Hill started from the pole and led in the rain until poor brake balance, set by him in dry practice conditions, caused a harrowing spin. A number of drivers would suffer the same fate, but Trips was faultless all day. Hill finished second, when Ginther moved over and waved him through near the finish. Hill now trailed his teammate by two points going to the Nürburgring, Trips' home track.

Again, Hill rose to the occasion, shattering the track record to claim pole position. But it was Moss who would win the German Grand Prix, driving masterfully and, it must be said, on a set of the new trick "wet" tires used only in practice on the Ferraris. Expected to do the same on the

Ginther in pursuit of Moss' winning Lotus in the experimental 120-degree V-6 Ferrari at Monaco in 1961. In one of the best drives of his career, Ginther qualified second, then shot off into the lead for 13 laps before Moss and Bonnier passed. By lap 24, Phil Hill had also gotten by. Ginther fell back at first, but passed Hill into second place on lap 74 to go after Moss. He closed the gap relentlessly and had pulled to within 2.8 seconds by the finish, in that time matching Stirling Moss' fastest lap of the race. *Dave Friedman photo collection*

Phil Hill at Monaco in the 60-degree V-6 Ferrari 156 Dino. Having passed Bonnier's No. 2 Porsche into second place on lap 25, Hill now chases the leader, Moss. At the 3/4 distance, Hill waived Ginther's faster 120-degree Ferrari by, settling for third place, two laps in front of their teammate von Trips. *Dave Friedman photo collection*

Lotus, Moss instead cleverly rubbed the markings off and ran them! Hill was running second, but gearbox troubles slowed him for half a lap, just long enough for Trips to catch up. The two battled furiously, one gaining an advantage here, the other passing again somewhere else. Near the end of the last tortuous lap, Hill held the advantage, but streaking toward the finish, they ran smack into a rainstorm. Without wet tires, both lost control—but hit nothing! Trips recovered a moment before Hill, and that proved decisive. Trips gained second place by a heartbeat. He now led Hill by four points. Then Enzo dropped a bombshell. As long as *any* Ferrari won the Italian Grand Prix, the team would not go to the U.S. Grand Prix. The Championship would be decided at Monza.

Phil Hill's moment had arrived, his chance to excel, to give tangible meaning to the strange and dangerous life he'd chosen. And with this

Hill leading von Trips through Le Source at Spa. Von Trips had defeated Hill at Zandvoort, the only F1 race ever in which not one starter retired, or even pitted. At Spa, Hill qualified fastest, sharing the front row with Ferrari teammates von Trips and, for the Belgian Grand Prix only, Olivier Gendebien. It was the Belgian, Gendebien, away first, but normal "works" drivers Hill, von Trips, and Ginther eventually went to the front, where a furious see-saw battle for the lead ensued between Hill and Trips. Finally, after 10 lead changes, Hill made it stick on lap 25, going on to win his second GP. *Dave Friedman photo collection*

Phil Hill and Ferrari team manager Romolo Tavoni (with the distinctive hat) check the time sheet after Hill's remarkable pole-winning qualifying lap, the first occasion on which the Nürburgring had been lapped in under nine minutes. Though Hill would also set the fastest race lap, without the option of using Dunlop's special wet tires (like Moss used) on their heavier Ferraris, Hill and teammate von Trips could only fight for second when the weather turned. Both spun on the final lap. Von Trips was faster to recover and ended up beating Hill to the flag by a second. *Road & Track*

right: Ginther's Ferrari under attack from Dan Gurney, in the Porsche, and Bruce McLaren's Cooper at the Nürburgring. While Hill and von Trips battled furiously for second behind Moss, Ginther slipped back to finish seventh, two minutes behind Gurney. *Road & Track*

exquisite moment, this once-in-a-lifetime opportunity, came excruciating pressure—and the fear of failure. Always a prerace worrier, Hill was a grenade waiting to self-destruct at Monza. Nothing seemed to go right. A faulty gearbox, a missed practice session while it was replaced, and finally, an inexplicable lack of speed. Monza was the track where Hill had set a lap record and won his first race, yet he was the slowest of the four factory Ferraris. Even newcomer Ricardo Rodriguez was faster in the old 60-degree car. The Commendatore himself is said to have chided Hill about this, and when Hill came in frustrated, complaining, saying the car wasn't right, Ferrari replied, "Are you sure it's not something wrong with your foot?"

In spite of continued resistance, even resentment, from the team, in the end, Hill ignored the pangs of doubt and guilt he felt and stuck to his guns. "Just change the damn engine," he flatly told his crew. "And so, they changed the engine," Hill recalled. "And God, it was really risky because of all the carburetion and the linkage and junk; it usually takes one session to get all that crap sorted out. So, I went out there early and drove up and

September 10, 1961: Phil Hill's Ferrari Dino 156 at full cry on the banking at Monza. After swapping the lead back and forth with teammate Ginther, Hill took over for good on lap 13, going on to win, and to be America's first Formula One World Champion. In a cruel twist of fate, the death of Hill's friend and teammate, von Trips, the only one capable of challenging him for the championship, cast a pall over what should have been Phil Hill's happiest day. By the most bizarre coincidence, 17 years later, Mario Andretti, America's second World Champion, would taste the same bittersweet mixture of triumph and tragedy at Monza. *Dave Friedman photo collection*

down the public roads near where we stayed and got it to what I thought was good. And I tried to do a couple of practice starts and it had a sort of stumble to it and everything, but, I mean, when the flag dropped, they never saw me. I was gone."

Long gone. Hill led convincingly coming off the banking for the first lap, with Ginther and a knot of six cars, inches apart, trailing. Trips had been slow off the line and desperately tried now to free himself of this group. He edged by Clark's Lotus on the banking, but approaching the Parabolica curve, Clark went deep to overtake on braking. Trips didn't see him and moved over as he too braked. The two cars touched and careened off the road. "I didn't know about the accident until the fol-

lowing lap around," said Hill, "and all these flags were waving and everything and Trips' car, I didn't even know it was his car except that it was a Ferrari, upside down."

Only after the race, in his moment of victory and vindication (but for Rodriguez's blown motor, *all* the other Ferraris experienced the valve spring failure of his first engine), did Hill learn that 14 people had died in the acciden. Among them was his teammate, rival, and friend, Wolfgang von Trips. Phil Hill had, through skill, intelligence and fierce determination, overcome every obstacle to gain the highest prize in motor racing. There was pride in that—and relief that the struggle was over. But on what should have been his greatest day, there was no joy.

A CHANGING OF THE GUARD
1962–1965

If there ever had been any doubts, Phil Hill's World Championship in 1961 served notice that America's best, given decent cars, could compete with anyone in Formula One. And Hill wasn't alone. Dan Gurney, who finished second to Hill in the Championship-clinching Italian Grand Prix, ended up tying Stirling Moss for third in points in the relatively slow, if reliable, Porsche. And despite not competing in the final 1961 Formula One race at Watkins Glen, another Californian, Richie Ginther, amassed enough points to finish fifth in the Championship, just behind Gurney. So, in 1961, there were three Americans among the top six Grand Prix drivers.

Even without Hill and Ginther, the season-ending U.S. Grand Prix featured no less than eight American drivers, with veterans Gurney and Masten Gregory joined by Jim Hall, in his second Formula One race, and first-timers Walt Hansgen, a four-time SCCA national champion, Lloyd Ruby, a wily veteran USAC sports car and circle-track racer, Hall's Chaparral partner Hap Sharp, and Roger Penske, who had just driven an RSK Porsche to the second of his four SCCA national championships. Hansgen, Sharp, and Penske were in year-old Coopers; Ruby, like Hall, was in a Lotus 18. Once again, Gurney was second. Penske and Sharp, eighth and tenth, were the only other American finishers, though Gregory made it to the end in relief of teammate Gendebien.

Over the winter, Ginther left Ferrari to drive for BRM. Though he and Hill were still friends—they shared an apartment in London—evidently Ginther harbored some feelings even then that he was being held back by Hill. If his move to BRM was in search of an opportunity to shine on his own, the reality was that Ginther was moving from the shadow of one teammate named Hill to another, Graham, who would win the 1962 World Championship. Phil Hill was persuaded to re-sign with Ferrari, only to find, to his dismay, that team director Tavoni and most of the engineers and mechanics had quit and joined a new racing concern called A.T.S., Automobili Turismo Sport.

"In effect, I was left without a team," said Hill. "Over the years I had grown comfortable with all these people. I mean, that was half of the reason I didn't go hopping from car to car. And suddenly, they were gone." It was just the beginning of Hill's problems.

Masten Gregory was the only American to contest the first three preseason Grands Prix of 1962, netting a fourth at the Cape GP in South Africa and DNFs at Brussells and at Snetterton. Two more American sports car drivers, both from California, made their Formula One debut at the non-points Lavant Cup GP at Goodwood, Tony Settember in an Emeryson-Climax and Jay Chamberlain in a Climax-powered Lotus 18. Financed by his wealthy young American friend Hugh Powell, Settember would campaign the Emeryson in eight Grands Prix in 1962, including two World Championship events. He was, unfortunately, physically too large for the car and had little success. His best result was a fifth place in the non-points Crystal Palace Trophy.

Chamberlain, an early U.S. Lotus distributor who had numerous successes in works sports cars and Formula Juniors, had, for business reasons, severed ties with Colin Chapman by 1962 and was strictly a privateer in Formula One. He owned, towed, wrenched on, and raced his Lotus, mostly in smaller, non-points Grands Prix. At the same time, Chamberlain also campaigned a

Phil Hill at Monaco in 1962. Clearly overmatched against the newest cars from Lotus, Cooper, Lola, and BRM, Hill could qualify no better than ninth and was lucky to finish second in the second World Championship round of 1962. *Dave Friedman photo collection*

Privateer Jay Chamberlain at Silverstone in his four-cylinder Climax-powered Lotus 18. In the non-points International Trophy race, Chamberlain qualified on the last row of a field that included works teams from Ferrari, Lotus, BRM, and Cooper, as well as some well-financed independents. Other Americans at Silverstone were Ginther, starting from the first row in a BRM; 8th, Gregory, in a BRP Lotus, and Tony Settember, in an Emeryson. Only the last two, and Chamberlain, would make it to the end, finishing, respectively, 8th, 14th, and 16th. *Jay Chamberlain collection*

Dan Gurney at Zandvoort, driving Porsche's new flat-8 for the first time. Gurney qualified the Porsche sixth and got as high as third before gear-change problems slowed and eventually stopped him. Third-place Phil Hill would be the only American to finish the 1962 Dutch Grand Prix. *Dave Friedman photo collection*

Cooper Formula Junior, with which he was much more competitive. Typically underfinanced and often pitted against faster eight-cylinder cars (like Settember's, his Climax was a four), Chamberlain's highest finish in seven Formula One races was a fifth at Goodwood.

"We worked our asses off," he remembered, "and towed a lot of miles. We had to make a living. It was hard being a single entry, like going back to midget racing, load up and go somewhere else after every race. But we had a lot of fun. And of course, now that it's 30 or 40 years later, I'm really glad I did it."

A New Game, New Players

From the first World Championship round of the season, at Zandvoort, it was clear that 1962 was not going to be another banner year for Ferrari or the defending American champion. The days of Maranello's domination were over, with new V-8 engines from Coventry-Climax and BRM powering the already advanced British racing chassis, including Colin Chapman's latest, the monocoque Lotus 25 driven by Jimmy Clark. At Zandvoort, Gurney, in the Porsche, and Ginther both outqualified Hill, but neither lasted and Hill held on to finish third in the race, 1 minute, 20 seconds behind Graham Hill's winning BRM.

"They'd increased the track on my car," explained Hill. "The car handled better, but there was more drag. See, they thought all that air between the wheels and the body was free, but it wasn't. It was all mixed-up air, so when they moved the wheels out, the turbulence was even greater and it wouldn't pull last year's gear when you got on a fast circuit like Zandvoort or Spa."

Not only were the British cars obviously superior to Hill's Ferrari, but his young countryman, Dan Gurney, with a full season of Formula One racing under his belt, had emerged as a real threat in the latest Porsche. A

strong third at the Dutch Grand Prix until his gearchange lever became detached, Gurney was eliminated, as was Ginther, in a first-lap crash at Monaco (Hill finished second) and sat on the sidelines when Porsche decided not to run the Belgian GP (another third for Hill). At the French Grand Prix, where Ferrari was absent because of a strike, Gurney outlasted the quicker cars of Clark and Graham Hill to give Porsche its first (and only) World Championship Grand Prix victory—and to become only the second American to win a Formula One race. Richie Ginther was third in the race, his best result yet in the BRM.

At Aintree, where Californians Settember (11th) and Chamberlain (15th) made their World Championship debut, Hill was never in the running, finally dropping out with ignition problems. Gurney ran third until a slipping clutch put him back to ninth. But at the German Grand Prix, Gurney started from the front row, dueling Graham Hill for the lead before a loose battery dropped him to third. Phil Hill, fastest of the Ferraris, could qualify no better than 12th, but was third at the end of lap one, only to slip back and ultimately retire with suspension problems. His season had disintegrated. It only got worse at Monza, where Hill's brilliant career with Ferrari ended ignominiously with an 11th-place finish, five laps behind the first- and second-place BRMs of Graham Hill and Richie Ginther.

"Oh, at Monza, Jesus! That was where I was just sabotaged. They just gave me a piece of crap. I heard about that later from the mechanics, who, years later, rolled their eyes about what that was all about." Turns out the cause was a meeting between Hill and his old friend, former Ferrari engineer Carlo Chiti, head of the group that had left to join ATS "Ferrari had heard that I had dinner with Chiti that weekend, and that was it," Hill says laughing. "And if you wonder why I came off so badly in all of Ferrari's books, that's when they were written." Just how bad was the Ferrari given to the reigning

Dan Gurney on his way to victory in the Porsche at Rouen. Qualifying sixth, Gurney outlasted the faster BRM of Graham Hill and Clark's Lotus to win his and Porsche's first Grand Prix. As it turned out, the 1962 French Grand Prix would be Porsche's only World Championship victory, but not its only GP win. A week later, Gurney won again, in the non-points Solitude Grand Prix. *Road & Track*

After two Grand Prix victories, Gurney sports a winning smile in the pits at Watkins Glen. He would finish fifth at the 1962 U.S. Grand Prix. *Dave Friedman photo collection*

behind Clark, Brabham, and Ireland, all in eight-cylinder cars, in the non-points Mexican Grand Prix. Sitting in for fellow Texan Hap Sharp, Homer Rader, in his only Grand Prix start, finished eighth in a Hall-entered Lotus 18. Tragically, young Ricardo Rodriguez lost his life in practice there in a borrowed Lotus.

Largely on the strength of his performance in the Mexican race, Hall was offered a seat for the 1963 season in the second Lotus-BRM of British Racing Partnership (BRP), a team run by Alfred Moss and Ken Gregory, Stirling's father and business manager, respectively.

"Of course, I said yes," Hall laughed. "At that point in my driving career, I thought I wanted to be World Champion! I dropped a lot of what I was doing, which was developing the rear-engine Chaparral. I just decided I would do it. I picked up and went to England for the season."

No longer feeling welcome at Ferrari, Phil Hill decided to go with the brilliant engineer Chiti, who had designed a new V-8 for the ATS Formula One car for 1963. It was a heroic, if less than successful, effort that effectively took Hill out of con-

Phil Hill may not have had a ride at Watkins Glen in 1962, but he was there and he did drive—Bonnier's Porsche in practice. Still camera in hand, Porsche racing director Huschke von Hanstein looks on as Hill is pushed back after hot-lapping the flat-8 Porsche. *Dave Friedman photo collection*

World Champion? "Oh, it was terrible. I was determined that I was going to blow the damn thing up and it was so bad I couldn't even blow it up!"

Phil Hill was not among the seven American drivers who lined up at Watkins Glen for the 1962 U.S. Grand Prix—Gurney, Ginther, Gregory, Penske, Sharp, and first-timers Formula Junior champion Tim Mayer, a real prospect, and Bob Schroeder, entered in a borrowed Rob Walker Lotus-Climax by fellow Texan John Mecom. Clark and Hill, in the latest from Lotus and BRM, were long gone and only Gurney, in Porsche's last official F1 entry, and, while he was running, Ginther, in the second BRM, were any threat at all. Gurney finished fifth, albeit a lap behind the two leaders, and one place ahead of Gregory's Cooper. Penske brought his Zerex-sponsored Lotus-Climax in ninth, four laps off the pace, with Schroeder and Sharp following in 10th and 11th. Both Mayer and Ginther were out about a third of the way through the race. Jim Hall had qualified in a Lotus bought from Jack Brabham, but never got to race due to engine problems. A month later, however, he finished an impressive fourth

tention for the year. His ill-fated ATS completed only one race in 1963, finishing seven laps behind the winner Clark for a humiliating 11th at Monza, the scene of Hill's past triumphs.

"No, it didn't work out," said Hill. "I don't think the horsepower was anything tremendous, but it had a marvelous little engine, and I have a great deal of respect for Chiti to be able to grind out amazing engines and things in quick order. I mean, he had to design the factory, the foundry, build the race team, do the whole thing. God, all in a year! But he was a little screwy, too. He tended to take on much too much and had a crazy temper. You know, tremendously productive, but tremendously neurotic and all, as well. I thought it was amazing that we were running with the store-bought BRMs at the end of the year. Remember, the BRMs were the ones that filled up the field that year."

With Porsche withdrawing from Formula One, British cars reigned supreme, especially Clark's Lotus. Ginther was well-placed on the 1962 Champion BRM team, but Gurney had little choice but to sign on with the fledgling team being fielded by two-time World Champion Jack Brabham. The year belonged to Jimmy Clark in the Lotus. But in 1963, in Gurney's hands especially, the Ron Tauranac-designed Brabham-Climax became a force to be reckoned with—in speed, if not reliability. Gurney got two seconds and a third, but was running second in four more races before the Brabham quit. Still, he ended up fifth in the World Championship behind Clark (who also finished second in his first Indy appearance), Graham Hill, Ginther, and Surtees in the latest Ferrari.

While Gurney's Brabham was still running, Ginther was rarely in front of him, but the diminutive Californian finished all but two races in the BRM. Three seconds, two thirds, and a fourth place added up to Ginther's best year ever in Formula One, as he tied teammate Graham Hill for second in the Championship.

Jim Hall contested the full season (except the last race at South Africa) in the BRP Lotus-BRM, finishing in the points twice, a fifth at the Nürburgring and a sixth in the British Grand Prix. Hall particularly remembered the Nürburgring, where he'd never raced before. "Boy, that was a really impressive deal," he recalled. "I'd gone up there a week early and I must have put in

---

Jim Hall is most often thought of as the innovative car-owner/engineer whose Chaparral sports racers of the 1960s and 70s featured advanced monocoque construction techniques, movable wings, and automatic transmissions, and in one case, the "sucker car," ground effects induced by a fan. He also brought true ground effects to Indianapolis in 1979. Sometimes overlooked is the fact that before a severe accident in 1968 ended his racing career (except for a turn in Trans-Am Camaros in 1970), Jim Hall was a fine driver himself.

Jim Hall
7/23/1935 to

James Ellis Hall was born in Abilene, Texas, in 1935, the second of four children of a wealthy family in the oil business. An interest in fast cars came early, and by 14 Hall had built a Ford-based V-8 hot rod. While studying engineering at the California Institute of Technology in 1954, Hall accompanied his brother to an SCCA race at Fort Sumner, New Mexico, borrowing his Austin Healey to run in the "novice" race. While Hall didn't finish, he had found a new passion. Within a year he had gone in with his brother on the ex-Hill/Shelby Sebring Ferrari Monza. Hall won his first race with the Ferrari at Fort Sumner, and over the next several years, in a variety of cars, including a Corvette, several Maseratis, and a Lister-Chevrolet, made a reputation for himself in SCCA racing.

In 1961, Hall commissioned Scarab builders Troutman and Barnes to construct a special, updated, space-framed front-engine car based on their experience. Hall called this car a Chaparral, and while it was undeniably fast and he managed to win a number of races with it, including the 1962 Road America 500, it was obvious that new mid-engine designs were the future. That year, with partner "Hap" Sharp, Hall began constructing his own mid-engine Chaparrals in Midland, Texas. With assistance from General Motors Research and Devopment, Hall won the U.S. Road Racing Championship in a Chaparral in 1964. The following year, co-driving with Sharp, he won the 12 Hours of Sebring. In the midst of building and testing the first mid-engine Chaparrals in 1963, Hall found the time and enthusiasm to drive an entire season in Europe in the markedly different 1,500-cc Formula One cars of the day.

Ironically, Hall, a trained engineer, was not permitted to communicate directly with his own mechanics on the team. "They were a little stodgy about that in my opinion. My mechanics and I couldn't work the car out amongst us. We always had to communicate through the team manager. And there was something lost there sometimes. I know one time I had afternoon tea with the mechanics and we were talking about the car. And I got chewed out about that."

Racing on wet tracks and in the rain was a particular problem, Hall admitted. "In my driving career up to that point, I probably hadn't run three races in the rain. It was a difficult year for me, because at almost every race meeting it rained either in practice or the race. That year was a particularly wet weekend year, I guess. It might not have happened in the race, but at some point it rained—you know, in practice or when you were trying to qualify."

Jim Hall.

Ultimately, Hall had to choose between Formula One and his Chaparral sports cars. "I was able to run Riverside and Laguna Seca at the end of 1963 with the new Chaparral and became, I guess, more interested in that. And after my experience in Europe, I realized that my career had been in large-displacement, torquey engines, and I was probably more competitive in them than with the 1,500-cc Formula One cars.

"And I realized, you know, it's all new circuits. I've got to learn the circuit every time in Europe and you don't get that many miles, so I realized it would take two or three years to get where I could get up in the field in Formula One. And I didn't particularly like the 1,500-cc Formula. And I didn't particularly like racing in the rain. So, I just made the decision at that point. I said, 'Gosh, if I can come home and build my own race car and run near the front of the pack, I'm gonna enjoy that more than Formula One.' So, I guess that's when I decided that the World Championship wasn't as important to me as I thought it was originally."

Jim Hall, of course, did come back to race his Chaparrals with great success against most of Europe's best F1 drivers at a time when the big U.S. cars were the fastest race cars in the world. With Phil Hill and Joakim Bonnier driving, Hall's long-distance Chaparrals won in Europe at the Nürburgring and at Brands Hatch, before an FIA rule change mandated engines no larger than 3.0 liters.

Hall's success as a car-owner continued long after he quit driving in 1968. A decade later, Chaparrals began to make their mark in Indy car racing with victories in three 500-mile races, the only time this Triple Crown has been accomplished. In 1980, Hall's car won the Indianapolis 500 again, also taking the PPG Indy car championship that year. Hall retired from racing altogether in 1986, but four years later, came back as an Indy car owner until 1996, when he announced his retirement again.

Pole- and race-winner Jimmy Clark goes around young Tim Mayer's Cooper in the 1962 U.S. Grand Prix. Mayer, who DNF'd with gear-selector problems at the Glen, had caught the eye of Cooper and after a season of Formula Two racing in Europe, was slated for a works drive for 1964. Sadly, he was killed in the final race of the Tasman series early that year. *Dave Friedman photo collection*

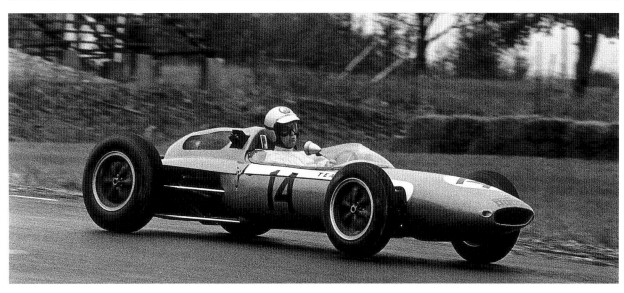

Roger Penske in a Lotus-Climax at Watkins Glen in 1962. Penske qualified 12th in a rented Lotus. While no threat to those at the front, he drove well to finish ninth. The future motor racing and business potentate also made F1 history, with the company name and livery of a nonracing sponsor, Zerex, represented on his car. "Those were some fun days, but, you know, I was way over my head," said Penske. "I remember pulling out of the pits at Watkins Glen and Graham Hill and the big guy from BRM, Stanley, were there. And I bumped into Hill's wheel. I about had a heart attack. You know, I turned a little bit too tight when I was going out and I touched his wheel." *Dave Friedman photo collection*

Hap Sharp in the 1962 U.S. Grand Prix. Driving what was reportedly Jack Brabham's backup Cooper at Indy, Sharp qualified 14th at Watkins Glen and finished 11th, behind fellow Americans Roger Penske and Bob Schroeder. The same year, Hap Sharp partnered with fellow Texan Jim Hall to build and drive the innovative Chaparral sports cars. Sharp won a number of important races in Chaparral cars, including the 1965 12 Hours of Sebring, co-driving with Hall. *Dave Friedman photo collection*

10 to 15 laps every day in the Mini Cooper S I drove around Europe. I'd run four or five laps, it's a long way around, you know, then I'd stop and think about it, then do it again. I did that every day that week until I knew the circuit. I can't tell you what a surprise it was after all that practice in the Mini Cooper, when I got in my race car, the height you sit in the car, my eye-height, was so different that what I was seeing that told me where the track was was *totally* different. And, of course, you're going faster, so not being able to see as far, it was a *big* surprise. I had to relearn the whole circuit."

Hall did have the opportunity to ride around in a sedan with Hill, Gurney, and Richie Ginther one morning. "That helped a lot, getting to see where they put the car, the lines. You know, the sport part of racing has changed a lot, but in those days the Americans tended to help each other out. It was a kind of a friendly deal."

Hall's considerably more experienced teammate, Innes Ireland, only scored three more points than he did in 1963, even though for a good part of the season, Ireland used a Lotus 25-like monocoque chassis, rather than the space frame Lotus 24 driven by Hall. "His car may have been a bit better, but the biggest difference was in the engines. They only had one set of engines with injection, so I got carburetors. I felt like that was a fairly big disadvantage because I couldn't come off the slow corners with the other guys at all. They could jump me off the corners almost every time." Interestingly, the one time Hall got to use an injected car, at the non-points Austrian Grand Prix, he outqualified Ireland to line up on the front row beside Jimmy Clark and Jack Brabham. "Yeah, they ran short of the carbureted engines. Up until that time, I didn't know how much better the injected one was." Hall's glory was short-lived, however. Injected or not, the engine disintegrated on lap three.

For one American, though, Austria was the high point of his Formula One career—at least in the record books. After one pre-season race at Pau in the old Emeryson, Tony Settember had campaigned his new Scirocco—in reality, the Emeryson made over and lengthened to accept a V-8 BRM. The venture was anything but successful. In six Grands Prix, four of them Championship rounds, the Scirocco never made it to the end of a race, except at the non-points Solitude GP, where Settember finished a distant 19th, too far back to be classified. At the Austrian Grand Prix, Settember qualified eighth, about midfield, but was already in trouble when the flag dropped. No clutch. While everybody else shot forward, Settember had to wait for a push-start to leave the line. But car after car dropped from the race and 1 hour and 40 minutes later, an astonished Settember found himself second of the three remaining survivors. It was the one bright moment in a nightmarish season for the American privateer.

A week later, at Monza, Settember qualified faster than Phil Hill's teammate, Baghetti, in the second ATS, but was passed over by the organizers in favor of the Italian, who was said to have a guaranteed spot. Gurney waged a thrilling duel with eventual winner (and World Champion) Clark until engine problems retired him two-thirds of the way home. Ginther ended up second, with fellow Americans Hall, eighth, and Hill, who had won twice at Monza, a pitiful 11th.

The last European Grand Prix of the season was the non-points International Gold Cup at Oulton Park. Other than Ginther, who finished second, most of the Americans should have stayed home, as an ill Jim Hall did.

Gurney, Gregory, and Settember were all out a quarter of the way through, but one new American face did manage to finish. Cosmetics heir Peter Revson made his Grand Prix debut at Oulton Park in a Lotus-BRM, even outqualifying Dan Gurney, who was admittedly, struggling to sort out his Brabham that day. Though never a threat to the front runners, Revson finished a conservative ninth, about two minutes behind winner Jim Clark.

At the 1963 U.S. GP, Rodger Ward had his second Formula One ride, this time in a proper Grand Prix car, albeit one of the "field-filling" Lotus-BRMs. He qualified 17th, two positions behind Phil Hill, who was mercifully just two DNFs away from freedom from the ATS. At Watkins Glen, Hill lasted only nine laps. Ward raced longer, but never made it to the end. Gearbox problems put him out on lap 45. Many believe Ward might have been successful in Grand Prix racing, had he gotten a reasonable opportunity—and perhaps had less of an attitude about "sporty car" driving the first time around. But if he had underestimated road-racers earlier, the two-time Indy winner felt differently in 1963.

"It was a real eye-opener for me in terms of the skill required to drive those cars," Ward admitted. "I mean, I was used to a big brute of an engine that, if you made a little mistake, it didn't matter. You could make it up. Well, that little BRM, you ran it between 10 or 12,000 rpm. And, man, if you missed a shift or if you just goofed a little bit, you lost a bunch. I gained a lot of respect for the guys running in Formula One. And I really enjoyed that race. It whetted my appetite. But I realized, by then, I was a little old to make a trek to Europe."

At 36, Phil Hill was at a crossroads. It had been two years since his last victory and, through no fault of his, the 1963 season with ATS had been a dismal failure. For too long, the lack of a competitive ride, if not time, had prevented Hill from regaining the form necessary to run at the front with younger men like Clark, Gurney, Surtees, or Graham Hill. Still, he was determined to try again in 1964. In the absence of a better offer, Hill signed with Cooper—a company that had produced World Championship cars in 1959 and 1960, but was now on the way down. In 1964, Hill finished only four races, with a sixth at the British GP his best. It was the last time that Phil Hill would score points in the Grand Prix World Championship.

"Yeah, it was awful," said Hill. "Terrible. I mean, ATS was a bit humiliating, but at least we had a fair amount of fun doing it. You know, we were

Jim Hall in the BRP Lotus-BRM at the Nürburgring in 1963. During the German GP, Hall was never passed on the track and ended up fifth, his best finish in a World Championship round. "Those 1500-cc F1 cars were a lot like a Formula Junior. I mean, you just kept your foot in it all the time and tried not to scrub off the speed," explained Hall. "You couldn't really control the attitude of the car very much with the throttle because they didn't have much torque. And I felt like I could race with those guys that were at the front in Formula One in sports cars. I didn't have any trouble with them at all. I felt like I ought to beat 'em. And yet, I certainly couldn't do it in a Formula One car." *Road & Track*

Rodger Ward and Phil Hill at the 1963 U.S. Grand Prix. Having again won the Indianapolis 500, Ward at least would drive a Formula One car for his second GP, albeit a less-than-front-line rented Reg Parnell Lotus-BRM. With little time to get acclimated, Ward qualified almost six seconds slower than pole-winner Graham Hill and retired from the race with gearbox problems. Phil Hill would fare no better, retiring even sooner with oil pump problems in the hopeless ATS. *Dave Friedman photo collection*

Richie Ginther's BRM at Watkins Glen in 1963. After starting from the third row, Ginther had a fine race and was in the lead group all the way. The only American to finish, Ginther ended up second, about a half minute behind BRM teammate Graham Hill. He and Hill would tie for second in points behind World Champion Jimmy Clark in 1963. *Dave Friedman photo collection*

brand new and what can you expect? Who can become competitive in one season? But even in the face of all that, it was nowhere near as bad as Cooper in '64. I had a hateful mechanic. How can you possibly go racing that way? And the cars were worse. Bruce McLaren was unhappy, too. I think Bruce and I were even on the back row one race. God, it was awful! Uprights, everything breaking. Just nothing was right. That was the pits. It soured me."

For Gurney, in his second year with Brabham, 1964 was his most successful and yet, most frustrating season so far, with only three points finishes. At Monaco, Gurney led Graham Hill and Clark at the halfway mark, having lapped all but fourth-place Ginther, before slowing for a fuel leak, then retiring with a broken gearbox. Ginther ultimately finished second. Gurney put the Brabham on the pole at Zandvoort and was running near the front when his steering wheel broke. Incredibly, the notoriously parsimonious Brabham had no spare in the pits, and Gurney was forced to retire. Worse, at Spa, after qualifying on the pole by two full seconds and pulling out to a huge lead, Gurney's Brabham began to run out of fuel in the closing laps. Again, he pitted for help, but this time, there was no fuel! The hapless Californian barely was able to hold on for sixth.

"Well," chuckled Gurney, "you know, it was kind of a hand to mouth then, very austere. Jack was always pretty careful with the money."

Richie Ginther, whom Gurney had just lapped before running out of fuel, ended up fourth at Spa. Peter Revson, now in a Lotus-BRM entered by Revson

Racing, had run four non-points Grands Prix in 1964, his best result being a fourth-place finish at Solitude. After failing to qualify at Monaco, Revson was at Spa where, armed with a newer spec BRM motor from the Reg Parnell team, he qualified to start from the fourth row in his first World Championship Grand Prix. That's as good as it got for the 25-year old, who was forced to make several pit stops during the race and was ultimately disqualified for a push start.

Making History for Brabham and Honda

Finally, at Rouen, Gurney's Brabham held together for a whole race and he scored his second World Championship Grand Prix victory. It was a historic occasion for the Brabham team, being the first World Championship win for that marque.

At the following British Grand Prix, where Revson made his second championship start (again, not finishing), Gurney qualified on the front row, but ignition problems forced him to pit early on after running second. Likewise, at the Nürburgring, Gurney exchanged the lead with Surtees in the fast new Ferrari until paper clogged the Brabham's radiator, eventually forcing a pit stop. He finished the race, but no better than 10th, three places behind Ginther in the BRM. Neither Phil Hill nor Peter Revson, in his third start, made it to the finish. Nor did another American, who was making history in his first Grand Prix start, Ronnie Bucknum.

Phil Hill in the ATS at the 1963 U.S. Grand Prix. Hill's disastrous first post-Ferrari season was almost at an end. At Watkins Glen, he qualified 15th in the slow and unreliable ATS. And, as was the case in every race but one in that car, his race ended in a DNF. *Dave Friedman photo collection*

Bucknum was a product of the same West Coast sports car scene that had produced Hill, Gurney, and Ginther. Though it was widely reported in the foreign press that his experience was limited to production MGs and Austin Healeys, Bucknum had a number of overall wins in Max Balchowsky's ugly but fast *Ol' Yeller*, bettering, in the process, most of the lap records of his three famous predecessors. However, no one was more surprised than the young Californian when he was contacted and asked to drive Honda's first Grand Prix car.

In 1991, nine months before he succumbed to complications from diabetes, Ronnie Bucknum seemed to enjoy reminiscing about his Honda adventure. "They first approached me early in 1964, around Sebring. Someone telephoned me, said it was Mr. Okumoto from American Honda, and he said Honda was interested in having me test their Formula One car. And at first, I thought it was one of the guys kidding me. You know, 'Come on, [Hollywood Sports Car

driver Jim] Adams, you know you don't sound Japanese.' It's a miracle I didn't say something."

Bucknum was asked to meet Okumoto at a restaurant to discuss the matter. He went fully prepared to be stood up. "But there was a guy there, sure enough, and I ended up flying to Japan." At the airport to meet Bucknum (who'd been given a Honda cap to wear so he could be recognized), was the man responsible for Honda's Formula One effort, Yoshio Nakamura.

It had never been Nakamura's intention for Honda to build a chassis for Formula One, just engines. So in September 1963 he had made a quick trip to Europe to look for a suitable partner for his radical 1,500-cc transverse V-12. Two weeks later, Colin Chapman came to Japan and met with Nakamura and Soichiro Honda. The result was an agreement to put the Honda in Jimmy Clark's Lotus for 1964. In January 1964, much too late for the Japanese to make other arrangements, Chapman cabled Honda that the deal was off. Offended and angry, Nakamura wired Chapman back, "I read your telegram and Honda will go our own way," and immediately set out to design and build a Formula One chassis from scratch. Seven months later, well into the 1964 season, Honda's first Grand Prix car, the RA271 was taken to the Nürburgring to race for the first time.

Peter Revson preparing to practice his Lotus-BRM at the 1964 British Grand Prix. In his second World Championship Grand Prix, Revson qualified on the last row, more than five seconds behind pole- and race-winner Jimmy Clark. Still learning, the 25-year old cosmetics heir did not impress at Brands Hatch, retiring with differential problems on lap 43. In 1964, good results would come only in a couple of non-championship Grands Prix, but nine years later, a much improved Peter Revson would win the British Grand Prix. *Dave Friedman photo collection*

California sports car racer Ronnie Bucknum and Honda motor racing headman Yoshio Nakamura at the 1964 German Grand Prix. Bucknum seemed an odd choice to debut Honda's first Grand Prix car but no "name" driver was available. "Somebody in motor sports department suggest a young American who is capable, but not well known. I am interested, so I ask if he will come to Japan," recalled Nakamura. "I wait for him in airport. We don't know each other so I ask him to have a Honda cap on his head. And when this American guy with a Honda cap appear, I met Ronnie Bucknum." *Dave Friedman photo collection*

Open-wheel rookie Ronnie Bucknum is pushed out to practice in his still-numberless Honda RA271 at the Nürburgring in 1964. Not yet race-ready, Bucknum's Honda was granted an extra practice session just to complete the minimum laps necessary to run. The first real development of the Formula One Honda began with the start of the German Grand Prix. It was widely reported that Bucknum crashed four laps from the finish. Rarely, however, was the reason given: broken steering resulting from metal failure. *Dave Friedman photo collection*

"Originally," recalled Bucknum, "they wanted to run it at Spa. They were going to debut there, but they didn't quite have it together." Indeed, other than a short session at Willow Springs in California, there had been little testing and the car was nowhere near ready to compete anywhere, much less in a Grand Prix. "They missed two more races then, finally, the timing was the Nürburgring. You know, I didn't know any better, so I . . . well, I realized the obvious drawbacks, but I said, 'Sure, what the heck!'"

Ronnie Bucknum was game and he was skilled, but admittedly an unlikely candidate to race a highly unconventional and virtually untested Grand Prix car for the first time—at one of the most difficult and daunting racetracks in the world. And what's more, to do this with a team with no experience and very little grasp of the English language in a foreign country. "I'd never been to Europe. I'd never raced an open-wheel car. We went to a Formula One race at Brands Hatch, Nakamura, myself, and my wife, and saw that race, so the second Formula One race I saw was the one I was in." Typically, the young Californian just got on with it.

"We went a few days early, and you could rent Volkswagens and drive around the track," he recalled, "so that's what we did. My wife sat there knitting, and I drove. And the day before practice opened, Gurney took me around in a Mercedes sedan, which helped a great deal. We did two or three laps. You know, he just kind of talked to me." Good thing he did, as there were so many teething, not to mention communications problems, Bucknum got very little track time in the Honda. In fact, an extra practice session was granted by race organizers the evening before the Grand Prix to permit Bucknum to get the minimum five laps required to start. As if the young American needed evidence of how treacherous this 14-mile tree-lined course

Brash, bigger than life, and fiercely American, A. J. Foyt is undeniably one of the greatest drivers in history and a genuine American hero. Before he retired from the cockpit, Foyt won 12 major championships, was the first four-time Indy winner, and remains the only driver ever to win at Indianapolis, Daytona, and Le Mans. When the offer to drive a Formula One BRM came, Foyt was 29 and at the height of his career. While BRM was by no means the leading team in 1964, it is hard to imagine someone with Foyt's iron will and prodigious skills not making an impact in any kind of racing. Did he ever seriously consider driving in Grands Prix?

A. J. Foyt the Formula One Driver?

"No," says Super Tex. "I never cared about goin' Formula One racin' 'cause I was runnin' the sprints and the midgets and stock cars and everything here. And I always felt that the American people is what made A. J. Foyt, and I just wanted to race here. I was approached by a good team and offered big money, but I just blowed 'em off. Just forgot about it.

"You know, over there it's a different kind of racin'. Over there, you're like number one, two, three. So, say the number one driver is off a little bit, the number two driver, well, the way it used to be, you'd run second, regardless. And that to me isn't racin'. That's kind of like barnstorm racin'. And I don't believe in it. And like I said, my name was made here and the American people is what made A. J. Foyt. And that's one reason I'm happy to have American boys drivin' for me. I got a lot of friends of mine that's foreigners, but they're still foreigners."

Dan Gurney, who drove both with Foyt (Le Mans) and against him (Daytona) in sports cars, would like to have seen Foyt in Formula One. "You know, that was a time in the mid-sixties where Mario—mid-to late-sixties—where Mario and A. J. Foyt were locking horns. And A. J. was also a legitimate superstar at the time. He was not a roadrace specialist, but he was, nevertheless, a great racing driver. And a great character. You know, we used to call him Cassius, after Cassius Clay. You know, the mouth. And A. J. has always been a consummate politician, a real talk-the-shirt-off-your-back kind of a guy. It would have been very interesting." Indeed.

A. J. Foyt.
Indianapolis Motor Speedway

was, it was during this added session that the popular Dutch privateer, Carol de Beaufort, was fatally injured in a crash.

Bucknum did start, albeit from the back of the grid, his "qualifying lap" about one minute off the pace of Surtees's pole-winning Ferrari. To his credit, in the race, Bucknum got the Honda going and had passed a number of cars before the steering broke, fortunately, on a low-speed corner, ending his and Honda's first historic race.

So, why did Honda hire an inexperienced and virtually unknown driver? "Oh, I knew I wasn't a big star," said Bucknum. "Really, they had nothing to lose and everything to gain." Phil Hill agreed, "Sure, why would they want to get Stirling Moss or somebody to come and say it's a piece of . . . it can't get out of its own way. Whereas, with sort of an unknown guy, it doesn't matter what happens. If it's fast, all the better for them, you know. And if it doesn't go, 'Well, what did you expect, the poor fellow has never even been here.' The fact of the matter is I think he did well for them."

continued on page 125

Watkins Glen, 1964: Phil Hill in a works Cooper, obviously not assuaged by whatever he's being told about his balky, underpowered engine in practice. South African mechanic Hughie Franklin, with whom Hill did not get along, leans over the car on the right. For Hill, 1964 was a nightmare. The Cooper was never right, making it to the end of only three of nine World Championship races. Hill finished in the points once. "I was on the tail end of Cooper's last gasp. It was horrible," said Hill. "Twenty-five years later I saw John Cooper at Fangio's 80th birthday in London. And we had a nice little chat. I think he wondered why I was speaking to him. But, you know, time cures lots of things." *Dave Friedman photo collection*

COLOR GALLERY

OFFICIAL
PROGRAM, SCORE CARD & GUIDE
FOR THE
GRAND PRIZE
OF THE
AUTOMOBILE CLUB
OF AMERICA

INTERNATIONAL ROAD RACE
SAVANNAH GA. NOV. 26 1908

25 CENTS

While the Vanderbilt Cup races, particularly those before 1908 and the revivals in 1936 and 1937, were virtually Grands Prix, America's first true GP, the American Grand Prize, took place in Savannah, Georgia, in 1908. The hugely successful event occurred again in Savannah in 1910 and 1911. The American Grand Prize continued in Milwaukee in 1912 but never with the success or international prestige of the earlier races. It was held again in Santa Monica in 1914 and San Francisco in 1915. The final American Grand Prize was run in Santa Monica in 1916. *The Schroeder collection*

Harry Schell in a works Maserati 250F at the 1957 Grand Prix of Modena. Schell finished third in both heats and on aggregate in this non-championship Grand Prix near the Maserati factory. Sadly, this would be the last European appearance for the financially beleaguered Maserati team, which would field cars only once more, at the Moroccan Grand Prix five weeks later. *Jim Sitz*

America's first Formula One car, Lance Reventlow's Scarab, in its first preliminary test at an airport near Bakersfield, California, in the summer of 1959. As Chuck Daigh (left) and team leader Warren Olson (center) look on, Reventlow readies himself for the first run in his temporarily Offy-powered Grand Prix car. Note the tow rope and jury-rigged release at the top of the right, front coil spring. *Cheryl Reventlow Post collection*

Lance Reventlow leads Chuck Daigh in practice at Monaco. Note the low-speed understeer on Daigh's car, just one of the Scarab's serious handling vices. Barely finished in time and virtually untested, neither car would qualify at Monaco. *Dean Batchelor*

Dan Gurney in the BRM at Monaco in 1960. In his first two (non-championship) races for BRM, Gurney completed only nine laps in the new mid-engine car, though he did manage a front-row start in one of them. At Monaco, Gurney's BRM was never right, but he nursed it home to officially "finish" 10th, albeit 52 laps behind former teammate Phil Hill, whose third-place Ferrari was the last car to finish on the same lap as Moss in the winning Lotus 18. Nineteen-sixty would prove to be a long year for Gurney. *Dave Friedman photo collection*

Roger Penske in the "Zerex Special" Lotus-Climax at the non-championship 1962 Mexican Grand Prix. Penske would DNF at Mexico, his third and final foray into Formula One. "To be quite honest, it would've been very interesting if Roger Penske had driven a proper Formula One car," said Tyler Alexander. "He was good. Oh, yeah, he was bloody good. He really was. He's still good—just at something else." *Dave Friedman photo collection*

The undeniably beautiful, if ill-conceived, Scarabs of Reventlow (#28) and Daigh (#30) attract attention in the pits at Spa in 1960. Both cars would qualify, with Reventlow being the fastest. In fact, Daigh, testing Reventlow's car, was mistaken for the young American millionaire, who was admittedly never at ease on the extremely fast and dangerous Belgian course. Reventlow's engine gave way on lap one. Daigh's lasted only 15 laps longer, ending a spectacular if not lead-threatening race for the Californian. *Dean Batchelor*

Dan Gurney at Rouen in 1962 on his way to becoming the second American to win a Grand Prix. Gurney's victory at the 1962 French GP was the first and only Formula One World Championship win for Porsche, although one week later, Gurney would also win with a Porsche at the non-championship Solitude GP. *Road & Track*

American sports car ace Walt Hansgen at Mexico in a rented Lotus-Climax in 1962. Hansgen would suffer his second Formula One DNF at the first (and as yet, non-championship) Mexican Grand Prix after qualifying 13th. His best—and final—F1 result would come a year later in the U.S. Grand Prix, where he'd finish fifth. *Dave Friedman photo collection*

Ronnie Bucknum at Watkins Glen in 1964 in Honda's ill-handling, but extremely powerful, first Grand Prix car. After starting 10th and climbing as high as 7th in the Italian Grand Prix, Bucknum could qualify no better than 14th at the 1964 U.S. GP, the third open-wheel race in which he'd ever taken part. He got up to 10th before head gasket problems struck, causing yet another DNF. *Dave Friedman*

right: The first lap of the historic 1965 Grand Prix of Mexico, the final World Championship round of the 1500-cc engine formula. Richie Ginther leads already in the Honda. Jackie Stewart's BRM is second, followed by Mike Spence in the Lotus, then Gurney's #8 Brabham in fourth, at the apex of the hairpin turn. Two other Americans are visible, Ronnie Bucknum, 12th, in the other white Honda, and last away, Bob Bondurant, in the Reg Parnell Lotus-BRM. Ginther would go on to win his, Honda's, and Goodyear's first Grand Prix victory. Firestone tires were making their Formula One debut on Ricardo Rodriguez' #14 Ferrari, seen here in 8th place. *Pete Biro*

Bob Bondurant takes his Ferrari out in practice for the 1965 U.S. Grand Prix. During the race, rain and loose-fitting goggles forced one-handed driving, but he still finished ninth. It was, as it turned out, a one-off drive for Ferrari, given to Bondurant because of his role in the 1965 GT World Manufacturers Championship—won by Cobra at the expense of Ferrari. At Watkins Glen, Bondurant became the sixth of seven Americans (and the fifth American-born driver) who would drive a works Ferrari in Formula One. *Dean Batchelor*

114

Gurney, in his last race for Brabham, on the way to second place at Mexico. Gurney closed on Ginther near the end of the race, and the two Californians swapped fastest laps. Finally, that honor went to Gurney, but when the flag fell, he was just under three seconds behind the winning Honda. Ronnie Bucknum made it three Americans in the points with a fifth-place finish, his best in Formula One. *Pete Biro*

At last, the Eagle flies! Dan Gurney on the way to victory in the Eagle-Weslake in the 1967 Belgian Grand Prix. *Pete Biro*

Gurney after his historic win at Spa in 1967. Celebrating with him is noted photographer Bernard Cahier (left). No American had won a Grand Prix in an American car since Jimmy Murphy and the Duesenberg in 1921. And no American has since. *Pete Biro*

Mario Andretti in his first works Ferrari ride at the 1971 South African Grand Prix. Andretti scored his first World Championship victory at Kyalami. He would repeat three weeks later at the non-championship Questor Grand Prix, but after that, more than five years would pass before Andretti would again taste victory in Formula One. *Dave Friedman photo collection*

Shadow driver George Follmer at Watkins Glen, the last stop in his one-season Formula One stint. After a brilliant start, two points finishes in his first two World Championship Grands Prix and a podium finish in his third, Follmer's season was all downhill. A combination of car problems and conflicts with his teammate and effective team manager Jackie Oliver sealed his fate. "Oh, sure, I would liked to have stayed in it, but I wanted to be with a good team," explained Follmer. "I couldn't continue with Shadow because of the problem with Oliver, and I was 39 years old. You know, the Europeans like everybody to be 20 years old. I didn't fit that niche. Too old, too late." *Pete Biro*

Peter Revson, blessed with good looks and wealth, came to be regarded as a dedicated and skillfull racer in Can-Am cars, at Indianapolis, and finally, in Formula One. Tragically, at the height of his career, Revson would die testing a Shadow-Cosworth at Kyalami early in 1974. He had just turned 35. *Pete Biro*

Andretti and Colin Chapman, one of the most successful pairings in Formula One. But for a spate of unreliable engines in 1977, Andretti might have scored two World Championships in Chapman's brilliant Lotus ground-effect cars. *Pete Biro*

Peter Revson at Monaco in the McLaren-Cosworth in 1973. He would finish fifth on the winding streets of Monaco but before the year was over would score two wins and become America's next real Formula One threat. *Pete Biro*

Mario Andretti in the ill-fated Parnelli-Cosworth fielded by Parnelli Jones and partner Vel Miletich at the 1976 U.S. Grand Prix West. Unbeknownst to Andretti, Long Beach (where he DNF'd) would be his final race in the Parnelli—a circumstance that would cause him to cast his lot with Lotus headman Colin Chapman. *Pete Biro*

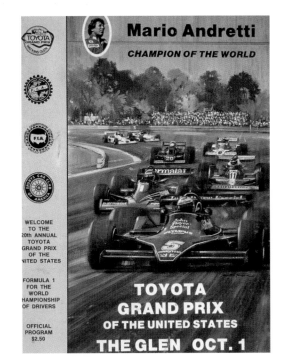

Andretti, Champion of the World. *Mike Martin collection*

Andretti on the grid at Long Beach in the Alfa Romeo. In the 1981 U.S. Grand Prix West, Andretti finished fourth, his only points finish that year. Andretti's Formula One career was nearing an end, and 1981 would be the last full season he would contend. *Pete Biro*

Mario Andretti at Monaco in 1978. Andretti would finish 11th at Monaco, but would dominate Formula One in the Lotus in 1978, winning six Grands Prix to become America's second World Champion. *Pete Biro*

Twenty-two-year old Eddie Cheever in an Osella-Cosworth at the 1980 U.S. Grand Prix West. Long Beach was the third Formula One race (and one of many DNFs that year) for Cheever, who would go on to start more Grands Prix (130) than any other American. *Dave Friedman*

Michael Andretti waits to qualify. Because of his unfamiliarity with the tracks, new rules limiting practice, and nagging technical problems with the McLaren, qualifying was unusually nerve-wracking for Andretti. *Terry Griffin*

Michael Andretti's McLaren-Ford at the Hungarian Grand Prix. Hungary was one of several races where Andretti put in a fine drive but, ultimately, DNF'd because of electrical or mechanical failures. After Hungary, Ron Dennis announced that Häkkinen would sit in for Andretti for three races in order to be evaluated. It was clear to Andretti that he was finished at McLaren. *Paul-Henri Cahier*

Danny Sullivan on his way to eighth place in his second Grand Prix at Long Beach in 1983. Rather than attempt another year in Formula One with the naturally-aspirated, Cosworth-powered Tyrrell (in the turbo era), Sullivan opted to go Indy car racing at home, where he would win the Indianapolis 500 in 1985. *Dave Friedman*

Michael Andretti's finest hour in Formula One. Last after stopping in the pits for new tires after a brake-problem-induced spin (the exact same thing put teammate Senna out), Andretti carved his way through the field at Monza to finish third in his final race for McLaren. *Paul-Henri Cahier*

Continued from page 107

Bucknum and Honda skipped the Austrian Grand Prix. Gurney and Hill might as well have. After leading for nearly half the race and setting fastest lap, Gurney went out with a broken front suspension. Phil Hill crashed, managing to scramble out of his Cooper as it burst into flames. Once again, Ginther brought the BRM home second.

For Gurney, Monza was much the same story—front row, vying with Surtees for the lead until a misfire dropped him eventually to 10th, three places ahead of Revson in his first World Championship Grand Prix finish. Steady Ginther held on for fourth. Honda was back and this time, Bucknum qualified a respectable 10th, with the same time as Ginther's BRM. To everyone's astonishment, Bucknum worked the shrieking V-12 car all the way up to fifth in the race before brake problems forced him to retire on lap 12. (Those who read the entry list for the 1964 U.S. Grand Prix at Watkins Glen must have raised their eyebrows when they came to the driver officially listed in BRM's third car, one Anthony Joseph Foyt. No, it didn't happen, but talks between Foyt, who had just won his second Indianapolis 500, and BRM apparently went far enough for BRM to enter Foyt at Watkins Glen and in the Mexican Grand Prix, as well. If only!)

At Watkins Glen, in what had become a pattern, Gurney soon pushed his way toward the front after a poor start, but eventually dropped out with falling oil pressure. Ginther snagged another fourth, one ahead of Walt Hansgen, who finally finished a Grand Prix, and in the points. Bucknum's Honda never did run right, finally retiring with persistent overheating. The only other Yanks fared even worse. Hap Sharp was running at the end, but too far back to be classified. A by-now thoroughly disgusted Phil Hill was out with ignition problems after only five laps.

It was a surprise to see Hill in the Cooper three weeks later at the season-ending Mexican Grand Prix. "Well," he shrugged, "they couldn't find anyone else to drive the damn thing!" For once, Gurney's luck was good—and Clark's, bad. The Scotsman led easily until his engine seized on the last lap, leaving the victory to Gurney, who became only the second American to win three World Championship Grands Prix. Phil Hill, the man whose record Gurney equaled, did not finish the race, his last in Formula One.

Not that Hill didn't have at least one interesting offer for the 1965 season.

Having broken the ice with three exploratory races in 1964, Honda wanted a front-line driver with experience, a veteran who could develop the chassis over the winter and hopefully win races the following season—the last for the 1,500-cc formula. Honda wanted Phil Hill to team with its driver of the future, Ronnie Bucknum.

"Yeah, they approached me," said Hill, "but, God, even by the time that 1964 season was half over, I had had it. I'd been on the tail end of Cooper's last gasp and the beginnings of ATS, both of which were horrible, and I just didn't really need another year of it. Of course," the former World Champion added with a smile, "you know, in retrospect, I would have loved it. There's nothing like a good car to get you going."

After Hill took himself out of the picture, Honda, at Bucknum's suggestion, approached Richie Ginther, a friend from California racing and a damn good chassis man. At BRM, Ginther had once again become frustrated with playing second fiddle to another driver. He had seen the Honda's raw power—from behind—at Monza and gladly left BRM for the new Japanese team. Ostensibly, there was to be no number-one or number-two at Honda, but from the first winter test sessions in Japan, Ginther began to assert himself and to take control. He also worked magic on the Honda chassis. Still, in spite of the progress made, and even more horsepower from the Honda V-12, it would take a good part of the 1965 season to make the car competitive.

Reliability problems continued to plague Gurney's Brabham in 1965, particularly in the first several races. It began at South Africa, where Gurney's car was shod with Goodyear's first "purpose-built" Grand Prix tires. But, if a DNF in this opening GP was a harbinger of Gurney's season, so, too, was Jimmy Clark's flag-to-flag victory. Unlike the previous year, when Clark's winning ways were stopped more by the fragility of his Lotus than the Ferrari of 1964 World Champion John Surtees, Clark and the Lotus were virtually unstoppable in 1965—even at Indy, where the popular Scotsman finally got the victory he so deserved. Third in the 500 that year was a 25-year-old rookie phenom named Mario Andretti. He'd seen his first Grand Prix in Italy at 14—and had dreamed about racing in Formula One ever since.

"Yeah," said Andretti, "I made it my business to get to know Colin Chapman at the Speedway that year. I was doing pretty well right off, actually. I was running quick in practice, and he kind of took notice. And it was easy for me to approach him then, and he was very warm. When I expressed a desire to do Formula One, you know, he really perked up. He told me

Richie Ginther in the BRM at Watkins Glen. Ginther was the highest-place American at the 1964 U.S. Grand Prix, finishing fourth, his best result since runner-up finishes at Monaco and Austria. He would end up fourth in the World Championship in 1964, but thanks in part to a recommendation by fellow Californian Ronnie Bucknum, Ginther would finally achieve a Formula One win almost exactly a year later with Honda. *Dave Friedman photo collection*

125

With Watkins Glen campers in the background, ace American sports car driver Walt Hansgen wheels his rented Team Lotus car to fifth place, about 30 seconds behind Ginther, in his only F1 finish in four tries. *Dave Friedman photo collection*

clearly, he says, 'Mario, whenever you decide,' he says, 'just give me a call.'" A few years later, Andretti would do just that.

In 1964, Gurney's Brabham had been a real threat to Jimmy Clark in the Lotus. Now, the gap between them had widened, and Gurney found himself scrambling even to match the BRMs of Hill and Ginther's replacement, Jackie Stewart. Only once in 1965 would Gurney start from the front row. Like Clark, Gurney also skipped Monaco to race in the 500, but he would

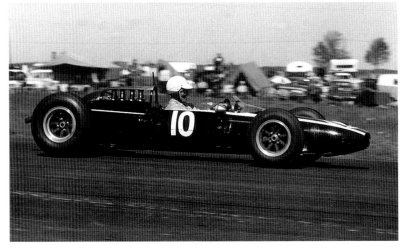

Phil Hill in his next-to-last Formula One start, in the 1964 U.S. Grand Prix. Hill's Cooper-Climax wasn't around long. Ignition problems sidelined America's first World Champion after only four laps. *Dave Friedman photo collection*

Dan Gurney at the 1964 Mexican Grand Prix. If there'd been any doubt before, Gurney's second year with Brabham established him as one of the fastest men in Formula One. In 1964 World Championship Grands Prix, while he still DNF'd on four occasions, Gurney managed to put the Brabham on the front row eight times, won two Grands Prix (including Mexico), and had the fastest race lap twice. *Dave Friedman photo collection*

score no Championship points before a sixth at Silverstone, midway through the year. After that, the Brabham was sound, if not blindingly fast, and Gurney finished third at Holland, Germany, and Italy, ending the season with seconds at the U.S. and Mexican GPs for fourth in the World Championship.

Masten Gregory, who had finished sixth in the non-points Syracuse GP in his only start in 1964, signed on to drive the BRM of Centro Sud again in 1965. But it was a pale effort for this pioneer, character, and one-time contender. His only classified finish was an eighth at the Nürburgring. Gregory's last Grand Prix was Monza, a DNF.

Best Laid Plans

Encouraged by the showing at Monza, Bucknum couldn't wait to work with Ginther in the off-season. "I just thought it would be ideal. You know, Richie had done a lot of development driving for Ferrari and was pretty well known for that. And I was the first to concede that I needed somebody, because I had no benchmark to go by. Nothing." Whatever Bucknum had anticipated, the plan began to unravel in Japan.

"Richie just took over the testing. I hardly got to drive at all. Eventually, I got a little bitchy about it and finally, at the very end, they put me in. And that set of laps is when the steering broke. Again." It was the same overstressed part that had given away in the German Grand Prix, inexplicably, never changed. This time, it happened at speed and the Honda flew off the road and slammed into a wall. Bucknum suffered painful leg injuries, including multiple fractures in one foot, but he refused to be taken away. "I made them carry me over to the wreckage and I got that piece out and sure

Two happy drivers on the podium at the 1964 Grand Prix of Mexico. With his victory in Mexico, Dan Gurney has become the second American to win three World Championship Grands Prix. Second-place finisher John Surtees clinched the World Championship, becoming the first—and only—man to win World Championships on two wheels and four wheels. *Dave Friedman photo collection*

Ronnie Bucknum in the Honda at Watkins Glen in 1965. The Honda was definitely improved, thanks to Richie Ginther's development. But Bucknum's lack of testing, due in part to Ginther, then an off-season crash in Japan (the same steering part failed as in a previous crash) put him at a disadvantage. During the season, he was overshadowed by and ultimately pushed aside by his admittedly more experienced teammate. At the U.S. Grand Prix, Bucknum finished for the first time in 1965 (13th). "It was missing a cylinder or two most of the time. To tell the truth, in the rain, it ran better on 11 cylinders than 12. It was easier to control," said Bucknum. *Dave Friedman photo collection*

enough, it had fatigued, just like at the Nürburgring. So, I had the part in my hand and I said, 'I don't want any excuses,' and I gave it to Richie to give to Nakamura."

By the time Bucknum recovered from surgery, the winter sessions were virtually over. Still, he couldn't help being enthusiastic about Ginther's improvements to the car. "He developed the car to where it was going twelve to fifteen seconds quicker. So, we figured, 'Boy, have we got a winner on our hands!'" Honda passed on the South African GP, but at Monte Carlo, the team got a rude shock. Bucknum and Ginther barely made the field, next to last and last, respectively. Neither finished. Obviously, there was work yet to do. At Spa, Ginther qualified fourth, Bucknum, 11th. It was his first time at the notoriously fast and dangerous track.

Richie Ginther's Honda at the 1965 U.S. Grand Prix. Ginther qualified well, starting third, but spun early on. By this time, the Honda was putting out more horsepower than any engine in Formula One. Not that it did much good at Watkins Glen in the rain. Ginther struggled to finish seventh, two laps behind Graham Hill's winning BRM. *Dave Friedman photo collection*

Bob Bondurant making his Formula One debut in a Ferrari at Watkins Glen in 1965. Bondurant ran as high as seventh before the rains came down and finished the race, ending up ninth. *Dave Friedman photo collection*

Ginther on the way to winning the 1965 Grand Prix of Mexico. Driving the car qualified by teammate Ronnie Bucknum, Ginther led flag to flag. "I had changed setups at Watkins Glen because of the rain," explained Bucknum. "I changed the sparkplugs setup. It didn't particularly help at the Glen, but when they unloaded that car down in Mexico, it just screamed." *Pete Biro*

Second-place finisher Dan Gurney in the Brabham has just passed Mike Spence's Lotus and now goes after Ginther. While he did gain ground and set the fastest lap of the race, Gurney could get no closer than three seconds to the flying Honda. *Dave Friedman photo collection*

"I spent a couple of days going around as fast as I could in a rented Chevy Bel Air to try and learn the track," Bucknum remembered, "but it was nothing like the Formula One car." To make matters worse, a heavy rain fell during the race, flooding the high-speed track with treacherous puddles. Bucknum's car blew on lap 10—to his great relief. "Yeah, it was a blessing in disguise," he admitted. "God, it was awful! The Honda was just diabolical, steering all over the world. And every time you'd hit a puddle, it would just go sideways. It was just a nightmare." In a heroic drive, Ginther held on to finish sixth, scoring Honda's first Formula One World Championship point.

Ginther was anything but satisfied. This was to be his year to win, to show he was no backup driver, yet, the car was still not ready. An agonizing marital split only intensified his increasingly desperate need to succeed. Old friends had already begun to notice a change. With each failure, Ginther was becoming more impatient, more demanding, more determined—even ruthless. At the difficult Clermont-Ferrand circuit, Bucknum struggled with a balky engine in practice for the French Grand Prix. Nakamura told him to take out the training car and get some laps in while they sorted out his car. Ginther was waiting for Bucknum when he came in.

"He says, 'Don't *ever* get in my backup car.' And I says, 'Well, what do you mean, this is the trainer. And the electrics went out on my car and I was just trying to get some seat time in.' And he says, 'From now on, there's *my* car and my *backup* car. You've got your own car and you stay in it.' And I said, 'Okay.'" After neither car finished at the French Grand Prix, Ginther convinced Honda team officials that they needed to concentrate on one car, not two, for now. Bucknum would have no ride for the next three races.

Richie Ginther was a little guy, wirey and freckle-faced. He was a clever and meticulous mechanic, who was confident enough to try new ideas. That helped him as both a tester and a driver. Most of all, he was quick. Quicker in fact than all but the very best. Trouble was, second-best to anyone wasn't good enough for Richie Ginther, particularly when he began to emerge from the shadow of his heroes. It was that insistence on perfection that made the diminutive Ginther so formidable—and damn quick.

Richie Ginther

8/5/1930 to 9/20/1989

Paul Richard "Richie" Ginther was born the youngest of three children in Los Angeles and raised in Santa Monica. Ginther was already into hot-rodding his own 1932 Chevy, when he met a friend of his older brother who had real knowledge about fast cars and racing. Taken by Ginther's little brother-like enthusiasm and willingness to work, Phil Hill became his friend and sort of mentor—a characterization that both would probably dispute for different reasons.

In 1951, Ginther entered his first competition, a 10-lap preliminary race at Pebble Beach, where he was to pit for Hill during the main event. In the short race, Ginther drove a hybrid Ford-engined MG TC to third behind Hill's Alfa and another Ford Special. The Korean War intervened and Ginther spent two years as an airplane mechanic, but afterwards, renewed his friendship with Hill, who was now racing other people's Ferraris. Ginther rode with Hill in a Ferrari in the Carrera Panamericana in 1953 and 1954. The first year they crashed, but in 1954 finished an impressive second behind Maglioli's works Ferrari.

Ginther's own driving career resumed at Bakersfield in 1955. He drove an Austin Healey for the dealership that employed him as a mechanic. After work, Ginther would help Phil Hill prepare the Ferraris he raced for VW/Porsche dealer John von Neumann. In gratitude, von Neumann gave Ginther a Porsche Spyder to race at Santa Barbara in September 1955. It was the break Ginther needed, and the beginning of a long and fruitful relationship with von Neumann, for whom Ginther would go to work. In that first race with the Porsche Spyder, Ginther finished third to West Coast standout Ken Miles and von Neumann. Soon, Miles was the only driver to outpace Ginther, who began to get rides in bigger cars, as well. With von Neumann's Ferraris in particular, Ginther became a force in West Coast events, especially when Hill, Shelby, Gregory, and Gurney began to spend more time in Europe.

In 1957, with Howard Hively, Ginther won his class in a two-liter Ferrari at Sebring. In his second international race, at Le Mans, Ginther's Ferrari was running second in class when it went out. His most important victory to that date came later the same year at Riverside Raceway. There, in John Edgar's big 4.9 Ferrari, Ginther dueled with Bob Drake in another 4.9 and Chuck Daigh in the Troutman-Barnes Special, outlasting both to win Riverside's inaugural event. John von Neumann became western distributor for Ferrari, and as general manager of that business, Ginther was no stranger at the factory. With a little help from talent scout Luigi Chinetti and Phil Hill, Ginther's on-track achievements finally resulted in a works ride in the 1960 1,000-Kilometers of Argentina, co-driving with von Trips. They finished second, and after a brief test in an F1 car, Ginther was offered a contract to be Ferrari's development driver, and importantly, to drive in three Grands Prix in 1960.

Ginther contributed greatly to the development of Ferrari's new mid-engine F1 car, in the process gaining valuable seat time. He also made engineer Carlo Chiti's midengine Tipo 246 sports car handle with a clever idea from his airplane mechanic days, mounting a vertical "trim tab" across the back to stabilize the car at high speed. It was the first use of the now almost universal rear spoiler.

Ginther's finest hour at Ferrari came at Monaco in 1961 when he put on a tremendous charge from way back to almost catch winner Moss. Ironically, Ginther came to regard this as more of a sore point than a matter of pride. Like many who drove for the Commendatore, Ginther felt underappreciated. But

Richie Ginther.
Dave Friedman photo collection

even years later, he claimed that he had been held back by Phil Hill at Monaco in 1961.

Unfortunately, it wasn't much different at BRM. Despite some great results, particularly in 1963, when he finished second in the World Championship, he was once again in the shadow of a teammate named Hill. It is no wonder that, given the opportunity, Ginther unabashedly seized the opportunity to be a number-one at Honda. There, his gifts were finally rewarded with a Grand Prix victory. Though Ginther notched only one win, a glance at his record is more revealing. In 68 Grands Prix (52 of them World Championship events), Ginther started from the front row 14 times. He finished second nine times, in the top three 16 times, and in the points 32 times. This against the likes of Moss, Clark, Gurney, Phil Hill, Brabham, Surtees, Hulme, Gregory, McLaren, and Graham Hill.

After retiring from driving, Ginther stayed involved in racing for several years, managing the efforts of others. But in the mid-1970s, he virtually dropped from sight for a decade. During this period, Ginther lived in a motor home and traveled extensively, eventually settling in Mexico. In 1989, Ginther attended a track reunion with his old Grand Prix car at Donington on the occasion of the 40th anniversary of BRM. He was not in good health but typically, drove hard—and fast—enough to exhaust himself, and had to be assisted out of the car. Days later, while vacationing in France, Richie Ginther's great heart gave out. He was 59.

Richie Ginther, winner of the 1965 Grand Prix of Mexico. Ginther's historic victory was the first for him, for Honda, and for Goodyear. Firestone tires, on Pedro Rodriguez's Ferrari, made their first Formula One appearance in the same race. With Ginther first, Gurney second, and Bucknum fifth, three Americans finished in the points at the last Grand Prix of the 1.5-liter formula. *Dave Friedman photo collection*

As if to prove his point, at Silverstone Ginther gave Honda its first front-row start, qualifying third, and leading for part of lap one, before Clark, Hill, and Surtees pushed by. But Ginther stayed with the leaders, passing Surtees back into third again, before ignition problems caused a long stop and finally retired the Honda. Ginther again qualified third at Zandvoort and, despite a spin, finished sixth. Progress was being made.

Honda skipped the German Grand Prix to prepare for Monza, where, ironically, Bucknum returned to qualify faster (6th) than Ginther (17th). Neither finished, but at Watkins Glen, Ginther got back on track, qualifying third behind Hill and Clark, with Bucknum several rows back. A first-lap spin dropped him back to eighth and once again, the Honda proved a handful when rain began to fall. Ginther finished a grim 7th. Bucknum's car never did run right and he ended a frustrating day 13th, many laps behind.

Watkins Glen saw another American driver make a memorable, if not particularly successful, Formula One debut. Ferrari's number one, John Surtees, had been injured in a Can-Am race. In his place at Watkins Glen was none other than Cobra driver Bob Bondurant. After vanquishing Ferrari earlier in international GT racing, he was now trying out for the Ferrari team in his first Grand Prix. Bondurant qualified on the seventh row, just behind Bucknum. He was moving up through the field when the rains came. "An oddball thing happened," Bondurant recalled. "We wore goggles then, and I was wearing a pair of goggles I'd had for years. The straps started to stretch and they blew down on my face going down the straightaway. Well, I couldn't see! I had another pair in my helmet bag, but I figured I'd lose too much time going in the pits, you know, trying to communicate to the Italians where they were. But,

I found if I turned sideways when I went down the straightaway, it'd blow the goggles back up on my face. So I'd hold them up with my hand and then, when I'd go to shift, I'd turn my head, shift, then grab them with my other hand. I drove most the race with one hand, like that. Ended up finishing ninth!"

Ferrari didn't ask him back, but Bondurant's second Formula One ride came three weeks later at Mexico—by accident. He'd gone down just to watch, with helmet bag in hand, of course, and ended up driving the Lotus-BRM intended for Innes Ireland, who had been fired on the spot for showing up late at the track. Bondurant lasted only 30 laps before a tie-rod broke, but the historic 1965 Mexican Grand Prix, the last for 1,500-cc engines, would find three Americans in the top five places.

No More Second Best

For the first time that season, Gurney put his Brabham on the front row. In Mexico City's high altitude, the fuel-injected Hondas were fast right off the transporter. Ginther qualified third and Bucknum 10th, though in the last practice session, Bucknum suddenly found some new speed, actually passed his teammate, then simply powered away from him. When the cars were lined up on the grid the next day, the numbers had been switched and Ginther sat in Bucknum's car.

"We switched cars a lot," said Bucknum with a smile. "He used to come and take mine at the last minute. And in all fairness, he should've had that car on that day, because he was the quickest of the two of us and my car was clearly faster. On that last lap of practice, I just drove by him, just drove off down the main straight and left him." But, when it happened, Bucknum was less than thrilled with the switch, or at least, when and how it was made—at the team breakfast on raceday morning.

"At breakfast, with all the mechanics around, Richie says, 'Boy, I've been up all night,' he says, 'I've got a hell of a cold—cough—and I don't know if I'm going to be able to make it through the whole race—cough—so, Bucknum's car has a lot of miles on it and I'd rather take it and give Bucknum the fresher car, cause he's feeling okay and it would give him a chance to race.'" After a frustrating season with Ginther, it was the last straw. "I got really hot," Bucknum laughed, "and I says, 'Oh, don't pull that shit on me!' But, that's the excuse that was used and that's what happened. They took my car and put it up in the second row and gave me his."

Ginther made the most of it, with a perfect start that shot him to the front immediately. He would never relinquish the lead, despite the determined efforts of second-place Dan Gurney. Finally, Richie Ginther had his victory, a well-earned win that was the first for Honda and Goodyear and, as it turned out, the only one of his Formula One career. Ronnie Bucknum also scored points, with a fifth-place finish, his best effort in Grand Prix racing.

The 1965 Mexican Grand Prix was pivotal in the history of Formula One. It marked the end of an important era, that of the high-revving, 1.5-liter, multicylinder, rear-engine Formula One cars. It was an era that saw the first American Grand Prix World Champion, an era in which American drivers won all-important first Grand Prix victories for Porsche, Brabham, and Honda, and one in which two famous American industrial giants, Goodyear and Firestone (on Rodriguez's Ferrari for the first time at Mexico City) introduced their technology to Formula One. Every end is a beginning, though, and the next era of Grand Prix racing would see even greater American involvement.

GOING FOR THE GOLD

1966–1968

The 1966 season ushered in a new era in Formula One racing. Gone were the delicate, if highly developed, 1,500-cc engines of the previous five years, replaced by a new generation of more powerful 3.0-liter engines. Formula One also benefited, both in terms of technology and financial support, from the struggle for supremacy by American tire companies Goodyear and Firestone, the latter committing to a full Grand Prix program for the first time in 1966.

Unquestionably, the fastest American in Formula One in the early- to mid-1960s had been Dan Gurney. Always a threat, Gurney had been deprived of more than his three victories only by poor luck and lack of reliability in the cars he drove. No one knew the frustrations of developing a new car more than Gurney after his stints with BRM, Porsche, and Brabham. Yet, more than anything else, what the Californian wanted to do was to field his own car, an American Grand Prix car.

"Grand Prix racing included that Olympic element," Gurney said later, "You know, that you were racing on behalf of your country. And that always meant a little bit extra to me."

Gurney's other goal was to win America's greatest race, the Indianapolis 500. To achieve both aims , Gurney enlisted Goodyear's support in 1965 and teamed with Carroll Shelby to form All American Racers. Lotus engineer Len Terry was hired, and the sleek Eagle race car, with its distinctive bill-like nose, was the result. Terry penned two versions, one for Indy and a slightly lighter model for F1. The latter was to be powered by a 3.0-liter V-12 designed by ex-BRM engineer Aubrey Woods and manufactured in England by Weslake. Though it was obvious the V-12 wouldn't be completed when the new season opened, Gurney was committed to the Eagle and left Brabham's employ at the end of 1965—ready or not. "I just felt it was an opportunity, as slim as the chances were, that I had to take," he explained.

Gurney and the Eagle missed Monaco, the first World Championship Grand Prix run under the new formula. Honda was also late with its new car, so Richie Ginther signed on to drive with Cooper, now powered by V-12 Maserati engines. At Monaco, Ginther ran as high as fourth, but, like most of the field, did not finish. The only other American in the race, Bob Bondurant, ended up fourth—and last to be classified—in an independent, ex-works 2.0-liter BRM, that concern's complicated new H-16 still being under development.

Two engines with American roots appeared at Monaco, one of them making its Formula One debut. Bruce McLaren had mounted a modified four-cam Indy Ford in the back of his new car. The experiment was not a success. The ill-suited Ford failed two out of the three times it was used (at Monaco and the Mexican GP). On the one occasion McLaren managed to make it last, appropriately, at the U.S. Grand Prix, he finished fifth, scoring the first—and so far, only, Grand Prix World Championship points by a truly American-made engine.

Jack Brabham also brought an American, or more accurately, American-derived engine to Monaco. In early 1965, engineers Frank Hallam and Phil Irving (of Vincent and Velocette motorcycle fame) had taken existing all-aluminum Oldsmobile F85 V-8 blocks and crafted single overhead cam heads for them, making a light and quite efficient 2.5-liter "Repco" engine for

Richie Ginther in the three-liter Honda in the 1966 Mexican Grand Prix. Once again, Ginther nailed the start and led lap one. But the Honda was more powerful than agile, and Ginther had to settle for fourth in what would be his final World Championship Grand Prix. *Pete Biro*

135

Dan Gurney's new Eagle at the Le Source hairpin in the rain at Spa. While way down on power due to the stop-gap use of a four-cylinder Climax engine, Gurney survived the first-lap carnage in which no less than seven cars were eliminated and an unplanned stop for, uh, "loss of fluids," to finish seventh (unclassified) on the Eagle's debut, in the 1966 Belgian Grand Prix. A week later, in the French Grand Prix, Gurney would finish fifth to score the first World Championship points for an American car. *Pete Biro*

Look closely. It's Phil Hill practicing the four-cylinder Eagle at Monza in 1966. Gurney had the untested Weslake V-12 in an Eagle for the first time at the Italian Grand Prix, but entered the four-cylinder just in case. Though he was by no means through racing, it would be the last time the American champion Hill would ever drive a Formula One car on a Grand Prix weekend. Appropriately, it was at Monza, where Hill had become the first American to win a Formula One race and where he had won again in 1961, to clinch the World Championship. *Robert Young collection*

The AAR team at Mexico in 1966, left to right, Mike Daniel, technical director, Weslake & Co.; Bill Dunne, AAR team manager; Mike Lowman, mechanic; Joaquin Ramirez, mechanic; Tim Wall, AAR chief mechanic; and seated, Carroll Shelby, vice-president, AAR. In the cars are Gurney in the 12-cylinder No. 15 car and Bob Bondurant in the No. 16 four-cylinder car. Gurney decided to switch cars for the race, a wise choice as he finished fifth. The V-12 quit after 24 laps, ending Bob Bondurant's short Grand Prix career with a DNF. *Pete Biro*

Brabham's cars in the Australia-New Zealand Tasman series. Brabham had debuted a 3.0-liter version of this compact and reliable engine in pre-season races at South Africa, Syracuse, and Silverstone, where he won the International Trophy GP. Though gearbox troubles sidelined him at Monaco, the American-Australian hybrid Repco V-8 would emerge as the dominant engine of 1966, powering Jack Brabham to wins at the French, British, Dutch, and German GPs, as well as both Drivers and Constructors World Championship.

The Belgian Grand Prix marked the first appearance of Dan Gurney's beautiful blue-and-white Eagle, albeit with an old Climax four-cylinder punched out to 2.7 liters (the Weslake was still not ready). Ginther, in the Cooper-Maserati, would be the only American to finish (fifth) the rain and accident-marred race—or at least, to be classified. Many cars spun on the first lap, among them the BRMs of Stewart, Hill, and Bondurant, whose Team Chamaco Collect BRM was repainted to look like the nonstarting McLaren's car for the movie *Grand Prix*. Though Bondurant's car landed upside down, he wasn't hurt, but Stewart, who'd also flipped, was trapped underneath and being soaked with leaking fuel until Hill and Bondurant managed to free him.

Gurney had trouble in the Eagle, too, but of a different kind. After suffering for an hour from his Climax four-cylinder's throbbing vibration, the lanky American was forced to make an unscheduled stop out on the rain-swept course. Leaving his engine to idle, Gurney scrambled out of the car,

Spa, Belgium, 1967: Jimmy Clark's Lotus leads up the hill from Eau Rouge on lap one. In hot pursuit are Rindt's Cooper, Stewart in the BRM, and the Ferrari of Michael Parkes, who would suffer a career-ending crash before the end of the lap. Caught out of gear when the flag fell, Gurney's Eagle lies ninth. *Pete Biro*

quickly wedged a rock under one tire, and stepped gingerly to the roadside—to relieve himself!

Gurney laughed when recalling the episode, "You'd think you'd be able to wet your pants, right? Could not do it. Absolutely could not do it. No way. So, the next thing that happens is you say, 'If I don't stop, something's gonna burst.' I mean, you're talking about a lot of pain. So, you stop. Finished seventh, though," he added with a grin.

Three weeks later, at Reims, Gurney drove the Eagle-Climax—nonstop—to fifth, scoring the first World Championship points ever by an American Formula One car. Gurney soldiered on with the underpowered old Climax for the next three races, even managing to put the Eagle on the front row with a bravura performance at Brands Hatch. "That four-cylinder lasted a lot longer than we thought it would and, in fact, ran pretty damn decently." But, though running as high as second at Brands (behind winner Brabham) and fourth at Zandvoort and the Nürburgring, Gurney was able to finish only at the German Grand Prix (seventh), even then, slowed by mechanical problems. Bondurant ran only at Brands Hatch, hanging on for ninth in the 2.0-liter BRM.

At Monza, the 12-cylinder was finally installed in a new Eagle. "The Weslakes weren't happy with the engine performance on the dyno, but they felt we should put the darn thing in the car anyway so that we'd learn something." Gurney never did get the car sorted out, retiring after only eight laps. "It didn't really do particularly well, but we got an attempt under our belt with the 12-cylinder."

Also making its first appearance of the year was Honda's new 3.0-liter car. Though the overweight chassis was obviously not right yet, Ginther pushed the powerful—and deafening—V-12 car up to second place before a

Gurney's Eagle flies through Eau Rouge. By lap three, Gurney caught and passed third-place Rindt's Cooper and set his sights on Stewart. Relentlessly, he closed the gap until the 10th lap, when he was on the BRM's gearbox. "Very few drivers were prepared to drive all-out at Spa," said Jackie Stewart. "Remember, we're talking about the old Spa. Not a lot of guard rails or barriers, just a narrow, winding strip of macadam through the Ardennes forest, and very, very fast. But Dan Gurney was always quick there." *Dave Friedman photo collection*

tire shredded at over 100 miles per hour in the Curva Grande, hurling the racer off course into a tree. Ginther was lucky to emerge with just a broken collarbone, as the Honda was destroyed. Bondurant was the only American to finish (seventh) three laps off the pace, in his last ride in the BRM.

"They weren't taking care of my car very well," remembered Bondurant. "I took a handful of wrenches and went around the car and found a lot of nuts and bolts half a turn loose and things. And I thought about it after the race and said, 'Well, my life's more valuable,' and I quit."

There was one American triumph at Monza. Ludovico Scarfiotti's winning Ferrari was shod with Firestone tires, giving that company its first victory in Formula One. The tire war was heating up and Dunlop, who had dominated Grand Prix racing since 1958 (winning 67 consecutive races before bowing to Ginther's Goodyear-equipped Honda at Mexico in 1965), was now losing ground to the two American tire companies. At Monza, only one car, Siffert's Cooper-Maserati, was on Dunlops. By the end of 1966, Goodyear tires had won five Grands Prix (all on Brabham's cars); Firestone, three; and Dunlop, two.

Gurney's problems continued at Watkins Glen. He retired the V-12 car on lap 14 with an overheating engine. Bondurant, driving the old Eagle-Climax, had been disqualified eight laps earlier for "outside assistance" after driving off-course to avoid an accident. In all, it was a bad day for American drivers, as neither the still-aching Ginther nor Ronnie Bucknum, making his first start in 1966 in the other Honda, finished—the former out with gearbox troubles, the latter with engine.

At Mexico, the high altitude proved less of a problem for the four-cylinder Climax, so Gurney and Bondurant switched cars. Sure enough, fuel-feed problems sidelined the V-12 after only a third of the race had been run. Gurney finished fifth with the old car. Ginther, duplicating his start the year before, rocketed into the lead from the second row. He led the first lap but was unable to keep the ill-handling, if powerful, Honda at the front, eventually finishing fourth after setting the fastest lap. An electrical short and resulting fire dropped Bucknum back to eighth in what was to be his last Grand Prix. Mexico was also the last Formula One race for Bondurant—and, as it turned out, the last World Championship race for Richie Ginther.

The diminutive Californian left Honda after Mexico and signed on with Gurney to drive the second Eagle in 1967. In January, at the season-opening South African GP, Gurney took only the old Climax engined-car, retiring with suspension failure after dicing for second. Both V-12 Eagles were ready for the non-points Race of Champions at Brands Hatch, and ran one-two (Gurney in front) until brake problems forced Ginther out. Gurney went on to win over Bandini's Ferrari, so progress was being made with the Formula One Eagles. When organizers limited the field at Monaco, however, Ginther had difficulty sorting out his chassis and, embarrassingly, failed to make the cut. Gurney lasted only five laps (fuel pump) in a race marred by the fiery and ultimately, fatal crash of Lorenzo Bandini.

At Indy, while bossman Gurney qualified his Eagle second to pole-winner Mario Andretti (neither finished), Ginther had more problems. He was never really comfortable on the narrow, high-speed oval and did not qualify. "He probably didn't have enough time to get acclimated," offered Gurney. "It's so difficult. At least, it was in those days. You'd be amazed how many

obstacles there are to just getting out onto the track and not having yellows or rains or other car problems that sort of steal the necessary time." At Zandvoort, Ginther abruptly announced his retirement, feeling no longer able to compete at the level he felt necessary. "I felt it was something that was private with Richie, and I didn't question it. I figured, hey, look, if he has enough guts to say that's it, then I tip my hat to him."

Official records showing only one Grand Prix victory belie Richie Ginther's driving skill, as well as the meaningful contributions he made to Formula One and all kinds of racing and high-performance driving. Ginther was an innovator who not only tested extensively—more like today's top Formula One drivers than his contemporaries—but heavily influenced the development and engineering of Ferrari's pivotal first

Gurney on the charge again after both he and leader Clark have pitted. Gurney's stop was momentary, Clark's more serious. In spite of a high-speed miss, the Eagle once more began to reel in Stewart, passing him for good with seven laps to go. *Dave Friedman photo collection*

rear-engine cars, a fact that World Champion Phil Hill is the first to admit. "Oh, yeah," said Hill of Ginther's effect on his Championship season, "Trips and I really owed Richie a lot." So did BRM and Honda later. And, to this day, so does every manufacturer and race car-builder who has ever utilized the now ubiquitous rear spoiler, an aerodynamic device Ginther pioneered when he was testing Ferrari's sports prototypes in 1961.

Now the only American driver in Formula One, Gurney put his newly lightened Eagle-Weslake on the front row at Zandvoort, just behind Graham Hill's Lotus. Both Hill and teammate Clark were debuting Colin Chapman's latest, the Lotus 49, and a brand new engine, the 3.0-liter Cosworth V-8 funded by Ford of Europe. "We broke down early on at Zandvoort," Gurney recalled, "but they had us covered on power, probably by 20 horses, maybe 25. And, the car was a pretty good car. I don't think it was a bit better than ours, but, you know, the handwriting was on the wall. I mean, that was the beginning of a reign that the Cosworth had for a long time." Clark went on to win the first of that remarkable engine's all-time record 155 Grand Prix victories between 1966 and 1985.

The Eagle Flies

At Spa, Gurney split the two Lotus cars on the front row, but was caught out of gear when the green flag dropped. Later, he thought it might have had something to do with Spa's downhill starting grid. "You want to be in gear with the clutch in and your foot on the gas. What you normally do is put a wad of something, like a rag, under your tire so it won't roll away. Well, sometimes that doesn't quite work or you have trouble getting it in gear or, you know, to keep from heating up the clutch, you just wait too long to do it. I honestly don't remember."

A solemn moment on the podium at Spa—Jackie Stewart, Dan Gurney, and third-place Chris Amon listen as The Star Spangled Banner is played. For the first time in 46 years, an American has won a Grand Prix driving an American car. *Dave Friedman photo collection*

Clark was away like a shot in the Lotus-Ford, followed by Jochen Rindt, Jackie Stewart, then Michael Parkes and Chris Amon in the Ferraris, and finally, Gurney heading the rest of the pack. Before the first lap had ended, Parkes crashed, injuring himself badly enough to end his Formula One career. But the Eagle was flying, and by the end of lap two, Gurney had passed Rindt and Amon and began to reel in Stewart.

He was on the BRM's gearbox by lap 10, two laps before Clark had to relinquish his lead to change plugs. Instead of challenging for the lead, Gurney also dove into the pits. "Well," he explained, "I had a persistent misfire up high, and I didn't know what to do about it. It didn't feel as though it was going to go the distance. But, honestly, I don't remember the pit stop." In fact, he didn't stop, but drove straight through the pits and out again. "I haven't got a clue why!" he laughed. "Maybe there was no one there and there wasn't anything to do. I mean, what are you going to do!?"

Now 15 seconds back, Gurney once again set sail. High-speed misfire or no, the gap began to close. The Eagle was definitely the fastest car on the

---

Comparing drivers in different cars and at different times is much like comparing apples and oranges, but many believe that in terms of pure speed, Dan Gurney may have been the fastest American Grand Prix driver ever. Faster than World Champion Phil Hill, faster than World Champion Mario Andretti. And like the latter, Gurney was an all-rounder. He won in sports cars, he won in stock cars, he won in Indy cars, and he won in Grand Prix cars. Gurney gave three different Formula One makes their first World Championship win, including his own All-American Eagle, the first—and only—modern American car to win a Grand Prix.

Dan Gurney
4/13/1931 to

Daniel Sexton Gurney was born in Port Jefferson, New York, in 1931, the son of an opera singer. He became enamored of motor racing as a boy in the early 1940s watching midget and stock car races at the 1/5-mile oval in nearby Freeport, and reading about exotic European Grand Prix racing in books by George Monkhouse and Floyd Clymer. "Oh, yeah," said Gurney, "I used to read about those prewar races, heck, sometimes two and three years after they happened. But there was something, you know, a contrast between the racing I could see, which was mostly all oval racing, and the ones that Caracciola and Rosemeyer and Nuvolari and all those guys did." Indeed, even at the age of 12, Dan Gurney showed interest in that "other" kind of racing.

When Gurney's father retired, the family moved west, settling in Riverside, California, in 1948. While still in school, Gurney took his Mercury flathead-powered hot rod to Bonneville in 1950 and ran 138 miles per hour. Because of the Korean War, his first road race would be delayed until 1955, when he raced a Triumph TR2 at Torrey Pines. After just one more race in the Triumph, Gurney bought a Porsche Speedster. With the Porsche, Gurney was immediately competitive in West Coast events, winning three races in 1956. The following year, Gurney was driving for someone else, at Riverside, easily winning the Production Class in a Corvette. Even more impressively, he finished sixth overall against Ferraris and Maseratis and the like in the Modified main event.

Gurney's next mount was a California-modified short-wheelbase 4.9 Ferrari owned by Frank Arciero. In Arciero's Ferrari, Gurney finished a strong second at Riverside in 1957 to Carroll Shelby, besting many of the most prominent drivers in America. "Yeah, big break," remembers Gurney. "Every break is important, you know, but that one sort of burst it out beyond California, beyond even the U.S. and it led to an invitation, through Luigi Chinetti, to run Le Mans." Once again, Chinetti had spotted an American with real promise, helped him get international exposure, then a chance with Ferrari. Gurney didn't disappoint him. After joining the Ferrari team in 1959, he quickly became a real Formula One threat, no matter what car he was driving.

The fact that Gurney never finished better than second in the World Driving Championship (1961) was certainly more a function of the cars he was driving than any measure of his skill. To this day, Gurney and Stirling Moss are widely regarded as the most talented and deserving of the Grand Prix drivers who never won a Championship. And no one except Jack Brabham and Bruce McLaren has ever won a World Championship Grand Prix in a car of his own manufacture. Actually, Gurney won one in a Brabham before Jack. But perhaps what is most amazing about Gurney is what he was able to accomplish outside Formula One, much of it while he was still active as a Grand Prix driver.

While Jack Brabham is rightfully given credit for bringing the first modern midengine car to Indianapolis in 1961, it was Dan Gurney who put Colin Chapman

Dan Gurney. *Dave Friedman photo collection* and Ford together in 1963 to field the first competitive midengine car at the Speedway—and that's when the real revolution started. That same year, Gurney won against the best stock car drivers at Riverside Raceway, as he would do four more times in the next five years. Then, of course, there was the founding of All-American Racers with Carroll Shelby in 1964, builders of three Indy 500 winners, not to mention the car that scored America's first Formula One victory. With a victory at the Rex Mays 300 in 1967, Gurney became the first driver ever to win championship races in the four major disciplines of motor racing; Formula One, sports cars, stock cars, and Indy cars.

Before he retired as a driver in 1970, Gurney would finish second twice and third once at Indy, win Le Mans, and win a Can-Am race. Aside from the many victories his Eagles scored in Indy car racing, Gurney also fielded championship Toyota GTO and GTP cars in the 1980s and 1990s, and in 1995, he fielded a new Toyota-powered Eagle Indy car. As ever, Dan Gurney remains a winner and a great American hero.

track. "I ended up getting the lap record. At that time, it was far and away the quickest Formula One record. A hundred and forty-eight or something." Still, Gurney was anything but confident. On Spa's long straightaways, the Weslake's misfire sounded terminal.

"It was like running the engine on the dyno, and it's going, 'Deeee-de-deeeee-de-deeeeeee-de-deeeeeeeeee-de-deeeee,' like that, and you know it's just torturing it. And I was trying to figure out, 'Is it better if I do full throttle or part throttle or what?' But then, I could see Jackie Stewart with that 16. I saw a wisp of oil coming out of his car and I said to myself, 'Oop, this guy may have himself a problem,' and I said, 'Either my car's going to blow or it's not going to blow, but it's no use blowing it if I'm not gassing it all the way.' And, so, I went after it and, maybe two laps later, I went by him. He was having gearbox trouble."

By now, Stewart had to hold his car in gear and Gurney increased his lead. When the checkered flag fell, the Eagle was just over a minute ahead of Stewart and the BRM. Forty-six years after Jimmy Murphy's Duesenberg took the checkered flag in the 1921 French Grand Prix, Dan Gurney had become only the second U.S. driver to win a European Grand Prix in an American car. Indeed, coming just a week after he and A. J. Foyt had won the 24 Hours of Le Mans in a Ford, it was America's proudest moment in motor racing and the pinnacle of Gurney's fine driving career. Typically, Gurney himself would only say, "Well, you can call it whatever you want, but honestly, in terms of just pure driving virtuosity, it was more nursing this thing and hoping and crossing your fingers. Oh, yeah, the lap records show that I was gassing it. And, as a personal milestone and achievement for the whole team, it meant a great deal. It said, hey, despite all the odds, despite what all the pundits said, we'd done it."

Bruce McLaren joined Gurney to drive a second Eagle for the British, French, and German Grands Prix, but neither finished any of them, although Gurney came close to winning again at the Nürburgring. Ahead by more than 45 seconds and having set the fastest lap, Gurney's Eagle coasted to a stop just three laps from the finish with a broken U-joint. At Canada, where American Mike Fisher, in a Lotus-BRM, finished 11th in his only Formula One start, Gurney came home third. These were to be the last World Championship points ever scored in an Eagle, for neither Gurney nor Scarfiotti, who started the second car at Monza, even finished another race in 1967.

And Down to Earth

Gurney began the next season with another DNF, at the South African Grand Prix. Nineteen sixty-eight was not to be a good year for him—or for racing. Tragically, the brilliant Jimmy Clark lost his life in a Formula Two race at Hockenheim in early April. Within a month, teammate Mike Spence—sitting in for Clark—was killed practicing the Lotus turbine at Indianapolis. Then, in June, Gurney's Monza number-two, Ludovico Scarfiotti, died at a hillclimb. A month later, Jo Schlesser lost his life at the French Grand Prix.

While Bobby Unser and Gurney finished first and second at the Speedway in Eagles, problems continued to mount with the Formula One effort. Gurney's main sponsor, Goodyear, was losing interest. Why? Many years later, Gurney could only smile. "Well, the director of Goodyear Racing took a fair amount of advice from my former partner, Carroll Shelby. And I think, in their infinite wisdom, they decided that they'd dry up the

And then the joy! "Well, yes, there's a special feeling of putting something in the history books," said Gurney in 1992. " Once it's in there, that's it, you know. There isn't anything you can do about it. It's in there and nobody can take that away. It's almost as though, if I get knocked off tomorrow, it's there, you know." *Pete Biro*

Nürburgring, 1968. After limping 7 miles around the course on a flat tire and an extended pit stop, Gurney persevered through miserable conditions to finish a gritty ninth. The 1968 German Grand Prix was the last for Formula One. "I think that was one of my better drives," recalled Gurney. "My guys told me after the stop I was faster than the leader [Jackie Stewart] for the whole race. He always says that was his best drive. Someday I hope I can verify my laptimes . . . . so I can smoke that turkey!" *Pete Biro*

Dan Gurney in a McLaren-Cosworth at the 1968 Canadian Grand Prix. With no funds to continue the Eagle effort, Gurney signed on with McLaren. With his Olsonite and Harvey Titanium Eagle sponsors now displayed on the McLaren, Gurney pulls out of the pits at Mont Tremblant. Second from the right, standing next to Bruce McLaren's car, American mechanic and McLaren principal Tyler Alexander can be seen turning back to look at Gurney. *Pete Biro*

Shelby. And I think, in their infinite wisdom, they decided that they'd dry up the stream. They wanted me to come back and try and help them more in their Indy efforts." Then, he added with a laugh, "And the best way to get me back was to cut off Formula One funding, right?"

In an attempt to find more reliability and speed up development on the Weslake, Gurney had opened his own shop in England to build and test engines. But, it was too little, too late. There simply was no way All American Racers could compete with well-funded factory teams and the Ford-backed Cosworth juggernaut. "Didn't have enough money," he said flatly. "Didn't have enough engines. Didn't have enough anything." Gurney skipped the Spanish Grand Prix and, after qualifying at the back of the grid, went out early with engine problems at Monaco. There was no Eagle ready for the Belgian, Dutch, and French GPs, though Gurney did get a ride in a Brabham at Zandvoort (DNF).

With the newest, obviously more powerful, V-12, Gurney posted the fourth best time in the first qualifying session at Brands Hatch. But then the gremlins returned. That engine later dropped a valve, and in the race, he lasted only eight laps before retiring with fuel pump trouble.

Gurney's bad luck continued at the Nürburgring, where Stewart won convincingly in miserable weather. "I cut a tire on the first lap," Gurney remembered, "and I had to drive a little over 7 miles with a flat. And then, we had to change one of these old fashioned—what do you call them—six, probably six nuts holding the wheel on, so I was *way* back. Now, my pit told me at the time that I ran almost every lap after that faster than the leader, for the whole race. I would say that that might have been one of my better drives. Finished ninth. It was raining like nobody's business—a terrific race." Historic, too, for it was at the Nürburgring that Dan Gurney introduced the first full-coverage helmet to Formula One, the California motorcycle racing-derived Bell Star.

Unfortunately, the German Grand Prix was also the last finish for a Formula One Eagle. At Monza, one month later, Gurney would drive the Eagle one last time—to another DNF.

The first Monza practice session was enlivened by the appearance of two more Americans, Mario Andretti and Bobby Unser. These two classic track racers were locked in a battle for the USAC national championship that would be undecided until the last race of 1968, a road course at Riverside. There, Unser would finish second to Gurney, edging Mario for the title in the closest points race ever. But at Monza, clearly, Andretti had the better horse. Unser, who had also won the Indianapolis 500, was entered in a works BRM, not only at Monza, but at the Canadian and U.S. Grands Prix, as well. Andretti, Lotus-mounted, had taken Colin Chapman up on his "whenever you're ready" offer made at Indianapolis three years earlier.

"By 1968," recalled Mario, "I'd gathered quite a bit of roadracing experience with the Ford Le Mans program, so I called him. And true to his word, boom, I went to Italy and did a test at Monza. I broke the track record. Bobby and I had to come back to the States for the Hoosier 100 that Saturday, then go right back to Monza for the Grand Prix. So I was only able to run the first 20 minutes of official practice, but when I left on Friday, I was the quickest by quite a bit." In fact, even though the track got faster and everyone had two full days to improve their times,

Andretti's time was good enough for a third row starting position, ahead of Gurney's Eagle, among others. Unser's time wasn't as fast, but he still made the grid. Or *should* have.

Officials disqualified both Andretti and Unser, invoking an obscure rule that prohibited drivers from taking part in two races in a 24-hour period. The trouble was, they didn't bother to say anything until after the Americans had made the arduous roundtrip across the Atlantic. The always-colorful Unser could still get wound up about it nearly three decades later.

"Aw, that was all political, that crap they pulled on us in Monza. They let us fly all that way for nothin'," he said, warming to the tale. "And then, we drove all the way to the racetrack like idiots, maniacs, tryin' to make [it]. I risked both Mario's and my lives just getting to the racetrack. We ran on sidewalks through towns. Italian cops were wavin' their arms and yellin' at us. Lucky they were on foot. If there'd been a way to shoot us, they would have. We just went and went. Mario'd read the signs, tell me where to go, and I'm drivin'. Stupidest thing I've done in my life. And all the time, we wasn't gonna have a chance to run anyway!"

Dan Gurney's Eagle did run at Monza, but not far and not fast. Never higher than ninth, the Eagle's engine gave out after 19 laps. The writing was on the wall. Gurney had already tried a new McLaren-Ford in practice, the car he would drive for the last three races in 1968. Without funding, the All American Racing Formula One Eagle could go no further.

"You know," Gurney said later of that stressful time, "there comes a point where the old college try and the never-give-up kind of stuff becomes, uh, just really hard to justify and reality starts raising its head. The Grand Prix thing involved a lot. I had to make a decision whether to continue on over there or continue over here. And I couldn't do both any longer. Never could do both efficiently. Plus, I had a marital problem that, uh, just added fuel to that little fire. So, that's where it just got to be too much."

In the McLaren, Gurney scored his best finish—and only points of the 1968 season—at the U.S. Grand Prix at Watkins Glen, where America's next Formula One World Champion made his spectacular, if abbreviated, debut. Mario Andretti stunned everybody by claiming the pole in a Lotus-Ford. What's more, he dueled with Stewart for the lead until a broken support bracket caused the nose section of the Lotus to drag on the ground. After losing a full minute in the pits, Andretti rejoined the race, but eventually went out with a bad clutch. Nevertheless, he had certainly managed to get everyone's attention. Years later, Gurney remembered clearly how shocked the Grand Prix fraternity was when "rookie" Andretti made his qualifying run. "Oh, in a situation like that the competitors are mad at him because he's making them look bad, right? But, that's the most fun you could possibly have, to come in there and do something like that."

"Yeah, it was great," recalled Andretti. "You know, a lot of people said, 'Yeah, well, the Glen,' you know, 'it's your home track.' I had never seen the place!" Andretti had, of course, raced against Gurney at Indy, but long before that was an admirer of the Californian. "Honestly," he added, "Gurney was the one who inspired me through my career. With his talent, if he would have concentrated on just driving rather than worrying about

Mario Andretti's Lotus at the 1968 U.S. Grand Prix. After an astonishing pole-position qualifying effort, Mario Andretti's Formula One debut quickly headed downhill. Here he's dueling with Stewart for the lead, but already, the nose of the Lotus is coming apart. Soon it was dragging on the ground and Andretti was forced to stop for repairs. Clutch problems put him out for good on lap 31. *Dave Friedman photo collection*

1968 Indianapolis-winner Bobby Unser's first and last World Championship Grand Prix. Unser's GP debut at Watkins Glen was less spectacular than Andretti's. Hampered by a broken ankle, a big-time crash in practice, and a car that was midfield at best, Unser qualified 19th, more than five seconds off Andretti's pole time. Attrition helped him get as high as 10th before transmission woes ended the effort on lap 35. *Dave Friedman photo collection*

Dan Gurney at the 1968 U.S. Grand Prix. At Watkins Glen, Gurney would qualify the McLaren seventh, ahead of team leader Bruce McLaren, then work his way up to third until a tire went down. Gurney ended up fourth, his only points finish of 1968. *Dave Friedman photo collection*

manufacturing his own car and flying the American flag so much, he would've been the second American World Champion, not me."

Most would agree, pointing to the two World Championships won by Brabham and Hulme after Gurney left as Brabham's number-one driver to launch the Eagle project. But, Gurney himself has no regrets. For him, the effort to build an American Grand Prix car was a noble crusade—and, given the circumstances, anything but a failure. "Listen," he said later, "we knew we were stretching it and asking for a great deal, but it was an opportunity we had, and we all wanted to do it—and we bloody

well did it. We won two Formula One races and achieved much more success than most of the pundits thought was possible. I mean, we whipped the Ferrari factory and everybody else at Brands Hatch there. And then at Spa, why, we whipped them all. I look back on the whole Eagle experience as being more miraculous than it was disappointing. I thought it was very, very good." So was Dan Gurney.

How good? Mario Andretti put it this way, "The guy was a phenomenal race driver to my way of thinking. Dan Gurney could drive anything. He could drive stock cars, could drive sports cars, Indy cars, could drive Formula One. He should've been World Champion, no question." The great Jimmy Clark may have paid Gurney the best compliment of all—posthumously. At the two-time World Champion's funeral in Scotland, Clark's father took Gurney aside and said, "You know, Jimmy told me that you were the only driver that he feared."

A NEW AMERICAN CHAMPION
Into the 1970s and 80s

No less than 26 Americans entered Grands Prix in the 1960s, a decade that saw California's Phil Hill become the first American Formula One winner and a year later, the first American World Champion. Three Californians, Hill, Dan Gurney, and Richie Ginther, accounted for all nine American World Championship victories in Formula One's second decade. One of Gurney's four wins, at Spa in 1967 with the Eagle, marked the first time an American car had ever won in Formula One. From 1960 to 1967, Hill, Gurney, and Ginther also claimed nine of the 10 American pole positions in the decade (Mario Andretti got another in 1968), 40 of the 42 Yankee front-row starts (Masten Gregory and Andretti had the others), 15 fastest laps, and led a total of 481 laps of World Championship Grands Prix. Andretti would eventually eclipse all these marks—once he finally committed to a full-time GP effort.

After Andretti's spectacular debut at the 1968 U.S. Grand Prix, Mario had time for only three Formula One races in 1969, all DNFs. Instead, he concentrated on winning the U.S. Indy car national championship. Mario finished first in nine races, including the Indianapolis 500 (two laps ahead of Dan Gurney in second). Gurney stayed home. The only other American driver to take part in a Grand Prix in 1969, much less finish one, was privateer Pete Lovely, back to take a last fling at Formula One. It had been almost a decade since he'd driven in a Grand Prix.

"Well," laughed the personable Lovely, "it took that long to save enough money." Literally. Lovely and wife Nevele put every penny they had saved into a Lotus 49. "After we did the deal with Chapman, they upped the price a couple of times. Finally, it cost us $36,000—more than our house was worth. They took the money, rolled it off the transporter at Brands Hatch, and that was the last we saw of Lotus. Nevele was my pitcrew and we used a six-pence to open the dzus-fasteners. When we first took delivery, that was our toolbox.

"We didn't even know how to start the thing. Of course, the battery went dead right away, so we were towing it around the paddock trying to get it to start. Finally, Ken Tyrrell came over and said, 'I say, do you know how to start that, then?' I said, 'Not really.' He said, 'You put it on full rich.' I said, 'Well, how do you do that?' And he said, 'Well, here, then,' and he called over his own mechanic to get us going. It was Alan McHall, who was Jimmy Clark's mechanic for years. Tyrrell was very nice to us." Lovely did get the Lotus going well enough the next day at Brands Hatch to finish sixth in the non-championship Race of Champions.

Mario Andretti's first race in 1969 was at South Africa, just before going to Indy. As he was challenging Lotus teammate Graham Hill for second, his transmission failed on the 32nd lap. Three months later, there was more frustration at the Nürburgring, where Andretti broke two engines practicing Chapman's new four-wheel drive Lotus 63, only to crash on the first lap of the race.

The highest finish for an American in a World Championship round all year was Pete Lovely's seventh at the Canadian GP. That race also marked the last Formula One appearance of an Eagle, the now hopelessly overmatched original four-cylinder Climax-powered car driven by Canadian Al Pease. At the U.S. Grand Prix, in stark contrast to the previous year, Andretti's Lotus was last away

Mario Andretti leads Jody Scheckter's Wolf, Lotus teammate Ronnie Peterson, and Gilles Villeneuve's Ferrari at Monaco in 1978. Three unplanned pit stops would ultimately take Andretti out of contention at Monaco, but starting at the next Grand Prix, Belgium, he would dominate in Colin Chapman's new Lotus 79. Most often, when he finished with the Lotus 79, Andretti won in 1978, on his way to the World Championship. *Pete Biro*

149

Through the efforts of Goodyear, Bobby Unser was contracted to drive for BRM for the last three Formula One World Championship races of 1968, a season in which the 34-year old charger would win not only the Indianapolis 500, but the USAC national championship, as well. BRM director Louis Stanley pledged to provide Unser with a car equal to that driven by works driver Pedro Rodriguez. At Monza, of course, Unser was not permitted to run the race, but in practice, was surprised that he wasn't quicker than Rodriguez.

"I mean," said Unser, "I was was a very cocky race driver in those days. I couldn't understand how any race driver could run faster than I could, number one. Number two, especially in the same car on the same team and all. It just couldn't happen. Somethin' wasn't right"

Unser missed the Canadian round but had every intention of running in the U.S. Grand Prix—that is, until the night before practice opened at Watkins Glen. That evening, Unser took part in a drivers versus press charity basketball game in Indianapolis and broke his right ankle.

"I went up to Watkins Glen," says Unser, "and I remember sittin' in the limousine with Lou Stanley, the guy that owned BRM. And I just told him, I says, 'Lou, I hate to tell you this, but I really can't run. I've got a broken ankle.' He says, 'Oh, that can't be. You must run. I've got obligations.'" Unser laughs, "Really, what that meant was they was payin' him a lot of money. I was a big-name draw.

"So, Lou gives me this sad story, 'You gotta run. It just makes no difference what, you have to run.' So, I go to the doctor; I'm gonna go and get some Novocain shots. I mean, what else can you do? It isn't gonna heal up. So, I go down to the damn doctor. And I don't know why, maybe he didn't know who I was, but instead of giving me Novocain, he gave me pills. Now, I didn't know anything about drugs. I mean, I had no idea. And he gave me some of the worst painkillers you ever saw. Something like Darvon or something like that. Big powerful ones. So, I just went over to the watercooler and chucked them things down and went out to practice.

And I'll tell you, I wrecked that race car soooo bad it was just unbelievable. And I had no pain. I remember getting out of that race car and it was just junk. Gasoline everywhere. They didn't even know what fuel bladders were, those cars were so unsafe. Anyway, the car's wrecked. There's no tires or wheels on it. I mean, there's nothing. It's just all on the ground, totally destroyed. And I felt nothing.

"So, I went over and says, 'You got another car?' Well, the spare car was made up for Pedro, so they had to make me a seat. There wasn't anything left of my car, so they made me a seat. So, I got into that car and went out, and the transmission was bad, but I found out that engine must've had 30 percent more power than mine! So, I made a few laps with the car and come in. I told 'em about the gearshift and then walked right back over to that limousine and told Lou Stanley, I says, 'I thought there was somethin' goin' on before.' I says, 'You promised me that we would have equal stuff and no matter what, my car would be as fast as Pedro's.' I says, 'I'm gonna tell you something, my engine is down at least 30% on power compared to his.' And I says, 'I'm not buyin' this program. I been had.'

"And so, that was my last deal. I drove the car in that one race. And, of course, the transmission wouldn't work."

Bobby Unser.
Indianapolis Motor Speedway

Team Lovely and Gold Leaf Team Lotus in the paddock at Clermont-Ferrand for the 1970 French Grand Prix. In the tradition of sporting independents of the 1950s and early 1960s, self-financed privateer Pete Lovely drove in as many Grands Prix, if not World Championship rounds, in 1969 and 1970 as his admittedly better-known fellow American, Mario Andretti. "I was very lucky to have been able to be there," said Lovely. "But sometimes the English press had no appreciation for the fact that we were out there doing the best we could. Maybe two seconds off the leaders, but we were still beating ourselves up, working just as hard. And, of course, on a pretty limited budget." *Pete Lovely collection*

after tangling with Brabham at the start. Four laps later he was out with a broken rear suspension. Lovely also failed to finish and two weeks later scored a ninth-place finish at Mexico. It had been a terrible season for Americans.

In 1970, Andretti drove an STP-sponsored March-Cosworth in five Formula One races, but managed to finish only once, placing third at the Spanish Grand Prix. After Bruce McLaren was killed testing his Can-Am car, Dan Gurney was persuaded to come back and drive the second Team McLaren car for three races. It was not a satisfying experience. "Well, you know," he recalled, "once you've had your own team, it's very difficult to go and drive for someone else." Particularly in the middle of a season, when you've been away for a year. Gurney managed to finish only once, scoring his last World Championship point with a sixth place at the French Grand Prix. Two weeks later at Brands Hatch, where Pete Lovely would be the only American to finish—albeit 11 laps behind, Gurney struggled for 61 laps with his overheating McLaren before finally switching off. "Hey," he laughed, "an air-cooled Cosworth will only go so far!" In fact, an era had ended. Dan Gurney, one of the most skillful and popular Yanks ever to pull on a helmet, had just driven in his last Grand Prix.

Were it not for the fact that privateer Gus Hutchison qualified a Brabham-Cosworth at Watkins Glen in 1970 in his one and only Formula One appearance (a DNF), there would have been no American starting in the U.S. Grand Prix, for the first time in its 11-year history. About the closest thing to an American Formula One victory in 1970 was the total domination by Goodyear and Firestone in the tire wars, acknowledged finally by Dunlop's pullout at the end of the season. But early in 1971, Yankee fortunes took a sudden turn for the better.

In his first start for Ferrari, Mario Andretti won the South African Grand Prix. Even with Andretti's storied career, it was a special moment. "Oh, well," he recalled, "it was probably my biggest high, that first Grand Prix win. And for Ferrari!" What's more, Andretti kept up the momentum with another win at the non-championship Questor Grand Prix. There, racing against all the major works Formula One cars were most of the fastest U.S. Formula 5000 driver/car combinations, including such American Indy car stalwarts as A. J. Foyt and Bobby and Al Unser. The other F5000 drivers making their "Grand Prix" debut at Ontario were Mark Donohue, George Follmer, Ron Grable, Sam Posey, Swede Savage, Tony Adamowicz, and Lou Sell. The American V-8-powered F5000 cars were no match for the F1 cars, and the highest placed, Donohue's Lola-Chevrolet, was only ninth. Up front, Andretti won again in the Ferrari.

"Yeah, we beat Stewart at Ontario, too," remembered Andretti. "Finished ahead of him in both heats there." But conflicting USAC races would make Andretti miss five Grands Prix that year, and he had just one more points result in 1971, a fourth at the Nürburgring. The one other race that Andretti finished that year was the Grand Prix of Canada, where another American made a most impressive World Championship Formula One debut. Mark Donohue finished third in Roger Penske's McLaren-Cosworth, while Andretti limped home 13th.

Two other Americans drove in their first Formula One races in 1971. One, future racing-school owner Skip Barber in a March-Cosworth, had been sixth in the non-championship Rhein-Pokalrennen Grand Prix at Hockenheim. A week later, in the Dutch Grand Prix, Barber managed to finish, but too far back to be classified. He was out with engine trouble after 13 laps in the Canadian Grand Prix and at Watkins Glen, was again not classified. In the "mixed" Questor Grand Prix at Ontario, Sam Posey had qualified his Formula 5000 Surtees-Chevrolet ninth, behind only Donohue and Follmer's F5000 cars, but then DNF'd. But it was at the Glen that Posey made his true Formula One debut.

Widely known later as a writer and television broadcaster, Sam Posey was, in the late 1960s and early 1970s, very competitive in the Trans-Am series, where he drove for Roger Penske, and in Formula 5000. In the latter series, driving a Surtees-Chevrolet, Posey finished second in the championship in 1971 and 1972. Naturally, he had lobbied John Surtees to run his third car in the U.S. Grand Prix, a possibility that became real when Surtees driver Rolf Stommelen was

Four laps from the end, Denis Hulme's McLaren suffers a suspension failure, and Mario Andretti takes the lead in the South African Grand Prix. *Robert Young*

Dan Gurney in his final F1 ride (DNF, overheating) at the 1970 British Grand Prix. Heavily involved at Indy as a builder and driver, Gurney could no longer commit fully to F1, and he knew it. "I remember one point in the race, there was a place the car got light coming over the crest of this hill, and then there was a right-hand turn," recalled Gurney. "I'm already in trouble with the water, but I'm trying to hustle. And I backed off, and Ronnie Peterson went by me on the inside and gave that thing a gigantic pitch and went through there just like he was on dirt and was gone. It was an extraordinary moment, because you could see, man, that guy really knew what he was doing. It was a beautiful piece of driving." *LaFollette Archives, Vintage Motorphoto*

injured. The problem was, the sponsor of that car had nominated Le Mans winner Gijs van Lennep to sit in. To his credit, Surtees let both drivers compete for the ride in early practice sessions.

"I tried harder than I've ever tried in a race car," Posey remembered of the head-to-head tryouts. He also employed a clever strategy to show his speed in the best light. "Every time I went out and did a four- or five-lap group, if I felt the next lap was slower, I'd pit. Even though I might want to stay out. I wanted my learning curve to be unbroken and look good, with progressively faster and faster lap times. In fact, everybody on the team remarked that it was a terrific learning curve." Posey was clearly faster than van Lennep and earned his Formula One ride. "It took a lot for Surtees to pick me. There was no money involved and he could've had a sponsored driver. I've always been proud of the way the whole thing happened. It was a real highlight of my life."

Posey qualified 17th, less than 0.3 of a second behind Surtees himself. "I blew the start, because I hadn't made a grid start in years. And Surtees didn't want me to practice starts. He said, 'We don't have any clutches, so just get it off the grid.' Well, I almost stalled it. And, of course, I didn't last long, so there wasn't much chance to really race in that one." Posey was out with engine trouble after 15 laps. Peter Revson, returning to Formula One after a seven-year absence, didn't even last that long. His Tyrrell-Cosworth lost its clutch on the first lap.

Somewhat surprisingly, it would be Revson, not Andretti, who emerged as the most successful American Grand Prix driver in the next two seasons. While always saddled with the image of "rich playboy heir to the Revlon cosmetics fortune," Revson had earned the respect of those he drove against. "Oh, Peter was good," said Andretti, "and good all around. You know, he was one of the very few that could really do well on the ovals, too." Indeed, in 1969, the year Mario won at Indy, Revson had come all the way from last place to finish fifth in his first 500. In 1971, he set a new track record, qualifying for the pole, and came home second in a McLaren-Offy.

Revson drove his first full Formula One World Championship season in 1972 for McLaren. "When he came back, it was with us," remembered then-McLaren headman Teddy Mayer. "And he was really pretty damned good at that stage. In the top six drivers, I would say." Feverish from an infection, Revson failed to finish at the Argentine GP after qualifying third, but scored his first World Championship points with a third at South Africa, just ahead of Andretti's Ferrari.

Once again choosing USAC over Formula One, Andretti missed four months in the middle of the Grand Prix season, managing only one more points finish all year—a sixth at Watkins Glen, where Posey (12th) and Barber (16th) were the only other Americans classified. In contrast, aside from his two DNFs, Revson scored points in every race except the Belgian GP, where he was seventh. His best result was a second place at the Canadian Grand Prix, after starting from the pole, and in the final tally of World Championship points for the year, Revson finished an impressive fifth.

Revson's exploits came into even sharper focus in 1973, when Andretti opted not to drive at all in Formula One. Engine and gearbox problems

Mario Andretti celebrates his first World Championship victory after winning the 1971 South African Grand Prix in a Ferrari. He would win again three weeks later in the non-championship Questor Grand Prix in California. Despite these successes, Andretti's next win wouldn't come for three years. *Dave Friedman photo collection*

caused an eighth-place finish and a DNF at Argentina and Brazil, but in South Africa, Revson finished second behind Jackie Stewart.

Also of interest at Kyalami was the debut of America's next Formula One car, the Universal Oil Products-sponsored Shadow-Cosworth penned by Tony Southgate. Two were entered by California-based Don Nichols for his Shadow Can-Am drivers, Jackie Oliver and George Follmer. Oliver had considerable experience in Formula One, but 39-year-old Follmer—while a proven champion sports car driver in the United States—was an F1 rookie (not counting his F5000 start in the 1971 Questor Grand Prix). What's more, the Shadow-Cosworth had never turned a wheel before that time.

"We finished those cars in South Africa," remembered Follmer two decades later. "They were shipped straight from Wolverhampton, England, to South Africa. And that's where we finished them and ran them. It was one of those things where you just go out and run. I didn't have any problem with it." Apparently not. Oliver DNF'd, but rookie Follmer finished a creditable sixth, scoring a point in his first ever Grand Prix. In his second, a month later at Silverstone's non-championship International Trophy race, Follmer notched another sixth-place finish. Remarkably, he would finish third, a minute in front of Revson, at the Spanish Grand Prix, after spirited duels with Jackie Ickx's Ferrari (12th after an unscheduled pit stop) and François Cevert's second-place Tyrrell. Those first three races and, in particular, Spain, would be the high point of Follmer's first—and last—season in Formula One.

"Yeah, there were good finishes in the beginning. But we had a lot of teething problems within the team because it was new. And we wrecked some cars and we didn't have replacements quick enough. New-team problems. And then it kind of fell apart. There was a bunch of friction between Oliver and myself. And the team was basically run by Oliver. He called the shots. It was a political problem. Ego got into play, and I didn't get the cars, didn't get the engines. That's the way it goes."

Follmer would liked to have raced more in Formula One, but at 39 he knew his chances of being hired by another team were slim. Even before the season's end, he was making plans to return to U.S. racing. In contrast, Revson's Formula One prospects were on the upswing.

At Silverstone, where Follmer and Oliver were both taken out in a first-lap multicar accident, Revson came into his own. Starting from the front row, he drove his McLaren-Cosworth to victory in the British Grand Prix to become the fifth American winner in Formula One. With another win at the Canadian Grand Prix and five more points finishes in 1973, Revson again placed fifth in the World Championship.

With the arrival of 1972 World Champion Emerson Fittipaldi at McLaren, however, Revson opted to drive for the American Shadow team for 1974. "Yes, that was sort of a sad thing," recalled Teddy Mayer. "We were struggling to make ends meet. And to do that, we had to run a third car. Two cars were going to be sponsored by Marlboro and Texaco and the third one by Yardley. And we decided Peter would be best in the Yardley car. And he felt, I hate to say this, but I blame this more on his manager than on Peter's decision, he thought that that car might not get the same effort as the other two. It turned out it probably got a better effort in many ways. But that was the decision they made, and he went off to run for Shadow. And, of course, unfortunately, there was a failure in the car and . . . It was a great shame."

Andretti, here behind Ferrari teammate Regazzoni, scored one of only two 1972 points finishes at the U.S. Grand Prix, inheriting sixth when an ignition wire broke in Revson's McLaren five laps from the finish. *Pete Biro*

Sam Posey makes his second appearance in a World Championship Grand Prix at Watkins Glen in 1972. Once again in a Surtees-Cosworth, Posey qualified on the ninth row but this time made it to the end. "I was a little tentative. It rained, and I wanted to finish a Grand Prix. And I did," said Posey. "I was running 10th with one lap to go, and I got caught up in the last turn. A guy spun in front of me, and there was nowhere for me to go. And Hill and Reine Wisell were right behind me and snuck by on the inside. I would've liked a top 10 finish, but, you know, hey, I used to sit in the stands and cheer Graham Hill. I was thrilled." *Dave Friedman photo collection*

Peter Revson, race driver. It took almost a decade, but Revson paid his dues, and when he drove for McLaren, there was no doubt he was for real. "He was good. I ran his car at a lot of races. The guy was as quick as hell, and he could drive anything," said Tyler Alexander. "He was quick in a Can-Am car, quick in an Indy car, and he was quick in a Formula One car. Not too shabby, really." *Pete Biro*

Tragically, what could well have been Revson's strongest year in Formula One ended before it began. After DNF's at Argentina and Brazil and a sixth in the non-championship Brands Hatch Race of Champions, Peter Revson was killed practicing his Shadow at Kyalami eight days before the 1974 South African Grand Prix. Among his peers, Revson is remembered as a burgeoning world-class driver, not the rich dilettante he has often been portrayed as in print. "You know," says Andretti, "he wasn't racing just for the hell of it like in the days of de Portago and people like that. Sure, he liked to play, liked the social side, but there's nothing wrong with that if you know where your priorities are. Peter was a total professional—and very accomplished. Champion material, no question."

Andretti missed most of 1974, but appeared at the Grand Prix of Canada in one of two more American Formula One cars making their debut, the VPJ4 Parnelli-Cosworth fielded by Parnelli Jones and partner Vel Miletich. Also present was the new Penske-Cosworth, which Roger Penske's Can-Am and Indy champion Mark Donohue had come out of retirement to drive. Andretti finished seventh and Donohue 12th at Canada. Though he would be disqualified for "outside assistance" after an

He was young, Hollywood handsome, and as an heir to the Revlon cosmetics fortune, able to do virtually anything he wanted. That's the way most people saw Peter Revson. Motor racing had certainly seen enough rich playboys to be skeptical, but ultimately Revson came to be respected and admired for what he was: a committed and skilled professional racer, taken, unfortunately, just as he was reaching his prime.

Peter Revson
2/27/1939 to 3/22/1974

Peter Revson was born in New York in 1939, the nephew of the founder of Revlon, the giant cosmetics empire. Not surprisingly, Revson received a good education, though he was always a better athlete than student. After knocking around Eastern prep schools, there were turns at Cornell, Columbia, and finally, the University of Hawaii. It was in Hawaii that Revson got a Morgan Plus 4. In 1961, Revson raced the Morgan in SCCA club events, winning his second time out.

In the next few years, Revson would become progressively more involved in racing—and less interested in pursuing a career. In 1962, Revson, Tim Mayer, and Bill Smith Jr. (later the owner of McLaren Engines in Detroit) ran a three-car Formula Junior team wrenched by Tyler Alexander. Finally in 1963, Revson chucked it all and moved to England to campaign a Formula Junior. For a whole season, he toured the continent with his privately entered Cooper, often living out of the transporter. In that time, there were a number of promising results, the best of which was a win at the Copenhagen Grand Prix.

Near the end of 1963, Revson got the chance to run an independent F1 Lotus-BRM, finishing a steady if undistinguished ninth in the non-points International Gold Cup at Oulton Park. He ran virtually the entire season the next year, his two best results coming in non-championship races, a fourth at Solitude and a sixth at the Mediterranean GP. In 1965, Revson concentrated on Formula Two and Formula Three races, winning impressively in the latter at Monaco.

Revson returned home for the 1966 season, getting rides from Ford in their GT40s and big-bore Can-Am cars. The latter were then the world's fastest race cars, and competing against the best drivers from the United States and Europe, Revson began to gain respect from the racing community. He tried Indianapolis in 1967, but did not qualify. In 1969, Revson just made the field, managing to qualify last in an underpowered Repco-Brabham. In the race, however, Revson hung on and worked his way up to fifth at the finish. It was enough to get the attention of McLaren, in whose car he qualified 16th for the 1970 500. That effort ended with magneto trouble after only 87 laps, but in 1971, Revson really turned some heads, setting a new Indy qualifying record to put his McLaren on the pole and finishing second. The same year, Revson was Can-Am champion in a McLaren. In no way due to good looks, wealth, or social status, Peter Revson had arrived as a professional racer—and a damn good one at that.

Revson's fifth-place finish in the 1972 World Championship is even more admirable, considering that his USAC Indy car commitments forced him to miss five points-paying Grands Prix. In the 10 Formula One races in which he did compete that year, Revson scored points in six and made the podium four times. Despite some mechanical misfortunes, he did even better the next season, scoring points in nine races, with four podium finishes, including two outright wins.

Peter Revson.
Indianapolis Motor Speedway

To Revson and his management, despite Teddy Mayer's assurances, the chances for equal support for the third car on a team with two past World Champions backed exclusively by Marlboro and Texaco did not seem good. Revson joined the Shadow team for 1974. He raced with the American team only three times. Then, in a prerace test before the South African Grand Prix, a suspension piece broke on Revson's car and he was fatally injured in the resulting crash. Peter Revson was 35.

Peter Revson leads McLaren teammate Denny Hulme in the first World Championship round of 1973, the Grand Prix of Argentina. Revson finished behind Hulme at Argentina and at Brazil two weeks later, but in the South African Grand Prix, Revson began to impress, coming home second. Amazingly, countryman George Follmer, in his and the "American" Shadow-Cosworth's debut, finished sixth in the same race. *Dave Friedman photo collection*

left: Shadow driver George Follmer on his way to a podium finish in only his third Formula One race, the Spanish Grand Prix. Follmer finished third, 2 seconds behind François Cevert, who complained later that the American was hard to get around. "Fuckin' A, I was! He wanted me to pull over and get out of the way, I guess. Lots of luck!" laughed Follmer. "Yeah, that would've given me a second place if he hadn't gotten by me, so I don't think I am going to move over. You know, that isn't what I got paid for." *Dave Friedman photo collection*

1974 Canadian Grand Prix. Mark Donohue debuting the new Penske PC-1. Donohue came out of retirement to drive the first car ever produced by Penske. Fuel-pressure problems with the Cosworth engine sidelined Donohue on Saturday, but his Friday practice time was fast enough to put him on the grid near the back. Donohue finished 12th at Mosport and DNF'd at the U.S. Grand Prix two weeks later when the rear suspension broke. *Dave Friedman photo collection*

electrical problem on lap four of the U.S. Grand Prix, Andretti had shown enough pace in the Parnelli to qualify third. For the first time, resolved to contest the full Grand Prix season, Andretti signed on to drive for the promising new American team in 1975 and 1976. Then, Firestone, a heavy backer of the Vel's Parnelli Jones team, dropped a bombshell by abruptly withdrawing from Formula One. This effectively crippled development on the new VPJ car, and Andretti struggled through all of 1975 to make the Parnelli competitive. Despite Andretti's efforts, he made only two points finishes all year, with his best a fourth at the Swedish Grand Prix.

Shadow drivers Jean-Pierre Jarier and Tom Pryce had some good results in 1975, but Donohue experienced nothing but grief with the other American car, the Penske PC1, his best finish coming at Sweden behind Andretti. By the British Grand Prix, Penske had purchased a March-Cosworth to use while a new car was being built. Donohue finished fifth at Silverstone in the March, but a month later disaster struck at the Austrian Grand Prix. About halfway through the prerace warm-up session, Donohue's March crashed heavily, after what is believed to have been a front tire failure. Donohue regained consciousness and appeared fine except for a severe headache. But on the way to the hospital for a checkup, he lost consciousness again. Emergency brain surgery was unsuccessful, and Mark Donohue died two days later.

Unnoticed in the pall cast at Austria by Donohue's tragic death was the first race of American privateer Brett Lunger, who would be a fixture in Formula One over the next two seasons, contesting a total of 38 Grands Prix.

Andretti, after being released for a one-off Lotus drive at Brazil for the first 1976 Grand Prix (DNF), soldiered on with his only slightly improved and now unsponsored Parnelli. The sixth Andretti managed at South Africa, behind John Watson in the Penske, was to be the last point ever scored by the Parnelli. In the partnership, Parnelli Jones had never been enthusiastic about Formula One. Now, with business problems at home,

Monza, 1976. Ferrari Director of Sport Daniele Audetto presents Brett Lunger a special trophy in gratitude for his part in rescuing Niki Lauda. It's on the occasion of Lauda's return, amazingly, only six weeks after his fiery crash. "They just told me they wanted to give me something after practice one day," explained Lunger. "It meant a lot to me because I wasn't one to, you know, seek out the PR thing on that. I happened to be there. It was an incident that happened. And I just did it and walked away. But to have them take a moment and say thank you, it meant a lot." *Pete Biro*

Miletich also began to lose interest. It was all to end at the U.S. Grand Prix at Long Beach. Fourth fastest in Friday's practice sessions, Andretti lost an engine and then suffered a broken rear suspension on Saturday, to end up 15th on the starting grid. In the race, he clawed his way up to eighth before retiring the Parnelli with a water leak. The memory of what happened next still angered Andretti many years later.

"Chris Economaki sticks a mike in my face and says, 'Hey, Mario, how about this being your last race in Formula One?' I said, 'What the hell are you talking about?' And he says, 'Well, that's what Vel told me,' and this and that. I said, 'Well, it may be *his* last race in Formula One, but it won't be *mine*.' And here, after I had a shitty day, the freakin' car broke, we had a water line or something go, I gotta get the news from Economaki!" Needless to say, Andretti terminated his relationship with Miletich and Jones that day.

The next morning, quite by accident, Andretti ran into Colin Chapman on the way to breakfast and the two decided to eat together. Chapman, too, was at a low point, his once-powerful Lotus team now in disarray. At Long Beach, neither Lotus had even qualified—an embarrassing first in Chapman's career as a Formula One constructor. "And we're sitting there," Andretti remembered, "just slopping over our cereal or whatever, and I'm looking at him looking at me and we were talking. And I said, 'You know something?' I said, 'Maybe out of a total negative for you can come a positive.' And he perked up and I said, 'How about I join you?' And I explained the situation and he says, 'You're on.' And I said, '*But*, you're coming back *racing*. Get rid of all your boats. Get rid of all your toys,' I said, 'You're coming back racing with me one-hundred percent.' He says, 'Done.' And so it

Like Rodgers and Hammerstein, indeed, like Jimmy Clark and Colin Chapman, Andretti and Chapman were a perfect combination. Chapman was a visionary, an innovator, Andretti, a driver who was not only very quick, but, because of years of oval-track racing could first, accurately perceive what a car was doing, and second, could suggest and quickly evaluate specific changes at a race. Each complemented the strengths of the other. The results were amazing. *Pete Biro*

was that one of the most productive alliances of the 1970s in Formula One was formed in a Long Beach hotel coffee shop. But success didn't come right away.

The Quest

Andretti laughed when he recalled his first impression of the latest iteration of Chapman's odd, variable-wheelbase Lotus Type 77. "I told him, 'This car is the biggest piece of shit I ever laid my hands on, but we're going to win a race before the year is out.'"

Andretti was right, but before that, Irishman John Watson would score the next "American" Formula One victory in a Penske-Cosworth. The newest Penske PC4 first appeared at Sweden, where Andretti qualified his Lotus second and led convincingly before losing an engine. Watson was knocked out of the race in a first-lap accident, but at France, showed that the PC4 was much improved and finished a strong third. Andretti was fifth in the Lotus. Watson followed with another third at the British Grand Prix—Andretti lasted only five laps because of ignition problems. Watson was seventh at the Nürburgring and Andretti, forced to stop with a loose battery, was classified 12th. That race had to be restarted after Niki Lauda's horrifying and nearly fatal accident on the second lap. American Brett Lunger came around a flat-out fourth-gear blind corner to find the Austrian's Ferrari blocking the track and on fire.

"I locked 'em up and slid into him," remembered Lunger, "and the impact set my on-board extingushers off. [Harald] Ertl and [Guy] Edwards came round after me. They saw the smoke and both stopped safely. Then [Arturo] Merzario stopped, too. I think Ertl, or maybe it was Edwards, grabbed a fire extinguisher and Merzario and I got him out. Merzario was the most important. The Ferrari seat belts were different. And he managed to get Lauda's belt undone. I was standing on top of the car and pulled him out by his shoulders, but Merzario's the guy that got his belt undone."

The actions of Brett Lunger, Merzario, Ertl and Edwards no doubt saved Nicki Lauda's life that day.

Two weeks later at Austria, a year after Mark Donohue was mortally injured there, Watson put the red-white-and-blue Penske on the front row and after one of the most exciting races of the season, won in front of Jacques Laffite's Ligier-Matra, with Andretti fifth in the Lotus. Watson would score

Mario Andretti in his final ride in the VPJ 4B Parnelli-Cosworth at Long Beach in 1976. The weekend of the 1976 U.S. Grand Prix West was historic. It was the first time a World Championship GP was held on the streets of Long Beach, the first time the Lotus team failed to qualify a car in a World Championship GP, and the last time that Mario Andretti—or anyone else—would drive a Parnelli in a Formula One race. Ironically, the disasters of Andretti and Colin Chapman (Lotus headman) drew them together at Long Beach, and the result was one of the most successful partnerships in Formula One. *Bob Tronolone*

only one more point in the Penske, with a sixth at the U.S. Grand Prix; at the end of the season, Roger Penske was to withdraw from Formula One. In the meantime, Mario Andretti's enthusiasm and set-up expertise had put Chapman's Lotus program back on track—and, in a way, Chapman, too.

"You know," recalled Andretti, "Hazel [Mrs. Chapman] many times remarked that I changed the man, I mean, at that point, anyway. He'd been distracted, uninterested. But then, he started really going. It was a typical Chapman resurgence. You know, he was full of peaks and valleys in his career, and after hitting the lowest low, he was ready to go boom, like a rocket. And I was right on that same rocket with him."

After a spate of DNFs early on, things began to look better, particularly in the second half of the season, where Andretti scored a fifth and two thirds. Then, in the season finale, the Japanese Grand Prix, Andretti won, scoring the first Lotus Formula One victory in two years. Colin Chapman was back. What's more, he had an exciting new car for Andretti to drive for 1977, the revolutionary Lotus 78 "wing-car."

The Lotus 78 bristled with innovation. It introduced the now ubiquitous side-pods, which were shaped like inverted wings and, importantly, equipped with "skirts" of a brush material at the outside edges to form ground-sucking tunnels that produced downforce. In other words, ground effects—the first in Formula One. Andretti also contributed greatly, not only by his chassis set-up skills in testing, but by incorporating American track-racing practices like driver-adjustable suspension (McLaren, with its American braintrust and Indy experience, used this, too) and what was vir-

After scoring in Indy car racing and IMSA sports car racing in 1977, Hawaiian-born, former drag racer Danny Ongais tried Formula One in a Penske-Cosworth in 1977. At Watkins Glen, Ongais lasted only seven laps before a crash ended his F1 debut. But at Mosport a week later, in the Canadian GP, Ongais survived a late-race spin on oil to finish seventh. After two DNF's and several failures to qualify in 1978, Ongais returned to Indy car and sports car racing. *Pete Biro*

What a difference a year makes! Mario Andretti in the Lotus-Cosworth at Long Beach in 1977 on his way to becoming the first American ever to win the U.S. Grand Prix. Andretti would win three more Grands Prix in Chapman's Lotus 78 that year. Indeed, were it not for the failure of many Cosworth development engines, Andretti might well have been World Champion in 1977. *Bob Tronolone*

engineering mind behind it on his part. You know, it paid off."

The season began with a bizarre practice accident in Argentina, when Andretti's on-board fire extinguisher exploded, doing enough damage to deny him time for a good qualifying run. But Andretti showed speed in the race and fought his way to second before tangling with a lapped car, only to make his way back up to second again, when a rear-wheel bearing seized. Even though he wasn't running at the finish, Andretti was classified fifth, scoring points the first time out with the new Lotus. Ignition problems and a crash eliminated Andretti in the Brazilian and South African Grands Prix.

What had looked to be a good omen for the American Shadow team at Brazil, where new driver Renzo Zorzi lucked into a sixth-place finish, turned sour on lap 23 of the Kyalami race. In a strange and tragic series of events, Zorzi's engine blew, and as he pulled to a stop, spilled fuel ignited. Without looking, a young fire marshal then dashed across the track—just as British number-one Shadow driver Tom Pryce appeared, flat out. In the ensuing collision, both were killed—Pryce by the heavy fire extinguisher the teenager had carried.

With a new, shorter-wheelbase Lotus 78, Andretti qualified second at Long Beach, and after a race-long battle with Lauda (Ferrari) and Jodi Scheckter (Wolf-Cosworth) gave the wing-car its first victory. In so doing, Mario Andretti also became the first American ever to win the U.S. Grand Prix, celebrating with not one, but *two* victory laps—quite a turnaround from the year before! He followed this with another win, flag to flag from the pole, in Spain. At Monaco, using a special new Cosworth engine, Andretti finished fifth, one place ahead of the Shadow-Cosworth of Alan Jones, who had replaced Tom Pryce.

At Zolder, Andretti and the Lotus simply overwhelmed the competition in practice, qualifying one and one-half seconds faster than Watson's Brabham. But Watson jumped ahead at the start and Andretti rammed the back of the Brabham on braking, eliminating himself on the

tually a "locked" rear end. Ordinarily, this would cause understeer, but noting the Type 78's incredible downforce-aided grip at the front, Andretti deduced that a near zero-slip rear end would provide extra acceleration off the corners. He was right. If the 1977 Lotus was somewhat slower on the straightaways, it cornered faster than other cars and almost shot out of the turns. The relationship between Chapman and Andretti was becoming much like the one that Chapman had enjoyed with Jimmy Clark: close and extremely productive.

"It was almost like a storybook," said Andretti, "because there was a real human effort there that paid off on both sides. There was a total commitment on my part and a commitment on his part that jelled. Not luck by any means. It was hard work and a good solid approach, and a good, sound

Long Beach, 1978 U.S. Grand Prix. Mario Andretti in the Lotus 78 on his way to a second-place finish behind Carlos Reutemann's Ferrari. *Dave Friedman*

first lap. Andretti sat on the pole again at Sweden and led 68 of 72 laps before he was forced to stop for fuel. A fuel-metering unit had vibrated all the way open. Nevertheless, Andretti finished sixth and at Dijon, started on the pole again and passed Watson's Brabham on the last lap to win the French Grand Prix. Obviously, Andretti's Lotus had become the car to beat—when it stayed together.

The Championship season that might have been began to unravel at the British Grand Prix. Andretti blew one of the new "development" engines in practice, replaced it with a normal one, and then blew that one in the race. He also failed to finish the next two Grands Prix, losing engines at Hockenheim and Austria, where Alan Jones won in the American Shadow—a first for both. Incredibly, Andretti blew his fifth straight Cosworth at the Dutch Grand Prix, for yet another DNF.

A decade and a half later, Andretti still felt the frustration. "The biggest, the *only* mistake we made, we were too ambitious. We went into a Cosworth engine development program in 1977. That year should've been an easier, more clear-cut victory in the World Championship for us than '78, but we just couldn't finish the freaking races. The engines just, I mean, just babying the stupid things. . . . You know, Cosworth was just dismal with their development. Terrible, terrible setups! I mean, we were breaking rings, we were consuming oil, doing everything wrong, and we didn't need those stupid development engines, you know, to win."

Andretti had one more win in 1977, a particularly gratifying one at Monza. He was second at the U.S. Grand Prix at Watkins Glen. Indy car driver and former drag racer Danny Ongais debuted there in a new Interscope-sponsored Penske PC4—and crashed. He also failed to finish at Canada and Japan.

Though his Lotus won more races than Constructors Champion Ferrari, Andretti finished third in the Drivers Championship, behind Lauda and Scheckter. In truth, most times when Andretti didn't win, he didn't finish

and the lack of points finishes proved to be the difference. "Those development engines were our demise in '77," he said flatly. "We lost a lot of good races we were just going away leading. So, that should have been two Championships." Then, Andretti shrugged and smiled, "But, it's like anything else—*should* have been, right?"

With the talented young Swede Ronnie Peterson returning as Andretti's teammate, Lotus was even stronger in 1978. As if to prove the point, Andretti qualified on the pole and won at Argentina, with Peterson fifth. American Danny Ongais DNF'd there in an Ensign-Cosworth, while

Andretti in the Lotus at Long Beach in 1979. Again, what a difference a year makes, though this time for the worse. By 1979, others had caught up with and surpassed the performance of Colin Chapman's Lotus. Andretti finished fourth in the U.S. Grand Prix West in the Lotus 79. Things didn't improve with the new Lotus 80, and Andretti would not win a Formula One race all year. *Bob Tronolone*

Brett Lunger's McLaren-Cosworth during practice at Long Beach in 1978. While Lunger's final year in Formula One would bring him his best finishes in both non-points (fourth at Silverstone) and World Championship GPs (eighth at the British and Austrian Grands Prix), he did not qualify at Long Beach. Six months later, Lunger drove the last of his 38 Formula One races at Watkins Glen. "I was very forunate. I never would have had the chance to race at that level if it hadn't been for the business support I had," said Lunger. "I know what I was capable of doing and how far I could have gone with it. I wouldn't have had the chance. I loved the driving. I loved the people. I'm thankful that I had the chance to do it." *Bob Tronolone*

Brett Lunger, driving a McLaren-Cosworth in his fourth and last Grand Prix season, finished 13th. At South Africa, Andretti was second and closing on the leader, when he was forced to stop for fuel, but worked his way back up to seventh at the checkered flag. Also at Kyalami, a 20-year-old American expatriate living in Italy, Eddie Cheever, after failing to qualify at the Argentine and Brazilian GPs, made his World Championship debut in a Hesketh-Cosworth (DNF).

At the Brazilian GP, where Ongais again DNF'd in his final Formula One race, Andretti ended up fourth, still in last year's car. Only one more points finish, a second at Long Beach, would be accomplished before Belgium, where the newest—even more efficient and faster—Lotus 79 would appear. There at Zolder, Andretti won easily from the pole, as he would in Spain several weeks later. He would, in fact, win three of the next six races. Ironically, Lotus clinched the 1978 Constructor's championship at Austria, where Andretti DNF'd and Peterson finished first. Before that race, Andretti led the Driver's championship by 18 points. At the Dutch GP, Andretti won again, his last Formula One victory, as it turned out. Peterson, the only driver

If you go by the record, Mario Andretti is arguably the greatest all-around driver in the history of motor racing. Much like an Italian immigrant from another time, Ralph DePalma, Andretti won in almost every kind of racing, in midgets, sprinters, champ cars, sports cars, stock cars, and Grand Prix cars, on pavement, on dirt, on the high-banked speedways, at Pikes Peak (1969), and at Indianapolis, where he qualified on the pole three times and won in 1969. Only A. J. Foyt won more Indy car races than Andretti's 52, but Andretti is the only driver in history to have victories in four decades, and with his last win at Phoenix in 1993, become, at 53, the oldest driver ever to win an Indy car race. He was USAC Indy car champion in 1965, 1966, and PPG CART World Series champion in 1984. He won NASCAR's Daytona 500 in 1967. The same year, he won the 12 Hours of Sebring, which he would win again in 1970 and 1972. He was USAC Dirt Track Champion in 1974. He qualified on the pole in his first Grand Prix and scored 12 victories, six of them in 1978, when he became World Champion.

Mario Andretti
2/28/1940 to

Mario Andretti was born in Montona, Italy, near Trieste in 1940. After World War II, the Andrettis were forced to flee their home (now in Croatia) to escape Communist rule. The next seven years were spent in a displaced persons camp in Tuscani, Lucca. The Andretti family immigrated to the United States in 1955, but already Mario had been bitten by the racing bug. He'd seen his idol Ascari race at Monza the year before in the Italian Grand Prix.

"Well," said Mario, "I think that almost every kid that pursued a career had to have a hero to look up to. Someone to emulate later on, the inspiration, so to speak. You know, Ascari just happened to be the one during those formative years. He was the one who got me excited at the beginning, the one that I was rooting for."

Interestingly, Andretti was exposed to uniquely American circle-track racing before coming to the United States, not only by radio and newspaper coverage of the Indianapolis 500, but in the popular Clark Gable movie *To Please a Lady*. It was at a local "bullring" near their new home in Nazareth, Pennsylvania, that Mario and twin brother Aldo began their racing careers in 1959—unbeknownst to their father—running a 1948 Hudson in the modified sportsman class on weekends. Any hope of keeping their secret ended with a crash that put Aldo in the hospital.

Family approval came eventually, cemented by success on the track. Andretti would win more than 20 events in the next three years, his first victory "of consequence" coming on March 3, 1962, a 35-lap TQ feature race at Teaneck, New Jersey. The "legend" of Mario Andretti probably began on September 1, 1963, the day he won three midget features at two tracks.

Mario Andretti joined USAC in 1964, finishing third in the sprint car championships and scoring his first USAC sprint car victory at Salem, Indiana. He also drove in his first Indy car race that year. Andretti was offered a ride by Mickey Thompson at Indy in 1964, but on advice from legendary car-builder Clint Brawner, passed.

"Yeah," says Andretti, "that's when McDonald was killed [in the Thompson car, along with Eddie Sachs]. It was fate. I stayed in bed. I was awake all night. I said I want it, but I'm not ready and I felt it was too soon. Yes, I was raising hell with sprint cars and stuff like that, but I was not ready for Indy. I said I need to do some Championship racing outside of Indianapolis because I wasn't really acquainted with all the speed. And, you know,

Mario Andretti. Toyota Grand Prix of Long Beach

if Clint Brawner doesn't think I'm ready, then I shouldn't do it. And that was really a good move on my part. And I always appreciated the fact that, you know, I think Mickey Thompson would've given me the opportunity, even though we never came to terms or anything. Again, it's amazing how things in life, you know, there are just key moments that make a big difference." Indeed. Andretti went to Indy in 1965 in the Brawner-wrenched Dean Van Lines car, finishing third and being named Rookie of the Year, impressing, in the process, Lotus headman Colin Chapman.

In addition to his numerous other accomplishments, Andretti was Driver of the Year in 1967, 1978, and 1984. He is the only man to win the award in three different decades, and the first unanimous selection (1984). Longevity is another of Andretti's attributes. Amazing longevity. At 52, he became the oldest Indy car pole winner in history with a 230-plus-mile-per-hour run at Michigan. In 1993, with his victory on the mile at Phoenix International Raceway, Mario Andretti became the oldest driver ever to win an Indy car race—at age 53.

Rick Mears in the Brabham-Cosworth at Riverside Raceway. As Nelson Piquet is interviewed on the pit wall behind, Mears talks with Brabham boss Bernie Ecclestone (with the white Parmalat shirt) during the second of his two Formula One tests. *Dale von Trebra*

Twenty-two-year old Eddie Cheever in 1980. Though he'd won three races for Osella in Formula Two in 1979, that team—and Cheever—were to find it rough sledding in Formula One. He finished only one race in 1980, at Monza, where the European-raised American was 12th. *Pete Biro*

who could possibly catch Andretti in the World Championship, was second at Zandvoort. Monza would be critical.

As he had six times before in 1978, Andretti took the pole at Monza, but after the confusion following a long-delayed start, a multicar accident occurred in turn one, and Ronnie Peterson was pushed off, crashing head-on into a guardrail. He was pulled from his burning car and taken to the hospital with two badly broken legs. On the restart, Gilles Villeneuve in the Ferrari anticipated the green flag and Andretti tore out after him. Andretti set fastest lap and won the race—on the track, that is. In fact, he'd been penalized one minute for jumping the start and was classified sixth. Still, it was good enough to clinch the World Drivers Championship.

Mario Andretti had won the Indianapolis 500, he'd won in stock cars, he'd won in sports cars, he'd even won Pikes Peak, and now, he'd finally won the prize he'd fantasized about since he was a small boy—the Formula One World Championship. Yet, strangely—and cruelly, as in the case of America's first World Champion, Phil Hill—what should have been Andretti's day of triumph was shattered by tragedy. His friend and Lotus teammate Ronnie Peterson died that very night after surgery.

Years later, Andretti still shuddered when he recalled that fateful day. "Yeah, it was terrible. I didn't do much celebrating. Here, it should've been the most, the happiest, the most important day of my life, when that happened. And yet, it was marred by that tragedy. And I told my wife, 'It's just so unfair, first of all to Ronnie and then, secondly, to me.' Because that's not the way that things are supposed to be. But, you know, life is crazy." Andretti shrugged, "What life hands you sometimes!"

After reaching this bittersweet pinnacle, Andretti's Formula One fortunes and those of Lotus began to ebb. The last two races of 1978 were an omen—a DNF at Watkins Glen and a 10th at Canada. Those two races, the U.S. and Canadian Grand Prix, would be the first and last Formula One appearances of another American.

At 25, Bobby Rahal had impressed Walter Wolf enough with several Formula Three rides in Europe to earn a ride on his F1 team for the final races of the season. On his only Formula One test, at Brands Hatch, Rahal had actually been quicker than regular Wolf driver Jody Scheckter. But many years later, the popular American Indy winner questioned the timing of his Grand Prix debut.

"I wasn't ready," he admitted. "You know, Brands Hatch for a few laps, it wasn't enough, especially for a difficult car to drive. It had extremely heavy steering. It was Wolf's version of the ground-effects Lotus 79. But I don't think the heavy steering had anything to do with downforce. I think it was just a truck."

Rahal qualified 20th, about four seconds slower than pole-sitter Andretti and two seconds behind Scheckter in 10th. He had an uneventful race, finishing 12th, one place ahead of countryman Brett Lunger, who was plagued by a broken rear shock in the last of his 34 World Championship Grands Prix. A week later, at Montreal, Rahal found more speed, but it did not come cheaply.

"The first or second session, it's raining, and I'm like third or fourth quickest. Well, if Peter Warr, the team manager, had had any brains, he'd have said, 'Okay, get out of the car right now. You're fine. It's pissin' down rain.' I just overcooked it. Passed the catch-fencing and *boom*, took a corner off the car and broke the bulkheads on the front suspension. They couldn't fix the car."

What the Wolf crew did was to pluck an old show car, a 1977 WR-1, out of a local hotel display and install an engine in it overnight. With just a few laps of practice, Rahal managed to qualify 20th. "I don't even think they expected me to qualify. But the car was pretty good. It had a lot of grip. It wasn't a ground-effect car, but it put the power down and it turned into the corners well." Indeed, Rahal was on the move from the start.

"We passed a lot of people early in the race. I don't know, I want to say we got up to eighth or ninth, right behind Piquet. But as the fuel load lightened, we had a fuel pickup problem and the car began to misfire. And then the thing broke and that was that. That was the end of my Formula One season."

It was more than that. A promised ride in Wolf's second car for 1979 went away when Scheckter left Wolf for Ferrari—and a World Championship. His successor at Wolf, James Hunt, insisted on a one-car team. Bobby Rahal would never drive in another Grand Prix.

It was to be a long and dismal season for defending World Champion Andretti. As brilliant and ahead of its time as the Lotus 79 was, the opposition had by now begun to make their own ground-effects cars—some clearly

Mario Andretti in the Lotus 81 at Long Beach. The U.S. Grand Prix was a short one for Andretti in 1980. He was out on lap one with bent steering, one of nine DNF's in his final season with Lotus. *Bob Tronolone*

Long Beach, 1981. Andretti on his way to fourth in the V-12 Alfa Romeo. The U.S. Grand Prix West marked the beginning of Mario Andretti's last full season in Formula One. It would also be the only points finish for him that year. *Bob Tronolone*

faster than Chapman's once-dominant creations. In 1979, there were no pole positions and no front-row starts for Andretti. In fact, he only reached the podium once that year, finishing third at the Spanish Grand Prix. Two fourths and two fifths were his only other points finishes in 1979.

The next season was even worse, Andretti's Lotus finishing in the points only one time in 1980, a sixth at Watkins Glen. That year was young Eddie Cheever's first full season of Formula One. It was anything but a success. Though he'd won three Formula Two races in an Osella chassis in 1979, in the new Osella-Cosworth F1 car, Cheever failed to even make the field four times, and in the 10 races in which he did qualify, he finished only once, 12th at Imola in the Italian Grand Prix.

Early in the 1980 season, another American driver did a little known test with Brabham in Europe and another at Riverside Raceway not long before the 1980 U.S. Grand Prix at Long Beach.

In 1979, in his first full season with Roger Penske, Rick Mears not only won the Indianapolis 500, but the first CART championship. Still, with the trouble between CART and USAC ongoing, the future of Indy car racing was not clear.

"I wanted to get my foot in the door over there," said Mears, "just in case CART didn't go. I think Jackie Stewart was instrumental in putting me together with Bernie Ecclestone and Brabham. I did two tests at Paul Ricard, and I was within about a half-second of Nelson Piquet on their home ground. And I was making very sure, you know, that I didn't make any mistakes. And I knew where I could gain more time with a little more time in

the car, where I could go ahead and lean on it a little more. Then at River-side, on a track that I knew, I was two to three seconds a lap quicker than Nelson. It went well. Everything was fine. We came to terms, Bernie and I, and it was just a matter of me making the final decision whether I wanted to do it or not. Nelson would've been my teammate in '81. You know, that was the year of his first World Championship."

In fact, Ecclestone wanted Mears to drive at Long Beach in 1980, but there was a hitch. "I don't know, the FISA or somewhere along the line they ran into a problem and wouldn't allow me to do it. I wasn't really sure I was going to do it anyway at that point."

In the end, Mears opted to race in the United States. "I didn't want the travel. I didn't want to leave the team I was with. Roger had given me his full blessing. He said, 'It sounds like a hell of a deal. But it's up to you to make your decision.' I mean, he didn't have any problem with me going and doing the test and all that. But the more I thought about it, I just decided to stay, for a lot of reasons.

"I enjoyed the fact that we were getting to drive both ovals and road courses here. You wouldn't get that variety in Formula One. And really, I didn't want to move the family to Europe five months out of the year. I like a McDonalds on every corner, you know, that kind of thing. And partially, some of the attitudes there. I've always been pretty easygoing, and I didn't care for some of these people thinking they stood a foot taller than every-body else. And it was a little more cut-throat over there. And I got into this as a hobby and for fun, because I love the sport. Finally, what it boiled down to after I weighed all the facts, I said, 'Guys, I'm gonna do what makes me happy, 'cause that's why I'm doin' it.' And I felt the Penske orga-nization and running here in the States would make me happier than run-ning over there, even though the money was better." "Rocket Rick" Mears would never drive in a Grand Prix. Pity.

In 1981, Mario Andretti signed a lucrative contract to drive the promis-ing Alfa Romeo GP car. The year, Andretti's final complete season in For-mula One, was another disaster. His uncompetitive Alfa managed a points finish only once, a fourth at Long Beach. There, fellow Indy car driver Kevin Cogan, in a one-off ride for Ken Tyrrell, failed to qualify by a mere 0.06 of a second. Finishing one place back of Andretti in the other Tyrrell-Cosworth, was Eddie Cheever, scoring his first ever World Championship points. While Cheever's fortunes were on the rise—he'd finish in the points four more times in 1981—America's most successful Formula One driver was nearing the end of his Grand Prix career.

Mario Andretti raced only three times in 1982, once at Long Beach in a Williams-Cosworth and at Monza and Las Vegas in a Ferrari. Fittingly, it was at Monza—where he'd seen his first Grand Prix in 1954, where, in his first Formula One appearance, in 1968, he'd stunned onlookers with quick times on the first day of practice, where, in 1977, he'd passed into the lead on the *outside* of the vaunted Parabolica curve and won, and where he clinched his World Championship in 1978—that Andretti gave his last bravura F1 performance. To the delight of the *Tifosi*, Andretti, in a Ferrari turbo V-6, scorched Monza's track record. "Yeah," he recalled, "my last ride. I put that thing on the pole. I thought the house was going to come down. Unbelievable!" And appropriate. Andretti's first Formula One vic-tory had come in a Ferrari, in South Africa in 1971.

Eddie Cheever

1/10/1958 to

Eddie McKay Cheever was born in January 1958 in Phoenix, Arizona. He moved to Italy with his family and attended grade school and high school in Rome. Cheever began racing go-karts at the age of 13 and was 100-cc European and Ital-ian champion at 15. At 16, Cheever was second in the World Karting Championship and not long after, got his first rides in For-mula Ford cars. Indeed, Cheever was considered a prodigy, and by 17 he was competing in Formula Three in England, where, as teammate to Danny Sullivan, he won 4 of 11 starts.

Cheever was so impressive that in 1978 he was considered for a seat on the Ferrari Formula One team, a possibility that disappeared when the Canadian phenom Gilles Villeneuve was signed instead. Eddie Cheever's long F1 career did start that same year, but not without a struggle. After unsuccessful attempts to qualify a Theodore in Argentina and Brazil, Cheever finally managed to make the grid in South Africa in a Hesketh-Cosworth, but retired with engine problems.

Two years of Formula Two would pass before Cheever would return to Formula One with his 1979 F2 team, Osella. Though he'd won three races in the junior formula with them the year before, Cheever's experience with the unreliable Osella was hardly a success in 1980. Nine years later, after accumulating more Grand Prix starts than any Ameri-can in history, the articulate and popular Cheever left Formula One for Indy car racing. He was named Rookie of the Year at Indianapolis, where he finished eighth, and in the PPG CART Championship, where he was ninth in points.

Deprived of a couple of Indy car wins in 1995 only by bad luck, Cheever made the switch to the IRL later that year. Driving for his own team in 1997, he won the Indy 200 at Walt Disney World.

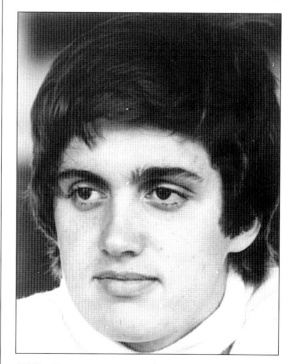

Eddie Cheever. *Toyota Grand Prix of Long Beach*

Mario Andretti is given thumbs up at Long Beach in his one-off ride for Williams in 1982. Wrong. He DNF'd. *Bob Tronolone*

"In fact," he added, "if one of the turbo linkages hadn't broken, I probably would've won that one in '82, too—finished second." Actually, third. It was the last pole and the last points finish for America's all-time F1 winner. In fact, it was to be Andretti's last Grand Prix finish. Two weeks later, at Las Vegas, on a weekend that would end up as the anticlimax to his brilliant Formula One career, Andretti's Ferrari went off with a broken rear suspension link on the 27th lap. Ironically, he was running right behind Eddie Cheever, on the way to his third podium finish of the year in a Ligier-Matra.

In his amazing 14-year Formula One career, Mario Andretti amassed 12 GP victories, 18 pole positions, 10 fastest laps, and 799 laps in the lead in World Championship Grands Prix.

Eddie Cheever, in Formula One through 1989, would set his own record, achieving more Grand Prix starts, 132, than any other American driver. At the 1982 U.S. Grand Prix in Detroit, Cheever scored his best finish yet, coming home second behind John Watson's McLaren.

Nineteen eighty-three looked to be a great year for Eddie Cheever. He would join Alain Prost on the works Renault team, whose turbocharged V-6 had so far shown ample power, if not reliability. And so went Cheever's season. His car failed on eight occasions, but in the seven remaining Grands Prix, Cheever missed the points only once, with a second at Canada and three thirds, France, Belgium, and Italy, his best finishes. Despite a truly impressive season, Cheever's accomplishments inevitably suffered in comparison to those of his phenomenal teammate, future four-time World Champion Alain Prost.

Eddie Cheever wasn't the only American in Formula One in 1983. Late in 1982, Danny Sullivan had been one of 10 drivers tested by Ken Tyrrell at the Paul Ricard circuit. Tyrrell was impressed enough to invite the American to Rio for another tryout while the team was doing preseason tire-testing. For a while, it looked like a wasted trip. "I stood there for nine-and-a-half days," remembered Sullivan, "and didn't do anything. And then they were about to leave and Ken says, 'Okay, jump in the car and you can get a few laps.' And I went out and was almost as quick as Alboreto in just a handful of laps. And he said, 'You've selected yourself. Welcome to the team.'"

170

September 25, 1982. After a near storybook race at Monza, where he qualified his Ferrari on the pole and finished third, Andretti's 134th—and final—Formula One race at the Las Vegas GP was an anticlimactic DNF. America's most prolific Grand Prix winner would retire afterwards. *Bob Tronolone*

Unlike Cheever, Sullivan, in the naturally aspirated Tyrrell-Cosworth, finished the first two Grands Prix of 1983, albeit with unspectacular 11th- and 8th-place results at Brazil and Long Beach, but in his third Grand Prix, the non-points Race of Champions at Brands Hatch, Sullivan staged a thrilling race-long duel with Keke Rosberg's Williams, which came to a head on the last lap.

"Rosberg and I went around Druids side by side. I was passing him on the outside and he drove me, well, not . . . You know how you say somebody closes the door? Well, he *opened* the door. I was on the outside of him and he just kind of drove me into the grass. You know, he said to me afterwards, because I got up alongside him a couple of other times, he said, 'Hey, I'm sorry.' I said, 'Don't be silly. If the situations had been reversed, you'd have had the same treatment.' You know, he didn't bang me or do anything like that. He just made himself real wide."

Sullivan's impressive second place would be his best result in Formula One. His best World Championship finish came a month later at Monaco, where he finished fifth from his last-place starting position. "It was a good season. You know, I qualified for every race. I had some good results. It was hard. We didn't do any testing. And Michele was the number-one, which was fine. But I proved, when they finally gave me the DFY, which was the trick version of the DFV, that I could hold my own."

With the newer Cosworth, Sullivan managed to outqualify his more experienced teammate in two of the last three races and put in a particularly strong performance at the last World Championship round of 1983, the South African Grand Prix. There, because of a last-moment car problem, Sullivan started last again but persevered to finish seventh, one place behind Eddie Cheever's Renault.

"Tyrrell thought that was possibly one of the best drives I had, because they had *gone* when I started. And because of the altitude at Johannesburg—normally aspirated engines really suffered there. So I was really, really down on power. So that was a bit of a deal."

Eddie Cheever in his second race with the turbocharged Renault at the 1983 U.S. Grand Prix West. Cheever DNF'd at Long Beach but would finish second three weeks later in the French Grand Prix. *Bob Tronolone*

The South African Grand Prix would be Sullivan's last Formula One race. Tyrrell was unable to secure a turbocharged engine for the 1984 season and at that point, the prospects of success with a normally aspirated engine were practically nil.

"I had a chance to stay with Ken for no money or to go with Doug Sheirson, who made me an offer to drive his Indy car. And I thought, 'Do I want to go back to Formula One just to be in Formula One? Or do I want to come back to America and race with a chance to win?' I'm a racer so I chose to come back where I had a chance to win. And in fact, I won three races that year and the next year, with Penske, won at Indy."

With no turbo motor, Tyrrell lost his Benetton sponsorship, which would then go to Alfa Romeo, for whom Eddie Cheever would drive for the next two seasons. It was to be a frustrating time for the expatriate American.

The turbocharged V-8 Alfa engine proved even less reliable than the Renault had been—and not nearly as fast. Incredibly, Cheever's fourth-place finish in the first race of 1984, the Brazilian Grand Prix, would be his *only* points finish in two full seasons. What's more, during those two years, there were three accident-related DNFs, but the other 22 times his Alfa failed to finish were due to engine or mechanical problems. It was a disaster. And in the fickle world of Formula One, Cheever was left without an F1 ride for 1986. He stayed busy, though, driving a TWR Jaguar in the World Sports Prototype Championship (he scored points in every race he finished and won outright at Silverstone). In the one Grand Prix in which Cheever did compete, he sat in for an ailing Patrick Tambay at Detroit in the latest "American" GP car, the Beatrice-sponsored Haas-Lola. There had even been talk of young Michael Andretti driving the car, but FISA wouldn't issue a "super-license." Though Cheever managed to jump right in after his long layoff and outqualify Haas-Lola number-one Alan Jones, neither he nor Jones made it to the finish.

Not finishing, unfortunately, was something that the Haas-Lolas did a lot of in their brief career, in spite of the best efforts of some of the most talented people in Formula One. Teddy Mayer, assisted, as usual, by Tyler Alexander, set up a new company for Carl Haas, called FORCE. What the car was to be called was another matter.

"Well, that was a moot point," laughed Alexander. "There was a funny argument amongst all of us. Carl was adamant that the thing be called a Lola. Why, I don't know. Lola had nothing to do with it. At one point, we had to sort of ask Eric Broadley, the Lola guy, to stay in Northampton or wherever he is. You know, he was very helpful, but you can't be a help unless you're there all the time. I think Carl was using him to keep an eye on us, because at that stage, Carl wasn't sure what we were doing. It was all happening pretty fast. We were equally adamant that the car should be a Haas. In the end, I think it was called a Beatrice Haas-Lola."

The effort was bankrolled by Beatrice Foods—at least, for 18 months. "It's pretty amazing," remembered Mayer, "when you think of the people we had assembled in that short time. We had Adrian Newey, chief designer at Williams; Ross Braun, chief designer at Benetton; and Neil Oatley, chief designer at McLaren. All of them worked in our drawing office."

The 1980 World Champion, Alan Jones, came out of retirement to drive the Haas-Lola in its debut at Monza late in 1985. He was joined the next season by Patrick Tambay, who would give the initial powerplant, a four-cylinder turbocharged Hart, its first and only finish, an eighth (albeit six laps down) at the 1986 Spanish Grand Prix. Whatever hopes there had been for the intended engine, a new Ford-Cosworth V-6 Turbo, faded when that motor was delivered in 1986.

"Unfortunately, its first year, it wasn't terribly successful," remembered Mayer. Alexander was more direct. "The engine was crap when we had it. I don't know, it was a lot of funny politics. We had one very good engine, at Monza in '86. You know, Tambay was like 15 kilometers per hour faster on the pit straightaway than with the other engine—a huge, huge amount. He was as quick as anyone on the racetrack. But we scuffed some pistons on it and had to change the thing. And that was the last we ever saw of that

---

In 1963, Teddy Mayer left law school to accompany his younger brother Tim to Europe for a season of Formula Two for Tyrrell. "I went with him because I had some engineering backround," says Mayer, "and because of my interest in it." Tim Mayer had won the SCCA Formula Junior national championship in a Cooper in 1962, qualified midpack at the U.S. Grand Prix that year (DNF), and shown sufficient promise to be offered a place on the works Cooper Formula One team in 1964. "Cooper asked me to come along as team manager," explained Mayer. First, however, would be the Tasman series, for which two special cars were constructed, one by Bruce McLaren, in whose name the two cars would be entered, the other by Teddy and Tim Mayer and fellow American Tyler Alexander.

Tragically, Tim Mayer was killed in the final Tasman race, but McLaren, Mayer, Alexander, and several others had already decided to join together and build their own racecars under the McLaren banner. "We started in the summer of 1964 by buying the Zerex," said Mayer, "and getting involved in the precursor of the Can-Am series." Alexander had, ironically, been one of the people involved in the construction of Roger Penske's successful Zerex Special, actually an extensively modified F1 Cooper with which Penske had won USAC's 1962 "sports car" championship. McLaren cars, of course, would eventually rule the Can-Am series for several years but success in Formula One would take some time.

"We had an abortive first season in 1966 with the Indy four-cam Ford," admitted Mayer. "It was a fairly bad choice for some technical reasons. We used 2-liter BRMs and the four-cam Ford off and on for that '66 season and in '67, we got a proper Cosworth-Ford V-8." Still, the McLaren team's first Grand Prix victory wouldn't come until March 1968, when Bruce won the non-championship Brands Hatch Race of Champions. Bruce won again at Spa and two more victories by Hulme and a number of points finishes allowed McLaren to finish second in the 1968 World Championship for makes. Ironically, Bruce McLaren would not live to see his team's greatest successes. He was killed testing a new McLaren Can-Am car in June 1970.

"Bruce and I were the two owners of McLaren, and Tyler Alexander had a bit of stock, too. When Bruce was killed in 1970, I bought most of the rest of it. I owned the majority of the stock and Tyler owned the rest." After New Zealander Phil Kerr left in the early 1970s, for nearly a decade McLaren would be run totally by Americans. "Yes, it was very American. I ran the Formula One team and Tyler ran the Indy car effort."

The ultimate success for a Grand Prix team came in 1974. McLaren driver Emerson Fittipaldi won the World Championship and McLaren was the World

Teddy Mayer and Tyler Alexander
The Americans at McLaren

Teddy Mayer and Tyler Alexander.
Pete Biro

Champion "make." To make things even sweeter, that same year Johnny Rutherford won the Indianapolis 500 in a McLaren.

There was another drivers World Championship two years later, with James Hunt. "Yes, we were very successful in 1974, '75, and '76. Then 1977, '78, and 1979 were not very good at all. And John Barnard was working for Ron Dennis at the time on sort of a pilot project with carbon fiber. Ron convinced both us and Marlboro that merging forces would be good. Which it was. And they, basically, brought the carbon fiber chassis to the team. We worked together for about three years after that. And at the end of '82, we sold out to Ron Dennis. He wanted to have control and made us a good offer that we decided was sensible to accept and we did."

Mayer and Alexander ran an Indy car team in 1983, coming very close to winning the Indy car championship with driver Tom Sneva. But in the mid-1980s, the two returned to Formula One to head up Carl Haas' short-lived FORCE company, which built and fielded the F1 Beatrice Haas-Lolas. By the 1990s, Teddy Mayer was Deputy Chairman of Penske Cars Ltd. and Tyler Alexander was Special Projects Manager at McLaren.

motor. After they refused to give us the engine anymore, the thing gained about 200 to 300 horsepower, which was what we needed. They had the thing. They just didn't want to give it to us. We got screwed by some people at Cosworth, and ultimately we got screwed by a corporate takeover."

Beatrice was bought out and the new owners shut FORCE down in 1986. "Well, that was the blow that killed the thing," said Alexander. "Because if we had had the money, we probably could have gone somewhere else and bought Renault engines or something. It's a shame, because the car itself was bloody good at the end." The Haas-Lola's last race was at Australia in October 1986. Jones DNF'd and Tambay finished, but far enough back not to be classified. Thus ended another ambitious American effort to field a Formula One car.

Eddie Cheever—One Last Chance

Eddie Cheever was back in Formula One in 1987, driving an Arrows-Megatron. It would be a long season for the American, who once again found himself in a car that was neither fast nor reliable. The Arrows failed to finish nine times, but in the seven races in which Cheever was around for the checkered flag, he finished in the points four times. His best results were fourth place at Belgium and Mexico. It was more of the same in 1988. An inspired third-place finish at Monza highlighted an otherwise dismal season, in which Cheever's only other points finish would be a sixth at Mexico.

Arrows changed to the Cosworth V-8 for 1989, but by then, Honda and Renault V-10s reigned supreme, followed by the Ferrari V-12. Cheever's Arrows was simply dead slow in comparison, particularly in qualifying. He failed to make the grid twice and in the 13 times he did, there were usually 20 or more cars starting ahead of him. Remarkably, Cheever still managed two points finishes and four others in seventh, just one position out of the points. The one bright spot of the year came at the U.S. Grand Prix, fittingly, at Phoenix, Arizona, where he was born. There, Cheever scored an impressive third-place finish and threatened Patrese's much faster second-place Williams-Renault to the end. It was to be Eddie Cheever's last podium finish in Formula One.

He had shown speed, enthusiasm, and great determination in motor racing since his teens, but Eddie Cheever knew that wasn't enough to win in Formula One. With no prospects for a ride of above midpack quality, Cheever left Formula One at the end of 1989. Though he had been on the podium nine times and had 22 finishes in the points, a Grand Prix victory eluded Cheever. Only once in his long Formula One career, had Cheever driven a truly competitive car—one capable of winning a Grand Prix—and that was the turbo Renault in 1983. It was fate that his role that year would be as number two to a French teammate who was a genuine superstar in ascendance, Alain Prost. Overshadowed and perhaps overlooked on an all-French team, Cheever saw his one opportunity to break out, to step up to the next level, slip away. He would never get another.

In Formula One, as elsewhere in life, timing is everything, a lesson America's next Grand Prix challenger would learn the hard way.

MICHAEL–PROMISE AND PROMISES GONE WRONG
1990–1993

In 1990, two of America's best drivers, Al Unser Jr. and Michael Andretti, finished one-two in the CART Indy car series. In January that year, Unser was in London to pick up *Autosport*'s "Sportsman of the Year" award. While there, Unser made inquiries at Benetton and in particular, Williams about driving in Formula One in 1991.

"I didn't have a contract for '91," said Unser later, "and we were tryin' to decide what we were going to do. It was mostly just talk. Frank Williams is a good man, and I like Patrick Head. They're real racers. They go to war. And I did ask them for a job and the comment they made, they said there was 'interest' in me."

Virtually raised behind the wheel of a race car, Unser had no worries about adapting to Grand Prix. "You know, I've always said Pikes Peak is the slickest road course I've ever raced. I'm just a race car driver, but an F1 car is nothin' but a race car. And just like any race car, you have to adapt to its characteristics to make it go the quickest."

Regardless, Williams hadn't called by the winter. "I was doin' a lot of calling over there, hustling for the ride. Finally, my father pretty much told me if they really wanted me, they would have already hired me." Uncle Bobby didn't mince words. "I told him, 'Little Al, don't go to Formula One. Don't go to England. You're just gonna get had if you go over there.'"

In the end, Unser signed to drive Indy cars for the next two years. "They were 'interested' is all," said Little Al, with typical candor, "and my heart was really in the Indianapolis 500, so it didn't bother me all that much." Of his longtime friend and competitor, Michael Andretti, Unser noted, "I think there's a little bit of pressure on Michael because of his father being a Formula One Champion and all that. Myself, I don't have that kind of pressure."

Andretti and his famous father also traveled to Europe to test the F1 waters in 1990. While Michael was committed to Indy car racing for Newman-Haas for the next two years, McLaren boss Ron Dennis seemed surprisingly enthusiastic, and definitely open to further discussions. Then, in October 1990, after Alessandro Nannini was seriously injured in a helicopter crash, Benetton called.

"The timing isn't very good," said papa Mario at the time. "Michael's got some moral obligations. He can't just pick up and go without Carl [Haas] having someone marketable to fill the seat." Michael, however, used the occasion to publicly re-affirm that he was definitely on his way to Formula One in the near future. At McLaren, an old family friend thought the younger Andretti was ready.

"Yes," remembered Tyler Alexander, "In fact, I probably instigated the conversation with Ron. I thought Michael should have a test drive." Early in 1991, it happened. After driving in the 24 hours of Daytona, Andretti flew to Portugal to test a McLaren-Honda V-10, the dominant car in Formula One. He was tired and because of constant rain, only man-

Andretti waits to qualify at Monaco. Typically, suspension problems (resulting in a crash for both McLaren drivers), have ensured that Andretti has had little practice, and, in truth, he knows neither the course nor the car. The pressure to perform to silence the critics, and to gain the confidence of his own team is mounting. Trouble with the auto-shifter would only further complicate a so-so starting position, but Andretti hung on until he became comfortable on the narrow, unforgiving Monaco streets, then began to move up, settle in, and actually, turn times comparable to the leaders—until a blocked track delayed him at Loews, ending him in eighth instead of with a points finish. *Paul-Henri Cahier*

Michael Andretti begins his Formula One career at the South African Grand Prix in 1993. Lack of practice in the new McLaren together with mechanical gremlins relegated Andretti to ninth in practice. Then a clutch problem saw him start from the pit lane a lap down. It got worse. After finally getting away, he made a couple of passes but then got balked, made contact, and ended up off course, minus a wheel. It would be the first of three straight contact-related DNFs. The nightmare of 1993 had begun. *Paul-Henri Cahier*

aged to get in about 12 laps, just four when it was dry, but Andretti felt good about his short test.

"I got a taste of the animal," he said afterwards, "and I don't foresee any major problems. You know, it's just another race car, with a different feel and different limits. It just takes miles to get there and I think if I can get some good testing in, we should get right down there. I mean, the conditions weren't the greatest and I never saw the track before, never drove the car before, but in my four dry laps, I was only about two seconds off Berger that day. I was pretty happy." So were American F1 fans, particularly when it was announced that Andretti had signed a "testing contract" with McLaren.

When asked shortly afterwards how he'd deal with the extraordinary pressure heaped on an F1 driver in Europe, Andretti had a ready answer, "Well, yeah, but that's maybe if you live there. But hopefully, I'll be able to do it without living there. I think it's very important to have a base to go home to. Look at what dad did. He not only did that, but he drove Indy cars here and I wouldn't be doing Indy cars. I'd just be coming home, so if he could do it, then I should be able to." Mario seemed to agree. "All he needs is one or two tests," said the 1978 World Champion. "He doesn't need to grind away. Michael's not a test driver like some of the other guys, you know, that do the donkey testing. He's there to go for it." Circumstances would seriously challenge those sentiments two years later.

Michael Andretti had a brilliant season in 1991, virtually overwhelming the competition to win the PPG Indy car championship with eight pole positions, a record eight victories, and records in the amount of laps led, points scored, and prize money won. Midway through the year, he found time for another McLaren test at Magny Cours, most of it with low downforce and a slightly detuned V-12 Honda to simulate the high altitudes at McLaren's next race, in Mexico. But with the car setup normalized, Andretti was up to racing speed in only 10 laps before rain stopped the session. In September, Michael and Mario visited Maranello, ostensibly, just to talk about buying a street car. Two weeks later, a Ferrari offer arrived for the 1992 Formula One season. Again, Michael's Newman-Haas commitment nixed the deal, but Formula One interest in American drivers seemed to be on the rise, and not just for Michael Andretti.

Before the year was over, Al Unser Jr. was testing a Formula One Williams-Renault. Flying directly from Indianapolis testing, Unser took part in a five-day session at Estoril in Portugal with regular works driver Riccardo Patrese and Williams test driver Damon Hill. In spite of jet-lag and lack of familiarity with the high-tech F1 cars or Estoril, the 29 year old Unser was up to speed on his third day. In fact, in a direct comparison test in the same FW14 Williams on race tires, Unser was 0.3 second faster than the experienced Patrese.

As he had thought, the lighter, grippier, and more nimble F1 car proved no problem for Unser. "It was a lot of fun," he enthused at the time, adding. "I feel I could definitely win races with that car and team." In the short run, Unser was committed to Indy car, but suddenly it appeared Formula One might soon have bright young stars from America's *two* most famous racing families. It appeared even more likely after Unser exercised the family birthright and won 1992's Indianapolis 500. Two months later, Unser attended the British Grand Prix as a guest of Benetton—and was later taken to the factory for seat fitting. But it would be Michael Andretti who would fire the first shot in Formula One.

In September 1992, Ron Dennis flew to Detroit and after a full day of negotiations, announced that Michael would drive for McLaren in 1993, with options for two more years. "I think he can win Grands Prix," said Dennis, "and in the process of winning those Grands Prix, he can become the World Champion," adding, "It's not a question of which country you come from. It's how you best demonstrate your desire to win. You've got to have that desire to win, and the aggression in traffic. And there are probably fewer than five drivers in the world that I consider to have the necessary aggression."

There were, however, some unanswered questions. Would Ayrton Senna return to McLaren? If not, who would be Andretti's teammate? And with Honda leaving Formula One, what engine would McLaren run? More pointedly, was Dennis' Andretti move a ploy to wrest exclusivity of the Ford "factory" engine from Benetton? Dennis vehemently denied the latter. To the contrary, in private, Andretti later recalled, Dennis maintained that he was 90 percent sure of Renault power for 1993. Andretti seemed set to realize his ultimate goal, a Formula One ride with a bonafide front-line team. "It's something I've always dreamed about," he said at the time, "carrying the American Flag is very important to me."

Andretti knew there was work to be done. He would have to acclimate himself to race cars vastly different than Indy cars. Much of the technology would be new, electronically managed active suspension, semi-automatic gearboxes, high-tech traction and braking systems, not to mention the tricky aerodynamics of a flat-bottom car. Michael acknowledged that seat time would play a critical role his learning curve. "I'll probably do a lot more testing than usual," he confirmed, "I have a feeling that I'll be doing most of the mileage." That part of the plan took a serious hit two weeks later.

In early October, the FISA World Council announced new regulations that virtually eliminated most testing once the season began, except in the team's own country. Preseason testing immediately assumed even greater importance, not only to become familiar with the new car to be campaigned, but with the tracks Andretti would be seeing for the first time. He got his first look at Barcelona in December. There, using the old car and the Honda motor, Andretti was quick. "Yeah," he said later, "at Spain I was just one-tenth of a second off Ayrton's qualifying time." Another test, also

Honda-powered, at Paul Ricard two weeks later was less encouraging. "The car was just hopeless there. It was the old car with the V-12."

By late November, Al Unser Jr. knew he wasn't headed for Formula One. Frank Williams had signed Alain Prost to replace Mansell (gone to Indy car to take Michael's seat with Newman-Haas) and wired Unser that he was loathe to take a chance with a Formula One rookie as Prost's teammate in 1993. Instead, Williams test driver Damon Hill would be nominated. Needless to say, Unser was disappointed, but in truth, Formula One was the loser.

Another question was answered in December. McLaren would not be using the anticipated Renault V-10, but a Ford V-8 for 1993—a "customer" engine, one spec behind that supplied Benetton. In an attempt to close the gap, McLaren would eschew Ford electronics for its own proprietary TAG-manufactured system. The problem was, this meant further delay for the new car—to the detriment of Andretti. Two other significant developments would occur before he ever saw his race car for 1993, both of them tainted with the brush of Formula One politics. Late in December, Ayrton Senna sent a warning message to Ron Dennis, conspicuously testing Roger Penske's Indy car at Phoenix. Message received, Dennis, in January, signed Mika Häkkinen, the promising young Finnish Lotus driver, to team with Michael—or to act as test driver if Senna *did* choose to come back.

Finally, in February, the new Ford-powered McLaren MP4/8 was ready to test. Well, almost ready. TAG's complicated electronics package proved particularly frustrating to Andretti—when it wasn't raining at Silverstone. "Every test, it rained," he remembered, "and whenever it was dry, we had electronics problems. I'd get out of the pits and the thing would stop." Ironically, only after Andretti had returned to the United States, did Mika Häkkinen get his first opportunity to drive—and the electronic gremlins disappeared. Though it was all according to a pre-arranged schedule, Tyler Alexander felt it was a fundamental mistake for Andretti to leave—in short, that he had chosen to commute instead of live in Europe.

"I mean," Alexander said later, "if you want to sum it up, that's it, really. He didn't live here. And, you know, because he wasn't here, he didn't test the car." The fact is, Häkkinen got some valuable seat time in the new car at Silverstone. Andretti got nothing, and as it turned out, never got to drive the car again until the first race of the season, the South African Grand Prix. To make things worse, FISA announced another rule change, this one limiting the number of tires sets to be used and cutting back the length of practice and qualifying sessions at a Grand Prix. This would be of particular significance to Andretti throughout the season. Going into his first Grand Prix, ironically, where his father had scored his first Formula One victory 22 years before, Michael Andretti was anything but comfortable in his new job.

"We went down to that first race, and I still had no feel of what was going on," he admitted later, "you know, with all the new electronics and the active suspension." He also didn't know who his teammate would be. Finally, just before the South African GP, Ayrton Senna agreed to drive for McLaren, albeit on a tentative, race-by-race basis. Quite naturally, a great deal of focus was on him, and on his car. Andretti began his new career in a strange car, on a strange racecourse, among strangers.

"On the first day, I think I was sixth, which wasn't too bad. But the second day, I had problems with the suspension. It was doing some weird things

Andretti and McLaren headman Ron Dennis. Relations between the two would cool after Michael's less-than-impressive Formula One start. *Paul-Henri Cahier*

on me." Because of software glitches, suspension problems would plague both McLaren drivers for nearly half the season. "I qualified ninth. I don't think I improved my time from the day before. I was way off what Senna was running, like three seconds. But some of that was because the track picked up on the second day and I was never able to take advantage of it."

It wouldn't have mattered if he had been on the pole. Just before the start, Andretti's car developed a clutch problem. "There *was* no clutch," he said later. "I'm sittin' on the line, I put it into gear, and it just goes, bluuuup. And that was it." Andretti's stalled car had to be pushed to the pit exit after everyone was gone. "When that happens with those cars, you're screwed, because they've got to hook up and get the pressure up." A thoroughly unsettled Andretti rejoined his first Grand Prix a lap down. He made a couple of passes, then, on the fourth lap, caught up to a group of cars, one of which bobbled and braked early. Andretti was caught out and slammed into Derek Warwick, knocking a corner off the McLaren. Not exactly the kind of debut Michael had in mind.

At Brazil, things seemed to go better. "Yeah, I was pretty happy with the car there. I qualified fifth, and I was only about nine-tenths of a second behind Senna, you know, on his home track." By comparison, the gap between Alain Prost and Williams number-two Damon Hill, in a car in which Hill had done much of the testing, was over a second. "Yeah, so I was pretty happy." At least until McLaren boss Ron Dennis gave him a sample of the all-or-nothing, cut-throat mentality of his new workplace. "He says, 'What the hell are you smiling about? You're only fifth on the grid.' I thought, 'Thanks a lot, Ron.'"

It got worse. Andretti blew the start. As the other cars leapt forward, Andretti's McLaren seemed to creep ahead, tire smoke—too much—the only evidence of motive power. "I never realized . . . The thing has an auto-upshift, but it doesn't do it from first to second. I didn't know it and ran it about 100 yards before I realized it wasn't shifting, that I had to do it. That's when the other guys had a run at me."

Andretti at full song in practice at Donington. With Mario watching for the first time, Michael put on a show, actually outpacing Senna in one session. This was the Michael Andretti everyone at home knew—and the one McLaren had hired. It all fell apart before the end of lap one of the race. Michael simply—and admittedly—reached for too much, made contact with (who else?) Wendlinger, and suffered his third DNF in a row. *Paul-Henri Cahier*

One of them, Karl Wendlinger, suddenly veered toward the side of Andretti, who swerved away—and into the path of Berger's overtaking Ferrari. A frightening crash ensued, with Andretti's car cartwheeling crazily against the turn-one barrier. It was a disaster, leaving Andretti shaken and his new team bewildered.

Two weeks later, at Donington, Andretti qualified sixth, but on race-day, in the morning warmup, everything came right. "Yeah," he recalled, "that was the best the car was all year. I was quicker than Senna." Mario was there, too, seeing his son at a Grand Prix for the first time. "Michael was awesome in the morning," said the former World Champion. "He was flying. He had quick time until just before the end of the session."

"I really thought we had a shot at winning," Michael said later. "I mean, I was real comfortable with the car. It would have come down to pit stops and all that. No question, I could've raced Senna." The juices were flowing and when the green light came on, Michael rocketed away, determined to take his rightful place up front. Too determined. Halfway through the lap, Andretti

tried what some might call a chancy pass, the kind, in fact, he'd made his reputation on. This one failed and instead, Michael ended up tangling with, who else, Wendlinger, and putting himself out of yet another Grand Prix.

"It was my screwup, completely," Andretti admitted. "I just went for too much." Mario agreed, "He tried to grab the whole cake in the beginning," adding, "like I've done, God knows." Yet another off, his third straight crash in three Grands Prix, only one of which did he manage to complete the first lap. The British press had a field day, and pressure was mounting on Andretti, from all sides.

"That's was when I started feeling, 'Okay, Ron's losing confidence in me.' I could just tell. You know, he'd say little things. And, there was this third guy floatin' around out there, Häkkinen, and Ron used that against me every chance he could, you know, saying that he was payin' Mika to do nothing, so he was the one that had to test. I didn't get to do hardly any testing, and that became the next problem."

"Well," said Tyler Alexander several years later, "I don't know, *that* part, that's some politics, and I don't know the facts. I could speculate on some things, but I'd rather not. I mean, one could draw the conclusion that someone didn't *want* him to test for some reason. But if I was Michael, I would have lived here in England, right near the factory. He didn't have to make a nuisance of himself, but he could've come in two or three times a week and, you know, chatted to the guys. Not wasted

Michael and then-wife Sandy Andretti who, fairly or not, would increasingly be subject to sniping from Andretti critics—and even team members. "Oh, yeah, there's no question about that," recalled Tyler Alexander. "Unfortunately, to some extent, when Michael came with Sandy—with her various outfits—that was it, the ugly American. 'What the hell is she doing here,' you know? The stupid thing is, if she'd paid a little attention and worn a white shirt and a pair of jeans and Gucci loafers, you know, she could have fit in perfectly. She just needed some jeans instead of some goddamn getup. . . . And that's where it was completely screwed up. Everybody was always taking the piss out of them all the time, because they do that. So he had two strikes going for him." *Paul-Henri Cahier*

people's time, but gotten himself *involved*. Well, he didn't do that."

It was a problem that Andretti never did quite understand, even years later. It is hard enough for any outsider to be accepted into Formula One, *ever*, let alone an American, and in particular, one with a famous name and a reputation as a hotshoe in another form of racing. Being just six hours away by plane and willing and ready to fly, day or night, on a moment's notice was commitment in Michael's eyes. It was considerably less to those involved in the self-consciously serious business of Grand Prix racing.

In fact, even to some within his own team, Michael's routine of "dropping in" on race weekends in a way trivialized their sport and their own commitment. It was also, obviously, a rejection of their culture. And inevitably, this bred resentment. Ironically, even the presence of Andretti's wife exacerbated his cultural-political problem. Sandy Andretti's requests for pit access and radio earphones, common practice for drivers' wives in Indy car racing, were regarded as pushy and offensive in the intense world of Formula One. Other such clashes in the norms of behavior and style, inadvertent or not, rankled those around him and made his acceptance even more difficult. Somehow, Andretti never saw it.

"I tried to explain some things to him early on," said Alexander. "For some reason, he didn't want to listen. It was like someone else was telling him what it was all about. Well, either they didn't or they were afraid to. I don't know."

As if it were not enough to struggle with mechanical and circumstantial problems on the track, there was now increasing public criticism and a growing undercurrent of resentment and rejection. But after only three Grands Prix, Andretti's biggest battle lay within, against his own personal devils, doubt and desperation. He would get little comfort at Imola. There, in practice, Andretti's McLaren suddenly seemed to jump sideways midway through a corner and he shot off-course. It was a computer software problem, which affected Senna, too, but it was Michael who got the drubbing.

"When you would hit a curb, the computer would tell the suspension to drop the car," Michael explained. "It was bottoming. Senna crashed two or three times because of that. I only did it once and Ron was reaming me out. I rode up on a curb once and it just dropped itself on the ground. That was it." But in the race, Andretti looked to be having a good run. After 32 laps, he was up to fifth, catching up to and momentarily slipping by fourth-place Karl Wendlinger into a corner before touching a curb on the way out, allowing the young Sauber driver by again. Moments later, Andretti spun off into the wet grass, his race over. It wasn't all Michael's fault. The brakes had been adjusted for the wet conditions early in the race. When the track dried, Andretti found himself unable to reach the knob that would back off his locking rears. He was trying to do just that when his brakes locked up again—and around he went. At fault or not, it was another off, another DNF, and again, Andretti was pilloried in the press.

"In my view," Mario Andretti said later, "the key race that he really blew was Imola. If he hadn't gotten stuck behind Wendlinger, you know, if he'd have been on the podium there, I think it would've been all downhill after that." As it was, the next time out, things got a little better.

At Spain, Andretti at last finished a Grand Prix, with a solid if unspectacular fifth. "All we did was finish, basically. The car was horrible. In all the other races, the car wasn't bad. I would've finished on the podium in every one of those races, had I finished. But that one, the car was so loose. But, you know, we were able to come home."

Two weeks later at Monaco, it looked like both McLaren drivers were in for another long weekend. Senna crashed heavily on the first day of practice, again, a suspension glitch that caused the car to bottom. Then on the first day of qualifying, in the wet, Andretti got into the wall. "I went to brake, and it locked the rears. And I hit the guardrail. It didn't cost me at all, because it was a wet qualifying session. And the next day was dry, anyway." What did matter was that rain took away valuable practice time. The result was a mediocre starting position, ninth, definitely a disadvantage on Monaco's narrow, hard-to-pass street circuit. Problems with the auto-shifter made it even worse for Andretti when the green light came on.

"I let the clutch out to go and it went, ching-ching, right up to third gear by itself—shifted right through second and went to third gear. And then it went, buh-buh-buh-buh, and that's the way it went off the line." By the time Michael got up to speed, he was nearly last. Worse, when he arrived at the Loews Hairpin, traffic was backed up. "Everything was stopped and I hit Barbazza or somebody in the back." His front wing broken, Andretti had to drive around to the pits for a new nose section before rejoining the race—dead last. From then on, he drove his best race yet, working through the field with well-timed, decisive passes.

"I went out and fought hard, and it was actually a fun race. I passed a lot of guys. I was doing better and better because I was learning the track." Now turning lap times equal to the leaders, Michael continued to move up, his progress slowed only by the notoriously obstructive Andrea De Cesaris. "I lost about 45 seconds before I finally got by him." More time was lost when Andretti found the road completely blocked at Loews. Gerhard Berger, after having already knocked one car aside to get by and then tagging his own teammate in another incident, had just slammed into Hill's Williams, which was still running, but now parked sideways across the road. But for that delay, Michael would surely have finished in the points. It was a good effort all around—except in the record books.

There were more car problems at Canada. Senna could qualify no better than eighth and Andretti, though he'd been faster than his teammate in a couple of practice sessions, was mired back in 12th at qualifying time. Then, in the morning warm-up, there was more trouble for Andretti. After only two laps, the McLaren's alternator failed. That problem was resolved, but when everyone else moved off for the parade lap, Michael's car remained in place, its motor silent. He was pushed to the pit and as McLaren mechanics furiously changed different electronic components, the race was started. Finally, the problem was identified—the starter battery was flat. This time, Andretti entered the race three laps down. Again, he drove well, turning lap times that would have put him in the points, but he was never a factor.

To Andretti's growing number of critics in Formula One, it was yet another poor result, gleefully compared to the success of F1 expatriate Nigel Mansell, already a major player in Indy cars, with two victories. While three straight finishes and competitive lap times had, no doubt, begun to rekindle some confidence, halfway through the season, Andretti's political situation seemed even more fragile. When Senna finally signed for the whole year, instead of ending Häkkinen's chances to drive in 1993, there were new statements from Dennis that the Finn would still get a shot. In whose seat? Then, at Magny Cours, an odd thing happened.

"That race," Andretti remembered later, "that weekend, in qualifying, that's when strange things started to happen to my car. There's a beacon that you have to go by every lap. It's how the car knows what position it's in on the racetrack. It resets every lap. Well, it's hard to believe, but for some reason, mine was shut off during qualifying. And what it was doing, it screwed up the downshifting, the auto downshift, where it would downshift in the middle of a corner on me. I had to qualify with the car like that and, I mean, it was horrible. I'd go into a corner and it'd go eeeeeeeeeh. I qualified 16th. I know I could've been way up on the grid there. That was like a very, very fishy thing."

Andretti got another poor start, entering the first turn toward the back of the field. "I just wasn't used to starting yet, but then I had a good race and some really good passes. I passed the Ferraris, and I passed Barrichello right near the end. You know, for a bad start, it was a good race." Indeed, it was, yielding Michael a well-earned sixth place, his second points finish.

"But, what was very interesting is we went testing at Magny Cours two weeks later. Both me and Senna tested. And I ran two and one-half seconds faster than I qualified and I was only a 10th slower than Ayrton at the test. But that was a track that I knew, now, and felt comfortable with, and I was only a 10th slower. . . ."

Michael also knew Silverstone, at least, in comparison to most of the tracks. With the benefit of a higher-spec pneumatic-valve Ford motor for the first time, he looked forward to the British Grand Prix. The seat time showed and in some practice sessions, Andretti was quicker than Senna. However, whether it was poor timing on McLaren's part or just bad luck, the American's qualifying effort was botched. "I don't know why they sent me out when they did. The only time it rained was just when I came through the stadium part, the last part, and it really screwed up my quickest lap. It cost me a few positions." Andretti easily made some of those up with his best Formula One start yet—but then went for too much. Pushed wide into the marbles, he slipped off the track, his race over. Once again, his own mistake overshadowed any bad hand he'd been dealt—and Andretti knew it.

At Hockenheim two weeks later, it didn't matter that he was quicker than Senna in an early practice session. It didn't matter that software problems with his car's suspension ruined later sessions, or that no one believed him until he came into the pits on three wheels—the other one just frozen in midair in full bump position. It didn't matter that it was Ayrton Senna who spun off on lap one (but continued). What mattered was that four laps later, Michael got pinched off by Berger, bent the steering, and was out, again. And what really mattered was that an obviously fed-up Ron Dennis told the press, "Michael made another mistake."

"My heart bleeds for him," said Mario two days later of his beleaguered son, "Michael's in a very difficult situation. He's got Mika hanging over him and that's part of the problem. But the thing at Germany, getting together with Berger, no matter how lightly, didn't help him at all. You know, one after the other."

Andretti's miseries seemed to continue at Hungary, with a couple of off-track excursions in practice and another poor qualifying effort. He lined up 11th. In the race, though, there was a glimmer of light. At the green light, Andretti virtually shot off the line, quickly gaining four positions. Comfortably in sixth, he looked quite confident. "Yeah, I was doing real well there. I was running right with the lead bunch, except for [winner] Hill. He just took off." Indeed, Andretti easily held off Schumacher in the Benetton and looked to be on his way to a good finish—until lap 15, when the McLaren's fly-by-wire throttle failed. The consensus was that he would certainly have made the podium, and possibly second place. But, yet again, instead of a good result, something positive to hold up to his critics, there was just another DNF. Andretti's situation was critical.

"Already, at that point, I started to get word that Ron was thinking about pulling me out of the car. He says, 'I gotta see how Häkkinen does and I gotta put him in race conditions for three races. And I can't renew your contract. I can't say that I will do anything until November.' He knew that I couldn't wait around. And so, he was saying he had to get Häkkinen in the car to evaluate and all that stuff. And so he was saying pick the races that you want."

Andretti didn't respond but went to the Belgian Grand Prix knowing he probably wouldn't last the season. The daunting high-speed, high-horsepower course at Spa was not ideal for the relatively anemic McLaren-Fords. Senna could finish no higher than fourth, almost two minutes behind winner Hill. Andretti was eighth, thanks in part to a disastrous first tire stop, where his motor died as soon as the neutral button was selected. "I had like a 30-second pit stop. I think I probably would've finished fifth."

It was ironic that Michael Andretti's last Formula One race—at least, in 1993—would occur at Monza, where so much American, and in particular Andretti, motor racing history had taken place. This was it. No matter what was said afterwards publicly, PR, BS, whatever, Andretti knew beforehand that this was his last race, his last chance. And he *damn* sure wasn't going to go out with a whimper.

"I missed the whole first day because of engine problems. Then I had a big fight because there was a series VIII engine and a series VII engine. They didn't want to give me the series VIII. It was worth a good three-tenths of a second. I fought hard and I finally got them convinced to give it to me for qualifying." He needed it. Between engine problems and the weather, Andretti had had very little practice. He qualified ninth, 1.2 seconds behind his teammate, who was fourth fastest. In the prerace warm-up, though, Michael was only 0.2 behind Senna, in spite of a persistent brake balance problem that would catch both of them out in the race. Michael first, on lap two.

"I spun going into the second chicane. Then a few laps later, Ayrton spun in the same place, when he took out Brundle. The rears would just lock up." Senna was out for good, but Andretti was able to get back on course and drive around to the pits for new tires and to have the grass removed from his radiators. He emerged from the pits 20th. "I was last, and the leaders weren't far behind me. So from then on it was just drive as hard

The McLaren crew performs an Andretti pit stop. When criticism began to mount from the outside, there was little personal support from within the team. *Marlboro*

as I can. I made some good passes." He made the kind of passes he'd been hired to make. Indeed it was vintage Michael Andretti. Nearly two hours later, he lunged past Patrese and, yes, Wendlinger, to claim third, just before the checkered flag. Redemption, at last.

How bittersweet it must have been on the podium. Michael Andretti's longtime dream, turned nightmare, was over, but at least he'd salvaged some pride at the end. And not only *on* the track. He had for months labored under the weight of unfulfilled expectations, frustration, and disappointment, and had never dropped his head. He had suffered withering public criticism and sniping, and had never complained. He had been ambushed by circumstance—official, mechanical, and political, and he had never given up.

How did it happen? How did the most exciting and successful American driver in recent times fall so short of what he and others had known was possible? Much was spoken and written of Andretti's mistakes. That he made them was never in question. To his credit, and the absolute astonishment of F1 colleagues, to whom the notion of culpability would never occur, Andretti admitted his errors. Most were rookie mistakes, born of inexperience and impatience. Seat time would have helped. Rule changes severely limited testing. And some opportunities were squandered by Michael's critical decision to commute between Europe and home. On that point, critics and supporters agree.

"Everybody here does," said Tyler Alexander from his office at McLaren. "Jackie Stewart, even Senna. Senna said to me, 'I like the kid. I

thought he was quite quick. But, you know, how could he not come over here? That's what you have to do to become involved in this business.' And Stewart said exactly the same thing. He said, 'If you had to say one mistake, 'He didn't come over here and live. You know, blend in with the people.'"

Nowhere near as worldly as his father, perhaps Andretti simply couldn't get comfortable outside his own environment. To be sure, his experience would've been better had he tried. And to be sure, with more seat time, there would've been fewer errors. That said, in fairness, too much emphasis was put on his failings. Yes, he had spins and crashes, but no more than F1 favorites like Gerhard Berger or Brundle or Andretti's own personal magnet, Wendlinger. Or in subsequent years, Häkkinen or Alesi or Irvine. Yet their transgressions, even when serious, were quickly forgiven and forgotten. They were family. Clearly, Andretti was not.

Cynics might wonder if it was accidental that in the smoke about Andretti's problems, the greatest failure of all was hardly mentioned, that of Formula One's formerly dominant team, McLaren. Simply put, Ron Dennis' inability to secure use of the V-10 Renault doomed not only Michael, but even the incandescent Senna to second-class status. Without it, McLaren's weakness was both ensured and exposed. Senna, of course, anticipated this and, had he not been outmaneuvered by Prost and French nationalism, would have had Renault power at Williams. As it was, he and Michael, were down some 60 to 80 horsepower all year long. This in a chassis that was late to begin with and plagued with its own problems, made worse by low-downforce setups to minimize the horsepower difference.

Another McLaren failure rarely mentioned that tormented both drivers most of the season was a bug-laden electronics system that affected not only

It is both a blessing and a curse to be the child of someone famous. As the son of Mario Andretti, a true legend, Michael Andretti has undoubtedly been presented with many opportunities in motor racing. But inevitable comparisons to his father and the relentless pressure of expectations, particularly his own, have been formidable adversaries throughout his racing career. To his credit, Michael Andretti's answer has always been speed and aggression.

Michael Andretti
5/10/1962 to-

Michael Mario Andretti was born in Bethlehem, Pennsylvania, the first of Mario's three children. At 10, he began racing go-karts and in 1980 moved up to Formula Fords. In 1981, Michael scored six Formula Ford victories to become SCCA Northeast Division champion. The following year, he was SCCA Super Vee champion and named SCCA Pro Rookie of the Year.

Along with the Formula Mondial (Atlantic) championship in 1983, Michael took two steps up the competition ladder, co-driving a Porsche with Mario to finish third at Le Mans, and making his Indy car debut at Caesar's Palace. Only one year later, Michael was Co-Rookie of the Year at Indianapolis after qualifying fourth with a fifth-place finish.

Michael Andretti won his first Indy car race at the Long Beach Grand Prix in 1986. Two more victories helped him finish second in the PPG CART championship. In the next six years, up to 1993, when he left to drive in Formula One, Andretti amassed 27 wins, placing him third in career victories, among active Indy car drivers, behind only Mario and Al Unser. His best year was 1991, when the younger Andretti dominated Indy car racing with a record eight wins.

Often during his harrowing year in Formula One, Michael's own lack of success was contrasted—always unfavorably—to World Champion Nigel Mansell's PPG championship the same year in Indy car racing. The fact is that Mansell won with the Lola chassis and Ford Cosworth engine that Michael had developed the previous year. While finishing only second in the PPG Championship in 1992, Michael won the same number of races and pole positions as Mansell in 1993, but led 533 more laps. Is it any wonder that Andretti considers his win over Mansell in their head-to-head match-up in the first Indy car race of 1994 among his favorites?

Speed was not the problem in Formula One. Michael was never slower than McLaren teammate Mika Häkkinen when they tested on the same day. Never. He even matched or was respectably close to Senna's times on occasions when he got enough laps to get comfortable.

But while he admired Senna's talent and was grateful to learn the Brazilian had given a press conference at Portugal to decry the raw deal Andretti had gotten, Michael remained convinced that had he been given the chance, and the car, things would've been different. Formula One holds no mystery for him.

"It's equal to over here, no better, no worse. Really, I think the top guys are just the same on both sides of the ocean. At one point, maybe, their field was a little deeper in terms of talent. But now, our field is very deep in talent. I don't think there's any difference."

Would he ever go back and try again? "I don't know. I'm really happy being back here. I did it. And I know I can do it. But it's such a screwed up atmosphere over there. So much politics, it's unbelievable. They're all control freaks." Andretti shook his head at the memory. Then, after a moment, he looked up and smiled, "But who knows?"

Michael Andretti.
Marlboro

the active suspension, but throttle, brakes, gearbox, and traction control. Yes, Senna, with his vast experience and superb ability to pinpoint trouble spots, managed to wade through these problems at the track faster than his rookie teammate, aided by the attention and qualifying priorities given a team's number-one. And yes, the Brazilian did manage to win five Grands Prix, three in the rain, where his legendary car control could even the odds, one at Monaco, where he was king—and had great luck—and at Australia, his emotional final race for McLaren. But notice, Senna didn't hesitate to leave for Williams. McLaren wouldn't win again until three years and 50 races later.

When Michael Andretti was just beginning to look to Formula One, Eddie Cheever, an American with a foot in both F1 and Indy cars, put it simply.

"Look, you are not *ordained* to be a Formula One driver. It's not like being the Pope. Racers are racers. If Michael has the right opportunity, he will do well. If he gets on a team that's on a downturn, he'll become history very quickly. He'll disappear like fog in the morning."

Indeed, he did. But it would have been a different story if Michael Andretti had gotten into Formula One in a Williams-Renault. As it was for another former Indy car champion three years later, young Jacques Villeneuve.

Alexander agreed. "Well, of course, the kid stepped into the best car on the grid and Michael didn't. I mean, there were a *lot* of things that had nothing to do with anybody screwing up. It was just the facts of life. That's what happened. You know, if he could have driven the car in the last three races, who knows what he would have done. He's quick. That's for sure. And he was starting to come around. He fought his way back at Monza. But for whatever political reasons, at that point, it was too late. I guess someone at McLaren had decided it was time for him to go."

America's Future in Formula One

Whoever is the next American to go to Formula One, be it Michael Andretti again or Little Al or the next Indy car champion or some young charger like Tony Stewart from this country's paved or dirt circle-tracks, they'd better be prepared to bump up against the same obstacles and, it must be said, the same prejudices American racers have faced for 100 years in Europe. It began when Frank Duryea's American car of the same name "won" the first London-to-Brighton Run in 1896. "Certainly, he must have cheated," claimed voices of doubt and disbelief. "He put his car on the train," they concluded, smugly. It was the same for Jimmy Murphy's Duesy in 1921. "Why, that car wouldn't last another lap," whined embarassed partisans. And America's World Champions, Phil Hill and Mario Andretti? "Only won because they had the fastest cars, and because their faster teammate was held back, and died," sniff doubters, even today.

As always, the next American Grand Prix threat will have to learn to ignore or endure such insults—or just flat overwhelm them with ability. Even then, they'll need patience and extraordinary determination. And above all, a good ride. When it happens, and it will, perhaps the next David Bruce-Brown, or Ralph DePalma, or Jimmy Murphy, or Hill or Gurney or Andretti will do us proud again—and Volume Two of *American Grand Prix Racing* will be underway.

APPENDIX

American Drivers in Grand Prix

The following conventions are used in this Driver Records Appendix:
Q = Qualified
F=Finished
DNF=Did Not Finish
DNS=Did Not Start
DQ=Disqualified
BOLDED UPPER CASE=a World Championship Grand Prix in post-1950 entries
#=car number

Entries are listed in the following order:
Name of Driver, birth & death dates if known: number of Grands Prix run (after 1950 number of Grands Prix run // **number of World C hampionship Grands Prix run**) *Italicized milestones*
Year- date name of race (car number car, qualifying position, result), date name of race, (car number car, qualifying position, result), *Italicized information about a race attended but not run - and why,* date name of race, (car number car, qualifying position, result), etc.
Year- date name of race, (car number car, qualifying position, result), etc.

Note: Driver, car number, car are not given in an entry if they remain unchanged from the previous entry in the same year.

Pre-World War Two

Emil Agraz: 1
1916- 11/18 American Grand Prize, Santa Monica (#10 Hercules, broken rod after 2 laps, DNF)

Johnny Aitken, ?-12/1918: 1
1916- 11/18 American Grand Prize, Santa Monica (#16 Peugeot, broken piston on 1st lap, DNF; Peugeot, in relief of Howdy Wilcox, F1)

Tom Alley, 1890-3/26/1953: 1
1915- 2/27 American Grand Prize, San Francisco (#2 Duesenberg, withdrawn due to weather after 89 laps, DNF)

Dave Anderson: 1
1916- 11/18 American Grand Prize, Santa Monica (#25 Kissell, broken valve after 5 laps, DNF)

Gil Anderson, 1880-7/26/1935 (or 9/1937?): 3
1912- 10/5 American Grand Prize, Milwaukee (#43 Stutz, F3)
1914- 2/28 American Grand Prize, Santa Monica (#3 Stutz, F5)
1915- 2/27 American Grand Prize, San Francisco (#5 Stutz, F4)

Guy Ball, 1888-?: 1
1914- 2/28 American Grand Prize, Santa Monica (#17 Marmon, F2)

Charlie Basle: 2
1910- 11/12 American Grand Prize, Savannah (#6 Pope-Hartford, seized piston after 19 laps, DNF)
1911- 11/30 American Grand Prize, Savannah (#43 Buick Hundred, engine failure after 10 laps, DNF)

Erwin Bergdoll, 1891-3/21/1965: 2
1911- 11/30 American Grand Prize, Savannah (#8 Benz, cracked cylinder after 8 laps, DNF)
1912- 10/5 American Grand Prize, Milwaukee (#40 Benz, F2)

Joe Boyer, 1890-9/1/1924: 1
1921- 7/26 A.C.F. Grand Prix, Le Mans (#16 Duesenberg, DNF)

Caleb S. Bragg, 1888-10/26/1947: 3
1911- 11/30 American Grand Prize, Savannah (#53 Fiat, F4)
1912- 10/5 American Grand Prize, Milwaukee (#41 Fiat, F1)
1915- 2/27 American Grand Prize, San Francisco (#14 Californian, broken crankshaft after 35 laps, DNF)

David Bruce-Brown, 1890-10/1/1912: 3 *1st American to win an international Grand Prix, 1st two-time Grand Prix winner*
1910- 11/12 American Grand Prize, Savannah (#15 Benz, F1)
1911- 11/30 American Grand Prize, Savannah (#48 Fiat, F1)
1912- 6/25-26 A.C.F. Grand Prix, Dieppe (#37 Fiat, DQ,*fastest lap), DNS 10/5 American Grand Prize, Milwaukee, fatal crash in practice

Bob Burman, 4/23/1884-4/8/1916: 4
1908- 11/26 American Grand Prize, Savannah (#4 Buick Special, retired after three laps, DNF)
1910- 11/12 American Grand Prize, Savannah (#17 Marquette-Buick, F3)
1911- 11/30 American Grand Prize, Savannah (#46 Marmon, magneto failure after 5 laps, DNF)
1912- 10/5 American Grand Prize, Milwaukee (#31 Benz, DNF; relieved Horan after 34 laps,F7)

George Buzane: 1
1916- 11/18 American Grand Prize, Santa Monica (#18 Duesenberg, piston after 27 laps, DNF)

William Carleton: 1
1916- 11/18 American Grand Prize, Santa Monica (#22 Owl Special, "broken pump" after 6 laps, DNF)

Billy Carlson, 1884-7/4/1915: 1
1915- 2/27 American Grand Prize, San Francisco (#32 Maxwell, withdrawn after 99 laps, DNF)

Arthur Chevrolet, 1886-4/16/1946: 1
1910- 11/12 American Grand Prize, Savannah (#3 Marquette-Buick, broken crankshaft after 9 laps, DNF)

J. Walter Christie, 1864-1/11/1944: 1 *Builder and driver of 1st American car to enter a Grand Prix*
1907- 7/2 A.C.F. Grand Prix, Le Mans (#WC-1 Christie WC-5, DNF)

George Clark: 1
1912- 10/5 American Grand Prize, Milwaukee (#39 Mercedes, F6)

Harry Cobe, 1881-8/22/1966: 1
1911- 11/30 American Grand Prize, Savannah (#49 Buick-Hundred, crashed after 3 laps, DNF)

W.M. "Bill" Cody: 1
1916- 11/18 American Grand Prize, Santa Monica (#23 National, engine failure after 33 laps, DNF)

Earl Cooper, 1886-10/22/1965: 4
1914- 2/28 American Grand Prize, Santa Monica (#8 Stutz, broken valve after 6 laps, DNF)
1915- 2/27 American Grand Prize, San Francisco (#8 Stutz, broken crankcase after 3 laps, DNF)
1916- 11/18 American Grand Prize, Santa Monica (#8 Stutz, F2)
1927- 9/4 European Grand Prix, Monza (#10 Cooper Special, turned car over to Kreis)

Joe Dawson, 1889-6/17/1947 (or 1946?): 1
1910- 11/12 American Grand Prize, Savannah (#8 Marmon, broken crankshaft afer 5 laps, DNF / 6th, in relief of Ray Harroun at 14 laps)

Ralph DePalma, 1883-3/31/1956: 8 *1st American driver to lead a Grand Prix & to set fastest lap*
1908- 11/26 American Grand Prize, Savannah (#18 Fiat, F9,*fastest lap)
1910- 11/12 American Grand Prize, Savannah (#19 Fiat, cracked cylinder after 23 laps, DNF)
1911- 11/30 American Grand Prize, Savannah (#55 Mercedes, F3)
1912- 6/25-26 A.C.F. Grand Prix, Dieppe (#42 Fiat, DNF), 10/5 American Grand Prize, Milwaukee (#35 Mercedes, crashed on last lap, classified F5)
1914- 2/28 American Grand Prize, Santa Monica (#12 Mercedes, F4); 7/4 A.C.F. Grand Prix, Lyons (#18 Vauxhall, DNF)
1915- 2/27 American Grand Prize, San Francisco (#22 Mercedes, withdrawn due to weather after 66 laps, DNF)
1921- 7/26 A.C.F. Grand Prix, Le Mans (#1 Ballot, F2),

9/4 Italian Grand Prix, Brescia (#4 Ballot, DNF)

Peter DePaolo, 4/5/1898-11/26/1980: *1st to drive a 4WD car in a Grand Prix*
1925- 9/6 Italian Grand Prix, Monza (#10 Alfa Romeo, F5)
1934- 5/6 Tripoli Grand Prix (#30 Miller 4WD, F6), 5/27 Avusrennen (Miller 4WD, DNF), *crashed #14 Maserati 8CM practicing for 6/17 Pena Rhin Grand Prix, Barcelona, DNS*

Lou Disbrow, ?-4/17/1947: 3
1910- 11/12 American Grand Prize, Savannah (#13 Pope-Hartford, cracked cylinder after 9 laps, DNF)
1911- 11/30 American Grand Prize, Savannah (#42 Pope-Hartford, F5)
1915- 2/27 American Grand Prize, San Francisco (#12 Simplex, F5)

Cliff Durant, ?-10/30/1937: 2
1915- 2/27 American Grand Prize, San Francisco (#20 Chevrolet, flagged off after 91 laps, DNF)
1916- 11/18 American Grand Prize, Santa Monica (#9 Stutz, broken valve after 17 laps, DNF)

Leon Duray (George Stewart), 4/30/1894-5/12/1956 (5/30?): 2
1929- 9/15 "non-formula" Monza Grand Prix (#20 Miller 91, DNF in 1.5 liter, #40 Miller 91 DNF in 3 liter event)
1932- 9/11 Monza Grand Prix (#44 Miller 91, DNF)

___ Fountain: 1
1912- 10/5 American Grand Prize, Milwaukee (#32 Lozier, steering failure after 22 laps, DNF)

Jack Gable: 1
1915- 2/27 American Grand Prize, San Francisco (#3 Tahis Special, flagged off after 92 laps, DNF)

____ Gandy: 1
1915- 2/27 American Grand Prize (#7 Edwards Special, accident after 21 laps, DNF)

Frank Goode, 1884-?: 1
1914- 2/28 American Grand Prize, Santa Monica (#11 Apperson, engine failure after 18 laps, DNF)

Huntley Gordon, 1884-?: 2
1914- 2/28 American Grand Prize, Santa Monica (#9 Mercer, F6)
1915- 2/27 American Grand Prize, San Francisco (#51 Gordon Special, withdrawn due to weather after 62 laps, DNF)

Harry Grant, 1878-10/8/1915: 2
1910- 11/12 American Grand Prize, Savannah (#7 Alco, stripped gears after 11 laps, DNF)

1915- 2/27 American Grand Prize, San Francisco (#30 Case, flagged off after 102 laps, DNF)

Hugh Harding: 1
1908- 11/26 American Grand Prize, Savannah (#11 National, broke camshaft after 5 laps, DNF)

Ray Harroun, 1/12/1879-1/19/1968: 1
1910- 11/12 American Grand Prize, Savannah (#14 Marmon, F6, after being relieved by Joe Dawson at 14 laps)

Willie Haupt, 1885-4/20/1966: 2
1908- 11/26 American Grand Prize, Savannah (#5 Chadwick, bearing failure after 5 laps, DNF)
1910- 11/12 American Grand Prize, Savannah (#18 Benz, leading when he crashed on lap 13, DNF,*fastest lap)

Eddie Hearne, ?-2/10/1955: 2
1911- 11/30 American Grand Prize, Savannah (#47 Benz, F2)
1915- 2/27 American Grand Prize, San Francisco (#21 Case, withdrawn due to weather after 64 laps, DNF)

George Heath: 3 *1st American to drive in a Grand Prix, 1st American driver on a "works" Grand Prix team*
1906- 6/26-27 A.C.F. Grand Prix, Le Mans (#10A Panhard, F6)
1907- 7/2 A.C.F. Grand Prix, Le Mans (#PL-1Panhard, DNF)
1908- 7/7 A.C.F. Grand Prix, Dieppe (#16 Panhard-Levassor, DNF)

Joe Horan, ?-9/16/1932: 2
1910- 11/12 American Grand Prize, Savannah (#12 Lozier, F5)
1912- 10/5 American Grand Prize, Milwaukee (#42 Benz, w/relief from Bob Burman, F7)

Hughie Hughes, ?-12/2/1916: 2
1912- 10/5 American Grand Prize, Milwaukee (#34 Mercer, severed fuel line after 8 laps, DNF)
1915- 2/27 American Grand Prize, San Francisco (#28 Ono, F3)

Lewis Jackson, ?-11/18/1916: 1 *1st American driver to die in a Grand Prix*
1916- 11/18 American Grand Prize, Santa Monica (#24 Marmon, crashed fatally after 13 laps, DNF)

Tony Janette, 1890-?: 1
1914- 2/28 American Grand Prize, Santa Monica (#19 Alco-6, cracked cylinder after 24 laps, DNF)

"Cap" Kennedy: 1
1915- 2/27 American Grand Prize, San Francisco (#11 Edwards Special, flagged off after 84 laps, DNF)

Arthur Klein: 1
1915- 2/27 American Grand Prize (#16 King, broken piston after 51 laps, DNF)

Peter Kreis, ?-5/25/1934:
1925- 9/6 Italian Grand Prix, Monza (#11 Duesenberg, DNF,*fastest lap)

1927- 9/4 European Grand Prix, Monza (#10 Cooper Special, DNF, F3 in Cooper's car)

Jack LeCain, ?-9/17/1931: 1
1915- 2/27 American Grand Prize, San Francisco (#18 Chevrolet, withdrawn due to weather after 81 laps, DNF)

Dave Lewis, 1882-5/13/1928: 1
1914- 2/28 American Grand Prize, Santa Monica (#16 Fiat, bearing failure after 22 laps, DNF)

Carl Limberg, ?-5/13/1916: 1
1911- 11/30 American Grand Prize, Savannah (#50 Abbot-Detroit, flagged off at 22 laps, F8)

J.B. "John" Marquis, 1883-?: 2
1914- 2/28 American Grand Prize, Santa Monica (#14 Sunbeam, accident after 33 laps, DNF)
1915- 2/27 American Grand Prize, San Francisco (#27 Bugatti, ingnition failure after 6 laps, DNF)

T. McKelvy: 1
1915- 2/27 American Grand Prize, San Francisco (#31 Overland, flagged off after 99 laps, DNF)

Tommy Milton, 1893-7/10/1962: 1
1925- 9/6 Italian Grand Prix, Monza (#7 Duesenberg, F4)

Al Mitchell: 1
1911- 11/30 American Grand Prize, Savannah (#44 Abbot-Detroit, F6)

Lou Moore, 9/12/1904-3/26/1956: 1
1934- 5/6 Tripoli Grand Prix (#24 Duesenberg-Miller, F7)

Mike Moosie: 1
1916- 11/18 American Grand Prize, Santa Monica (#11 Duesenberg, clutch failure after 5 laps, DNF)

Ralph Mulford, 1885-10/23/1973: 3
1908- 11/26 American Grand Prize, Savannah (#2 Lozier, retired after 11 laps, DNF)
1910- 11/12 American Grand Prize, Savannah (#4 Lozier, F4)
1911- 11/30 American Grand Prize, Savannah (#45 Lozier, retired with broken driveshaft after 23 laps, F7)

Jimmy Murphy, 1895-9/19/1924: 2 *1st American to win a European Grand Prix, drove 1st American car to win a European Grand Prix*
1921- 7/26 A.C.F. Grand Prix, Le Mans (#12 Duesenberg, F1,*fastest lap)
1923- 9/9 Italian Grand Prix, Monza (#5 Miller, F3)

Charles Muth, 1892-?: 1
1914- 2/28 American Grand Prize, Santa Monica (#15 Marmon, out of fuel and stranded after 25 laps, DNF)

Claude Newhouse: 1
1915- 2/27 American Grand Prize, San Francisco (#15 Delage, flagged off after 92 laps, DNF)

Louis Nikrent: 1
1915- 2/27 American Grand Prize, San Francisco (#10 Mercer, flagged off after 102 laps, DNF)

Eddie O'Donnell, ?-11/25/1920 (11/26?): 1
1915- 2/27 American Grand Prize (#19 Duesenberg, retired after 59 laps, DNF)

Berna Eli "Barney" Oldfield, 1/29/1878-10/4/1946: 3
1912- 10/5 American Grand Prize, Milwaukee (#44 Fiat, F4)
1914- 2/28 American Grand Prize, Santa Monica (#7 Mercer, bearing failure after 37 laps, DNF)
1915- 2/27 American Grand Prize, San Francisco (#1 Maxwell, piston after 31 laps, DNF)

Jim Parsons: 1
1915- 2/27 American Grand Prize (#24 Parsons Special, withdrawn due to weather after 55 laps, DNF)

Cyrus Patschke: 1 *1st driver to lead a Grand Prix in an American car*
1911- 11/30 American Grand Prize, Savannah (#51 Marmon, engine mount failure after 9 laps, DNF)

A.H. Patterson: 1
1916- 11/18 American Grand Prize, Santa Monica (#20 Hudson, F3)

Sterling Price: 1
1916- 11/18 American Grand Prize, Santa Monica (#14 Gandy Special, clutch failure after 10 laps, DNF)

Ed Pullen, 1888-?: 3 *driver of 1st American car to win an international Grand Prix*
1914- 2/28 American Grand Prize, Santa Monica (#4 Mercer, F1)
1915- 2/27 American Grand Prize, San Francisco (#4 Mercer, withdrawn after 71 laps due to weather, DNF)
1916- 11/18 American Grand Prize, Santa Monica (#4 Mercer, accident, DNF)

Eddie Rickenbacker, 10/8/1890-7/23/1973: 3
1914- 2/28 American Grand Prize, Santa Monica (#20 Mason, broken crankshaft after 34 laps, DNF)
1915- 2/27 American Grand Prize, San Francisco (#17 Maxwell, ignition after 41 laps, DNF)
1916- 11/18 American Grand Prize, Santa Monica (#17 Duesenberg, stripped gears after 27 laps, DNF; Duesenberg, in relief of Weightman, F5)

Clyde Roads: 1
1916- 11/18 American Grand Prize, Santa Monica (#6 Hudson, F4)

Glover Ruckstell: 2
1915- 2/27 American Grand Prize, San Francisco (#6 Mercer, witdrawn due to weather after 67 laps, DNF)
1916- 11/18 American Grand Prize, Santa Monica (#3 Mercer, broken valve after 39 laps, DNF,*fastest lap)

Laury Schell, ?-11/1939: 2
1936- 10/3 Donington Grand Prix w/"Alan Selbourne" (#22 Delahaye 135S, F12)
1938- 5/15 Tripoli Grand Prix (#12 Delehaye 145, DNF)

Lucy O'Reilly Schell: 4 *1st American woman to drive in a Grand Prix*
1927- 8/25 Baule Grand Prix (Bugatti 37, F12)
1928- 7/5 Marne Grand Prix (#8 Bugatti 37A, 1F4), 8/23 Baule Grand Prix (Bugatti 37A, F8)
1932- 8/17 Baule Grand Prix (#29 Alfa Romeo 6C, F10)

Joe Seymour: 1 *1st American to finish a Grand Prix in an American car*
1908- 11/26 American Grand Prize, Savannah (#3 Simplex, F11)

Phil "Red" Shafer: 1
1931- 7/19 German Grand Prix, Nürburgring (#38 Shafer-8 Special, DNF)

Elliot Shepard: 2
1906- 6/26-27 A.C.F. Grand Prix, Le Mans (#12C Hotchkiss, DNF)
1907- 7/2 A.C.F. Grand Prix, Le Mans (#BC-3 Clement-Bayard, F9)

George Souders, 1903-7/26/1976: 1
1927- 9/4 European Grand Prix, Monza (#8 Duesenberg, DNF)

Egbert "Babe" Stapp,?-9/17/1980: 1
1930- 9/7 Monza Grand Prix (#50 Duesenberg, 3rd in heat, F8 in final)

Michael Straight, 9/2/1916-___: 1
1934- 12/27 South African Grand Prix, East London (#16 Railton-Terraplane, F3)

Whitney Straight, 11/6/1912-4/5/1979: 18
1932- 2/29 Swedish Winter Grand Prix (#14 Maserati 26M, DNF)
1933- 7/2 Marne Grand Prix (#20 Maserati 26M, Q14,F4), 8/8 Swedish Summer Grand Prix (#22 Alfa Romeo 8C-2300, F4), 8/13 Coppa Acerbo, Pescara (#60 Maserati 26M, DNF), 8/20 Comminges Grand Prix, St. Gaudens (#32, DNF), 8/27 Albi Grand Prix (#6, F2), 9/10 Italian Grand Prix, Monza (#48, F11), 9/10 Monza Grand Prix (#12, F4)
1934- 4/2 Monaco Grand Prix (#4 Maserati 8CM, F7), 5/6 Tripoli Grand Prix (#54, DNF), 5/20 Morocco Grand Prix, Anfa (#12, Q4, F4), 6/3 Montreux Grand Prix (#10, Q2,F4), 7/8 Marne Grand Prix, Reims (#32, Q6, DNF), 7/15 Vichy Grand Prix (#26,F1), 8/19 Nice Grand Prix (#24, Q7,DNF-accident), 8/26 Comminges Grand Prix (#2, Q3,F3), 9/9 Italian Grand Prix, Monza (#26, Q13,F8), 10/6 Donington Park Trophy (#22, F1), 10/28 Algerian Grand Prix, Bouzerea (#16,F3), 12/27 South African Grand Prix, East London (#18, F1)

Lewis Strang, ?-7/20/1911: 1 *1st American to finish in the American Grand Prize at Savannah*
1908- 7/7 A.C.F. Grand Prix, Dieppe (#15 Thomas,

DNF), 11/26 American Grand Prize at Savannah (#16 Renault, F6)

William E. "Billy" Taylor, 1888-1918: 2
1914- 2/28 American Grand Prize, Santa Monica (#6 Alco, F3)
1915- 2/27 American Grand Prize, San Francisco (#29 Alco, flagged off, DNF)

"Terrible" Teddy Tetzlaff, 1887-12/16/1929: 2
1912- 10/5 American Grand Prize, Milwaukee (#33 Fiat, torque rod failure after 31 laps, DNF,*fastest lap)
1914- 2/28 American Grand Prize, Santa Monica (#1 Fiat, broken rod after 18 laps, DNF,*fastest lap)

Omar Toft, ?-1/12/1921: 1
1916- 11/18 American Grand Prize, Santa Monica (#27 Omar Special, clutch failure after 10 laps, DNF)

Ira Vail, 1894-4/21/1979: 1
1916- 11/18 American Grand Prize, Santa Monica (#19 Hudson, bearing failure after 9 laps, DNF)

Frank Verbeck, 1891-?: 1
1914- 2/28 American Grand Prize, Santa Monica (#18 Fiat, broken valve after 2 laps, DNF)

William Weightman: 1
1916- 11/18 American Grand Prize, Santa Monica (#21 Duesenberg, w/relief from Eddie Rickenbacker, F5)

Howard "Howdy" Wilcox, 1889-9/4/1923: 2
1915- 2/27 American Grand Prize, San Francisco (#26 Stutz, F2)
1916- 11/18 American Grand Prize, Santa Monica (#26 Peugeot, w/Johnny Aitken in relief, F1)

Spencer Wishart, 1890-8/21/1914 (8/22?): 3
1911- 11/30 American Grand Prize, Savannah (#54 Mercedes, cracked cylinder after 9 laps, DNF)
1912- 10/5 American Grand Prize, Milwaukee (#36 Mercedes, broken rod after 4 laps, DNF)
1914- 2/28 American Grand Prize, Santa Monica (#2 Mercer, bearing failure after 22 laps, DNF)

Len Zengle, ?-9/25/1963: 1
1908- 11/26 American Grand Prize, Savannah (#7 Acme-6, broken spring after 7 laps, DNF)

Post-World War Two

Tony Adamowicz, 5/2/1941-____: 1
1971- 3/28 Questor Grand Prix at Ontario (#34 Lola-Chevrolet F5000, Q25, DNF in heat 1, 10th in heat 2, F17 on aggregate)

Mario Andretti, 2/28/1940-____: 134 // **128** *2nd American World Champ., most poles, 18, 2/28/40- most wins - 13 (12 World Championship), most points finishes, 38, most laps in lead, 799, most fastest laps, 10*
1968- ....DNS 9/8 ITALY in #18 Lotus-Cosworth because of "24-hr. Rule"....10/6 **USA** (#12 Q1,DNF)
1969- 3/1 **SOUTH AFRICA** (#3 Lotus-Cosworth, Q6,DNF), 8/3 **GERMANY** (#3, Q12,DNF-

accident), 10/5 **USA** (#9, Q13,DNF)
1970- 3/7 **SOUTH AFRICA** (#8 March-Cosworth,Q11,DNF), 4/19 **SPAIN** (#18 Q16,F3), 7/19 **GREAT BRITAIN** (#26, Q9,DNF), 8/2 **GERMANY** (#11, Q9,DNF), 8/16 **AUSTRIA** (#5, Q18, DNF-accident)
1971- 3/6 **SOUTH AFRICA** (#6 Ferrari, Q4,F1), 3/28 Questor Grand Prix at Ontario (#5, Q11, 1st in heat 1, 1st in heat 2, F1 on aggregate), 4/18 **SPAIN** (#6, Q8,DNF), 6/20 **HOLLAND** (#4, Q18,DNF), 8/1 **GERMANY** (#5, Q11,F4), 9/19 **CANADA** (#6, Q13,F13)
1972- 1/23 **ARGENTINA** (#10 Ferrari, Q9,DNF), 3/4 **SOUTH AFRICA** (#7, Q6,F4), 5/1 **SPAIN** (Q5,DNF), 9/10 **ITALY** (#3, Q7,F7), 10/8 **USA** (#9, Q10,F6)
1974- 9/22 **CANADA** (#55 Parnelli-Cosworth, Q16,F7), 10/6 **USA** (Q3, DQ-outside assistance)
1975- 1/12 **ARGENTINA** (#27 Parnelli-Cosworth, Q10,DNF), 1/26 **BRAZIL** (Q18,F7), 3/1 **SOUTH AFRICA** (Q6,F17-not running at finish), 4/13 Daily Express International Trophy, Silverstone (Q10,F3), 4/27 **SPAIN** (Q4,DNF), 5/11 **MONACO** (Q13,DNF), 6/8 **SWEDEN** (Q15,F4), 7/6 **FRANCE** (Q15,F5), 7/19 **GREAT BRITAIN** (Q12,F12), 8/3 **GERMANY** (Q13,DNF), 8/17 **AUSTRIA** (Q19,DNF), 9/7 **ITALY** (Q15,DNF-accident), 10/5 **USA** (Q5,DNF)
1976- 1/25 **BRAZIL** (#6 Lotus-Cosworth, Q16,DNF-accident), 3/6 **SOUTH AFRICA** (#27 Parnelli-Cosworth, Q14,F6), 3/28 **USA-WEST** (Q15, DNF), 4/11 Daily Express International Trophy, Silverstone (#24 Williams-Cosworth, Q9,F7), 5/2 **SPAIN** (#5 Lotus-Cosworth, Q10,DNF), 5/16 **BELGIUM** (Q11,DNF), 6/13 **SWEDEN** (Q2,DNF), 7/4 **FRANCE** (Q7,F5), 7/18 **GREAT BRITAIN** (Q3,DNF), 8/1 **GERMANY** (Q12,F12), 8/15 **AUSTRIA** (Q9,F5), 8/29 **HOLLAND** (Q6,F3), 9/12 **ITALY** (Q14,DNF), 10/3 **CANADA** (Q5,F3), 10/10 **USA-EAST** (Q11,DNF), 10/24 **JAPAN** (Q1,F1)
1977- 1/9 **ARGENTINA** (#5 Lotus-Cosworth, Q8, F5-not running at finish), 1/23 **BRAZIL** (Q3,DNF), 3/5 **SOUTH AFRICA** (Q6,DNF-accident), 4/3 **USA-WEST** (Q2,F1), 5/8 **SPAIN** (Q1,F1), 5/22 **MONACO** (Q10,F5), 6/5 **BELGIUM** (Q1,DNF-accident), 6/19 **SWEDEN** (Q1,F6), 7/3 **FRANCE** (Q1,F1,*fastest lap), 7/16 **GREAT BRITAIN** (Q6, F14-not running at finish), 7/31 **GERMANY** (Q7,DNF), 8/14 **AUSTRIA** (Q3,DNF), 8/28 **HOLLAND** (Q1,DNF), 9/11 **ITALY** (Q4,F1,*fastest lap), 10/2 **USA-EAST** (Q4,F2), 10/9 **CANADA** (Q1,DNF), 10/23 **JAPAN** (Q1,DNF-accident)
1978- 1/15 **ARGENTINA** (#5 Lotus-Cosworth, Q1,F1), 1/29 **BRAZIL** (Q3,F4), 3/4 **SOUTH AFRICA** (Q2,F7,*fastest lap), 3/19 International Trophy, Silverstone (Q3,DNF-accident), 4/2 **USA-WEST** (Q4,F2), 5/7 **MONACO** (Q4,F11), 5/21 **BELGIUM** (Q1,F1), 6/4 **SPAIN** (Q1,F1,*fastest lap), 6/17 **SWEDEN** (Q1,DNF), 7/2 **FRANCE** (Q2,F1), 7/16 **GREAT BRITAIN** (Q2,DNF), 7/30 **GERMANY** (Q1,F1), 8/13

AUSTRIA (Q2, accident on lap 1, race stopped and restarted,DNS), 8/27 **HOLLAND** (Q1,F1), 9/10 **ITALY** (Q1, race stopped and restarted after accident, 1-min. penalty for jumping start, F6,*fastest lap), 10/1 **USA-EAST** (Q1,DNF), 10/8 **CANADA** (Q9, F10)
1979- 1/21 **ARGENTINA** (#1 Lotus-Cosworth, Q8,F5), 2/4 **BRAZIL** (Q4,DNF), 3/3 **SOUTH AFRICA** (Q8,F4), 4/8 **USA-WEST** (Q6,F4), 4/15 Marlboro-Daily Mail Race of Champions at Brands Hatch (#1, Q1,F3), 4/29 **SPAIN** (Q3,F3), 5/13 **BELGIUM** (Q5, DNF), 5/27 **MONACO** (Q13,DNF), 7/1 **FRANCE** (Q12,DNF), 7/14 **GREAT BRITAIN** (Q9,DNF), 7/29 **GERMANY** (Q11,DNF), 8/12 **AUSTRIA** (Q15,DNF), 8/26 **HOLLAND** (Q17,DNF), 9/9 **ITALY** (Q10,F5), 9/30 **CANADA** (Q10,F-10-not running at finish), 10/7 **USA-EAST** (Q17,DNF)
1980- 1/13 **ARGENTINA** (#11 Lotus-Cosworth, Q6,DNF), 1/27 **BRAZIL** (Q11,DNF), 3/1 **SOUTH AFRICA** (Q15,F12), 3/30 **USA-WEST** (Q15,DNF-accident), 5/4 **BELGIUM** (Q17,DNF), 5/18 **MONACO** (Q19,F7), 6/1 Spanish Grand Prix, Jarama (Q8,F7), 6/29 **FRANCE** (Q12,DNF), 7/80 **GREAT BRITAIN** (Q9,DNF), 8/10 **GERMANY** (Q9,F7), 8/17 **AUSTRIA** (Q17,DNF), 8/31 **HOLLAND** (Q10,F8-not running at finish), 9/14 **ITALY** (Q10,DNF), 9/28 **CANADA** (Q18,DNF), 10/5 **USA-EAST** (Q11,F6)
1981- 3/15 **USA-WEST** (#22 Alfa Romeo,Q6,F4), 3/29 **BRAZIL** (Q9,DNF-accident on lap 1), 4/12 **ARGENTINA** (Q17,F8), 5/3 **SAN MARINO** (Q12,DNF), 5/17 **BELGIUM** (Q18,F10), 5/31 **MONACO** (Q12,DNF-accident), 6/21 **SPAIN** (Q8,F8), 7/5 **FRANCE** (Q10,F8), 7/18 **GREAT BRITAIN** (Q11,DNF), 8/2 **GERMANY** (Q12,F9), 8/16 **AUSTRIA** (Q13,DNF), 8/30 **HOLLAND** (Q7,DNF-accident), 9/13 **ITALY** (Q13,DNF), 9/27 **CANADA** (Q16,F7), 10/17 **LAS VEGAS** (Q10,DNF)
1982- 4/4 **USA-WEST** (#5 Williams-Cosworth, Q14,DNF), 9/12 **ITALY** (#28 Ferrari, Q1,F3), 9/25 **LAS VEGAS** (Q7,DNF)

Michael Andretti, 5/10/1962-____: // 13
1993- 3/14 **SOUTH AFRICA** (#7 McLaren-Ford, Q9,DNF-accident), 3/28 **BRAZIL** (Q5,DNF-accident), 4/11 **EUROPE**, Donington (Q6,DNF-accident), 4/25 **SAN MARINO** (Q7,F5), 5/9 **SPAIN** (Q7,F5), 5/23 **MONACO** (Q9,F8), 6/13 **CANADA** (Q12 [started from pits on lap 3],F4), 7/4 **FRANCE**, Magny-Cours (Q16,F6), 7/11 **GREAT BRITAIN**, Silverstone (Q11,DNF-accident), 7/25 **GERMANY** (Q12,DNF-accident), 8/15 **HUNGARY** (Q11,DNF), 8/29 **BELGIUM** (Q14,F8), 9/12 **ITALY** (Q9,F3)

Skip Barber, 11/16/1936-____: 6 // 5
1971- ....DNQ #28 March-Cosworth at 5/23 MONACO....6/13 Rhein Pokalrennen Grand Prix at Hocken-

heim (#19 March-Cosworth, Q15,F6), 6/20 **HOLLAND** (#22, Q24,F14-not classified), 9/19 **CANADA** (#33, Q25,DNF), 10/3 **USA** (Q25,F18-not classified)
1972- 9/24 **CANADA** (#33 March-Cosworth, Q22,F18-not classified), 10/8 **USA** (Q20,F16)

Harry Blanchard, 6/30/1929-1/31/1960: // 1
1959- 12/12 **USA**, Sebring (#17 Porsche RSK Formula Two, Q16,F7)

Bob Bondurant, 4/27/1933-____: 10 // 9
1965- 10/3 **USA** (#24 Ferrari, Q14,F9), 10/24 **MEXICO** (#22 Lotus-BRM, Q17,DNF)
1966- 5/22 **MONACO** (#19 BRM, Q16,F4), 6/13 **BELGIUM** (#8, Q11,DNF-accident), 7/16 **GREAT BRITAIN** (#25, Q3,F9), 8/7 **GERMANY** (#14, Q11,DNF), 9/4 **ITALY** (#48, Q18,F7), 10/2 **USA** (#16 Eagle-Climax, Q16,DQ-outside assistance), 10/23 **MEXICO** (#16, Q18, swapped cars w/Gurney before start,DNF)
1971- 3/28 Questor Grand Prix at Ontario (#35 Lola-Chevrolet F5000, Q23, DNF in heat 1 - engine)

Ronnie Bucknum, 4/5/1936-4/14/1992: // 11
1964- 8/2 **GERMANY** (#20 Honda, Q22,DNF-accident), 9/6 **ITALY** (#28, Q10,DNF), 10/4 **USA** (#25, Q14,DNF)
1965- 5/30 **MONACO** (#19 Honda, Q15,DNF), 6/13 **BELGIUM** (#11, Q11,DNF), 6/27 **FRANCE** at Charade, Clermont-Ferrand (#28, Q16,DNF), 9/12 **ITALY** (#22, Q6,DNF), 10/3 **USA** (#14, Q12,F13-not classified), 10/24 **MEXICO** (#12, Q10,F5)
1966- 10/2 **USA** (#14, Q18,DNF), 10/23 **MEXICO** (#14, Q13,F8)

Jay Chamberlain, 12/29/1925-____: 8 // 1
1962- 4/23 Lavant Cup, Goodwood (#16 Lotus-Climax, Q5,F5), 4/23 Glover Trophy, Goodwood (#16, Q12,DNF), 4/29 B.A.R.C. 200, Aintree (#20, Q18,DQ-push start), 5/12 International Trophy, Silverstone (#24, Q22,F16), ...DNQ at 5/20 Naples Grand Prix...., 6/11 Crystal Palace Trophy (#7, Q12,DNF), 7/21 **GREAT BRITAIN** (#46, Q20,F15-not classified), ...DNQ at 8/5 GERMANY..., 8/26 Danish Grand Prix (Q10, DNF heat 1, DNS heat 2, 9th in heat 3, not classified in aggregate), ...DNQ at 9/16 ITA..., 11/4 Mexican Grand Prix (#52, Q16,F9-not classified)

Eddie Cheever, 1/10/1958-____: 134 // **132** *most F1 starts for an American*
1978- ...DNQ #32 Theodore-Cosworth at 1/15 ARGENTINA..., ...DNQ at 1/29 BRAZIL...., 3/4 **SOUTH AFRICA** (#24 Hesketh-Cosworth, Q25,DNF)
1980- ...DNQ #31 Osella-Cosworth at 1/13 ARGENTINA..., DNQ at 1/27 BRAZIL..., 3/1 **SOUTH AFRICA** (#31 Osella-Cosworth, Q22,DNF-accident), 3/30 **USA-WEST** (Q19,DNF), ...DNQ at 5/4 BELGIUM..., ...DNQ at 5/18 MONACO..., 6/1 Spanish Grand Prix, Jarama (Q10,DNF), 6/29 **FRANCE** (Q21,DNF), 7/13 **GREAT BRITAIN** (Q20,DNF), 8/10 **GERMANY**

(Q18,DNF), 8/17 **AUSTRIA** (Q19,DNF), 8/31 **HOLLAND** (Q19,DNF), 9/14 **ITALY** (Q17,F12), 9/28 **CANADA** (Q14,DNF), 10/5 **USA-WEST** (Q16,DNF-accident)

1981- 2/7 Nashua Grand Prix of South Africa (#3 Tyrrell-Cosworth, Q12,F7), 3/15 **USA-WEST** (Q8,F5), 3/29 **BRAZIL** (Q14,-not classified), 4/12 **ARGENTINA** (Q13,DNF), 5/3 **SAN MARINO** (Q19,DNF), 5/17 **BELGIUM** (Q8,F6), 5/31 **MONACO** (Q15,F5), 6/21 **SPAIN** (Q20,-not classified), 7/5 **FRANCE** (Q19,F13), 7/18 **GREAT BRITAIN** (Q21,F4), 8/2 **GERMANY** (Q18,F5), 8/30 **HOLLAND** (Q22,DNF-accident), 9/13 **ITALY** (Q17,DNF), 9/27 **CANADA** (Q14,F12,-not running at finish), 10/17 **LAS VEGAS** (Q19,DNF)

1982- 1/23 **SOUTH AFRICA** (#25 Ligier-Matra, Q17,DNF), 3/21 **BRAZIL** (Q26,DNF), 4/4 **USA-WEST** (Q13,DNF), 5/9 **BELGIUM** (Q14,F3), 5/23 **MONACO** (Q16,DNF), 6/6 **USA-EAST** (Q9,F2), 6/13 **CANADA** (Q12,F10), ...*DNQ at 7/3 HOLLAND...*, 7/18 **GREAT BRITAIN** (Q24,DNF), 7/25 **FRANCE** (Q19,F16), 8/8 **GERMANY** (Q12,DNF), 8/15 **AUSTRIA** (Q22,DNF), 8/29 **SWITZERLAND** (Q16,-not classified), 9/12 **ITALY** (Q14,F6), 9/25 **LAS VEGAS** Ceasars Palace Grand Prix (Q4,F3)

1983- 3/13 **BRAZIL** (#16 Renault, Q8,DNF), 3/27 **USA-WEST** (Q15,DNF), 4/17 **FRANCE** (Q2,F3), 5/1 **SAN MARINO** (Q6,DNF), 5/15 **MONACO** (Q3,DNF), 5/22 **BELGIUM** (Q8,F3), 6/5 **USA-EAST** (Q7,DNF), 6/12 **CANADA** (Q6,F2), 7/16 **GREAT BRITAIN** (Q7,DNF), 8/7 **GERMANY** (Q6,DNF), 8/14 **AUSTRIA** (Q8,F4), 8/28 **HOLLAND** (Q11,DNF), 9/11 **ITALY** (Q7,F3), **EUROPE** at Brands Hatch (Q7,F10), 10/15 **SOUTH AFRICA** (Q14,F6)

1984- 3/25 **BRAZIL** (#23 Alfa Romeo, Q12,F4), 4/7 **SOUTH AFRICA** (Q16,DNF), 4/29 **BELGIUM** (Q11,DNF), 5/6 **SAN MARINO** (Q8,F8), 5/20 **FRANCE** (Q17,DNF-accident), ...*DNQ at 6/3 MONACO...*, 6/17 **CANADA** (Q11,F11-not running at finish), 6/24 **USA-EAST** (Q8,DNF), 7/8 **DALLAS** (Q14,DNF-accident), 7/22 **GREAT BRITAIN** (Q18,DNF-accident), 8/5 **GERMANY** (Q18,DNF-accident), 8/19 **AUSTRIA** (Q16,DNF), 8/26 **HOLLAND** (Q17,F13-not running at finish), 9/9 **ITALY** (Q10,F9-not running at finish), 10/7 **EUROPE** at the Nürburgring (Q13,DNF), 10/21 **PORTUGAL** (Q14,F17)

1985- 4/7 **BRAZIL** (#23 Alfa Romeo, Q18,DNF), 4/21 **PORTUGAL** (Q14-started from pit lane,DNF), 5/5 **SAN MARINO** (Q12,DNF), 5/19 **MONACO** (Q4,DNF), 6/16 **CANADA** (Q11,F17), 6/24 **USA-EAST** (Q7,F9), 7/7 **FRANCE** (Q17,F10), 7/21 **GREAT BRITAIN** (Q22,DNF), 8/4 **GERMANY** (Q18,DNF), 8/18 **AUSTRIA** (Q20,DNF), 8/25 **HOLLAND** (Q20,DNF), 9/8 **ITALY** (Q17,DNF), 9/15 **BELGIUM** (Q19,DNF), 10/6 **EUROPE** at Brands Hatch (Q18,F11), 10/19 **SOUTH AFRICA** (Q14,DNF-accident), 11/3 **AUSTRALIA** (Q13,DNF)

1986- 6/22 **USA-EAST** (#16 Team Haas Lola FORCE-Cosworth V6, Q10,DNF)

1987- 4/12 **BRAZIL** (#18 Arrows-Megatron, Q14,DNF), 5/3 **SAN MARINO** (Q9,DNF), 5/17 **BELGIUM** (Q11,F4), 5/31 **MONACO** (Q6,DNF), 6/21 **USA-EAST** (Q6,F6), 7/5 **FRANCE** (Q14,DNF), 7/12 **GREAT BRITAIN** (Q14,DNF), 7/26 **GERMANY** (Q15,DNF), 8/9 **HUNGARY** (Q11,F8), 8/16 **AUSTRIA** (Q12,DNF), 9/6 **ITALY** (Q13,DNF), 9/20 **PORTUGAL** (Q11,F6), 9/27 **SPAIN** (Q13,F8), 10/18 **MEXICO** (Q12,F4), 11/1 **JAPAN** (Q12,F9), 11/15 **AUSTRALIA** (Q11,DNF)

1988- 4/3 **BRAZIL** (#18 Arrows-Megatron, Q15,F8), 5/1 **SAN MARINO** (Q7,F7), 5/15 **MONACO** (Q9,DNF), 5/29 **MEXICO** (Q7,F6), 6/12 **CANADA** (Q8,DNF), 6/19 **USA-EAST** (Q15,DNF), 7/3 **FRANCE** (Q13,F11), 7/10 **GREAT BRITAIN** (Q13,F7), 7/24 **GERMANY** (Q15,F10), 8/7 **HUNGARY** (Q14,DNF), 8/28 **BELGIUM** (Q11,F8), 9/11 **ITALY** (Q5,F3), 9/25 **PORTUGAL** (Q18,DNF), 10/2 **SPAIN** (Q25,DNF), 10/30 **JAPAN** (Q15,DNF), 11/13 **AUSTRALIA** (Q18,DNF)

1989- 326 **BRAZIL** (#18 Arrows-Ford, Q24,DNF-accident), 4/23 **SAN MARINO** (Q21,F7), 5/7 **MONACO** (Q20,F7), 5/28 **MEXICO** (Q24,F7), 6/4 **USA** at Phoenix (Q17,F3), 6/18 **CANADA** (Q16,DNF), 7/9 **FRANCE** (Q25,F7), ...*DNQ at 7/16 GREAT BRITAIN...*, 7/30 **GERMANY** (Q25,DNF), 8/13 **HUNGARY** (Q16,F5), 8/27 **BELGIUM** (Q24,DNF), ...*DNQ at 9/10 ITALY...*, 9/13 **PORTUGAL** (Q26,DNF-accident), 10/1 **SPAIN** (Q22,DNF), 10/22 **JAPAN** (Q24,F8), 11/13 **AUSTRALIA** (Q22,DNF-accident)

Luigi Chinetti, 7/7/1901-8/17/1994: 1
1950- 10/29 Penya Rhin Grand Prix, Barcelona (Ferrari 125, Q19,DNF)

George Constantine, 2/22/1918-1/7/1968: // 1
1959- 12/12 USA Sebring (#16 Cooper-Climax, Q15,DNF)

Chuck Daigh, 11/29/1933-___: // 3
1960- ....*DNQ at 5/29 Monaco, ... DNS 6/6 HOLLAND, car withdrawn...*, 6/19 **BELGIUM** (#30 Scarab, Q17,DNF),....*DNS at 7/3 FRANCE at Reims, engine....*, **7/16 GREAT BRITAIN (#3 Cooper-Climax, Q19,DNF), 11/20 USA-WEST (#23 Scarab, Q18,F10)**

Mark Donohue, 3/18/1937-8/17/1975: 15 // 14
1971- 3/28 Questor Grand Prix at Ontario (#26 Lola-Chevrolet F5000, Q7, 9th in heat 1, DNF in heat 2, F14 on aggregate), 9/19 **CANADA** (#10 McLaren-Ford, Q8 ,F3)
1974- 9/22 **CANADA** (#66 Penske-Cosworth, Q24,F12), 10/6 **USA** (#31, Q14,DNF)
1975- 1/12 **ARGENTINA** (#28 Penske-Cosworth, Q16,F7), 1/26 **BRAZIL** (Q16,DNF),), 3/16 British Airways-Daily Mail Race of Champions, Brands Hatch (Q7,DNF), 4/13 Daily

Express International Trophy, Silverstone (Q11,F6), 5/1 **SOUTH AFRICA** (Q18,F8), **SPAIN** (Q17,DNF-accident), 5/11 **MONACO** (Q16,DNF-accident), 5/25 **BELGIUM** (Q21,F11), 6/8 **SWEDEN** (Q16,F5), 6/22 **HOLLAND** (Q18,F8), 7/6 **FRANCE** (Q17,DNF), 7/19 **GREAT BRITAIN** (#28 March-Cosworth, Q15,F5-not running at finish), 8/3 **GERMANY** (Q19,DNF), *Q20 but DNS at 8/17 AUSTRIA because of accident in warmup, died later in hospital*

Bob Drake, 12/14/1919-April, 1990: // 1
1960- 11/20 **USA** (#20 Maserati 250F, Q22,F13)

Dale Duncan, 5/13/1925-10/81: 1
1959- 4/18 B.A.R.C. 200, Aintree (#4 Maserati 250F, Q27,F15-not classified)

Mike Fisher, 3/13/1943-___: // 1
1967- 8/27 **CANADA** (#6 Lotus-BRM, Q18,F11), *Q18 but DNS at 10/22 MEXICO after mechanical problem*

John Fitch, 8/4/1917-___: 3 // 2
1953- 7/26 Circuit du Lac, Aix-les-Bains (#24 Cooper-Bristol, 8th in heat 1, 4th in heat 2, F4 in final), 9/13 **ITALY** (#18 HWM-Alta, Q26,DNF)
1955- 9/11 **ITALY** (#40 Maserati 250F, F9)

George Follmer, 1/27/1934-___: 14 // 12
1971- 3/28 Questor Grand Prix at Ontario (#27 Lotus-Ford F5000, Q10, DNF-engine in heat 1)
1973- 3/3 **SOUTH AFRICA** (#23 Shadow-Ford, Q21,F6), 3/31 International Trophy at Silverstone (#8, Q17,F6), 4/29 **SPAIN** (#20, Q14,F3), 5/20 **BELGIUM** (#16, Q12,DNF), ...*DNS in 6/3 MONACO.....*, 6/17 **SWEDEN** (Q19,F14), 7/1 **FRANCE** (Q20,DNF), 7/14 **GREAT BRITAIN** (Q25, lap-one accident, did not re-start), 7/29 **HOLLAND** (Q22,F10), 8/5 **GERMANY** (Q22,DNF-accident), 8/19 **AUSTRIA** (Q20,DNF), 9/9 **ITALY** (Q21,F10), 9/23 **CANADA** (Q13,F17), 10/7 **USA** (Q20,F14)

A.J. Foyt, 1/16/1935-___: 1
1971- 3/28 Questor Grand Prix at Ontario (#28 McLaren-Chevrolet F5000, Q30, DNF in heat 1, DNF in heat 2)

Fred Gamble, 3/17/1932-___: // 1
1960- 9/4 **ITALY** (#28 Porsche-Behra Formula Two, Q14,F10)

Richie Ginther, 8/5/1930-9/20/1989: 67 // **52**
1960- **5/29 MONACO** (#34 Ferrari Dino 246P, Q9,F6), 6/6 **HOLLAND** (#3, Q12,F6),....*DNS in Scarab at 7/3 FRANCE at Reims, engine,....* 8/1 Silver City Trophy, Brands Hatch, (#42 Ferrari Dino 246, Q13,F9), **9/4 ITALY** (#18, Q2,F2)
1961- 5/14 **MONACO** (#36 Ferrari Dino 156, Q2,F2,*fastest lap), 5/22 **HOLLAND** (#2, Q3,F5), 6/18 **BELGIUM** (#6, Q5,F3,*fastest lap), 7/2 **FRANCE** (#18, Q3,DNF), 7/15 **GREAT BRITAIN** (#6, Q2,F3), 8/6 **GERMANY** (#5, Q14,F8), 9/10, **ITALY** (#6, Q3,DNF)

1962- 4/23, Glover Trophy, Goodwood (#2 BRM, Q6,F9 - car refused to start for two laps), 4/29 B.A.R.C. 200, Aintree (#12, Q5,DNF), 5/12 International Trophy, Silverstone (#2, Q4,DNF), 5/20 **HOLLAND** (#18, Q7,-not classified), 6/3 **MONACO** (#8, Q13,DNF-accident), 6/17 **BELGIUM** (#2, Q9,-not classified), 7/1 Reims Grand Prix (#4, Q9,DNF), 7/8 **FRANCE** (#10, Q10,F3), 7/21 **GREAT BRITAIN** (#14, Q8,F13), 8/5 **GERMANY** (#12, Q7,F8), 9/1 International Gold Cup, Oulton Park (#18, Q1,DNF), 9/16 **ITALY** (#12, Q3,F2), 10/7 **USA** (#4, Q2,DNF), 12/15 Rand Grand Prix, Kyalami (#4, Q5,DNF), 12/22 Natal Grand Prix, Westmead (#4, Q2, 1st in heat 1, F3), 12/29 **SOUTH AFRICA** at East London (#3, Q7,F7)
1963- 3/30 Lombank Trophy, Snetterton (#2 BRM, Q2,F5), 4/15 Glover Trophy, Goodwood (#2, Q5,DNF), 4/27 B.A.R.C. 200, Aintree (#2, Q5,F4), 5/11 International Trophy, Silverstone (#2, Q8,DNF), 5/26 **MONACO** (#5, Q4,F2), 6/9 **BELGIUM** (#8, Q9,F4), 6/23 **HOLLAND** (#14, Q6,F5), 6/30 **FRANCE** (#4, Q12,DNF), 7/20 **GREAT BRITAIN** (#2, Q9,F4), 8/4 **GERMANY** (#2, Q6,F3), 9/8 **ITALY** (#10, Q4,F2), 9/21 International Gold Cup, Oulton Park (#2, Q3,F2), 10/6 **USA** (#2, Q4,F2), 10/27 **MEXICO** (#2, Q5,F3), 12/28 **SOUTH AFRICA** (#6, Q7,DNF)
1964- 5/10 **MONACO** (#7 BRM, Q8,F2), 5/24 **HOLLAND** (#8, Q8,F11-not classified), 6/14 **BELGIUM** (#2, Q8,F4), 6/28 **FRANCE** (#10, Q9,F5), 7/11 **GREAT BRITAIN** (#4, Q14,F8), 8/2 **GERMANY** (#4, Q11,F7), 8/23 **AUSTRIA** (#4, Q5,F2), 9/6 **ITALY** (#20, Q9,F4), 10/4 **USA** (#4, Q13,F4), 10/25 **MEXICO** (#4, Q11,F8)
1965- 5/30 **MONACO** (#20 Honda, Q16,F6), 6/13 **BELGIUM** (#10, Q4,F6), 6/27 **FRANCE** at Charade, Clermont-Ferrand (#26, Q7,DNF), 7/10 **GREAT BRITAIN** (#11, Q3,DNF), 7/18 **HOLLAND** (#22, Q1,F6), 9/12 **ITALY** (#20, Q17,DNF), 10/3 **USA** (#11, Q3,F7), 10/24 **MEXICO** (#11, Q4,F1,*fastest lap)
1966- 1/1 South African Grand Prix (#7 BRM, Q6,DNF-crash), 5/14 International Trophy, Silverstone (#5 Cooper-Maserati, Q7,DNF), 5/22 **MONACO** (#9, Q9,F5-not classified), 6/13 **BELGIUM** (#18, Q8,F5), 9/4 **ITALY** (#18 Honda, Q7,DNF-crash), 10/2 **USA** (#12, Q8,F8-not classified), 10/23 **MEXICO** (#12, Q3,F4,*fastest lap)
1967- 3/12 Race of Champions, Brands Hatch (#6 Eagle-Gurney-Weslake, Q3, 3rd in heat 1, 2nd in heat 2,F10 in final),....*DNQ #22 Eagle-Gurney-Weslake at 5/7 MONACO...*

Ron Grable: 1
1971- 3/28 Questor Grand Prix at Ontario (#29 Lola-Chevrolet F5000, Q22, 10th in heat 1, 7th in heat 2, F7 on aggregate - 1st in F5000)

Masten Gregory, 2/29/1932-11/8/1985: 75 // **38** *1st American to score a World Championship podium finish, at 5/19/1957 MONACO*
1957- 1/27 Buenos Aires Grand Prix (relieved Collins in #12 Ferrari/Lancia D50, finished 7th in

heat 1, DNF in heat 2), 4/22 Pau Grand Prix (#22 Maserati 250F, Q3,F4), 4/28 Naples Grand Prix at Posillipo (#? Q6,F5), 5/19 MONACO (#2 Q10,F3), 7/14 Reims Grand Prix (#18 Q11,F7), 8/4 GERMANY (#16 Maserati 250F, Q10,F8), 8/18 PESCARA (#14 Q7,F4), 9/8 ITALY (#26 Q11,F4), 9/14 International Trophy, Silverstone (#2, 3rd in heat, F5 in final),

1958- 4/13 Syracuse Grand Prix (#22 Maserati 250F, Q5,DNF), 5/3 International Trophy, Silverstone (#3, Q10,F3), 5/25 HOLLAND (#12, Q14,DNF), 6/15 BELGIUM (#30, Q10,DNF), 9/7 ITALY (#32, Q11,-relieved by Shelby, F4), 10/19 MOROCCO (#22, Q13,F6)

1959- 3/30 Glover Trophy, Goodwood (#9 Cooper-Climax, Q7,F5), 4/18 B.A.R.C. 200, Aintree (#11, Q1,DNF), 5/10 MONACO (#26 Q11,DNF), 5/31 HOLLAND (#9, Q7,F3), 7/5 FRANCE at Reims (#6, Q7,DNF), 7/18 GREAT BRITAIN (#14, Q5,F7), 8/2 GERMANY at Avus (#3, Q4,DNF), 8/23 PORTUGAL at Monsanto (#9, Q3,F2)

1960- 2/6 ARGENTINA (#2 Porsche-Behra Formula Two, Q16,F12), 5/14 International Trophy, Silverstone (#9 Cooper-Maserati, Q12,F6), ..DNQ at 5/29 MONACO.......Qualified at 6/6 HOL, but DNS in absense of starting money..., 7/3 FRANCE at Reims (#40 Cooper-Climax, Q17,F9), 7/16 GREAT BRITAIN (#16, Q14,F14), 8/1 Silver City Tophy, Brands Hatch, (#28 Cooper-Maserati, Q21,DNF), 8/14 PORTUGAL (#30, Q11,DNF), 9/24 International Gold Cup, Oulton Park (#21, Q17,DNF),

1961- 4/22 B.A.R.C. 200, Aintree (#15 Cooper-Climax, Q26,F5), 6/18 BELGIUM (#44, Q12,F10), 7/2 FRANCE (#36, Q16,F12), 7/15 GREAT BRITAIN (#42, Q16,F11), 8/26-27 Danish Grand Prix at Roskilde (#8 Lotus-Climax, Q8, 8th in heat 1, DNF in heat 2, DNF), 9/3 Modena Grand Prix (#32, Q7,F11-not classified), 9/10 ITALY (#22, Q17,DNF), 9/23 International Gold Cup, Oulton Park (#14, Q8,F5), 10/8 USA (#22, Q10,DNF-took over Gendebien's #21, F11), 12/9 Rand Grand Prix, Kyalami (#6 Lotus-Climax, Q3,DNF), 12/17 Natal Grand Prix at Westmead (#6, Q4,DNF), 12/26 South African Grand Prix at East London (#6, Q5,DNF)

1962- 2/1 Cape Grand Prix at Killarney (#6 Lotus-Climax, Q4,F4), 4/1 Brussels Grand Prix (#3, Q9,DNF), 4/14 Lombank Trophy, Snetterton (#8, Q5,DNF-accident), 4/23 Glover Trophy, Goodwood (#9, Q8,F5), 4/29 B.A.R.C. 200, Aintree (#9, Q7,DNF), 5/12 International Trophy, Silverstone (#8, Q8,F5), 5/20 HOLLAND (#10, Q18, -not classified), ...DNQ at 6/3 MONACO in Lotus-BMW...6/11 2000 Guineas Grand Prix at Mallory Park (#7 Lotus-Climax, Q7,F5), 6/17 BELGIUM (#21 Lotus-BRM, Q8,DNF), 7/1 Reims Grand Prix (#32, Q6,DNF), 7/8 FRANCE (#34, Q7,DNF), 7/21 GREAT BRITAIN (#34 Lotus-Climax, Q12,F7), 8/12 Kanonloppet Grand Prix, Karlskoga (#3 Lotus-BRM, Q6,F1), 8/26

Danish Grand Prix (Q2, 2nd in heat 1, 4th in heat 2, second in heat 3, F2), 9/1 International Gold Cup, Oulton Park (#15, Q13,F6), 9/16 ITALY (#38, Q6,F12), 10/7 USA (#16, Q7,F6), 11/4 Mexican Grand Prix (#16, Q9,F5),

1963- 6/30 FRANCE (#48 Lotus-BRM, Q17,DNF), 7/20 GREAT BRITAIN (#21, Q22,F11), 8/11 Kanonloppet Grand Prix, Karlskoga (#1, Q7, 7th in heat 1, 6th in heat 2, F6 on aggregate), 9/8 ITALY (#42, Q12,DNF), 9/21 International Gold Cup, Oulton Park (#17, Q14,DNF), 10/6 USA (#17 Lola-Climax, Q8,DNF), 10/27 MEXICO (#2, Q14,DNF)

1964- 4/12 Syracuse Grand Prix (#30 BRM, Q11,F6)

1965- 3/13 Race of Champions, Brands Hatch (#14 BRM, Q18,DNF), 4/4 Syracuse Grand Prix (#8, Q9,F11-not classified), 6/13 BELGIUM (#29, Q20,DNF), 7/10 GREAT BRITAIN (#12, Q19,F12-not classified), 8/1 GERMANY (#24, Q18,F8), 8/15 Mediterranean Grand Prix, Pergusa (#38, Q13,DQ-shared car w/Biscaldi), 9/12 ITALY (#48, Q22,DNF)

Dan Gurney, 4/13/1931-____: 101 // 86 *1st American driver to win a Grand Prix in a car of his own manufacture*

1959- 7/5 FRANCE at Reims (#28 Ferrari Dino 246, Q12,DNF), 8/2 GERMANY at Avus (#6, Q3, 2nd in heat 1, 3rd in heat 2, 2nd in final), 8/23 PORTUGAL at Monsanto (#16, Q6,F3), 9/13 ITALY (#36, Q4,F4)

1960- 4/18 Glover Trophy, Goodwood (#4 BRM, Q7,DNF-accident), 5/14 International Trophy, Silverstone (#3, Q3,DNF), 5/29 MONACO (#4, Q14,F10), 6/6 HOLLAND (#15, Q6,DNF), 6/19 BELGIUM (#8, Q11,DNF), 7/3 FRANCE at Reims (#10, Q7,DNF), 7/16 GREAT BRITAIN (#5, Q6,F10), 8/1 Silver City Tophy, Brands Hatch, (#8 Cooper-Climax, Q10,F7), 8/14 PORTUGAL (#24 BRM, Q2,DNF),.....DNS at 9/17 Lombank Trophy, Snetterton, engine....., 9/24 International Gold Cup, Oulton Park (#15, Q8,F6), 11/20 USA (#16, Q3,DNF)

1961- 4/9 Brussels Grand Prix, (#32 Porsche, Q3,DNF), 4/22 B.A.R.C. 200, Aintree (#23 Lotus-Climax, Q15,F14), 4/25 Syracuse Grand Prix, (#30 Porsche, Q1,F2,*fastest lap), 5/14 MONACO (#4, Q10,F5), 5/22 HOLLAND (#7, Q6,F10), 6/3 Silver City Tophy, Brands Hatch, (#32, Q12,F5), 6/18 BELGIUM (#20, Q10,F6), 7/2 FRANCE (#12, Q9,F2), 7/15 GREAT BRITAIN (#10, Q12,F7), 7/23 Solitude Grand Prix (#11, Q2,F3,*fastest lap), 8/6 GERMANY (#9, Q7,F7), 9/3 Modena Grand Prix (#12, Q3,F3), 9/10 ITALY (#46, Q12,F2), 10/8 USA (#12, Q7,F2)

1962- 5/20 HOLLAND (#12 Porsche, Q8,DNF), 6/3 MONACO (#4, Q5,DNF- crash), ...no Porsche at 6/17 BEL, tried Seidel's Lotus, declined to drive..... 7/8 FRANCE at Rouen (#30, Q6,F1), 7/15 Solitude Grand Prix (#10, Q2,F1,*fastest lap), 7/21 GREAT BRITAIN (#8, Q6,F9), 8/5 GERMANY (#7, Q1,F3), 9/16 ITALY (#16, Q7,DNF), 10/7 USA

(#10, Q4,F5)

1963- 5/26 MONACO (#4 Brabham-Climax, Q6,DNF), 6/9 BELGIUM (#18, Q2,F3), 6/23 HOLLAND (#18, Q14,F2), 6/30 FRANCE (#8, Q3,F5), 7/20 GREAT BRITAIN (#9, Q2,DNF), 8/4 GERMANY (#10, Q11,DNF), 9/8 ITALY (#24, Q5,DNF), 9/21 International Gold Cup, Oulton Park (#16, Q16,DNF), 10/6 USA (#16, Q6,DNF), 10/27 MEXICO (#6, Q4,F6), 12/28 SOUTH AFRICA (#9, Q3,F2,*fastest lap)

1964- 4/18 B.A.R.C. 200, Aintree (#6 Brabham-Climax, Q20,DNF), 5/2 International Trophy, Silverstone (#6, Q1,DNF), 5/10 MONACO (#6, Q5,DNF), 5/24 HOLLAND (#16, Q1,DNF), 6/14 BELGIUM (#15, Q1,F6,*fastest lap), 6/28 FRANCE (#22, Q2,F1), 7/11 GREAT BRITAIN (#6, Q3,F13), 8/2 GERMANY (#5, Q3,F10), 8/23 AUSTRIA (#5, Q4,DNF,*fastest lap), 9/6 ITALY (#16, Q2,F10), 10/4 USA (#6, Q3,F9-not classified), 10/25 MEXICO (#6, Q2,F1)

1965- 1/1 SOUTH AFRICA (#8 Brabham-Climax, Q9,DNF), 3/13 Race of Champions, Brands Hatch (#7, Q13, 2nd in heat 1,*fastest lap, DNF in heat 2, F12 on aggregate), 6/13 BELGIUM (#15, Q5,F10), 6/27 FRANCE at Charade, Clermont-Ferrand (#14, Q5,DNF), 7/10 GREAT BRITAIN (#7, Q7,DNS..took over Brabham's #8,F6), 7/18 HOLLAND (#16, Q4,F3), 8/1 GERMANY (#5, Q5,F3), 9/12 ITALY (#12, Q9,F3), 10/3 USA (#8, Q8,F2), 10/24 MEXICO (#8, Q2,F2)

1966- 6/13 BELGIUM (#27 Eagle-Climax, Q15,F7-not classified), 7/3 FRANCE (#26, Q14,F5), 7/16 GREAT BRITAIN (#16, Q3,DNF), 7/24 HOLLAND (#10, Q4,DNF), 8/7 GERMANY (#12, Q8,F7), 9/4 ITALY (#30 Eagle-Gurney-Weslake, Q19,DNF), 10/2 USA (#15, Q14,DNF), 10/23 MEXICO (#15, Q9, swapped cars w/Bondurant before start,F5)

1967- 1/2 SOUTH AFRICA (#9 Eagle-Climax, Q11,DNF), 3/12 Race of Champions, Brands Hatch (#5 Eagle-Gurney-Weslake, Q1, 1st in heat 1,*fastest lap, 1st in heat 2,*fastest lap, F1 in final), 5/7 MONACO (#23, Q7,DNF), 6/4 HOLLAND (#15, Q2,DNF), 6/18 BELGIUM (#36, Q2,F1,*fastest lap), 7/1 FRANCE at Le Mans (#9, Q3,DNF), 7/15 GREAT BRITAIN (#9, Q5,DNF), 8/6 GERMANY (#9, Q4,DNF,*fastest lap), 8/27 CANADA (#10, Q5,F3), 9/10 ITALY (#8, Q5,DNF), 10/1 USA (#11, Q3,DNF), 10/22 MEXICO (#11, Q3,DNF)

1968- 1/1 SOUTH AFRICA (#6 Eagle-Gurney-Weslake, Q12,DNF), 5/26 MONACO (#19, Q16,DNF), 6/23 HOLLAND (#18 Brabham-Repco, Q12,DNF), 7/20 GREAT BRITAIN (#24 Eagle-Gurney-Weslake, Q6,DNF), 8/4 GERMANY (#14, Q10,F9), 9/8 ITALY (#21, Q12,DNF), 9/22 CANADA (#11 McLaren-Cosworth, Q4,DNF), 10/6 USA (#14, Q7,F4), 11/3 MEXICO (#14, Q5,DNF)

1970- 6/21 HOLLAND (#32 McLaren-Cosworth, Q19,DNF), 7/5 FRANCE at Charade, Clermont-Ferrand (Q17,F6), 7/19 GREAT BRITAIN (#10, Q11,DNF)

Jim Hall, 7/23/1935-____: 17 // 11

1960- 11/20 USA (#24 Lotus-Climax, Q12,F7)
1961- 10/8, USA (#17, Lotus-Climax, Q18,DNF)
1962- *...DNS Lotus-Climax at 10/7 USA-engine...*, 11/4 Mexican Grand Prix (#25 Lotus-Climax, Q10,F4)
1963- 4/15 Glover Trophy, Goodwood (#5 Lotus-BRM, Q6,F4), 4/27 B.A.R.C. 200, Aintree (#9, Q8,DNF), 5/11 International Trophy, Silverstone (#14, Q11,DNF), 5/26 MONACO (#12, Q13,DNF), 6/9 BELGIUM (#5, Q12,DNF-accident), 6/23 HOLLAND (#42, Q18,F8), 6/30 FRANCE (#34, Q16,F11), 7/20 GREAT BRITAIN (#12, Q13,F6), 7/28 Solitude Grand Prix (#3, Q9,F6), 8/4 GERMANY (#20, Q16,F5), 9/1 Austrian Grand Prix at Zeltweg (#5, Q3,DNF), 9/8 ITALY (#30, Q16,F8), 10/6 USA (#16, Q16,DNF), 10/27 MEXICO (#16, Q15,F8)

Walt Hansgen, 10/18/1919-4/7/1966: 4 // 3
1961- 10/8 USA (#60 Cooper-Climax, Q14,DNF-accident)
1962- 10/7 USA (#60 Lotus-Climax, Q13,DNF), 11/4 Mexican Grand Prix (#60, Q13,DNF)
1964- 10/4 USA (#17 Lotus-Climax, Q17,F5)

Phil Hill, 4/20/1927-____: 55 // 48 *1st American to win a Formula One Grand Prix, last driver to win an international Grand Prix in a front-engine car, 1st American World Champion*

1958- 7/6 FRANCE at Reims (#36 Maserati 250F, Q13,F7), 8/3 GERMANY (#23 Formula Two Ferrari, Q10,F9-4th in Formula Two), 9/7 ITALY (#18, Q7,F3,*fastest lap), 10/19 MOROCCO (#4, Q5,F3)

1959- 5/2 International Trophy at Silverstone (#9 Ferrari Dino 246, Q8,F4), 5/10 MONACO (#48, Q5,F4), 5/31 HOLLAND (#3, Q5,F6), 7/5 FRANCE at Reims (#26, Q3,F2), 8/2 GERMANY at Avus (#5, 3rd in heat 1, 2nd in heat 2,*fastest lap, F3 on aggregate), 8/23 PORTUGAL at Monsanto (#15, Q7,DNF), 9/13 ITALY (#32, Q5,F2,*fastest lap), 12/12 USA (#5 Q8,DNF)

1960- 2/6 ARGENTINA (#26 Ferrari Dino 246, Q6,F8), 5/14 International Trophy, Silverstone (#25, Q4,F5), 5/29 MONACO (#36, Q10,F3), 6/6 HOLLAND (#1, Q5,F3), 6/19 BELGIUM (#24, Q3,F4), 7/3 FRANCE at Reims (#2, Q2,DNF), 7/16 GREAT BRITAIN (#10, Q10,F7), 8/1 Silver City Tophy, Brands Hatch, (#40, Q18,F4), 8/14 PORTUGAL (#26, Q5,DNF-accident), 9/4 ITALY (#20, Q1,F1,*fastest lap), 11/20 USA (#9 Cooper-Climax, Q13,F6)

1961- 5/14, MONACO (#38 Ferrari Dino 156, Q5,F3), 5/22, HOLLAND (#1, Q1,F2), 6/18, BELGIUM (#4, Q1,F1), 7/2, FRANCE (#16, Q1,F9,*fastest lap), 7/15 GREAT BRITAIN (#2, Q1,F2), 8/6, GERMANY (#4, Q1,F3,*fastest lap), 9/10, ITALY (#2, Q4,F1),

1962- 4/29, B.A.R.C. 200, Aintree (#1 Ferrari Dino 156, Q6,F3), 5/20 **HOLLAND** (#1, Q9,F3), 6/3 **MONACO** (#36, Q9,F2), 6/17 **BELGIUM** (#9, Q4,F3), ... *no cars for 7/8 FRANCE because of strike*... 7/21 **GREAT BRITAIN** (#2, Q12,DNF), 8/5 **GERMANY** (#1, Q12,DNF), 9/16 **ITALY** (#10, Q15,F11)
1963- 6/9 **BELGIUM** (#26 ATS, Q17,DNF), 6/23 **HOLLAND** (#24, Q13,DNF), 6/30 **FRANCE** (#42 Lotus-BRM, Q13,F14-not classified), 7/28 Solitude Grand Prix (#14, Q16,DNF), ... *ATS transporter crashed, missed GERMANY Grand Prix*.... 9/8 **ITALY** (#16, Q14,F11), 10/6 **USA** (#25, Q15,DNF), 10/27 **MEXICO** (#25, Q17,DNF)
1964- 3/14 Daily Mirror Trophy, Snetterton (#11 BRM, Q8,F4), 4/18 B.A.R.C. 200, Aintree (#10 Cooper-Climax, Q9,DNF), 5/2 International Trophy, Silverstone (#10, Q9,F4), 5/10 **MONACO** (#9, Q9,DNF), 5/24 **HOLLAND** (#22, Q9,F8), 6/14 **BEL-GIUM** (#21, Q15,DNF), 6/28 **FRANCE** (#14, Q10,F7), 7/11 **GREAT BRITAIN** (#10, Q15,F6), 8/2 **GERMANY** (#10, Q8,DNF), 8/23 **AUSTRIA** (#10, Q20,DNF-accident), 10/4 **USA** (#10, Q19,DNF), 10/25 **MEXICO** (#10, Q15,F9)
1966- ...*DNQ #34 Eagle-Climax at 9/4 ITALY*...

Gus Hutchison, 4/26/1937-___: 2 // **1**
1970- 10/4 **USA** (#31 Brabham-Ford, Q22,DNF)
1971- 3/28 Questor Grand Prix at Ontario (#36 ASD-Chevrolet F5000, Q28, 17th in heat 1 - not classified, 14th in heat 2, F19 on aggregate),

Pete Lovely, 4/11/1926-___: 11 // **7**
1959- ...*Entered at 3/30/1959 Glover Trophy, Goodwood in Lotus 16-Climax by Team Lotus, car not ready,DNA*,.... *Entered in 4/18 B.A.R.C. 200 in Lotus 16-Climax By Team Lotus, car not ready,DNA*....5/2 International Trophy at Silverstone (#12 Lotus 16-Climax, Q7,F15-not classified),.. *Entered at 5/10 MONACO in Lotus 16-Climax by Team Lotus, DNQ*
1960- 11/20 **USA** (#25 Cooper-Ferrari, Q20,F11)
1969- 3/16 Race of Champions, Brands Hatch (#15 Lotus-Cosworth, Q9,F6), 3/30 International Trophy, Silverstone (#17, Q12,DNF-accident), 9/20 **CANADA** (#25, Q16,F7), 10/5 **USA** (#21, Q16,DNF), 10/19 **MEXICO** (#21, Q16,F9)
1970- 3/22 Race of Champions, Brands Hatch (#10 Lotus-Cosworth, Q12,DNF), 4/26 International Trophy, Silverstone (#17, Q20, 17th in heat 1, 13th in heat 2, F13 on aggregate), ...*DNQ at 6/21 HOL... DNQ at 7/5 FRANCE at Charade, Clermont-Ferrand*...7/19 **GREAT BRITAIN** (#29, Q23,F10-not classified),... *DNQ at 4/10 USA*...
1971- ....*DNQ #40 Lotus-Cosworth at 3/28 Questor Prix at Ontario*..., 9/19 **CANADA** (#35, Q24,F18-not classified), 10/3 **USA** (#30, Q29,F21-not classified)

Robert Brett Lunger, 11/14/1945-___: 38 // **34**
1972- 10/22 World Championship Victory Race, Brands Hatch (#35 Lola-Chevrolet F5000, Q30,F17- 6th in F5000)

1973- 3/18 Race of Champions, Brands Hatch (#19 Lola-Chevrolet F5000, Q12,DNF), 4/8 International Trophy, Silverstone (Q10,DNF-accident)
1975- 8/17 **AUSTRIA** (#25 Hesketh-Cosworth, Q17,F13), 9/7 **ITALY** (Q21,F10), 10/5 **USA** (Q18,DNF)
1976- 3/6 **SOUTH AFRICA** (#18 Surtees-Cosworth, Q19,F11), ...*DNQ at 3/28 USA-WEST*..., Q16-accident, DNS at 4/11 Daily Express International Trophy, Silverstone..., DNQ at 5/2 SPAIN...., 5/16 **BELGIUM** (Q26,DNF), 6/13 **SWEDEN** (Q24,F15), 7/4 **FRANCE** (Q23,F16), 7/18 **GREAT BRITAIN** (Q18,DNF), 8/1 **GERMANY,** (Q24,DNF-accident), 8/15 **AUSTRIA** (Q16,F10-not running at finish), 9/12 **ITALY** (Q24,F14), 10/3 **CANADA** (Q21,F15), 10/10 **USA-EAST** (Q24,F11)
1977- 3/5 **SOUTH AFRICA** (#30 March-Cosworth,Q23,F14), 4/3 **USA-WEST** (Q21,DNF), 5/8 **SPAIN** (Q25,F10), ...*DNS at 6/5 BELGIUM, Q22-engine problem in warmup*..., 6/19 **SWEDEN** (Q22,F11), ...*DNQ at 7/3 FRANCE*... , 7/16 **GREAT BRITAIN** (Q19,,DNF), **GERMANY** (Q19,,DNF), 8/14 **AUSTRIA** (Q17,F10), 8/28 **HOLLAND** (Q20,F9), 9/11 **ITALY** (Q22,DNF), 10/2 **USA-EAST** (Q17,F10), **CANADA** (Q20,F11-not running at finish)
1978- 1/15 **ARGENTINA** (#30 McLaren-Cosworth, Q24,F13), 1/29 **BRAZIL** (Q13,DNF), 3/4 **SOUTH AFRICA** (Q20,F11), 3/19 Daily Express International Trophy, Silverstone (Q5,F4), ...*DNQ at 4/2 USA-WEST*..., ...*Did not pre-qualify at 5/7 MONACO*..., 5/21 **BEL-GIUM** (Q24,F7), ...*DNQ at 6/4 SPAIN*..., ..*DNQ at 6/17 SWEDEN*..., 7/2 **FRANCE** (Q24,DNF), 7/16 **GREAT BRITAIN** (Q24,F8), ...*Did not pre-qualify at 7/30 GER-MAN*..., 8/13 **AUSTRIA** (Q17,F8), 8/27 **HOLLAND** (Q21,DNF), 9/10 **ITALY** (Q21,DNF-accident on lap 1, did not restart), 10/1 **USA-EAST** (#23 Ensign-Cosworth, Q24,F13)

Herbert Mackay-Fraser, 6/22/1925-7/14/1957: // **1**
1957- 7/7 **FRANCE** at Rouen (#28 BRM, Q12,DNF)

Tim Mayer, 2/22/1938-2/28/1964: // **1**
1962- 10/7 **USA** (#23 Cooper-Climax, Q11,DNF)

Robert O'Brien: 2 // **1** *1st American-born driver to race in a Formula One Grand Prix*
1952- 6/22 **BELGIUM** (#44 Gordini, Q22-last,F14-not classified), 8/31 Grenzlandring Rennen (#130 Simca-Gordini, not classified)

Danny Ongais, 5/21/1942-___: // **4**
1977- 10/2 **USA-EAST** (#14 Penske-Cosworth, Q22,DNF-accident), 10/9 **CANADA** (Q22,F7)
1978- 1/15 **ARGENTINA** (#22 Ensign-Cosworth, Q21,DNF), 1/29 **BRAZIL** (Q23,DNF), ...*Did not pre-qualify #39 Shadow-Cosworth at 4/2 USA-WEST*..., ...*Did not pre-qualify four weeks before 8/27 HOLLAND*....

Roger Penske, 2/20/1937-___: 3 // **2**
1961- 10/8 **USA** (#6 Cooper-Climax, Q16,F8)
1962- 10/7 **USA** (#14 Lotus-Climax, Q12,F9), 11/4 Mexican Grand Prix (Q5,DNF)

Sam Posey, 5/26/1944-___: 3 // **2**
1971- 3/28 Questor Grand Prix at Ontario (#30 Surtees-Chevrolet F5000, Q9, DNF in heat 1), 10/3 **USA** (#10 Surtees-Cosworth, Q17,DNF)
1972- 10/8 **USA** (#34 Surtees-Cosworth, Q23,F12)

Homer Rader, ?-?: 1
1962-11/4 Mexican Grand Prix (#24 Lotus-Climax, Q14,F8)

Bobby Rahal, 1/10/1953-___: // **2**
1978- 10/1 **USA-EAST** (#21 Wolf-Cosworth, Q20,F12), 10/8 **CANADA** (Q20,DNF)

Peter Revson, 2/27/1939-3/22/1974: 41 // **30**
1963- 9/21 International Gold Cup, Oulton Park (#18 Lotus-BRM, Q15,F9)
1964- 3/14 Daily Mirror Trophy, Snetterton (#18 Lotus-BRM, Q11,DNF-accident), 3/3 News of the World Trophy, Goodwood (#18, Q13,F10-not classified), 4/12 Syracuse Grand Prix (#36, Q8,DNF-accident), 5/2 International Trophy, Silverstone (#22, Q14,F9), ...*DNQ at 5/10 MONACO*... 6/14 **BELGIUM** (#29, Q10,DQ-push start), 7/11 **GREAT BRITAIN** (#24, Q22,DNF), 7/19 Solitude Grand Prix (#12, Q15,F4), 8/2 **GERMANY** (#27, Q18,DNF-accident), 8/16 Mediterranean Grand Prix, Pergusa (#12, Q9,F6), 9/6 **ITALY** (#38, Q18,F13)
1971- 3/28 Questor Grand Prix at Ontario (#31 Surtees-Chevrolet F5000, Q24, DNF in heat 1), 10/3 **USA** (#10 Tyrrell-Cosworth, Q19,DNF)
1972- 1/23 **ARGENTINA** (#18 McLaren-Cosworth, Q4,DNF),), 3/4 **SOUTH AFRICA** (#14, Q12,F3), 3/19 Race of Champions, Brands Hatch (#56, Q5,F8), 4/23 International Trophy, Silverstone (#4, Q5,F5), 5/1 **SPAIN** (#20, Q11,F5), 6/4 **BELGIUM** (#10, Q7,F7), 7/15 **GREAT BRITAIN** (#19, Q3,F3), 8/13 **AUSTRIA** (#14, Q4,F3), 9/10 **ITALY** (#15, Q8,F4), 9/24 **CANADA** (#19, Q1,F2), 10/8 **USA** (#20, Q2,F18)
1973- 1/28 **ARGENTINA** (#16 McLaren-Cosworth, Q11,F8), 2/11 **BRAZIL** (#8, Q12,DNF), 3/3 **SOUTH AFRICA** (#6, Q6,F2), 4/8 International Trophy, Silverstone (#10, Q4,F4), 4/29 **SPAIN** (#6, Q5,F4), 5/20 **BEL-GIUM** (#8, Q10,DNF), 6/3 **MONACO** (Q15,F5), 6/17 **SWEDEN** (Q7,F7), 7/14 **GREAT BRITAIN** (Q3, F1-after restart), 7/29 **HOLLAND** (Q6,F4), 8/5 **GERMANY** (Q7,F9), 8/19 **AUSTRIA** (Q4,DNF), 9/9 **ITALY** (Q2,F3), 9/23 **CANADA** (Q2,F1),

10/7 **USA** (Q7,F5)
1974- 1/13 **ARGENTINA** (#16 Shadow-Cosworth, Q4,DNF-accident), 1/27 **BRAZIL** (Q6,DNF), 3/17 Race of Champions, Brands Hatch (Q9,F6),....*killed 3/22 at Kyalami in pre-race test-ing the week before the 3/30 SOUTH AFRICA Grand Prix*

Lloyd Ruby, 1/12/1928-___: // **1**
1961- 10/8 **USA** (#26 Lotus-Climax, Q19,DNF)

Troy Ruttman, 3/11/1930-5/19/1997: // **1** *1st Indianapolis 500 winner to race in a World Championship Formula One Grand Prix*
1958- 7/6 **FRANCE** (#30 Maserati 250F, Q18,F10), ...*DNQ at 8/3 GERMANY, blown engine*

Boris "Bob" Said, 5/5/1932-___: // **1**
1959- 12/12 **USA** Sebring, (#18 Connaught, Q13, DNF)

Swede Savage, 8/26/1946-7/2/1973: 1
1971- 3/28 Questor Grand Prix at Ontario (#32 Eagle-Plymouth F5000, Q29, DNF in heat 1 - acci-dent)

Harry Schell, 6/29/1921-5/13/1960: 128 // **55** *1st American to score points in the Formula One World Championship, drove more makes than any other American (8), first American to die in Formula One*
1946- 4/22 Nice Grand Prix (#40 Maserati 6CM, Q20,DNF-accident), 5/13 Marseilles Grand Prix (#32, 5th in heat, DNQ final), 6/9 Coupe Rene Le Begue (#12, Q12,DNF-gear-box), 6/30 Rousillon Grand Prix (#16, DNF-accident), 7/21 Grand Prix of Nations (#30, 10th in heat, DNQ final)
1947- 6/8 Swiss Grand Prix (#62 Cisitalia D46, 7th in heat, DNQ final), 7/13 Albi Grand Prix (#54, Q13,DNF), 8/10 Comminges Grand Prix (#48, F12)
1949- 4/18 Pau Grand Prix (#26 Talbot 26, Q11,DNF), 5/21,22 Marseille Grand Prix (#46 Cisitalia D46, DNF in heat, DNQ final), 7/3 Swiss Grand Prix (#48 Talbot 26, Q17,F16), 7/10 Albi Grand Prix (#40, 8th in heat, DNF final), 10/9 Salon Grand Prix (#7, Q5,F2)
1950- 5/21 **MONACO** (#8 Cooper-J.A.P., Q20,DNF-accident), 6/4 **SWITZERLAND**, Bremgarten (#44 Talbot-Lago, Q18,F8), 7/3 Grand Prix of Nations, Geneva (#32 Maserati 4CLT48, Q12,DNF)
1951- 3/11 Syracuse Grand Prix (#22 Maserati 4CLT48, Q10,DNF), 3/26 Pau Grand Prix (#24, Q14,DNF), 4/22 San Remo Grand Prix (#8, Q8,F4), 4/29 Bordeaux Grand Prix (#12, Q3,DNF), 5/5 International Trophy, Silverstone (#20, 9th in heat, not classified in final), 5/20 Paris Grand Prix (#28, F7 in car shared w/De Graffenried), 5/27 **SWITZERLAND**, Bremgarten (#32, Q17,F12), 7/1 **FRANCE** (#20, Q22,DNF), 8/15 Pescara Grand Prix (#12, Q11,F7), 9/2 Bari Grand Prix (#24, Q19,DNF)
1952- 6/1 Albi Grand Prix (#32 Simca-Gordini, Q10,DNF), 8/2 Daily Mail Trophy, Boreham (#35 Maserati 4CLT48, DNF), 5/10 International Trophy, Silverstone (#37, 8th

in heat, DNF in final), 5/18 **SWITZER-LAND** (#40, Q16,DNF), 5/22 Paris Grand Prix (#18, Q18,DNF), 6/8 Circuit du Lac at Aix-les-Bains (#10, 5th in heat 1, 4th in heat 2, F4), 6/29 Marne Grand Prix (#24, Q23,DNF), 7/6 **FRANCE**, Rouen (#18, Q11,DNF), 7/13 Sables D'Olonne Grand Prix (Q10,DNF), 7/19 **GREAT BRITAIN** (#33, Q32,F17), 7/27 Caen Grand Prix (#10 Simca-Gordini, DNF), 8/2 Daily Mail Trophy (#35 Maserati 4CLT48, DNF), 8/10 Comminges Grand Prix (#38 Simca-Gordini, Q16,DNF), 8/24 Baule Grand Prix (#14, Q14,DNF), 9/1 Circuit De Cadours Grand Prix (#28 Gordini, 1st in heat, F2)

1953- 4/6 Pau (#22 Gordini, Q11,F3), 5/3 Bordeaux Grand Prix (#22, Q15,F4), 5/9 International Trophy, Silverstone (#4, 7th in heat, DNS final), 5/31 Albi Grand Prix (DNF in heat), 6/7 **HOLLAND** (#20, Q10, blew engine, given Wacker's engine, not classified, transmission), 6/21 **BELGIUM** (Q12,F8), 6/28 Rouen Grand Prix (#14, Q7,F4, 1st Formula Two car), 7/5 **FRANCE** at Reims (#6, Q20,DNF), 7/18 **GREAT BRITAIN** at Silverstone (#28, Q9,DNF), 7/26 Circuit du Lac at Aix-les-Bains (#6, 7th in heat, DNF in final), 8/2 **GERMANY** (#11, Q10,DNF), 8/9 Sables d'Olonne Grand Prix (#6, 5th in heat, DNF in final), 8/30 Circuit de Cadours (#34, 1st in heat, F2 in final), 9/13 **ITALY** (#38, Q15,F12), 9/20 Modena Grand Prix (#18, Q11, F6-not classified)

1954- 1/17 **ARGENTINA** (#28 Maserati A6GCM, Q10,F6), 4/19 Pau Grand Prix (#22, Q7,DNF), 5/9 Bordeaux Grand Prix (Q8,DNF), 5/22 Bari Grand Prix (F5), 6/6 Rome Grand Prix (#14, Q6,F2), 7/4 **FRANCE** at Reims (#48, Q21,DNF), 7/11 Rouen Grand Prix (#24, Q10,DNF), 7/17 **GREAT BRITAIN** (#3, Q16,F12), 7/25 Caen Grand Prix (#18, Q5,DNF), 8/1 **GERMANY** (#15, Q14,F7), 8/15 Pescara Grand Prix (#24, Q8,F3), 8/22 **SWITZERLAND** (#34 Maserati 250F Q13,DNF), 9/12 Circuit de Cadours Grand Prix (Maserati A6GCM 1st in heat, DNF in final), 9/19 Berlin Grand Prix (#22, Q11-last,F8-not classified), 10/2 Daily Telegraph Trophy, Aintree (#15 Maserati 250F, Q4,F3), 10/26 **SPAIN** (#24, Q4,DNF)

1955- 1/16 **ARGENTINA** (#28 Maserati 250F, Q7,F6 with Behra in relief), 3/27 Valentino Grand Prix (#20 Ferrari 625, Q9,F5), 5/22 **MONACO** (#46 Ferrari 555, Q18,DNF), 7/16 **GREAT BRITAIN** (#30 Vanwall,

Q7,DNF, took over #28 for Ken Wharton,F9-not classified), 7/30 London Trophy, Crystal Palace (#2 Vanwall, 1st in heat, F2 in final), 8/13 Redex Trophy, Snetterton (#142, Q2,F1), 9/11 **ITALY** (#42, Q13,DNF), 9/24 International Trophy, Oulton Park (#7, Q5,DNF), 10/1 Avon Trophy, Castle Combe (#26, Q1,F1), 10/23 Syracuse Grand Prix (#18 Maserati 250F, Q5,F6)

1956- 5/5 International Trophy, Silverstone (#4 Vanwall, Q2,DNF), 5/13 **MONACO** (#16, Q5,DNF), 6/3 **BELGIUM** (#10, Q6,F4), 7/1 **FRANCE** at Reims (#22, Q4,DNF..relieved Hawthorn in #24, F10), 7/14 **GREAT BRITAIN** (#16 Q5,DNF), 8/5 **GERMANY** (#12, Maserati 250F, Q12,DNF), 8/26 Caen Grand Prix (#?, Q5,F1), 9/2 **ITALY** (#18, Vanwall, Q10,DNF)

1957- 1/13 **ARGENTINA** (#22 Maserati 250F, Q9,F4), 1/27 Buenos Aires Grand Prix (#10, Q12,DNF), 4/7 Syracuse Grand Prix (#24, Q5,DNF), 4/22 Pau Grand Prix (#20, Q2,F2), 5/19 **MONACO** (#38, Q8,DNF...relieved Scarlatti in #34, DNF), 7/7 **FRANCE** at Rouen (#6, Q4,F5), 7/14 Reims Grand Prix (#14, Q10,F4), 7/20 **GREAT BRITAIN** (#6, Q7,DNF), 7/28 Caen Grand Prix (#4 BRM, Q5,DNF), 8/4 **GERMANY** (#3 Maserati 250F, Q6,F7), 8/18 **PESCARA** (#6, Q5,F3), 9/8 **ITALY** (#4, Q6,DNF), 9/14 International Trophy, Silverstone (#7 BRM, 1st in heat, F2), 9/22 Modena Grand Prix (#6, 3rd in heat 1, 3rd in heat 2, F3 in final), 10/27 Moroccan Grand Prix (#10, Q7,F5)

1958- 1/19 **ARGENTINA** (#8 Maserati 250F, Q8,F6), 4/7 Glover Trophy, Goodwood (#4, Q5,DNF), 4/19 B.A.R.C. 200, Aintree (#2 Formula Two Cooper-Climax, Q14,F6 - 3rd in Formula Two), 5/18 **MONACO** (#8 BRM, Q11,F6), 5/25 **HOLLAND** (#15, Q7,F2), 6/15 **BELGIUM** (#10 Q7,F5), 7/6 **FRANCE** at Reims (#16, Q3,F12-not classified), 7/19 **GREAT BRITAIN** at Silverstone (#20, Q2,F5), 7/20 Caen Grand Prix (#?, Q8,DNF), 8/3 **GERMANY** (#6, Q8,DNF), 8/24 **PORTUGAL** at Oporto (#10, Q7,F6), 9/7 **ITALY** (#10, Q9,DNF), 10/19 **MOROCCO** (#16, Q10,F5)

1959- 3/30 Glover Trophy, Goodwood (#1 BRM, Q1,F3), 4/18 B.A.R.C. 200, Aintree (#14, Q3,DNF), 5/10 **MONACO** (#16, Q9,DNF), 5/31 **HOLLAND** (#6, Q6,DNF), 7/5 **FRANCE** at Reims (#6, Q9,F7), 7/18 **GREAT BRITAIN** (#8, Q3,F4), 8/2 **GERMANY** at Avus (#10, Q8, 5th in heat 1, 7th in heat 2 - not classified, F7 in final - not

classified), 8/23 **PORTUGAL** at Monsanto (#6, Q9,F5), 9/13 **ITALY** (#2, Q7,F7), 12/12 **USA** (#19, Q3,DNF)

1960- 2/6 **ARGENTINA** (#34 Cooper-Climax, Q9,DNF), 4/18 Glover Trophy, Goodwood (#8, Q3,DNF),... *killed in practice in #22 Yeoman Credit Cooper-Climax the day before 5/14 International Trophy at Silverstone...*

Bob Schroeder, 5/11/1926-___: 2 // 1
1962- 10/7 **USA** (#26 Lotus-Climax, Q16,F10), 11/4 Mexican Grand Prix (#77, Q11,F6)

Lou Sell: 1
1971- 3/28 Questor Grand Prix at Ontario (#37 Lola-Chevrolet F5000, Q21, 14th in heat 1, 12th in heat 2, F13 on aggregate)

Tony Settember, 7/10/1926-___: 17 // 7
1962- 4/23, Lavant Cup, Goodwood (#10 Emeryson-Climax, Q4,DNF), 4/23, Glover Trophy, Goodwood (#10, Q9,F8), 4/29 B.A.R.C. 200, Aintree (#24, Q19,F8), 5/20, Naples Grand Prix (#24, Q8, - not classified), 6/11 Crystal Palace Trophy (#11, Q5,F5), 7/15 Solitude Grand Prix (#16, Q9,DNF), 7/21 **GREAT BRITAIN** (#40, Q19,F11), ... DNS at 9/1 International Gold Cup at Oulton Park ... 9/16 **ITALY** (#48, Q21,DNF)

1963- 4/15 Pau Grand Prix (#12 Emeryson-Climax, Q7,DNF), 6/9 **BELGIUM** (#24 Scirocco-BRM, Q19,DNF-accident), 6/23 **HOLLAND** (#38, Q18,DNF), 6/30 **FRANCE** (#38, Q18,DNF), 7/20 **GREAT BRITAIN** (#15, Q18,DNF), 7/28 Solitude Grand Prix (#26, Q15,F19-not classified), 8/4 **GERMANY** (#23, Q22,DNF-accident), 9/1 Austrian Grand Prix at Zeltweg (#11, Q8,F2) [lost clutch at start, push-started, no clutch for race], ...DNQ at 9/8 ITALY... 9/21 International Gold Cup, Oulton Park (#24, Q22,DNF)

James R. "Hap" Sharp, 1/1/1928-5/1993: // 6
1961- 10/8 **USA** (#3 Cooper-Climax, Q17,F10)
1962- 10/7 **USA** (#24 Cooper-Climax, Q14,F11)
1963- 10/6 **USA** (#22 Lotus-BRM, Q18,DNF), **MEXICO** (Q16,F7)
1964- 10/4 **USA** (#23 Brabham-Climax, Q18,F10-not classified), **MEXICO** (Q19,F13)

Carroll Shelby, 1/11/1923-___: 10 // 8
1955- 10/23 Syracuse Grand Prix (#28 Maserati 250F, Q6,F5)
1958- 7/6 **FRANCE** at Reims (#28 Maserati 250F, Q17,DNF), 7/19 **GREAT BRITAIN** at Silverstone (#5, Q15,F9), 8/24 **PORTUGAL** (#28, Q10,F9), 9/7 **ITALY** (#34, Q17, out on

lap 1,DNF-took over Gregory's car, F4), ...*Alternate driver at 10/8 MOROCCO, DNS*
1959- 5/2 International Trophy, Silverstone (#2 Aston Martin, Q6,F6), 5/31 **HOLLAND** (#5, Q10,DNF), 7/18 **GREAT BRITAIN** (#4, Q6,F11), 8/23 **PORTUGAL**, Monsanto (#9, Q11,F8), 9/13 **ITALY** (#26, Q19,F10)

Danny Sullivan, 3/9/1950-___: 16 // 15
1983- 3/13 **BRAZIL** (#4 Tyrrell-Ford, Q21,F11), 3/27 **USA-WEST** (Q9,F8), 4/10 Race of Champions, Brands Hatch (Q6,F2), 4/17 **FRANCE** (Q24,DNF), 5/1 **SAN MARINO** (Q22,DNF-accident), 5/15 **MONACO** (Q20,F5), 5/22 **BELGIUM** (Q23,F12), 6/5 **USA-EAST** (Q16,DNF), 6/12 **CANADA** (Q22,DQ-underweight after losing coolant), 7/16 **GREAT BRITAIN** (Q23,F14), 8/7 **GERMANY** (Q21,F12), 8/14 **AUSTRIA** (Q23,DNF-accident), 8/28 **HOLLAND** (Q26,DNF), 9/11 **ITALY** (Q22,DNF), **EUROPE** at Brands Hatch (Q20,DNF), 10/15 **SOUTH AFRICA** (Q19,F7)

Alfonso Thiele: // 1
1960- 9/4 **ITALY** (#34 Cooper-Maserati, Q9,DNF)

Al Unser, 5/29/1939-___: // 1
1971- 3/28 Questor Grand Prix at Ontario (#33 Lola-Chevrolet F5000, Q26, DNF in heat 1 - engine)

Bobby Unser, 2/20/1934-___: 2 // 1
1968- 10/6 USA (#9 BRM, Q19,DNF)
1971- 3/28 Questor Grand Prix at Ontario (#38 Lola-Chevrolet F5000, Q27, 12th in heat 1, DNF in heat 2, F16 on aggregate)

Fred Wacker, 7/10/1918-___: 7 // 3 *1st American-born driver to achieve a podium finish in a Formula One Grand Prix.*
1953- 5/24 Frontieres Grand Prix at Chimay (#4 Gordini, Q6,F3), 5/31 Eifelrennen at the Nürburgring (#9, F9),....Entered in 6/7 HOLLAND in #40 Gordini, DNS - car taken over by Schell..., 6/21 **BELGIUM** (#38 Gordini, Q15,F10).....*crashed #44 Gordini in practice for 8/23 Swiss Grand Prix, Bremgarten, DNS*
1954- 8/22 SWITZERLAND (#14 Gordini, Q15,DNF), 9/5 **ITALY** (#42, Q18,F6), 9/12 Circuit de Cadours Grand Prix (#3, 2nd in heat, 3 seconds behind Schell, 4th in final), 9/19 Berlin Grand Prix (#16, Q9,F6)

Rodger Ward, 1/10/1921-___: // 2 1st American to drive an American car in Formula One
1959- 12/12 **USA** Sebring (#1 Kurtis Kraft-Offy, Q19-last, broken clutch lap 21)
1963- 10/6 USA (#18 Lotus-BRM, Q17,DNF)

191

American Cars in Grand Prix

Note: the following conventions are used in this Car Records Appendix:
Q = Qualified
F=Finished
DNF=Did Not Finish
DNS=Did Not Start
BOLD UPPER CASE=a World Championship Grand Prix in post-1950 entries
#=car number
underlined=car designation (if the driver, car#, car, or car designation are not given in an entry, they remain the same as the preceding entry in that year)

Entries are listed in the following order:

Name of Car-Engine: (designer) *Italicized milestones*
Year- underlined model designation date name of 1st race (car number driver, qualifying position, result), date name of race, (different model designation car number driver, qualifying position, result), *Italicized information about a race attended but not run - and why*, date name of race, (different model designation car number driver, qualifying position, result), etc.
Year- model designation date name of race (different models designation car number driver, qualifying position, result), etc.

Note: Car number, driver are not given in an entry if they remain unchanged from the previous entry in the same year. Model designation is given inside the parenthesis only when it differs from the model designation raced previously.

Pre-World War Two

Abbott-Detroit:
1911- 11/30 American Grand Prize, Savannah (#44 Al Mitchell, F6; #50 Carl Limberg, F8)

Acme:
1908- 11/26 American Grand Prize, Savannah (#7 Len Zengle, DNF)

Alco:
1910- 11/12 American Grand Prize, Savannah (#7 Harry Grant, DNF)
1914- 2/28 American Grand Prize, Santa Monica (#6 Billy Taylor, F3; #19 Tony Janette, DNF)
1915- 2/27 American Grand Prize, San Francisco (#29 Billy Taylor, DNF)

Apperson:
1914- 2/28 American Grand Prize, Santa Monica (Frank Goode, DNF)

Buick:
1932- 2/29 Swedish Winter Grand Prix, Ramen (#7 Eric Bake, F3)

Marquette-Buick:
1910- 11/12 American Grand Prize, Savannah (#17 Bob Burman, F3; #3 Arthur Chevrolet, DNF)
1911- 11/30 American Grand Prize, Savannah (#43 Charles Basle, DNF; #49 Harry Cobe, DNF)

Californian:
1915- 2/27 American Grand Prize, San Francisco (#14 Caleb Bragg, DNF)

Case:
1915- 2/27 American Grand Prize, San Francisco (#21 Eddie Hearne, DNF; Harry Grant, DNF)

Chadwick Big Six: *1st supercharged car in a Grand Prix*
1908- 11/26 American Grand Prize, Savannah (#5 Willie Haupt, DNF)

Chevrolet:
1915- 2/27 American Grand Prize, San Francisco (#20 Cliff Durant, DNF; #18 LeCain, DNF)
1932- 2/29 Swedish Winter Grand Prix, Ramen (#16 Clemens Bergström, F7; #24 Folke Hjelm, DNF; #28 Per Nas, F6; #30 Martin Strömberg, F11)
1933- 8/8 Swedish Summer Grand Prix, Vram (#18 Martin Strömberg, DNF; #21 Gosta Askergren, -not classified)

Christie WC-5: *1st American car to enter a Grand Prix, largest engine in a Grand Prix, 1st front-drive in a Grand Prix, 1st transverse engine in a Grand Prix, 1st V4 in a Grand Prix*
1907- 7/2 A.C.F. Grand Prix, Dieppe (#WC-1 J. Walter Christie, DNF)

Chrysler:
1932- 2/29 Swedish Winter Grand Prix, Ramen (#12 Sulo Pàavo Keinänen, F2; #20 Johan Ramsay, DNF; #29 Anders Olsson, F10), 5/15 Frontieres Grand Prix, Chimay (Freddy Thélussen, F5)

Cooper Special:
1927- 9/4 European Grand Prix, Monza (#10 Peter Kreis, DNF; #2 Earl Cooper, F3-with Kreis in relief)

De Soto:
1930- 5/18 Picardie Grand Prix at Perrone (#65 Pesato, F9-2nd in 5-liter Sports Car Class)
1933- 2/29 Swedish Winter Grand Prix, Ramen (#18 Erik Lafrenz, DNF)

Duesenberg: *1st American car to win a European Grand Prix, first four-wheel hydraulic brakes in a Grand Prix, first detachable heads, first American-made tires to win a Grand Prix - Oldfield tires made by Firestone*
1915- 2/27 American Grand Prize, San Francisco (#2 Tom Alley, DNF; #19 Eddie O'Donnell, DNF)
1916- 11/18 American Grand Prize, Santa Monica (#21 William Weightman- with relief from Eddie Rickenbacker, F5; #17 Eddie Rickenbacker, DNF; #11 Mike Moosie, DNF; #18 George Buzane, DNF)
1921- 7/6 A.C.F. Grand Prix, Le Mans (#12 Jimmy Murphy, F1,*fastest lap*; #19 André Dubonnet, F4; #6 Albert Guyot, F6; #16 Joe Boyer, DNF)

Californian:

1925- 9/6 Italian Grand Prix, Monza (#7 Tommy Milton, F4; #11 Peter Kreis, DNF,*fastest lap*)
1927- 9/4 European Grand Prix, Monza (#8 George Souders, DNF)
1930- 9/7 Monza Grand Prix (#50 Babe Stapp, 3rd in heat, F8 in final)
1933- 9/10 Monza Grand Prix (#4 Count Carlo Trossi, DNF)

Duesenberg-Miller 255:
1934 5/6 Tripoli Grand Prix (#24 Lou Moore, F7)

Edwards Special:
1915- 2/27 American Grand Prize, San Francisco (#7 Gandy, DNF; #11 "Cap" Kennedy, DNF)

Ford Model T:
1911- 7/29 Grand Prix of France, LeMans

Ford:
1932- 2/29 Swedish Winter Grand Prix, Ramen (#11 Thure Johansson, DNF; #15 Carl-Gustav Johansson, DNF; #15 Harry Larsson, DNF; #23 Olle Bennström, F1)
1933- 8/8 Swedish Summer Grand Prix, Vram (#2 Olle Bennström, DNF-accident; #6 Carl-Gustav Johansson, DNF; #7 Asser Wallenius, DNF-accident; #11 John Forsberg, DNF-accident; #20 Walter Görtz, F7; #24 Harry Larsson, F6; #26 Morian Hansen, DNF; #27 Paul Tholstrup, DNF)

Montier Ford Special:
1929- 7/7 Dieppe Grand Prix (#60 Charles Montier, -not classified; #62 Ferdinand Montier, -not classified)
1930- 5/18 Picardie Grand Prix at Perrone (#60 Ferdinand Montier, F10, 3rd in 5-liter Sports Car Class), 10/5 Spanish Grand Prix at San Sebastion (Ferdinand Montier, F8; Charles Montier, DNF)
1931- 7/12 Belgian Grand Prix, Spa (#20 Ferdinand Montier, DNF; #22 Charles Montier & Ducolombier, F8), 7/26 Dieppe Grand Prix (#72 Ferdinand Montier, F11; #70 Charles Montier, F10)
1932- 5/5 Picardie Grand Prix at Peronne (#29 Ferdinand Montier, F6; #27 Charles Montier, F9), 8/17 Baule Grand Prix (#2 Ford V8, Ferdinand Montier, F6)
1934- 7/29 Belgian Grand Prix (#24 Charles Montier, F5), 9/9 U.M.F. Grand Prix, Montlhéry (#19 Charles Montier, -not classified)
1935- 6/30 Lorraine Grand Prix, Nancy (#12 Charles Montier, F10)

Ford V8 Special:
1934- 12/27 South African "Border 100" Grand Prix, East London (#9 James Herbert Case, F2, #15 S. McKenzie, DNF)
1936- 1/1 South African Grand Prix, East London (#14 James Herbert Case, DNF; #12 Vernon Celliers Berrange, DNF; #13 G. Billiet, DNF; #15 J.Whitehead, DNF)
1937- 1/1 South African Grand Prix, East London (#11 James Herbert Case, F8)

Gordon Special (Mercer):
1915- 2/27 American Grand Prize, San Francisco (#51 Huntley Gordon, DNF)

Hercules Special:
1916- 11/18 American Grand Prize, Santa Monica (#10 Emil Agraz, DNF)

Hudson:
1916- 11/18 American Grand Prize, Santa Monica (#20 A.H. Patterson, F3; #6 Clyde Roads, F4; #19 Ira Vail, DNF)
1937- 1/1 South African Grand Prix, East London (#11 K. Walter, DNF)

Hudson Terraplane Six:
1934- 12/27 South African "Border 100" Grand Prix, East London (#14 W. Ross, F4; #13 Emilio Rosingana, DNF-accident)
1937- 1/1 South African Grand Prix, East London (#6 H.Bruce, DNF)

King:
1915- 2/27 American Grand Prize, San Francisco (#16 Arthur Klein, DNF)

Kissell:
1916- 11/18 American Grand Prize, Santa Monica (#25 Dave Anderson, DNF)

Lozier:
1908- 11/26 American Grand Prize, Savannah (#2 Ralph Mulford, DNF)
1910- 11/12 American Grand Prize, Savannah (#4 Ralph Mulford, F4; #12 Joe Horan, F5)
1911- 11/30 American Grand Prize, Savannah (Ralph Mulford, F7)
1912- 10/5 American Grand Prize, Milwaukee (#45 Fountain, DNF)

Marmon: *1st American car to lead a Grand Prix, 1911 American Grand Prize, Cyrus Patschke*
1910- 11/12 American Grand Prize, Savannah (#8 Joe Dawson, DNF; #14 Ray Harroun-with Joe Dawson in relief, F6)
1911- 11/30 American Grand Prize, Savannah (#46 Bob Burman, DNF, #51 Cyrus Patshke, DNF)
1914- 2/28 American Grand Prize, Santa Monica (#17 Guy Ball, F2; #15 Charlie Muth, DNF)
1916- 11/18 American Grand Prize, Santa Monica (#24 Lewis Jackson, DNF)

Mason:
1914- 2/28 American Grand Prize, Santa Monica (#20 Eddie Rickenbacker, DNF)

Maxwell:
1915- 2/27 American Grand Prize, San Francisco (#1 Barney Oldfield, DNF; #17 Eddie Rickenbacker, DNF, #32 Billy Carlson, DNF)

Mercer:
1912- 10/5 American Grand Prize, Milwaukee (#34 Hughie Hughes, DNF)
1914- 2/28 American Grand Prize, Santa Monica (#7 Barney Oldfield, DNF; #4 Ed Pullen, F1; #9 Huntley Gordon, F6; #2 Spencer Wishart, DNF)

1915- 2/27 American Grand Prize, San Francisco (#10 Louis Nikrent, DNF; #4 Ed Pullen, DNF; #6 Grover Ruckstell, DNF)
1916- 11/18 American Grand Prize, Santa Monica (#4 Ed Pullen, DNF, #3 Grover Ruckstell, DNF,*fastest lap)

Miller 122:
1923- 9/9 Italian Grand Prix, Monza (#5 Jimmy Murphy, F3; #16,*modified w/2 seats, Martin de Alzaga, F6; #11 Zboroski, DNF), 10/28 Spanish Grand Prix, Sitges-Terramar (#1 Zboroski, F2,*fastest lap)
1924- 8/3 European Grand Prix at Lyons (#6 Zboroski, DNF)

Miller 91:
1929- 9/15 "non-formula" Monza Grand Prix (#20 Leon Duray, DNF in 1.5 liter event, *fastest lap; #40 Leon Duray, DNF in 3 liter event)

Miller 91 (rear-wheel drive):
1932- 9/11 Monza Grand Prix (#44 Leon Duray, DNF)

Miller 4WD: *1st 4WD car in a Grand Prix*
1934- 5/6 Tripoli Grand Prix (#30 Peter DePaolo, F6); 5/27 Avusrennen Grand Prix (#25 Peter DePaolo, DNF)

National:
1908- 11/26 American Grand Prize, Savannah (#11 Hugh Harding, DNF)
1916- 11/18 American Grand Prize, Santa Monica (#23 W.M. "Bill" Cody, DNF)

Omar Special:
1916- 11/18 American Grand Prize, Santa Monica (#27 Omar Toft, DNF)

Ono:
1915- 2/27 American Grand Prize, San Francisco (#28 Hughie Hughes, F3)

Overland:
1915- 2/27 American Grand Prize, San Francisco (#31 T. McKelvy, DNF)

Owl Special:
1916- 11/18 American Grand Prize, Santa Monica (#22 William Carleton, DNF)

Packard Indy:
1922- 10/22 Autumn Grand Prix, Monza (#24 Caiselli, F9)

Parsons Special:
1915- 2/27 American Grand Prize, San Francisco (#24 Jim Parsons, DNF)

Plymouth:
1936- 1/1 South African Grand Prix, East London (#8 W.F. Mills, F8)

Pope-Hartford:
1910- 11/12 American Grand Prize, Savannah (#6 Charlie Basle, DNF)
1911- 11/30 American Grand Prize, Savannah (#42 Lou Disbrow, F5)

Railton-Terraplane (Hudson 8):
1934- 12/27 South African "Border 100" Grand Prix, East London (#16 Michael Straight, F3)

Shafer-8 Special:
1931- 7/19 German Grand Prix, Nürburgring (#38 Phil "Red" Shafer, DNF)

Simplex:
1908- 11/26 American Grand Prize, Savannah (#3 Joe Seymour, F11)
1915- 2/27 American Grand Prize, San Francisco (#12 Lou Disbrow, F5)

Studebaker:
1933- 2/29 Swedish Winter Grand Prix, Ramen (#8 Ernst Timar, F12)

Stutz:
1912- 10/5 American Grand Prize, Milwaukee (#43 Gil Anderson, F3)
1914- 2/28 American Grand Prize, Santa Monica (#3 Gil Anderson, F5; #8 Earl Cooper, DNF)
1915- 2/27 American Grand Prize, San Francisco (#8 Earl Cooper, DNF; #5 Gil Anderson, F4; #26 Howard "Howdy" Wilcox, F2)
1916- 11/18 American Grand Prize, Santa Monica (#9 Cliff Durant, DNF; #8 Earl Cooper, F2)
1928- 8/23 Baule Grand Prix, France (Eduardo Brisson, F9)

Tahis Special:
1915- 2/27 American Grand Prize, San Francisco (#3 Jack Gable, DNF)

Thomas:
1908- 7/7 A.C.F. Grand Prix, Dieppe (#15 Strang, DNF)

Willys:
1936- 1/1 South African Grand Prix, East London (#7 J.G. Clarke, DNF)
1937- 1/1 South African Grand Prix, East London (#10 Vernon Celliers Berrange, DNF)

Post-World War Two

Beatrice Haas-Lola-Hart: (designed by Neil Oatley)
1985- THL-1 9/8 **ITALY** (#33 Alan Jones, Q25,DNF), 10/6 **EUROPE** at Brands Hatch (Q22,DNF), *...Qualified 18th but Jones taken ill, DNS at 10/19 SOUTH AFRICA...,* 11/3 **AUSTRALIA** (Q19,DNF)
1986- THL-1 3/23 **BRAZIL** (#15 Alan Jones, Q19,DNF; #16 Patrick Tambay, Q13,DNF), 4/13 **SPAIN** (#15 Jones, Q17,DNF-accident; #16 Tambay, Q18,F8-six laps down), 4/27 **SAN MARINO** (#16 Tambay, Q11,DNF)

Beatrice Haas-Lola-Ford V-6: (designed by Neil Oatley)
1986- THL-2 4/27 **SAN MARINO** (#15 Alan Jones, Q21,DNF), 5/11 **MONACO** (#15 Jones, Q18,DNF-accident; #16 Tambay, Q8,DNF-accident; 5/25 **BELGIUM** (#15 Jones, Q16,F11-not running at finish; #16 Tambay, Q10,DNF-accident), 6/15 **CANADA** (#15 Jones, Q14,F10; ...#16 *Tambay Qualified 14th, DNS, accident in warm-up..*), 6/22 **USA-EAST**

(#15 Jones, Q21,DNF; #16 Eddie Cheever, Q10,DNF), 7/6 **FRANCE** (#15 Jones, Q20,DNF-accident;#16 Tambay, Q13,DNF), 7/13 **GREAT BRITAIN** (#15 Jones, Q14,DNF; #16 Tambay, Q17,DNF), 7/27 **GERMANY** (#15 Jones, Q19,started from back of grid,F9; #16 Tambay, Q13,8), 8/10 **HUNGARY** (#15 Jones, Q10,DNF; #16 Tambay, Q6,F7), 8/17 **AUSTRIA** (#15 Jones, Q16,F4; #16 Tambay, Q13,F5), 9/7 **ITALY** (#15 Jones, Q18,F6; #16 Tambay, Q15,DNF-accident), 9/21 **PORTUGAL** (#15 Jones, Q17,DNF-spun, stalled; #16 Tambay, Q14,-not classified), 10/12 **MEXICO** (#15 Jones, Q15,DNF; #16 Tambay, Q8,DNF-accident), 10/26 **AUSTRALIA** (#15 Jones, Q15,DNF; #16 Tambay, Q17,F11-not classified)

Eagle-Climax: (Designed by Len Terry)
1966- 6/13 **BELGIUM** (#27 Dan Gurney, Q15,F7-not classified), 7/3 **FRANCE** (#26 Gurney, Q14,F5), 7/16 **GREAT BRITAIN** (#16 Gurney, Q3,DNF), 7/24 **HOLLAND** (#10 Gurney, Q4,DNF), 8/7 **GERMANY** (#12 Gurney, Q8,F7), ...#34 *Phil Hill DNQ at 9/4 ITALY...,* 10/2 **USA** (#16 Bob Bondurant, Q16,DQ-outside assistance), 10/23 **MEXICO** (#15 Gurney, Q9,F5-swapped cars with Bondurant before start)
1967- 1/2 **SOUTH AFRICA** (#9 Dan Gurney, Q11,DNF), 8/27 **CANADA** (#11 Al Pease, Q16,F14-not classified)
1969- 9/20 **CANADA** (#69 Al Pease, Q16,DQ-too slow)

Eagle-Plymouth (F5000):
1971- 3/28 Questor Grand Prix at Ontario (#32, Savage, Q29, DNF in heat one - accident)

Eagle-Gurney-Weslake: (Designed by Len Terry)
1966- 9/4 **ITALY** (#30 Dan Gurney, Q19,DNF), 10/2 **USA** (#15 Gurney, Q14,DNF), 10/23 **MEXICO** (#16 Bob Bondurant, Q18,DNF-swapped cars w/Gurney before start)
1967- 3/12 Race of Champions, Brands Hatch (#5 Dan Gurney, Q1, 1st in heat one, 1st in heat two,F1 in final; #6 Richie Ginther, Q3, 3rd in heat one, 2nd in heat two,F10 in final), 5/7 **MONACO** (#23 Gurney, Q7,DNF), 6/4 **HOLLAND** (#15 Gurney, Q2,DNF), 6/18 **BELGIUM** (#36 Gurney, Q2,F1,-*fastest lap), 7/1 **FRANCE** at Le Mans (#9 Gurney, Q3,DNF; #8 Bruce McLaren, Q5,DNF), 7/15 **GREAT BRITAIN** (#9 Gurney, Q5,DNF; #10 McLaren, Q10,DNF), 8/6 **GERMANY** (#9 Gurney, Q4,DNF: #10 McLaren, Q5,DNF), 8/27 **CANADA** (#10 Gurney, Q5,DNF), 9/10 **ITALY** (#8 Gurney, Q5,DNF: #10 Ludovico Scarfiotti, Q10,DNF), 10/1 **USA** (#11 Gurney, Q3,DNF), 10/22 **MEXICO** (#11 Gurney, Q3,DNF)
1968- 1/1 **SOUTH AFRICA** (#6 Dan Gurney, Q12,DNF), 5/26 **MONACO** (#19 Gurney, Q16,DNF), 7/20 **GREAT BRITAIN** (#24 Gurney, Q6,DNF), 8/4 **GERMANY** (#14 Gurney, Q10,F9), 9/8 **ITALY** (#21 Gurney, Q12,DNF)

Kurtis Kraft-Offenhauser midget: *1st American car to run in a post-war Grand Prix*
1959- 12/12 **USA**, Sebring (#1 Ward, Q19,DNF)

Parnelli-Ford: (designed by Maurice Phillippe):
1974- VPJ4 9/22 **CANADA** (#55 Mario Andretti, Q16,F7), 10/6 **USA** (Q3, DQ-outside assistance)
1975- VPJ4 1/12 **ARGENTINA** (#27 Mario Andretti, Q10,DNF), 1/26 **BRAZIL** (Q18,F7), 3/1 **SOUTH AFRICA** (Q6,F17-not running at finish), 4/13 Daily Express International Trophy, Silverstone, (Q10,F3), 4/27 **SPAIN** (Q4,DNF,*fastest lap), 5/11 **MONACO** (Q13,DNF), 6/8 **SWEDEN** (Q15,F4), 7/6 **FRANCE** (Q15,F5), 7/19 **GREAT BRITAIN** (Q12,F12), 8/3 **GERMANY** (Q13,DNF), 8/17 **AUSTRIA** (Q19,DNF), 9/7 **ITALY** (Q15,DNF-accident), 10/5 **USA** (Q5,DNF)
1976- VPJ4B 3/6 **SOUTH AFRICA** (#27 Mario Andretti, Q14,F6), 3/28 **USA-WEST** (Q15, DNF)

Penske-Cosworth: (PC1 designed by Geoff Ferris; PC3 & PC4 by Ferris and Don Cox):
1974- PC1 9/22 **CANADA** (#66 Mark Donohue, Q24,F12), 10/6 **USA** (Q14,DNF)
1975- 1/12 **ARGENTINA** (#28 Mark Donohue, Q16,F7), 1/26 **BRAZIL** (Q16,DNF), 3/1 **SOUTH AFRICA** (Q18,F8), 3/16 British Airways-Daily Mail Race of Champions, Brands Hatch (Q7,DNF), 4/13 Daily Express International Trophy, Silverstone, (PC1 #28 Donohue, Q11,F6), 4/27 **SPAIN** (Q17,DNF-accident), 5/11 **MONACO** (Q16,DNF-accident), 5/25 **BELGIUM** (Q21,F11), 6/8 **SWEDEN** (Q16,F5), 6/22 **HOLLAND** (Q18,F8), 7/6 **FRANCE** (Q17,DNF), 10/5 **USA** (#28 John Watson Q12- engine problem with new PC3 in warmup, started backup PC1 at the back of the field,F9)
1976- PC3 1/25 **BRAZIL** (#28 John Watson, Q8,DNF), 3/6 **SOUTH AFRICA** (Q3,F5), 3/14 Daily Mail Race of Champions, Brands Hatch, (Q8,DNF), 3/28 **USA-WEST** (Q10,-not classified), 5/2 **SPAIN** (Q13,DNF), 5/16 **BELGIUM** (Q17,F7), 5/30 **MONACO** (Q18,F10), PC4 6/13 **SWEDEN** (Q17,DNF), 7/4 **FRANCE** (Q8,F3), 7/18 **GREAT BRITAIN** (Q11,F3), 8/1 **GERMANY** (Q19,F7), 8/15 **AUSTRIA** (Q2,F1), 8/29 **HOLLAND** (Q4,DNF), 9/12 **ITALY** (Q27,F11), 10/3 **CANADA** (Q14,F10), 10/10 **USA-EAST** (Q8,F6), 10/24 **JAPAN** (Q4,DNF)
1977- PC3 3/20 Marlboro-Daily Mail Race of Champions, Brands Hatch (#24 Bob Evans, Q11,F11), 4/3 **USA-WEST** (PC4 #34 Jean-Pierre Jarier, Q10,F6), 5/22 **MONACO** (Q12,F11), 6/5 **BELGIUM** (Q26,F11), 6/19 **SWEDEN** (Q18,F8), 7/3 **FRANCE** (Q19,DNF-accident), 7/16 **GREAT BRITAIN** (Q20,F9), 7/31 **GERMANY** (Q12,DNF; PC4 #35 Hans Heyer, Q-third reserve,DNF), 8/14 **AUSTRIA** (Q18,F14; PC4 #33 Hans Binder, Q19,F12), 8/28 **HOLLAND** (Jarier Q21,DNF; #35 Binder Q18,F8), 9/11 **ITALY** (Jarier Q18,DNF; ...#33 Binder DNQ), 10/2 **USA-EAST** (PC4 #14 Danny Ongais, Q26,DNF-accident), 10/9 **CANADA** (Ongais Q22,F7)

Scarab: *America's 1st ground-up Formula One car, 1st car to run Goodyear tires in a Grand Prix*

1960- ....*Daigh & Reventlow DNQ at 5/29 MONACO...,
...Daigh & Reventlow DNS at 6/6 HOLLAND, car withdrawn...,* 6/19 **BELGIUM** (#30 Chuck Daigh, Q17,DNF; #28 Lance Reventlow, Q15,DNF), ...*Daigh DNS at FRANCE, engine...,* 11/20 **USA-WEST** (#23 Daigh, Q18,F10)

Scirocco-BRM:

1963- 6/9 **BELGIUM** (#24 Tony Settember, Q19,DNF-accident), 6/23 **HOLLAND** (#38 Settember, Q18,DNF), 6/30 **FRANCE** (#38 Settember, Q18,DNF), 7/20 **GREAT BRITAIN** (#15 Settember, Q18,DNF; #16 Ian Burgess, Q20,DNF), 7/28 Solitude Grand Prix (#26 Settember, Q15,F19-not classified; #27 Burgess, Q27,DNF), 8/4 **GERMANY** (#23 Settember, Q22,DNF-accident; #24 Burgess, Q19,DNF-accident), 9/1 Austrian Grand Prix at Zeltweg (#11 Settember, Q8,F2; #12 Burgess, Q13,DNF), ...*#36 Settember DNQ at 9/8 ITALY...* 9/21 International Gold Cup, Oulton Park (#24 Settember, Q22,DNF; #23 Burgess, Q18,F8)

Shadow-Cosworth: (Designed by Tony Southgate)

1973- DN1 3/3 **SOUTH AFRICA** (#22 Jackie Oliver, Q14,DNF-engine on lap 15; #23 George Follmer, Q23,F6), 4/8 International Trophy, Silverstone (#7 Oliver, Q14,DNF; #8 Follmer, Q17,F6), 4/29 **SPAIN** (#19 Oliver, Q13,DNF; #20 Follmer, Q14,F3; #25 Graham Hill, Q22,DNF), 5/20 **BELGIUM** (#17 Oliver, Q21,DNF-accident; #16 Follmer, Q12,DNF; #12 Hill (Q23,F9), 6/3 **MONACO** (#17 Oliver, Q22,F10; #12 Hill, Q25,DNF; ...*#16 Follmer Q20 but DNS, accident in practice...*), 6/17 **SWEDEN** (#17 Oliver, Q17,DNF; #16 Follmer, Q19,F14; #12 Hill, Q18,DNF), 7/1 **FRANCE** 9#17 Oliver, Q21,DNF); #16 Follmer, Q20,DNF; #12 Hill, Q16,F10), 7/14 **GREAT BRITAIN** (#17 Oliver, Q26,-accident at start, race restarted, DNS; #16 Follmer, Q25,-accident at start, race restarted, DNS; #12 Hill, Q27,DNF), 7/29 **HOLLAND** (#17 Oliver, Q10,DNF-accident; #16 Follmer, Q22,F10; #12 Hill, Q17,-not classified), **GERMANY** Oliver (Q17,F8; #16 Follmer, Q21,DNF-accident; #12 Hill, Q20,F13), 8/19 **AUSTRIA** (#17 Oliver, Q18,DNF; #16 Folmer, Q20,DNF; #12 Hill, Q22,DNF), 9/9 **ITALY** (#17 Oliver, Q19,F11; #16 Follmer, Q21,F10; #12 Hill, Q22,F14), 9/23 **CANADA** (#17 Oliver, Q14,F3; #16 Follmer, Q13,F17; #12 Hill, Q17,F16), 10/7 **USA** (#17 Oliver, Q22,F15; #16 Follmer, Q20,F14; #12 Hill, Q18,F13)

1974- DN3 1/13 **ARGENTINA** (#16 Peter Revson, Q4,DNF-accident; #17 Jean-Pierre Jarier, Q16,DNF-accident), 1/27 **BRAZIL** (#16 Revson, Q6,DNF; DN1 7/Jarier, Q20,DNF), DN3 3/17 Race of Champions, Brands Hatch (#16 Revson, Q9,F6;... *#17 Jarier DNS, accident....*), 4/7 Daily Express International Trophy, Silverstone, (#17 Jarier, Q10,F3), 4/28 **SPAIN** (#17 Jarier, Q12,-not classified; #16 Brian Redman, Q21,F7), 5/12 **BELGIUM** (#17 Jarier, Q17,F13; #16 Redman, Q18,F18-not running at finish), 5/26 **MONACO** (#17 Jarier, Q6,F3; #16 Redman, Q16,DNF-accident), 6/9 **SWEDEN** (#17 Jarier, Q8,F5; #16 Bertil Roos, Q23,DNF; #16 Bertil Roos, Q23,DNF; 6/23 **HOLLAND** (#17 Jarier, Q7,DNF; #16 Tom Pryce, Q9,DNF-accident), 7/7 **FRANCE** (#17 Jarier, Q12,F12; #16 Pryce, Q3,DNF-accident), 7/20 **GREAT BRITAIN** (#17 Jarier, Q16,DNF; #16 Pryce, Q5,F8), 8/4 **GERMANY** (#17 Jarier, Q18,F8; #16 Pryce, Q11,F6), 8/18 **AUSTRIA** (#17 Jarier, Q23,F8; #16 Pryce, Q16,DNF), 9/8 **ITALY** (#17 Jarier, Q9,DNF; #16 Pryce, Q22,F10), 9/22 **CANADA** (#17 Jarier, Q5,DNF; #16 Pryce, Q13,DNF), 10/6 **USA** (#17 Jarier, Q10,F10; #16 Pryce, Q18,-not classified)

1975- DN5 1/12 **ARGENTINA** (.....*#17 Jean-Pierre Jarier, Q1 but DNS,-stripped rear end gears on simulated start on warmup lap....* ; DN3b #16 Tom Pryce, Q14,F12-not running at finish), 1/26 **BRAZIL** (DN5 #17 Jarier, Q1,DNF,-leading easily when fuel metering unit failed on lap 33,*fastest lap;* DN3b #16 Pryce, Q14,DNF-accident on lap 32), 3/1 **SOUTH AFRICA** (DN5 #17 Jarier, Q13,DNF; DN5 #16 Pryce, Q17,F9),), 3/16 British Airways-Daily Mail Race of Champions, Brands Hatch (#19 Jarier, Q3,F8; #16 Pryce, Q1,F1,*fastest lap),* 4/13 Daily Express International Trophy, Silverstone (DN5 #16 Pryce, Q5,F9), 4/27 **SPAIN** (#17 Jarier, Q10,F4; #16 Pryce, Q8,DNF-accident on lap 20), 5/11 **MONACO** (#17 Jarier, Q3,DNF-accident on lap one; #16 Pryce, Q2,DNF-accident on lap 39), 5/25 **BELGIUM** (#17 Jarier, Q10,DNF-accident, spun on lap 14; #16 Pryce, Q5,F6), 6/8 **SWEDEN** (#17 Jarier, Q4,DNF; #16 Pryce, Q8,DNF-accident, spun on lap 54), 6/22 **HOLLAND** (#17 Jarier, Q10,DNF-accident, tire failure caused spin on lap 45 while in third; #16 Pryce, Q12,F6), 7/6 **FRANCE** (#17 Jarier, Q4,F8; #16 Pryce, Q6,DNF), 7/19 **GREAT BRITAIN** (#17 Jarier, Q11,F14-not running at finish; #16 Pryce, Q1,DNF-accident on lap 21 while leading), 8/3 **GERMANY** (#17 Jarier, Q10,DNF-accident, tire failed on lap 8; #16 Pryce, Q14,F4), 8/17 **AUSTRIA** (#16 Pryce, Q15,F3), 8/24 Swiss Grand Prix at Dijon-Prenois, France (#17 Jarier, Q1,DNF,*fastest lap;* #16 Pryce, Q8,F7), 9/7 **ITALY** (#16 Pryce, Q14,F6), 10/5 **USA** (#17 Jarier, Q4,DNF; #16 Pryce, Q9,-not classified)

1976- DN5b 1/25 **BRAZIL** (#17 Jean-Pierre Jarier, Q3,DNF-accident,*fastest lap;* #16 Tom Pryce, Q12,F3), 3/6 **SOUTH AFRICA** (#17 Jarier, Q16,DNF; #16 Pryce, Q8,F7), 3/14 Daily Mail Race of Champions, Brands Hatch, (#16 Price, Q9,F6), 3/28 **USA-WEST** (#17 Jarier, Q8,F7; #16 Pryce, Q6,DNF), 4/11 BRDC International Trophy, Silverstone (#17 Jarier, Q6,F5; #16 Pryce, Q3,F4), 5/2 **SPAIN** (#17 Jarier, Q15,DNF; #16 Pryce, Q18,F8), 5/16 **BELGIUM** (#17 Jarier, Q14,F9; #16 Pryce, Q13,F10), 5/30

MONACO (#17 Jarier, Q9,F8; #16 Pryce, Q16,F7), 6/13 **SWEDEN** (#17 Jarier, Q14,F12; #16 Pryce, Q12,F9), 7/4 **FRANCE** (#17 Jarier, Q15,F12; #16 Pryce, Q16,F8), 7/18 **GREAT BRITAIN** (#17 Jarier, Q24,F9; #16 Pryce, Q20,F4), 8/1 **GERMANY** (#17 Jarier, Q23,F11; #16 Pryce, Q18,F8), 8/15 **AUSTRIA** (#17 Jarier, Q18,DNF; #16 Pryce, Q6,DNF), 8/29 **HOLLAND** (#17 Jarier, Q20,F10; DN8 #16 Pryce,Q3,F4), 9/12 **ITALY** (DN5 #17 Jarier, Q17,F19; DN8 #16 Pryce, Q15,F8), 10/3 **CANADA** (DN5 #17 Jarier, (Q18,F18; DN8 #16 Pryce, Q13,F11), 10/10 **USA-EAST** (DN5 #17 Jarier, Q16,F10; DN8 #16 Pryce Q9,DNF), 10/24 **JAPAN** (DN5 #17 Jarier, Q15,F10; DN8 #16 Pryce, Q14,DNF)

1977- 1/9 **ARGENTINA** ; DN8 #16 Tom Pryce, Q9,-not classified; DN5b #17 Renzo Zorzi, Qlast,DNF), 1/23 **BRAZIL** (DN8 #16 Pryce, Q12,DNF; DN5b #17 Zorzi, Q18,F6), 3/5 **SOUTH AFRICA** (DN8 #16 Pryce, Q16,DNF- fatal accident on lap 23; DN8 #17 Zorzi, Q20,DNF), 3/20 Race of Champions, Brands Hatch (DN8 #16 Jackie Oliver, Q7,DNF), 4/3 **USA-WEST** (DN8 #17 Alan Jones, Q14,DNF; DN8 #16 Zorzi, Q20,DNF), 5/8 **SPAIN** (DN8 #17 Jones, Q14,DNF-accident; DN8 #16 Zorzi, Q24,DNF), 5/22 **MONACO** (DN8 #17 Jones, Q11,F6; DN8 #16 Ricardo Patrese, Q13,F9), 6/5 **BELGIUM** (DN8 #17 Jones, Q18,F5; DN8 #16 Patrese, Q16,DNF-accident), 6/19 **SWEDEN** (DN8 #17 Jones, Q11,F17; DN8 #16 Jackie Oliver, Q16,F9), 7/3 **FRANCE** (DN8 #17 Jones, Q10,DNF; DN8 #16 Patrese, Q17,DNF), 7/16 **GREAT BRITAIN** (DN8 #17 Jones, Q12,F7; DN8 #16 Patrese, Q25,DNF), 7/31 **GERMANY** (DN8 #17 Jones, Q17,DNF-accident; DN8 #16 Patrese, Q16,F10-not running at finish), 8/14 **AUSTRIA** (DN8 #17 Jones, Q14,F1; DN8 #16 Arturo Merzario, Q21,DNF), 8/28 **HOLLAND** (DN8 #17 Jones, Q13,DNF; DN8 #16 Patrese, Q16,DNF), 9/11 **ITALY** (DN8 #17 Jones, Q16,F3; DN8 #16 Patrese, Q6,DNF-accident), 10/2 **USA-EAST** (DN8 #17 Jones, Q13,DNF-accident; DN8 #16 Jean-Pierre Jarier, Q16,F9), 10/9 **CANADA** (DN8 #17 Jones, Q7,F4; DN8 #16 Patrese, Q8,F10-not running at finish), 10/23 **JAPAN** (DN8 #17 Jones, Q12,F4; DN8 #16 Patrese, Q13,F6)

1978- DN8 1/15 **ARGENTINA** (#17 Gianclaudio "Clay" Regazzoni, Q16,F15; #16 Hans-Joachim Stuck, Q18,F17), 1/29 **BRAZIL** (#17 Regazzoni, Q15,F5; #16 Stuck, Q9,F9), ...*Regazzoni & Stuck DNQ at 3/4 SOUTH AFRICA...,* 3/19 International Trophy, Silverstone (#17 Regazzoni, Q16,DNF-accident; #16 Stuck, Q7,F6-not classified), 4/2 **USA-WEST** (#17 Regazzoni, Q20,F10; ...*Stuck DNQ* DN9*-accident...;* ....*Danny Ongais did not pre-qualify* DN9 *#29...),* 5/7 **MONACO** (... *Regazzoni DNQ* DN9 *... ;* DN9 #16 Stuck, Q17,DNF-accident), 5/21 **BELGIUM** (DN9 #17 Reggazoni, Q18,DNF; DN9 #16 Stuck, Q20,DNF-accident), 6/4 **SPAIN** (DN9 #17 Reggazoni, Q22,F15-not running at finish; DN8 #16 Stuck, Q24,DNF), 6/17 **SWEDEN**

(DN9 #17 Reggazoni, Q16,F5; DN9 #16 Stuck, Q20,F11), 7/2 **FRANCE** (DN9 #17 Reggazoni, Q17,DNF; DN9 #16 Stuck, Q18,F11), 7/16 **GREAT BRITAIN** (DN9 #17 Reggazoni, Q17,DNF; DN9 #16 Stuck, Q18,F5), 7/30 **GERMANY** (...*Regazzoni DNQ* DN9 *#17...* ; DN9 #16 Stuck, Q24,DNF-accident), 8/13 **AUSTRIA** (DN9 #17 Reggazoni, Q22,-not classified; DN9 #16 Stuck, Q23,DNF-accident), 8/27 **HOLLAND** (...*Regazzoni DNQ* DN9 *#17...* ; ...*Ongais did not pre-qualify* DN9 *#39 four weeks before...* ; DN9 #16 Stuck, Q18,DNF), 9/10 **ITALY** (DN9 #17 Reggazoni, Q15,-not classified; DN9 #16 Stuck, Q17,DNF-accident), 10/1 **USA-EAST** (DN9 #17 Reggazoni, Q17,F14; DN9 #16 Stuck, Q14,DNF), 10/8 **CANADA** (...*Regazzoni DNQ* DN9 *#17...* ; DN9 #16 Stuck, Q8,DNF-accident)

1979- DN9 1/21 **ARGENTINA** (#17 Jan Lammers, Q21,DNF; #18 Elio de Angelis, Q16,F7), 2/4 **BRAZIL** (#17 Lammers, Q21,F14; #18 de Angelis, Q20,F12), 3/3 **SOUTH AFRICA** (#17 Lammers, Q21,DNF-accident; #18 de Angelis, Q15,DNF-accident), 4/8 **USA-WEST** (#17 Lammers, Q14,DNF-accident; #18 de Angelis, Q20,F7), 4/15 Marlboro-Daily Mail Race of Champions, Brands Hatch (#18 de Angelis, Q6,F6), 4/29 **SPAIN** (#17 Lammers, Q24,F12; #18 de Angelis, Q22,DNF), 5/13 **BELGIUM** (#17 Lammers, Q21,F10; #18 de Angelis, Q22,DNF-accident), ...*#17 Lammers and #18 de Angelis DNQ at 5/27 MONACO... ,* 7/1 **FRANCE** (#17 Lammers, Q21,F18; #18 de Angelis, Q24,F16), 7/14 **GREAT BRITAIN** (#17 Lammers, Q21,F11; #18 de Angelis, Q12,F12), 7/29 **GERMANY** (#17 Lammers, Q20,F10; #18 de Angelis, Q21,F11), 8/12 **AUSTRIA** (#17 Lammers, Q23,DNF-accident; #18 de Angelis, Q22,DNF), 8/26 **HOLLAND** (#17 Lammers, Q23,DNF; #18 de Angelis, Q22,DNF), 9/9 **ITALY** (...*#17 Lammers DNQ... #18 de Angelis, Q24,DNF),* 9/16 Dino Ferrari Grand Prix, Imola (#18 de Angelis, Q14,DNF-accident; ... *Beppe Gabbiani DNS #18,-engine...*), 9/30 **CANADA** (#17 Lammers, Q21,F9; #18 de Angelis, Q23,DNF), 10/7 **USA-EAST** (....*#17 Lammers DNQ...* ; #18 de Angelis, Q20,F4)

1980- DN11 ....*#17 Stefan Johansson and #18 D. Kennedy DNQ at 1/13 ARGENTINA...,* ...*#17 Johansson and #18 Kennedy DNQ at 1/27 Brazil...,* 3/1 **SOUTH AFRICA** (#17 Geoff Lees, Q24,F13-not running at finish; ...*#18 Kennedy DNQ..),* ...*#17 Lees and #18 Kennedy DNQ* 4/30 *USA-WEST...,* ...DN12 *#17 Lees and* DN11 *#17 Kennedy DNQ at 5/4 BELGIUM...,* DN12 *#17 Lees and* DN11 *#18 Kennedy DNQ at 5/18 MONACO...,* 6/2 Spanish Grand Prix (DN12 #17 Lees Q20,DNF; DN11 #18 Kennedy, Q22,DNF), ...DN12 *#17 Lees and* DN12 *#18 Kennedy DNQ at 6/29 FRANCE...*

Shadow-Matra: (designed by Tony Southgate)

1975- 8/17 **AUSTRIA** (DN7 #17 Jean-Pierre Jarier, Q14,DNF), 9/7 **ITALY** (#17 Jarier, Q13,DNF)

INDEX

196